# KL-KWX

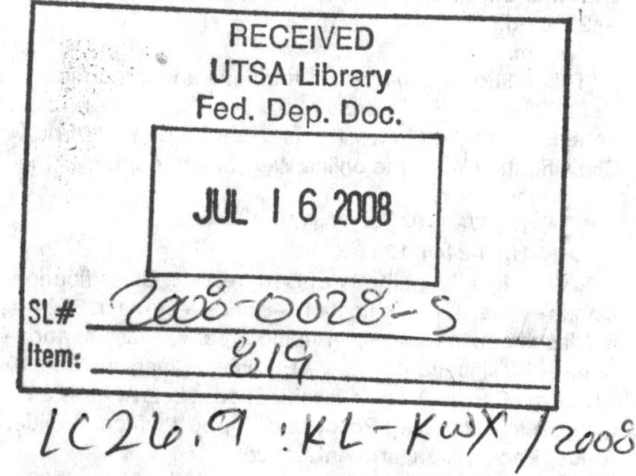




# Law of Asia and Eurasia, Africa, Pacific Area, and Antarctica

## Library of Congress Classification
## 2008

Prepared by the Cataloging Policy and Support Office
Library Services

LIBRARY OF CONGRESS
Cataloging Distribution Service
Washington, D.C.

This edition cumulates all additions and changes to subclasses KL-KWX through Weekly List 2008/08, dated February 20, 2008. Additions and changes made subsequent to that date are published in weekly lists posted on the World Wide Web at

**<http://www.loc.gov/aba/cataloging/classification/weeklylists/>**

and are also available in *Classification Web*, the online Web-based edition of the Library of Congress Classification.

**Library of Congress Cataloging-in-Publication Data**

Library of Congress.
Library of Congress classification. KL-KWX. Law of Asia and Eurasia, Africa, Pacific Area, and Antarctica / prepared by the Cataloging Policy and Support Office Library Services. — 2008 ed.
p. cm.
"This edition cumulates all additions and changes to subclasses KL-KWX through Weekly List 2008/08, dated February 20, 2008. Additions and changes made subsequent to that date are published in weekly lists posted on the World Wide Web ... and are also available in Classification Web, the online Web-based edition of the Library of Congress classification."
Includes index.
ISBN-13: 978-0-8444-1204-7
ISBN-10: 0-8444-1204-X
1. Classification, Library of Congress. 2. Classification—Books—Law. 3. Classification—Books—Asia. 4. Classification—Books—Eurasia. 5. Classification—Books—Africa. 6. Classification—Books—Pacific Area. 7. Classification—Books—Antarctica. 8. Law—Asia—Classification. 9. Law—Eurasia—Classification. 10. Law—Africa—Classification. 11. Law—Pacific Area—Classification. 12. Law—Antarctica—Classification. I. Library of Congress. Cataloging Policy and Support Office. II. Title. III. Title: Law of Asia and Eurasia, Africa, Pacific Area, and Antarctica.
Z696.U5K75 2008 025.4'634—dc22 2008000530



For sale by the Library of Congress Cataloging Distribution Service,
101 Independence Avenue, S.E., Washington, DC 20541-4912.
Product catalog available on the Web at **www.loc.gov/cds**.

# PREFACE

The first edition of subclasses KL-KWX, *Law of Asia and Eurasia, Africa, Pacific Area, and Antarctica*, was published in 1993. A 2001 edition cumulated additions and changes that were made during the period 1993-2001. This 2008 edition cumulates additions and changes made since the publication of the 2001edition. Captions for place names and other proper names in subclasses KNN, KNP, and KNQ now include Chinese characters in addition to their Latin-script counterparts. The Library of Congress gratefully acknowledges the assistance of William B. McCloy, University of Washington Gallagher Law Library, and Nongji Zhang, Harvard Law School Library, in providing the Chinese characters for these proper names.

Classification numbers or spans of numbers that appear in parentheses are formerly valid numbers that are now obsolete. Numbers or spans that appear in angle brackets are optional numbers that have never been used at the Library of Congress but are provided for other libraries that wish to use them. In most cases, a parenthesized or angle-bracketed number is accompanied by a "see" reference directing the user to the actual number that the Library of Congress currently uses, or a note explaining Library of Congress practice.

Access to the online version of the full Library of Congress Classification is available on the World Wide Web by subscription to *Classification Web*. Details about ordering and pricing may be obtained from the Cataloging Distribution Service at

**<http://www.loc.gov/cds/>**

New or revised numbers and captions are added to the L.C. Classification schedules as a result of development proposals made by the cataloging staff of the Library of Congress and cooperating institutions. Upon approval of these proposals by the weekly editorial meeting of the Cataloging Policy and Support Office, new classification records are created or existing records are revised in the master classification database. Weekly lists of newly approved or revised classification numbers and captions are posted on the World Wide Web at

**<http://www.loc.gov/aba/cataloging/classification/weeklylists/>**

Jolande Goldberg, law classification specialist in the Cataloging Policy and Support Office, and Paul Weiss, senior cataloging policy specialist, are responsible for coordinating the overall intellectual and editorial content of class K and its various subclasses. Kent Griffiths, assistant editor, creates new classification records and their associated index terms, and maintains the master database.

**This printed edition of KL-KWX must be used in conjunction with the separately published K Tables: Form Division Tables for Law,** available for purchase from the Cataloging Distribution Service. This classification schedule includes references to form division tables within the range K1 to K24, which are found only in that publication.

Barbara B. Tillett, Chief
Cataloging Policy and Support Office

March 2008

# OUTLINE OF SCHEDULE

| | |
|---|---|
| KL2-9299 | History of law. The ancient orient |
| KL2-135 | General |
| KL147-177 | Ancient legal systems compared |
| KL190-420 | Sources |
| KL701-2215 | Mesopotamia. Assyro-Babylonian law |
| KL1001-1299 | Sumer |
| KL1601-1899 | Assyria |
| KL2201-2499 | Babylonia |
| KL2801-3099 | Egypt |
| KL3501-3799 | Elam |
| KL4101-4399 | Greek law |
| KL4701-4999 | Hittite law |
| KL5301-5599 | Persia |
| KL5901-6199 | Phoenicia |
| KLA-KLW | Eurasia |
| | Turkey, see KKX |
| KLA1-9999 | Russia, Soviet Union |
| KLA85-248 | History of law |
| KLA122-248 | By period |
| KLA474-478 | Regional division. Subregions |
| KLA2020-2025 | Public law |
| KLA2050-2260 | Constitutional law |
| KLB1-5780 | Russia (Federation, 1992- ) |
| KLD1-(490) | Armenian SSR (to 1991) |
| KLE1-490 | Azerbaijan |
| KLF1-490 | Belarus (Republic) |
| | Estonia, see KJS |
| KLH1-490 | Georgia (Republic) |
| | Latvia, see KKI |
| | Lithuania, see KKJ |
| KLM1-490 | Moldova |
| KLN1-489 | Russian S.F.S.R. (to 1991) |
| KLP1-4989 | Ukraine |
| KLP9001-9499 | Zakavkazskai͡a Sot͡sialisticheskai͡a Federativnai͡a Sovetskai͡a Respublika (to 1936) |
| KLQ1-499 | Bukharskai͡a Narodnai͡a Sovetskai͡a Respublika (to 1924) |
| KLR1-490 | Kazakhstan |
| KLR1001-1499 | Khorezmskai͡a Sovetskai͡a Sot͡sialisticheskai͡a Respublika (to 1924) |
| KLS1-490 | Kyrgyzstan |
| KLT1-490 | Tajikistan |

| | |
|---|---|
| | Eurasia - Continued |
| KLV1-490 | Turkmenistan |
| KLW1-490 | Uzbekistan |
| | |
| KM-KPW | Asia |
| KM1-999 | General |
| KMC1-KMY489 | Middle East. Southwest Asia |
| KMC1-849 | Regional comparative and uniform law |
| KMF1-489 | Armenia (Republic) |
| KMF1001-1490 | Bahrain |
| KMG1-489 | Gaza |
| KMH1-4990 | Iran |
| KMJ1-4990 | Iraq |
| KMK1-4990 | Israel |
| KML1-490 | Jerusalem |
| KMM1-490 | Jordan |
| KMM501-994 | West Bank |
| KMN1-499 | Kuwait |
| KMP1-490 | Lebanon |
| KMQ1-490 | Oman |
| KMQ1001-1499 | Palestine (to 1948) |
| KMS1-490 | Qatar |
| KMT1-4990 | Saudi Arabia |
| | Southern Yemen, see KMY |
| KMU1-490 | Syria |
| KMV1-9870 | United Arab Emirates |
| KMX1001-1526 | Yemen |
| KMY1-489 | Yeman (People's Democratic Republic) (to 1990) |
| KNC1-KPW489 | South Asia. Southeast Asia. East Asia |
| KNC1-999 | Regional comparative and uniform law |
| KNE10-499 | Regional organization and integration |
| KNF1-4990 | Afghanistan |
| KNG1-4990 | Bangladesh |
| KNH1-490 | Bhutan |
| KNK1-490 | Brunei |
| KNL1-4990 | Burma |
| KNM1-4990 | Cambodia |
| KNN | China |
| KNN9-80 | Sources |
| KNN88-93 | Legal education |
| KNN94-96 | Legal profession |
| KNN132-460 | By period |
| KNN5101-7599 | Provinces (Sheng) |

## OUTLINE OF SCHEDULE

OUTLINE

# OUTLINE OF SUBJECT DIVISION TABLES

| | |
|---|---|
| | Regional Comparative and Uniform Law |
| | Constitutional law - Continued |
| KL-KWX2 582-608 | Organs of government |
| KL-KWX2 615-619 | State and religion |
| KL-KWX2 620-627 | Administrative law |
| KL-KWX2 628-628.5 | Civil service |
| KL-KWX2 630-(641) | Police and public safety |
| KL-KWX2 643-680 | Public property |
| KL-KWX2 682-691.5 | Public health. Sanitation |
| KL-KWX2 692-702 | Medical legislation |
| KL-KWX2 705-716.5 | Environmental law |
| KL-KWX2 717-736 | Cultural affairs |
| KL-KWX2 720-725.5 | Education |
| KL-KWX2 738-763 | Economic law |
| KL-KWX2 750-758 | Competition rules |
| KL-KWX2 760-762.5 | Standards. Norms. Quality control |
| KL-KWX2 763 | Labeling |
| KL-KWX2 764-852 | Regulation of industry, trade, and commerce |
| KL-KWX2 768-805 | Agriculture. Forestry. Rural law |
| KL-KWX2 808-813 | Fishery |
| KL-KWX2 815-826 | Mining. Quarrying |
| KL-KWX2 827-832 | Manufacturing industries |
| KL-KWX2 833-836 | Food processing industries |
| KL-KWX2 838-839 | Building and construction industry |
| KL-KWX2 842-844 | International trade |
| KL-KWX2 845-850.5 | Domestic trade |
| KL-KWX2 852 | Artisans |
| KL-KWX2 853-860 | Energy policy. Power supply |
| KL-KWX2 861-876 | Transportation |
| KL-KWX2 878-896 | Communication. Mass media |
| KL-KWX2 879-889 | Postal services. Telecommunication |
| KL-KWX2 890-892 | Radio and television communication |
| KL-KWX2 893-896 | Press law |
| KL-KWX2 896.5 | Weather bureau |
| KL-KWX2 897-899 | Professions |
| KL-KWX2 900-955 | Public finance |
| KL-KWX2 916-943.5 | Taxation |
| KL-KWX2 945-949 | Customs. Tariff |
| KL-KWX2 956 | Government measures in time of war, national emergency, or economic crisis |
| KL-KWX2 962-973 | National defense. Military law |
| KL-KWX2 974-982 | Criminal law |
| KL-KWX2 983-998.8 | Criminal courts and procedure |

OUTLINE OF SUBJECT DIVISION TABLES

| | |
|---|---|
| KL-KWX4 | Civil Law (5000 numbers) |
| KL-KWX4 2 | General |
| KL-KWX4 9.5 | Legislation |
| KL-KWX4 18 | Court decisions |
| KL-KWX4 38 | Trials |
| KL-KWX4 50 | Legal education |
| KL-KWX4 54 | Bar associations |
| KL-KWX4 56 | Public registers. Registration |
| KL-KWX4 85 | History of law |
| KL-KWX4 440 | Philosophy, jurisprudence, and theory of law |
| KL-KWX4 479 | Private law |
| KL-KWX4 480 | Private international law |
| KL-KWX4 491 | Civil law |
| KL-KWX4 511 | Persons |
| KL-KWX4 512 | Natural persons |
| KL-KWX4 521 | Juristic persons |
| KL-KWX4 531 | Domestic relations. Family law |
| KL-KWX4 542 | Marriage |
| KL-KWX4 569 | Matrimonial property |
| KL-KWX4 583 | Consanguinity and affinity |
| KL-KWX4 587 | Parent and child |
| KL-KWX4 622 | Guardian and ward |
| KL-KWX4 631 | Property. Law of things |
| KL-KWX4 654 | Ownership |
| KL-KWX4 655 | Acquisition and loss of ownership |
| KL-KWX4 683 | Real property. Land law |
| KL-KWX4 685 | Concepts of customary (native) land rights |
| KL-KWX4 687 | Ownership |
| KL-KWX4 717 | Hypothecation |
| KL-KWX4 726 | Pledges |
| KL-KWX4 737 | Land register and registration |
| KL-KWX4 761 | Inheritance. Succession upon death |
| KL-KWX4 777 | Intestate succession |
| KL-KWX4 785 | Wills |
| KL-KWX4 801 | Obligations |
| KL-KWX4 811 | Debtor and creditor |
| KL-KWX4 817 | Extinction of obligation |
| KL-KWX4 824 | Nonperformance |
| KL-KWX4 828 | Damages |
| KL-KWX4 834 | Delicts. Torts |
| KL-KWX4 842 | Individual torts |
| KL-KWX4 858 | Contracts and transactions |
| KL-KWX4 860 | Declaration of intention |

| | |
|---|---|
| | Civil Law (5000 numbers) |
| | Civil law |
| | Obligations |
| | Contracts and transactions - Continued |
| KL-KWX4 869 | Formation of contract |
| KL-KWX4 874 | Individual contracts and transactions |
| KL-KWX4 911 | Commercial law. Commercial transactions |
| KL-KWX4 921 | Merchant and business enterprise |
| KL-KWX4 926 | Commercial sale |
| KL-KWX4 931 | Freight forwarders and carriers. Carriage of passengers and goods |
| KL-KWX4 937 | Negotiable instruments. Titles of credit |
| KL-KWX4 940 | Banking. Stock exchange |
| KL-KWX4 970 | Maritime law |
| KL-KWX4 998 | Insurance law |
| KL-KWX4 1040 | Business associations |
| KL-KWX4 1043 | Personal companies |
| KL-KWX4 1050 | Stock companies |
| KL-KWX4 1120 | Cooperative societies |
| KL-KWX4 1155 | Intellectual and industrial property |
| KL-KWX4 1160 | Copyright |
| KL-KWX4 1185 | Author and publisher |
| KL-KWX4 1194 | Patent law and trademarks |
| KL-KWX4 1234 | Unfair competition |
| KL-KWX4 1261 | Labor law |
| KL-KWX4 1279 | Labor contract and employment |
| KL-KWX4 1326 | Prohibition of discrimination in employment |
| KL-KWX4 1330 | Wages |
| KL-KWX4 1347 | Labor-management relations |
| KL-KWX4 1376 | Collective bargaining and labor agreements |
| KL-KWX4 1408 | Protection of labor |
| KL-KWX4 1440 | Labor courts and procedure |
| KL-KWX4 1468 | Social legislation |
| KL-KWX4 1472 | Social insurance. Social security |
| KL-KWX4 1520 | Social services. Public welfare |
| KL-KWX4 1552 | Social courts and procedure |
| KL-KWX4 1572 | Courts and procedure |
| KL-KWX4 1580 | Courts |
| KL-KWX4 1600 | The legal profession |
| KL-KWX4 1650 | Procedure in general |
| KL-KWX4 1695 | Civil procedure |
| KL-KWX4 1834 | Noncontentious (ex parte) jurisdiction |
| KL-KWX4 1885 | Insolvency |

Civil Law (5000 numbers)
Courts and procedure
Insolvency - Continued

| | |
|---|---|
| KL-KWX4 1942 | Bankruptcy |
| KL-KWX4 1976 | Costs |
| KL-KWX4 2000 | Public law |
| KL-KWX4 2050 | Constitutional law |
| KL-KWX4 2240 | Modern constitutional principles |
| KL-KWX4 2400 | Foreign relations |
| KL-KWX4 2430 | Individual and state |
| KL-KWX4 2500 | Organs of national government |
| KL-KWX4 2685 | State and religion |
| KL-KWX4 2711 | Administrative law |
| KL-KWX4 2820 | Indemnification for acts performed by government |
| KL-KWX4 2860 | Administrative organization |
| KL-KWX4 2875 | Juristic persons of public law |
| KL-KWX4 2937 | Municipal government |
| KL-KWX4 2970 | Civil service |
| KL-KWX4 3000 | Police and public safety |
| KL-KWX4 3022 | Control of individuals |
| KL-KWX4 3034 | Control of social activities |
| KL-KWX4 3040 | Public property |
| KL-KWX4 3043 | Roads and highways |
| KL-KWX4 3046 | Water resources |
| KL-KWX4 3056 | Public land law |
| KL-KWX4 3075 | Public health |
| KL-KWX4 3090 | Drug laws |
| KL-KWX4 3098 | Medical legislation |
| KL-KWX4 3124 | Birth control. Family planning |
| KL-KWX4 3127 | Environmental law |
| KL-KWX4 3137 | Cultural affairs |
| KL-KWX4 3138 | Education |
| KL-KWX4 3160 | Science and the arts |
| KL-KWX4 3176 | Public collections |
| KL-KWX4 3183 | Historic buildings and monuments |
| KL-KWX4 3190 | Economic law |
| KL-KWX4 3195 | Government control and policy |
| KL-KWX4 3220 | Control of contracts and combinations in restraint of trade |
| KL-KWX4 3254 | Standards. Norms |
| KL-KWX4 3272 | Regulation of industry, trade, and commerce |
| KL-KWX4 3295 | Primary production. Extractive industries |
| KL-KWX4 3295 | Agriculture. Forestry. Rural law |

Civil Law (5000 numbers)
Economic law
Regulation of industry, trade, and commerce
Primary production. Extractive industries - Continued

KL-KWX4 3340 Fishery
KL-KWX4 3344 Mining and quarrying
KL-KWX4 3372 Manufacturing industries
KL-KWX4 3377 Food processing industries. Food products
KL-KWX4 3402 Building and construction industry
KL-KWX4 3405 International trade
KL-KWX4 3415 Domestic trade
KL-KWX4 3426 Artisans
KL-KWX4 3431 Energy policy. Power supply
KL-KWX4 3440 Transportation
KL-KWX4 3442 Road traffic
KL-KWX4 3459 Railroads
KL-KWX4 3467 Aviation
KL-KWX4 3469 Space law
KL-KWX4 3470 Water transportation
KL-KWX4 3482 Communication. Mass media
KL-KWX4 3485 Postal services. Telecommunication
KL-KWX4 3491 Radio communication
KL-KWX4 3500 Press law
KL-KWX4 3515 Professions. Intelligentsia
KL-KWX4 3525 Public finance
KL-KWX4 3534 Money
KL-KWX4 3540 National revenue
KL-KWX4 3541 Taxation
KL-KWX4 3573 Income tax
KL-KWX4 3616 Property tax. Taxation of capital
KL-KWX4 3627 Excise taxes. Taxes on transactions
KL-KWX4 3645 Customs. Tariff
KL-KWX4 3655 State and local finance
KL-KWX4 3660 Taxation
KL-KWX4 3663 Property tax. Taxation of capital
KL-KWX4 3674 Business tax
KL-KWX4 3682 Tax and customs courts and procedure
KL-KWX4 3693 Tax and customs crimes and delinquency. Procedure
KL-KWX4 3709 Government measures in time of war, national emergency, or economic crisis
KL-KWX4 3727 War damage compensation
KL-KWX4 3730 Military occupation

Civil Law (5000 numbers) - Continued

| | |
|---|---|
| KL-KWX4 3735 | National defense. Military law |
| KL-KWX4 3738 | The armed forces |
| KL-KWX4 3752 | Civil defense |
| KL-KWX4 3758 | Military criminal law and procedure |
| KL-KWX4 3790 | Criminal law |
| KL-KWX4 3824 | Concepts and principles |
| KL-KWX4 3840 | Criminal offense |
| KL-KWX4 3946 | Punishment |
| KL-KWX4 4048 | Individual offenses |
| KL-KWX4 4601 | Criminal procedure |
| KL-KWX4 4632 | Pretrial procedures |
| KL-KWX4 4664 | Procedure at first instance |
| KL-KWX4 4795 | Execution of sentence |
| KL-KWX4 4855 | Victimology |

| | |
|---|---|
| KL-KWX5 | Civil Law (500 numbers) |
| KL-KWX5 1 | General |
| KL-KWX5 1.75 | Legislation |
| KL-KWX5 2.2 | Court decisions |
| KL-KWX5 3.4 | Trials |
| KL-KWX5 5 | Legal education |
| KL-KWX5 5.5 | Bar associations |
| KL-KWX5 5.53 | Public registers. Registration |
| KL-KWX5 8.5 | History of law |
| KL-KWX5 12 | By period |
| KL-KWX5 44 | Philosophy, jurisprudence, and theory of law |
| KL-KWX5 48.2 | Private law |
| KL-KWX5 48.3 | Private international law |
| KL-KWX5 49 | Civil law |
| KL-KWX5 51 | Persons |
| KL-KWX5 51.2 | Natural persons |
| KL-KWX5 53 | Juristic persons |
| KL-KWX5 54 | Domestic relations. Family law |
| KL-KWX5 54.2 | Marriage |
| KL-KWX5 56.9 | Matrimonial property |
| KL-KWX5 58.3 | Consanguinity and affinity |
| KL-KWX5 59 | Parent and child |
| KL-KWX5 62.4 | Guardian and ward |
| KL-KWX5 63 | Property. Law of things |
| KL-KWX5 65.7 | Ownership |
| KL-KWX5 65.8 | Acquisition and loss of ownership |
| KL-KWX5 68.3 | Real property. Land law |
| KL-KWX5 68.6 | Concepts of customary (native) land rights |
| KL-KWX5 68.8 | Ownership |
| KL-KWX5 72 | Hypothecation |
| KL-KWX5 73 | Pledges |
| KL-KWX5 74.4 | Land register and registration |
| KL-KWX5 76 | Inheritance. Succession upon death |
| KL-KWX5 76.7 | Intestate succession |
| KL-KWX5 78.5 | Wills |
| KL-KWX5 80 | Obligations |
| KL-KWX5 80.2 | Debtor and creditor |
| KL-KWX5 81.5 | Extinction of obligation |
| KL-KWX5 82.4 | Nonperformance |
| KL-KWX5 82.8 | Damages |
| KL-KWX5 83.5 | Delicts. Torts |
| KL-KWX5 85 | Individual torts |

| | |
|---|---|
| | Civil Law (500 numbers) |
| | Civil law |
| | Obligations - Continued |
| KL-KWX5 87.6 | Contracts and transactions |
| KL-KWX5 87.9 | Declaration of intention |
| KL-KWX5 89.5 | Formation of contract |
| KL-KWX5 89.75 | Individual contracts and transactions |
| KL-KWX5 97 | Commercial law. Commercial transactions |
| KL-KWX5 97.2 | Merchant and business enterprise |
| KL-KWX5 97.5 | Commercial sale |
| KL-KWX5 98.2 | Freight forwarders and carriers. Carriage of |
| KL-KWX5 | passengers and goods |
| KL-KWX5 99 | Negotiable instruments. Titles of credit |
| KL-KWX5 99.5 | Banking. Stock exchange |
| KL-KWX5 101.6 | Maritime law |
| KL-KWX5 104.3 | Insurance law |
| KL-KWX5 107.5 | Business associations |
| KL-KWX5 108 | Personal companies |
| KL-KWX5 108.9 | Stock companies |
| KL-KWX5 112 | Cooperative societies |
| KL-KWX5 115 | Intellectual and industrial property |
| KL-KWX5 115.2 | Copyright |
| KL-KWX5 118.5 | Author and publisher |
| KL-KWX5 119 | Patent law and trademarks |
| KL-KWX5 123 | Unfair competition |
| KL-KWX5 126 | Labor law |
| KL-KWX5 127 | Labor contract and employment |
| KL-KWX5 131 | Prohibition of discrimination in employment |
| KL-KWX5 132 | Wages |
| KL-KWX5 134 | Labor-management relations |
| KL-KWX5 137.5 | Collective bargaining and labor agreements |
| KL-KWX5 140 | Protection of labor |
| KL-KWX5 144 | Labor courts and procedure |
| KL-KWX5 146 | Social legislation |
| KL-KWX5 146.5 | Social insurance. Social security |
| KL-KWX5 152 | Social services. Public welfare |
| KL-KWX5 155 | Social courts and procedure |
| KL-KWX5 157 | Courts and procedure |
| KL-KWX5 158 | Courts |
| KL-KWX5 160 | The legal profession |
| KL-KWX5 165 | Procedure in general |
| KL-KWX5 169.5 | Civil procedure |
| KL-KWX5 183.4 | Noncontentious (ex parte) jurisdiction |

Civil Law (500 numbers)
Courts and procedure - Continued

KL-KWX5 188.5 Insolvency
KL-KWX5 194 Bankruptcy
KL-KWX5 197.6 Costs
KL-KWX5 200 Public law
KL-KWX5 205 Constitutional law
KL-KWX5 224 Modern constitutional principles
KL-KWX5 240 Foreign relations
KL-KWX5 243 Individual and state
KL-KWX5 250 Organs of national government
KL-KWX5 268.7 State and religion
KL-KWX5 272 Administrative law
KL-KWX5 282 Indemnification for acts performed by government
KL-KWX5 285 Administrative organization
KL-KWX5 287 Juristic persons of public law
KL-KWX5 293.7 Municipal government
KL-KWX5 297.4 Civil service
KL-KWX5 300 Police and public safety
KL-KWX5 302 Control of individuals
KL-KWX5 303.3 Control of social activities
KL-KWX5 304 Public property
KL-KWX5 304.7 Roads and highways
KL-KWX5 305 Water resources
KL-KWX5 306.5 Public land law
KL-KWX5 308.5 Public health
KL-KWX5 310 Drug laws
KL-KWX5 310.8 Medical legislation
KL-KWX5 313.4 Birth control. Family planning
KL-KWX5 313.7 Environmental law
KL-KWX5 315 Cultural affairs
KL-KWX5 315.3 Education
KL-KWX5 318.8 Science and the arts
KL-KWX5 319.9 Public collections
KL-KWX5 320.4 Historic buildings and monuments
KL-KWX5 320.7 Economic law
KL-KWX5 321 Government control and policy
KL-KWX5 322 Control of contracts and combinations in restraint of trade
KL-KWX5 325.4 Standards. Norms
KL-KWX5 327 Regulation of industry, trade, and commerce
KL-KWX5 328.5 Primary production. Extractive industries
KL-KWX5 328.5 Agriculture. Forestry. Rural law

Civil Law (500 numbers)
Economic law
Regulation of industry, trade, and commerce
Primary production. Extractive industries - Continued

KL-KWX5 334 Fishery
KL-KWX5 334.4 Mining and quarrying
KL-KWX5 337.45 Manufacturing industries
KL-KWX5 337.7 Food processing industries. Food products
KL-KWX5 340.2 Building and construction industry
KL-KWX5 340.5 International trade
KL-KWX5 341.5 Domestic trade
KL-KWX5 342.6 Artisans
KL-KWX5 343.2 Energy policy. Power supply
KL-KWX5 344 Transportation
KL-KWX5 344.2 Road traffic
KL-KWX5 346 Railroads
KL-KWX5 346.7 Aviation
KL-KWX5 347 Water transportation
KL-KWX5 348.2 Communication. Mass media
KL-KWX5 348.5 Postal services. Telecommunication
KL-KWX5 349.2 Radio communication
KL-KWX5 350 Press law
KL-KWX5 352 Professions. Intelligentsia
KL-KWX5 352.8 Public finance
KL-KWX5 353.55 Money
KL-KWX5 353.9 National revenue
KL-KWX5 354 Taxation
KL-KWX5 356.6 Income tax
KL-KWX5 360.4 Property tax. Taxation of capital
KL-KWX5 361.25 Excise taxes. Taxes on transactions
KL-KWX5 364 Customs. Tariff
KL-KWX5 365 State and local finance
KL-KWX5 365.5 Taxation
KL-KWX5 366.2 Property tax. Taxation of capital
KL-KWX5 367.5 Business tax
KL-KWX5 368 Tax and customs courts and procedure
KL-KWX5 370 Tax and customs crimes and delinquency. Procedure
KL-KWX5 370.9 Government measures in time of war, national
KL-KWX5 emergency, or economic crisis
KL-KWX5 373 War damage compensation
KL-KWX5 373.5 Military occupation
KL-KWX5 374 National defense. Military law
KL-KWX5 374.5 The armed forces

| | |
|---|---|
| | Common Law (5000 numbers) |
| | Economic constitution. Economic legislation - Continued |
| KL-KWX6 975 | Government-owned industry |
| KL-KWX6 981 | Standards. Norms. Quality control |
| KL-KWX6 982 | Regulation of industry, trade, and commerce |
| KL-KWX6 985 | Primary production. Extractive industries |
| KL-KWX6 985 | Agriculture. Forestry. Rural law |
| KL-KWX6 1004 | Fishing industry |
| KL-KWX6 1006 | Mining. Quarrying |
| KL-KWX6 1016 | Manufacturing industries |
| KL-KWX6 1020 | Food processing industries |
| KL-KWX6 1023.5 | Construction and building industry |
| KL-KWX6 1024 | Trade |
| KL-KWX6 1025 | International trade. Foreign trade |
| KL-KWX6 1026.7 | Retail trade |
| KL-KWX6 1032 | Public utilities |
| KL-KWX6 1034 | Power supply |
| KL-KWX6 1039 | Transportation and communication |
| KL-KWX6 1040 | Road traffic |
| KL-KWX6 1044 | Railroads |
| KL-KWX6 1050 | Aviation |
| KL-KWX6 1055 | Space law |
| KL-KWX6 1056 | Water transportation |
| KL-KWX6 1062 | Postal service |
| KL-KWX6 1065 | Press law |
| KL-KWX6 1066 | Telecommunication |
| KL-KWX6 1070 | Professions. Intelligentsia |
| KL-KWX6 1100 | Intellectual and industrial property |
| KL-KWX6 1104 | Copyright |
| KL-KWX6 1125 | Author and publisher |
| KL-KWX6 1134 | Patent law and trademarks |
| KL-KWX6 1174 | Unfair competition |
| KL-KWX6 1205 | Social legislation |
| KL-KWX6 1211 | Labor law |
| KL-KWX6 1229 | Labor contract and employment |
| KL-KWX6 1276 | Prohibition of discrimination in employment |
| KL-KWX6 1280 | Wages |
| KL-KWX6 1297 | Labor-management relations |
| KL-KWX6 1336 | Collective bargaining and labor |
| KL-KWX6 1348 | Collective labor disputes |
| KL-KWX6 1368 | Protection of labor |
| KL-KWX6 1400 | Practice and procedure. Courts |

Common Law (5000 numbers) - Continued

| | |
|---|---|
| KL-KWX6 1410 | Social insurance. Social security |
| KL-KWX6 1430 | Health insurance |
| KL-KWX6 1440 | Workers' compensation |
| KL-KWX6 1446 | Old age, survivors and disability insurance |
| KL-KWX6 1451 | Unemployment insurance |
| KL-KWX6 1456 | Social services. Public welfare |
| KL-KWX6 1462 | Social service beneficiaries |
| KL-KWX6 1482 | Human reproduction |
| KL-KWX6 1488 | Public health |
| KL-KWX6 1493 | Contagious and infectious diseases |
| KL-KWX6 1502 | Mental health |
| KL-KWX6 1504 | Drug addiction |
| KL-KWX6 1507 | Environmental law |
| KL-KWX6 1520 | Medical legislation |
| KL-KWX6 1536 | Drug laws. Liquor laws |
| KL-KWX6 1550 | Police and public safety |
| KL-KWX6 1562 | Hazardous articles and processes |
| KL-KWX6 1572 | Control of individuals |
| KL-KWX6 1582 | Control of social activities |
| KL-KWX6 1600 | Cultural affairs |
| KL-KWX6 1610 | Education |
| KL-KWX6 1670 | Science and the arts |
| KL-KWX6 1692 | Public collections |
| KL-KWX6 1700 | Historic buildings and monuments |
| KL-KWX6 1710 | Public law |
| KL-KWX6 1734 | Constitutional law |
| KL-KWX6 1895 | Modern constitutional principles |
| KL-KWX6 2060 | Foreign relations |
| KL-KWX6 2090 | Individual and state |
| KL-KWX6 2095 | Human rights. Civil and political rights |
| KL-KWX6 2140 | Nationality and citizenship |
| KL-KWX6 2162 | Religion and state |
| KL-KWX6 2172 | Organs of national government |
| KL-KWX6 2295 | Administrative departments of federal states, etc. |
| KL-KWX6 2320 | Municipal government |
| KL-KWX6 2400 | Civil service |
| KL-KWX6 2450 | Administrative law |
| KL-KWX6 2500 | Public property |
| KL-KWX6 2510 | Roads and highways |
| KL-KWX6 2522 | Water resources |
| KL-KWX6 2550 | Public land law |
| KL-KWX6 2562 | Native (customary) land |

| | |
|---|---|
| | Common Law (5000 numbers) |
| | Public land law - Continued |
| KL-KWX6 2570 | Regional planning |
| KL-KWX6 2600 | Government property |
| KL-KWX6 2650 | Government measures in time of war, national |
| KL-KWX6 | emergency, or economic crisis |
| KL-KWX6 2686 | War damage compensation |
| KL-KWX6 2715 | Public finance |
| KL-KWX6 2760 | Money. Monetary policy |
| KL-KWX6 2778 | National revenue |
| KL-KWX6 2781 | Taxation |
| KL-KWX6 2810 | Tax administration. Revenue service |
| KL-KWX6 2832 | Income tax |
| KL-KWX6 3100 | Property tax. Taxation of capital |
| KL-KWX6 3145 | Excise taxes. Taxes on transactions |
| KL-KWX6 3190 | Customs. Tariff |
| KL-KWX6 3220 | State and local finance |
| KL-KWX6 3230 | Taxation |
| KL-KWX6 3315 | Tax and customs crimes and delinquency |
| KL-KWX6 3350 | National defense. Military law |
| KL-KWX6 3354 | The armed forces |
| KL-KWX6 3380 | Military criminal law and procedure |
| KL-KWX6 3407 | Courts and procedure |
| KL-KWX6 3441 | Courts |
| KL-KWX6 3492 | Judicial officers. Court employees |
| KL-KWX6 3520 | Procedure in general |
| KL-KWX6 3557 | Civil procedure |
| KL-KWX6 3572 | Procedural principles |
| KL-KWX6 3617 | Procedure at first instance |
| KL-KWX6 3790 | Criminal law |
| KL-KWX6 3812 | Philosophy of criminal law |
| KL-KWX6 3827 | Applicability and validity of the law |
| KL-KWX6 3840 | Criminal offense |
| KL-KWX6 3946 | Punishment |
| KL-KWX6 4049 | Individual offenses |
| KL-KWX6 4601 | Criminal procedure |
| KL-KWX6 4619 | Procedural principles |
| KL-KWX6 4632 | Pretrial procedures |
| KL-KWX6 4664 | Procedure at first instance |
| KL-KWX6 4770 | Remedies |
| KL-KWX6 4795 | Execution of sentence |
| KL-KWX6 4855 | Victimology |

| | |
|---|---|
| KL-KWX7 | Common Law (500 numbers) |
| KL-KWX7 1 | General |
| KL-KWX7 1.8 | Legislation |
| KL-KWX7 2.2 | Law reports and related materials |
| KL-KWX7 3.4 | Trials |
| KL-KWX7 5 | Legal education |
| KL-KWX7 5.43 | The legal profession |
| KL-KWX7 5.5 | Bar associations |
| KL-KWX7 5.52 | Notaries |
| KL-KWX7 5.53 | Public registers. Registration |
| KL-KWX7 8.5 | History of law |
| KL-KWX7 44 | Philosophy, jurisprudence, and theory of law |
| KL-KWX7 47.9 | Private law |
| KL-KWX7 48 | Conflict of laws |
| KL-KWX7 51 | Persons |
| KL-KWX7 51.2 | Natural persons |
| KL-KWX7 54 | Domestic relations. Family law |
| KL-KWX7 54.4 | Marriage. Husband and wife |
| KL-KWX7 58.4 | Consanguinity and affinity. Kinship |
| KL-KWX7 63 | Property |
| KL-KWX7 66 | Real property. Land law |
| KL-KWX7 66.3 | Land tenure |
| KL-KWX7 72 | Personal property |
| KL-KWX7 73.8 | Trusts and trustees |
| KL-KWX7 76 | Succession upon death |
| KL-KWX7 77 | Testamentary succession. Wills |
| KL-KWX7 78.3 | Intestate succession |
| KL-KWX7 81 | Contracts |
| KL-KWX7 81.7 | Formation of contracts |
| KL-KWX7 84.6 | Public contracts. Government contracts |
| KL-KWX7 85 | Individual contracts |
| KL-KWX7 96 | Torts. Extracontractual liability |
| KL-KWX7 97 | Particular torts |
| KL-KWX7 97.3 | Strict liability |
| KL-KWX7 97.74 | Compensation to victims of crime |
| KL-KWX7 97.75 | Agency |
| KL-KWX7 97.8 | Associations |
| KL-KWX7 97.8 | Unincorporated associations |
| KL-KWX7 97.85 | Incorporated associations. Corporations |
| KL-KWX7 98.3 | Insolvency and bankruptcy |
| KL-KWX7 99 | Economic constitution. Economic legislation |
| KL-KWX7 99.6 | Economic assistance |
| KL-KWX7 99.7 | Prices and price control |

Common Law (500 numbers)
Economic constitution. Economic legislation - Continued

| | |
|---|---|
| KL-KWX7 99.8 | Government-owned industry |
| KL-KWX7 99.9 | Standards. Norms. Quality control |
| KL-KWX7 100 | Regulation of industry, trade, and commerce |
| KL-KWX7 100.2 | Primary production. Extractive industries |
| KL-KWX7 100.2 | Agriculture. Forestry. Rural law |
| KL-KWX7 101.4 | Fishing industry |
| KL-KWX7 101.6 | Mining. Quarrying |
| KL-KWX7 103 | Manufacturing industries |
| KL-KWX7 103.7 | Food processing industries |
| KL-KWX7 104.5 | Construction and building industry |
| KL-KWX7 104.7 | Trade |
| KL-KWX7 104.8 | International trade. Foreign trade |
| KL-KWX7 105.4 | Public utilities |
| KL-KWX7 105.6 | Power supply |
| KL-KWX7 106.2 | Transportation and communication |
| KL-KWX7 106.3 | Road traffic |
| KL-KWX7 106.6 | Railroads |
| KL-KWX7 107 | Aviation |
| KL-KWX7 107.45 | Space law |
| KL-KWX7 107.5 | Water transportation |
| KL-KWX7 108 | Postal service |
| KL-KWX7 108.5 | Press law |
| KL-KWX7 109 | Telecommunication |
| KL-KWX7 110.2 | Professions. Intelligentsia |
| KL-KWX7 112 | Intellectual and industrial property |
| KL-KWX7 112.2 | Copyright |
| KL-KWX7 115.5 | Author and publisher |
| KL-KWX7 116 | Patent law and trademarks |
| KL-KWX7 121 | Unfair competition |
| KL-KWX7 123 | Social legislation |
| KL-KWX7 125 | Labor law |
| KL-KWX7 125.5 | Labor contract and employment |
| KL-KWX7 130 | Prohibition of discrimination in employment |
| KL-KWX7 131 | Wages |
| KL-KWX7 133 | Labor-management relations |
| KL-KWX7 137 | Collective bargaining and labor |
| KL-KWX7 138 | Collective labor disputes |
| KL-KWX7 140 | Protection of labor |
| KL-KWX7 143.3 | Practice and procedure. Courts |
| KL-KWX7 143.8 | Social insurance. Social security |

Common Law (500 numbers)
Social insurance. Social security - Continued

| | |
|---|---|
| KL-KWX7 145 | Health insurance |
| KL-KWX7 146 | Workers' compensation |
| KL-KWX7 148.4 | Old age, survivors and disability insurance |
| KL-KWX7 148.7 | Unemployment insurance |
| KL-KWX7 149 | Social services. Public welfare |
| KL-KWX7 149.6 | Social service beneficiaries |
| KL-KWX7 152 | Human reproduction |
| KL-KWX7 153 | Public health |
| KL-KWX7 153.6 | Contagious and infectious diseases |
| KL-KWX7 154.7 | Mental health |
| KL-KWX7 155 | Environmental law |
| KL-KWX7 157.3 | Medical legislation |
| KL-KWX7 159.2 | Drug laws. Liquor laws |
| KL-KWX7 160 | Police and public safety |
| KL-KWX7 160.5 | Hazardous articles and processes |
| KL-KWX7 160.9 | Control of individuals |
| KL-KWX7 161.2 | Control of social activities |
| KL-KWX7 162 | Cultural affairs |
| KL-KWX7 162.5 | Education |
| KL-KWX7 166 | Science and the arts |
| KL-KWX7 168.5 | Public collections |
| KL-KWX7 169.3 | Historic buildings and monuments |
| KL-KWX7 169.5 | Public law |
| KL-KWX7 170 | Constitutional law |
| KL-KWX7 181 | Modern constitutional principles |
| KL-KWX7 206 | Foreign relations |
| KL-KWX7 209 | Individual and state |
| KL-KWX7 209.5 | Human rights. Civil and political rights |
| KL-KWX7 214 | Nationality and citizenship |
| KL-KWX7 216.2 | Religion and state |
| KL-KWX7 217 | Organs of national government |
| KL-KWX7 229.5 | Administrative departments of federal states, etc. |
| KL-KWX7 232 | Municipal government |
| KL-KWX7 240 | Civil service |
| KL-KWX7 245 | Administrative law |
| KL-KWX7 250 | Public property |
| KL-KWX7 250.2 | Roads and highways |
| KL-KWX7 251 | Water resources |
| KL-KWX7 253 | Public land law |
| KL-KWX7 254 | Native (customary) land |
| KL-KWX7 254.23 | Regional planning |

Common Law (500 numbers)

| | |
|---|---|
| | Public property - Continued |
| KL-KWX7 256 | Government property |
| KL-KWX7 262 | Government measures in time of war, national emergency, or economic crisis |
| KL-KWX7 266 | War damage compensation |
| KL-KWX7 268 | Public finance |
| KL-KWX7 272 | Money. Monetary policy |
| KL-KWX7 274 | National revenue |
| KL-KWX7 275 | Taxation |
| KL-KWX7 277 | Tax administration. Revenue service |
| KL-KWX7 279 | Income tax |
| KL-KWX7 298 | Property tax. Taxation of capital |
| KL-KWX7 301 | Excise taxes. Taxes on transactions |
| KL-KWX7 305 | Customs. Tariff |
| KL-KWX7 308 | State and local finance |
| KL-KWX7 309 | Taxation |
| KL-KWX7 316 | Tax and customs crimes and delinquency |
| KL-KWX7 319 | National defense. Military law |
| KL-KWX7 320 | The armed forces |
| KL-KWX7 324 | Military criminal law and procedure |
| KL-KWX7 328 | Courts and procedure |
| KL-KWX7 332 | Courts |
| KL-KWX7 341 | Judicial officers. Court employees |
| KL-KWX7 346 | Procedure in general |
| KL-KWX7 352 | Civil procedure |
| KL-KWX7 353.2 | Procedural principles |
| KL-KWX7 360 | Procedure at first instance |
| KL-KWX7 379 | Criminal law |
| KL-KWX7 380.2 | Philosophy of criminal law |
| KL-KWX7 381.2 | Applicability and validity of the law |
| KL-KWX7 384 | Criminal offense |
| KL-KWX7 394.6 | Punishment |
| KL-KWX7 404 | Individual offenses |
| KL-KWX7 460 | Criminal procedure |
| KL-KWX7 461 | Procedural principles |
| KL-KWX7 463.2 | Pretrial procedures |
| KL-KWX7 466.4 | Procedure at first instance |
| KL-KWX7 477 | Remedies |
| KL-KWX7 479.5 | Execution of sentence |
| KL-KWX7 487 | Victimology |

# OUTLINE OF SUBJECT DIVISION TABLES

| | |
|---|---|
| | States, Territories, etc. |
| | Cultural affairs - Continued |
| KL-KWX8 68-68.7 | Public collections |
| KL-KWX8 69 | Historic buildings |
| KL-KWX8 70-82.4 | Economic law. Regulation of industry, trade, and commerce |
| KL-KWX8 71.3-76.3 | Agriculture |
| KL-KWX8 77 | Fishery |
| KL-KWX8 77.3-77.4 | Mining and quarrying |
| KL-KWX8 78-78.3 | Manufacturing industries |
| KL-KWX8 78.5-78.6 | Food processing industries |
| KL-KWX8 79 | Construction and building industry |
| KL-KWX8 79.3 | International trade |
| KL-KWX8 79.5-80.5 | Domestic trade |
| KL-KWX8 81-81.3 | Artisans |
| KL-KWX8 81.5-81.6 | Public utilities |
| KL-KWX8 82.5-83.7 | Transportation |
| KL-KWX8 82.6-83.3 | Road traffic |
| KL-KWX8 83.4-83.5 | Railroads |
| KL-KWX8 83.6-83.7 | Water transportation |
| KL-KWX8 84-84.7 | Communication. Mass media |
| KL-KWX8 85-85.4 | Professions |
| KL-KWX8 85.5-88 | Public finance |
| KL-KWX8 86.5-88 | State revenue |
| KL-KWX8 86.6-87.6 | Taxation |
| KL-KWX8 87.7-87.8 | Customs. Tariff |
| KL-KWX8 88.3-89.5 | Government measures in time of war, national emergency, or economic crisis |
| KL-KWX8 89.6-90.5 | Military law |
| KL-KWX8 91-96.4 | Criminal law |
| KL-KWX8 92.3-96.4 | Criminal courts and procedure |

| | |
|---|---|
| KL-KWX9 | Cities, etc. (One number) |
| KL-KWX9 .A1-.A8 | General |
| KL-KWX9 .A85-.A9 | History |
| KL-KWX9 .12-.29 | Private law |
| KL-KWX9 .3-.33 | Labor law. Social insurance. Public welfare |
| KL-KWX9 .34-.46 | City constitution and government |
| KL-KWX9 .47-.5 | Public property |
| KL-KWX9 .54-.58 | Public health. Medical legislation |
| KL-KWX9 .6 | Environmental laws |
| KL-KWX9 .63-.68 | Cultural affairs |
| KL-KWX9 .7-.78 | Industry, trade, and commerce |
| KL-KWX9 .8 | Public utilities |
| KL-KWX9 .83-.85 | Public finance |
| KL-KWX9 .86 | Offenses and administration of criminal justice |

# OUTLINE OF SUBJECT DIVISION TABLES

| | |
|---|---|
| KL-KWX9a | Cities, etc. (Cutter number) |
| KL-KWX9a .x | Legislation |
| KL-KWX9a .x2 | Decisions |
| KL-KWX9a .x3 | General works |

History of law. The ancient orient
Class here works on the ancient/early and defunct legal systems of the Middle East, including Asia Minor (Anatolia), that are not clearly identified with a particular modern jurisdiction, and including historico-legal works on ancient/early nations (civilizations) in the region
For the ancient/early periods of legal history of an individual jurisdiction, see the jurisdiction, e.g., India, China
For the colonial periods, see the jurisdiction
2 Bibliography
6 Periodicals
For periodicals consisting predominantly of articles on Roman law see KJA6
54 Encyclopedias. Law dictionaries
56 Terms and phrases. Vocabularies
Methodology see KL190
Auxiliary sciences
74 General works
75 Diplomatics
76 Paleography
(77) Papyrology
see KL190
78 Archaeology. Symbolism in law
80 Linguistics. Semantics
83 Seals. Flags. Insignia. Armory
Law and lawyers in literature
see subclasses PB - PZ
Biography of lawyers
122 Collective
124 Collections of portraits
135 Congresses. Seminars. By date of the congress or seminar
Ancient legal systems compared. General works
Class here general works on law development and comparisons of ancient legal systems in the region
Including compends, essays, festschriften, etc.
For works on the law development of national systems, see the appropriate region
For general works on the colonial periods, see the appropriate jurisdiction
For comparisons of particular subjects, see KL8015+
147 General
Particular systems compared
Including general works on groups of systems treated as a whole
Roman law compared with ancient legal systems see KJA168+
170 Babylonian and Egyptian

Ancient legal systems compared. General works
Particular systems compared -- Continued
172 Egyptian and Greek
174 Semitic legal systems (General)
175 Indo-Europeans
(176) Mosaic (Jewish) and other ancient legal systems (e.g. Babylonian law)
see KB201+
177 Other (not A-Z)
Philosophy, jurisprudence, and theory of law
see the appropriate place in KL700+
Sources
190 Studies on sources
Including history and methodology (e.g., epigraphy, papyrology, etc.)
For philological studies, see classes P, PJ, PK, and PL
Collections. Compilations. Lists of specimens. Selections
195 Comprehensive
197 Indexes. Chronologies. Concordances, etc.
Sources in cuneiform script
Class here collections and selections of legal sources in cuneiform characters on stone, metal, and other hard surfaces, and on clay tablets, of two or more ancient jurisdictions in the region
200 Texts
Including facsimiles and originals; and including typographical reproductions of the text entirely in ancient type, or transliterated in Roman characters
210 Translations (without edition of original text)
220 Indexes. Chronologies. Concordances, etc.
Sources in Egyptian script
Class here collections and selections of legal sources in hieroglyphic, hieratic, or demotic script on stone, ostraca, or papyri, of two or more ancient jurisdictions in the region
300 Texts
Including facsimiles and originals; and including typographical reproductions of the text entirely in ancient type, or transliterated in Roman characters
310 Translations (without edition of original text)
320 Indexes. Chronologies. Concordances, etc.
Sources in Mediterranean script
Class here collections of selections in ancient Mediterranean characters on hard surfaces, clay tablets, etc., of two or more ancient jurisdictions in the region

Sources
Collections. Compilations. Lists of specimens. Selections
Sources in Mediterranean script -- Continued
400 Texts
Including facsimiles and originals; and including typographical reproductions of the text entirely in ancient type, or transliterated in Roman characters
410 Translations (without edition of original text)
420 Indexes. Chronologies. Concordances, etc.
Individual sources or groups of sources
see the jurisdiction
Cuneiform laws (Keilschriftrecht) see KL200+
Mesopotamia. Assyro-Babylonian law
701-999 General (Table KL-KWX1)
1001-1299 Sumer (General) (Table KL-KWX1)
1601-1899 Assyria (General) (Table KL-KWX1 modified)
Sources
Individual sources and groups of sources. By period
1611 Early (to ca. 2000 B.C.)
1612 Later (to ca. 1780 B.C.). Age of Hammurabi
1613 Kassite period (to ca. 689 B.C.)
1614 Neo-Babylonian and Persian period (to ca. 100 B.C.)
2201-2499 Babylonia (General) (Table KL-KWX1 modified)
Sources
Individual sources and groups of sources. By period
2211 Early (to ca. 2000 B.C.)
2212 Later (to ca. 1780 B.C.). Age of Hammurabi
Royal statutes. Codes of law
2212.1 Code of Hammurabi
2213 Kassite period (to ca. 689 B.C.)
2214 Neo-Babylonian and Persian period (to ca. 100 B.C.)
2215.A-Z Sources of particular states and city states, territories, cities, and colonies. By state, city state, etc., A-Z
Including inscriptions (Stelae), clay tablets, papyri, etc. in ancient character
2215.A77 Assur
2215.A78 Arrapha
2215.B33 Babylon
2215.L36 Larsa
2215.N56 Nippur
2215.N89 Nuzi
Cretan law see KL4115.C74
2801-3099 Egypt (General) (Table KL-KWX1 modified)
Sources
Individual sources and groups of sources. By period
2811 Old Egyptian (Dynasties I-VIII, ca. 3400-2400 B.C.)
2812 Middle Egyptian (Dynasties IX-XVIII, ca. 2400-1350 B.C.)

Egypt (General)
Sources
Individual sources and groups of sources. By period -- Continued
2813 Late (New) Egyptian (Dynasties XIX-XXIV, ca. 1580-710 B.C.)
2814 Demotic (Dynasties XXV to end, ca. 700 B.C - 332 B.C.)
2814.5 Ptolemaic and Roman periods, ca. 332 B.C.-639 A.D.
2815.A-Z Particular states and city states, territories, cities, colonies, etc. A-Z
2815.A64 Aphrodito
3501-3799 Elam (General) (Table KL-KWX1)
4101-4399 Greek law (General) (Table KL-KWX1 modified)
Class here sources of, and treatises on, the ancient periods
Including treaties and interstate arbitration
For medieval Greece (Byzantine Empire), see class KJA
Sources
Individual sources and groups of sources. By period
4111 Archaic periods (to ca. 500 B.C.)
4112 Polis (city states) (to ca. 360 B.C.)
4113 Macedonian Hellenic periods (to ca. 146 B.C.)
4114 Roman period (to ca. 323 A.D.)
4115.A-Z Particular states and city states (Polis), territories, cities, colonies, etc., A-Z
Including peace treaties and treaties of territorial settlements e.g.
4115.A75 Athens
4115.C74 Crete (Mycenaean and Minoan civilizations)
4115.C97 Cyrene
4115.D4 Delphi
4115.E65 Ephesus
4115.E83 Euboea Island
4115.I84 Ithake
4115.M33 Macedonia
4115.M55 Milet
4115.S63 Sparta
4115.T54 Thebes
4115.T56 Thrace
Constitutional law
By period
4361 Archaic periods (to ca. 500 B.C.)
Including age of tyrants (ca. 560-510 B.C.)
Period of the Polis (city states) and Macedonian Hellenic Periods (to ca. 146 B.C.)
4361.3 General
4361.32.A-Z Particular city states, A-Z
4361.32.A75 Athens

Greek law (General)
Individual sources and groups of sources. By period
Constitutional law
By period
Period of the Polis (city states) and Macedonian Hellenic Periods (to ca. 146 B.C.)
Particular city states, A-Z -- Continued
4361.32.S63 Sparta
4361.5 Roman period (to ca. 323 A.D.)
4701-4999 Hittite law (General) (Table KL-KWX1)
5301-5599 Persia (General) (Table KL-KWX1 modified)
Sources
Individual sources or groups of sources. By period
5311 Median empire (640-558 B.C.)
5312 Persian empire (558-330 B.C.)
5313 Parthian empire (246 B.C.-226 A.D.)
5314 Sassanian empire (226-651 A.D.)
5315.A-Z Particular states and city states, territories, cities, colonies, etc., A-Z
Macedonian law see KL4115.M33
5901-6199 Phoenicia (General) (Table KL-KWX1 modified)
Sources
5915.A-Z Sources of particular states and city states, territories, cities, and colonies. By state, city state, etc., A-Z
5915.B33 Baalbek
5915.S37 Sarepta
5915.S54 Sidon
5915.T97 Tyre
Sumer see KL1001+
Thracian law see KL4115.T56
6901-7199 Syria. Asia Minor (Table KL-KWX1)
Including all Roman provinces in Asia unless otherwise provided for
For Jewish law in Palestine see KBM
8015-8299 Comparative works on particular subjects
Subarrange by Table KL-KWX1 using only numbers 15-299. Add number from table to KL8000
For comparisons of Roman law and another legal system, see KJA
For comparisons of legal systems not limited to a subject, see KL170+

Eurasia: Regional comparative and uniform law

9001-9999 General (Table KL-KWX2)

# EURASIA: TURKEY

Eurasia: Turkey
see KKX1+

Eurasia: Russia, Soviet Union

Class here Russian statutory and decree law and the socialist law of the Soviet Union to 1991

Class here also works on the law of two or more former Soviet republics, and works on the law of the Commonwealth of Independent States

For the law of a particular republic or state after independence, see the jurisdiction in KLB - KLW

0-4999 General (Table KL-KWX4 modified)

Add number in table to KLA0

History of law

85 Bibliography

86 Encyclopedias

86.2 Law dictionaries. Terms and phrases. Vocabularies

Including early works

Law dictionaries. Vocabularies. Terms and phrases see KLA86.2

Auxiliary sciences

87 General works

90 Paleography

92 Linguistics. Semantics

Archaeology. Folklife studies

94 General works

96.5.A-Z By place or nation, A-Z

100 Heraldry. Seals. Flags. Insignia

120 General works. Treatises

By period

Ancient/early to ca. 1480

Including Kievan Rus' (to 1237) and Mongol domination (Golden Horde) (to 1480)

For the history of a subject, see the subject

122 General works

Sources

For the sources of a territory or town, see the appropriate jurisdiction

123 Studies on sources

Including history and methodology (e.g. epigraphy, papyrology, etc.)

For philological studies, see class PG

124 Collections. Compilations. Selections

Class here comprehensive collections of legal sources in various vernacular scripts

125.A-Z Individual sources and groups of sources, A-Z

125.R87 Russkaia Pravda. Rus'ka pravda (Table K21)

Late medieval and imperial periods (to 1917)

Including Muscovy (to ca. 1689) and the Empire (to 1917)

130 General works

General
History of law
By period
Late medieval and imperial periods (to 1917) -- Continued
Sources
For sources of a territory or town, see the appropriate territory or town
132 Studies on sources
Including history and methodology, e.g. epigraphy, papyrology, etc.
For philological studies, see class P
134 Collections. Compilations. Selections
Class here comprehensive collections of legal sources
Individual sources and groups of sources
135 Sudebnik 1497 (code of law in Muscovy) (Table K20b)
136 Sudebnik 1550 (code of law, compiled 1550) (Table K20b)
136.3 Sudebnik 1589 (code of law, compiled 1589; Theodore I, 1584-1598) (Table K20b)
137 Ulozhenĭe Aleksi͡ei͡a Mikhaĭlovicha 1649 (code of Czar Alexis Mikhaĭlovich) (Table K20b)
Ukazy. Prikazy. Decrees. Orders
140 Ukaznye knigi prikazov
Including compilations of boyar duma decisions, and tsar's decrees from the second half of the 16th and first half of the 17th centuries in Muscovy (ukazy gosudarskii)
(140.2<date>) This number from Table KL-KWX4 is not used with subclass KLA
142 Stateinye knigi
Including books of laws and decrees between 1550 and 1649
The span 144-146.2 from Table KL-KWX4 is not used with subclass KLA
(144) This number not used
(146.2<date>) This number not used
Imennye ukazy. Decrees signed by the emperor (Imperial period)
148 General (two or more emperors/reigns)
149.A-Z By individual emperor/reign, A-Z
150 Individual ukazy
By emperor and date of ukaz
(150.2<date>) This number from Table KL-KWX4 is not used with subclass KLA
The Crown. Princes and rulers

General
History of law
By period
Late medieval and imperial periods (to 1917)
The Crown. Princes and rulers -- Continued
246 General (Table K11)
248.A-Z Special topics, A-Z
Dynastic succession see KLA248.S93
248.D95 Dynastic house rules
248.I45 Imperium
248.L36 Legal status of the Imperial house
248.R53 Rights and prerogatives
248.S93 Succession to the crown
474 Regional divisions. Subregions
Class here general works on the law or legal systems in force within a single subregion of Imperial Russia or the Soviet Union
For works on a particular subject, see the subject in KLA479+
475 Baltic states
475.5 Caucasus Region. Transcaucasia
476 Siberia
For Siberia (Provisional government, 1917-1918) see KLN1+
476.2 Northeastern Siberia
476.4 Eastern Siberia
476.6 Western Siberia
477 Central Asia
478 Far East
Dal'nevostochnaia Respublika (to 1922) see KLN293.55.D35
Public law
Class here works on all aspects of public law, including early works
The State
Centralization of powers see KLA2260
Rule of law
2020 General works
Socialist state. Democratic centralism
2025 General works
(2030) This number from Table KL-KWX4 not used with subclass KLA
(2035) This number from Table KL-KWX4 not used with subclass KLA

General -- Continued
Constitutional law
Class here works on constitutional law of the USSR and Russia beginning with the constitution of 1918
For works on the constitutional aspects of a subject, see the subject
For works on constitutional law prior to 1918 see KLA2101+
History see KLA2101+
2050 Constitutional reform. Criticism. Polemic
For works on a particular constitution, see the constitution
Sources
Including 19th century sources
For earlier sources see KLA123+
2064 Collections. Compilations. By date
Including imperial sources, federal and state (republic) sources and sources of several jurisdictions
2064.5<date> Individual constitutions
Arrange chronologically by appending the date of adoption to the number KLA2064.5 and deleting any trailing zeros
Subarrange each by Table K17
2064.51918 Constitution of July 5, 1918 (Table K17)
2064.51924 Constitution of January 31, 1924 (Table K17)
2064.51936 Constitution of December 15, 1936 (Table K17)
2064.51977 Constitution of October 7, 1977 (Table K17)
2064.6<date> Individual sources other than constitutions
Arrange chronologically by appending the date of adoption to the number KLA2064.6 and deleting any trailing zeros
2064.61905 Manifesto 1905, August 6
2064.61905a Manifesto 1905, October 17
2064.61905b Imperial decree 1905, December 11
Constitutional history
For individual constitutions see KLA2064.5<date>
By period
Ancient/early to ca. mid 19th century see KLA122+
From ca. mid 19th century to Soviet constitution (1918)
2101 General (Table K11)
Constitutional principles
Rule of law see KLA2020+
2130 Rulers, princes, dynasties
For dynastic rules and works on legal status and juristic personality of the imperial house (Romanov) see KLA248.A+
2140 Privileges of classes and particular groups (Table K11)

General
Constitutional law
Constitutional history
By period
From ca. mid 19th century to Soviet constitution (1918)
Constitutional principles -- Continued
2150 Privileges, prerogatives, and immunities of estates (Table K11)
Legislative power
2196 General (Table K11)
2196.5 State council
2197 State Duma
2197.3 First, 1906
2197.4 Second, 1907
2197.5 Third, 1907-1912
2197.6 Fourth, 1912-1917
The Czar
2198 General (Table K11)
2198.3.A-Z Special topics, A-Z
Dynastic rules see KLA248.D95
2198.3.P68 Powers and prerogatives of the Czar
Succession to the crown see KLA248.S93
2200.A-Z Special topics, A-Z
Class here works on topics not provided for elsewhere
For the history of a particular subject, see the subject
2200.S4 Serfdom. Emancipation of the serfs, 1861 (Table K12)
Modern constitutional principles
2240 Legitimacy
2250 Legality. Socialist legality
Rule of law see KLA2020+
2260 Centralization of powers. Democratic centralism
5001-9999 Historic (defunct) jurisdictions
For the Soviet Republics, see KLD-KLW

Eurasia: Russia (Federation, 1992- )
For the Russian S.F.S.R. (1917-1991) see KLN1+
0-4999 General (Table KL-KWX4)
Add number in table to KLB0
Autonomous republics
5002 Adygea (Table KL-KWX9)
5008 Bashkortostan (Table KL-KWX9)
5010 Buri͡atii͡a (Table KL-KWX9)
5012 Chechni͡a (Table KL-KWX9)
5014 Chuvashia (Table KL-KWX9)
5016 Dagestan (Table KL-KWX9)
5020 Gorno-Altay (Table KL-KWX9)
5025 Ingushetia (Table KL-KWX9)
5027 Kabardino-Balkarii͡a (Table KL-KWX9)
5029 Kalmykii͡a (Table KL-KWX9)
5032 Karachay-Cherkessia (Table KL-KWX9)
5035 Karelia (Table KL-KWX9)
5037 Khakasskai͡a respublika (Table KL-KWX9)
5040 Komi (Table KL-KWX9)
5044 Mari El (Table KL-KWX9)
5046 Mordovii͡a (Table KL-KWX9)
5050 North Ossetia (Table KL-KWX9)
5060 Sakha (Table KL-KWX9)
5064 Tatarstan (Table KL-KWX9)
5066 Tuva (Table KL-KWX9)
5070 Udmurtii͡a (Table KL-KWX9)
Cities, communities, etc. in Russia
Subarrange each by Table KL-KWX9
5100 Arkhangel'sk (Table KL-KWX9)
5145 Ekaterinburg (Table KL-KWX9)
5200 I͡Aroslavl' (Table KL-KWX9)
5210 Kaliningrad (Table KL-KWX9)
5215 Khabarovsk (Table KL-KWX9)
5320 Kirov (Table KL-KWX9)
Leningrad see KLB5700
5350 Moscow (Table KL-KWX9)
5370 Murmansk (Table KL-KWX9)
5375 Nizhniĭ Novgorod (Table KL-KWX9)
5376 Noril'sk (Table KL-KWX9)
5378 Novocherkassk (Table KL-KWX9)
5420 Pskov (Table KL-KWX9)
5450 Rostov-na-Donu (Table KL-KWX9)
5700 Saint Petersburg (Table KL-KWX9)
5710 Samara (Table KL-KWX9)
5720 Smolensk (Table KL-KWX9)
5750 Stavropol' (Table KL-KWX9)
5760 Syktyvkar (Table KL-KWX9)

Cities, communities, etc. in Russia -- Continued

5780 Vladimir (Table KL-KWX9)

5800 Vologda (Table KL-KWX9)

Eurasia: Armenian SSR (to 1991)

From 1921-1936 part of the Transcaucasian Federation (S.F.S.R.), and from 1936-1991 constituent republic of the U.S.S.R.

For Armenia (Republic) see KMF1+

1-489 General (Table KL-KWX5)

(490) Cities, communities, etc.

see KMF490.A+

Eurasia: Azerbaijan

Azerbaijan S.S.R., from 1921-1936, part of the Transcaucasian Federation (S.F.S.R.), and from 1936-1991 constituent republic of the U.S.S.R.

1-489 General (Table KL-KWX5 modified)

Administrative law

Administrative organization

Administrative and political divisions. Local government other than municipal

Including those of centralized national governments or federal governments

293.5.A-Z Oblasts and autonomous S.S.R.'s, A-Z

Including official gazettes, bylaws, statutory orders, regulations, and general works, as well as works on specific legal topics

293.5.N35 Nagorno-Karabakhskai͡a avtonomnai͡a oblast'

293.5.N36 Nakhichevanskai͡a A.S.S.R.

490.A-Z Cities, communities, etc., A-Z

Subarrange each by Table KL-KWX9a

490.B35 Baku (Table KL-KWX9a)

490.N35 Nakhichevan (Table KL-KWX9a)

Eurasia: Belarus (Republic)

Byelorussian S.S.R., from 1919-1991, constituent republic of the U.S.S.R.

Previously White Russian S.S.R.

1-489 General (Table KL-KWX5 modified)

Administrative law

Administrative organization

Administrative and political divisions. Local government other than municipal

Including those of centralized national governments or federal governments

293.5.A-Z Oblasts, A-Z

Including official gazettes, bylaws, statutory orders, regulations, and general works, as well as works on specific legal topics

293.5.B74 Brestskaia͡ oblast'

293.5.G66 Gomel'skaia͡ oblast'

293.5.G76 Grodnenskaia͡ oblast'

293.5.M56 Minskaia͡ oblast'

293.5.M65 Mogilevskaia͡ oblast'

293.5.V57 Vitebskaia͡ oblast'

490.A-Z Cities, communities, etc., A-Z

Subarrange each by Table KL-KWX9a

490.M55 Minsk (Table KL-KWX9a)

490.V57 Vitebsk (Table KL-KWX9a)

Eurasia: Bessarabia (to 1918)
see KLM492

Eurasia: Estonia
see KJS1+

Eurasia: Georgia (Republic)

Georgian S.S.R., from 1921-1936 part of the Transcaucasian Federation (S.F.S.R.), and from 1936-1991 constituent republic of the U.S.S.R.

1-489 General (Table KL-KWX5 modified)

Administrative law

Administrative organization

Administrative and political divisions. Local government other than municipal

Including those of centralized national governments or federal governments

293.5.A-Z Autonomous republics and oblasts, A-Z

Including official gazettes, bylaws, statutory orders, regulations, and general works, as well as works on specific legal topics

293.5.A33 Abkhazskai͡a A.S.S.R.

293.5.A48 Adzharskai͡a A.S.S.R.

293.5.I85 I͡Ugo-Osetinskai͡a avtonomnai͡a oblast'

490.A-Z Cities, communities, etc., A-Z

Subarrange each by Table KL-KWX9a

490.K87 Kutaisi (Table KL-KWX9a)

490.T35 Tbilisi (Table KL-KWX9a)

Eurasia: Karelo-Finskai͡a S.S.R.
see KLN293.5.K37

Eurasia: Krymskai͡a A.S.S.R.
see KLP2935.5.K78

Eurasia: Latvia
see KKI1+

Eurasia: Lithuania
see KKJ5001+

Eurasia: Moldavia (Principality)
see KLM494

Eurasia: Moldova

Moldavian S.S.R., until 1991 a constituent republic of the U.S.S.R.

For Moldavia (Romania), a region of eastern Romania see KKR4931+

For the historical feudal region of Bessarabia see KLM492

For the historical principality of Moldavia see KLM494

For Moldavian A.S.S.R. (Ukraine) see KLP4870

1-489 General (Table KL-KWX5)

492 Bessarabia (Table K11)

Class here works on the historical region of Bessarabia. From 1812-1918 part of Russia, and in 1918 incorporated into Romania except for the left bank of the Dniester, which later became the Moldavian A.S.S.R. (Ukraine). Ceded in 1940 to the U.S.S.R. and merged in 1947 with the Moldavian S.S.R.

494 Moldavia (Table K11)

Class here works on the historical principality of Moldavia

496.A-Z Cities,A-Z

496.B35 Balti (Table KL-KWX9a)

496.C45 Chisinau (Table KL-KWX9a)

496.T57 Tiraspol (Table KL-KWX9a)

Eurasia: Moldavian S.S.R.
see KLM1+

Eurasia: Russian S.F.S.R. (to 1991)
For Russia (Federation (1992- ) see KLB0+

1-489 General (Table KL-KWX5 modified)
Administrative law
Administrative organization
Administrative and political divisions. Local government other than municipal
Including those of centralized national governments or federal governments

293.5.A-Z Autonomous republics, A-Z
Including historic (defunct) jurisdictions, e.g. A.S.S.R. Nemt͡sev Povolzh'i͡a
Including official gazettes, bylaws, statutory orders, regulations, and general works, as well as works on specific legal topics

293.5.B37 Bashkirskai͡a A.S.S.R.
293.5.B87 Buriatskai͡a A.S.S.R.
293.5.C54 Checheno-Ingushskai͡a A.S.S.R.
293.5.C58 Chuvashskai͡a A.S.S.R.
293.5.D35 Dagestanskai͡a A.S.S.R.
293.5.I35 I͡Akutskai͡a A.S.S.R.
293.5.K33 Kabardino-Balkarsklai͡a A.S.S.R.
293.5.K35 Kalmyt͡skai͡a A.S.S.R.
293.5.K37 Karel'skai͡a A.S.S.R.
293.5.K66 Komi A.S.S.R.
293.5.M37 Mariiskai͡a A.S.S.R.
293.5.M67 Mordovskai͡a A.S.S.R.
293.5.N46 A.S.S.R. Nemt͡sev Povolzh'i͡a (Volga German A.S.S.R.)
293.5.S48 Severo-Osetinskai͡a A.S.S.R.
293.5.T37 Tatarskai͡a A.S.S.R.
293.5.T88 Tuvinskai͡a A.S.S.R.
293.5.U46 Udmurtskai͡a A.S.S.R.

293.55.A-Z Krais, A-Z
Including official gazettes, bylaws, statutory orders, regulations, and general works, as well as works on specific legal topics

293.55.A57 Altaĭskiĭ kraĭ
293.55.D35 Dal'nevostochnyi kraĭ
293.55.K53 Khabarovskiĭ kraĭ
293.55.K73 Krasnodarskiĭ kraĭ
293.55.K74 Krasnoiarskiĭ kraĭ
293.55.P75 Primorskiĭ kraĭ
293.55.S73 Stavropol'skiĭ kraĭ

General
Administrative law
Administrative organization
Administrative and political divisions. Local government other than municipal

293.57.A-Z Oblasts, A-Z

Including historic (defunct) jurisdictions, e.g., Evreiskai͡a a tonomnai͡a oblast'

Including official gazettes, bylaws, statutory orders, regulations, and general works, as well as works on specific legal topics

293.57.A68 Amurskai͡a oblast'
293.57.A75 Arkhangelskai͡a oblast'
293.57.A78 Astrakhanskai͡a oblast'
293.57.B45 Belgorodskai͡a oblast'
293.57.B75 Bri͡anskai͡a oblast'
293.57.C45 Cheli͡abinskai͡a oblast'
293.57.C58 Chitinskai͡a oblast'
293.57.E87 Evreiskai͡a avtibinbai͡a oblast' (Jewish autonomous oblast)
293.57.G67 Gor'kovskai͡a oblast'
293.57.I37 I͡Aroslavskai͡a oblast'
293.57.I75 Irkutskai͡a oblast'
293.57.I83 Ivanovskai͡a oblast'
293.57.K34 Kaliningradskai͡a oblast'
293.57.K35 Kalininskai͡a oblast'
293.57.K37 Kaluzhskai͡a oblast'
293.57.K38 Kamchatskai͡a oblast'
293.57.K46 Kemerovskai͡a oblast'
293.57.K57 Kirovskai͡a oblast'
293.57.K67 Kostromskai͡a oblast'
293.57.K85 Kurganskai͡a oblast'
293.57.K86 Kurskai͡a oblast'
293.57.K87 Kuĭbyshevskai͡a oblast'
293.57.L45 Leningradskai͡a oblast'
293.57.L57 Lipetskai͡a oblast'
293.57.M35 Magadanskai͡a oblast'
293.57.M77 Moscow (Oblast')
293.57.M87 Murmanskai͡a oblast'
293.57.N67 Novgorodskai͡a oblast'
293.57.N68 Novosibirskai͡a oblast'
293.57.O57 Omskai͡a oblast'
293.57.O74 Orenburgskai͡a oblast'
293.57.O75 Orlovskai͡a oblast'
293.57.P45 Penzenskai͡a oblast'
293.57.P47 Permskai͡a oblast'
293.57.P75 Pskovskai͡a oblast'

General
Administrative law
Administrative organization
Administrative and political divisions. Local government other than municipal
Oblasts, A-Z -- Continued

| | |
|---|---|
| 293.57.R53 | Rīazanskaīa oblast' |
| 293.57.R67 | Rostovskaīa oblast' |
| 293.57.S35 | Sakhalinskaīa oblast' |
| 293.57.S37 | Saratovskaīa oblast' |
| 293.57.S66 | Smolenskaīa oblast' |
| 293.57.S84 | Sverdlovskaīa oblast' |
| 293.57.T36 | Tambovskaīa oblast' |
| 293.57.T58 | Tīumenskaīa oblast' |
| 293.57.T66 | Tomskaīa oblast' |
| 293.57.T85 | Tul'skaīa oblast' |
| 293.57.U55 | Ul'īanovskaīa oblast' |
| 293.57.V53 | Vladimirskaīa oblast' |
| 293.57.V64 | Volgogradskaīa oblast' |
| 293.57.V65 | Volgogodskaīa oblast' |
| 293.57.V67 | Voronezhskaīa oblast' |

Cities, communities, etc. see KLB5100+

Eurasia: Ukraine (1919-1991)
From 1919 to 1991 a republic of the U.S.S.R.
For Ukraine (1991- ) see KKY1+

0-4890 General (Table KL-KWX4 modified)
Add number in table to KLP0
Administrative law
Administrative organization
Administrative and political divisions. Local government other than municipal
Including those of centralized national governments or federal governments

2935.5.A-Z Oblasts, A-Z
Including official gazettes, bylaws, statutory orders, regulations, and general works, as well as works on specific legal topics

2935.5.C45 Cherkasskai͡a oblast'
2935.5.C46 Chernigovskai͡a oblast'
2935.5.C47 Chernovitskai͡a oblast'
2935.5.D54 Dnepropetrovskai͡a oblast'
2935.5.D66 Donetskai͡a oblast'
2935.5.I73 Ivano-Frankovskai͡a oblast'
2935.5.K53 Khar'kovskai͡a oblast'
2935.5.K54 Khersonskai͡a oblast'
2935.5.K56 Khmel'nitskai͡a oblast'
2935.5.K64 Kievskai͡a oblast'
2935.5.K67 Kirovogradskai͡a oblast'
2935.5.K78 Krymskai͡a oblast'
2935.5.L86 L'vovskai͡a oblast'
2935.5.N55 Nikolaevskai͡a oblast'
2935.5.O44 Odesskai͡a oblast'
2935.5.P65 Poltavskai͡a oblast'
2935.5.R68 Rovenskai͡a oblast'
2935.5.S86 Sumskai͡a oblast'
2935.5.T47 Ternopolskai͡a oblast'
2935.5.V56 Vinnitskai͡a oblast'
2935.5.V65 Volynskai͡a oblast'
2935.5.V67 Voroshilovgradskai͡a oblast'
2935.5.Z35 Zakarpatskai͡a oblast'
2935.5.Z37 Zaporozhskai͡a oblast'
2935.5.Z55 Zhitomirskai͡a oblast'

4870 Moldavian A.S.S.R. (Table K11)
Cities, communities, etc. see KKY4984+

Eurasia: White Russian S.S.R.
see KLF1+

9001-9499 Eurasia: Zakavkazskai͡a Sot͡sialisticheskai͡a Federativnai͡a Sovetskai͡a Respublika (to 1936) (Table KL-KWX5)

Also known as Transcaucasian Federation (S.F.S.R.)

Was dissolved in 1936 when Azerbaijan, Armenia, and Georgia became constituent republics of the U.S.S.R.

1-499 Eurasia: Bukharskai͡a Narodnai͡a Sovetskai͡a Respublika (to 1924) (Table KL-KWX5)

Incorporated into the central Asian Soviet Republics of Uzbek S.S.R., Turkmen S.S.R., and Tajik S.S.R.

Eurasia: Kazakhstan

Kazakh S.S.R., from 1936-1991, a constituent republic of the central Asian U.S.S.R.

1-489 General (Table KL-KWX5 modified)

Administrative law

Administrative organization

Administrative and political divisions. Local government other than municipal

Including those of centralized national governments or federal governments

293.5.A-Z Oblasts, A-Z

Including official gazettes, bylaws, statutory orders, regulations, and general works, as well as works on specific legal topics

293.5.A57 Akt͡iubinskai͡a oblast'
293.5.A65 Alma-Atinskai͡a oblast'
293.5.C55 Chimkentskai͡a oblast'
293.5.D95 Dzhambulskai͡a oblast'
293.5.G87 Gur'evskai͡a oblast'
293.5.K37 Karagandinskai͡a oblast'
293.5.K67 Kokchetavskai͡a oblast'
293.5.K87 Kustanaiskai͡a oblast'
293.5.K98 Kzyl-Ordinskai͡a oblast'
293.5.M36 Mangyshlakskai͡a oblast'
293.5.P39 Pavlodarskai͡a oblast'
293.5.S46 Semipalatinskai͡a oblast'
293.5.S48 Severo-Kazakhstanskai͡a oblast'
293.5.T35 Taldy-Kurganskai͡a oblast'
293.5.T74 Tselinogradskai͡a oblast'
293.5.T87 Turgaiskai͡a oblast'
293.5.U73 Ural'skai͡a oblast'
293.5.V67 Vostochno-Kazakhstanskai͡a oblast'

490.A-Z Cities, communities, etc., A-Z

Subarrange each by Table KL-KWX9a

490.A55 Alma-Ata (Table KL-KWX9a)
490.K37 Karaganda (Table KL-KWX9a)

1001-1499 Eurasia: Khorezmskai͡a Sovetskai͡a Sot͡sialisticheskai͡a Respublika (to 1924) (Table KL-KWX5)

Incorporated into the central Asian Soviet Republics of Uzbek S.S.R., Turkmen S.S.R., and Kara-Kalpakskai͡a. A.O.

Eurasia: Kyrgyzstan

Kirgiz S.S.R., from 1936-1991 a constituent republic of the central Asian U.S.S.R.

1-489 General (Table KL-KWX5 modified)

Administrative law

Administrative organization

Administrative and political divisions. Local government other than municipal

Including those of centralized national governments or federal governments

293.5.A-Z Oblasts, A-Z

Including official gazettes, bylaws, statutory orders, regulations, and general works, as well as works on specific legal topics

293.5.I77 Issyk-Kul'skai͡a oblast'

293.5.N37 Narynskai͡a oblast'

293.5.O75 Oshskai͡a oblast'

293.5.T35 Talasskai͡a oblast'

490.A-Z Cities, communities, etc., A-Z

Subarrange each by Table KL-KWX9a

490.B57 Bishkek (Table KL-KWX9a)

Between 1926 and 1991 known as Frunze

(490.F78) Frunze

see KLS490.B57

490.O75 Osh (Table KL-KWX9a)

Eurasia: Tajikistan

Tadzhik S.S.R., from 1929-1991 a constituent republic of the central Asian U.S.S.R.

1-489 General (Table KL-KWX5 modified)

Administrative law

Administrative organization

Administrative and political divisions. Local government other than municipal

Including those of centralized national governments or federal governments

293.5.A-Z Oblasts, A-Z

Including official gazettes, bylaws, statutory orders, regulations, and general works, as well as works on specific legal topics

293.5.G67 Gorno-Badakhshanskai͡a avtonomnai͡a oblast'

293.5.K85 Kuli͡abskai͡a oblast'

293.5.K87 Kurgan-Ti͡ubinskai͡a oblast'

293.5.L46 Leninabadskai͡a oblast'

490.A-Z Cities, communities, etc., A-Z

Subarrange each by Table KL-KWX9a

490.D87 Dushanbe (Table KL-KWX9a)

490.L46 Leninabad (Table KL-KWX9a)

Eurasia: Turkmenistan

Turkmen S.S.R., from 1925-1991 a constituent republic of the central Asian U.S.S.R.

1-489 General (Table KL-KWX5 modified)

Administrative law

Administrative organization

Administrative and political divisions. Local government other than municipal

Including those of centralized national governments or federal governments

293.5.A-Z Oblasts, A-Z

Including official gazettes, bylaws, statutory orders, regulations, and general works, as well as works on specific legal topics

293.5.A75 Ashkhabadskai͡a oblast'

293.5.C53 Chardzhouskai͡a oblast'

293.5.K73 Krasnovodskai͡a oblast'

293.5.M37 Maryiskai͡a oblast'

293.5.T37 Tashauzskai͡a oblast'

490.A-Z Cities, communities, etc., A-Z

Subarrange each by Table KL-KWX9a

490.A75 Ashkhabad (Table KL-KWX9a)

490.C53 Chardzhov (Table KL-KWX9a)

Eurasia: Uzbekistan

Uzbek S.S.R., from 1925-1991 a constituent republic of the central Asian U.S.S.R.

1-489 General (Table KL-KWX5)

Administrative law

Administrative organization

Administrative and political divisions. Local government other than municipal

Including those of centralized national governments or federal governments

293.5.A-Z A.S.S.R., A-Z

Including official gazettes, bylaws, statutory orders, regulations, and general works, as well as works on specific legal topics

293.5.A64 Andizhanskai͡a oblast'

293.5.B86 Bukharskai͡a oblast'

293.5.D94 Dzhizakskai͡a oblast'

293.5.F47 Ferganskai͡a oblast'

293.5.K37 Kashkadar'inskai͡a oblast'

293.5.K46 Khorezmskai͡a oblast'

293.5.N36 Namanganskai͡aa oblast'

293.5.N38 Navoiĭskai͡a oblast'

293.5.S36 Samarkandskai͡a oblast'

293.5.S87 Surkhandar'inskai͡a oblast'

293.5.S96 Syrdar'inskai͡a oblast'

293.5.T37 Tashkentskai͡a oblast'

490.A-Z Cities, communities, etc., A-Z

Subarrange each by Table KL-KWX9a

490.S35 Samarkand (Table KL-KWX9a)

490.T37 Tashkent (Table KL-KWX9a)

1-999 Asia (General) (Table KL-KWX2)
86 History (General)
Law of indigenous peoples
88 General
88.5.A-Z Specific indigenous peoples, A-Z
88.5.B44 Bedouins
Cf. KQ9000.B44 Africa

Asia (Middle East. Southwest Asia): Regional comparative and uniform law

1-999 General (Table KL-KWX2 modified)

Legal systems compared

Including comparisons of law and legal systems of Arab countries and peoples (e.g. Bedouins), or Arab countries and other countries in the region

For comparisons of subjects, see the subject

112 General works

(114) Modern legal systems (civil or common law systems) compared with religious law (e.g., Islamic law)

see KB250

Regional divisions. Subregions

116 Asia Minor

117 Arabian Peninsula. (Arabia)

118 Persian Gulf States

119 Persian Gulf region

120 Palestine (Region)

For Palestine to 1948 see KMQ1001+

Asia (Middle East. Southwest Asia): Regional comparative and uniform law: Regional organization and integration

Class here works on treaties establishing, and laws governing, the organizations and their legal activity

Including subregional organizations

For official acts or legal measures on a particular subject, see the subject in KMC

For organizations governing a particular subject activity, see the subject in KMC (Table 2), e.g. Arab Iron and Steel Union KMC831.8.A83

10 General

51-99 League of Arab States, 1945 (Table KL-KWX3)

151-199 Majlis al-Wahdah al-Iqtis adiyah al-'Arabiyah. Council of Arab Economic Unity, 1964 (Table KL-KWX3)

451-499 Arab Common Market. Sūq al-ʻArabīyah al-Mushtarakah (Table KL-KWX3)

551-599 Arab Cooperation Council (Table KL-KWX3)

751-799 Gulf Cooperation Council, 1981 (Table KL-KWX3)

801-849 Central Treaty Organization (CENTO) (to 1979) (Table KL-KWX3)

Asia (Middle East. Southwest Asia): Armenia (Republic)

From 1921-1936 part of the Transcaucasian Federation (S.F.S.R.), and from 1936-1991 constituent republic of the U.S.S.R.

For Armenian SSR see KLD1+

1-489 General (Table KL-KWX5)

490.A-Z Cities, A-Z

Subarrange each by Table KL-KWX9a

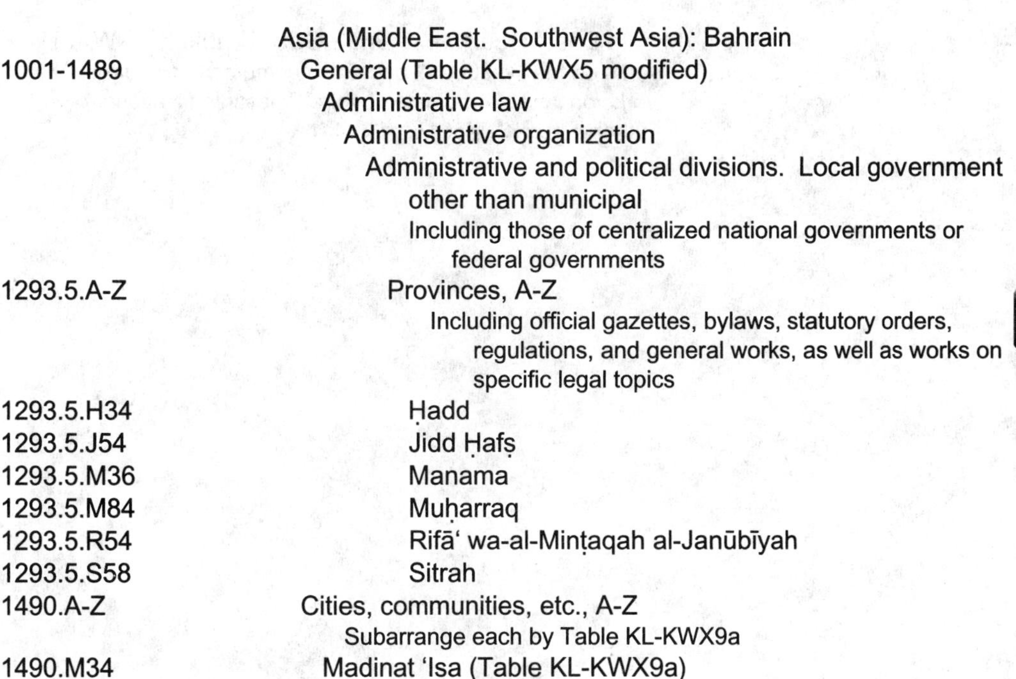

Asia (Middle East. Southwest Asia): Bahrain

1001-1489 General (Table KL-KWX5 modified)

Administrative law

Administrative organization

Administrative and political divisions. Local government other than municipal

Including those of centralized national governments or federal governments

1293.5.A-Z Provinces, A-Z

Including official gazettes, bylaws, statutory orders, regulations, and general works, as well as works on specific legal topics

1293.5.H34 Ḥadd

1293.5.J54 Jidd Ḥafṣ

1293.5.M36 Manama

1293.5.M84 Muḥarraq

1293.5.R54 Rifāʻ wa-al-Minṭaqah al-Janūbīyah

1293.5.S58 Sitrah

1490.A-Z Cities, communities, etc., A-Z

Subarrange each by Table KL-KWX9a

1490.M34 Madinat ʻIsa (Table KL-KWX9a)

1490.M36 Manama (Table KL-KWX9a)

1-489 Asia (Middle East. Southwest Asia): Gaza (Table KL-KWX5)

For works on the West Bank and Gaza combined, including works on laws promulgated by the Palestinian National Authority see KMM501+

Asia (Middle East. Southwest Asia): Iran

0-4890 General (Table KL-KWX4 modified)

Add number in table to KMH0

Administrative law

Administrative organization

Administrative and political divisions. Local government other than municipal

Including those of centralized national governments or federal governments

2935.A-Z Provinces (Ostāns), A-Z

Including official gazettes, bylaws, statutory orders, regulations, and general works, as well as works on specific legal topics

2935.A93 Āzarbāyjān-i Bākhtarī

2935.A94 Āzarbāyjān-i Khavari

2935.B34 Bākhtarān

2935.B69 Boyer Ahmadi and Kohkiluyeh (Bovīr Aḥmadī va Kohkīlūyeh)

2935.B87 Būshehr

2935.C53 Chahār Mahal and Bakhtiāri (Chahār Maḥall va Bakhtiārī)

2935.F38 Fārs

2935.G45 Gīlān

2935.H36 Hamadān

2935.H87 Hurmuzgān

2935.I53 Ilām and Poshtkuh

2935.I74 Iṣfahān

2935.K57 Khurasan

2935.K58 Khūzestān

2935.K59 Kirmān

2935.K67 Kordestān

2935.L87 Luristān

2935.M37 Markazī

2935.M39 Māzandarān

2935.S46 Semnān

2935.S57 Sīstān va Balūchestān

2935.T45 Tehran

2935.Y39 Yazd

2935.Z36 Zanjān

Cities, communities, etc.

4980 Ahvāz (Table KL-KWX9)

4981 Iṣfahān (Table KL-KWX9)

4982 Kermānshāh (Table KL-KWX9)

4983 Mashhad (Table KL-KWX9)

4985 Shīrāz (Table KL-KWX9)

4986 Tabrīz (Table KL-KWX9)

4987 Tehran (Table KL-KWX9)

Cities, communities, etc. -- Continued
4988 Zāhedān (Table KL-KWX9)
4990.A-Z Other cities, A-Z
Subarrange each by Table KL-KWX9a
4990.B36 Bandar Abbas (Table KL-KWX9a)
4990.K57 Kirmān (Table KL-KWX9a)
4990.R37 Rasht (Table KL-KWX9a)
4990.R49 Rezayeh (Table KL-KWX9a)
4990.S36 Sanandaj (Table KL-KWX9a)
4990.S37 Sari (Table KL-KWX9a)

Asia (Middle East. Southwest Asia): Iraq

0-4890 General (Table KL-KWX4 modified)

Add number in table to KMJ0

Administrative law

Administrative organization

Administrative and political divisions. Local government other than municipal

Including those of centralized national governments or federal governments

2935.A-Z Provinces (Muḥāfaẓāt or Alwiyah), A-Z

Including official gazettes, bylaws, statutory orders, regulations, and general works, as well as works on specific legal topics

2935.A52 Anbār

2935.B32 Bābil

2935.B33 Baghdād

2935.B38 Baṣrah

2935.D35 Dahūk

2935.D55 Dhī Qār

2935.D58 Diyāla

2935.I72 Irbīl

2935.K37 Karbalā'

2935.M38 Maysān

2935.M88 Muthanná

2935.N35 Najaf

2935.N55 Nīnawá

2935.Q33 Qādisīyah

2935.S35 Ṣalāḥ al-Dīn

2935.S94 Sulaymānīyah

2935.T35 Ta'mīm

2935.W38 Wāsit

4881-4979 Kurdistan (Table KL-KWX8)

Cities

4980 Baghdad (Table KL-KWX9)

4981 Baṣrah (Table KL-KWX9)

4982 Hillah (Table KL-KWX9)

4983 Irbīl (Table KL-KWX9)

4984 Karbalā' (Table KL-KWX9)

4985 Kirkuk (Table KL-KWX9)

4986 Mosul (Table KL-KWX9)

4987 Najaf (Table KL-KWX9)

4988 Sulaymānīyah (Table KL-KWX9)

4990.A-Z Other cities, A-Z

Subarrange each by Table KL-KWX9a

Asia (Middle East. Southwest Asia): Israel

For Palestine after 1948 see KMC120

For Palestine to 1948 see KMQ1001+

1-4890 General (Table KL-KWX6 modified)

Administrative and political divisions. Local government other than municipal

2315.A-Z Districts (Mehozot), A-Z

Including official gazettes, bylaws, statutory orders, regulations, and general works, as well as works on specific legal topics

2315.D37 Darom

2315.H35 Haifa

2315.M47 Merkaz

2315.T35 Tel Aviv

2315.T73 Tsafon

Cities, communities, etc., A-Z

4980 Beersheba (Table KL-KWX9)

4981 Haifa (Table KL-KWX9)

Jerusalem see KML1+

4983 Nazareth (Table KL-KWX9)

4985 Ramla (Table KL-KWX9)

4987 Tel Aviv (Table KL-KWX9)

4990.A-Z Other cities, A-Z

Subarrange each by Table KL-KWX9a

1-490 Asia (Middle East. Southwest Asia): Jerusalem (Table KL-KWX5)

Asia (Middle East. Southwest Asia): Jordan

1-489 General (Table KL-KWX5 modified)

Administrative law

Administrative organization

Administrative and political divisions. Local government other than municipal

Including those of centralized national governments or federal governments

293.5.A-Z Provinces (Muḥāfaẓāt), A-Z

Including official gazettes, bylaws, statutory orders, regulations, and general works, as well as works on specific legal topics

293.5.A55 Amman

293.5.B34 Balqā'

293.5.I72 Irbid

293.5.K37 Karak

293.5.M32 Ma'ān

293.5.Z37 Zarqā'

490.A-Z Cities, communities, etc., A-Z

Subarrange each by Table KL-KWX9a

490.A66 Amman (Table KL-KWX9a)

490.A73 'Aqabah (Table KL-KWX9a)

490.I73 Irbid (Table KL-KWX9a)

490.K37 Karak (Table KL-KWX9a)

490.S36 Salṭ (Table KL-KWX9a)

490.Z37 Zarqā' (Table KL-KWX9a)

Asia (Middle East. Southwest Asia): West Bank
Palestinian territory governed by Jordan from 1948 to 1967
Class here works on the West Bank, and on the West Bank and Gaza combined, including works on laws promulgated by the National Palestinian Authority
For works limited to Gaza see KMG1+

501-989 General (Table KL-KWX5 modified)
Administrative law
Administrative organization
Administrative and political divisions. Local government other than municipal
Including those of centralized national governments or federal governments

793.5.A-Z Administrative divisions (Muḥāfaẓāt), A-Z
Including official gazettes, bylaws, statutory orders, regulations, and general works, as well as works on specific legal topics

793.5.K45 Khalil

793.5.N32 Nablus

Cities, communities, etc.

990 Bi'r Zayt (Table KL-KWX9)

Jerusalem see KML1+

991 Kahlil (Table KL-KWX9)

992 Nablus (Table KL-KWX9)

993 Ram Allah (Table KL-KWX9)

994 Tul Karim (Table KL-KWX9)

Asia (Middle East. Southwest Asia): Kuwait

1-499 General (Table KL-KWX5 modified)

Administrative law

Administrative organization

Administrative and political divisions. Local government other than municipal

Including those of centralized national governments or federal governments

293.5.A-Z Administrative divisions (Baladīyāt), A-Z

Including official gazettes, bylaws, statutory orders, regulations, and general works, as well as works on specific legal topics

293.5.A56 Aḥmadī

293.5.H38 Ḥawallī

293.5.J35 Jahrā'

293.5.K88 Kuwait

Asia (Middle East. Southwest Asia): Lebanon

1-489 General (Table KL-KWX5 modified)

Administrative law

Administrative organization

Administrative and political divisions. Local government other than municipal

Including those of centralized national governments or federal governments

293.5.A-Z Provinces (Muḥāfaẓāt), A-Z

Including official gazettes, bylaws, statutory orders, regulations, and general works, as well as works on specific legal topics

293.5.B44 Beirut

293.5.B57 Biqāʻ

293.5.J32 Jabal Lubnan

293.5.J35 Janub

293.5.N33 Nabaṭīyah

293.5.S45 Shamal

490.A-Z Cities, A-Z

Subarrange each by Table KL-KWX9a

490.B35 Baʻlabakk (Table KL-KWX9a)

490.B45 Beirut (Table KL-KWX9a)

490.S54 Sidon (Table KL-KWX9a)

490.S87 Ṣūr (Table KL-KWX9a)

490.T75 Tripoli (Table KL-KWX9a)

490.Z34 Zaḥlah (Table KL-KWX9a)

Asia (Middle East. Southwest Asia): Oman

1-489 General (Table KL-KWX5 modified)

Administrative law

Administrative organization

Administrative and political divisions. Local government other than municipal

Including those of centralized national governments or federal governments

293.5.A-Z Provinces (Alwiyah), A-Z

Including official gazettes, bylaws, statutory orders, regulations, and general works, as well as works on specific legal topics

293.5.B38 Bāṭinah

293.5.D46 Dhofar

293.5.H34 Ḥajar al-Gharbī

293.5.H35 Ḥajar al-Sharqī

293.5.J35 Ja'lān

293.5.M87 Muscat

293.5.R88 Ru'ūs al-Jibāl

293.5.S53 Sharqīyah

293.5.U53 'Umān al-Wusṭa

293.5.Z35 Zāhirah

490.A-Z Cities, communities, etc., A-Z

Subarrange each by Table KL-KWX9a

490.M87 Muscat (Table KL-KWX9a)

490.N59 Nizwa (Nazwa) (Table KL-KWX9a)

490.R37 Rasut (Table KL-KWX9a)

490.S35 Ṣalālah (Table KL-KWX9a)

490.S85 Ṣuḥar (Table KL-KWX9a)

1001-1499 Asia (Middle East. Southwest Asia): Palestine (to 1948) (Table KL-KWX5)

For Palestine after 1948 see KMC120

Cf. KMG1+ Gaza

Cf. KMK1+ Israel

Cf. KMM501+ West Bank

Asia (Middle East. Southwest Asia): Qatar

1-489 General (Table KL-KWX5)

490.A-Z Cities, communities, etc., A-Z

Subarrange each by Table KL-KWX9a

490.D38 Dawḥah (Table KL-KWX9a)

490.D43 Dhakhīrah (Table KL-KWX9a)

490.M34 Madīnat al-Shamāl (Table KL-KWX9a)

490.R88 Ruways (Table KL-KWX9a)

490.U53 Umm Bāb (Table KL-KWX9a)

490.U56 Umm Saʻīd (Table KL-KWX9a)

490.U57 Umm Ṣilāl ʻAlī (Table KL-KWX9a)

490.W35 Wakrah (Table KL-KWX9a)

Asia (Middle East. Southwest Asia): Saudi Arabia

0-4890 General (Table KL-KWX4 modified)

Add number in table to KMT0

Administrative law

Administrative and political divisions. Local government other than municipal

Including those of centralized national governments or federal governments

2935.A-Z Provinces (Manāṭiq), A-Z

Including official gazettes, bylaws, statutory orders, regulations, and general works, as well as works on specific legal topics

2935.A45 ʻAfīf
2935.A85 ʻAsīr
2935.B34 Bāḥah
2935.B57 Bīshah
2935.H35 Ḥā'il
2935.H84 Hudūd al-Shamālīyah
2935.J38 Jawf
2935.J58 Jīzān
2935.K43 Khāsirah
2935.M42 Mecca
2935.M44 Medina
2935.M85 Muqāṭaʻah al-Shamālīyah
2935.N35 Najrān
2935.Q37 Qasīm
2935.Q87 Qurayyāt
2935.R35 Rānyah
2935.R58 Riyadh
2935.S53 Sharqīyah

Cities, communities, etc.

4980 Abhā (Table KL-KWX9)
4981 Dammān (Table KL-KWX9)
4982 Dhahran (Table KL-KWX9)
4983 Ḥā'il (Table KL-KWX9)
4985 Jiddah (Table KL-KWX9)
4986 Mecca (Table KL-KWX9)
4987 Medina (Table KL-KWX9)
4988 Riyadh (Table KL-KWX9)
4989 Ṭā'if (Table KL-KWX9)

4990.A-Z Other cities, A-Z

Subarrange each by Table KL-KWX9a

4990.A63 Anaiza (Table KL-KWX9a)
4990.B87 Buraida (Bū Raida) (Table KL-KWX9a)
4990.H64 Hofuf (Table KL-KWX9a)
4990.J38 Jawf (Table KL-KWX9a)

Other cities, A-Z -- Continued

4990.K46 Khobar (Khubār) (Table KL-KWX9a)

4990.S35 Sakata (Table KL-KWX9a)

Asia (Middle East. Southwest Asia): Southern Yemen
see KMY1+

Asia (Middle East. Southwest Asia): Syria

1-489 General (Table KL-KWX5 modified)

Administrative law

Administrative organization

Administrative and political divisions. Local government other than municipal

Including those of centralized national governments or federal governments

293.5.A-Z Provinces (Muḥāfaẓāt), A-Z

Including official gazettes, bylaws, statutory orders, regulations, and general works, as well as works on specific legal topics

293.5.A54 Aleppo

293.5.D36 Damascus

293.5.D37 Dar'ā

293.5.D38 Dayr al-Zawr

293.5.H36 Ḥamāh

293.5.H37 Ḥasakah

293.5.H56 Ḥimṣ

293.5.I45 Idlib

293.5.L37 Latakia

293.5.Q86 Qunaytirah

293.5.R36 Raqqah

293.5.S88 Suwaydā'

293.5.T37 Ṭarṭūs

490.A-Z Cities, communities, etc., A-Z

Subarrange each by Table KL-KWX9a

490.A54 Aleppo (Table KL-KWX9a)

490.D36 Damascus (Table KL-KWX9a)

490.D38 Dayr al-Zawr (Table KL-KWX9a)

490.H36 Ḥamāh (Table KL-KWX9a)

490.H56 Ḥimṣ (Table KL-KWX9a)

490.L38 Latakia (Table KL-KWX9a)

| | |
|---|---|
| | Asia (Middle East. Southwest Asia): United Arab Emirates |
| 0-4999 | General (Table KL-KWX4) |
| | Add number in table to KMV0 |
| | Emirates |
| 5051-5149 | Abū Zaby (Table KL-KWX8) |
| 5251-5349 | ʻAjmān (Table KL-KWX8) |
| 5451-5549 | Dubayy (Table KL-KWX8) |
| 5651-5749 | Fujayrah (Table KL-KWX8) |
| 5851-5949 | Ra's al-Khaymah (Table KL-KWX8) |
| 6051-6149 | Shāriqah (Table KL-KWX8) |
| 6251-6349 | Umm al-Qaywayn (Table KL-KWX8) |
| | Cities, communities, etc. |
| 9850 | Abū Zaby (Table KL-KWX9) |
| 9851 | ʻAjmām (Table KL-KWX9) |
| 9852 | ʻAyn (Table KL-KWX9) |
| 9853 | Dubayy (Table KL-KWX9) |
| 9854 | Fujayrah (Table KL-KWX9) |
| 9855 | Jumayrah (Table KL-KWX9) |
| 9856 | Ra's al-Khaymah (Table KL-KWX9) |
| 9857 | Shāriqah (Table KL-KWX9) |
| 9858 | Umm al-Qaywayn (Table KL-KWX9) |
| 9870.A-Z | Other cities, A-Z |
| | Subarrange each by Table KL-KWX9a |

Asia (Middle East. Southwest Asia): Yemen
Including People's Democratic Republic of Yemen after 1990
1001-1489 General (Table KL-KWX5 modified)
Administrative law
Administrative organization
Administrative and political divisions. Local government other than municipal
Including those of centralized national governments or federal governments
1293.5.A-Z Provinces (Muḥāfaẓāt, Alwiyah), A-Z
Including official gazettes, bylaws, statutory orders, regulations, and general works, as well as works on specific legal topics
1293.5.A38 Abyan
1293.5.A43 ‘Adan
1293.5.B38 Bayḍā’
1293.5.D43 Dhamār
1293.5.H34 Ḥaḍramawt
1293.5.H35 Ḥajjah
1293.5.H84 Ḥudayadah
1293.5.I33 Ibb
1293.5.J38 Jawf
1293.5.L34 Laḥij
1293.5.M34 Mahrah
1293.5.M35 Maḥwīt
1293.5.M37 Ma’rib
1293.5.S34 Ṣa‘dah
1293.5.S36 Ṣan‘ā’
1293.5.S43 Shabwah
1293.5.T35 Ta‘izz
Cities, communities, etc.
1500 Abyan (Table KL-KWX9)
1502 Aden (Table KL-KWX9)
1504 Bayḍā’ (Table KL-KWX9)
1506 Dhamār (Table KL-KWX9)
1508 Ḥajjah (Table KL-KWX9)
1509 Ḥudaydah (Table KL-KWX9)
1512 Ibb (Table KL-KWX9)
1515 Mukalla (Table KL-KWX9)
1516 Mukhā (Table KL-KWX9)
1517 Mulla (Table KL-KWX9)
1518 Ridā‘ (Table KL-KWX9)
1520 Ṣa‘dah (Table KL-KWX9)
1522 Ṣan‘ā’ (Table KL-KWX9)
1524 Ṣheikh Othman (Table KL-KWX9)
1526 Ta‘izz (Table KL-KWX9)

Asia (Middle East. Southwest Asia): Yemen (People's Democratic Republic) (to 1990)

Previously Southern Yemen

1-489 General (Table KL-KWX5 modified)

Administrative law

Administrative organization

Administrative and political divisions. Local government other than municipal

Including those of centralized national governments or federal governments

293.5.A-Z Provinces (Muḥāfaẓāt), A-Z

Including official gazettes, bylaws, statutory orders, regulations, and general works, as well as works on specific legal topics

293.5.A38 Abyan

293.5.A43 ʻAdan

293.5.H34 Ḥaḍramawt

293.5.L34 Laḥij

293.5.M34 Mahrah

293.5.S43 Shabwah

Cities, communities, etc. see KMX1500+

Asia (South Asia. Southeast Asia. East Asia): Regional comparative and uniform law

1-999 General (Table KL-KWX2)

116 Regional divisions. Subregions

For Soviet Central Asia, Soviet Far East see KLA0+

Asia (South Asia. Southeast Asia. East Asia): Regional organization and integration

Class here works on treaties establishing, and laws governing, the organization and their organs, and works on their legal activity

Including subregional organizations

For official acts or legal measures on a particular subject, see the subject in KNC

For organizations governing a particular subject or activity, see the subject in KNC



10 General works

151-199 ASEAN (Table KL-KWX3)

351-399 COLOMBO Plan (Table KL-KWX3)

451-499 South Asian Association for Regional Cooperation (SAARC) (Table KL-KWX3)

Asia (South Asia. Southeast Asia. East Asia): Afghanistan

0-4890 General (Table KL-KWX4 modified)

Add number in table to KNF0

Administrative law

Administrative organization

Administrative and political divisions. Local government other than municipal

Including those of centralized national governments or federal governments

2935.A-Z Provinces (Valāyāt), A-Z

Including official gazettes, bylaws, statutory orders, regulations, and general works, as well as works on specific legal topics

2935.B34 Badakhshān
2935.B35 Bādghīs
2935.B36 Baghlān
2935.B37 Balkh
2935.B38 Bāmīān
2935.F37 Farāh
2935.F38 Faryāb
2935.G53 Ghaznī
2935.G56 Ghowr
2935.H45 Helmand
2935.H47 Herāt
2935.J68 Jowzjān
2935.K33 Kabul
2935.K66 Kondūz
2935.L35 Laghmān
2935.L68 Lowgar
2935.N36 Nangarhār
2935.N56 Nimrūz
2935.O78 Orūzgān
2935.P35 Paktīā
2935.P37 Parvān
2935.Q36 Qandahār
2935.S36 Samangān
2935.S38 Sar-e Pol
2935.T35 Takhār
2935.V37 Vardak
2935.Z33 Zābol

Cities, communities, etc.

4982 Baghlan (Table KL-KWX9)
4983 Charikar (Table KL-KWX9)
4984 Cheghcheran (Table KL-KWX9)
4985 Faizabad (Table KL-KWX9)
4986 Gardez (Table KL-KWX9)

Cities, communities, etc. -- Continued

4987 Herat (Table KL-KWX9)

4988 Jalalabad (Table KL-KWX9)

4989 Kabul (Table KL-KWX9)

4990.A-Z Other cities, A-Z

Subarrange each by Table KL-KWX9a

4990.K36 Kandahar (Table KL-KWX9a)

4990.M39 Mazār-i-Sharīf (Table KL-KWX9a)

4990.M48 Meterlam (Table KL-KWX9a)

4990.P85 Pulialam (Table KL-KWX9a)

4990.Q35 Qala-i-nau (Table KL-KWX9a)

Qandahār see KNF4990.K36

4990.S54 Sherberghan (Table KL-KWX9a)

4990.T35 Taluqan (Table KL-KWX9a)

4990.U53 Uiback (Table KL-KWX9a)

## ASIA (SOUTH ASIA. SOUTHEAST ASIA. EAST ASIA): ANNAM

Asia (South Asia. Southeast Asia. East Asia): Annam
see KNV1+ ; KPV1+

Asia (South Asia. Southeast Asia. East Asia): Bangladesh

1-4890 General (Table KL-KWX6 modified)

Administrative and political divisions. Local government other than municipal

2315.A-Z Administrative districts, A-Z

Including official gazettes, bylaws, statutory orders, regulations, and general works, as well as works on specific legal topics

2315.B34 Bāgerhāt District
2315.B36 Bāndarban District
2315.B38 Barisāl District
2315.B46 Bhola District
2315.B64 Bogra District
2315.B67 Borguna District
2315.B73 Brāhmanbāria District
2315.C43 Chāndpur District
2315.C44 Chapai Nawābganj District
2315.C45 Chattagram District
2315.C48 Chuādānga District
2315.C66 Comilla District
2315.C69 Cox's Bāzār District
2315.D43 Dhaka District
2315.D56 Dinājpur District
2315.F37 Farīdpur District
2315.F46 Feni District
2315.G35 Gaibandha District
2315.G39 Gāzipur District
2315.G66 Gopālganj District
2315.H33 Habiganj District
2315.J35 Jaipurhāt District
2315.J36 Jamālpur District
2315.J47 Jessore District
2315.J53 Jhālakāti District
2315.J55 Jhenaidah District
2315.K53 Khagrāchari District
2315.K58 Khulna District
2315.K66 Kishorganj District
2315.K87 Kurīgrām District
2315.K88 Kushtia District
2315.L35 Laksmipur District
2315.L36 Lalmonirhat District
2315.M34 Mādārīpur District
2315.M35 Māgura District
2315.M36 Mānikganj District
2315.M44 Meherpur District
2315.M68 Moulavibāzār District

General
Administrative and political divisions. Local government other than municipal
Administrative districts, A-Z -- Continued

2315.M86 Munshiganj District
2315.M95 Mymensingh District
2315.N34 Naogaon District
2315.N35 Narail District
2315.N36 Nārāyanganj District
2315.N37 Narsingdi District
2315.N38 Nator District
2315.N47 Netrakona District
2315.N55 Nilphāmāri District
2315.N63 Noākhāli District
2315.P33 Pābna District
2315.P36 Panchāgar District
2315.P37 Parbattya Chattagram District
2315.P38 Patuākhāli District
2315.P57 Pirojpur District
2315.R34 Rājbāri District
2315.R35 Rājshāhi District
2315.R36 Rangpur District
2315.S37 Sātkhira District
2315.S43 Shariyatpur District
2315.S47 Sherpur District
2315.S57 Sirājganj District
2315.S86 Sunamganj District
2315.S94 Sylhet District
2315.T34 Tangail District
2315.T43 Thākurgaon District
4980-4989 Cities, communities, etc.
4980 Barisal (Table KL-KWX9)
4982 Chittagong (Table KL-KWX9)
4985 Dhaka (Table KL-KWX9)
4987 Khulna (Table KL-KWX9)
4988 Narayanganj (Table KL-KWX9)
4989 Rajshahi (Table KL-KWX9)
4990.A-Z Other cities, A-Z
Subarrange each by Table KL-KWX9a

Asia (South Asia. Southeast Asia. East Asia): Bhutan

1-489 General (Table KL-KWX7 modified)

Administrative and political divisions. Local government other than municipal

231.5.A-Z Districts, A-Z

Including official gazettes, bylaws, statutory orders, regulations, and general works, as well as works on specific legal topics

490.A-Z Cities, communities, etc., A-Z

Subarrange each by Table KL-KWX9a

490.T55 Thimphu (Table KL-KWX9a)

Asia (South Asia. Southeast Asia. East Asia): Brunei

1-489 General (Table KL-KWX7 modified)

Administrative and political divisions. Local government other than municipal

231.5.A-Z Districts, A-Z

Including official gazettes, bylaws, statutory orders, regulations, and general works, as well as works on specific legal topics

231.5.B45 Belait

231.5.B78 Brunei and Muara

231.5.T46 Temburong

231.5.T88 Tutong

490.A-Z Cities, communities, etc., A-Z

Subarrange each by Table KL-KWX9a

490.B36 Bandar Seri Begawan (Table KL-KWX9a)

Asia (South Asia. Southeast Asia. East Asia): Burma

1-4890 General (Table KL-KWX6 modified)

Administrative and political divisions. Local government other than municipal

2315.A-Z States and divisions, A-Z

Including official gazettes, bylaws, statutory orders, regulations, and general works, as well as works on specific legal topics

Arakan State see KNL2315.R35

2315.C45 Chin State

2315.I77 Irrawaddy Division

2315.K33 Kachin State

2315.K36 Karan State

2315.K38 Kawthule State

2315.K39 Kayah State

2315.M35 Magwe Division

2315.M36 Mandalay

2315.M66 Mon State

2315.P45 Pegu District

2315.R35 Rakhine State

2315.R36 Rangoon Division

2315.S35 Sagaing

2315.S43 Shan State

2315.T46 Tenasserim Division

Cities, communities, etc.

Akyab see KNL4989

4981 Bassein (Table KL-KWX9)

4982 Henzada (Table KL-KWX9)

4983 Mandalay (Table KL-KWX9)

4984 Moulmein (Table KL-KWX9)

4985 Myingyan (Table KL-KWX9)

4986 Pegu (Table KL-KWX9)

4987 Prome (Table KL-KWX9)

4988 Rangoon (Table KL-KWX9)

4989 Sittwe (Table KL-KWX9)

4990.A-Z Other cities, A-Z

Subarrange each by Table KL-KWX9a

Asia (South Asia. Southeast Asia. East Asia): Cambodia

0-4890 General (Table KL-KWX4 modified)

Add number in table to KNM0

Administrative law

Administrative organization

Administrative and political divisions. Local government other than municipal

Including those of centralized national governments or federal governments

2935.A-Z Provinces (Khêt), A-Z

Including official gazettes, bylaws, statutory orders, regulations, and general works, as well as works on specific legal topics

2935.B38 Khêt Batdâmbâng
2935.K36 Khêt Kâmpóng Cham
2935.K37 Khêt Kâmpóng Chhnăng
2935.K38 Khêt Kâmpóng Spóè
2935.K385 Khêt Kâmpóng Thun
2935.K39 Khêt Kâmpôt
2935.K395 Khêt Kândal
2935.K42 Khêt Kaôh Kŏng
2935.K43 Khêt Krâchéh
2935.M66 Khêt Môndól Kiri
2935.P68 Khêt Poŭthĭsăt
2935.P74 Khêt Prey Vêng
2935.S54 Khêt Siĕmréab-O-Târ Méachey
2935.S86 Khêt Stœng Trêng
2935.S93 Khêt Svay Riĕng
2935.T35 Khêt Takêv

Cities, communities, etc.

4983 Battambang (Table KL-KWX9)
4987 Phnom Penh (Table KL-KWX9)
4990.A-Z Other cities, A-Z

Subarrange each by Table KL-KWX9a

Asia (South Asia. Southeast Asia. East Asia): China

KNN2-KNN460 is arranged as shown below. KNN479-4999 is arranged by Table KL-KWX4 using only the numbers KL-KWX4 479+ and adding the appropriate number from the table to KNN0

Class here works on Chinese law, including all periods, beginning with ancient periods to ca. 1949

For the law of Taiwan see KNP1+

For for the law of the People's Republic of China 中華人民共和國 from 1949 on see KNQ0+

General

Bibliography

For bibliography of special topics, see the topic

2 Bibliography of bibliography

3 General bibliography. Bibliography of secondary sources

3.4 Chinese

3.5 Japanese

3.6 Western

Bibliography of primary sources

Library and archive catalogs

Including both Chinese and foreign

4 General

4.3 Union catalogs

4.4 Catalogs of published catalogs

Indexes and tables. Concordances

For indexes to a particular publication, see the publication

4.5 General

4.6 Chronological indexes

5 Indexes to periodical literature, society publications, and collections

For indexes to a particular publication, see the publication

<6> Periodicals

For periodicals consisting predominantly of legal articles, regardless of subject matter and jurisdiction, see K1+

For periodicals consisting primarily of informative material (newsletters, bulletins, etc.) relating to a special subject, see the subject and form division tables for periodicals

For law reports, official bulletins or circulars intended chiefly for the publication of laws and regulations, see appropriate entries in the text or form division tables

6.5 Monographic series

Official gazettes

7 General

Provincial or city gazettes

see the issuing province or city

General
Official gazettes -- Continued
Departmental gazettes
see the issuing department or agency
8 Indexes (General)
Sources
For the sources of a territory or town, see the appropriate jurisdiction
Studies on sources
Including methodology
9 General works
9.5 Classification of sources
Including codes (lü 律); edicts (chi 敕); statutes (ling 令); decrees (ge 格); regulations, ordinances (shi 式); etc.
Indexes and tables. Concordances see KNN4.5+
Collections. Compilations. Selections
General
Class here collections of legal sources from all branches of the law, arranged in chronological order, beginning with the earliest works, and covering all periods
Including all types, as codes (lü 律); edicts (chi 敕); statutes (ling 令); decrees (ge 格); ordinances, regulations (shi 式); etc.
10 Collections covering all periods to 1912
11 Collections covering the period 1912-1949. By date
Named collections
12 Qin lü. 秦律 (221 B.C. to 207 B.C.) (Table K20b)
13 Jiu chao lü kao. 九朝律考 (collected fragments of the codes from Han 漢 to Sui 隋 Dynasties, 202 B.C.-618 A.D.) (Table K20b)
13.3 Kaihuang lü. 開皇律 (between 581 and 600) (Table K20b)
14 Tang lü. 唐律 (7th century A.D.) (Table K20b)
Song hui yao ji gao. 宋會要輯稿 (960 A.D.) see KNN57
14.5 Dazhong xing lü tong lei. 大中刑律統類 (835 A.D.?) (Table K20b)
15 Qingtai bian chi. 清泰編敕 (935 A.D.) (Table K20b)
15.3 Tianfu bian chi. 天福編敕 (939 A.D.) (Table K20b)
15.5 Xü bian chi. 續編敕 (951 A.D.) (Table K20b)
16 Jianlong bian chi. 建隆編敕 (963 A.D.) (Table K20b)
16.5 Shaoxing chi ling ge shi. 紹興敕令格式 (1131.A.D.) (Table K20b)
17 Chunxi chi ling ge shi. 淳熙敕令格式 (before 1170) (Table K20b)

General
Sources
Collections. Compilations. Selections
General
Named collections -- Continued
Qiandao chi ling ge shi. 乾道敕令格式 (1170/72 .A.D.) see KNN31.3
17.6 Chunxi tiao fa shi lei. 淳熙條法事類 (1172.A.D.) (Table K20b)
18 Qing yuan chi ling ge shi. 慶元敕令格式 (1198.A.D.) (Table K20b)
25 Zhonghua lü ling ji cheng. Qing juan. 中華律令集成. 清卷 (Table K20b)
By subject
Criminal law. Criminal procedure. Penalties
30 Tang lü shu yi. 唐律疏議 (737 A.D.) (Tang penal code with commentary) (Table K20b)
30.2 Da Zhou xing tong. 大周刑統 (10th century A.D.) (Table K20b)
30.5 Song xing tong. 宋刑統 (963 A.D.) (Repertory of penal law) (Table K20b)
30.7 Zhe yu gui jian. 折獄龜鑑. The Grand Mirror for Judging Criminal Cases (Zheng, Ke, jin shi, 1124. 鄭克, 進士, 1124) By date
Class here editions of the original work as well as editions (reconstructions of the original work) by Xu Lian 許槤 (comp., 1787-1862)
30.72 Zhe yu gui jian bu. . 折獄龜鑑補. Supplement to The Grand Mirror for Judging Criminal Cases (Hu Wenbing 胡文炳, comp.)
31 Qiandao chong xiu chi ling ge shi. 乾道重修敕令格式 (1168 A.D.) (Table K20b)
31.3 Qiandao chi ling ge shi. 乾道敕令格式 (1170/72 A.D.) (Table K20b)
31.5 Huang Ming tiao fa shi lei zuan. 皇明條法事類纂 (1531-1533 A.D.) (Table K20b)
32 Da Ming lü. 大明律 (1373/74 A.D.) (Ming code) (Table K20b)
33 Geng ding Da Ming lü. 更定大明律 (1397 A.D.) (revised edition of the Ming code) (Table K20b)
34 Da Qing lü li. 大清律例 (1740 A.D.) (Ming/Qing code and precedences) (Table K20b)
Administrative law
39 Tang liu dian. 唐六典 (738 A.D.) (Compendium of administrative law of the Tang) (Table K20b)

General
Sources
Collections. Compilations. Selections
By subject
Administrative law -- Continued
39.3 Qingyuan tiao fa shi lei. 慶元條法事類 (1195-1202 A.D.) (Table K20b)
39.7 Yuan dian zhang. 元典章 (1322 A.D.) (Table K20b)
40 Shen ke Yuan dian zhang jiao. 沈刻元典章校 (Table K20b)
40.3 Da Yuan tong zhi tiao ge. 大元通制條格 (Table K20b)
40.5 Jing shi da dian. 經世大典 (Compendium for the administration of the empire) (Table K20b)
41 Huang Ming zhi shu. 皇明制書 (1579 A.D.) (Table K20b)
41.2 Da Ming ling. 大明令 (1368 A.D.) (Table K20b)
41.3 Zhu si zhi zhang. 諸司職掌 (1393-1458 A.D.) (Statutes of the central administration) (Table K20b)
42 Xian gang shi lei. 憲綱事類 (1371 A.D.) (Regulations for the censorate) (Table K20b)
42.3 Da Ming hui dian. 大明會典 (1503 A.D.) (Collected statutes of the Ming) (Table K20b)
42.8 Wanli hui dian. 萬曆會典 (1585-1587 A.D.) (Table K20b)
43 Da Qing hui dian. 大清會典 (Table K20b)
By type of source
Including edicts, decrees, regulations, etc.
49 Tang da zhao ling ji. 唐大詔令集. Edicts of the Tang (Table K20b)
49.5 Song da zhao ling ji. 宋大詔令集. Edicts of the Song (Table K20b)
50 Huang Ming zhao ling. 皇明詔令 (1367-1539 A.D.). Edicts of the Ming (Table K20b)
51 Da Qing shi chao sheng xun. 大清十朝聖訓 (1616-1874 A.D.). Edicts of the Qing (Table K20b)
52 Yongzheng zhu pi yu zhi. 雍正硃批諭旨 (to 1741 A.D.). Edicts of the Yongzheng Emperor (Table K20b)
52.5 Shang yu ba qi. 上諭八旗 (1741 A.D.) (Table K20b)
55 Tang hui yao. 唐會要 (Table K20b)
56 Song hui yao. 宋會要 (Table K20b)
57 Song hui yao ji gao. 宋會要輯稿 (Table K20b)
58 Song hui yao yan jiu. 宋會要研究 (Table K20b)
Treaties
62 General

General
Sources
Treaties -- Continued
Treaties on international public law
see KZ
Treaties on uniform private law
see K524
Court decisions. Cases. Precedence
Including decisions of the national (imperial) court and decisions of two or more provinces and national (imperial) and provincial decisions combined
For decisions of an individual province, see the respective jurisdiction (e.g. Hunan Sheng. 湖南省)
For list of sources in vernacular script, see Appendix
62.5 Indexes. Registers. By date
For indexes relating to a particular collection, see the publication
Collections. Older collections of precedences (gu shi 故事; li 例)
63 Song li. 宋例 (11th century A.D.). By date
63.3 Tang yin bi shi. 棠陰比事 (1211 A.D.). By date
63.4 Ming gong shu pan qing ming ji. 名公書判清明集. By date
By subject (not A-Z)
Penal cases
64 Xing an hui lan. 刑案滙覽 (1834; 1886) (Table K20b)
By court or court system
National (Imperial) court
Constitutional court
see KNN2620+
65 Highest court of appeal. Supreme (imperial) court (Table K19)
Lower courts
66 Various courts (Table K19)
Including highest court and lower courts (e.g. national (imperial) court and courts of two or more provinces combined)
Intermediate appellate courts
67 Collective (Table K19)
68.A-Z Particular courts, A-Z
Courts of first instance. District courts
69 Collective (Table K19)
70.A-Z Particular courts, A-Z
Provincial courts

General
Sources
Court decisions. Cases. Precedence
By court or court system
Provincial courts -- Continued
72 Collections (Reports) covering all provinces or selected provinces (Table K19)
73 Collections (Reports) covering national (imperial) decisions and decisions of the courts of two or more provinces (Table K19)
Decisions (Reports) of an individual province
see the province
75 Decisions of central (imperial) administrative agencies
Trials
77 General collections
Criminal trials and judicial investigations
For military trials, see KNN3770+
78 Collections. Compilations
79.A-Z Particular offenses, A-Z
79.A78 Arson
79.F73 Fraud
79.P64 Political crimes
80.A-Z Other trials. By plaintiff, defendant, or best known (popular) name, A-Z
Including records, commentaries, and stories on a particular trial
Legal research. Auxiliary sciences
82 General works
83 Epigraphy
84 Linguistics
Archaeology. Folklife studies. Symbolism
85 General works
86.A-Z Special topics, A-Z
87 Heraldry. Seals. Flags. Insignia. Armory
Legal education
88 General works
89 Study and teaching. Teaching methods
90 Law teachers
91 Law students
Law schools
92 General works
93.A-Z Particular law schools. By name, A-Z
Including constitution and bylaws, statutes, regulations, degrees, and general works (history)
The legal profession

General
The legal profession -- Continued
General
see KNN1600+
Law and lawyers in literature
see classes PB-PH
Biography of lawyers
Collective
94 General
95 Collections of portraits
96.A-Z Individual, A-Z
Subarrange each by Table KL-KWX11
Law societies and institutes
Class here works on, and journals by, individual societies and their activities, e.g., annual reports, proceedings, incorporating statutes, bylaws, handbooks, and works (history) about the society
Including courts of honor and disbarment
For publications of associations on special subjects, see the subject
For biography (collective) see KNN94+
For biography (individual) see KNN96.A+
97 General works
Particular types of organizations
98.A-Z National associations, A-Z
99.A-Z Provincial societies, etc., A-Z
For biography see KNN94+
100.A-Z Local associations, lawyers' clubs, etc.. By county, city, A-Z
For biography see KNN94+
Notarial law. Public instruments
see KNN1842+
Public registers. Registration
102 General (Table K11)
Civil registry
see KNN1854+
Registration of juristic persons in civil law
see KNN523.5
Commercial registers
see KNN925
104 Registration of miscellaneous titles and documents
Property registration. Registration of pledges
106 General (Table K11)
Land register
see KNN737+

General
Public registers. Registration
Property registration. Registration of pledges -- Continued
Mining registration
see KNN3350
Aircraft registration
see KNN935.4
Law societies and institutes
see KNN97+
107.A-Z Congresses. Conferences. By name of congress or conference, A-Z
108.A-Z Academies. By name of academy, A-Z
Encyclopedias
109 General
Specialized encyclopedic histories
110 Institutional histories
e.g. Tongdian 通典 (801)
112 Dictionaries. Words and phrases. Glossaries. Encyclopedic phrase dictionaries
Including bilingual and multilingual dictionaries
For dictionaries on a particular subject, e.g. administrative law, see the subject
114 Maxims. Quotations
116 Form books (General). Formularies
For form books on a particular subject, see the subject
Judicial statistics
118 General
120.A-Z Other. By subject, A-Z
122 General works. Treatises
Including all historic periods
123 Compends, outlines, etc.
124 Addresses, essays, lectures
125 Indexes to festschriften
Manuals and other works for particular groups of users
126 Compilations. Collections (General)
127.A-Z By user, A-Z
127.B36 Bankers
127.C46 Censors
127.C54 Clerks
127.C67 Coroners
127.L63 Local officials
Officials, Local see KNN127.L63
Semantics and language
see KNN84
Legal symbolism
see KNN94+

General -- Continued
Legal anecdotes, wit and humor
see K184.4
Law and lawyers in literature
see classes PB - PH
Law and art
see K487.C8
Law and history
see K487.C8



129.A-Z Works on diverse aspects of a particular subject and falling within several branches of the law. By subject, A-Z
By period
To ca. 618 A.D.
Including ancient/early periods to Zhou 周 Dynasty (1122 B.C. to 221 B.C.); and pre-Tang periods: Qin 秦 (221 B.C. to 207 B.C.); Han 漢 (202 B.C. to 220 A.D.); and Wei 魏, Jin 晉, Six Dynasties 六朝, and Sui 隋Dynasty (220 A.D. to 618 A.D.)
For sources and general works, see KNN2+
The state and its constitution
132 General (Table K11)
Social status. Estates. Classes
134 General (Table K11)
135.A-Z Particular classes, A-Z
135.A78 Artisans (gong 工)
135.B87 Burghers (free)
135.C66 Commoners
135.E96 Eunuchs
135.F37 Farmers (nong 農)
Functionaries see KNN135.O55
135.L68 Lowly (jian nu 賤奴)
135.M47 Merchants (shang 商)
135.O55 Officials. Functionaries (shi 士)
135.S53 Slaves (nu 奴)
Including state-owned and privately owned slaves
137.A-Z Special topics, A-Z
137.B57 Birth rights
137.D94 Dynastic rules
Feudal capacity see KNN149
137.P44 Peerage, Rights of
State and religion
see KNN2685+
138 Territory (Table K22)
139 Foreign relations (Table K22)
Feudal law
140 General (Table K22)

General
By period
To ca. 618 A.D.
The state and its constitution
Feudal law -- Continued
Sources
142 Collections. Compilations
143.A-Z Individual sources or groups of sources, A-Z
Subarrange each by Table K21
Feudal institutes
144 General (Table K11)
Feudal lords. Provincial (regional) lords. Governorships
145 General (Table K22)
147 Vassalage. Peers (Table K22)
Including individuals, towns, and villages, and regions
148 Fief. Feoffment (Table K22)
149 Feudal capacity (Table K22)
150 Feudal succession (Table K22)
Rural (peasant) land tenure and peasantry. Land law
152 General (Table K22)
Manorial estates. Landlords. Landed gentry. Land holders
153 General (Table K22)
155.A-Z Special topics, A-Z
Leasehold for years and inheritance
157 General (Table K22)
158.A-Z Special topics, A-Z
159 Succession to rural holdings (Table K22)
The imperial house. Dynasty. Princes and rulers
160 General (Table K22)
162.A-Z Special topics, A-Z
162.D95 Dynastic house rules
Imperial powers see KNN162.R53
Legal status. Juristic personality of ruling dynasty see KNN162.D95
Prerogatives see KNN162.R53
162.R53 Rights and prerogatives
State goods and dynastic estates see KNN176
162.S93 Succession and legitimation
The court. Court officials and councils
164 General (Table K22)
165.A-Z Particular, A-Z
167 Legislation. State and crown councils. Legislative advisors

General
By period
To ca. 618 A.D. -- Continued
169 Military organization and administration (Table K22)
Finance. Revenue and expenditure
173 General (Table K22)
174 Organization and administration (Table K22)
176 State goods and dynastic house goods (Table K22)
Taxes
178 General (Table K22)
179.A-Z Particular taxes, A-Z
Administration (Civil)
Class here works on subjects not represented elsewhere in the schedule
For works on the history of subjects, see the subject
183 General (Table K22)
Administrative organization. Bureaucracy. Hierarchy
184 General (Table K22)
185.A-Z Particular departments, ministries, etc., A-Z
186 Administrative divisions. Local government (Table K22)
187 Municipal government. Urban administration (Table K22)
For particular cities, see the city
Organs of government. Civil service. Officials
188 General (Table K22)
189.A-Z Particular, A-Z
189.C46 Censors
190.A-Z Special topics, A-Z
State and religion
see KNN2685+
Public order and welfare
192 General (Table K22)
Social legislation. Social (urban) services
194 General (Table K22)
195.A-Z Particular, A-Z
195.B37 Bath houses
195.F66 Food distribution
Hospitals (State) see KNN195.M44
195.M44 Medical care (Public)
195.O76 Orphanages
Sumptuary laws
197 General (Table K22)
198.A-Z Particular, A-Z
198.A73 Architecture. Buildings
Including allotted floor space for head

General
By period
To ca. 618 A.D.
Public order and welfare
Sumptuary laws
Particular, A-Z -- Continued
198.D74 Dress code
200 Private law. Special topics, A-Z
Class here works on subjects not represented elsewhere in the schedule
Including early works
For works on the history of other subjects, see the subject
Judiciary. Court organization
225 General (Table K22)
230 Administration of justice. Officials (Table K22)
235.A-Z Particular courts, tribunals, etc., A-Z
Procedure
240 General (Table K22)
255.A-Z Special topics, A-Z
Criminal law and procedure
Class here works on topics not represented elsewhere in the schedule
For works on the history of other subjects, see the subject
265 General (Table K22)
275.A-Z Particular crimes, A-Z
Procedure
277 General (Table K22)
279.A-Z Particular procedures, A-Z
281.A-Z Particular penalties, A-Z
281.A66 Amputation of limbs
281.B36 Banishment
281.B73 Branding
281.C37 Castration
281.F66 Flogging
281.L68 Lowering of civil status
281.M87 Mutilation
281.S87 Strangling (by silk rope)
618 A.D. to 1644 A.D. Tang and post-Tang periods
Including Tang 唐 Dynasty (618 A.D. to 907 A.D.); Five Dynasties and Ten Kingdoms 五代十國 (907 A.D. to 979 A.D.); Song 宋 (960 A.D. to 1279 A.D.); Yuan 元 (1260 A.D. to 1368 A.D.); and Ming 明 Dynasties (1368 A.D. to 1644 A.D.)
For sources and general works, see KNN2+
The state and its constitution
282 General (Table K11)

General
By period
618 A.D. to 1644 A.D. Tang and post-Tang periods
The state and its constitution -- Continued
Social status. Estates. Classes
284 General (Table K11)
285.A-Z Particular classes, A-Z
285.A78 Artisans (gong 工)
285.B87 Burghers (free)
285.C66 Commoners
285.F37 Farmers (nong 農)
Functionaries see KNN285.O55
285.L68 Lowly (jian nu 賤奴)
285.M47 Merchants (shang 商)
285.O55 Officials. Functionaries (shi 士)
285.S53 Slaves (nu 奴)
287.A-Z Special topics, A-Z
287.B57 Birth rights
287.D94 Dynastic rules
Feudal capacity see KNN299
287.P44 Peerage, Rights of
State and religion
see KNN2685+
288 Territory (Table K22)
289 Foreign relations (Table K22)
Feudal law
290 General (Table K22)
Sources
292 Collections. Compilations
293.A-Z Individual sources or groups of sources, A-Z
Subarrange each by Table K21
Feudal institutes
294 General (Table K11)
Feudal lords. Provincial (regional) lords. Governorships
295 General (Table K22)
297 Vassalage. Peers (Table K22)
Including individuals, towns, and villages, and regions
298 Fief. Feoffment (Table K22)
299 Feudal capacity (Table K22)
300 Feudal succession (Table K22)
Rural (peasant) land tenure and peasantry. Land law
302 General (Table K22)
Manorial estates. Landlords. Landed gentry. Land holders

General
By period
618 A.D. to 1644 A.D. Tang and post-Tang periods
Rural (peasant) land tenure and peasantry. Land law
Manorial estates. Landlords. Landed gentry. Land holders -- Continued
303 General (Table K22)
305.A-Z Special topics, A-Z
Leasehold for years and inheritance
307 General (Table K22)
308.A-Z Special topics, A-Z
309 Succession to rural holdings (Table K22)
The imperial house. Dynasty. Princes and rulers
310 General (Table K22)
312.A-Z Special topics, A-Z
312.D95 Dynastic house rules
Imperial powers see KNN312.R53
Legal status. Juristic personality of ruling dynasty see KNN312.D95
Prerogatives see KNN312.R53
312.R53 Rights and prerogatives
State goods and dynastic estates see KNN326
312.S93 Succession and legitimation
The court. Court officials and councils
314 General (Table K22)
315.A-Z Particular, A-Z
317 Legislation. State and crown councils. Legislative advisors
319 Military organization and administration (Table K22)
Finance. Revenue and expenditure
323 General (Table K22)
324 Organization and administration (Table K22)
326 State goods and dynastic house goods (Table K22)
Taxes
328 General (Table K22)
329.A-Z Particular taxes, A-Z
Administration (Civil)
Class here works on subjects not represented elsewhere in the schedule
For works on the history of subjects, see the subject
333 General (Table K22)
Administrative organization. Bureaucracy. Hierarchy
334 General (Table K22)
335.A-Z Particular departments, ministries, etc., A-Z
336 Administrative divisions. Local government (Table K22)

General
By period
618 A.D. to 1644 A.D. Tang and post-Tang periods
Administration (Civil)
Administrative organization. Bureaucracy. Hierarchy -- Continued
337 Municipal government. Urban administration (Table K22)
For particular cities, see the city
Organs of government. Civil service. Officials
338 General (Table K22)
339.A-Z Particular, A-Z
339.C46 Censors
340.A-Z Special topics, A-Z
State and religion
see KNN2685+
Public order and welfare
342 General (Table K22)
Social legislation. Social (urban) services
344 General (Table K22)
345.A-Z Particular, A-Z
345.B37 Bath houses
345.F66 Food distribution
Hospitals (State) see KNN345.M44
345.M44 Medical care (Public)
345.O76 Orphanages
Sumptuary laws
347 General (Table K22)
348.A-Z Particular, A-Z
348.A73 Architecture. Buildings
Including allotted floor space for head
348.D74 Dress code
350 Private law. Special topics, A-Z
Class here works on subjects not represented elsewhere in the schedule
Including early works
For works on the history of other subjects, see the subject
Judiciary. Court organization
375 General (Table K22)
380 Administration of justice. Officials (Table K22)
385.A-Z Particular courts, tribunals, etc., A-Z
Procedure
390 General (Table K22)
405.A-Z Special topics, A-Z

General
By period
618 A.D. to 1644 A.D. Tang and post-Tang periods -- Continued
Criminal law and procedure
Class here works on topics not represented elsewhere in the schedule
For works on the history of other subjects, see the subject
415 General (Table K22)
425.A-Z Particular crimes, A-Z
Procedure
427 General (Table K22)
429.A-Z Particular procedures, A-Z
431.A-Z Particular penalties, A-Z
431.A66 Amputation of limbs
431.B36 Banishment
431.B73 Branding
431.C37 Castration
431.F66 Flogging
431.L68 Lowering of civil status
431.M87 Mutilation
431.S87 Strangling (by silk rope)
1644 to 1949
Including Qing 清 Dynasty (1644 -1912) and the Republic of China 中華民國 (1912-1949)
For sources and general works, see KNN2+
For history of a particular subject, see the subject
For works comparing history of a particular subject with modern doctrine, see the subject in KNQ
Philosophy, jurisprudence, and theory of law
Including all periods of Chinese history to 1949
For works on the philosophy of a particular branch of the law (e.g. criminal law), see the branch
For works on the philosophy of law in general see K237+
For works comparing recent legal thought with legal thought relating to one or several periods of Chinese history see KNQ440+
440 General works
Schools of philosophy and legal theory
455 General works
Confucianism
456 General works
458 Wang An-shih school (Wang Anshi school) (State control advocates)
460 Sung school (Song school). Neo-Confucianism

General
By period
1644 to 1949 -- Continued
469-4999 Other topics (Table KL-KWX4)
Add number in table to KNN0
5000 Manchoukuo. Manzhouguo. 滿洲國 (Manchuria) (1932-1946) (Table KL-KWX9)
Class here works on the law of the historic region of Manchoukuo created by Japan in 1932, comprising the provinces (sheng 省)Liaoning Sheng 遼寧省, Jilin Sheng 吉林省, and Heilongjiang Sheng 黑龍江省
Provinces (Sheng 省)
Class here historic/defunct provinces, prefectures, etc. not listed as a present day jurisdiction of the same name in KNQ
For present day jurisdictions see KNQ5000+
5101-5199 An-tung sheng. Andong Sheng. 安東省 (Table KL-KWX8)
5201-5299 Ch'a-ha-erh sheng. Chaha'er Sheng. 察哈爾省 (Table KL-KWX8)
Fukien Province. Fujian Sheng. 福建省 see KNQ5301+
5401-5499 Hsi-k'ang sheng. Xikang Sheng. 西康省 (Table KL-KWX8)
5501-5599 Ho-Chiang sheng. Hejiang Sheng. 合江省 (Table KL-KWX8)
5601-5699 Hsing-an sheng. Xing'an Sheng. 興安省 (Table KL-KWX8)
5901-5999 Je-ho sheng. Rehe Sheng. 熱河省 (Table KL-KWX8)
Kwangsi Province. Kuang-hsi sheng. Guangxi Sheng. 廣西省 see KNQ8201+
Kwangtung Province. Guangdong Sheng. 廣東省 see KNQ6801+
6001-6099 Liao-pei sheng. Liaobei Sheng. 遼北省 (Table KL-KWX8)
6101-6199 Nen-Chiang sheng. Nenjiang Sheng. 嫩江省 (Table KL-KWX8)
6201-6299 Ning-hsia sheng. Ningxia Sheng. 寧夏省 (Table KL-KWX8)
6301-6399 Pin-Chiang sheng. Binjiang Sheng. 濱江省 (Table KL-KWX8)
Sikang Province. Xikang Sheng. 西康省 see KNN5401+
7301-7399 Sui-yüan sheng. Suiyuan Sheng. 綏遠省 (Table KL-KWX8)
7401-7499 Sung-Chiang sheng. Songjiang Sheng. 松江省 (Table KL-KWX8)
7501-7599 T'ai-wan sheng. Taiwan Sheng. 臺灣省 (Table KL-KWX8)
9000.A-Z Prefectures (zhou 州 or fu 府), sub-prefectures, etc., A-Z
Cities, communities, etc.
see KNQ8100+

Asia (South Asia. Southeast Asia. East Asia): China (Republic, 1949- ). 中華民國 Taiwan. 臺灣

Class here works on the law of the Nationalist government after its retreat to Taiwan (Formosa) and on the period of Chinese administration beginning in 1945; and on works on the preceding period of Japanese rule (1895-1945)

For the Republic of China. 中華民國 (1912-1949) see KNN1+

1-489 General (Table KL-KWX5 modified)

Administrative law

Administrative organization

Administrative and political divisions. Local government other than municipal

Including those of centralized national governments or federal governments

293.5.A-Z Counties (Hsien. Xian. 縣), A-Z

Including official gazettes, bylaws, statutory orders, regulations, and general works, as well as works on specific legal topics

293.5.C43 Chang-hua hsien. Zhanghua Xian. 彰化縣

293.5.C45 Chia-i hsien. Jiayi Xian. 嘉義縣

293.5.H75 Hsin-chu hsien. Xinzhu Xian. 新竹縣

293.5.H83 Hua-lien hsien. Hualian Xian. 花蓮縣

293.5.I23 I-lan hsien. Yilan Xian. 宜蘭縣

293.5.K36 Kao-hsiung hsien. Gaoxiong Xian. 高雄縣

293.5.M53 Miao-li hsien. Miaoli Xian. 苗栗縣

293.5.N36 Nan-t'ou hsien. Nantou Xian. 南投縣

293.5.P46 P'eng-hu hsien. Penghu Xian. 澎湖縣

293.5.P56 P'ing-tung hsien. Pingdong Xian. 屏東縣

293.5.T34 Tai-chung hsien. Taizhong Xian. 臺中縣

293.5.T35 T'ai-nan hsien. Tainan Xian. 臺南縣

293.5.T36 T'ai-pei hsien. Taibei Xian. 臺北縣

293.5.T37 T'ai-tung hsien. Taidong Xian. 臺東縣

293.5.T38 T'ao-yüan hsien. Taoyuan Xian. 桃園縣

293.5.Y86 Yün-lin hsien. Yunlin Xian. 雲林縣

Cities, communities, etc., A-Z

Subarrange each by Table KL-KWX9a

490.C55 Chi-lung shih. Jilong Shi. 基隆市 (Table KL-KWX9a)

490.K36 Kao-hsiung shih. Gaoxiong Shi. 高雄市 (Table KL-KWX9a)

490.T35 T'ai-chung shih. Taizhong Shi. 臺中市 (Table KL-KWX9a)

490.T36 T'ai-nan shih. Tainan Shi. 臺南市 (Table KL-KWX9a)

490.T364 T'ai-pei shih (Taipei). Taibei Shi. 臺北市 (Table KL-KWX9a)

490.T38 Tan-shui chen. Danshui Zhen. 淡水鎮 (Table KL-KWX9a)

501-599 Taiwan Province. T'ai-wan sheng. Taiwan Sheng. 臺灣省 (Table KL-KWX8)

For the province of Taiwan before 1895 see KNN7501+

Asia (South Asia. Southeast Asia. East Asia): China (People's Republic, 1949- ). 中华人民共和国

0-4999 General (Table KL-KWX4 modified)

Add number in table to KNQ0

350 Customary law for ethnic minorities

For materials relating to the periods to 1644 A.D. see KNN132+

For materials relating to the Qing Dynasty 清 (1644-1912) and the Republic of China 中華民國 (1912-1949) see KNN440+

Philosophy, jurisprudence, and theory of law

Including works comparing recent legal thought with legal thought relating to one or several periods of Chinese history

440 General works

Constitutional law

For works on the constitutional aspects of a subject, see the subject

Constitutional history

2090 General (Table K11)

By period

Ancient/Early to ca. 1800

see KNN132+

Provinces (Sheng 省)

5001-5099 Anhwei Province. Anhui Sheng. 安徽省 (Table KL-KWX8)

Canton Province. 广东省 see KNQ6801+

5201-5299 Chekiang Province. Zhejiang Sheng. 浙江省 (Table KL-KWX8)

5301-5399 Fukien Province. Fujian Sheng. 福建省 (Table KL-KWX8)

Gansu Province. 甘肃省 see KNQ6201+

Guangdong Province. 广东省 see KNQ6801+

Guizhou Province. 贵州省 see KNQ6901+

5401-5499 Hainan Province. Hainan Sheng. 海南省 (Table KL-KWX8)

Hebei Province. 河北省 see KNQ5801+

5501-5599 Heilungkiang Province. Heilongjiang Sheng. 黑龙江省 (Table KL-KWX8)

5601-5699 Honan Province. Henan Sheng. 河南省 (Table KL-KWX8)

5801-5899 Hopeh Province. Hebei Sheng. 河北省 (Table KL-KWX8)

5901-5999 Hunan Province. Hunan Sheng. 湖南省 (Table KL-KWX8)

6101-6199 Hupeh Province. Hubei Sheng. 湖北省 (Table KL-KWX8)

Jiangsu Province. 江苏省 see KNQ6301+

Jiangxi Province. 江西省 see KNQ6501+

Jilin Province. 吉林省 see KNQ6701+

6201-6299 Kansu Province. Gansu Sheng. 甘肃省 (Table KL-KWX8)

6301-6399 Kiangsu Province. Jiangsu Sheng. 江苏省 (Table KL-KWX8)

6501-6599 Kiangsi Province. Jiangxi Sheng. 江西省 (Table KL-KWX8)

Provinces (Sheng 省) -- Continued
6701-6799 Kirin Province. Jilin Sheng. 吉林省 (Table KL-KWX8)
6801-6899 Kwangtung Province. Canton Province. Guangdong Sheng. 广东省 (Table KL-KWX8)
6901-6999 Kweichow Province. Guizhou Sheng. 贵州省 (Table KL-KWX8)
7101-7199 Liaoning Province. Liaoning Sheng. 辽宁省 (Table KL-KWX8)
Qinghai Province. 青海省 see KNQ7801+
7201-7299 Shensi Province. Shaanxi Sheng. 陕西省 (Table KL-KWX8)
7301-7399 Shantung Province. Shandong Sheng. 山东省 (Table KL-KWX8)
7401-7499 Shansi Province. Shanxi Sheng. 山西省 (Table KL-KWX8)
7601-7699 Szechwan Province. Sichuan Sheng. 四川省 (Table KL-KWX8)
7801-7899 Tsinghai Province. Qinghai Sheng. 青海省 (Table KL-KWX8)
7901-7999 Yunnan Province. Yunnan Sheng. 云南省 (Table KL-KWX8)
Zhejiang Province. 浙江省 see KNQ5201+
Autonomous regions (Zizhiqu 自治区)
Guangxi Zhuangzu Zizhiqu. 广西壮族自治区 see KNQ8201+
8101-8199 Inner Mongolia. Nei Monggol. 内蒙古 (Table KL-KWX8)
8201-8299 Kwangsi Chuang Autonomous Region. Guangxi Zhuangzu Zizhiqu. 广西壮族自治区 (Table KL-KWX8)
Nei Monggol. 内蒙古 see KNQ8101+
8401-8499 Ningsia Hui Autonomous Region. Ningxia Huizu Zizhiqu. 宁夏回族自治区 (Table KL-KWX8)
8501-8599 Sinkiang Uighur Autonomous Region. Xinjiang Uygur Zizhiqu. 新疆维吾尔自治区 (Table KL-KWX8)
8701-8799 Tibet. Xizang Zizhiqu. 西藏自治区 (Table KL-KWX8)
Including historic periods before 1956
Xinjiang Uygur Zizhiqu. 新疆维吾尔自治区 see KNQ8501+
Xizang Zizhiqu. 西藏自治区 see KNQ8701+
Autonomous municipalities
Beijing. 北京 see KNQ8901+
8901-8999 Peking. Beijing. 北京 (Table KL-KWX8)
9001-9099 Shanghai. 上海 (Table KL-KWX8)
9201-9299 Tientsin. Tianjin Shi. 天津市 (Table KL-KWX8)
Special administrative regions
9301-9399 Hong Kong. Xianggang Tebie Xingzhengqu. 香港特别行政区 (Table KL-KWX8)
9401-9499 Macau. Aomen Tebie Xingzhengqu. 澳门特别行政区 (Table KL-KWX8)
Cities, communities, etc.
9510 Canton. Guangzhou. 广州 (Table KL-KWX9)
9512 Ch'ang-sha. Changsha. 长沙 (Table KL-KWX9)
9518 Ch'ang-ch'un. Changchun. 长春 (Table KL-KWX9)
9520 Cheng-chou. Zhengzhou. 郑州 (Table KL-KWX9)

Cities, communities, etc. -- Continued
9522 Ch'eng-tu. Chengdu. 成都 (Table KL-KWX9)
9524 Fu-chou. Fuzhou. 福州 (Table KL-KWX9)
Guilin. 桂林 see KNQ9546
Guiyang. 贵阳 see KNQ9548
Guangzhou. 广州 see KNQ9510
9531 Hang-chou. Hangzhou Shi. 杭州市 (Table KL-KWX9)
9533 Harbin. Ha-erh-bin. Haerbin. 哈尔滨 (Table KL-KWX9)
9538 Ho-fei. Hefei. 合肥 (Table KL-KWX9)
9540 Hsi-ning. Xining. 西宁 (Table KL-KWX9)
9544 Hu-ho-hao-t'e. Huhehaote. 呼和浩特 (Table KL-KWX9)
Jinan. 济南 see KNQ9586
9546 Kuei-lin. Guilin. 桂林 (Table KL-KWX9)
9548 Kuei-yang. Guiyang. 贵阳 (Table KL-KWX9)
9550 K'un-ming. Kunming. 昆明 (Table KL-KWX9)
9552 Lan-chou. Lanzhou. 兰州 (Table KL-KWX9)
9556 Lhasa. La-sa. Lasa. 拉萨 (Table KL-KWX9)
9562 Nan-ch'ang. Nanchang. 南昌 (Table KL-KWX9)
9564 Nan-ching. Nanjing. 南京 (Table KL-KWX9)
Nanking. 南京 see KNQ9564
9566 Nan-ning. Nanning. 南宁 (Table KL-KWX9)
9575 Shen-yang. Shenyang. 沈阳 (Table KL-KWX9)
9578 Shih-Chia-chuang. Shijiazhuang. 石家庄 (Table KL-KWX9)
9580 Sian. Xi'an. 西安 (Table KL-KWX9)
9584 T'ai-yüan. Taiyuan. 太原 (Table KL-KWX9)
9586 Tsinan. Jinan. 济南 (Table KL-KWX9)
9590 Urumchi. Ürümqi. Wulu Muqi. 乌鲁木齐 (Table KL-KWX9)
9594 Wu-han. Wuhan. 武汉 (Table KL-KWX9)
Wulu Muqi. 乌鲁木齐 see KNQ9590
Xi'an. 西安 see KNQ9580
Xining. 西宁 see KNQ9540
9598 Yin-ch'uan. Yinchuan. 银川 (Table KL-KWX9)
Zhengzhou. 郑州 see KNQ9520
9665.A-Z Other cities, A-Z
Subarrange each by Table KL-KWX9a

Asia (South Asia. Southeast Asia. East Asia): Cochin China
see KNV1+ ; KPV1+

Asia (South Asia. Southeast Asia. East Asia): East Timor
see KNW5001+

Asia (South Asia. Southeast Asia. East Asia): Hong Kong (to 1997)

For Hong Kong (Special administrative region of China) see KNQ9301+

1-489 General (Table KL-KWX7 modified)

Administrative and political divisions. Local government other than municipal

231.5.A-Z Urban area districts and new territories districts, A-Z

Including official gazettes, bylaws, statutory orders, regulations, and general works, as well as works on specific legal topics

231.5.C46 Central and Western (Table KL-KWX9a)

231.5.E37 Eastern (Table KL-KWX9a)

231.5.I75 Islands (Table KL-KWX9a)

Islands District see KNR231.5.I75

231.5.K68 Kowloon (Table KL-KWX9a)

231.5.K87 Kwun Tong (Table KL-KWX9a)

231.5.M66 Mong Kok (Table KL-KWX9a)

231.5.N67 North (Table KL-KWX9a)

231.5.S35 Sai Kung. Xigong (Table KL-KWX9a)

231.5.S52 Sha Tin (Table KL-KWX9a)

231.5.S54 Sham Shui Po (Table KL-KWX9a)

231.5.S67 Southern (Table KL-KWX9a)

231.5.T35 Tai Po (Table KL-KWX9a)

231.5.T78 Tsuen Wan (Table KL-KWX9a)

231.5.T84 Tuen Mun (Table KL-KWX9a)

231.5.W36 Wan Chai (Table KL-KWX9a)

231.5.W66 Wong Tai Sin (Table KL-KWX9a)

231.5.Y38 Yau Ma Tei (Table KL-KWX9a)

231.5.Y84 Yuen Long (Table KL-KWX9a)

Asia (South Asia. Southeast Asia. East Asia): India

1-4999 General (Table KL-KWX6 modified)

Official gazettes

7 Gazette of India

Law reports and related materials

Class here national (Federal) and regional reports, and reports of older courts prior to independence (1947- )

For reports of an individual state or territory, see the appropriate jurisdiction

For reports relating to a particular subject, and for reports of courts of limited jurisdiction other than those listed below, see the appropriate subject

17.8 Privy Council Law reports. Privy Council cases (Table K18)

National (Federal) courts

18 Federal Court (1936-1950). Federal Court reports (Table K18)

18.5 Supreme Court of India (1950- ) (Table K18)

Presidencies' Law Reports, and reports from the North West Provinces (to 1866)

Class here Supreme Court reports of the Presidencies of Bombay, Calcutta, and Madras, and lesser courts, including the decision of the Sadar or Suddar Diwani Adalats, Sadar Nizamat Adalats, Sadar Fordari Adalats, and other courts of these three areas, from 1727 to approximately 1861 (Indian High Courts Act)

19 General reports covering more than one Presidency (Table K18)

Bombay Presidency

19.1 Collective (Table K18)

19.15 Supreme Court of Bombay (1823-1862) (Table K18)

19.16 Suddar Diwani Adalats & Sadar Fozdari Adalats (Bombay) (Table K18)

19.19 Royal Courts. Recorder's Courts (1753-1823) (Table K18)

Calcutta/Bengal Presidency (Fort William Presidency)

19.2 Collective (Table K18)

19.25 Supreme Court of Calcutta (Bengal) (1774-1862) (Table K18)

19.27 Sadar Diwani Adalats (civil) & Sadar Nizamat Adalats (criminal) (Bengal) (1791-1871 (Table K18)

19.28 Small Causes Court. East India Company's Justice of the peace (Zemindar's court). Mayor's court. Court of the Quarter Sessions (Table K18)

19.29 Zillah Courts (Bengal) (1846-1861) (Table K18)

General
Law reports and related materials
Presidencies' Law Reports, and reports from the North West Provinces (to 1866)
Calcutta/Bengal Presidency (Fort William Presidency) -- Continued
19.3 Admiralty and ecclesiastical precedents. Combined reports (Table K18)
Madras Presidency
19.33 Collective (Table K18)
19.35 Supreme Court of Madras (1801-1862) (Table K18)
19.37 Suddar Diwani Adalats (civil cases) & Sadar Fozdari Adalats (criminal cases) (1802-1862) (Table K18)
19.38 Choulty Court, Royal Courts, Mayor's Court, Court of Requests, Recorder's Courts (1727-1801) (Table K18)
19.39 Zillah Courts (Madras) (1851-1855) (Table K18)
North West Provinces
19.4 Collective (Table K18)
19.42 Sadar or Suddar Diwani Adalats (1843-1866) (Table K18)
19.44 Nizamut Adalat (1851-1866) (Table K18)
19.46 Zillah Courts (1848-1855) (Table K18)
Princely States' Law Reports (to 1947)
20 Collective (Table K18)
20.15 Ajmar (Table K18)
20.2 Kathiawar (Table K18)
20.3 Mayurbhanj (Table K18)
20.4 Mysore (Table K18)
20.5 Travancore (Table K18)
20.6.A-Z Other Princely States, A-Z
Subarrange by main entry
(21.A-Z) This number not used
Law reports from areas and territories prior to independence in 1947
e.g. Burma, Sind, and parts of the Punjab, not any longer Indian jurisdictions
Burma
21.15 Collective (Table K18)
21.16 High Court (Table K18)
21.17 Lower Burma (Table K18)
21.18 Upper Burma (Table K18)
Northwest Frontier Province
21.2 Collective (Table K18)

General
Law reports and related materials
Law reports from areas and territories prior to independence in 1947 -- Continued
Punjab
Including Delhi Civil Decisions, 1848-1951, and pre-1947 cases from Lahore and revenue rulings
21.3 Collective (Table K18)
21.31 Chief Court or High Court (Table K18)
21.36 District Court/Sessions Court (Table K18)
21.38 Revenue rulings (Table K18)
Sind
Class here pre-1947 cases of the area, now in Pakistan
21.4 Collective (Table K18)
21.41 High Court (Table K18)
(22) Digests and indexes to federal decisions
see KNS18
State courts. High courts
For reports of an individual state, see the state, subdivided by Table KL-KWX7, 2.2-2.25, e.g. Assam, KNT2002.2-KNT2002.25
23 Reports covering all states, including territories, or selected states (Table K18)
25.A-Z High court cases originating from the province or state after 1861. By province or state, A-Z
Subarrange by main entry
Including High Court of Agra (1866-1868), and High Court of Allahabad (1869-1875)
25.3 Digests of Supreme Court and State High Court reports
25.4 Citators
25.45.A-Z Other auxiliary publications
e.g. conversion tables, chronological tables, etc.
25.48 Decisions of national administrative agencies
For decisions of particular administrative agencies, see the subject
64.A-Z Academies. Institutes. By name, A-Z
64.I54 Indian Law Institute, New Delhi
64.N37 National Academy of Administration
History of law
By period
Ancient/early and medieval India
Class here works on the pre-colonial periods, including the Sanskrit literature (Hindu jurisprudence) and the literature of the Mughal period to ca. 1761
Including ancient people
For the history of a subject, see the subject

General
History of law
By period
Ancient/early and medieval -- Continued
121 Bibliography
122 General works. Theory
Sources
For sources of a territory or town, see the appropriate jurisdiction
123 Studies on sources
Including history and methodology, epigraphy, papyrology, etc.
For philological studies, see classes P, PJ, and PK-PL, etc.
Collections. Compilations. Selections
Class here comprehensive collections of legal sources in various vernacular scripts (e.g. Nagari, Grantha, etc.)
Vedic texts see BL1112.2+
125 Dharma literature. By author or title
Including Sutras, Smrtis, Nibandhas, and commentaries
Individual sources or groups of sources
Dharma literature
Sutras, Smrtis, and Sastras
(126) Manu, Code of. Mānavadharmaśāstra
see KNS127.3
126.2 Āpastambasmr̥ti (Table K20b)
126.3 Aṅgirassmr̥ti (Table K20b)
126.4 Atrismr̥ti (Table K20b)
126.45 Bhavadeva, 11th cent. Dattakatilaka (Table K20b)
126.5 Bhr̥gusmr̥ti (Table K20b)
126.6 Br̥hadyogiyajñavalkyasmr̥ti (Table K20b)
126.7 Br̥haspatismr̥ti (Table K20b)
126.8 Devalasmr̥ti (Table K20b)
127 Gautamadharmaśāstra (Table K20b)
127.2 Haritasmr̥ti (Table K20b)
127.25 Laghudharmaprakāśikā. Śāṅkarasmr̥tiḥ (Table K20b)
127.3 Mānavadharmaśāstra. Code of Manu. Manusmr̥ti (Table K20b)
127.4 Paraśarasmr̥ti (Table K20b)
127.5 Śaṅkhalikitasmr̥ti (Table K20b)
127.6 Vāsiṣthasmr̥ti (Table K20b)
127.76 Viṣṇusmr̥ti (Table K20b)

General
History of law
By period
Ancient/early and medieval
Sources
Individual sources or groups of sources
Dharma literature
Sutras, Smrtis, and Sastras -- Continued
127.8 Yājñavalkyasmṛti (Table K20b)
Nibandhas see KNS125
130.A-Z Special topics, A-Z
Class here sources grouped by subject and not represented elsewhere
Muslim rule (997-1761)
130.5 General works
Sources
130.7 Collections. Compilations. Selections
Individual sources and groups of sources
131 Royal privileges
Including privileges for particular classes, groups, communities, courts of justice, etc.
131.2 Royal mandates, decrees, orders, etc.
Court decisions. Cases. Advisory opinions
Including digests, etc.
131.3 Several courts
131.4.A-Z Individual courts. By place, A-Z
131.5 Trials
131.6 Contemporary legal literature
Portuguese period (ca. 1500-1961) see KNT5001+
French period (1664-1954) see KNU5001+
British period (1761-1947)
For British government (1858-1947) see KNS1754.12+
132 General works
Sources
For sources of a territory or town, see the appropriate territory or town
Studies on sources
Including history and methodology (e.g. epigraphy, papyrology, etc.)
For philological studies, see classes P, PJ, PK, and PL
133 General works
133.5 Classification of sources
134 Collections. Compilations. Selections
Class here coprehensive collection of legal sources in various native (vernacular) scripts

General
History of law
By period
British period (1761-1947) -- Continued
East India Company (1761-1857)
Sources
139 Collections. Compilations
Individual sources and groups of sources
National (imperial) laws and legislation
Including constitutional legislation
Collected see KNS139
142 East India Company Act, 1784
Royal (imperial) privileges
Including privileges for particular classes, groups, communities, courts of justice, etc.
144 Collections. Compilations
146 Individual. By date
Subarrange each by Table K20b
Royal (imperial) mandates. Decrees, orders, etc., of princes and rulers
Collections. Compilations
Individual. By date
Subarrange each by Table K20b
Treaties
Treaties on international public law
see KZ
Treaties on international uniform law
see K524+ KJC38+ KMC, KNC, KQC, and KVC
Court decisions
see KNS19+
(160) This number not used
(164.A-Z) This number not used
Trials
Criminal trials and judicial investigations
Collections. Compilations
170 General
172.A-Z Particular offenses, A-Z
172.W58 Witchcraft
174.A-Z Individual trials. By defendant, or best known (popular) name, A-Z
Including records, briefs, commentaries, and stories on a particular trial
Other trials
176 Collections. Compilations
178.A-Z Individual trials. By plaintiff, defendant, or best known (popular) name, A-Z

General
History of law
By period
British period (1761-1947)
East India Company (1761-1857)
Sources
Individual sources or groups of sources -- Continued
180 Contemporary legal literature. Documents. Public and private records
Class here general collections
For collections or individual documents on a topic, see the topic
The State and its constitution
202 General (Table K22)
Classes. Castes
204 General works
205.A-Z Special topics, A-Z
205.B57 Birth rights
205.D94 Dynastic rules
205.E62 Equality of birth
Feudal capacity see KNS228
205.M37 Marriage, Inter-varna
205.O87 Outlawry. Outcasts
209 Territory (Table K22)
212 Foreign relations (Table K22)
Feudal law
213 General (Table K22)
Sources
214 Collections. Compilations
220.2<date> Individual sources
Arrange chronologically by appending the date of the source to the number KNS220.2 and deleting any trailing zeros. Subarrange each by Table K20b
Feudal institutes
221 General (Table K22)
Feudal lords and vassalage
222 General (Table K22)
223 Peers (Table K22)
Fief
224 General (Table K22)
226.A-Z Special topics, A-Z
226.C65 Commendation. Hommage
Hommage see KNS226.C65
226.L3 Land

General
History of law
By period
British period (1761-1947)
East India Company (1761-1857)
The State and its constitution
Feudal law
Feudal institutes
Fief
Special topics, A-Z -- Continued
226.V5 Villages. Towns
228 Feudal capacity (Table K22)
230 Feudal succession (Table K22)
Rural (peasant) land tenure and peasantry
232 General (Table K22)
Leashold for years and inheritance
238 General (Table K22)
240.A-Z Special topics, A-Z
242 Succession to rural holdings (Table K22)
Kings. Princes and rulers. Chiefs
246 General (Table K22)
248.A-Z Special topics, A-Z
Crown goods and dynastic estates see KNS263
248.E43 Election
Prerogatives see KNS248.R53
248.R53 Rights and prerogatives
248.S93 Succession and designation
250 The court. Court officials and councils (Table K22)
254 Legislature (Table K22)
256 Military organization (Table K22)
Finance
Class here works on topics not represented elswhere in the schedule
For works on the history of particular subjects, see the subject
259 General (Table K22)
263 Crown goods and dynastic house goods (Table K22)
268.A-Z Special topics, A-Z
The judiciary. Court organization and procedure
Class here general works on the development of the judiciary, and on a defunct court or court system
For the history of a particular court, see the jurisdiction
For reports see KNS19+
283 General works

General
History of law
By period
British period (1761-1947)
East India Company (1761-1857)
The State and its constitution
The judiciary. Court organization and procedure -- Continued



285 Suddar Adalat Courts of the East India Company (1772-1862)
286.A-Z Supreme court (General). By name, A-Z
286.B66 Bombay (1823-1862)
286.C35 Calcutta (1774-1862)
286.M34 Madras (1801-1862)
288.A-Z Special topics, A-Z
Criminal law and procedure
Class here works on topics not represented elsewhere in the schedule
For works on the history of other subjects, see the subject
292 General (Table K22)
294.A-Z Particular crimes, A-Z
296.A-Z Particular procedures, A-Z
298.A-Z Particular penalties, A-Z
299.A-Z Particular branches and subjects of the law, A-Z
Class here works on topics not represented elsewhere
For works on the history of a subject, see the subject
Indic peoples. Ethnic groups
Class here works on the law of Indic peoples regardless of whether they are identified with a particular state or the region at large
For particular subjects, see the subject
Collections of laws and customs. Codes of indigenous laws. Treaties
For court rules, trial practice in customary (native) courts, etc., see the court
350 General
352.A-Z By region or state, A-Z
352.P86 Punjab
354 General works. Treatises
Including history
Particular peoples or ethnic groups
For particular subjects, see the subject
356 Ahoms (Table KL-KWX12)
357 Aos (Table KL-KWX12)
358 Angami (Table KL-KWX12)

General
Indic peoples. Ethnic groups
Particular peoples or ethnic groups -- Continued

360 Bharia (Table KL-KWX12)
361 Buxas (Table KL-KWX12)
362 Cheros (Table KL-KWX12)
363 Dafla (Table KL-KWX12)
364 Deori (Table KL-KWX12)
365 Dhodias (Table KL-KWX12)
366 Didayi (Table KL-KWX12)
367 Dogros (Table KL-KWX12)
368 Dorla (Table KL-KWX12)
370 Gadaba (Table KL-KWX12)
372 Gaddos (Table KL-KWX12)
373 Garo (Table KL-KWX12)
375 Gond (Table KL-KWX12)
376 Gujaratis (Table KL-KWX12)
377 Ho (Table KL-KWX12)
379 Kanarese (Table KL-KWX12)
380 Kandh (Table KL-KWX12)
382 Khasi (Table KL-KWX12)
383 Koknas (Table KL-KWX12)
384 Koltas (Table KL-KWX12)
385 Konkans (Table KL-KWX12)
386 Koragas (Table KL-KWX12)
387 Kuku (Table KL-KWX12)
390 Lalungs (Table KL-KWX12)
392 Lodha (Table KL-KWX12)
393 Lushai (Table KL-KWX12)
394 Malayalis (Table KL-KWX12)
396 Maring (Table KL-KWX12)
397 Meithei (Table KL-KWX12)
398 Meos (Table KL-KWX12)
399 Miri (Table KL-KWX12)
402 Munda (Table KL-KWX12)
403 Muria (Table KL-KWX12)
406 Oraan (Table KL-KWX12)
410 Pengo (Table KL-KWX12)
412 Purum (Table KL-KWX12)
415 Sausi (Table KL-KWX12)
416 Savara (Table KL-KWX12)
418 Siddhi (Table KL-KWX12)
420 Soligas (Table KL-KWX12)
421 Tamil (Table KL-KWX12)
424 Telugus (Table KL-KWX12)
426 Tulus (Table KL-KWX12)

General
Indic peoples. Ethnic groups
Particular peoples or ethnic groups -- Continued
430 Warlis (Table KL-KWX12)
439.A-Z Other, A-Z
Subarrange each by Table KL-KWX12
Conflict of laws
480 General (Table K11)
481 Plurality of laws conflict. Two or more legal systems in operation
Including common law and religious law (Hindu and Islamic law), or common law, customary and religious law
Public law
Class here works on all aspects of public law, including early works
The state
Including philosophy and theory of the state
For nonlegal works on political theory, see class J
1724 Sovereignty. Sovereignty of Parliament
Federalism
see KL-KWX6 2035
1726 Rule of law
Constitutional law
For works on the constitutional aspects of a subject, see the subject
History
see KL-KWX6 1751+
1734 Constitutional reform. Criticism. Polemic
For works on a particular constitution, see the constitution
Sources
Including early constitutions and related materials
1744.5<date> Individual constitutions
Arrange chronologically by appending the date of adoption to the number KNS1744.5 and deleting any trailing zeros. Subarrange each by Table K17
1744.51948.A2 India Draft Constitution, 1948
1744.5195 Constitution of 1950 (Table K17)
1744.6<date> Individual sources other than constitutions. By date
Arrange chronologically by appending the date of adoption to the number KNS1744.6 and deleting any trailing zeros
East India Company Act 1784 see KNS142
1744.61858 India Act 1858
1744.61915 Government of India Act 1915
1744.61919 Government of India Act 1919
1744.61935 Government of India Act 1935

General
Constitutional law -- Continued
Constitutional history
By period
Ancient/early and medieval India to ca. second half of the 19th century see KNS121+
Medieval
see KNS121+
Mid-nineteenth century to most recent constitution
1760 General (Table K11)
Constitutional principles
Rule of law see KNS1726
1780 Sovereignty of parliament (Table K11)
1800 Rulers. Princes. Viceroys (Table K11)
Including dynastic rules and works on legal constitutional status

Asia (South Asia. Southeast Asia. East Asia): India: States and union territories (A-L)

Included in this list are modern jurisdictions (States and Union territories), subarranged by Table KL-KWX7 , and historic/extinct jurisdictions (presidencies, princely states, etc.), subarranged by Table KL-KWX8

1-499 Andaman and Nicobar Islands (Table KL-KWX7 modified)

Law reports and related materials

For reports relating to a particular subject, and for reports of courts of limited jurisdiction other than those listed below, see the appropriate subject

State courts

2.2 Highest court of appeal. Supreme court. Court of Cassation (Table K18)

Lower courts

2.23 Various courts (Table K18)

Including highest court and lower courts

Intermediate appellate courts. Courts of appeals

2.24 Collective (Table K18)

2.25.A-Z Particular courts, A-Z

(2.27) Digests and indexes to state court decisions

see KNT2.2 ; KNT2.23 ; etc.

Local courts

2.3 General (Table K18)

2.35.A-Z Particular courts. By city, etc., A-Z

2.4 Decisions of state administrative agencies

For decisions of particular agencies, see the subject

501-999 Andhra Pradesh (Table KL-KWX7 modified)

Law reports and related materials

For reports relating to a particular subject, and for reports of courts of limited jurisdiction other than those listed below, see the appropriate subject

State courts

502.2 Highest court of appeal. Supreme court. Court of Cassation (Table K18)

Lower courts

502.23 Various courts (Table K18)

Including highest court and lower courts

Intermediate appellate courts. Courts of appeals

502.24 Collective (Table K18)

502.25.A-Z Particular courts, A-Z

(502.27) Digests and indexes to state court decisions

see KNT502.2 ; KNT502.23 ; etc.

Local courts

502.3 General (Table K18)

502.35.A-Z Particular courts. By city, etc., A-Z

Andhra Pradesh -- Continued
502.4 Decisions of state administrative agencies
For decisions of particular agencies, see the subject
1001-1499 Arunāchal Pradesh (Table KL-KWX7 modified)
Law reports and related materials
For reports relating to a particular subject, and for reports of courts of limited jurisdiction other than those listed below, see the appropriate subject
State courts
1002.2 Highest court of appeal. Supreme court. Court of Cassation (Table K18)
Lower courts
1002.23 Various courts (Table K18)
Including highest court and lower courts
Intermediate appellate courts. Courts of appeals
1002.24 Collective (Table K18)
1002.25.A-Z Particular courts, A-Z
(1002.27) Digests and indexes to state court decisions
see KNT1002.2 ; KNT1002.23 ; etc.
Local courts
1002.3 General (Table K18)
1002.35.A-Z Particular courts. By city, etc., A-Z
1002.4 Decisions of state administrative agencies
For decisions of particular agencies, see the subject
2001-2499 Assam (Table KL-KWX7 modified)
Law reports and related materials
For reports relating to a particular subject, and for reports of courts of limited jurisdiction other than those listed below, see the appropriate subject
State courts
2002.2 Highest court of appeal. Supreme court. Court of Cassation (Table K18)
Lower courts
2002.23 Various courts (Table K18)
Including highest court and lower courts
Intermediate appellate courts. Courts of appeals
2002.24 Collective (Table K18)
2002.25.A-Z Particular courts, A-Z
(2002.27) Digests and indexes to state court decisions
see KNT2002.2 ; KNT2002.23 ; etc.
Local courts
2002.3 General (Table K18)
2002.35.A-Z Particular courts. By city, etc., A-Z
2002.4 Decisions of state administrative agencies
For decisions of particular agencies, see the subject
Bengal (pre-1905) see KNT3101+

2501-2999 Bihar (Table KL-KWX7)
Law reports and related materials
For reports relating to a particular subject, and for reports of courts of limited jurisdiction other than those listed below, see the appropriate subject
State courts
2502.2 Highest court of appeal. Supreme court. Court of Cassation (Table K18)
Lower courts
2502.23 Various courts (Table K18)
Including highest court and lower courts
Intermediate appellate courts. Courts of appeals
2502.24 Collective (Table K18)
2502.25.A-Z Particular courts, A-Z
(2502.27) Digests and indexes to state court decisions
see KNT2502.2 ; KNT2502.23 ; etc.
Local courts
2502.3 General (Table K18)
2502.35.A-Z Particular courts. By city, etc., A-Z
2502.4 Decisions of state administrative agencies
For decisions of particular agencies, see the subject
3101-3199 Calcutta/Bengal Presidency (Table KL-KWX8)
3501-3599 Chandigarh (Table KL-KWX7 modified)
Law reports and related materials
For reports relating to a particular subject, and for reports of courts of limited jurisdiction other than those listed below, see the appropriate subject
State courts
3502.2 Highest court of appeal. Supreme court. Court of Cassation (Table K18)
Lower courts
3502.23 Various courts (Table K18)
Including highest court and lower courts
Intermediate appellate courts. Courts of appeals
3502.24 Collective (Table K18)
3502.25.A-Z Particular courts, A-Z
(3502.27) Digests and indexes to state court decisions
see KNT3502.2 ; KNT3502.23 ; etc.
Local courts
3502.3 General (Table K18)
3502.35.A-Z Particular courts. By city, etc., A-Z
3502.4 Decisions of state administrative agencies
For decisions of particular agencies, see the subject
4001-4499 Dadra and Nagar Haveli (Table KL-KWX7 modified)

Dadra and Nagar Haveli -- Continued
Law reports and related materials
For reports relating to a particular subject, and for reports of courts of limited jurisdiction other than those listed below, see the appropriate subject
State courts
4002.2 Highest court of appeal. Supreme court. Court of Cassation (Table K18)
Lower courts
4002.23 Various courts (Table K18)
Including highest court and lower courts
Intermediate appellate courts. Courts of appeals
4002.24 Collective (Table K18)
4002.25.A-Z Particular courts, A-Z
(4002.27) Digests and indexes to state court decisions
see KNT4002.2 ; KNT4002.23 ; etc.
Local courts
4002.3 General (Table K18)
4002.35.A-Z Particular courts. By city, etc., A-Z
4002.4 Decisions of state administrative agencies
For decisions of particular agencies, see the subject
4501-4999 Delhi (Table KL-KWX7 modified)
Law reports and related materials
For reports relating to a particular subject, and for reports of courts of limited jurisdiction other than those listed below, see the appropriate subject
State courts
4502.2 Highest court of appeal. Supreme court. Court of Cassation (Table K18)
Lower courts
4502.23 Various courts (Table K18)
Including highest court and lower courts
Intermediate appellate courts. Courts of appeals
4502.24 Collective (Table K18)
4502.25.A-Z Particular courts, A-Z
(4502.27) Digests and indexes to state court decisions
see KNT4502.2 ; KNT4502.23 ; etc.
Local courts
4502.3 General (Table K18)
4502.35.A-Z Particular courts. By city, etc., A-Z
4502.4 Decisions of state administrative agencies
For decisions of particular agencies, see the subject
5001-5499 Goa, Daman, and Diu (Table KL-KWX7 modified)

Goa, Daman, and Diu -- Continued
Law reports and related materials
For reports relating to a particular subject, and for reports of courts of limited jurisdiction other than those listed below, see the appropriate subject
State courts
5002.2 Highest court of appeal. Supreme court. Court of Cassation (Table K18)
Lower courts
5002.23 Various courts (Table K18)
Including highest court and lower courts
Intermediate appellate courts. Courts of appeals
5002.24 Collective (Table K18)
5002.25.A-Z Particular courts, A-Z
(5002.27) Digests and indexes to state court decisions
see KNT5002.2 ; KNT5002.23 ; etc.
Local courts
5002.3 General (Table K18)
5002.35.A-Z Particular courts. By city, etc., A-Z
5002.4 Decisions of state administrative agencies
For decisions of particular agencies, see the subject
5501-5999 Gujarat (Table KL-KWX7 modified)
Law reports and related materials
For reports relating to a particular subject, and for reports of courts of limited jurisdiction other than those listed below, see the appropriate subject
State courts
5502.2 Highest court of appeal. Supreme court. Court of Cassation (Table K18)
Lower courts
5502.23 Various courts (Table K18)
Including highest court and lower courts
Intermediate appellate courts. Courts of appeals
5502.24 Collective (Table K18)
5502.25.A-Z Particular courts, A-Z
(5502.27) Digests and indexes to state court decisions
see KNT5502.2 ; KNT5502.23 ; etc.
Local courts
5502.3 General (Table K18)
5502.35.A-Z Particular courts. By city, etc., A-Z
5502.4 Decisions of state administrative agencies
For decisions of particular agencies, see the subject
6001-6499 Haryana (Table KL-KWX7 modified)

Haryana -- Continued
Law reports and related materials
For reports relating to a particular subject, and for reports of courts of limited jurisdiction other than those listed below, see the appropriate subject
State courts
6002.2 Highest court of appeal. Supreme court. Court of Cassation (Table K18)
Lower courts
6002.23 Various courts (Table K18)
Including highest court and lower courts
Intermediate appellate courts. Courts of appeals
6002.24 Collective (Table K18)
6002.25.A-Z Particular courts, A-Z
(6002.27) Digests and indexes to state court decisions
see KNT6002.2 ; KNT6002.23 ; etc.
Local courts
6002.3 General (Table K18)
6002.35.A-Z Particular courts. By city, etc., A-Z
6002.4 Decisions of state administrative agencies
For decisions of particular agencies, see the subject
6501-6999 Himachal Pradesh (Table KL-KWX7 modified)
Law reports and related materials
For reports relating to a particular subject, and for reports of courts of limited jurisdiction other than those listed below, see the appropriate subject
State courts
6502.2 Highest court of appeal. Supreme court. Court of Cassation (Table K18)
Lower courts
6502.23 Various courts (Table K18)
Including highest court and lower courts
Intermediate appellate courts. Courts of appeals
6502.24 Collective (Table K18)
6502.25.A-Z Particular courts, A-Z
(6502.27) Digests and indexes to state court decisions
see KNT6502.2 ; KNT6502.23 ; etc.
Local courts
6502.3 General (Table K18)
6502.35.A-Z Particular courts. By city, etc., A-Z
6502.4 Decisions of state administrative agencies
For decisions of particular agencies, see the subject
Hyderabad (Andhra Pradesh) see KNT501+
Hyderabad (Karnataka) see KNT8001+
Hyderabad (Maharashtra) see KNU1001+
7201-7299 Jaipur (Table KL-KWX8)

7501-7999 Jammu and Kashmir (Table KL-KWX7 modified)
Law reports and related materials
For reports relating to a particular subject, and for reports of courts of limited jurisdiction other than those listed below, see the appropriate subject
State courts
7502.2 Highest court of appeal. Supreme court. Court of Cassation (Table K18)
Lower courts
7502.23 Various courts (Table K18)
Including highest court and lower courts
Intermediate appellate courts. Courts of appeals
7502.24 Collective (Table K18)
7502.25.A-Z Particular courts, A-Z
(7502.27) Digests and indexes to state court decisions
see KNT7502.2 ; KNT7502.23 ; etc.
Local courts
7502.3 General (Table K18)
7502.35.A-Z Particular courts. By city, etc., A-Z
7502.4 Decisions of state administrative agencies
For decisions of particular agencies, see the subject
8001-8499 Karnataka (Table KL-KWX7 modified)
Law reports and related materials
For reports relating to a particular subject, and for reports of courts of limited jurisdiction other than those listed below, see the appropriate subject
State courts
8002.2 Highest court of appeal. Supreme court. Court of Cassation (Table K18)
Lower courts
8002.23 Various courts (Table K18)
Including highest court and lower courts
Intermediate appellate courts. Courts of appeals
8002.24 Collective (Table K18)
8002.25.A-Z Particular courts, A-Z
(8002.27) Digests and indexes to state court decisions
see KNT8002.2 ; KNT8002.23 ; etc.
Local courts
8002.3 General (Table K18)
8002.35.A-Z Particular courts. By city, etc., A-Z
8002.4 Decisions of state administrative agencies
For decisions of particular agencies, see the subject
8501-8999 Kerala (Table KL-KWX7)

Kerala -- Continued
Law reports and related materials
For reports relating to a particular subject, and for reports of courts of limited jurisdiction other than those listed below, see the appropriate subject
State courts
8502.2 Highest court of appeal. Supreme court. Court of Cassation (Table K18)
Lower courts
8502.23 Various courts (Table K18)
Including highest court and lower courts
Intermediate appellate courts. Courts of appeals
8502.24 Collective (Table K18)
8502.25.A-Z Particular courts, A-Z
(8502.27) Digests and indexes to state court decisions
see KNT8502.2 ; KNT8502.23 ; etc.
Local courts
8502.3 General (Table K18)
8502.35.A-Z Particular courts. By city, etc., A-Z
8502.4 Decisions of state administrative agencies
For decisions of particular agencies, see the subject
9301-9399 Kumaon (Table KL-KWX8)
9501-9999 Lakshadweep (Table KL-KWX7 modified)
Law reports and related materials
For reports relating to a particular subject, and for reports of courts of limited jurisdiction other than those listed below, see the appropriate subject
State courts
9502.2 Highest court of appeal. Supreme court. Court of Cassation (Table K18)
Lower courts
9502.23 Various courts (Table K18)
Including highest court and lower courts
Intermediate appellate courts. Courts of appeals
9502.24 Collective (Table K18)
9502.25.A-Z Particular courts, A-Z
(9502.27) Digests and indexes to state court decisions
see KNT9502.2 ; KNT9502.23 ; etc.
Local courts
9502.3 General (Table K18)
9502.35.A-Z Particular courts. By city, etc., A-Z
9502.4 Decisions of state administrative agencies
For decisions of particular agencies, see the subject

Asia (South Asia. Southeast Asia. East Asia): India: States and union territories (M-Z)

Included in this list are modern jurisdictions (States and Union territories), subarranged by Table KL-KWX7 , and historic/extinct jurisdictions (presidencies, princely states, etc.), subarranged by Table KL-KWX8

1-499 Madhya Pradesh (Table KL-KWX7 modified)

Law reports and related materials

For reports relating to a particular subject, and for reports of courts of limited jurisdiction other than those listed below, see the appropriate subject

State courts

2.2 Highest court of appeal. Supreme court. Court of Cassation (Table K18)

Lower courts

2.23 Various courts (Table K18)

Including highest court and lower courts

Intermediate appellate courts. Courts of appeals

2.24 Collective (Table K18)

2.25.A-Z Particular courts, A-Z

(2.27) Digests and indexes to state court decisions

see KNU2.2 ; KNU2.23 ; etc.

Local courts

2.3 General (Table K18)

2.35.A-Z Particular courts. By city, etc., A-Z

2.4 Decisions of state administrative agencies

For decisions of particular agencies, see the subject

501-599 Madras Presidency (Table KL-KWX8)

1001-1499 Maharashtra (Table KL-KWX7 modified)

Including former Presidency, Province and State

Law reports and related materials

For reports relating to a particular subject, and for reports of courts of limited jurisdiction other than those listed below, see the appropriate subject

State courts

1002.2 Highest court of appeal. Supreme court. Court of Cassation (Table K18)

Lower courts

1002.23 Various courts (Table K18)

Including highest court and lower courts

Intermediate appellate courts. Courts of appeals

1002.24 Collective (Table K18)

1002.25.A-Z Particular courts, A-Z

(1002.27) Digests and indexes to state court decisions

see KNU1002.2 ; KNU1002.23 ; etc.

Local courts

Maharashtra
Law reports and related materials
Local courts -- Continued
1002.3 General (Table K18)
1002.35.A-Z Particular courts. By city, etc., A-Z
1002.4 Decisions of state administrative agencies
For decisions of particular agencies, see the subject
1501-1999 Manipur (Table KL-KWX7 modified)
Law reports and related materials
For reports relating to a particular subject, and for reports of courts of limited jurisdiction other than those listed below, see the appropriate subject
State courts
1502.2 Highest court of appeal. Supreme court. Court of Cassation (Table K18)
Lower courts
1502.23 Various courts (Table K18)
Including highest court and lower courts
Intermediate appellate courts. Courts of appeals
1502.24 Collective (Table K18)
1502.25.A-Z Particular courts, A-Z
(1502.27) Digests and indexes to state court decisions
see KNU1502.2 ; KNU1502.23 ; etc.
Local courts
1502.3 General (Table K18)
1502.35.A-Z Particular courts. By city, etc., A-Z
1502.4 Decisions of state administrative agencies
For decisions of particular agencies, see the subject
2501-2999 Meghalaya (Table KL-KWX7 modified)
Law reports and related materials
For reports relating to a particular subject, and for reports of courts of limited jurisdiction other than those listed below, see the appropriate subject
State courts
2502.2 Highest court of appeal. Supreme court. Court of Cassation (Table K18)
Lower courts
2502.23 Various courts (Table K18)
Including highest court and lower courts
Intermediate appellate courts. Courts of appeals
2502.24 Collective (Table K18)
2502.25.A-Z Particular courts, A-Z
(2502.27) Digests and indexes to state court decisions
see KNU2502.2 ; KNU2502.23 ; etc.
Local courts
2502.3 General (Table K18)

Meghalaya
Law reports and related materials
Local courts -- Continued
2502.35.A-Z Particular courts. By city, etc., A-Z
2502.4 Decisions of state administrative agencies
For decisions of particular agencies, see the subject
3001-3499 Mizoram (Table KL-KWX7 modified)
Law reports and related materials
For reports relating to a particular subject, and for reports of courts of limited jurisdiction other than those listed below, see the appropriate subject
State courts
3002.2 Highest court of appeal. Supreme court. Court of Cassation (Table K18)
Lower courts
3002.23 Various courts (Table K18)
Including highest court and lower courts
Intermediate appellate courts. Courts of appeals
3002.24 Collective (Table K18)
3002.25.A-Z Particular courts, A-Z
(3002.27) Digests and indexes to state court decisions
see KNU3002.2 ; KNU3002.23 ; etc.
Local courts
3002.3 General (Table K18)
3002.35.A-Z Particular courts. By city, etc., A-Z
3002.4 Decisions of state administrative agencies
For decisions of particular agencies, see the subject
Mysore see KNT8001+
3501-3999 Nāgāland (Table KL-KWX7 modified)
Law reports and related materials
For reports relating to a particular subject, and for reports of courts of limited jurisdiction other than those listed below, see the appropriate subject
State courts
3502.2 Highest court of appeal. Supreme court. Court of Cassation (Table K18)
Lower courts
3502.23 Various courts (Table K18)
Including highest court and lower courts
Intermediate appellate courts. Courts of appeals
3502.24 Collective (Table K18)
3502.25.A-Z Particular courts, A-Z
(3502.27) Digests and indexes to state court decisions
see KNU3502.2 ; KNU3502.23 ; etc.
Local courts
3502.3 General (Table K18)

Nāgāland
Law reports and related materials
Local courts -- Continued
3502.35.A-Z Particular courts. By city, etc., A-Z
3502.4 Decisions of state administrative agencies
For decisions of particular agencies, see the subject
4501-4999 Orissa (Table KL-KWX7 modified)
Law reports and related materials
For reports relating to a particular subject, and for reports of courts of limited jurisdiction other than those listed below, see the appropriate subject
State courts
4502.2 Highest court of appeal. Supreme court. Court of Cassation (Table K18)
Lower courts
4502.23 Various courts (Table K18)
Including highest court and lower courts
Intermediate appellate courts. Courts of appeals
4502.24 Collective (Table K18)
4502.25.A-Z Particular courts, A-Z
(4502.27) Digests and indexes to state court decisions
see KNU4502.2 ; KNU4502.23 ; etc.
Local courts
4502.3 General (Table K18)
4502.35.A-Z Particular courts. By city, etc., A-Z
4502.4 Decisions of state administrative agencies
For decisions of particular agencies, see the subject
5001-5499 Pondicherry (Table KL-KWX7 modified)
Law reports and related materials
For reports relating to a particular subject, and for reports of courts of limited jurisdiction other than those listed below, see the appropriate subject
State courts
5002.2 Highest court of appeal. Supreme court. Court of Cassation (Table K18)
Lower courts
5002.23 Various courts (Table K18)
Including highest court and lower courts
Intermediate appellate courts. Courts of appeals
5002.24 Collective (Table K18)
5002.25.A-Z Particular courts, A-Z
(5002.27) Digests and indexes to state court decisions
see KNU5002.2 ; KNU5002.23 ; etc.
Local courts
5002.3 General (Table K18)
5002.35.A-Z Particular courts. By city, etc., A-Z

Pondicherry -- Continued
5002.4 Decisions of state administrative agencies
For decisions of particular agencies, see the subject
5501-5999 Punjab (Table KL-KWX7 modified)
Law reports and related materials
For reports relating to a particular subject, and for reports of courts of limited jurisdiction other than those listed below, see the appropriate subject
State courts
5502.2 Highest court of appeal. Supreme court. Court of Cassation (Table K18)
Lower courts
5502.23 Various courts (Table K18)
Including highest court and lower courts
Intermediate appellate courts. Courts of appeals
5502.24 Collective (Table K18)
5502.25.A-Z Particular courts, A-Z
(5502.27) Digests and indexes to state court decisions
see KNU5502.2 ; KNU5502.23 ; etc.
Local courts
5502.3 General (Table K18)
5502.35.A-Z Particular courts. By city, etc., A-Z
5502.4 Decisions of state administrative agencies
For decisions of particular agencies, see the subject
6001-6499 Rajasthan (Table KL-KWX7 modified)
Law reports and related materials
For reports relating to a particular subject, and for reports of courts of limited jurisdiction other than those listed below, see the appropriate subject
State courts
6002.2 Highest court of appeal. Supreme court. Court of Cassation (Table K18)
Lower courts
6002.23 Various courts (Table K18)
Including highest court and lower courts
Intermediate appellate courts. Courts of appeals
6002.24 Collective (Table K18)
6002.25.A-Z Particular courts, A-Z
(6002.27) Digests and indexes to state court decisions
see KNU6002.2 ; KNU6002.23 ; etc.
Local courts
6002.3 General (Table K18)
6002.35.A-Z Particular courts. By city, etc., A-Z
6002.4 Decisions of state administrative agencies
For decisions of particular agencies, see the subject
6501-6999 Sikkim (Table KL-KWX7 modified)

Sikkim -- Continued
Law reports and related materials
For reports relating to a particular subject, and for reports of courts of limited jurisdiction other than those listed below, see the appropriate subject
State courts
6502.2 Highest court of appeal. Supreme court. Court of Cassation (Table K18)
Lower courts
6502.23 Various courts (Table K18)
Including highest court and lower courts
Intermediate appellate courts. Courts of appeals
6502.24 Collective (Table K18)
6502.25.A-Z Particular courts, A-Z
(6502.27) Digests and indexes to state court decisions
see KNU6502.2 ; KNU6502.23 ; etc.
Local courts
6502.3 General (Table K18)
6502.35.A-Z Particular courts. By city, etc., A-Z
6502.4 Decisions of state administrative agencies
For decisions of particular agencies, see the subject
7001-7499 Tamil Nadu (Table KL-KWX7 modified)
Law reports and related materials
For reports relating to a particular subject, and for reports of courts of limited jurisdiction other than those listed below, see the appropriate subject
State courts
7002.2 Highest court of appeal. Supreme court. Court of Cassation (Table K18)
Lower courts
7002.23 Various courts (Table K18)
Including highest court and lower courts
Intermediate appellate courts. Courts of appeals
7002.24 Collective (Table K18)
7002.25.A-Z Particular courts, A-Z
(7002.27) Digests and indexes to state court decisions
see KNU7002.2 ; KNU7002.23 ; etc.
Local courts
7002.3 General (Table K18)
7002.35.A-Z Particular courts. By city, etc., A-Z
7002.4 Decisions of state administrative agencies
For decisions of particular agencies, see the subject
7501-7999 Tripura (Table KL-KWX7 modified)

Tripura -- Continued
Law reports and related materials
For reports relating to a particular subject, and for reports of courts of limited jurisdiction other than those listed below, see the appropriate subject
State courts
7502.2 Highest court of appeal. Supreme court. Court of Cassation (Table K18)
Lower courts
7502.23 Various courts (Table K18)
Including highest court and lower courts
Intermediate appellate courts. Courts of appeals
7502.24 Collective (Table K18)
7502.25.A-Z Particular courts, A-Z
(7502.27) Digests and indexes to state court decisions
see KNU7502.2 ; KNU7502.23 ; etc.
Local courts
7502.3 General (Table K18)
7502.35.A-Z Particular courts. By city, etc., A-Z
7502.4 Decisions of state administrative agencies
For decisions of particular agencies, see the subject
8001-8499 Uttar Pradesh (Table KL-KWX7 modified)
Including United Provinces of Agra and Oudh
Law reports and related materials
For reports relating to a particular subject, and for reports of courts of limited jurisdiction other than those listed below, see the appropriate subject
State courts
8002.2 Highest court of appeal. Supreme court. Court of Cassation (Table K18)
Lower courts
8002.23 Various courts (Table K18)
Including highest court and lower courts
Intermediate appellate courts. Courts of appeals
8002.24 Collective (Table K18)
8002.25.A-Z Particular courts, A-Z
(8002.27) Digests and indexes to state court decisions
see KNU8002.2 ; KNU8002.23 ; etc.
Local courts
8002.3 General (Table K18)
8002.35.A-Z Particular courts. By city, etc., A-Z
8002.4 Decisions of state administrative agencies
For decisions of particular agencies, see the subject
8501-8999 West Bengal (Table KL-KWX7 modified)

West Bengal -- Continued
Law reports and related materials
For reports relating to a particular subject, and for reports of courts of limited jurisdiction other than those listed below, see the appropriate subject
State courts
8502.2 Highest court of appeal. Supreme court. Court of Cassation (Table K18)
Lower courts
8502.23 Various courts (Table K18)
Including highest court and lower courts
Intermediate appellate courts. Courts of appeals
8502.24 Collective (Table K18)
8502.25.A-Z Particular courts, A-Z
(8502.27) Digests and indexes to state court decisions
see KNU8502.2 ; KNU8502.23 ; etc.
Local courts
8502.3 General (Table K18)
8502.35.A-Z Particular courts. By city, etc., A-Z
8502.4 Decisions of state administrative agencies
For decisions of particular agencies, see the subject
Other states
9005 Chhattīsgarh (Table KL-KWX9)
9012 Jharkhand (Table KL-KWX9)
9022 Uttaranchal (Table KL-KWX9)

Asia (South Asia. Southeast Asia. East Asia): India: Cities, communities, etc.

9500 Agra (Table KL-KWX9)
9505 Ahmedabad (Table KL-KWX9)
9507 Allahabad (Table KL-KWX9)
9510 Bangalore (Table KL-KWX9)
9511 Bombay. Mumbai (Table KL-KWX9)
9515 Calcutta. Kolkata (Table KL-KWX9)
9519 Delhi (Table KL-KWX9)
9523 Gangtok (Table KL-KWX9)
9528 Hyderabad (Table KL-KWX9)
9530 Indore (Table KL-KWX9)
9540 Jabalpur (Table KL-KWX9)
9545 Jaipur (Table KL-KWX9)
9549 Kanpur (Table KL-KWX9)
Kolkata see KNU9515
9557 Lucknow (Table KL-KWX9)
9565 Madras (Table KL-KWX9)
9570 Madurai (Table KL-KWX9)
Mumbai see KNU9511
9576 Nagpur (Table KL-KWX9)
9580 Pune (Table KL-KWX9)
9590 Varanasi (Table KL-KWX9)
9665.A-Z Other cities, A-Z
Subarrange each by Table KL-KWX9a

Asia (South Asia. Southeast Asia. East Asia): French Indochina. Indochina (Federation)

Comprised from ca. 1883/1899 to 1946 the French colony of Cochin-China, the protectorates of Annam, Cambodia, Tonkin, and Laos

For Cambodia see KNM0+

For Laos see KPE0+

For Vietnam see KPV0+

1-489 General (Table KL-KWX5)

Cities, communities, etc.

see the present day jurisdictions, e.g., Louang Prabang (Laos)

Asia (South Asia. Southeast Asia. East Asia): Indonesia
Previously Dutch East Indies
0-4890 General (Table KL-KWX4 modified)
Add number in table to KNW0
Customary law for ethnic minorities
Class here works on the law of peoples regardless of whether they are identified with a particular province or region at large
For particular subjects, see the subject
Collections of laws and customs. Codes of customary law. Treaties
For court rules, trial practice in customary (native) courts, see the court
350 General
352.A-Z By region or state, A-Z
354 General works. Treatises
Including history
Particular peoples or ethnic groups
For particular subjects, see the subject
395 Minangkabau (Table KL-KWX12)
398 Uhunduni (Table KL-KWX12)
Administrative law
Administrative organization
Administrative and political divisions. Local government other than municipal
Including those of centralized national governments or federal governments
2935.A-Z Provinces (Propinsi-propinsi), A-Z
Including official gazettes, bylaws, statutory orders, regulations, and general works, as well as works on specific legal topics
2935.A33 Aceh. Nanggroe Aceh Darussalam
2935.B35 Bali
Bangka Belitung see KNW2935.K47
2935.B46 Bengkulu
2935.G67 Gorontalo
2935.I75 Irian Jaya. Papua
2935.I77 Irian Jaya Barat
2935.J34 Jakarta Raya
Cf. KNW4982 Jakarta (City)
2935.J35 Jambi
2935.J36 Jawa Barat
2935.J37 Jawa Tengah
2935.J38 Jawa Timur
2935.K34 Kalimantan Barat
2935.K35 Kalimantan Selatan

General
Administrative law
Administrative organization
Administrative and political divisions. Local government other than municipal
Provinces (Propinsi-propinsi), A-Z -- Continued

2935.K36 Kalimantan Tengah
2935.K37 Kalimantan Timur
2935.K47 Kepulauan Bangka Belitung
2935.L36 Lampung
Loro Sae see KNW2935.T56
2935.M35 Maluku Utara
Nanggroe Aceh Darussalam see KNW2935.A33
2935.N86 Nusa Tenggara Barat
2935.N87 Nusa Tenggara Timur
Papua see KNW2935.I75
2935.R53 Riau
2935.S83 Sulawesi Selatan
2935.S84 Sulawesi Tengah
2935.S85 Sulawesi Tenggara
2935.S86 Sulawesi Utara
2935.S87 Sumatera Barat
2935.S88 Sumatera Selatan
2935.S89 Sumatera Utara
2935.T56 Timor Timur (to 2002)
For East Timor, see KNW5001+
2935.Y65 Yogyakarta
2936.A-Z Daerah Tingkat II (Level II regions. Districts), A-Z
Including regencies (kabupaten) and municipalities (kotamadya)
2936.A25 Aceh Barat
2936.J39 Jaipur District
2936.K87 Kupang
2936.M36 Manokwari
2936.S47 Serang

Cities, communities, etc.

4980 Bandung (Table KL-KWX9)
4981 Banjarmasin (Table KL-KWX9)
4982 Jakarta (Table KL-KWX9)
For Jakarta Raya (Propinsi) see KNW2935.J34
4984 Medan (Table KL-KWX9)
4985 Padang (Table KL-KWX9)
4986 Palu (Table KL-KWX9)
4987 Semarang (Table KL-KWX9)
4988 Surabaya (Table KL-KWX9)
4989 Ujung Padang (Table KL-KWX9)

4990.A-Z Other cities, A-Z
Subarrange each by Table KL-KWX9a
4990.A63 Ambon (Table KL-KWX9a)
4990.B35 Balikpapan (Table KL-KWX9a)
4990.B36 Banda Aceh (Table KL-KWX9a)
4990.B38 Bandar Lampung (Table KL-KWX9a)
4990.B46 Bengkulu (Table KL-KWX9a)
4990.D46 Denpasar (Table KL-KWX9a)
4990.J35 Jaipur (Table KL-KWX9a)
4990.J36 Jambi (Table KL-KWX9a)
4990.K46 Kendari (Table KL-KWX9a)
4990.M35 Manado (Table KL-KWX9a)
4990.M37 Mataram (Table KL-KWX9a)
4990.P35 Pakanbaru (Table KL-KWX9a)
4990.P36 Palangka Raya (Table KL-KWX9a)
4990.P37 Palembang (Table KL-KWX9a)
4990.P66 Pontianak (Table KL-KWX9a)
4990.S36 Samarinda (Table KL-KWX9a)
4990.T36 Tanjungkarang-Telukbetung (Table KL-KWX9a)
4990.T45 Telanaipura (Table KL-KWX9a)
4990.T47 Ternate (Table KL-KWX9a)
4990.Y64 Yogyakarta (Table KL-KWX9a)

| | |
|---|---|
| | Asia (South Asia. Southeast Asia. East Asia): East Timor |
| 5001-5499 | General (Table KL-KWX5 modified) |
| 5490.A-Z | Cities, communities, etc., A-Z |
| 5490.D55 | Dili (Table KL-KWX9a) |

Asia (South Asia. Southeast Asia. East Asia): Japan

0-4999 General (Table KL-KWX4 modified)

Add number in table to KNX0

History of law

By period

Ancient to Kamakura shogunate 1184

Clan society, to the Taika reform 646 A.D. Period of customary (proper) law

122 General (Table K11)

123.A-Z Special topics, A-Z

From Taika reform to Kamakura shogunate 1184.A.D.

Including Nara (710-794 A.D.) and Heian (794-1185 A.D.) periods

Sources

124 Collections. Compilations. Selections

Including transliterations and translations

125 Indexes. Chronologies

Individual sources or groups of sources

126 Omi codification of 661 A.D. (Table K20b)

126.5 Ritsu code of 678 A.D. (Table K20b)

126.7 Ryo code of 678 A.D. (Table K20b)

127 Kyaku. Compilations of amendments and abrogations of the ritsu and ryo codes. By date of original compilation

e.g. 819 A.D.; 869 A.D.; 905 A.D.

128 Shiki. Compilations of edicts and regulations for implementation of the ritsu, ryo, and kyaku. By date of original compilation

e.g. 869 A.D.; 925 A.D.

From 1185 to 1868 A.D. Shogunate. Feudal society

Including Kamakura and Ashikaga shogunates (1185 to 1600 A.D.); and Tokugawa period (1600-1868 A.D.)

Sources

134 Collections. Compilations

Including transliterations and translations

134.5 Indexes. Chronologies, etc.

Individual sources and groups of sources

Codes of law

135 Goseibai-Shikimoku (1232. A.D.) (Table K20b)

136 Kujikata-Osada-megaki (Osadamegaki-Hyakkajo) (1742 A.D.) (Table K20b)

160 Judicial precedents (Table K20b)

Including feudal cases

The state and its constitution

Classes. Warrior classes (Samurai). Peers

204 General (Table K22)

General -- Continued
Regional divisions. Subregions
474 Hokkeido
475 Tohoku region
476 Kanto region
476.5 Chubu region
477 Kinki region
477.5 Chugoku region
478 Shikoku region
478.3 Kyushu region
Formosa. Taiwan see KNP1+
Constitutional law
Class here works on constitutional law of Japan, beginning with the constitution of 1947
For works on the constitutional aspects of a subject, see the subject
For works on constitutional law prior to 1947 see KNX2100.2+
History see KNX2100.2+
Sources
Including 19th century sources
For earlier sources see KNX122+
2064 Collections. Compilations. By date
Including imperial (national) sources and sources of several jurisdictions
2064.5<date> Individual constitutions
Arrange chronologically by appending the date of adoption to the number KNX2964.5 and deleting any trailing zeros. Subarrange each by Table K17
2064.51889 Constitution of 1889 (Table K17)
2064.51947 Constitution of 3 May 1947 (Table K17)
2064.6<date> Individual sources other than constitutions
Arrange chronologically by appending the date of adoption to the number KNX2064.6 and deleting any trailing zeros
2064.61946 SWNCC - 228 (State-War-Navy-Coordinating Committee, January 11, 1946 - Document nr. 228; "Reform of Japanese Governmental System")
Constitutional history
For individual constitutions see KNX2064.5<date>
By period
Ancient (early to 1868) see KNX122+
Meiji restoration, 1868 to 1945
2101 General (Table K11)
Constitutional principles
2130 Rulers. Princes. Dynasties

General
Constitutional law
Constitutional history
By period
Meiji restoration, 1868 to 1945
Constitutional principles -- Continued
2140 Privileges of classes and particular groups. Rights of peerage (nobility)
Legislature. Legislative power
2196 General (Table K11)
2196.3 The Diet
Including House of Peers and House of Representatives
The Emperor. Nihon-Koku Tenno
2198 General (Table K11)
2198.3.A-Z Special topics, A-Z
2198.3.D58 Divinity
Dynastic succession to the throne see KNX2535.S92
Imperial House Law see KNX2535.I66
2198.3.P68 Powers and prerogatives
Japan under Allied Occupation, 1945-1952
2201 General (Table K11)
Supreme Commander for the Allied Powers (SCAP)
2202 General (Table K11)
General Headquarters (GHQ). Chief of Staff
2205 General (Table K11)
Particular policy sections
2206 Government Section
2207 Civil Information and Education Section
2208 Economic and Scientific Section
2209 Legal Section
2210 Public Health and Welfare Section
2211 Natural Resources Section
2212 Diplomatic Section
2213 Civil Transportation Section
2214 Civil Communication Section
2214.5 Civil Property Custodian Section
2215 Reparations Section
2216 Civilian Personnel Section
2217 Statistics and Reports Section
2218 International Prosecution Section
2219 Allied Council for Japan
2219.3 Far Eastern Commission
Constitutional principles
Executive privilege see KNX2300

General
Constitutional law
Constitutional principles
Separation and delegation of powers -- Continued
2290 No privileges for classes and particular groups.
Renunciation of rights of peerage (Table K11)
Including patent of nobility
2300 Privileges, prerogatives, and immunities of the Emperor (Table K11)
Organs of government
2500 General (Table K11)
The legislature. Legislative power
2511 Parliamentary supremacy
The Diet. Kokkai
2514 General (Table K11)
2515 Sangiin. House of Councillors
2515.3 Shugiin. House of Representatives
The head of state
The Emperor. Nihon-Koku Tennō
2532 General (Table K11)
2535.A-Z Special topics, A-Z
2535.D58 Divinity, Renunciation of (Table K12)
Dynastic rules. Legal status of dynasty see KNX2535.I66
2535.I66 Imperial House Law (16 January 1947) (Table K12)
2535.R45 Regency (Table K12)
2535.S92 Succession (dynastic) to the throne (Table K12)
State and religion. State Shinto
2697 Disestablishment of state Shinto
Administrative law
Administrative organization
Administrative and political divisions. Local government other than municipal
Including those of centralized national governments or federal governments
2920 General works
2935.A-Z Indivdual prefectures (Do, Fu, and Ken), A-Z
Including official gazettes, bylaws, statutory orders, regulations, and general works, as well as works on specific legal topics
2935.A43 Aichi-ken
2935.A55 Akita-ken
2935.A66 Aomori-ken
2935.C55 Chiba-ken
2935.E45 Ehime-ken
2935.F84 Fukui-ken

General
Administrative law
Administrative organization
Administrative and political divisions. Local government other than municipal
Individual prefectures (Do, Fu, and Ken), A-Z -- Continued

2935.F85 Fukuoka-ken
2935.F86 Fukushima-ken
2935.G54 Gifu-ken
2935.G66 Gunma-ken
2935.H57 Hiroshima-ken
Hokkai Dōchō see KNX2935.H75
2935.H75 Hokkaido
Hokkaidō-Chō see KNX2935.H75
2935.H96 Hyōgo-ken
2935.I33 Ibaraki-ken
2935.I75 Ishikawa-ken
2935.I83 Iwate-ken
2935.K35 Kagawa-ken
2935.K36 Kagoshima-ken
2935.K37 Kanagawa-ken
2935.K63 Kōchi-ken
2935.K86 Kumamoto-ken
2935.K95 Kyoto
Kyōto-fu see KNX2935.K95
2935.M54 Mie-ken
2935.M57 Miyagi-ken
2935.M58 Miyazaki-ken
2935.N34 Nagano-ken
2935.N35 Nagasaki-ken
2935.N37 Nara-ken
2935.N55 Niigata-ken
2935.O57 Ōita-ken
2935.O63 Okayama-ken
2935.O64 Okinawa-ken. Ryukyu Islands
2935.O73 Osaka
Osaka-fu see KNX2935.O73
Ryukyu Islands see KNX2935.O64
2935.S35 Saga-ken
2935.S36 Saitama-ken
2935.S55 Shiga-ken
2935.S56 Shimane-ken
2935.S59 Shizuoka-ken
2935.T63 Tochigi-ken
2935.T65 Tokushima-ken

General
Administrative law
Administrative organization
Administrative and political divisions. Local government other than municipal
Individual prefectures (Do, Fu, and Ken), A-Z -- Continued

2935.T66 Tokyo
Tōkyō-to see KNX2935.T66
2935.T68 Tottori-ken
2935.T69 Toyama-ken
2935.W36 Wakayama-ken
2935.Y36 Yamagata-ken
2935.Y365 Yamaguchi-ken
2935.Y37 Yamanashi-ken

Asia (South Asia. Southeast Asia. East Asia): Japan: Cities, communities, etc.

10 Akita-shi (Table KL-KWX9)
12 Aomori-shi (Table KL-KWX9)
16 Chiba-shi (Table KL-KWX9)
20 Fukui-shi (Table KL-KWX9)
24 Fukuoka-shi (Table KL-KWX9)
26 Fukushima-shi (Table KL-KWX9)
30 Gifu-shi (Table KL-KWX9)
34 Hiroshima-shi (Table KL-KWX9)
36 Kagoshima-shi (Table KL-KWX9)
42 Kanazawa-shi (Table KL-KWX9)
44 Kōbe-shi (Table KL-KWX9)
48 Kōfu-shi (Table KL-KWX9)
50 Kumamoto-shi (Table KL-KWX9)
53 Kyoto (Table KL-KWX9)
Kyōtō-shi see KNY53
55 Maebashi-shi (Table KL-KWX9)
63 Matsue-shi (Table KL-KWX9)
65 Masuyama-shi (Table KL-KWX9)
70 Mito-shi (Table KL-KWX9)
72 Miyazaki-shi (Table KL-KWX9)
74 Morioka-shi (Table KL-KWX9)
78 Nagano-shi (Table KL-KWX9)
80 Nagasaki-shi (Table KL-KWX9)
83 Nagoya-shi (Table KL-KWX9)
85 Naha-shi (Table KL-KWX9)
88 Nara-shi (Table KL-KWX9)
92 Niigata-shi (Table KL-KWX9)
96 Ōita-shi (Table KL-KWX9)
100 Okayama-shi (Table KL-KWX9)
104 Osaka (Table KL-KWX9)
Osaka-shi see KNY104
106 Otaru-shi (Table KL-KWX9)
108 Ōtsu-shi (Table KL-KWX9)
112 Saga-shi (Table KL-KWX9)
116 Sapporo-shi (Table KL-KWX9)
120 Sendai-shi (Table KL-KWX9)
122 Shizuoka-shi (Table KL-KWX9)
126 Takamatsu-shi (Table KL-KWX9)
130 Tokushima-shi (Table KL-KWX9)
134 Tokyo (Table KL-KWX9)
Tōkyō-shi see KNY134
136 Tottori-shi (Table KL-KWX9)
140 Toyama-shi (Table KL-KWX9)
143 Tsu-shi (Table KL-KWX9)

146 Urawa-shi (Table KL-KWX9)
149 Utsunomiya-shi (Table KL-KWX9)
153 Wakayama-shi (Table KL-KWX9)
156 Yamagata-shi (Table KL-KWX9)
160 Yamaguchi-shi (Table KL-KWX9)
163 Yokohama-shi (Table KL-KWX9)

220.A-Z Asia (South Asia. Southeast Asia. East Asia): Japan: Other cities, A-Z
Subarrange each by Table K9a
220.A53 Akashi-shi (Table KL-KWX9a)
220.A63 Amagasaki-shi (Table KL-KWX9a)
220.A73 Asahikawa-shi (Table KL-KWX9a)
220.F84 Fuji-shi (Table KL-KWX9a)
220.F845 Fujisawa-shi (Table KL-KWX9a)
220.F85 Fukuyama-shi (Table KL-KWX9a)
220.F86 Funabashi-shi (Table KL-KWX9a)
220.H33 Hachinohe-shi (Table KL-KWX9a)
220.H335 Hachiōji-shi (Table KL-KWX9a)
220.H35 Hakodate-shi (Table KL-KWX9a)
220.H36 Hamamatsu-shi (Table KL-KWX9a)
220.H54 Higashiōsaka-shi (Table KL-KWX9a)
220.H55 Himeji-shi (Table KL-KWX9a)
220.H56 Hirakata-shi (Table KL-KWX9a)
220.H58 Hitachi-shi (Table KL-KWX9a)
220.I33 Ibaraki-shi (Table KL-KWX9a)
220.I35 Ichihara-shi (Table KL-KWX9a)
220.I36 Ichikawa-shi (Table KL-KWX9a)
220.I37 Ichinomiya-shi (Table KL-KWX9a)
220.I83 Iwaki-shi (Table KL-KWX9a)
220.K35 Kakogawa-shi (Table KL-KWX9a)
220.K36 Kashiwa-shi (Table KL-KWX9a)
220.K37 Kasugai-shi (Table KL-KWX9a)
220.K38 Kawagoe-shi (Table KL-KWX9a)
220.K385 Kawaguchi-shi (Table KL-KWX9a)
220.K387 Kawasaki-shi (Table KL-KWX9a)
220.K57 Kitakyūshū-shi (Table KL-KWX9a)
220.K67 Kōriyama-shi (Table KL-KWX9a)
220.K68 Koshigaya-shi (Table KL-KWX9a)
220.K86 Kumagaya-shi (Table KL-KWX9a)
220.K865 Kurashiki-shi (Table KL-KWX9a)
220.K87 Kure-shi (Table KL-KWX9a)
220.K88 Kurume-shi (Table KL-KWX9a)
220.K885 Kushiro-shi (Table KL-KWX9a)
220.M33 Machida-shi (Table KL-KWX9a)
220.M37 Matsudo-shi (Table KL-KWX9a)
220.N49 Neyagawa-shi (Table KL-KWX9a)
220.N55 Niigata-shi (Table KL-KWX9a)
220.N56 Nishinomiya-shi (Table KL-KWX9a)
220.N86 Numazu-shi (Table KL-KWX9a)
220.O65 Ōmiya-shi (Table KL-KWX9a)
220.S34 Sagamihara-shi (Table KL-KWX9a)
220.S35 Sakai-shi (Table KL-KWX9a)

KM-KPW

| | |
|---|---|
| 220.S37 | Sasebo-shi (Table KL-KWX9a) |
| 220.S55 | Shimizu-shi (Table KL-KWX9a) |
| 220.S56 | Shimonoseki-shi (Table KL-KWX9a) |
| 220.S75 | Suita-shi (Table KL-KWX9a) |
| 220.T35 | Takamatsu-shi (Table KL-KWX9a) |
| 220.T36 | Takatsuki-shi (Table KL-KWX9a) |
| 220.T365 | Takasaki-shi (Table KL-KWX9a) |
| 220.T37 | Takeo-shi (Table KL-KWX9a) |
| 220.T65 | Tokorozawa-shi (Table KL-KWX9a) |
| 220.T67 | Toyohashi-shi (Table KL-KWX9a) |
| 220.T675 | Toyonaka-shi (Table KL-KWX9a) |
| 220.T68 | Toyota-shi (Table KL-KWX9a) |
| 220.Y36 | Yao-shi (Table KL-KWX9a) |
| 220.Y65 | Yokkaichi-shi (Table KL-KWX9a) |
| 220.Y66 | Yokosuka-shi (Table KL-KWX9a) |

# ASIA (SOUTH ASIA. SOUTHEAST ASIA. EAST ASIA): KAMPUCHEA

Asia (South Asia. Southeast Asia. East Asia): Kampuchea
see KNM1+

Asia (South Asia. Southeast Asia. East Asia): Korea. South Korea

0-4890 General (Table KL-KWX4 modified)

Add number in table to KPA0

Administrative law

Administrative organization

Administrative and political divisions. Local government other than municipal

Including those of centralized national governments or federal governments

2935.A-Z Provinces (Do), A-Z

Including official gazettes, bylaws, statutory orders, regulations, and general works, as well as works on specific legal topics

2935.C43 Cheju-do

2935.C45 Chŏlla-namdo

2935.C46 Chŏlla-pukto

2935.C55 Ch'ungch'ŏng-namdo

2935.C56 Ch'ungch'ŏng-pukto

2935.K36 Kwangwŏn-do

2935.K86 Kyŏnggi-do

2935.K87 Kyŏngsang-namdo

2935.K88 Kyongsang-pukto

2935.P87 Pusan

2935.S46 Seoul

Cities, communities, etc.

4980 Cheju-si (Table KL-KWX9)

4981 Ch'ŏngju-si (Table KL-KWX9)

4982 Chŏnju-si (Table KL-KWX9)

4983 Ch'unch'ŏn-si (Table KL-KWX9)

4984 Inch'ŏn (Table KL-KWX9)

4985 Kwangju-si (Table KL-KWX9)

4986 Suwŏn-si (Table KL-KWX9)

4987 Taegu (Table KL-KWX9)

4988 Taejŏn-si (Table KL-KWX9)

4990.A-.X Other cities, A-Z

Subarrange each by Table KL-KWX9a

Asia (South Asia. Southeast Asia. East Asia): Democratic People's Republic of Korea. North Korea

0-4890 General (Table KL-KWX4 modified)

Add number in table to KPC0

Administrative law

Administrative organization

Administrative and political divisions. Local government other than municipal

Including those of centralized national governments or federal governments

2935.A-Z Provinces (Do), A-Z

Including official gazettes, bylaws, statutory orders, regulations, and general works, as well as works on specific legal topics

2935.C53 Chagang-do

2935.C56 Ch'ŏngjin-si

2935.H35 Hamgyŏng-butko

2935.H36 Hamgyŏng-namdo

2935.H93 Hwanghae-namdo

2935.H94 Hwanghae-putko

2935.K33 Kaesŏng-si

2935.K34 Kangwŏn-do

2935.P95 P'yŏngan-namdo

2935.P96 P'yŏngan-pukto

2935.P97 P'yŏngyang

2935.Y36 Yanggang-do

Cities, communities, etc.

4985 Sinuiju-si (Table KL-KWX9)

4988 Wonsan (Table KL-KWX9)

4990.A-Z Other cities, A-Z

Subarrange each by Table KL-KWX9a

Asia (South Asia. Southeast Asia. East Asia): Laos

0-4890 General (Table KL-KWX4 modified)

Add number in table to KPE0

Administrative law

Administrative organization

Administrative and political divisions. Local government other than municipal

Including those of centralized national governments or federal governments

2935.A-Z Provinces, A-Z

Including official gazettes, bylaws, statutory orders, regulations, and general works, as well as works on specific legal topics

2935.A88 Attapu

2935.B64 Bokeo

2935.B65 Bolikhamsai

2935.C53 Champasak

Houaphán see KPE2935.X36

Khammouan see KPE2935.M83

2935.K56 Khouéng

2935.K57 Khouéng Louang Namtha

2935.L67 Louangphrabang

2935.M83 Muang Khammouan

2935.M84 Muang Khôngxédôn

2935.O84 Oudomxay

2935.P56 Phôngsali

Sam Neua see KPE2935.X36

2935.S36 Saravan

Sayabury see KPE2935.X34

2935.S39 Savannakhét

Sedone see KPE2935.M84

Sekong see KPE2935.X45

2935.V53 Viangchan

Vientiane see KPE2935.V53

2935.X34 Xaignabouri

2935.X36 Xam Nua

Xédôn see KPE2935.M84

2935.X45 Xehong

2935.X53 Xiangkhoang

Cities, communities, etc.

4985 Luangphrabang (Table KL-KWX9)

4986 Pakxe (Table KL-KWX9)

4987 Svannakhét (Table KL-KWX9)

4988 Vientiane (Table KL-KWX9)

4990.A-Z Other cities

Subarrange each by Table KL-KWX9a

Asia (South Asia. Southeast Asia. East Asia): Macau (to 1999)

Portuguese overseas territory (pessoa collectiva)

For Macau (Special administrative region of China) see KNQ9401+

1-489 General (Table KL-KWX5)

Asia (South Asia. Southeast Asia. East Asia): Malaysia
Including the different groupings of the Maylayan States
1-4890 General (Table KL-KWX6)
Straits Settlements (to 1942)
Including Singapore, Penang, and Malacca
For Singapore see KPP1+
5001-5499 General (Table KL-KWX7)
Federated Malay States (1896-1942)
Including Pahang, Perak, Negeri Sembilan, and Selangor
5501-5599 General (Table KL-KWX7)
Malayan Union (1946-1947)
Including Malayan States, Penang, and Malacca
6001-6499 General (Table KL-KWX7)
Malaya (1948-1962)
6501-6999 General (Table KL-KWX7)

Asia (South Asia. Southeast Asia. East Asia): Malaysia: States of East and West Malaysia (1957- ) (Part 1)

Brunei see KNK1+

7001-7499 Federal Territory (Kuala Lumpur) (Table KL-KWX7 modified)

Law reports and related materials

For reports relating to a particular subject, and for reports of courts of limited jurisdiction other than those listed below, see the appropriate subject

State courts

7002.2 Highest court of appeal. Supreme court. Court of Cassation (Table K18)

Lower courts

7002.23 Various courts (Table K18)

Including highest court and lower courts

Intermediate appellate courts. Courts of appeals

7002.24 Collective (Table K18)

7002.25.A-Z Particular courts, A-Z

(7002.27) Digests and indexes to state court decisions

see KPG7002.2 ; KPG7002.23 ; etc.

Local courts

7002.3 General (Table K18)

7002.35.A-Z Particular courts. By city, etc., A-Z

7002.4 Decisions of state administrative agencies

For decisions of particular agencies, see the subject

7501-7999 Johor (Table KL-KWX7 modified)

Law reports and related materials

For reports relating to a particular subject, and for reports of courts of limited jurisdiction other than those listed below, see the appropriate subject

State courts

7502.2 Highest court of appeal. Supreme court. Court of Cassation (Table K18)

Lower courts

7502.23 Various courts (Table K18)

Including highest court and lower courts

Intermediate appellate courts. Courts of appeals

7502.24 Collective (Table K18)

7502.25.A-Z Particular courts, A-Z

(7502.27) Digests and indexes to state court decisions

see KPG7502.2 ; KPG7502.23 ; etc.

Local courts

7502.3 General (Table K18)

7502.35.A-Z Particular courts. By city, etc., A-Z

7502.4 Decisions of state administrative agencies

For decisions of particular agencies, see the subject

8001-8499 Kedah (Table KL-KWX7 modified)
Law reports and related materials
For reports relating to a particular subject, and for reports of courts of limited jurisdiction other than those listed below, see the appropriate subject
State courts
8002.2 Highest court of appeal. Supreme court. Court of Cassation (Table K18)
Lower courts
8002.23 Various courts (Table K18)
Including highest court and lower courts
Intermediate appellate courts. Courts of appeals
8002.24 Collective (Table K18)
8002.25.A-Z Particular courts, A-Z
(8002.27) Digests and indexes to state court decisions
see KPG8002.2 ; KPG8002.23 ; etc.
Local courts
8002.3 General (Table K18)
8002.35.A-Z Particular courts. By city, etc., A-Z
8002.4 Decisions of state administrative agencies
For decisions of particular agencies, see the subject
8501-8999 Kelantan (Table KL-KWX7 modified)
Law reports and related materials
For reports relating to a particular subject, and for reports of courts of limited jurisdiction other than those listed below, see the appropriate subject
State courts
8502.2 Highest court of appeal. Supreme court. Court of Cassation (Table K18)
Lower courts
8502.23 Various courts (Table K18)
Including highest court and lower courts
Intermediate appellate courts. Courts of appeals
8502.24 Collective (Table K18)
8502.25.A-Z Particular courts, A-Z
(8502.27) Digests and indexes to state court decisions
see KPG8502. ; KPG8502.23 ; etc.2
Local courts
8502.3 General (Table K18)
8502.35.A-Z Particular courts. By city, etc., A-Z
8502.4 Decisions of state administrative agencies
For decisions of particular agencies, see the subject
Labuan see KPH4501+
9001-9499 Malacca (Table KL-KWX7 modified)

Malacca -- Continued
Law reports and related materials
For reports relating to a particular subject, and for reports of courts of limited jurisdiction other than those listed below, see the appropriate subject
State courts
9002.2 Highest court of appeal. Supreme court. Court of Cassation (Table K18)
Lower courts
9002.23 Various courts (Table K18)
Including highest court and lower courts
Intermediate appellate courts. Courts of appeals
9002.24 Collective (Table K18)
9002.25.A-Z Particular courts, A-Z
(9002.27) Digests and indexes to state court decisions
see KPG9002.2 ; KPG9002.23 ; etc.
Local courts
9002.3 General (Table K18)
9002.35.A-Z Particular courts. By city, etc., A-Z
9002.4 Decisions of state administrative agencies
For decisions of particular agencies, see the subject
9501-9999 Negeri Sembilan (Table KL-KWX7 modified)
Law reports and related materials
For reports relating to a particular subject, and for reports of courts of limited jurisdiction other than those listed below, see the appropriate subject
State courts
9502.2 Highest court of appeal. Supreme court. Court of Cassation (Table K18)
Lower courts
9502.23 Various courts (Table K18)
Including highest court and lower courts
Intermediate appellate courts. Courts of appeals
9502.24 Collective (Table K18)
9502.25.A-Z Particular courts, A-Z
(9502.27) Digests and indexes to state court decisions
see KPG9502.2 ; KPG9502.23 ; etc.
Local courts
9502.3 General (Table K18)
9502.35.A-Z Particular courts. By city, etc., A-Z
9502.4 Decisions of state administrative agencies
For decisions of particular agencies, see the subject

Asia (South Asia. Southeast Asia. East Asia): Malaysia: States of East and West Malaysia (1957- ) (Part 2)

1-499 Pahang (Table KL-KWX7 modified)

Law reports and related materials

For reports relating to a particular subject, and for reports of courts of limited jurisdiction other than those listed below, see the appropriate subject

State courts

2.2 Highest court of appeal. Supreme court. Court of Cassation (Table K18)

Lower courts

2.23 Various courts (Table K18)

Including highest court and lower courts

Intermediate appellate courts. Courts of appeals

2.24 Collective (Table K18)

2.25.A-Z Particular courts, A-Z

(2.27) Digests and indexes to state court decisions

see KPH2.2 ; KPH2.23 ; etc.

Local courts

2.3 General (Table K18)

2.35.A-Z Particular courts. By city, etc., A-Z

2.4 Decisions of state administrative agencies

For decisions of particular agencies, see the subject

501-999 Pinang (Table KL-KWX7 modified)

Law reports and related materials

For reports relating to a particular subject, and for reports of courts of limited jurisdiction other than those listed below, see the appropriate subject

State courts

502.2 Highest court of appeal. Supreme court. Court of Cassation (Table K18)

Lower courts

502.23 Various courts (Table K18)

Including highest court and lower courts

Intermediate appellate courts. Courts of appeals

502.24 Collective (Table K18)

502.25.A-Z Particular courts, A-Z

(502.27) Digests and indexes to state court decisions

see KPH502.2 ; KPH502.23 ; etc.

Local courts

502.3 General (Table K18)

502.35.A-Z Particular courts. By city, etc., A-Z

502.4 Decisions of state administrative agencies

For decisions of particular agencies, see the subject

1001-1499 Perak (Table KL-KWX7 modified)

Perak -- Continued
Law reports and related materials
For reports relating to a particular subject, and for reports of courts of limited jurisdiction other than those listed below, see the appropriate subject
State courts
1002.2 Highest court of appeal. Supreme court. Court of Cassation (Table K18)
Lower courts
1002.23 Various courts (Table K18)
Including highest court and lower courts
Intermediate appellate courts. Courts of appeals
1002.24 Collective (Table K18)
1002.25.A-Z Particular courts, A-Z
(1002.27) Digests and indexes to state court decisions
see KPH1002.2 ; KPH1002.23 ; etc.
Local courts
1002.3 General (Table K18)
1002.35.A-Z Particular courts. By city, etc., A-Z
1002.4 Decisions of state administrative agencies
For decisions of particular agencies, see the subject
1501-1999 Perlis (Table KL-KWX7 modified)
Law reports and related materials
For reports relating to a particular subject, and for reports of courts of limited jurisdiction other than those listed below, see the appropriate subject
State courts
1502.2 Highest court of appeal. Supreme court. Court of Cassation (Table K18)
Lower courts
1502.23 Various courts (Table K18)
Including highest court and lower courts
Intermediate appellate courts. Courts of appeals
1502.24 Collective (Table K18)
1502.25.A-Z Particular courts, A-Z
(1502.27) Digests and indexes to state court decisions
see KPH1502.2 ; KPH1502.23 ; etc.
Local courts
1502.3 General (Table K18)
1502.35.A-Z Particular courts. By city, etc., A-Z
1502.4 Decisions of state administrative agencies
For decisions of particular agencies, see the subject
2001-2499 Sabah (Table KL-KWX7 modified)
Previously North Borneo

Sabah -- Continued
Law reports and related materials
For reports relating to a particular subject, and for reports of courts of limited jurisdiction other than those listed below, see the appropriate subject
State courts
2002.2 Highest court of appeal. Supreme court. Court of Cassation (Table K18)
Lower courts
2002.23 Various courts (Table K18)
Including highest court and lower courts
Intermediate appellate courts. Courts of appeals
2002.24 Collective (Table K18)
2002.25.A-Z Particular courts, A-Z
(2002.27) Digests and indexes to state court decisions
see KPH2002.2 ; KPH2002.23 ; etc.
Local courts
2002.3 General (Table K18)
2002.35.A-Z Particular courts. By city, etc., A-Z
2002.4 Decisions of state administrative agencies
For decisions of particular agencies, see the subject
2501-2999 Sarawak (Table KL-KWX7 modified)
Law reports and related materials
For reports relating to a particular subject, and for reports of courts of limited jurisdiction other than those listed below, see the appropriate subject
State courts
2502.2 Highest court of appeal. Supreme court. Court of Cassation (Table K18)
Lower courts
2502.23 Various courts (Table K18)
Including highest court and lower courts
Intermediate appellate courts. Courts of appeals
2502.24 Collective (Table K18)
2502.25.A-Z Particular courts, A-Z
(2502.27) Digests and indexes to state court decisions
see KPH2502.2 ; KPH2502.23 ; etc.
Local courts
2502.3 General (Table K18)
2502.35.A-Z Particular courts. By city, etc., A-Z
2502.4 Decisions of state administrative agencies
For decisions of particular agencies, see the subject
3001-3499 Selangor (Table KL-KWX7 mdofied)

Selangor -- Continued
Law reports and related materials
For reports relating to a particular subject, and for reports of courts of limited jurisdiction other than those listed below, see the appropriate subject
State courts
3002.2 Highest court of appeal. Supreme court. Court of Cassation (Table K18)
Lower courts
3002.23 Various courts (Table K18)
Including highest court and lower courts
Intermediate appellate courts. Courts of appeals
3002.24 Collective (Table K18)
3002.25.A-Z Particular courts, A-Z
(3002.27) Digests and indexes to state court decisions
see KPH3002.2 ; KPH3002.23 ; etc.
Local courts
3002.3 General (Table K18)
3002.35.A-Z Particular courts. By city, etc., A-Z
3002.4 Decisions of state administrative agencies
For decisions of particular agencies, see the subject
4001-4499 Terengganu (Table KL-KWX7 modified)
Law reports and related materials
For reports relating to a particular subject, and for reports of courts of limited jurisdiction other than those listed below, see the appropriate subject
State courts
4002.2 Highest court of appeal. Supreme court. Court of Cassation (Table K18)
Lower courts
4002.23 Various courts (Table K18)
Including highest court and lower courts
Intermediate appellate courts. Courts of appeals
4002.24 Collective (Table K18)
4002.25.A-Z Particular courts, A-Z
(4002.27) Digests and indexes to state court decisions
see KPH4002.2 ; KPH4002.23 ; etc.
Local courts
4002.3 General (Table K18)
4002.35.A-Z Particular courts. By city, etc., A-Z
4002.4 Decisions of state administrative agencies
For decisions of particular agencies, see the subject
4501-4999 Labuan (Table KL-KWX7 modified)

Labuan -- Continued
Law reports and related materials
For reports relating to a particular subject, and for reports of courts of limited jurisdiction other than those listed below, see the appropriate subject
State courts
4502.2 Highest court of appeal. Supreme court. Court of Cassation (Table K18)
Lower courts
4502.23 Various courts (Table K18)
Including highest court and lower courts
Intermediate appellate courts. Courts of appeals
4502.24 Collective (Table K18)
4502.25.A-Z Particular courts, A-Z
(4502.27) Digests and indexes to state court decisions
see KPH4502.2 ; KPH4502.23 ; etc.
Local courts
4502.3 General (Table K18)
4502.35.A-Z Particular courts. By city, etc., A-Z
4502.4 Decisions of state administrative agencies
For decisions of particular agencies, see the subject

Asia (South Asia. Southeast Asia. East Asia): Malaysia: Cities, communities, etc.

4999.2 Alor Star (Table KL-KWX9)
4999.4 Georgetown (Table KL-KWX9)
4999.43 Ipoh (Table KL-KWX9)
4999.44 Johor Bharu (Table KL-KWX9)
4999.45 Kota Bahru (Table KL-KWX9)
4999.46 Kota Kinabalu (Table KL-KWX9)
4999.47 Kuala Lumpur (Table KL-KWX9)
4999.48 Kuala Trengganu (Table KL-KWX9)
4999.5 Kuantan (Table KL-KWX9)
4999.65 Kuching (Table KL-KWX9)
4999.75 Malacca (Table KL-KWX9)
4999.76 Seremban (Table KL-KWX9)
4999.77 Shah Alam (Table KL-KWX9)
4999.9.A-Z Other cities, A-Z

Subarrange each by Table KL-KWX9a

Asia (South Asia. Southeast Asia. East Asia): Maldives

5001-5489 General (Table KL-KWX7 modified)

Administrative and political divisions. Local government other than municipal

5231.5.A-Z Administrative divisions, A-Z

Including official gazettes, bylaws, statutory orders, regulations, and general works, as well as works on specific legal topics

5231.5.A55 Aliffa
5231.5.B33 Baa
5231.5.D35 Dalu
5231.5.F33 Faafu
5231.5.G33 Gaafu Aliff
5231.5.G335 Gaafu Daalu
5231.5.H33 Haa Aliff
5231.5.H335 Haa Daalu
5231.5.K33 Kaafu
5231.5.L33 Laamu
5231.5.L38 Laviyani
5231.5.M35 Male
5231.5.M44 Meenu
5231.5.N38 Naviyani
5231.5.N66 Noonu
5231.5.R33 Raa
5231.5.S44 Seenu
5231.5.S53 Shaviyani
5231.5.T53 Thaa
5231.5.W33 Waavu

5490.A-Z Cities, communities, etc., A-Z

Subarrange each by Table KL-KWX9a

5490.M35 Male (Table KL-KWX9a)

Asia (South Asia. Southeast Asia. East Asia): Mongolia

1-489 General (Table KL-KWX5 modified)

Administrative law

Administrative organization

Administrative and political divisions. Local government other than municipal

Including those of centralized national governments or federal governments

293.5.A-Z Provinces (Aĭmag), A-Z

Including official gazettes, bylaws, statutory orders, regulations, and general works, as well as works on specific legal topics

293.5.A75 Arkhangaĭ Aĭmag

293.5.B34 Baı͡an-Olgiĭ Aĭmag

293.5.B35 Baı͡ankhongor Aĭmag

293.5.B85 Bulgan Aĭmag

293.5.D67 Dornod Aĭmag

293.5.D68 Dornogov' Aĭmag

293.5.D86 Dundgov' Aĭmag

293.5.D93 Dzavkhan Aĭmag

293.5.G68 Gov'-Altai Aĭmag

293.5.K54 Khėntiĭ Aĭmag

293.5.K68 Kovd Aĭmag

293.5.K685 Kȯvsgȯl Aĭmag

293.5.O96 Ovȯrkhangaĭ Aĭmag

293.5.S45 Sėlėngė Aĭmag

293.5.S85 Su̇khbaatar Aĭmag

293.5.T68 Tȯv Aĭmag

293.5.U98 Uvs Aĭmag

490.A-Z Cities, municipalities, etc., A-Z

Subarrange each by Table KL-KWX9a

490.D37 Darkhan (Table KL-KWX9a)

490.E74 Erdenet (Table KL-KWX9a)

490.U53 Ulaanbaatar (Table KL-KWX9a)

ASIA (SOUTH ASIA. SOUTHEAST ASIA. EAST ASIA):
MYANMAR

Asia (South Asia. Southeast Asia. East Asia): Myanmar
see KNL1+

Asia (South Asia. Southeast Asia. East Asia): Nepal

1-489 General (Table KL-KWX7 modified)

Administrative and political divisions. Local government other than municipal

231.5.A-Z Administrative zones, A-Z

Including official gazettes, bylaws, statutory orders, regulations, and general works, as well as works on specific legal topics

231.5.B35 Bagmati Zone

231.5.B54 Bherī Zone

231.5.D53 Dhawalāgiri Zone

231.5.G36 Gandaki Zone

231.5.J36 Janakpur Zone

231.5.K37 Karnālī Zone

231.5.K68 Kosī Zone

231.5.L86 Lumbinī Zone

231.5.M35 Mahākālī Zone

231.5.M43 Mechī Zone

231.5.N37 Nārāyani Zone

231.5.R36 Rāptī Zone

231.5.S35 Sagarmāthā Zone

231.5.S47 Setī Zone

490.A-Z Cities, communities, etc., A-Z

Subarrange each by Table KL-KWX9a

490.B53 BhÕadgaon (Table KL-KWX9a)

490.K37 Kathmandu (Table KL-KWX9a)

490.M67 Morang (Table KL-KWX9a)

490.P37 PÕatan (Table KL-KWX9a)

Asia (South Asia. Southeast Asia. East Asia): Pakistan

1-4890 General (Table KL-KWX6 modified)

Administrative and political divisions. Local government other than municipal

2315.A-Z Provinces, A-Z

Including official gazettes, bylaws, statutory orders, regulations, and general works, as well as works on specific legal topics

2315.A93 Azad Kashmir

2315.B35 Balochistān

2315.N68 North-West Frontier Province

2315.P76 Punjab

2315.S56 Sindh

Cities, communities, etc.

4980 Islamabad (Capital Territory) (Table KL-KWX9)

4981 Karachi (Table KL-KWX9)

4982 Lahore (Table KL-KWX9)

4983 Faisalabad (Table KL-KWX9)

4984 Rawalpindi (Table KL-KWX9)

4985 Hyderabad (Table KL-KWX9)

4986 Multan (Table KL-KWX9)

4987 Gujranwala (Table KL-KWX9)

4990.A-Z Other cities, A-Z

Subarrange each by Table KL-KWX9a

4990.J43 Jhang (Table KL-KWX9a)

4990.K37 Kasur (Table KL-KWX9a)

4990.Q84 Quetta (Table KL-KWX9a)

4990.S37 Sargodha (Table KL-KWX9a)

4990.S85 Sukkur (Table KL-KWX9a)

Asia (South Asia. Southeast Asia. East Asia): Philippines

1-4999 General (Table KL-KWX6 modified)

Law of Philippine peoples

Class here works on the law of Philippine peoples regardless of whether they are identified with a particular territory, island, or with the region at large

For subjects, see the subject

350 Customals. Collections of laws and customs. Codes of customary law

For court rules, trial practice, etc., in native courts, see the court

352.A-Z By territory, or island, A-Z

354 General works. Treatises

Including history

Particular peoples or ethnic groups

For particular subjects, see the subject

356 Aeta

359 Bagobo

360 Batak

362 Bikols

364 Bontoks

366 Buhid

367 Bukidnon

369 Cebuano

375 Gaddang

378 Hiligaynon

385 Ibanag

386 Igorot

387 Ilokanos

388 Isneg

390 Itawis

391 Iwaak

395 Magindanaos

396 Mandaya

397 Mangyan

398 Manobos

399 Mansaka

400 Maranao

405 Palawan

408 Samals

409 Sulod

410 Tagalog

412 Tasaday

413 Tboli

415 Tinguian

416 Tiruray

General
Law of Philippine peoples
Particular peoples or ethnic groups -- Continued
420 Yakan
Administrative and political divisions. Local government other than municipal
2315.A-Z Provinces, A-Z
Including official gazettes, bylaws, statutory orders, regulations, and general works, as well as works on specific legal topics
2315.A37 Abra
2315.A47 Agusan del Norte
2315.A48 Agusan del Sur
2315.A54 Aklan
2315.A55 Albay
2315.A68 Antique
2315.B35 Basilan
2315.B36 Bataan
2315.B37 Batanes
2315.B38 Bantangas
2315.B46 Benguet
2315.B65 Bohol
2315.B84 Bukidnon
2315.B85 Bulacan
2315.C33 Cagayan
2315.C35 Camarines Norte
2315.C355 Camarines Sur
2315.C36 Camiguin
2315.C365 Capiz
2315.C37 Catanduanes Province
2315.C38 Cavite Province
2315.C43 Cebu
2315.D36 Davao del Sur
2315.D38 Davao Oriental
2315.E37 Eastern Samar
2315.I48 Ifugao
2315.I55 Ilocos Norte
2315.I56 Ilocos Sur
2315.I57 Iloilo
2315.I83 Isabela
2315.K35 Kalinga-Apayao
2315.L32 La Union
2315.L35 Laguna
2315.L36 Lanao del Norte
2315.L37 Lanao del Sur
2315.L49 Leyte

General
Administrative and political divisions. Local government other than municipal
Provinces, A-Z -- Continued

2315.M35 Maguindanao
2315.M37 Marinduque
2315.M38 Masbate
2315.M56 Mindoro Occidental
2315.M57 Mindoro Oriental
2315.M58 Misamis Occidental
2315.M585 Misamis Oriental
2315.M68 Mountain Province
2315.N44 Negros Occidental
2315.N45 Negros Oriental
2315.N67 North Cotabato
2315.N68 Northern Samar
2315.N84 Nueva Ecija
2315.N86 Nueva Vizcaya
2315.P35 Palawan
2315.P36 Pampanga
2315.P37 Pangasinan
2315.Q84 Quezon
2315.Q85 Quirino
2315.R59 Rizal
2315.R66 Romblon
2315.S36 Samar
2315.S56 Siquijor
2315.S66 Sorsogon
2315.S67 South Cotabato
2315.S68 Southern Leyte
2315.S85 Sultan Kudarat
2315.S86 Sulu
2315.S87 Surigao del Norte
2315.S88 Surigao del Sur
2315.T37 Tarlac
2315.T38 Tawitawi
2315.W47 Western Samar
2315.Z35 Zambales
2315.Z36 Zamboanga del Norte
2315.Z37 Zamboanga del Sur

Cities, communities, etc.

4980 Bacolod (Table KL-KWX9)
4981 Cebu (Table KL-KWX9)
4983 Davao (Table KL-KWX9)
4985 Iloilo (Table KL-KWX9)
4987 Manila (Table KL-KWX9)

Cities, communities, etc. -- Continued

4988 Pasay (Table KL-KWX9)

4989 Quezon City (Table KL-KWX9)

4990.A-Z Other cities, A-Z

Subarrange each by Table KL-KWX9a

4990.S36 San Carlos (Table KL-KWX9a)

4990.Z36 Zamboanga City (Table KL-KWX9a)

Asia (South Asia. Southeast Asia. East Asia): Singapore

Previously one of the Straits Settlements, together with Penang and Malacca

For 1957-1965, a State in the Federation of Malaysia see KPG5001+

| | |
|---|---|
| 1-498 | General (Table KL-KWX7) |
| 499.A-Z | Cities, communities, etc., A-Z<br>Subarrange each by Table KL-KWX9a |
| 499.C53 | Changi (Table KL-KWX9a) |
| 499.G48 | Geylang Serai (Table KL-KWX9a) |
| 499.J87 | Jurong (Table KL-KWX9a) |
| 499.P37 | Pasir Panjang (Table KL-KWX9a) |

Asia (South Asia. Southeast Asia. East Asia): Sri Lanka
Previously known as Ceylon

1-4890 General (Table KL-KWX6 modified)
Administrative and political divisions. Local government other than municipal
2315.A-Z Administrative districts, A-Z
Including official gazettes, bylaws, statutory orders, regulations, and general works, as well as works on specific legal topics
2315.A66 Amparai District
2315.B34 Badulla District
2315.B37 Baticaloa District
2315.C65 Colombo District
2315.G35 Galle District
2315.G37 Gampaha District
2315.H36 Hambantota District
2315.J34 Jaffna District
2315.K87 Kurunegala District
2315.M35 Mannar District
2315.M37 Matale District
2315.M38 Matara District
2315.M85 Mullattivu District
2315.N88 Nuwara Eliya District
2315.P65 Polonnaruwa District
2315.R37 Ratnapura District
2315.V38 Vavuniya District
Cities, communities, etc.
4980 Colombo (Table KL-KWX9)
4981 Dehiwela (Table KL-KWX9)
4982 Galle (Table KL-KWX9)
4983 Jaffna (Table KL-KWX9)
4984 Kandy (Table KL-KWX9)
4985 Kotte (Table KL-KWX9)
4986 Kurunegala (Table KL-KWX9)
4987 Moratuwa (Table KL-KWX9)
4988 Nuwara Eliya (Table KL-KWX9)
4990.A-Z Other cities, A-Z
Subarrange each by Table KL-KWX9a
4990.A68 Anuradhapura (Table KL-KWX9a)
4990.K35 Kalutara (Table KL-KWX9a)
4990.M38 Matara (Table KL-KWX9a)
4990.T75 Trincomalee (Table KL-KWX9a)

Asia (South Asia. Southeast Asia. East Asia): Taiwan
see KNP1+

Asia (South Asia. Southeast Asia. East Asia): Thailand
Previously Siam
0-4890 General (Table KL-KWX4 modified)
Add number in table to KPT0
Customary law for ethnic minorities
Class here works on the law of Thai peoples regardless of whether they are identified with a particular province or the region at large
For particular subjects, see the subject
Collections of laws and customs. Codes of customary law. Treaties
For court rules, trial practice in customary (native) courts, see the court
350 General
352.A-Z By region or state, A-Z
354 General works. Treatises
Including history
Administrative law
Administrative organization
Administrative and political divisions. Local government other than municipal
Including those of centralized national governments or federal governments
2935.A-Z Provinces (Changwat), A-Z
Including official gazettes, bylaws, statutory orders, regulations, and general works, as well as works on specific legal topics
2935.A64 Ang Thong
Ayuthia see KPT2935.P575
2935.B87 Buriram
2935.C43 Chachoengsao
2935.C44 Chai Nat
2935.C445 Chaiyaphum
2935.C45 Chanthaburi
2935.C46 Chiang Mai
2935.C465 Chiang Rai
2935.C47 Chon Buri
2935.C48 Chumphon
2935.K35 Kalasin
2935.K36 Kamphaeng Phet
2935.K37 Kanchanaburi
2935.K56 Khon Kaen
2935.K73 Krabi
2935.L36 Lampang
2935.L37 Lamphun
2935.L64 Loei

General
Administrative law
Administrative organization
Administrative and political divisions. Local government other than municipal
Provinces (Changwat), A-Z -- Continued

2935.L66 Lop Buri
2935.M34 Mae Hong Son
2935.M35 Maha Sarakham
2935.M85 Mukdahan
2935.N34 Nakhon Nayok
2935.N345 Nakhon Pathom
2935.N35 Nakhon Phanom
2935.N36 Nakhon Ratchasima
2935.N365 Nakhon Sawan
2935.N37 Nakhon Si Thammarat
2935.N38 Nan
2935.N66 Narathiwat
2935.N67 Nong Khai
2935.N68 Nonthaburi
2935.P37 Pathum Thani
2935.P38 Pattani
2935.P43 Phangnga
2935.P44 Phatthalung
2935.P45 Phayao
2935.P53 Phetchabun
2935.P56 Phichit
2935.P565 Phitsanulok
2935.P575 Phra Nakhon Si Ayutthaya
2935.P58 Phrae
2935.P59 Phuket
2935.P73 Prachin Buri
2935.P74 Prachuap Khiri Khan
2935.R36 Ranong
2935.R37 Ratchaburi
2935.R38 Rayong
2935.R65 Roi Et
2935.S34 Sakon Nakhon
2935.S345 Samut Prakan
2935.S35 Samut Sakhon
2935.S355 Samut Songkhram
2935.S36 Saraburi
2935.S37 Satun
2935.S54 Sing Buri
2935.S57 Sisaket
2935.S66 Songkhla

General
Administrative law
Administrative organization
Administrative and political divisions. Local government other than municipal
Provinces (Changwat), A-Z -- Continued

2935.S74 Sukhothai
2935.S75 Suphan Buri
2935.S76 Surat Thani
2935.S77 Surin
2935.T35 Tak
Thammarat see KPT2935.N365
2935.T56 Thon Buri
2935.T73 Trang
2935.T74 Trat
2935.U35 Ubon Ratchatani
2935.U46 Udon Thani
2935.U85 Uthai Thani
2935.U88 Uttaradit
2935.Y35 Yala
2935.Y37 Yasothon

Cities, communities, etc.

4980 Bangkok (Table KL-KWX9)
4981 Chiang Mai (Table KL-KWX9)
4982 Hat Yai (Table KL-KWX9)
4983 Kohn Kaen (Table KL-KWX9)
4984 Nakhon Ratchasima (Table KL-KWX9)
4985 Nakhon Sawan (Table KL-KWX9)
4986 Nakhon Si Thammarat (Table KL-KWX9)
4987 Phitsanulok (Table KL-KWX9)
4988 Songkhla (Table KL-KWX9)
4989 Udon Thani (Table KL-KWX9)
4990.A-Z Other cities, A-Z
Subarrange each by Table KL-KWX9a

Asia (South Asia. Southeast Asia. East Asia): Tibet
see KNQ8701+

# ASIA (SOUTH ASIA. SOUTHEAST ASIA. EAST ASIA): TONKIN

Asia (South Asia. Southeast Asia. East Asia): Tonkin
see KNV1+ ; KPV1+

Asia (South Asia. Southeast Asia. East Asia): Vietnam
Class here works on the law of Vietnam prior to 1945, the law of the Democratic Republic of Vietnam (North Vietnam) during the period 1945-1975, and the law of the reunified Vietnam (Socialist Republic of Vietnam) since 1975
Including Annam, Tonkin, and Cochin-China
For the law of the Republic of Vietnam (South Vietnam) during the period 1956-1975 see KPW1+



0-4999 General (Table KL-KWX4 modified)
Add number in table to KPV0
Customary law for ethnic minorities
Class here works on the law of Vietnamese peoples regardless of whether they are identified with a particular province or the region at large
For particular subjects, see the subject
Collections of laws and customs. Codes of customary law. Treaties
For court rules, trial practice in customary (native) courts, see the court
350 General
352.A-Z By region or state, A-Z
354 General works. Treatises
Including history
Particular peoples or ethnic groups
For particular subjects, see the subject
370 Mnong (Table KL-KWX12)
390 Rhade (Table KL-KWX12)
395 Tai (Table KL-KWX12)
Administrative law
Administrative organization
Administrative and political divisions. Local government other than municipal
Including those of centralized national governments or federal governments
2935.A-Z Provinces (Tinh), A-Z
Including autonomous municipalities
Including official gazettes, bylaws, statutory orders, regulations, and general works, as well as works on specific legal topics
2935.A63 An Giang
2935.B34 Bắc Thái
2935.B46 Bến Tre
2935.B54 Biên Hòa (To 1975)

General
Administrative law
Administrative organization
Administrative and political divisions. Local government other than municipal
Provinces (Tinh), A-Z -- Continued

2935.B55 Bình Định
Cf. KPV2935.Q827 Quang Bình
Cf. KPV2935.Q85 Quang Trị
Cf. KPV2935.T57 Thùa Thiên-Huế
2935.B56 Bình Trị Thiên (To 1989)
2935.C36 Cao-Bằng
2935.C88 Cuu Long
2935.D33 Đắc Lắc
2935.D66 Đồng Nai
2935.D67 Đồng Tháp
2935.G53 Gia Lai-Kon Tum
2935.H33 Hà Bắc
2935.H34 Hà Nam Ninh
2935.H35 Hà Sơn Bình
2935.H353 Hà Tây
2935.H355 Hà Tuyên
2935.H36 Hai Hung
2935.H365 Haiphong
2935.H37 Hanoi
2935.H38 Hậu Giang
2935.H63 Ho Chi Minh City
2935.H635 Hoàng Liên Sơn
2935.K43 Khán Hòa
2935.K54 Kiên Giang
2935.L35 Lai Châu
2935.L36 Lâm Đồng
Lạng Sơn see KPV2935.C36
2935.L66 Long An
2935.M56 Minh Hai
2935.N44 Nghệ Tĩnh
2935.N45 Nghĩa Bình (to 1989)
Cf. KPV2935.B55 Bình Định
Cf. KPV2935.Q838 Quang Ngãi
2935.P48 Phú Khánh (to 1989)
Cf. KPV2935.K43 Khán Hòa
Cf. KPV2935.P485 Phú Yên
2935.P485 Phú Yên
2935.Q827 Quang Bình
2935.Q83 Quang Nam
2935.Q838 Quang Ngãi

General
Administrative law
Administrative organization
Administrative and political divisions. Local government other than municipal
Provinces (Tinh), A-Z -- Continued
2935.Q84 Quang Ninh
2935.Q85 Quang Trị
2935.S66 Sơn La
2935.S665 Sông Bé
2935.T39 Tây Ninh
2935.T53 Thái Bình
2935.T54 Thanh Hóa
Thành phố Hồ Chí Minh see KPV2935.H63
2935.T57 Thùa Thiên-Huế
2935.T58 Thuận Hai
2935.T64 Tiền Giang
2935.V56 Vĩnh Phú
2935.V86 Vũng Tàu-Con Đao (Special zone)
6001-6499 Annam (Table KL-KWX8)
6501-6999 Tonkin (Table KL-KWX8)
7001-7499 Cochin-China (Table KL-KWX8)
Cities, communities, etc.
8083 Biên Hòa (Table KL-KWX9)
8084 Đà Nẵng (Table KL-KWX9)
8085 Haiphong (Table KL-KWX9)
8086 Hanoi (Table KL-KWX9)
8087 Ho Chi Minh City (Table KL-KWX9)
8089 Huế (Table KL-KWX9)
8090 Nha Trang (Table KL-KWX9)
8094 Qui Nhon (Table KL-KWX9)
Saigon see KPV8087

Asia (South Asia. Southeast Asia. East Asia): Vietnam (Republic). South Vietnam

Class here works on the law of the Republic of Vietnam (South Vietnam) from ca. 1956 to 1975

For the law prior to 1956, and for the law of the Social Republic of Vietnam (re-unified state from 1975 on), see KPV

1-489 General (Table KL-KWX5 modified)

Administrative law

Administrative organization

Administrative and political divisions. Local government other than municipal

Including those of centralized national governments or federal governments

293.5.A-Z Provinces (Tinh), A-Z (as of 1971)

Including autonomous municipalities

Including official gazettes, bylaws, statutory orders, regulations, and general works, as well as works on specific legal topics

293.5.A36 An Giang
293.5.A37 An Xuyên
293.5.B32 Ba Xuyên
293.5.B33 Bạc Liêu
293.5.B45 Bến Tre
293.5.B54 Biên Hòa
293.5.B55 Bình Định
293.5.B555 Bình Dương
293.5.B56 Bình Long
293.5.B57 Bình Thuận
293.5.B58 Bình Tuy
293.5.C35 Cam Ranh
293.5.C36 Cần Thơ
293.5.C43 Châu Dốc
293.5.C48 Chuông Thiên
293.5.D32 Đà Lạt
293.5.D33 Đà Nẵng
293.5.D34 Đắc Lắc
293.5.D56 Định Tường
293.5.G53 Gò Công
293.5.H38 Hậu Nghĩa
293.5.H84 Huế
293.5.K43 Khánh Hòa
293.5.K54 Kiên Giang
293.5.K55 Kiên Phong
293.5.K56 Kiến Tường
293.5.K66 Kon Tum
293.5.L36 Lâm Đồng

General
Administrative law
Administrative organization
Administrative and political divisions. Local government other than municipal
Provinces (Tinh), A-Z (as of 1971) -- Continued

293.5.L66 Long An
293.5.L67 Long Khánh
293.5.M93 Mỹ Tho
293.5.N53 Nha Trang
293.5.N56 Ninh Thuận
293.5.P46 Phong Dinh
293.5.P47 Phú Bốn
293.5.P475 Phú Yên
293.5.P48 Phước Long
293.5.P485 Phước Tuy
293.5.P54 Pleiku
293.5.Q83 Quang Duc
293.5.Q84 Quang Nam
293.5.Q845 Quang Ngãi
293.5.Q85 Quang Tin
293.5.Q86 Quang Trị
293.5.Q87 Qui Nhơn
293.5.R33 Rach Giá
293.5.S33 Sa Đéc
293.5.T39 Tây Ninh
293.5.T48 Thùa Thiên
293.5.T88 Tuyên Đúc
293.5.V56 Vĩnh Bình
293.5.V57 Vĩnh Hòa
293.5.V86 Vũng Tàu

Cities, communities, etc. see KPV0+

Africa: History of law

Class here general works on the ancient/early and defunct legal systems and customary law of Africa, that are clearly identified with a particular ethnic group

For the law of particular historic states (kingdoms, empires, etc.), see the states in KQ3000+

For the law of a particular ethnic group or people, see the ethnic group or people in KQ9000+

For the colonial periods, see the appropriate jurisdiction

2 Bibliography

6 Periodicals

For periodicals consisting predominantly of articles on Roman law see KJA6



54 Encyclopedias. Law dictionaries

Auxiliary sciences

74 General works

75 Diplomatics

76 Paleography

77 Papyrology

78 Archaeology. Folklife studies

80 Linguistics. Semantics

83 Seals. Flags. Insignia. Armory

Law and lawyers in literature

see classes PB - PZ

Biography of lawyers

122 Collective (General)

124 Collections of portraits

135 Congresses. Seminars

By date of the congress or seminar

Ancient legal systems compared. General works

Class here general works on law development and comparisons of ancient legal systems in the region

Including compends, essays, festschriften, etc.

For general works on the colonial periods, see the appropriate jurisdiction

For comparisons of particular subjects, see the subject

147 General

Particular systems compared

Roman law compared with ancient legal systems see KJA168+

Semitic legal systems (General) see KL174

177 Other (not A-Z)

Sources

190 Studies on sources

Including history and methodology (e.g., epigraphy, papyrology, etc.)

For philological studies, see class PL

Sources -- Continued

195 Collections. Compilations. Lists of specimens. Selections

197 Indexes. Chronologies. Concordances, etc.

Africa: Law of indigenous peoples

2010 Collections of laws and customs. Codes of indigenous law. Treaties

Class here general collections

For the laws, customs, codes, etc. identified with a particular region, state, or people, see the appropriate jurisdiction

2030 General works. Treatises

Individual peoples, chiefdoms, kingdoms and empires

Historic states

Class here legal works on the states of the pre-colonial periods (to ca. mid 19th century)

3001-3020 Ashanti (Table KL-KWX13)

Cf. KRX1+ Ghana

3041-3060 Ashanti State (ca. 1570-ca. 1680) (Table KL-KWX13)

3071-3090 Ashanti Empire (ca. 1680-1896) (Table KL-KWX13)

3401-3420 Barotseland. Lozi Empire (ca. 1550-1891) (Table KL-KWX13)

Cf. KTY1+ Zambia

3801-3820 Batlokwa Kingdom (ca. 1660-1885) (Table KL-KWX13)

Cf. KQK1+ Botswana

4401-4420 Batwanaland (Kingdom, ca. 1795-1885) (Table KL-KWX13)

Cf. KQK1+ Botswana

4501-4520 Benin Chiefdom (1170-1897) (Table KL-KWX13)

Cf. KQJ1+ Benin

4701-4720 Dahomey Kingdom (1730-1894) (Table KL-KWX13)

Cf. KQJ1+ Benin

5001-5020 Fante Kingdom (ca. 1670-1730) (Table KL-KWX13)

Cf. KRX1+ Ghana

5501-5520 Ghana Empire (350-1240) (Table KL-KWX13)

Cf. KST1+ Mali

5701-5720 Kangaba Kingdom ca. 1050-ca. 1237) (Table KL-KWX13)

Cf. KST1+ Mali

6001-6020 Mali Empire (ca. 1237-1464) (Table KL-KWX13)

Cf. KST1+ Mali

6201-6220 Hausa States. Hausaland (Table KL-KWX13)

6241-6260 Katsina (Kingdom ca. 1015-1806; Emirate to 1903) (Table KL-KWX13)

Cf. KTA1+ Nigeria

6261-6280 Daura (Table KL-KWX13)

6281-6300 Kano (Kingdom 998-1806; Emirate to 1903) (Table KL-KWX13)

Cf. KTA1+ Nigeria

6321-6340 Zaria (Zazzau) (Table KL-KWX13)

6341-6360 Gobir (Table KL-KWX13)

6361-6380 Rano (Table KL-KWX13)

6381-6400 Biram (Table KL-KWX13)

6421-6440 Zamfara (Table KL-KWX13)

Individual peoples, chiefdoms, kingdoms and empires
Historic states
Hausa States. Hausaland -- Continued
6441-6460 Kebbi (Table KL-KWX13)
6461-6480 Gwari (Table KL-KWX13)
6501-6520 Yauri (Table KL-KWX13)
Ilorin see KQ8661+
6561-6580 Kwararafa (Table KL-KWX13)
Imerina Kingdom (ca. 1300-1810) see KSR1+
Madagascar Kingdom (1810-1896) see KSR1+
7001-7020 Kanem Kingdom (784-ca. 1260) (Table KL-KWX13)
7101-7120 Bornu State (ca. 850-ca. 1260) (Table KL-KWX13)
7201-7220 Kanem Bornu (ca. 1256-ca. 1400) (Table KL-KWX13)
7301-7320 Bornu Empire (ca. 1400-1893) (Table KL-KWX13)
7401-7420 Fulani Empire (Caliphate; 1804-1903) (Table KL-KWX13)
Cf. KTA1+ Nigeria
7801-7820 Mwene Mutapa Empire ca. 1330-ca. 1888) (Table KL-KWX13)
7901-7920 Rozwi Empire (1480-1838) (Table KL-KWX13)
7961-7980 Matabeleland Empire (1837-1894) (Table KL-KWX13)
Cf. KSX0+ Mozambique
Cf. KTZ1+ Zimbabwe
7981-8000 Mossi States. Chiefdoms (Table KL-KWX13)
8001-8020 Wagadugu (ca. 1495-1896) (Table KL-KWX13)
8041-8060 Yatenga (1540-1895) (Table KL-KWX13)
8071-8090 Gurma (1204-1895) (Table KL-KWX13)
8121-8140 Dagomba Kingdom (1440-1896) (Table KL-KWX13)
8201-8220 Songhai States (Table KL-KWX13)
8241-8260 Songhai Kingdom (ca. 500-1464) (Table KL-KWX13)
8271-8290 Songhai Empire (1464-1640) (Table KL-KWX13)
8401-8420 Yoruba States. Yorubaland (Table KL-KWX13)
8441-8460 Oyo Empire (ca. 1400-1900) (Table KL-KWX13)
8501-8520 Lagos Empire (ca. 1700-1861) (Table KL-KWX13)
8601-8620 Ibadan Empire (ca. 1750-1893) (Table KL-KWX13)
8661-8680 Ilorin Kingdom (to 1829) (Table KL-KWX13)
8701-8720 Ilorin Emirate (1831-1897) (Table KL-KWX13)
Cf. KTA1+ Nigeria
8901-8920 Zeng Empire (Table KL-KWX13)
9000.A-Z Individual ethnic groups, A-Z
Ashanti see KQ3001+
9000.A67 Arusha (Table KL-KWX14)
9000.B33 Babua (Table KL-KWX14)
9000.B34 Bafokeng (Table KL-KWX14)
9000.B36 Baggara (Table KL-KWX14)
9000.B365 Bamileke (Table KL-KWX14)
9000.B37 Banjal (Table KL-KWX14)
9000.B375 Bantu (Table KL-KWX14)

Individual peoples, chiefdoms, kingdoms and empires
Individual ethnic groups, A-Z -- Continued

9000.B4 Batwa (Table KL-KWX14)
9000.B44 Bedouin (Table KL-KWX14)
Cf. KM88.5.B44 Asia
9000.B47 Berber (Table KL-KWX14)
9000.C53 Chaga (Table KL-KWX14)
9000.D56 Dinka (Table KL-KWX14)
9000.D57 Diola (Table KL-KWX14)
9000.E35 Ebira (Table KL-KWX14)
9000.F85 Fula (Table KL-KWX14)
9000.H36 Hamar (Table KL-KWX14)
Hausa see KQ6201+
9000.H38 Haya (Table KL-KWX14)
9000.H65 Holoholo (Table KL-KWX14)
9000.H87 Hutu (Table KL-KWX14)
9000.I53 Igbo (Table KL-KWX14)
9000.I54 Ila (Table KL-KWX14)
9000.J45 Jekri (Table KL-KWX14)
9000.K34 Kaffa (Table KL-KWX14)
Kalinga see KQ9000.H87; KQ9000.T87
9000.K36 Kamba (Table KL-KWX14)
9000.K365 Kanuri (Table KL-KWX14)
9000.K53 Kgatla (Table KL-KWX14)
9000.K57 Kipsigis (Table KL-KWX14)
9000.K65 Kongo (Table KL-KWX14)
9000.K75 Kuku (Table KL-KWX14)
9000.K76 Kunama (Table KL-KWX14)
9000.K77 Kuria (Table KL-KWX14)
9000.L69 Lozi (Table KL-KWX14)
9000.L86 Luo (Table KL-KWX14)
Mashona see KQ9000.S56
Mossi see KQ7981+
9000.M85 Murle (Table KL-KWX14)
9000.N56 Ngoni (Table KL-KWX14)
9000.N84 Nuer (Table KL-KWX14)
9000.S56 Shona (Table KL-KWX14)
9000.T54 Tigrinya (Table KL-KWX14)
9000.T58 Tiv (Table KL-KWX14)
9000.T65 Toka (Table KL-KWX14)
Tswana see KQ4401+
9000.T87 Tutsi (Table KL-KWX14)
9000.V46 Venda (Table KL-KWX14)
Yoruba see KQ8401+
9000.Z85 Zulu (Table KL-KWX14)

Africa: Regional comparative and uniform law

1-999 General (Table KL-KWX2 modified)

Regional divisions. Subregions

116 North Africa

Class here works on Algeria, Egypt, Libya, Morocco, and Tunisia combined; and on the Barbary States (Maghrib), i.e., Algeria, Morocco, and Tunisia

117 Eastern Africa

Class here works on Kenya, Tanzania, and Uganda combined

For British East Africa see KRL1+

For Italian East Africa see KSG1+

For Portuguese East Africa see KSX0+

118 Northeast Africa

Class here works on Djibouti, Ethiopia, Somalia, and Sudan combined

119 Southern Africa

Class here works on jurisdictions south of Zaire and Tanzania

For South Africa, Republic see KTL0+

Southwest Africa. Namibia see KSY1+

120 West Africa

121 British West Africa

Class here works on British law of the subregion and works on British Cameroon, Nigeria, British Togoland, Gold Coast, Ashanti, Northern Territories, Sierra Leone, Gambia, and the islands of Ascension, and Saint Helena, and Tristan da Cunha combined

Cf. Gambia, Ghana, Nigeria, and Sierra Leone

Spanish West Africa see KTN1+

French West Africa see KRS1+

Portuguese West Africa see KQH0+

Africa: Regional organization and integration
Class here treaties establishing, and laws governing, the organizations and their legal activity
Including subregional organizations
For official acts or legal measures on a particular subject, see the subject in KQC
For organizations governing a particular subject activity, see the subject in KQC

10 General works

101-149 Common Market for Eastern and Southern Africa. (COMESA) (Table KL-KWX3)
Including the Preferential Trade Area for Eastern and Southern Africa

200-249 East African Community (Table KL-KWX3)
Founded in 1967 and dissolved in 1977. Re-established in 1999

251-299 Economic Community of Central African States. Communauté Economique des Etats de l'Afrique Centrale (CEEAC), 1983 (Table KL-KWX3)

300-349 Economic Community of West African States. Communauté économique des Etats de l'Afrique de l'Ouest (Table KL-KWX3)

401-449 Mali Federation (1959-1960) (Table KL-KWX3)
Including the Sudanese Republic and Senegal
Cf. KST1+ Mali
Cf. KTG0+ Senegal

501-549 Federation of Rhodesia and Nyasaland (1953-1963) (Table KL-KWX3)
Including Northern Rhodesia, Southern Rhodesia and Nyasaland (Zambia, Zimbabwe, and Malawi)

601-649 Organisation Commune Africaine et Malagache (Table KL-KWX3)

701-749 Organization of African Unity. Organisation de l'Unité Africaine (Table KL-KWX3)

801-849 Ruanda-Urundi (Table KL-KWX3)
Including Burundi and Rwanda

901-949 Senegambia (Table KL-KWX3)

1201-1249 Arab Maghreb Union (AMU), 1989 (Table KL-KWX3)

1401-1449 West African Economic and Monetary Union. Union économique et monétaire ouest africaine (Table KL-KWX3)

Africa: Abyssinia
see KRP1+

Africa: Algeria
0-4999 General (Table KL-KWX4 modified)
Add number in table to KQG0
Administrative law
Administrative organization
Administrative and political divisions. Local government other than municipal
Including those of centralized national governments or federal governments
2935.A-Z Provinces (Wilayat), A-Z
Including official gazettes, bylaws, statutory orders, regulations, and general works, as well as works on specific legal topics
2935.A47 Adrar
2935.A54 Algiers
2935.A66 Annaba
2935.B38 Batna
2935.B43 Béchar
2935.B45 Bejaïa
2935.B48 Biskra
2935.B54 Blida
2935.B68 Bouira
2935.C45 Chlef
2935.C66 Constantine
2935.D54 Djelfa
2935.G74 Guelma
2935.J55 Jījil
2935.L35 Laghouat
2935.M37 Mascara
2935.M44 Médéa
2935.M67 Mostaganem
2935.M75 M'Sila
2935.O73 Oran
2935.O83 Ouargla
2935.O86 Oum el-Bouaghi
2935.S35 Saïda
2935.S47 Sétif
2935.S54 Sidi Bel Abbès
2935.S56 Skikda
2935.T36 Tamanghasset
2935.T53 Tiaret
2935.T56 Tipasa
2935.T59 Tizi Ouzou
2935.T64 Tlemcen
Cities, communities, etc.
4980 Al Asnam (Table KL-KWX9)
4981 Algiers (Table KL-KWX9)

| | |
|---|---|
| | Cities, communities, etc. -- Continued |
| 4982 | Annaba (Table KL-KWX9) |
| 4983 | Batna (Table KL-KWX9) |
| 4984 | Bejaia (Table KL-KWX9) |
| 4985 | Blida (Table KL-KWX9) |
| 4986 | Constantine (Table KL-KWX9) |
| 4987 | Médéa (Table KL-KWX9) |
| 4988 | Mostaganem (Table KL-KWX9) |
| 4989 | Oran (Table KL-KWX9) |
| 4990.A-Z | Other cities, A-Z<br>Subarrange each by Table KL-KWX9a |
| 4990.S47 | Sétif (Table KL-KWX9a) |
| 4990.S54 | Siddi-Bel-Abbès (Table KL-KWX9a) |
| 4990.S65 | Skikda (Table KL-KWX9a) |
| 4990.T59 | Tizi-Ouzou (Table KL-KWX9a) |
| 4990.T64 | Tlemcen (Table KL-KWX9a) |

Africa: Anglo-Egyptian Sudan
see KTQ1+

Africa: Angola
Previously Portuguese West Africa
0-4890 General (Table KL-KWX4 modified)
Add number in table to KQH0
Administrative law
Administrative organization
Administrative and political divisions. Local government other than municipal
Including those of centralized national governments or federal governments
2935.A-Z Provinces, A-Z
Including official gazettes, bylaws, statutory orders, regulations, and general works, as well as works on specific legal topics
2935.B46 Bengo
2935.B47 Benguela
2935.B54 Bié
2935.C33 Cabinda
2935.C83 Cuando Cubango
2935.C84 Cuanza Norte
2935.C845 Cuanza Sul
2935.C96 Cunene
2935.H83 Huambo
2935.H85 Huíla
2935.L83 Luanda
2935.L84 Lunda Norte
2935.L845 Lunda Sul
2935.M35 Malanje
2935.M69 Moxico
2935.N36 Namibe
2935.U55 Uíge
2935.Z35 Zaïre
Cities, communities, etc.
4980 Benguela (Table KL-KWX9)
4981 Huambo (Table KL-KWX9)
4982 Lobito (Table KL-KWX9)
4983 Luanda (Table KL-KWX9)
4984 Lubango (Table KL-KWX9)
4985 Malange (Table KL-KWX9)
Nova Lisboa see KQH4981
4990.A-Z Other cities, communities, etc., A-Z
Subarrange each by Table KL-KWX9a

## AFRICA: ASHANTI PROTECTORATE (1896-1901). ASHANTI COLONY (1901-1957)

Africa: Ashanti Protectorate (1896-1901). Ashanti Colony (1901-1957)
see KRX1+

Africa: Basutoland
see KSL1+

Africa: Bechuanaland Protectorate
see KQK1+

Africa: Belgian Congo
see KTX1+

Africa: Benin

Previously Dahomey (French West Africa)

1-489 General (Table KL-KWX5 modified)

Administrative law

Administrative organization

Administrative and political divisions. Local government other than municipal

Including those of centralized national governments or federal governments

293.5.A-Z Provinces, A-Z

Including official gazettes, bylaws, statutory orders, regulations, and general works, as well as works on specific legal topics

293.5.A83 Atakora

293.5.A85 Atlantique

293.5.B67 Borgou

293.5.M66 Mono

293.5.O84 Ouémé

293.5.Z68 Zou

490.A-Z Cities, communities, etc., A-Z

Subarrange each by Table KL-KWX9a

490.A36 Abomey (Table KL-KWX9a)

490.C68 Cotonou (Table KL-KWX9a)

490.K36 Kandi (Table KL-KWX9a)

490.N38 Natitingou (Table KL-KWX9a)

490.O85 Ouidah (Table KL-KWX9a)

490.P37 Parakou (Table KL-KWX9a)

490.P67 Porto-Novo (Table KL-KWX9a)

Africa: Botswana
Previously Bechuanaland Protectorate and High Commission Territory (1885-1964)
For the law of early historic states of the region see KQ3001+

1-489 General (Table KL-KWX7 modified)
Administrative and political divisions. Local government other than municipal
231.5.A-Z Districts and town councils, A-Z
Including official gazettes, bylaws, statutory orders, regulations, and general works, as well as works on specific legal topics
231.5.C45 Chobe District
231.5.C47 Central (Ngwato) District
231.5.G43 Ghanzi District
231.5.K53 Kgalagadi District
231.5.K54 Kgatleng District
231.5.K94 Kweneng District
231.5.N43 Ngamiland District
231.5.N67 North East District
231.5.S67 South East District
231.5.S68 Southern (Ngwaketse) District
490.A-Z Cities, communities, etc., A-Z
Subarrange each by Table KL-KWX9a
490.F73 Francistown (Town council) (Table KL-KWX9a)
490.G33 Gaborone (Town council) (Table KL-KWX9a)
490.L63 Lobatse (Town council) (Table KL-KWX9a)
490.S45 Selebi-Pikwe (Table KL-KWX9a)
490.S47 Serowe (Table KL-KWX9a)

Africa: British Cameroons
see KQW1+

Africa: British Central Africa Protectorate

Class here works on British colonial law of the subregion and works on Rhodesia and Nyasaland combined

For individual countries of British Central Africa Protectorate, see the individual country

For works on the Federation of Rhodesia and Nyasaland see KQE501+

1-499 General (Table KL-KWX7 modified)

Administrative and political divisions. Local government other than municipal

231.5.A-Z Administrative divisions, A-Z

Including official gazettes, bylaws, statutory orders, regulations, and general works, as well as works on specific legal topics

490.2 Cities, communities, etc.

see the appropriate present-day jurisdictions, Malawi, Zambia, and Zimbabwe

Africa: British East Africa
see KRL1+

Africa: British Indian Ocean Territory

Including Chagos Archipelago (Diego Garcia)

1-499 General (Table KL-KWX7)

Africa: British Somaliland

Class here works on British colonial law of the Somaliland Protectorate until its merger with the Italian trusteeship territory of Somalia in 1960

For Somalia see KTK1+

1001-1499 General (Table KL-KWX7 modified)

Administrative and political divisions. Local government other than municipal

1231.5.A-Z Administrative divisions, A-Z

Including official gazettes, bylaws, statutory orders, regulations, and general works, as well as works on specific legal topics

Cities, communities, etc. see KTK490.A+

Africa: British West Africa
see KQC121

Africa: Buganda (Kingdom, to 1962)
see KTW1+

Africa: Burkina Faso
Previously Upper Volta
1-489 General (Table KL-KWX5 modified)
Administrative law
Administrative organization
Administrative and political divisions. Local government other than municipal
Including those of centralized national governments or federal governments
293.5.A-Z Provinces, A-Z
Including official gazettes, bylaws, statutory orders, regulations, and general works, as well as works on specific legal topics
293.5.B36 Bam
293.5.B38 Bazéga
293.5.B67 Bougouriba
293.5.B68 Boulgou
293.5.B685 Boulkiemde
293.5.C66 Comoé
293.5.G36 Ganzourgou
293.5.G53 Gnagna
293.5.G68 Gourma
293.5.H68 Houet
293.5.K34 Kadiogo
293.5.K46 Kénédougou
293.5.K68 Kossi
293.5.K69 Kouritenga
293.5.M67 Mouhoun
293.5.N34 Naouri
293.5.N36 Namentenga
293.5.O83 Oubritenga
293.5.O84 Oudalan
293.5.P37 Passore
293.5.P66 Poni
293.5.S35 Sanguié
293.5.S36 Sanmatenga
293.5.S46 Séno
293.5.S57 Sissili
293.5.S67 Soum
293.5.S68 Sourou
293.5.T36 Tapoa
293.5.W37 Watenga
293.5.Z68 Zoundwéogo
490.A-Z Cities, communities, A-Z
Subarrange each by Table KL-KWX9a
490.B36 Banfora (Table KL-KWX9a)
490.B63 Bobo-Dioulasso (Table KL-KWX9a)

Cities, communities, A-Z -- Continued

490.F34 Fada N'Gourma (Table KL-KWX9a)
490.K39 Kaya (Table KL-KWX9a)
490.K68 Koudougou (Table KL-KWX9a)
490.O83 Ouagadougou (Table KL-KWX9a)
490.O84 Ouahigouya (Table KL-KWX9a)
490.T46 Tenkodogo (Table KL-KWX9a)

Africa: Burundi
Previously Ruanda-Urundi

1-489 General (Table KL-KWX5 modified)
Administrative law
Administrative organization
Administrative and political divisions. Local government other than municipal
Including those of centralized national governments or federal governments

293.5.A-Z Provinces, A-Z
Including official gazettes, bylaws, statutory orders, regulations, and general works, as well as works on specific legal topics

293.5.B83 Bubanza
293.5.B84 Bujumbura
293.5.B87 Bururi
293.5.C36 Cankuzo
293.5.C53 Cibitoke
293.5.G57 Gitega
293.5.K37 Karuzi
293.5.K39 Kayanza
293.5.K58 Kirundo
293.5.M35 Makamba
293.5.M87 Muramvya
293.5.M88 Muyinga
293.5.N56 Ngozi
293.5.R87 Rutana
293.5.R88 Ruyigi

490.A-.Z Cities, communities, etc., A-Z
Subarrange each by Table KL-KWX9a

490.B85 Bujumbura (Table KL-KWX9a)
490.G57 Gitega (Table KL-KWX9a)
490.M85 Mugina (Table KL-KWX9a)

Africa: Cameroon
Previously the French trusteeship of Cameroun (1919-1960) and British Southern Cameroons (1919-1961)
0-4999 General (Table KL-KWX4)
Add number in table to KQW0
Provinces
5001-5099 Centre Province (Table KL-KWX8)
Previously South-Central
5101-5199 South-Central Province (to 1983) (Table KL-KWX8)
Cf. KQW5001+ Centre Province
Cf. KQW6501+ South Province
5301-5399 East Province (Table KL-KWX8)
5401-5499 Littoral Province (Table KL-KWX8)
5501-5599 Adamaoua (Table KL-KWX8)
5601-5699 Far North Province (Table KL-KWX8)
5701-5799 North Province (Table KL-KWX8)
5801-5899 North-West Province (Table KL-KWX8)
5901-5999 West Province (Table KL-KWX8)
6501-6599 South Province (Table KL-KWX8)
6701-6799 South-West Province (Table KL-KWX8)
Cities, communities, etc.
8001 Yaoundé (Table KL-KWX9)
8002 Douala (Table KL-KWX9)
8003 Bafoussam (Table KL-KWX9)
8004 Edéa (Table KL-KWX9)
8005 Garoua (Table KL-KWX9)
8007 Foumban (Table KL-KWX9)
8008 Maroua (Table KL-KWX9)
8009 Ngaoundéré (Table KL-KWX9)
8020.A-Z Other cities, A-Z
Subarrange each by Table KL-KWX9a
8020.B84 Buea (Table KL-KWX9a)
8020.K86 Kumba (Table KL-KWX9a)
8020.L56 Limbe (Victoria) (Table KL-KWX9a)
8020.N56 Nkongsamba (Table KL-KWX9a)

Africa: Canary Islands
see KKT5861+

Africa: Cape Verde

Including island groups of Barlavento and Sotavento

1-489 General (Table KL-KWX5)

490.A-Z Cities, municipalities, etc., A-Z

Subarrange each by Table KL-KWX9a

490.M56 Mindelo (Table KL-KWX9a)

490.P73 Praia (Table KL-KWX9a)

Africa: Central African Empire
see KRB1+

Africa: Central African Republic

Previously Central African Empire (Ubangi Shari, a territory of French Equatorial Africa)

1-489 General (Table KL-KWX5 modified)

Administrative law

Administrative organization

Administrative and political divisions. Local government other than municipal

Including those of centralized national governments or federal governments

293.5.A-Z Prefectures and autonomous communes, A-Z

Including official gazettes, bylaws, statutory orders, regulations, and general works, as well as works on specific legal topics

293.5.B36 Bamingui-Bangoran

293.5.B37 Bangui

293.5.B38 Basse-Kotto

293.5.H36 Haut-M'bomou

293.5.H37 Haute-Kotto

293.5.H38 Haute-Sangha

293.5.K36 Kémo-Gribingui

293.5.L63 Lobaye

293.5.M36 M'bomou

293.5.N36 Nana-Mambéré

293.5.O63 Ombella-M'poko

293.5.O83 Ouaka

293.5.O84 Ouham

293.5.O85 Ouham-Pendé

293.5.V35 Vakaga

490.A-Z Cities, communities, etc., A-Z

Subarrange each by Table KL-KWX9a

490.B36 Bambari (Table KL-KWX9a)

490.B365 Bangui (Table KL-KWX9a)

490.B47 Berberati (Table KL-KWX9a)

490.B67 Bossangoa (Table KL-KWX9a)

490.B68 Bouar (Table KL-KWX9a)

490.B75 Bria (Table KL-KWX9a)

Africa: Chad
Previously part of French Equatorial Africa

1-489 General (Table KL-KWX5 modified)
Administrative law
Administrative organization
Administrative and political divisions. Local government other than municipal
Including those of centralized national governments or federal governments

293.5.A-Z Prefectures, A-Z
Including official gazettes, bylaws, statutory orders, regulations, and general works, as well as works on specific legal topics

293.5.B37 Batha
293.5.B55 Biltine
293.5.B67 Borkou-Ennedi-Tibesti
293.5.C43 Chari-Baguirmi
293.5.G84 Guéra
293.5.K36 Kanem
293.5.L33 Lac
293.5.L64 Logone Occidental
293.5.L65 Logone Oriental
293.5.M39 Mayo-Kebbi
293.5.M69 Moyen-Chari
293.5.O83 Ouaddai
293.5.S35 Salamat
293.5.T35 Tandjilé
Wadai see KRC293.5.O83

490.A-Z Cities, communities, etc., A-Z
Subarrange each by Table KL-KWX9a

490.A34 Abéché (Table KL-KWX9a)
490.A63 Am Timan (Table KL-KWX9a)
490.B66 Bongor (Table KL-KWX9a)
490.D63 Doba (Table KL-KWX9a)
490.F39 Faya-Largeau (Table KL-KWX9a)
Fort-Lamy see KRC490.N44
Fort-Archambault see KRC490.S37
490.K45 Kelo (Table KL-KWX9a)
490.L35 Laï (Table KL-KWX9a)
490.M36 Mao (Table KL-KWX9a)
490.M66 Mongo (Table KL-KWX9a)
490.M68 Moundou (Table KL-KWX9a)
490.N44 N'Djamena (Table KL-KWX9a)
490.S37 Sarh (Table KL-KWX9a)

| | |
|---|---|
| | Africa: Comoros |
| | Including Moheli Island, the Grande Comore, and Anjouan Island |
| 1-489 | General (Table KL-KWX5) |
| 490.A-Z | Cities, communities, etc., A-Z |
| | Subarrange each by Table KL-KWX9a |
| 490.M67 | Moroni (Table KL-KWX9a) |
| 490.M78 | Mutsamudu (Table KL-KWX9a) |
| 490.N53 | Njazidja (Table KL-KWX9a) |

Africa: Congo (Brazzaville)
Previously Middle Congo (Moyen-Congo), a territory of French Equatorial Africa
1-489 General (Table KL-KWX5 modified)
Administrative law
Administrative organization
Administrative and political divisions. Local government other than municipal
Including those of centralized national governments or federal governments
293.5.A-Z Regions, A-Z
Including official gazettes, bylaws, statutory orders, regulations, and general works, as well as works on specific legal topics
293.5.B68 Bouenza
293.5.C88 Cuvette
293.5.F44 Federal District (Brazzaville)
293.5.K68 Kouilou
293.5.L45 Lékoumou
293.5.L55 Likouala
293.5.N53 Niari
293.5.P53 Plateaux
293.5.P66 Pool
293.5.S36 Sangha
490.A-Z Cities, communities, etc., A-Z
Subarrange each by Table KL-KWX9a
490.B73 Brazzaville (Table KL-KWX9a)
Jacob see KRG490.N53
490.N53 N'Kayi (Table KL-KWX9a)
490.P65 Pointe-Noire (Table KL-KWX9a)

Africa: Congo (Democratic Republic)
see KTX1+

Africa: Congo Freestate
see KTX1+

Africa: Dahomey
see KQJ1+

Africa: Djibouti
Previously French Somaliland, and later French Territory of the Afars and Issas

1-489 General (Table KL-KWX5 modified)
Administrative law
Administrative organization
Administrative and political divisions. Local government other than municipal
Including those of centralized national governments or federal governments

293.5.A-Z Provinces, A-Z
Including official gazettes, bylaws, statutory orders, regulations, and general works, as well as works on specific legal topics

293.5.A55 ʻAli Sabīḥ
293.5.D45 Dikhil
293.5.D55 Djibouti
293.5.O36 Obock
293.5.T34 Tadjoura

490.A-Z Cities, communities, etc., A-Z
Subarrange each by Table KL-KWX9a

490.A55 ʻAli Sabīḥ (Table KL-KWX9a)
490.D54 Dikhil (Table KL-KWX9a)
490.D55 Djibouti (Table KL-KWX9a)
490.O36 Obock (Table KL-KWX9a)
490.T34 Tadjoura (Table KL-KWX9a)

Africa: East Africa Protectorate

Class here works on British colonial law of the subregion (to 1920); the law of Kenya Colony and Protectorate (to 1963), and works on Kenya and Tanzania combined

For individual countries of East Africa Protectorate, see the individual country

1-499 General (Table KL-KWX7 modified)

Administrative and political divisions. Local government other than municipal

231.5.A-Z Administrative divisions, A-Z

Including official gazettes, bylaws, statutory orders, regulations, and general works, as well as works on specific legal topics

Cities, communities, etc.

see the appropriate present-day jurisdictions in Kenya and Tanzania

Africa: Egypt (United Arab Republic)

0-4890 General (Table KL-KWX4 modified)

Add number in table to KRM0

Administrative law

Administrative organization

Administrative and political divisions. Local government other than municipal

Including those of centralized national governments or federal governments

2935.A-Z Governorates (Muḥāfaẓāt), A-Z

Including official gazettes, bylaws, statutory orders, regulations, and general works, as well as works on specific legal topics

2935.A54 Alexandria

2935.A78 Aswān

2935.A79 Asyūṭ

2935.B34 Bahr al-Ahmar

2935.B36 Banī Suwayf

2935.B84 Buhayrah

2935.B87 Būr Saʻīd

2935.C35 Cairo

2935.D36 Damietta

2935.D37 Daqahlīyah

2935.F39 Fayyūm

2935.G43 Gharbīyah

2935.I75 Ismailia

2935.J36 Janūb Sīnā'

Previously Sinai

2935.J59 Jīzah

2935.K34 Kafr al-Shaykh

2935.M37 Maṭrūḥ

2935.M56 Minūfīyah

2935.M57 Minyā

2935.Q35 Qalyubīyah

2935.Q56 Qinā

2935.S53 Shamāl Sīnā'

Previously Sinai

2935.S54 Sharqiyah

2935.S64 Suez

2935.S65 Sūhāj

2935.W34 Wadi al-Jadīd

4982-4989 Cities, communities, etc.

4982 Damanhūr (Table KL-KWX9)

4983 Fayyūm (Table KL-KWX9)

4984 Jīzah (Table KL-KWX9)

4985 Ismailia (Table KL-KWX9)

4986 Maḥallah al-Kubrá (Table KL-KWX9)

Cities, communities, etc. -- Continued

4987 Alexandria (Table KL-KWX9)

4988 Aswān (Table KL-KWX9)

4989 Cairo (Table KL-KWX9)

4990.A-Z Other cities, A-Z

Subarrange each by Table KL-KWX9a

4990.A79 Asyūṭ (Table KL-KWX9a)

4990.M36 Mansūra (Table KL-KWX9a)

4990.M56 Minyā (Table KL-KWX9a)

4990.S84 Suez (Table KL-KWX9a)

4990.T36 Ṭanṭā (Table KL-KWX9a)

Africa: Eritrea

Previously Italian colony, and from 1952-1993 an autonomous unit within the Federation of Ethiopia

1-499 General (Table KL-KWX5)

Africa: Ethiopia
Previously Abyssinia
0-4890 General (Table KL-KWX4 modified)
Add number in table to KRP0
Administrative law
Administrative organization
Administrative and political divisions. Local government other than municipal
Including those of centralized national governments or federal governments
2935.A-Z Provinces (Kifle Hāger), A-Z
Including official gazettes, bylaws, statutory orders, regulations, and general works, as well as works on specific legal topics
2935.A44 Addis Ababa
2935.A77 Ārsī Kifle Hāger
2935.A78 Arusi
Bagēmder see KRP2935.G66
2935.B35 Balē Kifle Hāger
2935.E75 Eritrea (to 1993)
Cf. KRN1+ Eritrea
2935.G36 Gamo Gofa Kifle Hāger
2935.G64 Gojam Kifle Hāger
2935.G66 Gonder Kifle Hāger
2935.H37 Hārergē Kifle Hāger
2935.I58 Īlubabur Kifle Hāger
2935.K44 Kefa Kifle Hāger
2935.K54 Sīdamo Kifle Hāger
2935.S44 Shewa
2935.T54 Tigray Kifle Hāger
2935.W45 Welega Kifle Hāger
2935.W455 Welo Kifle Hāger
Cities, communities, etc.
4980 Addis Ababa (Table KL-KWX9)
4982 Āsmera (Table KL-KWX9)
4983 Āwasa (Table KL-KWX9)
4984 Dirē Dawa (Table KL-KWX9)
4986 Hārer (Table KL-KWX9)
4987 Nazrēt (Table KL-KWX9)
4990.A-Z Other cities, A-Z
Subarrange each by Table KL-KWX9a

Africa: French Cameroun
see KQW1+

Africa: French Equatorial Africa

Class here works on French colonial rule of the subregion and works on Ubangi Shari, Middle Congo, Chad, and Gabon combined

For individual countries of French Equatorial Africa, see the individual country

1-499 General (Table KL-KWX5 modified)

Administrative law

Administrative organization

Administrative and political divisions. Local government other than municipal

Including those of centralized national governments or federal governments

293.5.A-Z Administrative divisions, A-Z

Including official gazettes, bylaws, statutory orders, regulations, and general works, as well as works on specific legal topics

Cities, communities, etc.

see the appropriate present-day jurisdiction

Africa: French Guinea
see KSA1+

Africa: French Somaliland
see KRK1+

Africa: French Sudan
see KST1+

# AFRICA: FRENCH TERRITORY OF THE AFARS AND ISSAS

Africa: French Territory of the Afars and Issas
see KRK1+

Africa: French West Africa

Class here works on French colonial law of the subregion and works on Dahomey, Upper Volta, French Guinea, Ivory Coast, French Sudan, Mauritania, Niger, and Senegal combined

For individual countries of French West Africa, see the individual country

1-499 General (Table KL-KWX5 modified)

Administrative law

Administrative organization

Administrative and political divisions. Local government other than municipal

Including those of centralized national governments or federal governments

293.5.A-Z Administrative divisions, A-Z

Including official gazettes, bylaws, statutory orders, regulations, and general works, as well as works on specific legal topics

Cities, communities, etc.

see the appropriate present-day jurisdiction

Africa: Gabon
1-489 General (Table KL-KWX5 modified)
Administrative law
Administrative organization
Administrative and political divisions. Local government other than municipal
Including those of centralized national governments or federal governments
293.5.A-Z Provinces, A-Z
Including official gazettes, bylaws, statutory orders, regulations, and general works, as well as works on specific legal topics
293.5.E77 Estuaire
293.5.H38 Haut-Ogooué
293.5.M69 Moyen-Ogooué
293.5.N56 Ngounié
293.5.N93 Nyanga
293.5.O55 Ogooué-Ivindo
293.5.O56 Ogooué-Lolo
293.5.O57 Ogooué-Maritime
293.5.W65 Woleu-Ntem
490.A-Z Cities, communities, etc., A-Z
Subarrange each by Table KL-KWX9a
Franceville see KRU490.M37
490.K68 Koulamoutou (Table KL-KWX9a)
490.L36 Lambaréné (Table KL-KWX9a)
490.L53 Libreville (Table KL-KWX9a)
490.M35 Makokou (Table KL-KWX9a)
490.M37 Masuku (Table KL-KWX9a)
490.M68 Mouila (Table KL-KWX9a)
490.O94 Oyem (Table KL-KWX9a)
490.P67 Port-Gentil (Table KL-KWX9a)
490.T34 Tchibanga (Table KL-KWX9a)

Africa: Gambia

1-489 General (Table KL-KWX7 modified)

Administrative and political divisions. Local government other than municipal

231.5.A-Z Administrative divisions, A-Z

Including official gazettes, bylaws, statutory orders, regulations, and general works, as well as works on specific legal topics

231.5.L69 Lower River Division

231.5.M33 MacCarthy Island Division

231.5.N67 North Bank Division

231.5.U66 Upper River Division

231.5.W47 Western Division

489.A-Z Cities, communities, etc., A-Z

Subarrange each by Table KL-KWX9a

489.B36 Banjul (Table KL-KWX9a)

489.B38 Bathurst (Table KL-LWX9a)

Africa: German East Africa

Class here works on German colonial law of the subregion and works on Tanganyika and Ruanda-Urundi combined

For individual countries of German East Africa, see the individual country

1-499 General (Table KL-KWX5 modified)

Administrative law

Administrative organization

Administrative and political divisions. Local government other than municipal

Including those of centralized national governments or federal governments

293.5.A-Z Administrative divisions, A-Z

Including official gazettes, bylaws, statutory orders, regulations, and general works, as well as works on specific legal topics

Cities, communities, etc.

see the appropriate present-day jurisdiction in Burundi, Rwanda, and Tanzania

Africa: German Southwest Africa
see KSY1+

Africa: Ghana

Including the former Northern Territories and Civil Protectorate of the Gold Coast (1899-1957), the (southern) Gold Coast Colony (from 1850-1953 with various names), and the Ashanti Protectorate and Colony (1896-1957) in middle Ghana

For Ashanti State and Ashanti Empire see KQ3001+

1-4890 General (Table KL-KWX6 modified)

Administrative and political divisions. Local government other than municipal

2315.A-Z Regions, A-Z

Including official gazettes, bylaws, statutory orders, regulations, and general works, as well as works on specific legal topics

2315.A74 Ashanti Region

2315.B76 Brong-Ahafo Region

2315.C46 Central Region

2315.E37 Eastern Region

2315.G74 Greater Accra Region

2315.N67 Northern Region

2315.U66 Upper East Region

2315.U67 Upper West Region

2315.V65 Volta Region

2315.W47 Western Region

Cities, communities, etc.

4980 Accra (Table KL-KWX9)

4981 Bolgatanga (Table KL-KWX9)

4982 Cape Coast (Table KL-KWX9)

4983 Keta (Table KL-KWX9)

4984 Kumasi (Table KL-KWX9)

4985 Obuasi (Table KL-KWX9)

4986 Tamale (Table KL-KWX9)

4987 Tarkwa (Table KL-KWX9)

4988 Tema (Table KL-KWX9)

4989 Winneba (Table KL-KWX9)

4990.A-Z Other cities, communities, etc., A-Z

Subarrange each by Table KL-KWX9a

Africa: Gibraltar

1-499 General (Table KL-KWX7)

Africa: Gold Coast
see KRX1+

# AFRICA: GOLD COAST, NORTHERN TERRITORIES OF THE (1899-1907)

Africa: Gold Coast, Northern Territories of the (1899-1907)
see KRX1+

## AFRICA: GOLD COAST, NORTHERN TERRITORIES OF THE (1907-1957)

Africa: Gold Coast, Northern Territories of the (1907-1957)
see KRX1+

Africa: Guinea
Previously French Guinea (a colony and territory of French West Africa)

1-489 General (Table KL-KWX5 modified)
Administrative law
Administrative organization
Administrative and political divisions. Local government other than municipal
Including those of centralized national governments or federal governments

293.5.A-Z Regions, A-Z
Including official gazettes, bylaws, statutory orders, regulations, and general works, as well as works on specific legal topics

293.5.B49 Beyla
293.5.B64 Boffa
293.5.B65 Boké
293.5.B65 Boké
293.5.C66 Conakry
293.5.D33 Dabola
293.5.D35 Dalaba
293.5.D56 Dinguiraye
293.5.D83 Dubréka
293.5.F37 Faranah
293.5.F67 Forécariah
293.5.F75 Fria
293.5.G36 Gaoual
293.5.G84 Guéckédou
293.5.K36 Kankan
293.5.K47 Kérouané
293.5.K56 Kindia
293.5.K57 Kissidougou
293.5.K68 Koundara
293.5.K685 Kouroussa
293.5.L33 Labé
293.5.L65 Lola
293.5.M33 Macenta
293.5.M35 Mali
293.5.M36 Mamou
293.5.N94 Nzérékoré
293.5.P57 Pita
293.5.S55 Siguiri
293.5.T45 Télimélé
293.5.T68 Tougué
293.5.Y66 Yomou

490.A-Z Cities, communities, etc., A-Z
Subarrange each by Table KL-KWX9a

Cities, communities, etc., A-Z -- Continued

490.C66 Conakry (Table KL-KWX9a)

490.K36 Kankan (Table KL-KWX9a)

490.K56 Kindia (Table KL-KWX9a)

490.L33 Labé (Table KL-KWX9a)

490.N94 N'Zékékoré (Table KL-KWX9a)

Africa: Guinea-Bissau
Previously Portuguese Guinea
1-489 General (Table KL-KWX5 modified)
Administrative law
Administrative organization
Administrative and political divisions. Local government other than municipal
Including those of centralized national governments or federal governments
293.5.A-Z Regions, A-Z
Including official gazettes, bylaws, statutory orders, regulations, and general works, as well as works on specific legal topics
293.5.B34 Bafatá
293.5.B56 Biombo
293.5.B65 Bolama-Bijagós
293.5.C33 Cacheu
293.5.G33 Gabu
293.5.O56 Oio
293.5.Q85 Quinara
293.5.T66 Tombali
490.A-Z Cities, communities, etc., A-Z
Subarrange each by Table KL-KWX9a
490.B57 Bissau (Table KL-KWX9a)
490.B65 Bolama (Table KL-KWX9a)
490.C33 Cacheu (Table KL-KWX9a)

Africa: Equatorial Guinea
Previously Spanish Guinea (Territorios Españoles del Golfo de Guinea)
1-489 General (Table KL-KWX5 modified)
Administrative law
Administrative organization
Administrative and political divisions. Local government other than municipal
Including those of centralized national governments or federal governments
293.5.A-Z Provinces, A-Z
Including official gazettes, bylaws, statutory orders, regulations, and general works, as well as works on specific legal topics
293.5.A66 Annobón
293.5.B56 Bioko Norte
293.5.B565 Bioko Sur
293.5.C46 Centro Sur
293.5.K54 Kié-Ntem
293.5.L57 Litoral
Pagalu see KSE293.5.A66
293.5.W45 Wele-Nzas
490.A-Z Cities, communities, etc., A-Z
Subarrange each by Table KL-KWX9a
490.B37 Bata (Table KL-KWX9a)
490.M35 Malabo (Table KL-KWX9a)
Santa Isabel see KSE490.M35
Cf. KSW0+ Morocco

601-699 Africa: Ifni
Previously Spanish overseas province (1958-1969)
601-699 General (Table KL-KWX8)

Africa: Italian East Africa

Class here works on Italian colonial law of the subregion and works on Ethiopia, Eritrea, and Somalia combined

For individual countries of Italian East Africa, see the country

1-499 General (Table KL-KWX5 modified)

Administrative law

Administrative organization

Administrative and political divisions. Local government other than municipal

Including those of centralized national governments or federal governments

293.5.A-Z Administrative divisions, A-Z

Including official gazettes, bylaws, statutory orders, regulations, and general works, as well as works on specific legal topics

Cities, communities, etc.

see the appropriate present-day jurisdictions in Ethiopia and Somalia

Cf. KTK1+ Somalia

Africa: Italian Somaliland

Class here works on Italian colonial law of the Italian Trusteeship Somalia until its merger with British Somaliland in 1960

1001-1499 General (Table KL-KWX5 modified)

Administrative law

Administrative organization

Administrative and political divisions. Local government other than municipal

Including those of centralized national governments or federal governments

1293.5.A-Z Administrative divisions, A-Z

Including official gazettes, bylaws, statutory orders, regulations, and general works, as well as works on specific legal topics

Cities, communities, etc.

see the appropriate present-day jurisdictions in Somalia

Africa: Côte d'Ivoire

0-4999 General (Table KL-KWX4 modified)

Add number in table to KSH0

Administrative law

Administrative organization

Administrative and political divisions. Local government other than municipal

Including those of centralized national governments or federal governments

2935.A-Z Departments, A-Z

Including official gazettes, bylaws, statutory orders, regulations, and general works, as well as works on specific legal topics

2935.A34 Abengourou
2935.A35 Abidjan
2935.A36 Aboisso
2935.A49 Adzopé
2935.A53 Agboville
2935.B53 Biankouma
2935.B66 Bondoukou
2935.B67 Bongouanou
2935.B68 Bouaflé
2935.B685 Bouaké
2935.B69 Bouna
2935.B695 Boundiali
2935.D33 Dabakala
2935.D35 Daloa
2935.D36 Danané
2935.D56 Dimbokro
2935.D59 Divo
2935.F47 Ferkéssédougou
2935.G35 Gagnoa
2935.G85 Guiglo
2935.I77 Issia
2935.K37 Katiola
2935.K67 Korhogo
2935.M36 Man
2935.M37 Mankono
2935.O45 Odienné
2935.O86 Oumé
2935.S37 Sassandra
2935.S45 Séguéla
2935.S68 Soubré
2935.T56 Tingréla
2935.T68 Touba
2935.Z84 Zuénoula

Cities, communities, etc.

| | |
|---|---|
| | Cities, communities, etc. -- Continued |
| 4980 | Abidjan (Table KL-KWX9) |
| 4982 | Bouake (Table KL-KWX9) |
| 4983 | Man (Table KL-KWX9) |
| 4984 | Yamoussoukro (Table KL-KWX9) |
| 4990.A-Z | Other cities, A-Z |
| | Subarrange each by Table KL-KWX9a |
| 4990.D35 | Daloa (Table KL-KWX9a) |
| 4990.G35 | Gagnoa (Table KL-KWX9a) |
| 4990.K67 | Korhogo (Table KL-KWX9a) |

Africa: Kenya

1-4890 General (Table KL-KWX6 modified)

Administrative and political divisions. Local government other than municipal

2315.A-Z Provinces, A-Z

Including official gazettes, bylaws, statutory orders, regulations, and general works, as well as works on specific legal topics

2315.C46 Central Province

2315.C63 Coast Province

2315.E37 Eastern Province

2315.N35 Nairobi Province

2315.N67 North-Eastern Province

2315.N93 Nyanza Province

2315.R54 Rift Valley Province

2315.W47 Western Province

Cities, communities, etc.

4980 Eldoret (Table KL-KWX9)

4982 Kisumu (Table KL-KWX9)

4983 Machakos (Table KL-KWX9)

4984 Mombasa (Table KL-KWX9)

4985 Nairobi (Table KL-KWX9)

4987 Nakuru (Table KL-KWX9)

4988 Thika (Table KL-KWX9)

4990.A-Z Other cities, communities, etc., A-Z

Subarrange each by Table KL-KWX9a

Africa: Lagos (Colony, 1886-1906)
see KTA1+

Africa: Lagos (Yoruba Kingdom, ca. 1700-1861)
see KQ8501+

Africa: Lagos Territory (1866-1886)
see KTA1+

Africa: Lesotho
Previously Basutoland (1822-1964)
1-489 General (Table KL-KWX7 modified)
Administrative and political divisions. Local government other than municipal
231.5.A-Z Districts, A-Z
Including official gazettes, bylaws, statutory orders, regulations, and general works, as well as works on specific legal topics
231.5.B87 Butha-Buthe
231.5.L47 Leribe
231.5.M34 Mafeteng
231.5.M37 Maseru District
231.5.M65 Mohales Hoek
231.5.M66 Mokhotlong
231.5.Q33 Qacha's Nek
231.5.Q87 Quthing
231.5.T49 Teyateyaneng
231.5.T53 Thaba-Tseka
490.A-Z Cities, communities, etc., A-Z
Subarrange each by Table KL-KWX9a
490.M37 Maseru (Table KL-KWX9a)

Africa: Liberia

1-489 General (Table KL-KWX7 modified)

Administrative and political divisions. Local government other than municipal

231.5.A-Z Counties, A-Z

Including official gazettes, bylaws, statutory orders, regulations, and general works, as well as works on specific legal topics

231.5.B65 Bomi County

231.5.B66 Bong County

231.5.G37 Grand Bassa County

231.5.G38 Grand Cape Mount County

231.5.G39 Grand Jide County

231.5.G42 Grand Kru County

231.5.L63 Lofa County

231.5.M37 Maryland County

231.5.M65 Montserrado County

231.5.N55 Nimba County

231.5.S55 Sino County

490.A-Z Cities, municipalities, etc., A-Z

Subarrange each by Table KL-KWX9a

490.C37 Caresburg (Table KL-KWX9a)

490.C39 Gbarnga (Table KL-KWX9a)

490.M65 Monrovia (Table KL-KWX9a)

490.N48 New Kru Town (Table KL-KWX9a)

490.R62 Robertsport (Table KL-KWX9a)

490.S23 Sagleipie (Table KL-KWX9a)

490.S26 Sanniquellie (Table KL-KWX9a)

490.T82 Tubmanburg (Table KL-KWX9a)

490.V64 Voinjama (Table KL-KWX9a)

490.Y44 Yekepa (Table KL-KWX9a)

490.Z67 Zorzor (Table KL-KWX9a)

490.Z93 Zwedru (Table KL-KWX9a)

Africa: Libya

0-4890 General (Table KL-KWX4 modified)

Add number in table to KSP0

Administrative law

Administrative organization

Administrative and political divisions. Local government other than municipal

Including those of centralized national governments or federal governments

2935.A-Z Provinces (Baladīyāt), A-Z

Including official gazettes, bylaws, statutory orders, regulations, and general works, as well as works on specific legal topics

2935.B36 Banghāzī

2935.B39 Bayḍā'

2935.D37 Darnah

2935.G53 Gharyān

2935.K58 Khums

2935.M57 Miṣrātah

2935.S33 Sabhā

2935.T37 Tarābulus

2935.Z38 Zāwiyah

Cities, communities, etc.

4984 Banghāzī (Table KL-KWX9)

4985 Miṣrātah (Table KL-KWX9)

4986 Tripoli (Table KL-KWX9)

4990.A-Z Other cities, communities, etc., A-Z

Subarrange each by Table KL-KWX9a

Africa: Madagascar
Previously Malagasy Republic
1-489 General (Table KL-KWX5 modified)
Administrative law
Administrative organization
Administrative and political divisions. Local government other than municipal
Including those of centralized national governments or federal governments
293.5.A-Z Provinces, A-Z
Including official gazettes, bylaws, statutory orders, regulations, and general works, as well as works on specific legal topics
293.5.A67 Antananarivo
293.5.A675 Antsiranana
293.5.F53 Fianarantsoa
293.5.M35 Mahajanga
293.5.T63 Toamasina
293.5.T65 Toliara
490.A-Z Cities, communities, etc., A-Z
Subarrange each by Table KL-KWX9a
490.A67 Antananarivo (Table KL-KWX9a)
490.A675 Antsirabe (Table KL-KWX9a)
490.A68 Antsiranana (Table KL-KWX9a)
490.M34 Mahajanga (Table KL-KWX9a)
490.M35 Maintirano (Table KL-KWX9a)
490.T63 Toamasina (Table KL-KWX9a)
490.T65 Toliara (Table KL-KWX9a)

Africa: Madagascar Colony (1896-1942)
see KSR1+

Africa: Madagascar Kindgom (1810-1896)
see KSR1+

Africa: Madeira
see KKQ2935.M33

Africa: Malagasy Republic
see KSR1+

Africa: Malawi

Previously Nyasaland and part of British Central Africa

| | |
|---|---|
| 1-489 | General (Table KL-KWX7 modified) |
| | Administrative and political divisions. Local government other than municipal |
| 231.5.A-Z | Administrative districts, A-Z |
| | Including official gazettes, bylaws, statutory orders, regulations, and general works, as well as works on specific legal topics |
| 231.5.B53 | Blantyre |
| 231.5.C55 | Chitipa |
| 231.5.D68 | Dowa |
| 231.5.K37 | Karonga District |
| 231.5.K375 | Kasungu District |
| 231.5.L55 | Lilongwe District |
| 231.5.M33 | Machinga District |
| 231.5.M35 | Mangochi |
| 231.5.M37 | Mchinji |
| 231.5.M95 | Mzimba District |
| 231.5.N54 | Nkhotakota District |
| 231.5.N73 | Nsanje District |
| 231.5.S35 | Salima District |
| 231.5.Z66 | Zomba District |
| 490.A-Z | Cities, communities, etc., A-Z |
| | Subarrange each by Table KL-KWX9a |
| 490.B53 | Blantyre (Table KL-KWX9a) |
| 490.C55 | Chitipa (Table KL-KWX9a) |
| 490.L55 | Lilongwe (Table KL-KWX9a) |
| 490.M34 | Magomero (Table KL-KWX9a) |
| 490.N54 | Nkhotakota (Table KL-KWX9a) |
| 490.N73 | Ntcheu (Table KL-KWX9a) |
| 490.T44 | Thekerani (Table KL-KWX9a) |
| 490.Z66 | Zomba (Table KL-KWX9a) |

Africa: Mali

Previously French Sudan, part of French West Africa; in 1958 it became the autonomous Sudanese Republic; in 1959, together with Senegal, it formed the Mali Federation; in 1960, after Senegal's withdrawal from the Federation, it assumed the name République du Mali

Cf. KQE401+ Mali Federation (1959-1960)

Cf. KRS1+ French West Africa

1-489 General (Table KL-KWX5 modified)

Administrative law

Administrative organization

Administrative and political divisions. Local government other than municipal

Including those of centralized national governments or federal governments

293.5.A-Z Regions, A-Z

Including official gazettes, bylaws, statutory orders, regulations, and general works, as well as works on specific legal topics

293.5.B36 Bamako

293.5.G36 Gao

293.5.K39 Kayes

293.5.K68 Koulikoro

293.5.M66 Mopti

293.5.S45 Ségou

293.5.S55 Sikasso

293.5.T66 Tombouctou

490.A-Z Cities, communities, etc., A-Z

Subarrange each by Table KL-KWX9a

490.B36 Bamako (Table KL-KWX9a)

490.D54 Djenné (Table KL-KWX9a)

490.G36 Gao (Table KL-KWX9a)

490.K37 Karangasso (Table KL-KWX9a)

490.K39 Kayes (Table KL-KWX9a)

490.K68 Koulikoro (Table KL-KWX9a)

490.M37 Markala (Table KL-KWX9a)

490.M66 Mopti (Table KL-KWX9a)

490.S45 Ségou (Table KL-KWX9a)

490.S55 Sikasso (Table KL-KWX9a)

490.T66 Tombouctou (Table KL-KWX9a)

490.V36 Vanékui (Table KL-KWX9a)

# AFRICA: MASHONALAND PROTECTORATE (1889-1894)

Africa: Mashonaland Protectorate (1889-1894)
see KTZ1+

## AFRICA: MATABELELAND. MATABELE EMPIRE (1837-1894)

Africa: Matabeleland. Matabele Empire (1837-1894)
see KQ7961+

KQ-KTZ

Africa: Mauritania

Previously part of French West Africa

Including part of the Sahara Español

1-489 General (Table KL-KWX5 modified)

Administrative law

Administrative organization

Administrative and political divisions. Local government other than municipal

Including those of centralized national governments or federal governments

293.5.A-Z Capital district and regions, A-Z

Including official gazettes, bylaws, statutory orders, regulations, and general works, as well as works on specific legal topics

293.5.A47 Adrar

293.5.B73 Brakna

293.5.D35 Dakhlet Nouadhibou

293.5.E53 El Acâba. ʻAcâba

293.5.G67 Gorgol

293.5.G85 Guidimaka

293.5.H63 Hodel Charbi

293.5.H64 Hodel Charqui

293.5.I63 Inchiri

293.5.T35 Tagant

293.5.T73 Tiris Zemmour

293.5.T77 Trarza

490.A-Z Cities, communities, etc., A-Z

Subarrange each by Table KL-KWX9a

490.A73 Atâr (Table KL-KWX9a)

490.K34 Kaédi (Table KL-KWX9a)

490.N67 Nouâdhibou (Table KL-KWX9a)

490.N675 Nouakchott (Table KL-KWX9a)

490.R67 Rossa (Table KL-KWX9a)

490.Z68 Zouérate (Table KL-KWX9a)

Africa: Mauritius
Including Rodrigues (former dependency) and the outer islands of Agalega and St. Brandon group

1-499 General (Table KL-KWX7 modified)

Administrative and political divisions. Local government other than municipal

231.5.A-Z Administrative districts (District councils and urban councils), A-Z

Including official gazettes, bylaws, statutory orders, regulations, and general works, as well as works on specific legal topics

231.5.B53 Black River

231.5.F53 Flacq

231.5.G73 Grand Port

231.5.M65 Moka

231.5.P36 Pamplemousses

231.5.P53 Plaines Wilhems

231.5.P67 Port Louis

231.5.R58 Rivière du Rempart

231.5.S38 Savanne

490.A-Z Cities, communities, etc., A-Z

Subarrange each by Table KL-KWX9a

490.B43 Beau Bassin-Rose Hill (Table KL-KWX9a)

490.C87 Curepipe (Table KL-KWX9a)

490.M34 Mahébourg (Table KL-KWX9a)

490.P67 Port Louis (Table KL-KWX9a)

490.Q83 Quatre Bornes (Table KL-KWX9a)

490.V33 Vacoas-Phoenix (Table KL-KWX9a)

Africa: Mayotte
Previously French Overseas Territory; since 1976 a Territorial Collectivity
Including Pamanzi Island
5001-5489 General (Table KL-KWX5 modified)
Administrative law
Administrative organization
Administrative and political divisions. Local government other than municipal
Including those of centralized national governments or federal governments
5293.5.A-Z Communes, A-Z
Including official gazettes, bylaws, statutory orders, regulations, and general works, as well as works on specific legal topics
5490.A-Z Cities, communities, etc., A-Z
Subarrange each by Table KL-KWX9a
5490.D93 Dzaoudzi (Table KL-KWX9a)
5490.M36 Mamoundzou (Table KL-KWX9a)

Africa: Morocco
Including the previous Spanish provinces of Ifni and Sahara Español
0-4890 General (Table KL-KWX4 modified)
Add number in table to KSW0
Administrative law
Administrative organization
Administrative and political divisions. Local government other than municipal
Including those of centralized national governments or federal governments
2935.A-Z Provinces (Wilāyāt), A-Z
Including official gazettes, bylaws, statutory orders, regulations, and general works, as well as works on specific legal topics



2935.A53 Agadir
2935.A95 Azilal
2935.B45 Ben Slimane
2935.B46 Beni Mellal
2935.B68 Boujadour
2935.B685 Boulemane
2935.C37 Casablanca
2935.C53 Chaouen
2935.E77 Essaouria
2935.F47 Fez
2935.F55 Figuig
2935.G84 Guelmim
2935.H63 Hoceïma
2935.I47 Ifrane
2935.J34 Jadida
2935.K45 Kelaa des Srarhna
2935.K46 Kenitra
2935.K54 Khemisset
2935.K545 Khenifra
2935.K56 Khouribga
2935.L33 Laâyoune
2935.M37 Marrakech
2935.M45 Meknes
2935.N34 Nador
2935.O83 Ouarzazate
2935.O84 Oued Eddahab
2935.O85 Oujda
2935.R33 Rabat-Salé
2935.R34 Rachidia
2935.S34 Safi
2935.S46 Semara
2935.S47 Settat

General
Administrative law
Administrative organization
Administrative and political divisions. Local government other than municipal
Provinces (Wilāyāt), A-Z -- Continued

2935.T33 Tan-Tan
2935.T35 Tangier
2935.T36 Taounate
2935.T37 Taroudant
2935.T38 Tata
2935.T39 Taza
2935.T47 Tétouan
2935.T59 Tiznet

Cities, communities, etc.

4981 Agadir (Table KL-KWX9)
4982 Casablanca (Table KL-KWX9)
4983 El Jadida (Table KL-KWX9)
4984 Fez (Table KL-KWX9)
4985 Marrakesh (Table KL-KWX9)
4986 Meknès (Table KL-KWX9)
4987 Rabat (Table KL-KWX9)
4988 Tangier (Table KL-KWX9)
4989 Tetuan (Table KL-KWX9)
4990.A-Z Other cities, A-Z
Subarrange each by Table KL-KWX9a
4990.K45 Kémitra (Table KL-KWX9a)
4990.K56 Khouribga (Table KL-KWX9a)
4990.M65 Mohammedia (Table KL-KWX9a)
4990.O85 Oujda (Table KL-KWX9a)
4990.S34 Safi (Table KL-KWX9a)
4990.S35 Salé (Table KL-KWX9a)

Africa: Mozambique
Previously Portuguese East Africa
0-4890 General (Table KL-KWX4 modified)
Add number in table to KSX0
Administrative law
Administrative organization
Administrative and political divisions. Local government other than municipal
Including those of centralized national governments or federal governments
2935.A-Z Provinces, A-Z
Including official gazettes, bylaws, statutory orders, regulations, and general works, as well as works on specific legal topics
2935.C33 Cabo Delgado
2935.G39 Gaza
2935.I65 Inhambane
2935.M36 Manica
2935.M37 Maputo
2935.N36 Nampula
2935.N53 Niassa
2935.S65 Sofala
2935.T47 Tete
2935.Z36 Zambézia
Cities, communities, etc.
4980 Beira (Table KL-KWX9)
4981 Chimoio (Table KL-KWX9)
4982 Inhambane (Table KL-KWX9)
4983 Lichinga (Table KL-KWX9)
Lourenço Marques see KSX4984
4984 Maputo (Table KL-KWX9)
4985 Nampula (Table KL-KWX9)
4986 Pemba (Table KL-KWX9)
4987 Quelimane (Table KL-KWX9)
4988 Tete (Table KL-KWX9)
4989 Xaixai (Table KL-KWX9)
4990.A-Z Other cities, communities, etc., A-Z
Subarrange each by Table KL-KWX9a

Africa: Namibia

Previously German Southwest Africa (protectorate) (to 1915), and South-West Africa (Mandate) (to 1967)

1-4890 General (Table KL-KWX6 modified)

Administrative and political divisions. Local government other than municipal

2315.A-Z Territories, districts, etc., A-Z

Including official gazettes, bylaws, statutory orders, regulations, and general works, as well as works on specific legal topics

2315.K37 Kavango

2315.K375 Karibib

2315.O79 Outjo

2315.O83 Owambo Territory

Cities, communities, etc.

4980 Windhoek (Table KL-KWX9)

4982 Rehoboth (Table KL-KWX9)

4984 Swakopmund (Table KL-KWX9)

4986 Lüderitz (Table KL-KWX9)

4987 Tsumeb (Table KL-KWX9)

4988 Otjiwarongo (Table KL-KWX9)

Pequena see KSY4986

4989 Rundu (Table KL-KWX9)

4990.A-Z Other cities, A-Z

Subarrange each by Table KL-KWX9a

Africa: Niger
1-489 General (Table KL-KWX5 modified)
Administrative law
Administrative organization
Administrative and political divisions. Local government other than municipal
Including those of centralized national governments or federal governments
293.5.A-Z Administrative districts (Départements), A-Z
Including official gazettes, bylaws, statutory orders, regulations, and general works, as well as works on specific legal topics
293.5.A43 Agadez
293.5.D54 Diffa
293.5.D68 Dosso
293.5.M37 Maradi
293.5.N54 Niamey
293.5.T35 Tahoua
293.5.Z56 Zinder
490.A-Z Cities, communities, etc., A-Z
Subarrange each by Table KL-KWX9a
490.A43 Agadèz (Table KL-KWX9a)
490.A56 Akouta (Table KL-KWX9a)
490.A75 Arlit (Table KL-KWX9a)
490.M37 Maradi (Table KL-KWX9a)
490.N53 Niamey (Table KL-KWX9a)
490.T35 Tahoua (Table KL-KWX9a)
490.Z56 Zinder (Table KL-KWX9a)

Africa: Nigeria

Previously Colony and Protectorate of Nigeria (Protectorate of Northern and Southern Nigeria combined)

1-4999 General (Table KL-KWX6)

States, territories, etc.

5200 Abia State (Table KL-KWX9)

Previously part of Imo State

5300 Abuja (Capital Territory) (Table KL-KWX9)

5400 Akwa Ibom State (Table KL-KWX9)

5500 Anambra State (Table KL-KWX9)

Previously part of East-Central State

5600 Bauchi State (Table KL-KWX9)

5700 Bendel State (Table KL-KWX9)

Cf. KTA6250 Delta State

Cf. KTA6310 Edo State

5800 Benue-Plateau State (to 1976) (Table KL-KWX9)

Cf. KTA5900 Benue State

Cf. KTA7800 Plateau State

5900 Benue State (Table KL-KWX9)

Previously part of Benue-Plateau State

6000 Borno State (Table KL-KWX9)

6200 Cross River State (Table KL-KWX9)

Previously South-Eastern State

6250 Delta State (Table KL-KWX9)

Previously part of Bendel State

6275 Eastern Region (1939-1965) (Table KL-KWX9)

6300 East-Central State (1967-1976) (Table KL-KWX9)

Cf. KTA5500 Anambra State

Cf. KTA6500 Imo State

6310 Edo State (Table KL-KWX9)

Previously part of Bendel State

6315 Ekiti State (Table KL-KWX9)

6320 Enugu State (Table KL-KWX9)

6400 Gongola State (Table KL-KWX9)

6500 Imo State (Table KL-KWX9)

Previously part of East-Central State

6600 Kaduna State (Table KL-KWX9)

Previously North-Central State

6700 Kano State (Table KL-KWX9)

6800 Katsina State (Table KL-KWX9)

6900 Kwara State (Table KL-KWX9)

7100 Lagos State (Table KL-KWX9)

7150 Mid-western State (Table KL-KWX9)

Including Mid-western Group of Provinces of Nigeria and Mid-western Nigeria

7200 Niger State (Table KL-KWX9)

Previously part of North-Western State

States, territories, etc. -- Continued
(7300) North-Central State
see KTA6600
North-Eastern State see KTA6000
7400 North-Western State (Table KL-KWX9)
Cf. KTA7200 Niger State
Cf. KTA8100 Sokoto State
7450 Northern Nigeria (1900-1966) (Table KL-KWX9)
Including former Protectorate, Northern Region, and Northern Provinces
For works on the law in northern Nigeria subsequent to the breakup of the jurisdiction of Northern Nigeria see the individual states
7500 Ogun State (Table KL-KWX9)
7600 Ondo State (Table KL-KWX9)
7650 Osun State (Table KL-KWX9)
7700 Oyo State (Table KL-KWX9)
7800 Plateau State (Table KL-KWX9)
7900 Rivers State (Table KL-KWX9)
8100 Sokoto State (Table KL-KWX9)
Previously part of North-Western State
South-Eastern State see KTA6200
8200 Western Region (1939-1965) (Table KL-KWX9)
9100-9125 Cities, communities, etc.
9100 Abeokuta (Table KL-KWX9)
9101 ado-Ekiti (Table KL-KWX9)
9102 Ibadan (Table KL-KWX9)
9103 Ilesha (Table KL-KWX9)
9104 Iwo (Table KL-KWX9)
9105 Ilorin (Table KL-KWX9)
9106 Kaduna (Table KL-KWX9)
9107 Kano (Table KL-KWX9)
9108 Lagos (Table KL-KWX9)
9109 Ogbomosho (Table KL-KWX9)
9110 Oshogbo (Table KL-KWX9)
9111 Onitsha (Table KL-KWX9)
9115 Port Harcourt (Table KL-KWX9)
9125 Zaria (Table KL-KWX9)
9150.A-Z Other cities, communities, etc., A-Z
Subarrange each by Table KL-KWX9a

Africa: Nyasaland
see KSS1+

Africa: Portuguese East Africa
see KSX1+

Africa: Portuguese Guinea
see KSC1+

Africa: Portuguese West Africa
see KQH1+

Africa: Réunion

French Overseas Department

1-489 General (Table KL-KWX5 modified)

Administrative law

Administrative organization

Administrative and political divisions. Local government other than municipal

Including those of centralized national governments or federal governments

293.5.A-Z Administrative divisions (Arrondissements), A-Z

Including official gazettes, bylaws, statutory orders, regulations, and general works, as well as works on specific legal topics

Africa: Rhodesia, Northern
see KTY1+

Africa: Rhodesia, Southern
see KTZ1+

Africa: Rio de Oro
see KTN1+

Africa: Ruanda-Urundi
see KTD1+

Africa: Rwanda
Previously Ruanda-Urundi
1-489 General (Table KL-KWX5 modified)
Administrative law
Administrative organization
Administrative and political divisions. Local government other than municipal
Including those of centralized national governments or federal governments
293.5.A-Z Prefectures, A-Z
Including official gazettes, bylaws, statutory orders, regulations, and general works, as well as works on specific legal topics
293.5.B87 Butare
293.5.B98 Byumba
293.5.C93 Cyangugu
293.5.G55 Gikongoro
293.5.G57 Gisenyi
293.5.G58 Gitarama
293.5.K53 Kibungo
293.5.K535 Kibuye
293.5.K54 Kigali
293.5.R85 Ruhengeri
490.A-Z Cities, communities, etc., A-Z
Subarrange each by Table KL-KWX9a
490.B87 Butare (Table KL-KWX9a)
490.G57 Gisenyi (Table KL-KWX9a)
490.K55 Kigali (Table KL-KWX9a)
490.R85 Ruhengeri (Table KL-KWX9a)

Africa: Saint Helena
Including the islands of Ascension and Tristan da Cunha
1-489 General (Table KL-KWX7)
490.A-Z Cities, communities, etc., A-Z
Subarrange each by Table KL-KWX9a
490.E45 Edinburgh (Table KL-KWX9a)
490.J36 Jamestown (Table KL-KWX9a)

Africa: Sao Tome and Principe
The archipelago includes the islands of Pedras Tinhosas and Rolas
1-489 General (Table KL-KWX5)
490.A-Z Cities, communities, etc., A-Z
Subarrange each by Table KL-KWX9a
490.S36 Sao Tomé (Table KL-KWX9a)

Africa: Senegal
Previously a territory of French West Africa
Cf. KQE401+ Mali Federation (1959-1960)
Cf. KRS1+ French West Africa

0-4890 General (Table KL-KWX4 modified)
Add number in table to KTG0
Administrative law
Administrative organization
Administrative and political divisions. Local government other than municipal
Including those of centralized national governments or federal governments

2935.A-Z Regions, A-Z
Including official gazettes, bylaws, statutory orders, regulations, and general works, as well as works on specific legal topics

2935.D35 Dakar
2935.D56 Diourbel
2935.F37 Fatick
2935.K36 Kaolack
2935.K65 Kolda
2935.L68 Louga
2935.S35 Saint Louis
2935.T36 Tambacounda
2935.T44 Thiès
2935.Z55 Zinguinchor

Cities, communities, etc.
4980 Dakar (Table KL-KWX9)
4981 Diourbel (Table KL-KWX9)
4982 Kaolack (Table KL-KWX9)
4983 Louga (Table KL-KWX9)
4984 Saint-Louis (Table KL-KWX9)
4986 Tambacounda (Table KL-KWX9)
4987 Thiès (Table KL-KWX9)
4988 Ziguinchor (Table KL-KWX9)
4990.A-Z Other cities, communities, etc., A-Z
Subarrange each by Table KL-KWX9a
4990.R84 Rufisque (Table KL-KWX9a)

Africa: Seychelles

The archipelago includes two island groups, the Mahé (Granitic) group and the Outer (Coralline) group

1-489 General (Table KL-KWX7)

490.A-Z Cities, communities, etc., A-Z

Subarrange each by Table KL-KWX9a

490.M34 Mahé (Table KL-KWX9a)

490.V53 Victoria (Table KL-KWX9a)

Africa: Sierra Leone

1-489 General (Table KL-KWX7 modified)

Administrative and political divisions. Local government other than municipal

231.5.A-Z Provinces, A-Z

Including official gazettes, bylaws, statutory orders, regulations, and general works, as well as works on specific legal topics

231.5.E37 Eastern Province

231.5.N67 Northern Province

231.5.S68 Southern Province

231.5.W47 Western area (Western Province)

490.A-Z Cities, communities, etc., A-Z

Subarrange each by Table KL-KWX9a

490.B62 Bo (Table KL-KWX9a)

490.F74 Freetown (Table KL-KWX9a)

490.K66 Kono (Table KL-KWX9a)

490.M35 Makeni (Table KL-KWX9a)

Africa: Somali Republic
see KTK1+

Africa: Somalia
Previously Somali Republic, incorporating British Somaliland and Italian Somalia
For works on French Somaliland (Territory of Afars and Issas) see KRK1+

1-489 General (Table KL-KWX7 modified)
Administrative and political divisions. Local government other than municipal
231.5.A-Z Regions (Gobolka), A-Z
Including official gazettes, bylaws, statutory orders, regulations, and general works, as well as works on specific legal topics
231.5.B35 Bakool
231.5.B36 Banaadir
231.5.B37 Bari
231.5.B39 Bay
231.5.G35 Galguduud
231.5.G44 Gedo
231.5.H55 Hiiraan
231.5.J83 Jubbada Dhexe
231.5.J84 Jubbada Hoose
231.5.M84 Mudug
231.5.N85 Nugaal
231.5.S36 Sanaag
231.5.S43 Shabeellaha Dhexe
231.5.S44 Shabeellaha Hoose
231.5.T64 Todgheer
231.5.W66 Woqooyi Galbeed
490.A-Z Cities, communities, etc., A-Z
Subarrange each by Table KL-KWX9a
490.B35 Baidoa (Table KL-KWX9a)
490.B87 Burao (Table KL-KWX9a)
490.H37 Hargeisa (Table KL-KWX9a)
490.K57 Kisimaio (Table KL-KWX9a)
490.M47 Merca (Table KL-KWX9a)
490.M67 Mogadishu (Table KL-KWX9a)

Africa: South Africa, Republic of
0-4999 General (Table KL-KWX4 modified)
Add number in table to KTL0
Trials
Criminal trials and judicial investigations
Individual trials
Including records, briefs, commentaries, and stories on a particular trial
41.A-Z By defendant, A-Z
42.A-Z By best known (popular) name, A-Z
42.R58 Rivonia Trial, 1964
42.T67 Treason Trial, 1956-1961
Provinces and self-governing territories
Including independent homelands
5000 Bophuthatswana (Table KL-KWX9)
5201-5299 Eastern Cape (Table KL-KWX8)
5301-5399 Northern Cape (Table KL-KWX8)
5401-5499 Western Cape (Table KL-KWX8)
5501-5599 Cape of Good Hope (Kaapland) (to 1994) (Table KL-KWX8)
6000 Ciskei (Table KL-KWX9)
Eastern Cape see KTL5201+
6101-6199 Mpulamanga (Table KL-KWX8)
Previously Eastern Transvaal
6301-6399 Gauteng (Table KL-KWX8)
6501-6599 KwaZulu-Natal (Table KL-KWX8)
Previously Natal
Including KwaZulu homeland areas
Natal see KTL6501+
6701-6799 North West (Table KL-KWX8)
Northern Cape see KTL5301+
6801-6899 Northern Province (Table KL-KWX8)
Previously Northern Transvaal
7001-7099 Free State (Table KL-KWX8)
Previously Orange Free State (Oranje Vrystaat)
7500 Transkei (Table KL-KWX9)
8001-8099 Transvaal (Table KL-KWX8)
8500 Venda (Table KL-KWX9)
9001-9499 Eastern Transvaal (Table KL-KWX5)
Western Cape see KTL5401+
Cities, communities, etc.
9500 Alberton (Table KL-KWX9)
9503 Benoni (Table KL-KWX9)
9506 Bloemfontein (Table KL-KWX9)
9509 Boksburg (Table KL-KWX9)
9512 Brakpan (Table KL-KWX9)
9515 Cape Town (Table KL-KWX9)
9518 Durban (Table KL-KWX9)

Cities, communities, etc. -- Continued

9522 East London (Table KL-KWX9)

9526 Germiston (Table KL-KWX9)

9530 Johannisburg (Table KL-KWX9)

9534 Kempton Park (Table KL-KWX9)

9537 Kimberley (Table KL-KWX9)

9540 Krugersdorp (Table KL-KWX9)

9543 Pietermaritzburg (Table KL-KWX9)

9546 Port Elizabeth (Table KL-KWX9)

9550 Pretoria (Table KL-KWX9)

9553 Vereeniging (Table KL-KWX9)

9555 Welkom (Table KL-KWX9)

9560.A-Z Other cities, A-Z

Subarrange each by Table KL-KWX9a

Africa: South-West Africa
see KSY1+

Africa: Spanish Guinea
see KSE1+

Africa: Spanish Sahara
see KTN601+

Africa: Spanish West Africa (to 1958)

Class here works on Spanish colonial law of the subregion and on the provincial laws of Spanish Sahara and Ifni combined

For individual countries of Spanish West Africa, see the country

For Ifni (Spanish Overseas Province) see KSE601+

For Spanish Sahara see KTN601+

1-499 General (Table KL-KWX5 modified)

Administrative law

Administrative organization

Administrative and political divisions. Local government other than municipal

Including those of centralized national governments or federal governments

293.5.A-Z Administrative divisions, A-Z

Including official gazettes, bylaws, statutory orders, regulations, and general works, as well as works on specific legal topics

Cities, communities, etc.

see the appropriate present-day jurisdictions in Morocco and Mauretania

Africa: Spanish Sahara (to 1975)

Spanish overseas province (Provincia de Sáhara), including Río de Oro and Seguia el Hamra

Cf. KSW0+ Morocco

601-699 General (Table KL-KWX8)

Administrative law

Administrative organization

Administrative and political divisions. Local government other than municipal

655.5 General (Table K11)

655.6.A-Z Administrative divisions (Districts), A-Z

655.6.A35 El Aaiún

655.6.V55 Villa Cisneros

Africa: Sudan

Previously Anglo-Egyptian Sudan (1898-1956)

1-4890 General (Table KL-KWX6 modified)

Administrative and political divisions. Local government other than municipal

2315.A-Z Provinces (Muhāfaẓāt), A-Z

Including official gazettes, bylaws, statutory orders, regulations, and general works, as well as works on specific legal topics

2315.A35 A'ālī al-Nīl

2315.B34 Baḥr al-Abyaḍ

2315.B35 Baḥr al-Aḥmar

2315.B36 Baḥr al Ghazāl

2315.B84 Buḥayrāt

2315.D37 Dārfūr al-Janūbīyah

2315.D38 Dārfūr al-Shamālīyah

2315.J39 Jazīrah

2315.J86 Jungalī

2315.K37 Kassalā

2315.K43 Khartoum

2315.K87 Kurdufān al Janūbīyah

2315.K88 Kurdufān al Shamālīyah

2315.M84 Murdīrīyah al-Istiwā'īyah al-Gharbīyah (to 1983)

Cf. KTQ2315.S67 Southern Region

2315.M85 Murdīrīyah al-Istiwā'īyah al-Sharqīyah (to 1983)

Cf. KTQ2315.S67 Southern Region

2315.N55 Nīl

2315.N56 Nīl al Azraq

2315.S53 Shamālīyah

2315.S67 Southern Region

Cities, communities, etc.

4981 Al-Qadarif (Table KL-KWX9)

4982 Atbara (Table KL-KWX9)

4983 El Obeid (Table KL-KWX9)

4984 Kassala (Table KL-KWX9)

4985 Khartoum (Table KL-KWX9)

4986 Khartoum North (Table KL-KWX9)

4987 Kosti (Table KL-KWX9)

4988 Port Sudan (Table KL-KWX9)

4990.A-Z Other cities, communities, etc., A-Z

Subarrange each by Table KL-KWX9a

4990.O64 Omdurman (Table KL-KWX9a)

4990.W34 Wadi Medain (Table KL-KWX9a)

Africa: Sudanese Republic (previously French Sudan)
see KST1+

Africa: Swaziland

1-489 General (Table KL-KWX7 modified)

Administrative and political divisions. Local government other than municipal

231.5.A-Z Regions (Districts), A-Z

Including official gazettes, bylaws, statutory orders, regulations, and general works, as well as works on specific legal topics

231.5.H56 Hhohho

231.5.L83 Lubombo

231.5.M36 Manzini District

231.5.S45 Shiselweni

490.A-Z Cities, communities, etc., A-Z

Subarrange each by Table KL-KWX9a

490.B54 Big Bend (Table KL-KWX9a)

490.H38 Havelock Mine (Table KL-KWX9a)

490.M36 Manzini (Table KL-KWX9a)

490.M42 Mbabane (Table KL-KWX9a)

490.M46 Mhlume (Table KL-KWX9a)

490.N55 Nhlangano (Table KL-KWX9a)

490.P55 Piggs Peak (Table KL-KWX9a)

490.S57 Siteki (Table KL-KWX9a)

Africa: Tanganyika
see KTT1+

Africa: Tanzania

Previously Tanganyika and (after inclusion of Zanzibar and Pemba) Tanganyika and Zanzibar

1-499 General (Table KL-KWX7, modified)

Constitutional law

Sources

Including early constitutions and related materials

171.A31<date> Individual constitutions

Arrange chronologically by appending the date of adoption to the number KTT171.A31 and deleting any trailing zeros. Subarrange each by main entry

Including constitutions of the former Tanganyika and of Zanzibar

171.A311984 Constitution of Zanzibar, 1984

Regions

5301-5399 Arusha Region (Table KL-KWX8)
5401-5499 Dar es Salaam (Table KL-KWX8)
5501-5599 Dodoma Region (Table KL-KWX8)
5601-5699 Iringa Region (Table KL-KWX8)
5701-5799 Kagera Region (Table KL-KWX8)
5801-5899 Kigoma Region (Table KL-KWX8)
5901-5999 Kilimanjaro Region (Table KL-KWX8)
6201-6299 Lindi (Table KL-KWX8)
6301-6399 Mara Region (Table KL-KWX8)
6501-6599 Mbeya Region (Table KL-KWX8)
6701-6799 Morogoro Region (Table KL-KWX8)
6901-6999 Mtwara (Table KL-KWX8)
7201-7299 Mwanza (Table KL-KWX8)
7301-7399 Pemba North (Table KL-KWX8)
7401-7499 Pemba South (Table KL-KWX8)
7501-7599 Pwani (Table KL-KWX8)
7601-7699 Rukwa Region (Table KL-KWX8)
7801-7899 Ruvuma Region (Table KL-KWX8)
8001-8099 Shinyanga Region (Table KL-KWX8)
8201-8299 Singida Region (Table KL-KWX8)
8301-8399 Tabora Region (Table KL-KWX8)
8501-8599 Tanga Region (Table KL-KWX8)
8601-8699 West Lake Region (Table KL-KWX8)
8701-8799 Zanzibar Central/South (Table KL-KWX8)
8901-8999 Zanzibar North (Table KL-KWX8)
9001-9099 Zanzibar Urban/West (Table KL-KWX8)

Cities, communities, etc.

9892 Arusha (Table KL-KWX9)
9894 Dar es Salaam (Table KL-KWX9)
9895 Dodoma (Table KL-KWX9)
9897 Iringa (Table KL-KWX9)
9899 Mbeya (Table KL-KWX9)

Cities, communities, etc. -- Continued

9900 Morogoro (Table KL-KWX9)

9901 Moshi (Table KL-KWX9)

9902 Mwanza (Table KL-KWX9)

9904 Tanga (Table KL-KWX9)

9906 Ujiji (Table KL-KWX9)

9908 Zanzibar (Table KL-KWX9)

9910.A-Z Other cities, communities, etc., A-Z

Subarrange each by Table KL-KWX9a

Africa: Togo
Previously Togoland (German)

1-489 General (Table KL-KWX5 modified)
Administrative law
Administrative organization
Administrative and political divisions. Local government other than municipal
Including those of centralized national governments or federal governments

293.5.A-Z Regions, A-Z
Including official gazettes, bylaws, statutory orders, regulations, and general works, as well as works on specific legal topics

293.5.C46 Centrale
293.5.K37 Kara
293.5.M37 Maritime
293.5.P53 Plateaux
293.5.S38 Savanes

490.A-Z Cities, communities, etc., A-Z
Subarrange each by Table KL-KWX9a

490.A64 Anécho (Table KL-KWX9a)
490.A73 Atakpamé (Table KL-KWX9a)
490.B37 Bassar (Table KL-KWX9a)
490.K53 Kpalimé (Table KL-KWX9a)
490.L66 Lomé (Table KL-KWX9a)
490.S65 Sokodé (Table KL-KWX9a)
490.T74 Tsévié (Table KL-KWX9a)

Africa: Togoland
see KTU1+

Africa: Tunisia

0-4890 General (Table KL-KWX4 modified)

Add number in table to KTV0

Administrative law

Administrative organization

Administrative and political divisions. Local government other than municipal

Including those of centralized national governments or federal governments

2935.A-Z Provinces (Wilayat), A-Z

Including official gazettes, bylaws, statutory orders, regulations, and general works, as well as works on specific legal topics

2935.B35 Bājah

2935.B49 Bezerte

2935.J86 Jundubah

2935.K34 Kāf

2935.M34 Madanīn

2935.M35 Mahdīyah

2935.M86 Munastir

2935.N33 Nabeul

2935.Q33 Qābis

2935.Q34 Qafṣah

2935.Q37 Qaṣrayn

2935.Q39 Qayrawān

2935.S34 Ṣafāqis

2935.S54 Sīdī Bū Zayd

2935.S55 Silyānah

2935.S87 Sūsah

2935.T38 Tawzar

2935.T86 Tunis

Cities, communities, etc.

4982 Béja (Table KL-KWX9)

4983 Bizerta (Table KL-KWX9)

4985 Djerba (Table KL-KWX9)

4986 Gabés (Table KL-KWX9)

4987 Kairouan (Table KL-KWX9)

4990.A-Z Other cities, communities, etc., A-Z

Subarrange each by Table KL-KWX9a

Africa: Uganda
Previously Protectorate of Uganda (1894-1962)

1-489 General (Table KL-KWX7 modified)

Administrative and political divisions. Local government other than municipal

231.5.A-Z Provinces, A-Z

Including official gazettes, bylaws, statutory orders, regulations, and general works, as well as works on specific legal topics

231.5.B85 Buganda Province (Buganda Kingdom to 1962)
231.5.B87 Busoga
231.5.C46 Central Province
231.5.E37 Eastern Province
231.5.K37 Karamoja District
231.5.N55 Nile Province
231.5.N67 North Buganda Province
231.5.N675 Northern Province
231.5.S67 South Buganda Province
231.5.S675 Southern Province
231.5.W47 Western Province

490.A-Z Cities, communities, etc., A-Z

Subarrange each by Table KL-KWX9a

490.A78 Arua (Table KL-KWX9a)
490.B66 Bombo (Table KL-KWX9a)
490.B87 Butebe (Table KL-KWX9a)
490.E68 Entebbe (Table KL-KWX9a)
490.G85 Gulu (Table KL-KWX9a)
490.J56 Jinja (Table KL-KWX9a)
490.K36 Kampala (Table KL-KWX9a)
490.M37 Masaka (Table KL-KWX9a)
490.M42 Mbale (Table KL-KWX9a)
490.M425 Mbarara (Table KL-KWX9a)
490.M67 Moroto (Table KL-KWX9a)

Africa: Upper Volta
see KQT1+

Africa: Congo (Democratic Republic)
Previously Congo Free State (Belgian Congo)
Previously Zaire (1971-1997)
0-4890 General (Table KL-KWX4 modified)
Add number in table to KTX0
Administrative law
Administrative organization
Administrative and political divisions. Local government other than municipal
Including those of centralized national governments or federal governments
2935.A-Z Regions, A-Z
Including official gazettes, bylaws, statutory orders, regulations, and general works, as well as works on specific legal topics
2935.B36 Bandundu
2935.B37 Bas-Zaire
2935.C67 Costermansville
2935.E68 Equateur
2935.H38 Haut-Zaïre
2935.K37 Kasai-Occidental
2935.K375 Kasai-Oriental
Katanga see KTX2935.S53
2935.K56 Kinshasa
Kongo-Central see KTX2935.B37
Province Oriental see KTX2935.H38
2935.S53 Shaba
Cities, communities, etc.
Bakwanga see KTX4989
4980 Bandundu (Table KL-KWX9)
Banningville see KTX4980
4981 Bukavu (Table KL-KWX9)
Costermansville see KTX4981
Coquilhatville see KTX4988
Elisabethville see KTX4987
Jadotville see KTX4986
4983 Kananga (Table KL-KWX9)
4983.2 Kikwit (Table KL-KWX9)
4984 Kinshasa (Table KL-KWX9)
4985 Kisangani (Table KL-KWX9)
Leopoldsville see KTX4984
4986 Likasi (Table KL-KWX9)
4987 Lubumbashi (Table KL-KWX9)
4988 Mbandaka (Table KL-KWX9)
4989 Mbuji-Mayi (Table KL-KWX9)
4990.A-Z Other cities, communities, etc., A-Z
Subarrange each by Table KL-KWX9a

Africa: Zaire
see KTX1+

Africa: Zambia
Previously Northern Rhodesia
1-489 General (Table KL-KWX7 modified)
Administrative and political divisions. Local government other than municipal
231.5.A-Z Provinces, A-Z
Including official gazettes, bylaws, statutory orders, regulations, and general works, as well as works on specific legal topics
231.5.C46 Central Province
231.5.C66 Copperbelt Province
231.5.E37 Eastern Province
231.5.L83 Luapula Province
231.5.L87 Lusaka Province
231.5.N67 North-Western Province
231.5.N675 Northern Province
231.5.S68 Southern Province
231.5.W47 Western Province
490.A-Z Cities, communities, etc., A-Z
Subarrange each by Table KL-KWX9a
490.C55 Chililabombwe (Table KL-KWX9a)
490.C56 Chingola (Table KL-KWX9a)
490.C57 Chipata (Table KL-KWX9a)
490.K33 Kabwe (Table KL-KWX9a)
490.K35 Kalulushi (Table KL-KWX9a)
490.K44 Kefa (Table KL-KWX9a)
490.K57 Kitwe (Table KL-KWX9a)
490.L58 Livingstone (Table KL-KWX9a)
490.L83 Luanshya (Table KL-KWX9a)
490.L87 Lusaka (Table KL-KWX9a)
490.M84 Mufulira (Table KL-KWX9a)
490.N46 Ndola (Table KL-KWX9a)

Africa: Zanzibar (to 1964)

Class here works on the Sultanate and Protectorate of Zanzibar until unification with Tanganyika to form the Republic of Tanganyika and Zanzibar

Including the island Pemba

1501-1599 General (Table KL-KWX8)

Cities, communities, etc.

see the appropriate present-day jurisdictions in Tanzania

Africa: Zanzibar and Pemba
see KTT1+

Africa: Zimbabwe
Previously Southern Rhodesia
1-489 General (Table KL-KWX7 modified)
Administrative law
Administrative organization
Administrative and political divisions. Local government other than municipal
Including those of centralized national governments or federal governments
293.5.A-Z Provinces, A-Z
Including official gazettes, bylaws, statutory orders, regulations, and general works, as well as works on specific legal topics
293.5.M36 Manicaland Province
293.5.M37 Mashonaland Central Province
293.5.M375 Mashonaland East Province
293.5.M38 Mashonaland West Province
293.5.M385 Masvingo Province
293.5.M387 Matabeleland North Province
293.5.M39 Matabeleland South Province
293.5.M54 Midlands Province
490.A-Z Cities, communities, etc., A-Z
Subarrange each by Table KL-KWX9a
490.B56 Bindura (Table KL-KWX9a)
490.B85 Bulawayo (Table KL-KWX9a)
490.H37 Harare (Table KL-KWX9a)
490.K34 Kadoma (Table KL-KWX9a)
490.M37 Masvingo (Table KL-KWX9a)
490.M87 Mutare (Table KL-KWX9a)

Pacific area: Australasia
see KVC116

Pacific area: Australia

1-4999 General (Table KL-KWX6 modified)

Law of Australian peoples. Aboriginal Australians

Class here works on the law of Australian peoples regardless of whether they are identified with a particular state, territory, island, or with the region at large

For subjects, see the subject

Collections of laws and customs. Codes of customary law. Treaties

For court rules, trial practice, etc., in customary (native) courts, see the court

350 General

352.A-Z By territory, state, or island, A-Z

354 General works. Treatises

Including history

Particular peoples or ethnic groups

For particular subjects, see the subject

356 Adnyamatana (Table KL-KWX12)

357 Alyawara (Table KL-KWX12)

358 Aranda (Table KL-KWX12)

360 Bindubi (Table KL-KWX12)

361 Buandik (Table KL-KWX12)

362 Burera (Table KL-KWX12)

363 Dangadi (Table KL-KWX12)

364 Diyari (Table KL-KWX12)

365 Euahlayi (Table KL-KWX12)

366 Gadjerong (Table KL-KWX12)

367 Gunwinggu (Table KL-KWX12)

368 Gurindji (Table KL-KWX12)

369 Jiman (Table KL-KWX12)

370 Kamilaroi (Table KL-KWX12)

371 Kaurna (Table KL-KWX12)

372 Kurnai (Table KL-KWX12)

373 Lardil (Table KL-KWX12)

374 Maung (Table KL-KWX12)

375 Murngin (Table KL-KWX12)

376 Muruwari (Table KL-KWX12)

380 Narangga (Table KL-KWX12)

382 Narrinyeri (Table KL-KWX12)

383 Nyunga (Table KL-KWX12)

387 Pintubi (Table KL-KWX12)

388 Pitjantjatjara (Table KL-KWX12)

390 Tiwi (Table KL-KWX12)

391 Wailpi (Table KL-KWX12)

392 Walbiri (Table KL-KWX12)

393 Walmatjari (Table KL-KWX12)

394 Wiradjuri (Table KL-KWX12)

General
Law of Australian peoples. Aboriginal Australians
Particular peoples or ethnic groups -- Continued
395 Wonnarua (Table KL-KWX12)
396 Worora (Table KL-KWX12)
397 Wurundjeri (Table KL-KWX12)
398 Yaburara (Table KL-KWX12)
399 Yangura (Table KL-KWX12)
Administrative and political divisions. Local government other than municipal
2315.A-Z Administered territories of islands, national preserves, etc., A-Z
Including official gazettes, bylaws, statutory orders, regulations, and general works, as well as works on specific legal topics
2315.A74 Ashmore and Cartier Islands
2315.C57 Christmas Island
2315.C63 Cocos (Keeling) Islands
2315.C67 Coral Sea Islands
2315.H43 Heard Island and McDonald Islands

1-499 Pacific area: Australia: States and territories: Australian Capital Territory (Table KL-KWX7 modified)

Law reports and related materials

For reports relating to a particular subject, and for reports of courts of limited jurisdiction other than those listed below, see the appropriate subject

State courts

2.2 Highest court of appeal. Supreme court. Court of Cassation (Table K18)

Lower courts

2.23 Various courts (Table K18)

Including highest court and lower courts

Intermediate appellate courts. Courts of appeals

2.24 Collective (Table K18)

2.25.A-Z Particular courts, A-Z

(2.27) Digests and indexes to state court decisions

see KUA2.2 ; KUA2.23 ; etc.

Local courts

2.3 General (Table K18)

2.35.A-Z Particular courts. By city, etc., A-Z

2.4 Decisions of state administrative agencies

For decisions of particular agencies, see the subject

# PACIFIC AREA: AUSTRALIA: STATES AND TERRITORIES: CENTRAL AUSTRALIA

Pacific Area: Australia: States and territories: Central Australia
see KUB1+

## PACIFIC AREA: AUSTRALIA: STATES AND TERRITORIES: NORTH AUSTRALIA

Pacific Area: Australia: States and territories: North Australia
see KUB1+

| | |
|---|---|
| 1-499 | Pacific area: Australia: States and territories: Northern Territory (Table KL-KWX7 modified) |
| | Law reports and related materials |
| | For reports relating to a particular subject, and for reports of courts of limited jurisdiction other than those listed below, see the appropriate subject |
| | State courts |
| 2.2 | Highest court of appeal. Supreme court. Court of Cassation (Table K18) |
| | Lower courts |
| 2.23 | Various courts (Table K18) |
| | Including highest court and lower courts |
| | Intermediate appellate courts. Courts of appeals |
| 2.24 | Collective (Table K18) |
| 2.25.A-Z | Particular courts, A-Z |
| (2.27) | Digests and indexes to state court decisions |
| | see KUB2.2 ; KUB2.23 ; etc. |
| | Local courts |
| 2.3 | General (Table K18) |
| 2.35.A-Z | Particular courts. By city, etc., A-Z |
| 2.4 | Decisions of state administrative agencies |
| | For decisions of particular agencies, see the subject |

1-499 Pacific area: Australia: States and territories: New South Wales (Table KL-KWX7 modified)

Law reports and related materials

For reports relating to a particular subject, and for reports of courts of limited jurisdiction other than those listed below, see the appropriate subject

State courts

2.2 Highest court of appeal. Supreme court. Court of Cassation (Table K18)

Lower courts

2.23 Various courts (Table K18)

Including highest court and lower courts

Intermediate appellate courts. Courts of appeals

2.24 Collective (Table K18)

2.25.A-Z Particular courts, A-Z

(2.27) Digests and indexes to state court decisions

see KUC2.2 ; KUC2.23 ; etc.

Local courts

2.3 General (Table K18)

2.35.A-Z Particular courts. By city, etc., A-Z

2.4 Decisions of state administrative agencies

For decisions of particular agencies, see the subject

1-499 Pacific area: Australia: States and territories: Queensland (Table KL-KWX7 modified)

Law reports and related materials

For reports relating to a particular subject, and for reports of courts of limited jurisdiction other than those listed below, see the appropriate subject

State courts

2.2 Highest court of appeal. Supreme court. Court of Cassation (Table K18)

Lower courts

2.23 Various courts (Table K18)

Including highest court and lower courts

Intermediate appellate courts. Courts of appeals

2.24 Collective (Table K18)

2.25.A-Z Particular courts, A-Z

(2.27) Digests and indexes to state court decisions

see KUD2.2 ; KUD2.23 ; etc.

Local courts

2.3 General (Table K18)

2.35.A-Z Particular courts. By city, etc., A-Z

2.4 Decisions of state administrative agencies

For decisions of particular agencies, see the subject

1-499 Pacific area: Australia: States and territories: South Australia (Table KL-KWX7 modified)

Law reports and related materials

For reports relating to a particular subject, and for reports of courts of limited jurisdiction other than those listed below, see the appropriate subject

State courts

2.2 Highest court of appeal. Supreme court. Court of Cassation (Table K18)

Lower courts

2.23 Various courts (Table K18)

Including highest court and lower courts

Intermediate appellate courts. Courts of appeals

2.24 Collective (Table K18)

2.25.A-Z Particular courts, A-Z

(2.27) Digests and indexes to state court decisions

see KUE2.2 ; KUE2.23 ; etc.

Local courts

2.3 General (Table K18)

2.35.A-Z Particular courts. By city, etc., A-Z

2.4 Decisions of state administrative agencies

For decisions of particular agencies, see the subject

1-499 Pacific area: Australia: States and territories: Tasmania (Table KL-KWX7 modified)

Law reports and related materials

For reports relating to a particular subject, and for reports of courts of limited jurisdiction other than those listed below, see the appropriate subject

State courts

2.2 Highest court of appeal. Supreme court. Court of Cassation (Table K18)

Lower courts

2.23 Various courts (Table K18)

Including highest court and lower courts

Intermediate appellate courts. Courts of appeals

2.24 Collective (Table K18)

2.25.A-Z Particular courts, A-Z

(2.27) Digests and indexes to state court decisions

see KUF2.2 ; KUF2.23 ; etc.

Local courts

2.3 General (Table K18)

2.35.A-Z Particular courts. By city, etc., A-Z

2.4 Decisions of state administrative agencies

For decisions of particular agencies, see the subject

1-499 Pacific area: Australia: States and territories: Victoria (Table KL-KWX7 modified)

Law reports and related materials

For reports relating to a particular subject, and for reports of courts of limited jurisdiction other than those listed below, see the appropriate subject

State courts

2.2 Highest court of appeal. Supreme court. Court of Cassation (Table K18)

Lower courts

2.23 Various courts (Table K18)

Including highest court and lower courts

Intermediate appellate courts. Courts of appeals

2.24 Collective (Table K18)

2.25.A-Z Particular courts, A-Z

(2.27) Digests and indexes to state court decisions

see KUG2.2 ; KUG2.23 ; etc.

Local courts

2.3 General (Table K18)

2.35.A-Z Particular courts. By city, etc., A-Z

2.4 Decisions of state administrative agencies

For decisions of particular agencies, see the subject

1-499 Pacific area: Australia: States and territories: Western Australia (Table KL-KWX7 modified)

Law reports and related materials

For reports relating to a particular subject, and for reports of courts of limited jurisdiction other than those listed below, see the appropriate subject

State courts

2.2 Highest court of appeal. Supreme court. Court of Cassation (Table K18)

Lower courts

2.23 Various courts (Table K18)

Including highest court and lower courts

Intermediate appellate courts. Courts of appeals

2.24 Collective (Table K18)

2.25.A-Z Particular courts, A-Z

(2.27) Digests and indexes to state court decisions

see KUH2.2 ; KUH2.23 ; etc.

Local courts

2.3 General (Table K18)

2.35.A-Z Particular courts. By city, etc., A-Z

2.4 Decisions of state administrative agencies

For decisions of particular agencies, see the subject

Pacific area: Australia: External territories
Territory of Cocos (Keeling) Islands see KU2315.C63
Australian Antarctic Territory see KWX1+
Christmas Island see KU2315.C57
501-999 Norfolk Island (Table KL-KWX7 modified)
Law reports and related materials
For reports relating to a particular subject, and for reports of courts of limited jurisdiction other than those listed below, see the appropriate subject
State courts
502.2 Highest court of appeal. Supreme court. Court of Cassation (Table K18)
Lower courts
502.23 Various courts (Table K18)
Including highest court and lower courts
Intermediate appellate courts. Courts of appeals
502.24 Collective (Table K18)
502.25.A-Z Particular courts, A-Z
(502.27) Digests and indexes to state court decisions
see KUN502.2 ; KUN2.23 ; etc.
Local courts
502.3 General (Table K18)
502.35.A-Z Particular courts. By city, etc., A-Z
502.4 Decisions of state administrative agencies
For decisions of particular agencies, see the subject
Heard Island and McDonald Islands see KU2315.H43
Territory of Ashmore and Cartier Islands see KU2315.A74
Territory of Coral Sea Islands see KU2315.C67

Pacific area: Australia: Cities, communities, etc.

3000 Adelaide (Table KL-KWX9)

3005 Brisbane (Table KL-KWX9)

3010 Canberra (Table KL-KWX9)

3015 Darwin (Table KL-KWX9)

3020 Hobart (Table KL-KWX9)

3030 Melbourne (Table KL-KWX9)

3035 Perth (Table KL-KWX9)

3040 Sydney (Table KL-KWX9)

3050.A-Z Other cities, etc., A-Z

Subarrange each by Table KL-KWX9a

Pacific area: New Zealand
Including North, South, and Stewart Islands
1-4890 General (Table KL-KWX6, modified)
Law of the Maori
Class here works on the law of aboriginal New Zealanders regardless of whether they are identified with a particular region, territory, or island
For subjects, see the subject
Collections of laws and customs. Codes of indigenous laws. Treaties
For court rules, trial practice in customary (native) courts, see the court
350 General
352.A-Z By region, territory, or island, A-Z
354 General works. Treatises
Including history
Particular peoples or ethnic groups
For particular subjects, see the subject
357 Ngaa Rauru (Table KL-KWX12)
359 Ngaitahu (Table KL-KWX12)
362 Ngati Mamoe (Table KL-KWX12)
365 Ngati Toa (Table KL-KWX12)
369 Tainui (Table KL-KWX12)
Administrative and political divisions. Local government other than municipal
2315.A-Z Regions (local government) and Overseas territories, A-Z
Including official gazettes, bylaws, statutory orders, regulations, and general works, as well as works on specific legal topics
Including (outside the regional structure) the two counties Great Barrier Island and Chatham Islands
2315.A67 Aorangi
2315.A83 Auckland
2315.B39 Bay of Plenty
2315.C36 Canterbury
2315.C53 Chatham Islands
2315.C58 Clutha-Central Otago
2315.C63 Coastal-North Otago
2315.E37 East Cape
2315.G74 Great Barrier Island
2315.H38 Hawke's Bay
2315.H67 Horowhenua
2315.M36 Manawatu
2315.M37 Marlborough
2315.N45 Nelson Bays
2315.N67 Northland
Ross Dependency see KWX1+

General
Administrative and political divisions. Local government other than municipal
Regions (local government), and Overseas territories, A-Z -- Continued
2315.S68 Southland
2315.T37 Taranaki
2315.T53 Thames Valley
2315.T65 Tokelau Islands
Including Atafu, Nukunonu, and Fakaofo
2315.T66 Tongariro
2315.W34 Waikato
2315.W35 Wairarapa
2315.W36 Wanganui County
2315.W45 Wellington
2315.W47 West Coast
Self-governing Territories Overseas
Cook Islands see KVL1+
Niue see KWA1+
Cities, municipalities, etc.
4980 Auckland (Table KL-KWX9)
4981 Christchurch (Table KL-KWX9)
4982 Dunedin (Table KL-KWX9)
4983 Hamilton (Table KL-KWX9)
4984 Napier-Hastings (Table KL-KWX9)
4987 Wellington (Table KL-KWX9)
4990.A-Z Other cities, A-Z
Subarrange each by Table KL-KWX9a
4990.B54 Blenheim (Table KL-KWX9a)
4990.G57 Gisborne (Table KL-KWX9a)
4990.G74 Greymouth (Table KL-KWX9a)
4990.I68 Invercargill (Table KL-KWX9a)
4990.N45 Nelson (Table KL-KWX9a)
4990.N48 New Plymouth (Table KL-KWX9a)
4990.W53 Whangarei (Table KL-KWX9a)

Pacific area: Pacific area jurisdictions: Regional comparative and uniform law: Australia and New Zealand

1-999 General (Table KL-KWX2)

Pacific area: Pacific area jurisdictions: Regional comparative and uniform law: Other Pacific area jurisdictions

1-999 General (Table KL-KWX2 modified)

Regional divisions. Subregions

Class here general works on the law or legal system in force within a single subregion

For works comparing the law on a particular subject, see the subject

116 Australasia

Class here works on the subregion composed of Australia, Tasmania, New Zealand, New Guinea, New Britain, New Caledonia, and Vanuatu collectively

For works limited to the law of Australia and New Zealand see KVB1+

Oceania

117 General works

118 Melanesia

Including New Caledonia, Vanuatu, Solomon Islands, Admiralty Islands, Bismarck Archipelago, and Fiji

119 Micronesia

Including Guam, Trust Territory of the Pacific Islands, Nauru, and Gilbert Islands

Cf. KVS501+ Micronesia (Federated States)

120 Polynesia

For French Polynesia see KVP1+

Pacific area: Pacific area jurisdictions: Regional comparative and uniform law: Regional organization and integration. Pacific area cooperation

Class here works on treaties establishing, and laws governing, the organizations and their legal activity

Including subregional organizations

For official acts or legal measures on a particular subject, see the subject in KVB or KVC

For organizations governing a particular subject, activity, see the subject in KVB or KVC

10 General works

201-249 South Pacific Forum (Table KL-KWX3)

ASEAN see KNE151+

301-349 Economic and Social Commission for Asia and the Pacific (ESCAP), 1974 (Table KL-KWX3)

401-449 Pacific Economic Cooperation Council (PECC) (Table KL-KWX3)

601-649 Asia Pacific Economic Cooperation (Table KL-KWX3)

Pacific area: Pacific area jurisdictions: American Samoa
U.S. Territory (unorganized and unincorporated)
1-489 General (Table KL-KWX7 modified)
Administrative and political divisions. Local government other than municipal
231.5.A-Z Districts, A-Z
Including official gazettes, bylaws, statutory orders, regulations, and general works, as well as works on specific legal topics
490.A-Z Cities, communities, etc., A-Z
Subarrange each by Table KL-KWX9a
490.F35 Fagatogo (Table KL-KWX9a)
490.T34 Tafuna (Table KL-KWX9a)

Pacific area: Pacific area jurisdictions: Austral Islands
see KVP1+

Pacific area: Pacific area jurisdictions: Australia
see KU+

Pacific area: Pacific area jurisdictions: Banks Islands
see KWR1+
Cf. KWH1+ Papua New Guinea

1001-1489 Pacific area: Pacific area jurisdictions: British New Guinea (Territory of Papua) (Table KL-KWX7)

Class here British/Australian law governing part of New Guinea

KU-KWW

PACIFIC AREA: PACIFIC AREA JURISDICTIONS:
BRITISH SOLOMON ISLANDS

Pacific area: Pacific area jurisdictions: British Solomon Islands
see KWL2001+

## PACIFIC AREA: PACIFIC AREA JURISDICTIONS: CAROLINE ISLANDS

Pacific area: Pacific area jurisdictions: Caroline Islands
see KWE1+ and KWG1+

1-490 Pacific area: Pacific area jurisdictions: Cook Islands
Self-governing overseas territory of New Zealand
Including Penrhyn island
1-489 General (Table KL-KWX7)

Pacific area: Pacific area jurisdictions: Easter Island

Chilean possession

1-489 General (Table KL-KWX5)

Pacific area: Pacific area jurisdictions: Ellice Islands
see KWQ1+

Pacific area: Pacific area jurisdictions: Fiji

1-489 General (Table KL-KWX7 modified)

Administrative and political divisions. Local government other than municipal

231.5.A-Z Administrative divisions, A-Z

Including official gazettes, bylaws, statutory orders, regulations, and general works, as well as works on specific legal topics

231.5.C46 Central Division

231.5.W47 Western Division

490.A-Z Cities, communities, etc., A-Z

Subarrange each by Table KL-KWX9a

490.N34 Nadi (Table KL-KWX9a)

490.N38 Nausori (Table KL-KWX9a)

490.S38 Savusavu (Table KL-KWX9a)

490.S88 Suva (Table KL-KWX9a)

Pacific area: Pacific area jurisdictions: French Polynesia

French overseas territory

Including the island groups of Austral, Society (Tahiti), Tuamotu, Gambier, and Marquesas

1-99 General (Table KL-KWX8)

100.A-Z Cities, communities, etc., A-Z

Subarrange each by Table KL-KWX9a

Pacific area: Pacific area jurisdictions: Gambier Islands
see KVP1+
Cf. KWH1+ Papua New Guinea

Pacific area: Pacific area jurisdictions: German New Guinea (to 1914)

Class here colonial law of the German part of New Guinea

1001-1099 General (Table KL-KWX8)

Pacific area: Pacific area jurisdictions: Gilbert and Ellice Islands Colony

see KVR1+ ; KWQ1+

Pacific area: Pacific area jurisdictions: Guam

American territory

1-489 General (Table KL-KWX7)

490.A-Z Cities, communities, etc., A-Z

Subarrange each by Table KL-KWX9a

490.A53 Agana (Table KL-KWX9a)

Pacific area: Pacific area jurisdictions: Kiribati
Including Gilbert, Phoenix, and Line Islands

1-489 General (Table KL-KWX7)

490.A-Z Cities, communities, etc., A-Z
Subarrange each by Table KL-KWX9a

Pacific area: Pacific area jurisdictions: Line Islands
see KVR1+

Pacific area: Pacific area jurisdictions: Marquesa Islands
see KVP1+

Pacific area: Pacific area jurisdictions: Marshall Islands

Free-associated state (USA). Previously part of the Trust Territory of the Pacific Islands

1-489 General (Table KL-KWX7)

490.A-Z Cities, communities, etc., A-Z

Subarrange each by Table KL-KWX9a

490.M35 Majuro (Table KL-KWX9a)

Pacific area: Pacific area jurisdictions: Micronesia (Federated States)

Freely-associated state (USA). Previously part of the Trust Territory of the Pacific Islands

501-989 General (Table KL-KWX7 modified)

Administrative and political divisions. Local government other than municipal

731.5.A-Z Administrative divisions, A-Z

Including official gazettes, bylaws, statutory orders, regulations, and general works, as well as works on specific legal topics

731.5.C58 Chuuk

Previously Truk

731.5.K67 Kosrae

Previously Kusaie

731.5.P65 Pohnpei

Previously Ponape

731.5.Y36 Yap

990.A-Z Cities, communities, etc., A-Z

Subarrange each by Table KL-KWX9a

990.A83 Auak (Table KL-KWX9a)

990.K65 Kolonia (Table KL-KWX9a)

990.N54 Nluul (Table KL-KWX9a)

990.W46 Wene (Table KL-KWX9a)

Pacific area: Pacific area jurisdictions: Midway Islands

U.S. Pacific Territory

2501-2989 General (Table KL-KWX7)

Pacific area: Pacific area jurisdictions: Nauru

1-489 General (Table KL-KWX7)

Pacific area: Pacific area jurisdictions: Netherlands New Guinea (to 1963)

Class here colonial law for the Netherlands part of New Guinea

Cf. KNW0+ Irian Jaya

1001-1099 General (Table KL-KWX8)

Pacific area: Pacific area jurisdictions: New Caledonia

French overseas territory

Including the Loyalty Islands, the Isle of Pines, and the Bélep Archipelago

1-489 General (Table KL-KWX5)

490.A-Z Cities, communities, etc., A-Z

Subarrange each by Table KL-KWX9a

490.N68 Nouméa (Table KL-KWX9a)

Pacific area: Pacific area jurisdictions: New Hebrides Condominium
see KWR1+

Pacific area: Pacific area jurisdictions: Niue
Self-governing overseas territory of New Zealand
1-489 General (Table KL-KWX8)

Pacific area: Pacific area jurisdictions: Northern Mariana Islands

Previously part of the Trust Territory of the Pacific Islands.

Commonwealth associated with U.S.

1-489 General (Table KL-KWX7)

490.A-Z Cities, communities, etc., A-Z

Subarrange each by Table KL-KWX9a

490.S35 Saipan (Table KL-KWX9a)

For Marshall Islands see KVS1+

For Federated States of Micronesia see KVS501+

For Northern Mariana Islands see KWC1+

For Palau see KWG1+

Pacific area: Pacific area jurisdictions: Pacific Islands (Trust Territory)

Including Mariana, Marshall, and Caroline groups (except Guam)

1-489 General (Table KL-KWX7)

Cities, communities, etc.

see the appropriate jurisdiction

Pacific area: Pacific area jurisdictions: Palau

Part of the Trust Territory of the Pacific Islands, U.S. administered

1-489 General (Table KL-KWX7)

490.A-Z Cities, communities, etc., A-Z

Subarrange each by Table KL-KWX9a

490.K67 Koror (Table KL-KWX9a)

Pacific area: Pacific area jurisdictions: Papua New Guinea
Comprises the previous German Colony of New Guinea (to 1914), later New Guinea (Territory) (1921), and British New Guinea, later Territory of Papua

1-489 General (Table KL-KWX7 modified)
Administrative and political divisions. Local government other than municipal
231.5.A-Z Provinces, A-Z
Including official gazettes, bylaws, statutory orders, regulations, and general works, as well as works on specific legal topics
231.5.B68 Bougainville Province
Formerly North Solomons Province
231.5.C46 Central Province
231.5.C55 Chimbu Province
231.5.E37 East New Britain Province
231.5.E375 East Sepik Province
231.5.E38 Eastern Highlands Province
231.5.E65 Enga Province
231.5.G85 Gulf Province
231.5.M34 Madang Province
231.5.M36 Manus Province
231.5.M55 Milne Bay Province
231.5.M67 Morobe Province
231.5.N37 National Capital District
231.5.N48 New Ireland Province
(231.5.N67) North Solomons Province
see KWH231.5.B68
231.5.N675 Northern Province
231.5.S36 Sandaun Province
231.5.S66 Southern Highlands Province
231.5.W47 West New Britain Province
West Sepik Province see KWH231.5.S36
231.5.W48 Western Province
231.5.W485 Western Highlands Province
490.A-Z Cities, communities, etc., A-Z
Subarrange each by Table KL-KWX9a
490.A56 Alotau (Table KL-KWX9a)
490.A73 Arawa (Table KL-KWX9a)
490.G67 Goroka (Table KL-KWX9a)
490.K56 Kimbe (Table KL-KWX9a)
490.K86 Kundiawa (Table KL-KWX9a)
490.L34 Lae (Table KL-KWX9a)
490.M34 Madang (Table KL-KWX9a)
490.M46 Mendi (Table KL-KWX9a)
490.M68 Mount Hagen (Table KL-KWX9a)

Cities, communities, etc., A-Z -- Continued

490.P67 Port Moresby (Table KL-KWX9a)

490.R33 Rabaoul (Table KL-KWX9a)

490.V36 Vanimo (Table KL-KWX9a)

490.W48 Wewak (Table KL-KWX9a)

Pacific area: Pacific area jurisdictions: Pitcairn Island

1-489 General (Table KL-KWX7)

# PACIFIC AREA: PACIFIC AREA JURISDICTIONS: SAMOA

Pacific area: Pacific area jurisdictions: Samoa
see KWW1+

Pacific area: Pacific area jurisdictions: Solomon Islands
Previously British Solomon Islands

2001-2489 General (Table KL-KWX7 modified)
Administrative and political divisions. Local government other than municipal
2231.5.A-Z Provinces, A-Z
Including official gazettes, bylaws, statutory orders, regulations, and general works, as well as works on specific legal topics
2231.5.C46 Central Province
2231.5.G83 Guadalcanal
2231.5.I73 Isabel
2231.5.M34 Makira and Ulawa
2231.5.M35 Malaita
2231.5.T46 Temotu
2231.5.W47 Western Province
2490.A-Z Cities, communities, etc., A-Z
Subarrange each by Table KL-KWX9a
2490.H66 Honiara (Table KL-KWX9a)

PACIFIC AREA: PACIFIC AREA JURISDICTIONS:
TAHITI

Pacific area: Pacific area jurisdictions: Tahiti
see KVP1+

# PACIFIC AREA: PACIFIC AREA JURISDICTIONS: TOKELAU

Pacific area: Pacific area jurisdictions: Tokelau
see KUQ2315.T65

Pacific area: Pacific area jurisdictions: Tonga

Including the island groups of Niuas, Vava'u, Ha'apai, Kotu, Nomuka, Otu Tolu, and Tongatapu

1-489 General (Table KL-KWX7)

490.A-Z Cities, communities, etc., A-Z

Subarrange each by Table KL-KWX9a

490.N85 Nuku'alofa (Table KL-KWX9a)

# PACIFIC AREA: PACIFIC AREA JURISDICTIONS: TUAMOTU ARCHIPELAGO

Pacific area: Pacific area jurisdictions: Tuamotu Archipelago
see KVP1+

Pacific area: Pacific area jurisdictions: Tubuai Islands
see KVP1+

Pacific area: Pacific area jurisdictions: Tuvalu

Formerly the Ellice Islands (as part of the British Protectorate, and later Gilbert and Ellice Islands Colony)

1-489 General (Table KL-KWX7 modified)

Administrative and political divisions. Local government other than municipal

231.5.A-Z Administrative divisions (island councils). By island (atoll), A-Z

Including official gazettes, bylaws, statutory orders, regulations, and general works, as well as works on specific legal topics

231.5.F86 Funafuti

231.5.N35 Nanumanga

231.5.N36 Nanumea

231.5.N58 Niutao

231.5.N85 Nui

231.5.N86 Nukufetau

231.5.N865 Nukulaelae

231.5.V35 Vaitupu

490.A-Z Cities, communities, etc., A-Z

Subarrange each by Table KL-KWX9a

490.F66 Fongafale (Table KL-KWX9a)

Pacific area: Pacific area jurisdictions: Vanuatu
Formerly the Anglo-French New Hebrides Condominum (Condominum des Nouvelle-Hébrides)
Including the islands of Santo, Malakula, Épi, Pentecôt, Aoba, Maewo, Paama, Ambrym, Éfate, Erromanga, Tanna, and Aneityum

1-489 General (Table KL-KWX7)
490.A-Z Cities, communities, etc., A-Z
Subarrange each by Table KL-KWX9a
490.L66 Longana (Table KL-KWX9a)
490.L85 Luganville (Table KL-KWX9a)
490.P67 Port-Vila (Table KL-KWX9a)

Pacific area: Pacific area jurisdictions: Wake Island

U.S. administered Pacific territory

1-489 General (Table KL-KWX7)

Pacific area: Pacific area jurisdictions: Wallis and Futuna Islands
Iles de Hoorn and Wallis Archipelago, a French overseas territory (Protectorate)

2001-2489 General (Table KL-KWX5 modified)
Administrative law
Administrative organization
Administrative and political divisions. Local government other than municipal
Including those of centralized national governments or federal governments

2293.5.A-Z Administrative districts, A-Z
Including official gazettes, bylaws, statutory orders, regulations, and general works, as well as works on specific legal topics

2293.5.A56 Alo

2293.5.S56 Sigavé

2293.5.U84 Uvéa

2490.A-Z Cities, communities, etc., A-Z
Subarrange each by Table KL-KWX9a

2490.M37 Mata-Uta (Table KL-KWX9a)

Pacific area: Pacific area jurisdictions: Samoa

Including Savai'i, Upolu, Manono, and Apolima Islands

Previously Western Samoa

1-489 General (Table KL-KWX7)

490.A-Z Cities, communities, etc., A-Z

Subarrange each by Table KL-KWX9a

490.A65 Apia (Table KL-KWX9a)

490.S55 Sili (Table KL-KWX9a)

Antarctica
Class here works on the Antarctic Treaty system and Antarctic legal regime, comprising the Antarctic Treaty law; the organization and legal measures of the Antarctic Consultative Powers; and agreements and conventions between the Antarctic Treaty Parties and other nations

1 Bibliography
3 Periodicals. Serials
For periodicals consisting primarily of informative material (newsletters, bulletins, etc.) relating to a particular subject, see the subject and form division for periodicals
For law reports, official bulletins or circulars, and official gazettes intended chiefly for the publication of laws and regulations, see the appropriate entries in the text or form division tables
4 Monographic series
6 Documentation
Intergovernmental congresses and conferences. By name of the congress
Including ad hoc conferences of heads of state
For conferences limited to a particular subject, see the subject
For other congresses, conferences, meetings, etc. see KWX60
Conference on Antarctica, 1959
10 Serials
10.2 Monographs. By date
Conference on Antarctic Resources policies, 1982
11 Serials
11.2 Monographs. By date
14.A-Z Other congresses and conferences. By name of the congress, A-Z
*Under each:*
*.xA12-.xA199* *Serials*
*.xA3* *Monographs. By date*
Official acts
18 Indexes and tables
19 Collections. Compilations (General)
Treaties and other international agreements
Class here treaties concluded by the Claimant Powers, and conventions between the Claimant Powers and other nations
For treaties establishing or expanding the Antarctic Treaty System, including treaties of association see KWX342+
20 Indexes and tables
22 Collections
Including either multilateral or bilateral treaties, or both

Official acts
Treaties and other international agreements -- Continued
Individual treaties
see the subject
Other official acts
Including recommendations (e. g. measures, decisions, and resolutions)
29 Indexes and tables
32 Abridgments and digests
Collections
34 Serials
36 Monographs. By date
Individual
see the appropriate subject
40 Official reports. Surveys on legal activity
44 Court decisions and related materials
For decisions and materials on a particular subject, see the subject
50 Dictionaries. Encyclopedias
52 Directories
60 Congresses. Conferences. By date of the congress
For conferences limited to a particular subject, see the subject
For intergovernmental congresses see KWX8+
70 General works
Including compends, essays, festschriften, etc.
Theory and principles
Including historical concepts
Class here works on concepts of international law as applied to Antarctica
(100) General works
see KWX70
Rule of law see KWX462
Intergovernmental legal regimes governing the Antarctic commons
General and comparative see KZ1322+
102 Res communes and common heritage of mankind doctrine
103 Organizations and their legal activities
Constitutional aspects of international cooperation see KWX467
Territorial division (Sectors). Territorial claims
By claimant power
125 Australian Antarctic Territory
Including Wilkes Land, Victoria Land, and Enderby Land
135 Tierra del Fuego. Sovereign Territories of Argentina in the Antarctic
Overlapping the Chilean and British claims

Territorial division (Sectors). Territorial claims
By claimant power -- Continued
145 British Antarctic Territory
Including South Orkney Islands and South Shetland Islands; Antarctic Peninsula (with Palmer Land and Graham Land), Coats Land and Ellsworth Land, overlapping both Chile's and Argentina's claims
155 Magallanes y Antártica. Chilean Antarctic Territory
Overlapping both Argentina's and Great Britain's claims
165 Terres australes et antarctiques françaises. French Southern and Antarctic Territories
Including the Kerguelen and Crozet archipelagoes, the islands of Saint Paul and Amsterdam (formerly Nouvelle Amsterdam), and Adélie Coast
175 Dronning Maud Land. Antarctic Territory under Norwegian sovereignty
185 Ross Dependency. New Zealand Antarctic Territory
Maritime boundaries. Delimination of southern sea areas.
National claims to marine areas see KZA1672
The Antarctic Treaty System
341 Bibliography
341.3 Periodicals
Including gazettes, yearbooks, bulletins, etc.
Treaties establishing or expanding the System
342 Indexes and tables
342.3 Collections
342.5 Proposed treaties. Drafts. By date
343.3<date> Individual treaties
Arrange chronologically by appending date of signature of the treaty to the number KWX343.3 and deleting any trailing zeros. Subarrange each by Table K5
343.31959 Antarctic Treaty, 1959 (Table K5 modified)
Texts of, and works on, the treaty
Related agreements
343.31959.Z52 Protocol on Environmental Protection, 1991
343.4<date> Treaties of Accession (adhesion) and association
Arrange chronologically by appending date of signature of the treaty to the number KWX343.4 and deleting any trailing zeros. Subarrange each by Table K5
344.8 Conferences. Symposia
General works see KWX70
450 Interpretation and construction
455 Constitutional principles
457 Sovereignty question. Claimant powers. Sector theory
460 Consultative status question
Including Contracting Powers and Consultative Powers
462 Rule of law

The Antarctic Treaty System -- Continued
Intergovernmental relations. Cooperation of states
Including activities, presence, or policy towards Antarctica
465 General (Table K14)
467 By region or country, A-Z
Accession of new states
470 General works
472 Legal problems of expansion of the Antarctic Treaty System
Antarctic Treaty institutions and organs
For organs, institutions, etc., with jurisdiction limited to a specific subject field, see the subject
478 General (Table K14)
480 Rules governing the official languages of the organs (Table K14)
Antarctic Treaty Consultative Meeting
484 General (Table K15)
487.A-Z Committees and commissions, A-Z
Subarrange each by Table K12
490.A-Z Meetings of experts. Advisory commissions, A-Z
Subarrange each by Table K12
494 Powers and duties. Jurisdiction
496 Parliamentary rules and procedures
Individual consultative meetings
500.2 Canberra, 1961 (Table K15)
500.3 Buenos Aires, 1962 (Table K15)
500.4 Brussels, 1964 (Table K15)
500.5 Santiago de Chile 1966 (Table K15)
500.6 Paris 1968 (Table K15)
500.7 Tokyo 1970 (Table K15)
500.8 Wellington 1972 (Table K15)
500.9 Oslo 1975 (Table K15)
501 London 1977 (Table K15)
501.2 Washington 1979 (Table K15)
501.3 Buenos Aires 1981 (Table K15)
501.4 Canberra 1983 (Table K15)
501.5 Brussels 1985 (Table K15)
501.6 Rio de Janeiro 1987 (Table K15)
501.7 Wellington 1988 (Table K15)
501.8 Paris 1990 (Table K15)
501.9 Bonn 1991 (Table K15)
502 Madrid 1991 (Table K15)
600 Administrative processes and provisions (Table K14)
Including management regimes
Public safety
630 General (Table K14)
Hazardous articles and processes

Public safety
Hazardous articles and processes -- Continued
634 General (Table K14)
635 Nuclear power (Table K14)
For radio active waste see KWX715
636 Scientific rockets (Table K14)
Social activities
638 General (Table K14)
Tourism see KWX732
International commons. Public domain
643 General (Table K14)
Res communes. Area designated as common heritage of mankind
For works on the doctrine of common heritage of mankind, etc. see KWX102
Cf. KWX457 Sovereignty question
644 General (Table K14)
645 Antarctica World Park. International marine sanctuary (Table K14)
Conservation of natural resources. Environmental planning see KWX706
653 Water resources. Ice (Table K14)
Shore protection. Coastal zone management see KWX707
Marine resources see KWX801+
(670) Public land use
see KWX644
682 Public health (Table K14)
692 Medical legislation (Table K14)
Antarctic environment. Code of environmental conduct. Protection against human impact
701-705 General (Table K7)
706 Environmental planning. Conservation of natural resources under common heritage commons management systems (Table K14)
707 Shore protection. Coastal zone management (Table K14)
Environmental pollution
708 General (Table K14)
709 Air pollution (Table K14)
Water pollution. Marine pollution
Including drainage, infiltration, and sewage control
711 General (Table K14)
712.A-Z Pollutants, A-Z
712.O55 Oil
712.R34 Radioactive substance
714-716 Refuse disposal (land and marine sites)
714 General (Table K14)
715 Radioactive waste (Table K14)

Antarctic environment. Code of environmental conduct.
Protection against human impact
Environmental pollution
Refuse disposal (land and marine sites) -- Continued

716 Human waste (Table K14)

Wilderness preservation. Conservation of Antarctic fauna and flora

717 General (Table K14)

Antarctic Protected Area System

718 General (Table K14)

719.A-Z Specially protected areas, A-Z

719.L85 Lynch Island (South Orkney Islands)

Sites of special scientific interest (land and marine sites)

Including management plans and guidelines; restrictions on pedestrian and vehicle traffic; sampling and killing; disturbance of breeding colonies; use of underwater explosives; etc.

720 General (Table K14)

721.A-Z Particular sites, A-Z

721.S68 South Shetland Islands

722 Sites and monuments of historic interest (Table K14)

723 Antarctic specially managed areas (Table K14)

Including tourism

Protection of native fauna

Including native mammals and birds

For marine life see KWX795+

723.3 General (Table K14)

Prohibition of Pelagic sealing

724-728 General (Table K7 modified)

Treaties and other international agreements. Conventions

726.3<date> Multilateral treaties

Arrange chronologically by appending date of signature of the treaty to the number KWX726.3 and deleting any trailing zeros. Subarrange each by Table K5

726.31972 Convention on the Conservation of Antarctic Seals, 1972 (Table K5)

729 Sealing zones and seal reserves

730.A-Z Protected species, A-Z

730.F87 Fur seal

730.R67 Ross seal

730.S68 Southern elephant seal

731 Prohibition of introducing non-indigenous species, parasites, and diseases

732 Tourism and non-government expeditions

Including commercial overflights in Antarctica

Antarctic scientific research
736 General (Table K14)
738 Scientific Committee on Antarctic Research (SCAR) (Table K15)
Siting of research stations
740 General (Table K14)
742.A-Z Stations, A-Z
742.M46 McMurdo
742.P35 Palmer
742.S68 South Pole
742.W67 World Park (Greenpeace)
Sites of special scientific or historic interest see KWX720
755 Antarctic meteorology (Table K14)
Fisheries. Harvesting activities in Antarctic waters
795 General (Table K14)
The Antarctic Marine Living Resources Regime. Antarctic marine ecosystem
801-805 General (Table K7, modified)
Treaties and other international agreements. Conventions
803.3<date> Multilateral treaties
Arrange chronologically by appending date of signature of the treaty to the number KWX803.3 and deleting any trailing zeros. Subarrange each by table K5
803.31980 Convention of the Conservation of Antarctic Marine Living Resources, 1980 (Table K5)
Commission for the Conservation of Antarctic Marine Living Resources
806 General (Table K15)
808 Scientific Committee (Table K15)
809 Secretariat (Table K15)
810 Rules of procedures (Table K15)
812.A-Z By region or sector, A-Z
813.A-Z By fish or marine fauna, A-Z
813.K85 Krill
The Antarctic Minerals Regime
Including mineral exploration, exploitation, and prospecting
821-825 General (Table K7, modified)
Treaties and other international agreements. Conventions
823.3<date> Multilateral treaties
Arrange chronologically by appending date of signature of the treaty to the number KWX823.3 and deleting any trailing zeros. Subarrange each by Table K5
823.31988 Convention on the Regulation of Antarctic Mineral Resources Activities, 1988 (Table K5)
Institutions and organs
826 General (Table K14)

The Antarctic Minerals Regime
Institutions and organs -- Continued
827 Antarctic Mineral Resources Commission (Table K15)
829 Scientific, Technical, and Environmental Advisory Committee (Table K15)
830 Regulatory Committees (Table K15)
832 Rules of procedures (Table K14)
834 Cooperation with International Organizations (Table K14)
836 Application for exploration permit. Management schemes (Table K14)
Dispute settlements
842 General (Table K14)
844 Arbitral tribunal and procedure (Table K15)
Transportation
861 General (Table K14)
Oversnow transport
863 General (Table K14)
865.A-Z Vehicles, A-Z
Air transport
868 General (Table K14)
870 Air fields (Table K14)
872 Air safety (Table K14)
Water transport
876 General (Table K14)
876.5 Coastwise shipping (Table K14)
877 Navigation (Table K14)
Meteorology. Meteorological stations see KWX755
Communication
878 General (Table K14)
Antarctic Postal services
879 General (Table K14)
885 Commemorative stamp issue (Table K14)
Telecommunication
886 General (Table K14)
887 Telegraph (Table K14)
888 Data transmission systems (Table K14)
Radio and television communication
890 General (Table K14)
892 Stations. Networks (Table K14)
Including frequency allocations and licensing
893 Radio aids to air navigation (Table K14)
895 Radio broadcasting (Table K14)
950 Criminal provisions (Table K14)

1 Bibliography
For bibliography of a particular author or work, see the author or title
For bibliography of special topics, see the topic
1.15 Indexes to periodical literature, society publications, collections, etc.
2 Periodicals
3 Encyclopedias. Law dictionaries
4 Terms and phrases. Vocabularies
Including early works
Methodology
see KL190
Auxiliary sciences
5 General works
Diplomatics
see KL75
Paleography (General)
see KL76
Papyrology
see KL77
Archaeology. Folklife studies
see KL78
6 Seals. Flags. Insignia. Armory
6.5 General works
Sources
7 Studies on sources
Including history of sources and methodology (e.g., epigraphy, papyrology, etc.)
For philological studies, see subclasses P, PJ, and PK
Collections. Compilations. Lists of specimens. Selections
Class here comprehensive collections of legal sources in ancient characters, i.e., ideographic; hieroglyphic (including hieratic and demotic); cuneiform inscriptions and scripts; and Mediterranean script
8 Texts (Inscriptions. Clay tablets. Papyri, etc.). By title, name, or other designation
Including facsimiles and originals; and including typographical reproductions of the text entirely in ancient type, or transliterated in Roman characters
9.A-Z Translations. By language, A-Z (without edition of original text)
10 Indexes. Chronologies. Concordances, etc.
Individual sources and groups of sources. By period
For sources originating from, or discovered at, a particular place, see the place
11 Earliest period (Table KL-KWX10)
12 Middle period (Table KL-KWX10)

Sources
Individual sources and groups of sources. By period -- Continued
13 Later period (Table KL-KWX10)
14 To Middle Ages (ca. 800 A.D.) (Table KL-KWX10)
15.A-Z Local (Provincial) and municipal law, colonial law, etc. By place, A-Z
Trials
15.3 General collections
Criminal trials and judicial investigations
Collections. Compilations
15.4 General
15.5.A-Z Particular offenses, A-Z
15.6.A-Z Individual trials. By defendant or best known name, A-Z
Including records, briefs, commentaries and stories on a particular trial
16 Legal education
17 The legal profession. Jurists. Notaries. Paralegals
e.g. orators, speakers
19 Interpretation and construction
Concepts and principles
21 General works
22 Private law and public law
23 Private international law. Conflict of laws
Private law
24 General works
Persons
25 General works
27 Personality. Capacity and incapacity. Status
28 Capacity to be a witness
Classes of persons
30 General works
32 Slaves and serfs
33 Outlaws
34 Women
34.5 Children
35 Peasants
36 Free men
37 Minorities
Including religious and ethnic minorities
38 Associations and groups of persons. Tribes
40 Family law. Family structure
42 Marriage
43 Betrothal
45 Marital status
Including age and capacity to contract marriage

Private law
Family law. Family structure
Marriage -- Continued
46 Marital contracts
Including consent, dowry, etc.
Particular types of marriages
47 Purchase marriage
49 Marriage among slaves
52 Mixed marriage (among slaves and free)
53 Marriage between brother and sister
55 Marriage between older and younger male
56 Multiple marriages
57 Polygamy
58 Polyandry
59 Conjugal community. Marriage bond
62 Marriages with or without jointly maintained household and domicile
Legal status of married women
63 General works
64 Equality. Emancipation and decision making
65 Woman follows personal status of husband (free or slave)
66 Clothing and dress laws
68 Guardianship over women
69 Civil liability
Crimes by or against married women see KL-KWX1 288.A+
72 Quasi marriage. Concubinage
Matrimonial action. Dissolution of marriage
74 General works
75 Divorce
77 Matrimonial property and regime
Including different forms, e.g., separation of property, community of property, etc.
78 Management and usufruct
79 Dower. Alimony
Consanguinity and affinity
80 General works
82 Cognates and agnates
Parent and child
83 General works
84 Support. Dowry
86 Adoption
Quasi-adoption see KL-KWX1 192
87 Parental power. Custody
88 Illegitimate children. Legitimation

Private law
Family law. Family structure
Consanguinity and affinity
Parent and child -- Continued
89 Children borne by slaves of the household
Guardian and ward
92 General works
93 Guardianship over minors
94 Guardianship over women
Inheritance. Succession upon death
96 General works
97 Universal succession
99 Intestate and testamentary succession
100 Estate. Inheritance
101 Heirs. Legal status
102 Masculine primogeniture
104 Sequence of heirs
106 Acceptance and disclaimer
107 Joint heirs
109 Wills. Testaments
110 Oral or written private will
111 Distribution of inheritance
113 Inheritance contracts
114 Disinheritance. Unworthiness of heir
115 Gift causa mortis
117 Funerary, priests; for tomb maintenance perpetual foundations
Law of things. Property
120 General works
122 Possession and ownership
Acquisition and loss
Including mobiles and immobiles
123 General works
124 Occupancy
125 Accessions
126 Prescription
127 Succession
128 Donation
130 Co-ownership
131 Claims and actions resulting from ownership or possession
133 Real property. Land law
Joint (communal) property of tribal or other local association see KL-KWX1 146
134 Private ownership of real property
135 Publicity of ownership
Rights incident to ownership of land

Private law
Law of things. Property
Real property. Land law
Rights incident to ownership of land
136 General works
137 Riparian rights. Water rights
138 Game and fishing rights
139 Law of adjoining landowners
140 Boundaries. Boundary stone (Kudurru)
141 Party walls
Rights to use of another's property
144 General works
King's land cultivated by officials, soldiers, and craftsmen in return for services see KL-KWX1 270+
146 Joint (communal) use of property by tribe or local association
Rural (peasant) land tenure. Peasantry see KL-KWX1 225
148 Servitudes
149 Right of way
150 Aquae ductus
152 Real securities. Pledges
Obligations. Contracts
154 General works
Debtor and creditor
155 General works
156 Obligations to perform and liability for enforcement
157 Plurality of debtors and creditors. Joint obligations
158 Types of obligations
159 Transfer and assumption of obligation
160 Secured transactions. Security
162 Extinction of obligation
163 Performance
Including enforcement (e.g., surrender of wife, children, or slaves instead of or as security for payment)
165 Non-performance. Default. Breach of contract
Penalties see KL-KWX1 295+
167 Consensual contract and real contract
Formation of contract
168 General works
169 Clauses
Contractual penalties see KL-KWX1 295+
171 Formalities. Documentation
Including written form, witnesses, seals, signatures, etc.
173 Parties to contract
Sale

Private law
Obligations. Contracts
Sale -- Continued
176 General works
Including warranty, default, etc.
177 Conditional sale
178 Sale in kind (species)
Commodities see KL-KWX1 240.A+
Price regulation see KL-KWX1 242
180 Exchange. Barter
182 Donations. Gifts
184 Lease. Landlords and tenant
Including buildings, rooms, and land
For agricultural lease see KL-KWX1 225
186 Commodatum. Loan (lease) of mobilia for use
Including domestic animals, ships, carriages, etc.
For loan (lease) of persons for service see KL-KWX1 190+
188 Mutuum. Loan of money. Credit
Including securities, bonds, etc.
Hire for service and labor
190 General works
191 Apprenticeship contract
192 Wetnurse contract
194 Agency. Negotiorum gestio. Mandat
196 Deposit. Depositum irregulare
198 Suretyship
200 Life annuities
202 Promise of debt. Promissory note
Commercial transactions. Industry, trade and commerce
204 General works
205 Consignment
206 Warehousing
Freightage
208 General works
209 Caravan traffic
211 Negotiable instruments
Banking
213 General works
214 Loan of money. Credit
Including suretyship and guaranty
Maritime law. Water transportation
216 General works
217 Affreightment. Carriage of goods at sea and inland waters
218 Carriage of passengers at sea
219 Average

Private law
Commercial transactions. Industry, trade and commerce
Maritime law. Water transportation -- Continued
220 Salvage
222 Partnerships. Companies. Associations and societies
Agricultural law
224 General works
225 Rural (peasant) land tenure. Peasantry
Including village communities
Mining. Quarrying
227 General works
228 Particular resources, A-Z (not A-Z)
230 Forestry. Timbering. Hunting
231 Fishery
233 Wine making
234 Horticulture
235 Apiculture
237.A-Z Occupations, professions, and trades, A-Z
237.A73 Architects
237.A78 Artisans
Including carpenters, metalsmiths, hairdressers, locksmiths, etc.
237.M47 Merchants
237.S87 Surgeons
237.V47 Veterinarians
240.A-Z Particular commodities A-Z
240.C47 Cereals
240.D66 Domestic animals
240.E63 Embroideries
240.F57 Fish
240.G53 Glass
240.L56 Linen
240.M47 Metalwork
240.O55 Oil
240.S35 Salt
240.S53 Slaves
240.W56 Wine
240.W66 Wood (Cedar; pine)
240.W67 Wool
242 Price regulation
Courts and procedure
244 General works
245 The administration of justice. Judiciary
Including criminal justice
246 Courts
Including courts of both criminal and civil justice

Courts and procedure -- Continued
The legal profession see KL-KWX1 17
Procedure
247 General works
248 Self-help and self-defense
248.2 Actions and defenses
249 Preliminary hearing
250 Evidence
Including witnesses, documentary evidence, oath, etc.
252 Decisions. Judgments
254 Insolvency
256 Execution
Including forced labor, imprisonment, etc.
257 Arbitration
Including commercial arbitration
Public law
258 General works
Constitutional law
General works see KL-KWX1 262
261 By period
262 General works
263 Territory
Nationality and citizenship. Class structure. Estates
264 General works
265 Nobles
266 Priests
267 Soldiers
268 Freemen
269 Slaves
Feudal law
270 General works
271 Fief. King's land cultivated by officials, soldiers, and craftsmen in return for service
272 Form of government
Including monarchy, tyranny (despotism), oligarchy, democracy, etc.
Organs of government
273 General works
274 Kings and rulers
Judiciary. Administration of justice see KL-KWX1 245
275 Councils of elders, senats, etc.
Administrative organization and process
Including administration of provinces, colonies, etc.
277 General works
277.3.A-Z Local government. By place, A-Z
277.3.A87 Attica

Public law
Constitutional law
Administrative organization and process -- Continued
277.5.A-Z Special topics, A-Z
277.5.A58 Aliens
Public finance
278 General works
279 Administration of public property
280 Taxes. Tithes. Duties
282 The military establishment
Foreign relations administration. International law
283 General works
284 Treaties. Confederations and alliances. Interstate arbitration
For text of treaties, see the sources in the appropriate period
Criminal law and procedure
285 General works
Administration of criminal justice and courts see KL-KWX1 245
286 Concepts and principles
287 Guilt
288.A-Z Individual offenses, A-Z
288.A36 Abortion
288.A48 Adultery
288.B37 Battery
288.B53 Blasphemy
288.B75 Bribery
288.D57 Displacing boundaries
288.E63 Embezzlement
288.E96 Expositio. Abandonment
288.F34 False accusation
288.F35 False testimony
288.I63 Incest
288.L48 Lewd acts
288.M87 Murder. Parracidium
288.P36 Pandering and pimping
288.P6 Political offenses
Including subversive activities
288.R63 Robbery. Theft
Subversive activities see KL-KWX1 288.P6
Theft see KL-KWX1 288.R63
Treason see KL-KWX1 288.P6
288.W57 Witchcraft
Criminal trial
289 General works
290 Compulsory measures against the accused
Evidence and burden of proof

Criminal law and procedure
Criminal trial
Evidence and burden of proof -- Continued
291 General works
292 Torture
293 Ordeal
Including fire and water ordeal
294 Judgment
Including ostracism
Punishment. Execution of sentence
295 General works
296 Talion
297 Human sacrifices
298.A-Z Particular penalties, A-Z
Amputation see KL-KWX1 298.M87
298.B43 Beating. Flogging
298.B73 Branding
298.D57 Disinheritance
298.E95 Exile
298.F56 Fines
Flogging see KL-KWX1 298.B43
298.F67 Forced labor. Penal servitude
298.M87 Mutilation. Amputation
Penal servitude see KL-KWX1 298.F67
298.S53 Slavery
298.S76 Stoning
Appeals. Remedies
299 General works
299.5.A-Z Special topics, A-Z
299.5.A46 Amnesty

Class here works on the law of, and treaties between, two or more countries or regional organizations in the region

For comparisons of the law of countries in the region with those of other regions, see class K

Bibliography

For bibliography of special topics, see the topic

1 Bibliography of bibliography

2 General bibliography

2.6 Library catalogs. Union lists

2.7 Indexes to periodical articles, society publications, collections, etc.

For indexes to a particular publication, see the publication

Periodicals

For periodicals consisting predominantly of legal articles, regardless of subject matter and jurisdiction, see K1+

For periodicals consisting primarily of informative material (newsletters, bulletins, etc.) relating to a special subject, see the subject and form division tables for periodicals

For law reports, official bulletins or circulars intended chiefly for the publication of laws and regulations, see appropriate entries in the text or form division tables

For indexes to periodical articles see KL-KWX2 2.7

4 Monographic series

Official gazettes

For official gazettes of an individual jurisdiction, see the subclass for the jurisdiction

For official gazettes of regional organizations, see the organization

6 Indexes (General)

7 Collections. Compilations

Regional organizations

see the subject

Legislative and executive papers. Documentation of the regional organizations

see the organization

8.A-Z Intergovernmental congresses and conferences. By name of the congress, A-Z

*Under each:*

*.xA15* *Serials*

*.xA2* *Monographs. By date*

Including ad hoc conferences of heads of state

For intergovernmental congresses on a particular subject, see the subject

Legislation

For legislation of a particular jurisdiction, see the subclass for the jurisdiction

For legislation on a particular branch of the law or subject, see the branch or subject

Indexes and tables. By date

For indexes limited to one jurisdiction, see the subclass for the jurisdiction

9 General

10 Chronological indexes

11 Indexes of translations

12 Summaries. Abridgements. Digests

Statutes. Statutory orders. Administrative regulations

Collections

Including official and private editions, and annotated editions

14 Serials

15 Monographs. By date

16 Codes and related materials

Treaties and other international agreements

Class here treaties between countries limited to the region, and treaties and other international agreements of regional organizations, including all bilateral treaties of an organization

For treaties between countries in different regions, see K524+

For treaties of public international law, see KZ

Collections. Compilations

Including either multilateral or bilateral treaties, or both, and related agreements (accessions, successions, amending agreements, protocols, etc.)

18 General

19.A-Z Collected treaties of an individual country limited to its region, and collected treaties of a regional organization. By country or organization, A-Z

Individual treaties

see the subject

Presidential messages and proclamations

see class J

Court decisions and related materials. Reports

19.5 Indexes. Digests. Analytical abstracts

For indexes, digests, etc. relating to a particular publication, see that publication

20 Several courts

21 Privy Council decisions

22 Highest court of appeals. Supreme Court

24 Encyclopedias

25 Dictionaries. Terms and phrases. Vocabularies
For bilingual and multilingual dictionaries, see K52+
For dictionaries on a particular branch of the law or subject, see the branch or subject
26 Legal maxims
27 Form books
Including graphic material, blanks, atlases, etc., and early works
For form books on a particular branch of the law or subject, see the branch or subject
Judicial statistics
31 General
32.A-Z By subject, A-Z
Directories
35 General
36.A-Z By specialization, A-Z
Trials
39 Collections. Compilations
Criminal trials and judicial investigations
Collections. Compilations
40 General
41.A-Z Particular offenses, A-Z
41.P66 Political crimes
Individual trials
see the subclass for the country
War crime trials
Trials by international tribunals
see KZ
Trials of aliens by national courts sitting at home or abroad
see KZ
Trials of nationals by the courts of their own country
Trials by the courts of a particular country
see the subclass for the country
Trials by the courts of countries in different regions
see K545
42 Collections. Compilations
Individual trials
see the subclass for the country
43 Legal research. Legal bibliography
44 Information retrieval systems. Electronic data processing
Legal education. Study and teaching
46 General
47.A-Z Particular subjects, A-Z
47.W65 Women. Women's rights
48 Law schools

50 The legal profession
Including law as a career
51 Judges (Table K8)
52.A-Z Particular classes of lawyers and types of careers, A-Z
52.L43 Legal assistants. Paralegals
Paralegals see KL-KWX2 52.L43
52.P83 Public interest law
Practice of law
54 General works
Directories see KL-KWX2 35+
54.7 Attorneys' and legal secretaries' handbooks, manuals, etc.
55 Legal aid. Legal services to the poor. Community legal services
56 Biography of lawyers
58 Bar associations
Cf. KL-KWX2 74.A+ International regional bar associations
Law and lawyers in literature
see classes PB-PZ
Legal anecdotes, wit, and humor
see K183+
60 Notarial law. Public instruments
62 The notarial profession (Table K8)
64 Public instruments (Table K8)
66 Public registers. Registration
Civil registry see KL-KWX2 147
Registers of will see KL-KWX2 220.3
Commercial registers see KL-KWX2 244.8
70 Registration of miscellaneous titles and documents. Public instruments
72.A-Z Other, A-Z
74.A-Z Comparative law societies. Regional bar associations, and other organizations. By name, A-Z
Class here works on, and journals of, individual societies and their activities, e.g. annual reports, proceedings, incorporating statutes, bylaws, handbooks, and works about the society
For works issued by individual societies on special subjects, see the subject
For journals devoted to legal subjects, wholly or in part, see K1+
For congresses and conferences sponsored by societies see KL-KWX2 76
76 Congresses. Conferences
For intergovernmental congresses and conferences see KL-KWX2 8.A+
78.A-Z Academies. Institutes. By name, A-Z

79 General works
Including popular works, civics, addresses, essays, lectures, festschriften, etc.
84.A-Z Manuals and other works for particular groups of users. By user, A-Z
84.B87 Businesspeople. Foreign investors
Foreign investors see KL-KWX2 84.B87
Semantics and language see KL-KWX2 106
Anecdotes, facetiae, satire, and humor
see K184.19
Law and lawyers in literature
see classes PB-PZ
Relation of law to other topics
see K486+
85.A-Z Works on diverse aspects of a particular subject falling within several branches of the law. By subject, A-Z
85.C65 Computers
Including the Internet and electronic commerce
Electronic commerce see KL-KWX2 85.C65
Internet see KL-KWX2 85.C65
86 History (General)
For the history of special subjects, see the subject
For the ancient Orient, see KL
For Roman law and Roman provincial law, see class KJA
For the law of the Byzantine Empire, see class KJA
<88> Indigenous people. Ethnic groups
For works on the law of indigenous peoples (aborigines) regardless of whether identified with one or more countries in the region, see KM, KN, KQ, or as indicated
For works on the constitutional status of indigenous people in the region see KL-KWX2 558+
Philosophy, jurisprudence, and theory of law
Class here works on doctrines peculiar to the legal institutions of the region
For works on the philosophy of a special branch or subject of the law of the region, see the branch or subject
For works on philosophy and jurisprudence of law in general, see K201+
90 General works
92 The concept of law
Including definition of law
93 The object of law
94 Ethics. Morality of law. Public policy
Including Repugnancy clause (British)
95 Law and the state. Legal order. Respect for law

Philosophy, jurisprudence, and theory of law
The concept of law -- Continued
96 Rights and duties. Sanction
96.5 Certainty of law
Including customary (indigenous law)
97.A-Z Other topics, A-Z
Sources of the law
98 General works
99 Custom and observance. Indigenous law
100 Methodology of uniform law development
Including unification, integration, and harmonization of both substantive law and conflict rules
For unification of different laws in force in a jurisdiction, see the jurisdiction
For unification of the law on a particular subject, see the subject
For works limited to the unification of conflict rules see KL-KWX2 128+
102 Congresses. Conferences. By date of the congress
For congresses, conferences, etc., devoted to unification or harmonization of the law on a particular subject, see the subject
103 Organizations and their legal activities. Cooperation
For organizations devoted to unification or harmonization of the law on a particular subject, see the subject
105 Reconciliation and integration of customary (indigenous, ethnic) law and civil law or common law, or multiple customary laws. Repugnancy clause
106 Semantics
108 Law reform and policies
109.A-Z Concepts applying to several branches of the law, A-Z
110 Intertemporal law. Retroactive law
Legal systems compared
Class here comparisons of legal systems, in the region, including historical development
For works not limited to the region, see K583+
For comparisons of subjects, see the subject
112 General works
Modern legal systems (civil or common law systems) compared with customary (indigenous, ethnic) law see KL-KWX2 105
114 Modern legal systems (civil or common law systems) compared with religious law (e.g., Islamic law)

Legal systems compared -- Continued

115 Modern legal systems (civil or common law systems) compared with ancient/early legal systems

Class here comparisons of ancient/early legal systems (e.g. Babylonia, Egyptian, etc.) with more than one modern legal system in the region

For comparisons of the legal system of an individual country with an ancient/early legal system, see the subclass for the country

Ancient legal systems compared

see KL147+

116 Regional divisions. Subregions

Class here general works on the law or the legal systems in force within a single subregion (e.g. North Africa (The Maghrib))

For works comparing the law on a particular subject, see the subject

Conflict of laws. Plurality of laws conflict

Class here works on the conflict rules of two or more countries in the region, including conflict rules of branches other than private law

For conflict of laws between countries in different regions, see K7000+

For conflict of laws between the United States and a country in the region, see KF416

For works on the conflict of laws of an individual country, see the country

126 General (Table K8)

127 Two or more different legal systems in force in the same territory

Class here works on domestic and/or international conflict of laws of two or more countries in the region, each with two coexisting legal systems, e.g., secular and religious, etc.

For works limited to a particular country, see the subclass for the country

Regional unification, approximation (alignment), and harmonization

Class here works on unification of conflict rules (activities and methods)

For unification of conflict rules relating to a special subject, see the subject

128 General (Table K8)

The Hague Conference on Private International Law

see K7053

128.5 Ordre Public. Public order

Choice of law

129 General (Table K8)

Conflict of laws. Plurality of laws conflict
Choice of law -- Continued
130 Points of contact (Table K8)
Including nationality and domicile as points of contact
131 Choice of law by the parties. Party autonomy (Table K8)
132 Renvoi (Table K8)
Limits of application of foreign law
133 General works
134 Public policy and order (Table K8)
135 Recognition of foreign penal, revenue, confiscatory, and political laws (Table K8)
136.A-Z Particular branches and subjects of the law, A-Z
Adoption see KL-KWX2 136.F35
136.A55 Aliens
Arbitral awards see KL-KWX2 136.P76
Bankruptcy and execution see KL-KWX2 136.P76
Capacity see KL-KWX2 136.P47
Caste see KL-KWX2 136.P4
136.C655 Commercial papers and negotiable instruments
136.C657 Commercial sales
136.D3 Defective and dissolved marriage
Divorce see KL-KWX2 136.D3
136.F35 Family. Parent and child. Adoption
Foreign judgments see KL-KWX2 474
136.M35 Marriage
136.M37 Matrimonial property
136.M85 Multiple marriage
Nationality of women see KL-KWX2 169
Negotiable instruments see KL-KWX2 136.C655
136.P4 Personal status. Caste
136.P47 Persons. Capacity. Incapacity
136.P76 Procedure. Bankruptcy and execution. Arbitral awards
Separation see KL-KWX2 136.D3
138 Private law. Civil law
Class here general works on the law other than public law
Juristic facts. Juristic acts and events
139 General (Table K8)
Illegal and unlawful acts see KL-KWX2 236+
139.5 Extinctive prescription (Table K8)
Persons
140 General (Table K8)
Natural persons
141 General (Table K8)
142 Civil status (Table K8)
143 Absence and presumption of death (Table K8)



KL-KWX2

Persons
Natural persons -- Continued
144 Capacity. Incapacity (Table K8)
For married women see KL-KWX2 169
145.A-Z Particular groups or classes of persons, A-Z
Aborigines see KL-KWX2 145.I64
145.A55 Aliens
145.E93 Ex-convicts
145.I64 Indigenous people. Aborigines
145.M55 Minors
145.W64 Women
Class here works on legal status under all aspects of law, e.g. religious, customary (indigenous), private, and public law
146 Citizenship (Table K8)
147 Recording and registration. Civil registry (Table K8)
Including registration of birth, marriage, death, and other vital statistics
Juristic persons
149 General (Table K8)
Associations
150 General (Table K8)
151 Incorporated societies (Table K8)
For business corporations see KL-KWX2 304+
152 Unincorporated societies
153 Foundations. Endowments (Table K8)
154 The state as a civil person (Table K8)
Including state liability in general
Domestic relations. Family law. Multiplicity of laws
156 General (Table K8)
158 Domestic relations courts and procedure (Table K8)
Including civil courts, religious courts, etc.
159 Domicile (Table K8)
Marriage. Husband and wife
160 General (Table K8)
161 Betrothal
Marriage impediments
162 General works
163 Caste
164 Widowhood
165 Premarital examinations
166 Common law marriage. Unwed cohabitation. Concubinage
166.5 Mixed marriages
Class here works on marriages between persons of different religions, castes, etc.

Persons

Domestic relations. Family law. Multiplicity of laws

Marriage. Husband and wife -- Continued

167 Multiple marriage. Polygamy. Polyandry

168 Void and voidable marriages. Nullity

169 Civil status of married women

170 Matrimonial property. Conjugal partnership

170 Matrimonial property. Conjugal partnership

Family property. Homestead law see KL-KWX2 192

171 Antenuptial contracts. Marriage settlements

Dissolution of marriage

173 General (Table K8)

Divorce. Separation

174 General (Table K8)

175 Divorce by mutual consent

176 Divorce of deserted wife

177 Dismissal of barren wife

Including women with daughters only

178 Particular grounds

Including adultery

179 Separate maintenance. Alimony

Consanguinity and affinity. Kinship

180 General (Table K8)

181 Maintenance and support

Parent and child

182 General (Table K8)

183 Legitimacy (Table K8)

183.3 Adoption

184 Illegitimacy. Unwed children

Including slaves' children

185 Affiliation (Matrilineal and patrilineal)

186 Parental rights and duties. Custody

187.A-Z Special topics, A-Z

187.A78 Artificial insemination

187.A78 Artificial insemination

188 Guardianship

Including guardianship over minors and adults, and including procedure

190 Curatorship

Including procedure

192 Family property. Homestead law

For government constituted homesteads see KL-KWX2 673+

Property. Real rights

194 General (Table K8)

Property. Real rights -- Continued
194.5 Right to property
195.A-Z Particular kinds of property or things, A-Z
195.F77 Fruits
Including civil, legal, agricultural, etc.
Tangible property see KL-KWX2 215.3
Property with respect to its owner
196 General works
Family property see KL-KWX2 192
Matrimonial property see KL-KWX2 170; KL-KWX2 170
Public property see KL-KWX2 640
Possession
Including acquisition and loss
197 General (Table K8)
198 Possessory actions. Protection of possession
Ownership
199 General (Table K8)
Acquisition and loss of real and personal property combined see KL-KWX2 202.5+
Restrictions and limitations of ownership. Restraint of alienation
200 General works
Family property. Homestead law see KL-KWX2 192
Fideicommissum. Fiduciary property see KL-KWX2 216+
Real property. Land law
For public land law see KL-KWX2 670+
201 General (Table K8)
Public and private restraint on real property
201.5 General (Table K8)
Eminent domain see KL-KWX2 648
Public policy. Land reforms and land policy legislation see KL-KWX2 672
Zoning laws see KL-KWX2 678
Concepts of customary (native) land rights
For new land system legislation (e.g. in African countries) see KL-KWX2 672
202 General (Table K8)
202.3 National collective patrimony. Areas of operation of customary land law, exercised collectively or individually
For co-operatives see KL-KWX2 788
Cf. KL-KWX2 672 Public land law
202.4 Group lands. Land possessed in common by ethnic groups (juristic persons) for use, but without shares in ownership

Property. Real rights
Real property. Land law -- Continued
Rural land tenure see KL-KWX2 772+
Acquisition and loss of ownership
Including works on real and personal property combined
202.5 General (Table K8)
203 Restoration of alienated land to customary ownership
203.3 Acquisitive prescription. Occupation of land by cultivator. Interruption of period of prescription
203.5 Transfer of title. Conveyancing
204 Abandonment
Expropriation see KL-KWX2 648
204.8 Underground space
Cf. KL-KWX2 208.3 Underground water
Cf. KL-KWX2 815.3 Ownership of mines and mineral resources
205 Airspace
Concurrent ownership. Co-ownership. Customary co-ownership
Including works on concurrent ownership in land and personal property combined
For communal property see KL-KWX2 202.4
206 General (Table K8)
207 Horizontal property. Condominium
207.5 Housing cooperatives
Party walls see KL-KWX2 211.6.P35
Tenancy. Landlord and tenant see KL-KWX2 235.L43
Rights and interests incident to ownership of land
208 General (Table K8)
208.3 Water rights. Riparian rights. Underground water
208.5 Hunting rights. Fishing rights
Commonage and pasture see KL-KWX2 210.3
Law of adjoining landowners
208.7 General works
209 Boundaries. Fences
Including actions to define boundary lines
Party walls see KL-KWX2 211.6.P35
Real rights upon things of another. Encumbrances
209.5 General (Table K8)
209.7 Emphyteusis
210 Usufruct. Use. Right of habitation
Fiefs see KL-KWX2 532+
210.3 Commonage and pasture. Grazing rights
210.5 Life annuities constituted on real property
Servitudes

Property. Real rights
Real property. Land law
Real rights upon things of another. Encumbrances
Servitudes -- Continued
211 General (Table K8)
Real servitudes. Easements
211.5 General works
211.6.A-Z Particular kinds of real servitudes, A-Z
211.6.L53 Light and air
211.6.P35 Party walls
211.6.R53 Right of way
211.6.W36 Water use
212 Public servitudes
Personal servitudes see KL-KWX2 210
Real rights of guaranty on real property. Hypothecation
For real rights of guaranty on real and personal property combined see KL-KWX2 235.S43
213 General (Table K8)
213.5 Mortgages. Land charges
Privileges. Liens see KL-KWX2 235.L54
Land registry
214 General (Table K8)
214.5 Cadasters. Land surveying
Personal property
215 General (Table K8)
Acquisition and loss of property see KL-KWX2 202.5+
215.3 Choses in action. Intangible property
Intellectual property see KL-KWX2 370+
Trusts and trustees
Including fideicommissum and fiduciary property
216 General (Table K8)
217 Trustees. Trust companies
Testamentary trusts see KL-KWX2 221.5
Transfer or ownership as security
Fiducia see KL-KWX2 235.S43
Charitable trusts see KL-KWX2 153
Succession upon death
Class here works on succession upon death and gifts combined
218 General (Table K8)
Testamentary succession. Wills
219 General (Table K8)
219.5 Capacity to make wills
219.7.A-Z Particular wills, A-Z
219.7.O73 Oral wills
220 Witnesses to wills

Succession upon death
Testamentary succession. Wills -- Continued
220.3 Registration of wills
221 Contracts of inheritance
221.5 Testamentary trusts
222 Intestate succession
223 Order of succession
Include succession of ascendants, of collaterals, unwed children, concubines, etc.
Heirs
224 General (Table K8)
224.3 Rights of surviving spouse(s)
Including usufruct, right of habitation, etc.
224.5 Relation among co-heirs
225 Probate courts and procedure
226 Administration of decedent's estate
Obligations and contracts
228 General (Table K8)
228.3.A-Z Types of obligations, A-Z
228.3.C5 Civil and natural obligations
Extinction of obligations
229 General works
230 Performance. Payment
232 Breach of contract. Liability. Damages
233 Arbitration agreement
Contracts
234 General (Table K8)
234.3 Government contracts. Public contracts
235.A-Z Particular contracts, A-Z
235.A54 Aleatory contracts
235.A77 Associations
Including non-profit associations, partnerships (civil companies), etc.
235.B37 Barter
235.C66 Contracts for work and labor
235.C67 Contracts for service and labor. Hire
Guaranty see KL-KWX2 235.S43
235.L43 Lease. Landlord and tenant
For farm tenancy see KL-KWX2 772+
For oil and gas leases see KL-KWX2 822
235.L53 Life annuity contract
Cf. KL-KWX2 210.5 Real rights
235.L54 Liens. Privileges
235.M36 Mandate. Agency
Pledge see KL-KWX2 235.S43



KL-KWX2

Obligations and contracts
Contracts
Particular contracts
Privileges see KL-KWX2 235.L54
235.S35 Sale
235.S43 Security
Including real rights of security (fiducia, pledges), suretyship, guaranty; liens, rights of retention, etc.
Suretyship see KL-KWX2 235.S43
235.5 Quasi contracts. Restitution
Torts. Delicts and quasi-delicts
236 General (Table K8)
237.A-Z Particular torts, A-Z
237.L53 Libel and slander
237.V56 Violation of privacy
Strict liability
238 General works
239.A-Z Ultrahazardous activities or occupations. By risk, A-Z
239.3 Products liability
239.5 Government torts
240 Damages for torts
Commercial contracts and transactions
242 General (Table K8)
243 Merchants (Table K8)
Auxiliaries and intermediaries of commerce
244 General works
244.3 Stock exchanges. Marketing of securities (Table K8)
Independent commercial agents and middlemen
244.4 General works
244.5 Brokers (Table K8)
244.6 Commercial travelers. Traveling salesmen (Table K8)
244.7 Accounting (Table K8)
Including inventory
244.8 Commercial registers
Commercial mandate and consignment
245 General works
246 Consignment of goods. Commission merchants (Table K8)
Commercial sale
247 General works
248 Conditional sale. Installment sale. Lease purchase (Table K8)
249 Export sale. International sale. Overseas sale (Table K8)
Including C.I.F. and F.O.B. clauses
Negotiable instruments. Title of credit
250 General (Table K8)

Commercial contracts and transactions
Negotiable instruments. Title of credit -- Continued
252 Bills of exchange (Table K8)
253.A-Z Special topics, A-Z
Checks
255 General (Table K8)
257.A-Z Special topics, A-Z
Banking
260 General (Table K8)
Particular types of banks and credit institutions
262 General works
263 National banks. Central banks (Table K8)
International regional banks for development and integration see KL-KWX2 908
265.A-Z Other banks, A-Z
Particular banking transactions
267 General works
268 Bank loans. Bank credit
270 Letters of credit (Table K8)
272 Commercial loans and credit (Table K8)
Pledge see KL-KWX2 235.S43
Investments
275 General (Table K8)
Marketing of securities see KL-KWX2 244.3
Foreign investments see KL-KWX2 747+
Carriers. Carriage of goods and passengers
277 General (Table K8)
280 Carriage by land and inland waterways (Table K8)
For motor carriers see KL-KWX2 865
For railroads see KL-KWX2 866
Carriage by air
Cf. KL-KWX2 870 Regulation of commercial aviation
Cf. KL-KWX2 870 Regulation of commercial aviation
282 General (Table K8)
284.A-Z Special topics, A-Z
284.M65 Aircraft mortgages
Carriage by sea see KL-KWX2 342+
Insurance
288 General (Table K8)
Particular lines of insurance
290 Life insurance (Table K8)
292 Health insurance. Medical care (Table K8)
Property insurance
294 General works
296 Multiple line insurance

Commercial contracts and transactions
Insurance
Particular lines of insurance
Property insurance -- Continued
297.A-Z Particular hazards, A-Z
297.F5 Fire
297.5 Investment guaranty insurance
Liability insurance
298 General (Table K8)
300.A-Z Particular risks, A-Z
300.A87 Automobiles
300.A88 Automotive transportation (General)
Including trucking, bus lines, etc.
300.A94 Aviation
Carriage of passengers at sea see KL-KWX2 345
Business associations. Commercial companies
304 General (Table K8)
Personal companies. Unincorporated business associations. Partnerships
305 General works
306 Joint ventures (Table K8)
307 Limited liability companies. Private companies (Table K8)
Stock companies. Incorporated business associations
309 General (Table K8)
310 Supervisors. Auditors (Table K8)
Corporate finance
312 General works
314 Issuance and sale of securities
Security exchange transactions see KL-KWX2 244.3
315 Stocks
Including bearer stock, common stock, preferred stock, etc.
317 Bonds
Stocks and stockholders' rights
319 General (Table K8)
320 Stock transfers (Table K8)
322 Foreign stockholders
324 Minority stockholders
Particular types of corporations
325 General works
327 Foreign corporations (Table K8)
Including nationality of corporations
329 Multinational corporations (Table K8)
Private companies see KL-KWX2 235.A77
330 Cooperative societies (Table K8)

Commercial contracts and transactions
Business associations. Commercial companies
Stock companies. Incorporated business associations -- Continued
332 Government-owned corporations and other business organizations
Including government monopolies in general
Maritime law
For regulatory aspects of water transportation, navigation, and pilotage see KL-KWX2 861+
340 General (Table K8)
Affreightment. Carriage of goods at sea and on inland waters
342 General works
343 Freight forwarders
344 Ocean bill of lading
345 Carriage of passengers at sea
346 Average
346.5 Bottomry and respondentia. Ship mortgages. Maritime liens
347 Salvage
348 Ship registers
350 Maritime courts
Prize courts
see KZ
Marine insurance. Liability insurance
352 General works
353.A-Z Particular risks, A-Z
354.A-Z Special topics, A-Z
354.A75 Arrest of ships
Including immunity of state-owned ships from arrest
Immunity of state-owned ships see KL-KWX2 354.A75
Maritime social legislation
356 General (Table K8)
357 Maritime labor law. Merchant mariners (Table K8)
359 Social insurance (Table K8)
Insolvency and bankruptcy. Creditors' rights
362 General (Table K8)
363 Execution
364 Bankruptcy
Special topics, A-Z
366 Debtors' relief. Composition
Commercial arbitration, International see KL-KWX2 136.P76
Commercial arbitration see KL-KWX2 500
Intellectual and industrial property
370 General (Table K8)

Intellectual and industrial property -- Continued
Copyright
371 General (Table K8, modified)
Intergovernmental congresses and conferences
Including unions and sponsoring organizations
International Union for the Protection of Literacy and Artistic Works (Bern Union)
see K1412+
Universal Copyright Convention
see K1414+
Authorship
Including multiple authorship and author cooperatives
371.2 General works
371.22 Anonyms and pseudonyms (Table K8)
371.23 Intangible property
371.3 Plagiarism
371.4 Formalities (Table K8)
Including registration of claim, transfer, licenses, deposit, and notice
371.5 Protected works (Table K8)
Including original works, subsequent rights, idea, and title
Scope of protection
371.6 General (Table K8)
371.62 Personality rights. Droit moral (Table K8)
Mechanical reproduction
371.623 General (Table K8)
371.64 Documentation and dissemination (Table K8)
Including fair use
371.65 Exhibition (Table K8)
Performing rights
Cf. KL-KWX2 385 Quasi copyright
371.7 General (Table K8)
371.72 Societies and industrial trusts (Table K8)
371.73 Broadcasting rights (Table K8)
371.75 Recording devices (Table K8)
Including phonographs, magnetic recorders, and jukeboxes
371.76 Filming and photographing (Table K8)
371.78 Translation (Table K8)
371.8 Employees' copyright (Table K8)
371.82 Duration and renewal (Table K8)
371.85 Delicts. Torts (Table K8)
371.9 Criminal provisions (Table K8)
Branches of copyright
373 Literary copyright (Table K8)
375 Musical copyright (Table K8)

Intellectual and industrial property
Copyright
Branches of copyright -- Continued
Fine art and photography
377 General (Table K8)
378 Designs and models (Table K8)
379 Prints and labels (Table K8)
Motion pictures and television shows
380 General (Table K8)
382.A-Z Special topics, A-Z
384 Computer programs (Table K8)
385 Quasi copyright and neighboring rights (Table K8)
387 Author and publisher (Table K8)
388 Litigation and execution (Table K8)
Patent law and trademarks
390 General (Table K8)
391.A-Z Patented processes, products, and engineering processes, A-Z
391.B56 Biotechnology
Including patents on genes
391.P55 Plants
392 Designs and utility models (Table K8)
393 Patent licenses. Foreign licensing agreements (Table K8)
395 Infringement. Patent litigation and procedure (Table K8)
Trademarks
396 General (Table K8)
397.A-Z Types of trademarks, A-Z
397.B73 Brand names
397.M37 Marks of origin
398 Licenses. Foreign licensing agreements
Unfair competition
399 General (Table K8)
400 Delicts. Torts
Labor law
403 General (Table K8)
Labor reform. National policy see KL-KWX2 429
Labor
International organization and international bureaus
see HD7801
405 Constitutional aspects (Table K8)
406 Conflict of laws (Table K8)
407 Labor contract and employment (Table K8)
408 Wages (Table K8)
Labor-management relations
409 General (Table K8)

Labor law
  Labor
    Labor-management relations -- Continued
410 Works councils (Table K8)
    Collective bargaining and labor agreements
412 General (Table K8)
413.A-Z By industry or occupation, A-Z
415 Collective labor disputes (Table K8)
416 Labor unions (Table K8)
    Protection of labor
417 General (Table K8)
418 Hours of labor (Table K8)
419 Youth labor (Table K8)
420 Women labor (Table K8)
422 Labor hygiene and industrial safety (Table K8)
424.A-Z Special topics, A-Z
426.A-Z Labor law for particular industries, occupations, or types of employment, A-Z
426.A34 Agricultural workers
426.A44 Alien labor
426.M53 Migrant workers
Social legislation
428 General (Table K8)
429 Social reform. National policy (Table K8)
  Including labor reform
  Social insurance
430 General (Table K8)
432 Health insurance (Table K8)
    Workers' compensation
434 General (Table K8)
436.A-Z By industry or group of workers, A-Z
438 Social security (Table K8)
440 Unemployment insurance (Table K8)
442 Social services. Public welfare. Charities. Public assistance (Table K8)
  Family planning. Population control. Birth control
445 General (Table K8)
450.A-Z Special topics, A-Z
Courts and procedure
455 General (Table K8)
  The administration of justice
    Cf. KL-KWX2 985+ Administration of criminal justice
457 General works
    Judicial statistics see KL-KWX2 31+
    Judicial assistance see KL-KWX2 473+

Courts and procedure -- Continued
Courts
459 General (Table K8)
Regular courts
460 General works
462 Supreme courts. Courts of last resort. Supreme peoples courts
Courts of special jurisdiction. Special tribunals
463 General works
Religious courts and councils
465 General (Table K8)
466 Sharia courts. Kadi courts
466.5 Rabbinical courts
467 Consular courts
469 Courts of human rights
470 Native customary courts of law
Including traditional councils, village arbitral tribunals, etc.
The legal profession see KL-KWX2 50
Judicial assistance
Including civil, criminal, and noncontentious jurisdiction matters
473 General (Table K8)
474 Foreign judgments (Conflict of laws)
475 Foreign letters rogatory
Procedure in general
Including all branches of the law
476 General (Table K8)
478.A-Z Special topics, A-Z
Civil procedure
480 General (Table K8)
482 Constitutional safeguards in civil procedure
Cf. KL-KWX2 495 Constitutional remedies. Judicial review
483 Jurisdiction. Venue
Trial. Procedure at first instance
485 General (Table K8)
Evidence. Burden of proof
486 General works
487 Admission of evidence
Witnesses
488 General works
Foreign letters rogatory see KL-KWX2 475
489 Privileged witnesses. Expert testimony
490.A-Z Special topics, A-Z
492 Jury and jurors

Courts and procedure
Civil procedure
Trial. Procedure at first instance -- Continued
493 Judicial decisions. Judgments
For recognition and enforcement of foreign judgments see KL-KWX2 474
Remedies and special proceedings
494 General (Table K8)
495 Constitutional remedies. Judicial review. Habeas corpus
497 Appellate procedure
498 Execution of judgment
Noncontentious jurisdiction. Notarial law. Registry see KL-KWX2 60
499 Negotiated settlement. Compromise
500 Arbitration and award
Including commercial arbitration
Cf. KL-KWX2 136.P76 Civil and commercial arbitration (Conflict of laws)
Public law
Class here works on all aspects of public law, including early works
510 General (Table K8)
The state
Including philosophy and theory of the state
511 General works
Law and the state see KL-KWX2 95
513 Sovereignty. Potestas (Table K8)
514 Rule of law (Table K8)
515 Succession of states (Table K8)
517.A-Z Special topics, A-Z
Constitutional law
For works on the constitutional aspects of a subject, see the subject
History see KL-KWX2 527+
522 Constitutional reform. Criticism
524.A12 Bibliography
Including bibliography of constitutional history
Sources
Including early and modern constitutions and related material
524.A44 Indexes and tables
524.A45 Collections and compilations
Including annotated editions and commentaries
524.A9-.Z9 General works. Treatises

Constitutional law -- Continued
Constitutional history
Class here general and comprehensive works on the constitutional development of a region or subregion
For sources (constitutions and related materials) see KL-KWX2 524.A44+
527 General works
Bibliography see KL-KWX2 524.A12
529 Peonage. Slavery (Table K8)
Including emancipation, prohibition, and criminal provisions
Feudal law
Class here general and comparative works on feudal law
For feudal law of an individual country, see the subclass for the country
532 General (Table K8)
Sources
533 Collections. Compilations
534.2<date> Individual sources or groups of sources
Arrange chronologically by appending the date of the source to this number and deleting any trailing zeros. Subarrange each by Table K21
535 Feudal institutes (Table K8)
537.A-Z Special topics, A-Z
537.F48 Feudal succession (Table K12)
537.F54 Fief (Table K12)
537.R55 Rights of escheat. Compulsory refeoffment (Table K12)
539 Interpretation and construction (Table K8)
Constitutional principles
542 Legitimacy (Table K8)
544 Legality (Table K8)
Rule of law see KL-KWX2 514
545 Centralization of power (Table K8)
Decolonization. Decentralization
546 General (Table K8)
547 Independence. Association or integration of states (Table K8)
Separation and delegation of power
548 General (Table K8)
549 Executive privilege (Table K8)
550 Judicial review of legislative acts (Table K8)
551 Privileges of classes and particular groups. Rights of peerage
552 Privileges, prerogatives, and immunities of states and estates
Sources and relationships of the law

KL-KWX2

Constitutional law
Constitutional principles
Sources and relationships of the law -- Continued
553 General works
553.5 International law and municipal law
554 Customary and religious law. Observance
555 National territory. Archipelagic territorial regimes (e.g. Pacific area)
Including territorial integrity (fragmentation, politically and ethnically) at independence
556 Foreign relations
Including foreign service
Individual and state
557 General works
Indigenous peoples. Aboriginals
558 General (Table K8)
Human rights. Civil and political rights see KL-KWX2 572+
Other nationals
562 General (Table K8)
Citizenship. Rule of indigenous ancestry
563 General works
Particular groups, A-Z
564.W64 Women
Aliens
Cf. KL-KWX2 136.A+ Conflict of laws
565 General (Table K8)
566 Immigration. Naturalization of aliens
567 Stateless persons. Refugees. Asylum seekers
Control of individuals see KL-KWX2 638
569 Internal security and control of subversive activities
Cf. KL-KWX2 982.P65 Political offenses
Human rights. Civil and political rights
572 General (Table K8)
573.A-Z Organization on, or for the protection of, human rights, A-Z
574.A-Z Courts for the protection of human rights, A-Z
Equality before the law. Antidiscrimination
575 General (Table K8)
576.A-Z Special topics, A-Z
576.L36 Language and culture
For language regulation in general see KL-KWX2 719
Freedom
578 General works
580.A-Z Particular, A-Z
Information, Freedom of see KL-KWX2 580.T56

Constitutional law
Individual and state
Human rights. Civil and political rights
Freedom
Particular, A-Z -- Continued
580.M68 Movement, Freedom of
Opposition to government, Right of see KL-KWX2 580.T56
Prohibition of censorship see KL-KWX2 580.T56
580.R45 Religion, Freedom of
580.T56 Thought and speech, Freedom of
Organs of government. Supreme organs of state power and state administration
582 General works
The people
583 General works
Election law
585 General (Table K8)
Suffrage
588 General works
590 Women
The legislature. Legislative power
593 General (Table K8)
Legislative process. Parliamentary process
595 General works
596 Committees. Consultative and advisory councils. Houses of chiefs (customary law), etc.
597.A-Z Particular legislative bodies, A-Z
Heads of state. Supreme organs
600 General works
Monarchs. Princes. Chiefs (traditional leaders), and other rulers
602 General (Table K8)
603.A-Z Special topics, A-Z
The presidents. Governors. Governors-General
604 General (Table K8)
605 War and emergency powers. Martial law
The executive branch. Government
606 General (Table K8)
607 Government departments, ministries, and other organizations of national government
608 The Judiciary. Judicial power
Class here constitutional status only
For courts, administration of justice, and organization of the judiciary see KL-KWX2 457+

Constitutional law -- Continued
610 Administrative departments of federal states
611 Administrative and political division. Local government other than municipal
Municipal government. Municipal corporations
613 General works
614 Municipal officials
Municipal civil service see KL-KWX2 628.5
State and religion
Class here works on the relationship of state and religion, regardless of denomination
For works on the internal law and government of religious corporations, sects, etc., see KB
615 General (Table K8)
616 Constitutional aspects. Human rights. Fundamental rights and constitutional guaranties
617 Religious corporations, institutions, organizations, etc.
Including membership
617.5 Legal schools
618 Lands of religious corporations, sects, etc.
Including taxation and tax assessment
619 Offenses against religion
Administrative law
620 General (Table K8)
623 Administrative organization
Judicial functions. Remedies
624 General works
626 Contentious-administrative jurisdiction and procedure. Administrative tribunals
627 Administrative responsibility. Indemnification for government acts
Cf. KL-KWX2 239.5 Government tort liability
Civil service
628 General (Table K8)
628.5 Municipal civil service
Police and public safety
630 General (Table K8)
632 Weapons. Firearms. Ammunition
Hazardous articles and processes
634 General works (Table K8)
634.5 Hazardous wastes
Including prevention of illegal international traffic in hazardous wastes

Police and public safety
Hazardous articles and processes -- Continued
635 Nuclear power. Reactors
Including protection from radiation and management of radioactive waste
636 Products safety
Cf. KL-KWX2 239.3 Products liability
638 Control of individuals and of social activities
639 Identification and registration
Including registration of residence
640 Passports
(641) Immigration and naturalization of aliens
see KL-KWX2 566
Public property. Domaine public
643 General (Table K8)
Government property. Powers and control
644 General (Table K8)
646 Records management. Access to public records
Including data bases and general data protection
For violation of privacy see KL-KWX2 237.V56
648 Expropriation. Nationalization. Eminent domain
For indemnification see KL-KWX2 627
Conservation and natural resources. Environmental planning see KL-KWX2 706
649 Roads and highways (Table K8)
Water resources
653 General (Table K8)
654 Development and conservation of water resources
Including water registers
Protection against pollution see KL-KWX2 708+
660.A-Z Particular bodies of water, river basins, etc., A-Z
662.A-Z Particular districts, A-Z
Shore protection. Coastal zone management see KL-KWX2 707
664 Marine resources
For fish protection see KL-KWX2 716
Public land law. Land use
670 General (Table K8)
672 Land reform and land policy. Legislation on new land systems
Including agrarian land policy legislation

Public property. Domaine public
Public land law. Land use -- Continued
Regional planning. Land development
Including expropriation, nationalization, and purchase of agricultural land holdings by the state and their redistribution; land grants; consolidation of land holdings; government constituted homesteads; and including resettlement and redistribution of population
For national collective patrimony see KL-KWX2 202.3
For group lands see KL-KWX2 202.4
673 General (Table K8)
674 Public land acquisition legislation
675 Ecological aspects
676 Public irrigation zones
City planning and redevelopment
677 General works
678 Zoning laws. Housing. Slum clearance
680 Building laws
Public health. Sanitation
682 General works
Contagious, infectious diseases. Parasitic diseases
684 General (Table K8)
Measures. Quarantine. Immunization. Vaccination
686 General works
687.A-Z Diseases, A-Z
687.A53 AIDS (Disease)
688 Drinking water standards
690-691.5 Drug laws
690 General (Table K8)
691 Intoxicating drugs. Opium legislation (Table K8)
691.5 Pharmacists and pharmacies (Table K8)
Medical legislation
692 General (Table K8)
693.A-Z The health professions, A-Z
Subarrange each by Table K12
Hospitals and other medical institutions or health services
695 General works
698 Institutions for the mentally ill
699 Artificial insemination
Cf. KL-KWX2 187.A78 Family law
Cf. KL-KWX2 187.A78 Family law
700.A-Z Special topics, A-Z
700.T73 Transplantation of organs, tissues, etc.
Including donation and sale of organs, tissues, etc.
702 Veterinary medicine and hygiene

Medical legislation -- Continued
Birth control see KL-KWX2 445+
Environmental law
705 General (Table K8)
706 Environmental planning. Conservation of natural resources
707 Shore protection. Coastal zone management
Environmental pollution
708 General (Table K8)
709 Air pollution
Including noxious gases, automobile emission control, etc.
711 Water and groundwater pollution
Including drainage, infiltration, and sewage control
712.A-Z Pollutants, A-Z
712.N65 Noise
Including traffic noise and noise control
712.R33 Radioactive substances, Control of
714 Recycling of refuse
Wilderness preservation
Including natural monuments, parks, ice, etc.
715 General (Table K8)
716 Wildlife conservation
For game laws see KL-KWX2 805
For fishery laws see KL-KWX2 808+
716.5 Plant protection (Table K8)
Cultural affairs
717 General (Table K8)
718 Cultural policy. State encouragement of science and the arts
719 Language
Including regulation of use, purity, etc.
Education
720 General (Table K8)
721 Education of children with disabilities (Table K8)
722 Vocational education
Higher education. Universities
723 General works
723.5 Academic degrees. International recognition
Adult education
724 General works
725 Religious education
725.5 Physical education
Education exchanges see KL-KWX2 736
Science and the arts. Research
726 General (Table K8)
728.A-Z The arts, A-Z
728.M67 Motion pictures

Cultural affairs -- Continued
Public collections
729 General (Table K8)
730 Museums and galleries
732 Libraries
734 Archives
735 Historical buildings and monuments. Archaeological excavations
Including preservation and protection of cultural property
736 Educational, scientific, and cultural exchanges
Economic law
738 General (Table K8)
739 Economic constitution
742 Economic cooperation
Class here general works
For works on a particular regional organization, see the region
For works on an organization in a particular geographic region devoted to a specific subject, see the region and the subject
Economic assistance
743 General (Table K8)
744 Finance. Subsidies
For economic assistance to a particular industry, see the industry
745.A-Z Economic assistance and development organizations, A-Z
For Arab industrial development organizations, see KME
Foreign investment
Cf. KL-KWX2 327 Foreign corporations
Cf. KL-KWX2 329 Multinational corporations
747 General works
Foreign exchange regulations see KL-KWX2 913
International capital movement regulations see KL-KWX2 914
747.5 Assistance to developing countries
748 Prices and price control
748.5 Government business enterprises
749 Licenses. Concessions
Competition rules. Control of contracts and combinations in restraint of trade
750 General (Table K8)
Horizontal and vertical combinations
752 General (Table K8)
753 Corporate consolidation, merger, etc.
Including fusion control
Cartels
755 General (Table K8)

Economic law
Competition rules. Control of contracts and combinations in restraint of trade
Horizontal and vertical combinations
Cartels -- Continued
756.A-Z Types of cartels, A-Z
756.E96 Export and import cartels
757 Exclusive dealing or use arrangements. Requirement contracts
758 Monopolies. Oligopolies. Antitrust law
759 Corporate representation of industry, trade, and commerce
Including chambers of commerce, trade associations, boards of trade, etc.
For regional representatives, see the region
Money, currency, and foreign exchange control see KL-KWX2 910+
Standards. Norms. Quality control
For standards and grading of agricultural or consumer products, see the product
760 General (Table K8)
761 Weight and measures. Containers
Standardization
762 General (Table K8)
762.5 Engineering standards
763 Labeling
For labeling of a particular product, see the product
Regulation of industry, trade, and commerce
764 General (Table K8)
765 Consumer protection (Table K8)
766 Advertising (Table K8)
Primary production. Extractive industries
767 General (Table K8)
Agriculture. Forestry. Rural law
768 General (Table K8)
769 Agricultural courts and procedure (Table K8)
770 Public lands
Rural (peasant) land tenure. Peasantry
772 General works
History
773 General works
774 Large estates. Feudal land grants
776 Classification of land. Dual systems of land rights. Native and non-native lands
780 Colonization. Agrarian colonies

Regulation of industry, trade, and commerce
Primary production. Extractive industries
Agriculture. Forestry. Rural law -- Continued
Land reform. Agrarian land policy legislation.
Transformation of the agricultural structure see KL-KWX2 672
Agricultural contracts
785 General (Table K8)
786 Leasing of rural property. Farm tenancy
787 Rural housing
788 Collective farming. Agricultural cooperatives
Agricultural laborers see KL-KWX2 426.A34
789 Field irrigation
791 Control of agricultural pests, plant diseases, etc.
Including control of plant imports
793 Economic legislation. Economic assistance
Agricultural production
Including marketing, standards, and grading
795 General (Table K8)
797.A-Z Field crops, A-Z
798 Livestock industry and trade. Cattle raising (Table K8)
For meat industry see KL-KWX2 836.D35
Dairy industry see KL-KWX2 836.D35
800 Forestry. Timber laws (Table K8)
802 Viticulture (Table K8)
Cf. KL-KWX2 836.W56 Wine and wine making
805 Game laws (Table K8)
Fishery law and legislation. Fishery resources
808 General (Table K8)
810 Conservation. Ecological aspects (Table K8)
812.A-Z By sea region, A-Z
Subarrange each by Table K12
For high seas fisheries and fisheries regimes, see K3866+
813.A-Z By fish or marine fauna, A-Z
Subarrange each by Table K12
Mining. Quarrying
Including registration of mining rights
815 General (Table K8)
815.3 Ownership of mines and mineral resources (Table K8)
Cf. KL-KWX2 824 Expropriation. Nationalization
816.A-Z Regional industrial organizations, A-Z
Petroleum. Oil and gas
817 General (Table K8)
818 Conservation. Ecological aspects (Table K8)

Regulation of industry, trade, and commerce
Primary production. Extractive industries
Mining. Quarrying
Petroleum. Oil and gas -- Continued
820 Submerged land legislation. Continental shelf. Offshore drilling (Table K8)
822 Oil and gas leases (Table K8)
Including registration
824 Expropriation. Nationalization. Government ownership (Table K8)
Cf. KL-KWX2 648 Public property
826.A-Z Particular oil fields, reserves, etc., A-Z
Manufacturing industries
Including light and heavy industries
827 General (Table K8)
Fertilizer industry
828 General works
829.A-Z Regional industrial organizations, A-Z
Iron and steel industry
830 General works
831.A-Z Regional industrial organizations, A-Z
832.A-Z Other. By type of manufacture, A-Z
Food processing industries
833 General (Table K8)
834.A-Z Regional industrial organizations, A-Z
835 Labeling. Purity (Table K8)
836.A-Z Particular industries and products, A-Z
836.A57 Agricultural products
836.B74 Brewing
836.D35 Dairy industry
836.D57 Distilling
836.M43 Meat industry
836.W56 Wine making
Building and construction industry
838 General works
839 Contracts and specifications
Including liability
International trade
For trade between individual countries in the region and the United States, see KF1975+
842 General works
Trade agreements see KL-KWX2 946
843 Export and import controls
Foreign exchange regulations see KL-KWX2 913
844.A-Z Particular commodities, A-Z

Regulation of industry, trade, and commerce -- Continued
Domestic trade
845 General (Table K8)
846 Wholesale trade (Table K8)
Retail trade
847 General (Table K8)
Conditions of trading
848 General (Table K8)
848.5 Sunday legislation (Table K8)
849.A-Z Modes of trading, A-Z
850.A-Z Particular products, A-Z
850.5 Service trades (Table K8)
852 Artisans (Table K8)
Energy policy. Power supply
Including publicly and privately owned public utilities
853 General (Table K8)
Particular sources of power
856 Electricity (Table K8)
857 Gas. Natural gas (Table K8)
Atomic energy
For protection from radiation see KL-KWX2 635
For ecological aspects see KL-KWX2 712.R33
858 General works
860.A-Z International agencies, A-Z
Transportation
861 General (Table K8)
Road traffic. Automotive transportation
862 General works
Traffic regulation and enforcement
863 General (Table K8)
864 Highway safety. Traffic signs
865 Carriage of passengers and goods. Motor carrier regulation
866 Railroads
867 Pipelines
Aviation. Air law
868 General (Table K8)
870 Commercial aviation. Airlines
870 Commercial aviation. Airlines
873 Space law
Water transportation. Navigation and shipping
875 General (Table K8)
Merchant mariners see KL-KWX2 357
876 Coastwise and inland shipping
Communication. Mass media

Communication. Mass media -- Continued
878 General (Table K8)
878.5 Constitutional aspects. Freedom of communication
Postal services. Telecommunication
879 General (Table K8)
Postal unions
For intergovernmental congresses and conventions of the Universal Postal Union (UPU), see K4247
880 General (Table K8)
881.A-Z Regional unions, A-Z
882 Classification of mail. Rates (Table K8)
884.A-Z Particular services, A-Z
884.A57 Airmail
Telecommunication
886 General (Table K8)
887 Telegraph (Table K8)
888 Teletype and data transmission systems. Transnational data flow (Table K8)
For data protection see KL-KWX2 646
889 Telephone (Table K8)
Radio and television communication
890 General (Table K8)
890.5 Stations. Networks
Including frequency allocation and licensing
891 Broadcasting
892 Criminal provisions. Pirate stations. Illegal operation of a station
Press law
893 General (Table K8)
Freedom of the press and censorship see KL-KWX2 878.5
895 Journalists. Correspondents
896 Press delicts
896.5 Weather bureau. Meteorological stations (Table K8)
Professions
897 General (Table K8)
898 Professional associations
899.A-Z Individual professions, A-Z
Health professions see KL-KWX2 693.A+
Lawyers see KL-KWX2 50
Notaries see KL-KWX2 62
Pharmacists see KL-KWX2 691.5
Veterinarians see KL-KWX2 702
Public finance
900 General (Table K8)
Finance reform and policies

Public finance
Finance reform and policies -- Continued
901 General works
Monetary policies see KL-KWX2 910+
Organization and administration
902 General (Table K8)
Budget. Government expenditures
903 General works
Expenditure control. Auditing
905 General (Table K8)
906 Financial courts
Public debts. Loans
Including war debts
907 General (Table K8)
908 External debts. International loan agreements
909.A-Z Regional and subregional banks for development and integration, A-Z
Money
Including control of circulation
910 General (Table K8)
910.5 Mint regulations
911 Bank notes. Banks of issue
912 Gold trading and gold standard
913 Foreign exchange control
914 International capital movement regulations
Taxation
916 General (Table K8)
917 Double taxation
918 Taxation as a measure of social or economic policy
919 Taxation of particular activities
920.A-Z Classes of taxpayers or lines of business (General), A-Z
920.A45 Aliens
Income tax
921 General (Table K8)
922 Taxable income. Exemptions
Including profits and capital gain
923 Capital investment. Foreign investment
924.A-Z Classes of taxpayers or lines of businesses, A-Z
Corporation tax
925 General (Table K8)
926 Nonprofit associations and corporations
926.5 Personal companies (Unincorporated business associations)
927 Cooperative societies
928 Stock companies (Incorporated business associations)

Public finance
Taxation
Income tax
Corporation tax -- Continued
929 Corporate reorganization
930.A-Z Lines of corporate businesses, A-Z
931 Foreign corporations
932 Multinational corporations
Property tax and taxation of capital
933 General (Table K8)
934 Personal property tax
935 Real property tax
936 Estate, inheritance, and gift taxes
937 Capital gains tax
Surtaxes
938 General (Table K8)
938.5 Excess profits tax
Excise taxes
939 General (Table K8)
940 Sales taxes
Including turnover tax and value-added tax
942.A-Z Commodities, services, and transactions, A-Z
Particular methods of assessment and collection
943 General (Table K8)
943.5 Stamp duties
Customs. Tariff
For multilateral trade agreements and related bilateral agreements not limited to a region, see K4600+
For trade agreements with the United States, see KF6665+
For foreign trade regulations see KL-KWX2 842+
945 General (Table K8)
946 Trade agreements. Particular tariffs
Including favored nations clause and reciprocity
Trade agreements not limited to a special commodity
947.A12 Bibliography
947.A13 Periodicals
947.A15 Monographic series
947.A3A-.A3Z Intergovernmental congresses and conferences. By name of the congress, A-Z
Contracting parties to the General Agreement on Tariffs and Trade (GATT)
see K4602+
Collections of trade agreements
Including either multilateral or bilateral treaties, or both
947.A35 General

Public finance
Customs. Tariff
Trade agreements. Particular tariffs
Trade agreements not limited to a special commodity
Collections of trade agreements -- Continued
947.A37A-.A37Z Collected treaties of an individual country or regional organization limited to its region. By country or regional organization, A-Z
947.A4<date> Multilateral treaties
Arrange chronologically by appending the date of signature of the treaty to this number and deleting any trailing zeros. Subarrange each by Table K6
947.A43A-.A43Z Bilateral treaties. By country or regional organization, A-Z, and date of signature of the treaty
For bilateral treaties relating to a multilateral treaty, see KL-KWX2 947.A4<date> and subdivision .xZ4-.xZ59 in Table K6
947.A9-.Z9 General works. Treatises
948.A-Z Trade agreements and tariffs limited to a particular commodity. By commodity, A-Z
949 Customs administration
Criminal provisions see KL-KWX2 954+
953 Tax and customs courts and procedure
Tax and customs crimes and delinquency
954 General (Table K8)
955.A-Z Individual offenses, A-Z
955.S58 Smuggling
956 Government measures in time of war, national emergency, or economic crisis
National defense. Military law
962 General (Table K8)
The armed forces
963 General works
964 Compulsory service
Including draft and selective service
Deferment
Including disqualification and exemptions
965 General works
966.A-Z Particular groups, A-Z
966.A55 Aliens
966.C65 Conscientious objectors
967 Civil defense
Military criminal law and procedure
968 General (Table K8)
970.A-Z Particular crimes, A-Z

National defense. Military law
Military criminal law and procedure -- Continued
972 Military courts
973 Military discipline
Criminal law
Including works on both criminal law and criminal procedure, and including works on conflict of rules of criminal law and procedure
974 General (Table K8)
975 History
976 Reform of criminal law, procedure, and execution
Including reform of criminal justice administration
For works limited to a particular subject, see the subject
Administration of criminal justice see KL-KWX2 985+
977 Philosophy of criminal law
978 Influence of foreign law on two or more legal systems in the region
979 Relationship of criminal law to other disciplines, subjects, or phenomena
980 Criminal offense. Criminal act
Punishment
981 General (Table K8)
981.3 Criminal policy of punishment
Causes barring prosecution or execution of sentence
Including pardon, amnesty, and clemency
981.5 General (Table K8)
Including pardon, amnesty, and clemency
982.A-Z Particular offenses, A-Z
982.A48 Adultery
982.C65 Commercial crimes
982.C67 Computer crimes
Crimes against women see KL-KWX2 982.W66
982.P65 Political offenses
982.T47 Terrorism
982.W66 Women, Crimes against
Criminal courts and procedure
For works on both criminal law and criminal procedure see KL-KWX2 974+
For criticism and reform see KL-KWX2 979
983 General works
984 History
Administration of criminal justice
985 General works
Criticism and reform see KL-KWX2 976
Judicial statistics see KL-KWX2 31+

Criminal courts and procedure
Administration of criminal justice -- Continued
Judicial assistance see KL-KWX2 473+
Criminal policy see KL-KWX2 981.3
Courts
986 General (Table K8)
986.3 Police magistrate's courts. Justice of the peace
986.5 Courts of assizes. Juries
Criminal procedure
987 General (Table K8)
Judicial assistance in criminal matters see KL-KWX2 473+
989 Compulsory and precautionary measures against suspects
Extradition
Including judicial assistance in criminal matters in general
990 General (Table K8)
990.5 Refusal of extradition
991 Rights of suspects
Including protection of human rights in criminal proceedings
Trial
992 General works
Evidence. Burden of proof
992.2 General (Table K8)
992.3 Witnesses
992.4 Particular proceedings
Procedure for juvenile delinquency
992.6 General (Table K8)
992.65 The juvenile delinquent. The young adult perpetrator (Table K8)
992.68 Juvenile crime (Table K8)
Punishment. Correctional or disciplinary measures
Including measures of rehabilitation and safety
992.7 General (Table K8)
992.72 Custodial education (Table K8)
992.74 Detention homes. Reformatories (Table K8)
993 Judicial decisions. Judgments
For recognition and enforcement of foreign judgments see KL-KWX2 474
994 Remedies. Appellate procedures
994.2 Post-conviction remedies
Execution of sentence
995 General (Table K8)
995.5 Capital punishment
996 Corporeal punishment. Whipping
997 Imprisonment
Including prison administration

Criminal courts and procedure
Criminal procedure
Execution of sentence -- Continued
997.5 Indeterminate sentence
998 Alternatives to imprisonment
998.2 Exile. Banishment. Punitive deportation
Pardon, amnesty, and clemency see KL-KWX2 981.5
998.3 Probation. Parole
Extradition see KL-KWX2 990+
998.8 Victimology

For a list of regional and subregional organizations and numbers assigned to them, see the appropriate region, e.g. KME the Middle East. To determine a subject division for a given organization, add the number or numbers in the table for the subject to the basic number for the organization

For works on official acts or legal measures on a particular subject, see the subject under the appropriate region subdivided by Table KL-KWX2

1 Bibliography

<3> Periodicals

For periodicals consisting predominantly of legal articles, regardless of subject matter and jurisdiction, see K1+

For periodicals consisting primarily of informative material (newsletters, bulletins, etc.) relating to a special subject, see the subject and form division tables for periodicals

For law reports, official bulletins or circulars intended chiefly for the publication of laws and regulations, see appropriate entries in the text or form division tables

4 Monographic series

5 Official gazettes

6 Legislative and executive papers. Documentation

Including legislative and executive papers of committees and councils

Intergovernmental congresses and conferences

see the appropriate region, using subdivision 8 from Table KL-KWX2

Non-intergovernmental congresses see KL-KWX3 17

Official acts

8 Indexes and tables

9 Collections. Compilations

Treaties and other international agreements

see the appropriate region, subdivided by Table KL-KWX2

Treaties (individual and collections) establishing and expanding the regional organization see KL-KWX3 23+

Legislation and legal measures

Including conclusions, resolutions, recommendations, decisions, opinions, etc.

10 Indexes and tables

11 Abridgments and digests

Collections

12 Serials

13 Monographs. By date

Individual

see the subject under the appropriate region subdivided by Table KL-KWX2

KL-KWX3

| | |
|---|---|
| 14 | Court decisions and related material |
| 15 | Dictionaries. Encyclopedias |
| 16 | Directories |
| 17 | Congresses. Conferences. By date of the congress |
| 18 | Surveys of legal activity |
| | Class here surveys concerning unification, approximation, cooperation, etc. |
| 21 | General works |
| | Including compends, essays, festschriften, etc. |
| | Organization law |
| 23.A12 | Bibliography |
| 23.A15 | Periodicals |
| | Including gazettes, yearbooks, bulletins, etc. |
| | Treaties establishing and governing the organization. Primary law |
| 23.A25 | Indexes and tables |
| 23.A3 | Collections |
| | Including either multilateral or bilateral treaties or both |
| 23.A35<date> | Multilateral treaties |
| | Arrange chronologically by appending the date of signature of the treaty to this number and deleting any trailing zeroes. Subarrange by Table K6 |
| 23.A43A-.A43Z | Bilateral treaties. By organization and date of signature of the treaty |
| | For bilateral treaties relating to a multilateral treaty, see .xZ4+ in Table K6 under Multilateral treaties, above |
| 23.A8 | Conferences. Symposia |
| 23.A9-.Z9 | General works. Treatises |
| 25 | Constitutional principles |
| | Foreign (External) relations. International cooperation |
| | Including membership in international organizations |
| 26 | General (Table K14) |
| | United Nations |
| | see KZ5003.A+ |
| 26.4 | Relations with other regional organizations (Table K14) |
| | For relations with European Economic Community, see KJE5060+ |
| 26.5 | Relations with other international organizations (Table K14) |
| 26.6 | Relations with non-member states (Table K14) |
| | Intergovernmental relations and cooperation |
| 28 | General (Table K14) |
| 28.5 | Jurisdiction (Table K14) |
| | Human rights. Civil and political rights |
| 28.6 | General (Table K14) |

KL-KWX3

Organization law
Human rights. Civil and political rights -- Continued
28.7 Freedom of movement (Table K14)
Including persons, capital, and goods
Organs of the organization
29 General (Table K14)
30 Rules governing the official language of the organs
Election law
32 General
32.5.A-Z Election to a particular office, A-Z
32.7.A-Z Expert committees and subcommittees, A-Z
36 Powers and duties (Table K14)
Legislative organ. Parliamentary assembly
38 General (Table K15)
38.5 Standing committee (Table K15)
39.A-Z Ordinary committees and subcommittees, A-Z
Subarrange each by Table K12
39.5 Powers and duties (Table K14)
39.7.A-Z Meeting of heads of governments. Intergovernmental councils, A-Z
Subarrange each by Table K12
39.8 Secretariat (Table K15)
39.9.A-Z Joint services, A-Z
Courts of justice. Tribunals
40 General (Table K15)
40.3 Jurisdiction (Table K14)
Civil service. Officials and functionaries
42 General works
43 Incompatibility of offices (Table K14)
43.5 Privileges and immunities (Table K14)
43.6 Appointment (Table K14)
43.8 Conditions of unemployment (Table K14)
Including discipline
44 Remuneration. Allowances (Table K14)
44.5 Retirement (Table K14)
44.6 Collective labor law (Table K14)
46 Finance. Budget (Table K14)
49.A-Z Other topics, A-Z

Bibliography
For bibliography of special topics, see the topic
For manuals on legal bibliography, legal research and the use of law books see KL-KWX4 47+
2 Bibliography of bibliography
3 General bibliography
4 Library catalogs
4.5 Sales catalogs
5 Indexes to periodical literature, society publications, and collections
For indexes to a particular publication, see the publication
<6> Periodicals
For periodicals consisting predominantly of legal articles, regardless of subject matter and jurisdiction, see K1+
For periodicals consisting primarily of informative material (newsletters, bulletins, etc.) relating to a special subject, see the subject and form division tables for periodicals
For law reports, official bulletins or circulars intended chiefly for the publication of laws and regulations, see appropriate entries in the text or form division tables
6.5 Monographic series
Official gazettes
7 General
State or city gazettes
see the issuing state or city
Departmental gazettes
see the issuing department or agency
8 Indexes (General)
Legislative documents
see class J
9 Other materials relating to legislative history
Including recommended legislation; legislation passed and vetoed
Legislation
For statutes, statutory orders, regulations, etc. on a particular subject, see the subject
Indexes and tables
Including indexes to statutes of several states
For indexes to a particular publication, see the publication; for indexes limited to one state, see the state
General
9.5 Serials
10 Monographs. By date
10.5 Chronological indexes. By date
10.6 Indexes to publisher editions (unannotated and annotated). By date
10.7 Other bibliographical aids

Legislation -- Continued
11 Abridgements and digests
Statutes
Including statutory orders and regulations, and decree law
Collections and compilations
Including official and private editions
12 Continuing resources
Including serials and updating loose-leafs
13 Monographs. By date
Including unannotated and annotated editions
Collected codes
Class here works consisting of private and public law codes, and customary law codes
For codes on a particular branch of law, see the branch of law
For works consisting of the civil and commercial codes see KL-KWX4 479
For collected public law codes see KL-KWX4 2000+
15 General
15.2 Legislative documents
15.4 Enactments
Class here collections of enactments of several states
For enactments of an individual state, see the state
For enactments of a particular code, see the code
15.6 Statute revision commission acts and reports. By date
Administrative and executive publications
Including statutory orders and regulations, orders in council, proclamations, etc.
For regulations on a particular subject, see the subject
17 Serials
17.5 Monographs. By date
17.6 Digests
17.7 Indexes. By date
Presidential proclamations, etc.
see class J
Treaties
For treaties on international public law, see class KZ
For treaties on international uniform law not limited to a region, see class K
For treaties on international uniform law of a particular region, see the region
Court decisions and related materials. Reports
Including decisions of national (federal) courts and decisions of two or more states, and national (federal) and state decisions combined. Class decisions of an individual state with the law of the respective jurisdiction
For decisions on a particular subject, see the subject

Court decisions and related materials. Reports -- Continued
National (Federal) courts
Constitutional court see KL-KWX4 2620+
18 Highest courts of appeal. Supreme courts. Courts of Cassation (Table K19)
Lower courts
19 Various courts (Table K19)
Including highest court and lower courts, or national (federal) courts of two or more state combined
Intermediate appellate courts. National (Federal) courts of appeal
20 Collective (Table K19)
21.A-Z Particular courts, A-Z
Courts of first instance. District courts
22 Collective (Table K19)
23.A-Z Particular courts, A-Z
State courts
24 Collections (Reports) covering all states or selected states (Table K19)
Decisions (Reports) of an individual state
see the state
24.3 Decisions of national (federal) administrative agencies
For decisions of particular agencies, see the subject
25 Encyclopedias
26 Dictionaries. Words and phrases
For bilingual and multilingual dictionaries, see K52+
For dictionaries on a particular subject, see the subject
27 Maxims. Quotations
28 Form books
For form books on a particular subject, see the subject
Judicial statistics
30 General
31 Criminal statistics
31.3 Juvenile crime
32.A-Z Other. By subject, A-Z
32.L34 Labor law
Directories
33 National and regional
34.A-Z By state, A-Z
35.A-Z Local. By administrative district or city, A-Z
36.A-Z By specialization, A-Z
Trials
38 General collections
Criminal trials and judicial investigations
For military trials see KL-KWX4 3770
39 Collections. Compilations

Trials
Criminal trials and judicial investigations
Collections. Compilations -- Continued
40.A-Z Particular offenses, A-Z
40.A78 Arson
40.F73 Fraud
40.M87 Murder
40.P64 Political crimes
40.R56 Riots
40.T73 Treason
War crimes see KL-KWX4 42.2+
Individual trials
Including records, briefs, commentaries, and stories on a particular trial
41.A-Z By defendant, A-Z
42.A-Z By best known (popular) name, A-Z
War crime trials
Trials by international military tribunals
see class KZ
43 Collections
44.A-Z Individual trials. By defendant or best known (popular) name, A-Z
Including records, briefs, commentaries, and stories on a particular trial
Other trials
45 Collections. Compilations
46.A-Z Individual trials. By plaintiff, defendant, or best known (popular) name, A-Z
Including records, briefs, commentaries, and stories on a particular trial
Legal research. Legal bibliography
Including methods of bibliographic research and how to find the law
47 General works
47.5 Electronic data processing. Information retrieval
47.7.A-Z By subject, A-Z
48 Systems of citation. Legal abbreviations
48.5 Surveys of legal research
48.7 Legal composition and draftsmanship
Legal education
50 General works
Study and teaching
General works see KL-KWX4 50
50.3 Teaching methods
Including clinical method, case method, etc.
51.A-Z By subject, A-Z
51.C65 Commercial law

Legal education
Study and teaching -- Continued
51.7 Students' guides
For introductory surveys of the law see KL-KWX4 50
51.8 Teachers' manuals
52 Pre-law school education
52.3 Law teachers
52.4 Law students
Including sociology and psychology of law students
Law schools
52.5 General works
53.A-Z Particular law schools. By name, A-Z
Including constitution and bylaws, statutes, regulations, degrees, and general works (history)
Post-law school education see KL-KWX4 1602
The legal profession see KL-KWX4 1600+
Bar associations. Law societies. Law institutes
Class here works on, and journals by, individual societies and their activities, e.g., annual reports, proceedings, incorporating statutes, bylaws, handbooks, and works (history) about the society
Including courts of honor and disbarment
For publications of associations on special subjects, see the subject
For journals devoted to legal subjects, either wholly or in part, see K1+
For membership directories see KL-KWX4 36.A+
For biography (Collective) see KL-KWX4 105
For biography (Individual) see KL-KWX4 110.A+
54 General works
Particular types of organizations
54.3.A-Z National associations. By name, A-Z
54.5.A-Z State associations. By state, A-Z
54.7.A-Z Local associations, lawyers' clubs, etc. By county, city, etc., A-Z
Notarial law. Public instruments see KL-KWX4 1846+
Public registers. Registration
56 General (Table K11)
Civil registry see KL-KWX4 1854+
Registration of juristic persons in civil law see KL-KWX4 523.5
Commercial registers see KL-KWX4 925
57 Registration of miscellaneous titles and documents
58 Property registration. Registration of pledges (Table K11)
Land register see KL-KWX4 737+
Mining registration see KL-KWX4 3350+
Aircraft registration see KL-KWX4 935+
Law societies and institutes see KL-KWX4 54+

62.A-Z Congresses. Conferences.
64.A-Z Academies. By name of academy, A-Z
68 General works. Treatises
70 Compends, outlines, examination aids, etc.
Forms, graphic materials, blanks, atlases see KL-KWX4 28
72 Popular works. Civics
74 Addresses, essays, lectures
Including single essays, collected essays of several authors, festschriften, indexes to festschriften, etc.
78.A-Z Manuals and other works for particular groups of users. By user, A-Z
78.A75 Armed Forces personnel
78.B87 Businesspeople. Foreign investors
78.C68 Communists
78.F37 Farmers
Foreign investors see KL-KWX4 78.B87
Semantics and language see KL-KWX4 92
Legal symbolism see KL-KWX4 94+
Legal anecdotes, wit and humor
see K184.4
Law and lawyers in literature
see classes PB-PH
Law and art
see K487.C8
Law and history
see K487.C8
80.A-Z Works on diverse aspects of a particular subject and falling within several branches of the law. By subject, A-Z
80.C65 Computers
80.P83 Public interest law
80.P85 Public relations
(80.W65) Women
see KL-KWX4 517.5
History of law
85 Bibliography
86 Periodicals
86.2 Encyclopedias
86.3 Law dictionaries. Vocabularies. Terms and phrases
Auxiliary sciences
87 General works
90 Paleography
92 Linguistics. Semantics
Archaeology. Folklife studies. Symbolism
94 General works
96.A-Z Special topics, A-Z
96.S76 Stool, Ancestral

History of law
Auxiliary sciences -- Continued
100 Heraldry. Seals. Flags. Insignia. Armory
Biography of lawyers
105 Collective
107 Collections of portraits
110.A-Z Individual, A-Z
Subarrange each by Table KL-KWX11
120 General works. Treatises
By period
<122> Ancient and early, including ancient people in the region
see KL, KQ, or particular jurisdiction, as specified (e.g. Russia, Japan)
Medieval and early modern (to second half of 19th century)
Including precolonial and early colonial periods
Sources
For sources of a territory or town, see the appropriate territory or town
132 Studies on sources
Including history and methodology, e.g. epigraphy, papyrology, etc.
For philological studies, see classes P, PJ, PK, and PL
133 Classification of sources
Including codes, statutes, ordinances, regulations, edicts, decrees, etc.
134 Collections. Compilations. Selections
Class here comprehensive collections of legal sources in various (native) scripts
Individual sources or groups of sources
National (imperial) laws and legislation
Including constitutional laws (leges fundamentales)
140 Collections. Compilations
140.2<date> Individual
Arrange chronologically by appending the date of the source to this number and deleting any trailing zeros. Subarrange each by Table K20b
Royal (imperial) privileges
Including privileges for particular classes, ecclesiastical rulers, religious groups, courts of justice, etc.
144 Collections. Compilations
146.2<date> Individual
Arrange chronologically by appending the date of the source to this number and deleting any trailing zeros. Subarrange each by Table K20b
Royal (imperial) edicts, etc. of princes and rulers. Decrees. Mandates

History of law
By period
Medieval and early modern (to second half of 19th century)
Sources
Individual sources or groups of sources
Royal (imperial) edicts, etc. of princes and rulers. Decrees. Mandates -- Continued
148 Collections. Compilations
150.2<date> Individual
Arrange chronologically by appending the date of the source to this number and deleting any trailing zeros. Subarrange each by Table K20b
Treaties
Treaties on international public law
see KZ118+
Treaties on international uniform law
see K524+ , KJC38+ , KMC , KNC , KQC and KVC
Court decisions. Cases. Precedents. Advisory opinions. Dooms. Digests
160 Several courts
164.A-Z Particular courts, A-Z
Law faculties
166 Several faculties
168.A-Z Individual faculties. By place, A-Z
Trials
Criminal trials and judicial investigations
170 Collections. Compilations
172.A-Z Particular offenses, A-Z
172.P64 Political offenses
Including treason, sedition, etc.
172.W58 Witchcraft
174.A-Z Individual trials. By defendant, or best known (popular) name, A-Z
Including records, briefs, commentaries, and stories on a particular trial
Other trials
176 Collections. Compilations
178 Individual trials. By plaintiff, defendant, or best known (popular) name, A-Z
Contemporary legal literature
Compends. Digests. Indexes
182 General
183.A-Z By subject, A-Z
Formularies
Including notarial art
184 Collections. Compilations

History of law
By period
Medieval and early modern (to second half of 19th century)
Sources
Contemporary legal literature
Formularies -- Continued
185 Particular clauses and formulae
187 Encyclopedic works
192 General works
195 Addresses, essays, lectures
The State and its constitution
202 General works (Table K22)
Estates. Classes. Castes
204 General works (Table K22)
205.A-Z Particular classes, A-Z
207.A-Z Special topics, A-Z
207.B57 Birth rights
207.D94 Dynastic rules
Feudal capacity see KL-KWX4 228
207.P44 Peerage, Rights of
State and religion see KL-KWX4 280+
209 Territory
212 Foreign relations
Feudal law
Class here works on feudal law beginning ca. 12th century
213 General works (Table K22)
Sources
214 Collections. Compilations
220.2<date> Individual sources or groups of sources
Arrange chronologically by appending the date of the source to this number and deleting any trailing zeros. Subarrange each by Table K20b
Feudal institutes
222 General (Table K22)
Feudal lords. Provincial (regional) lords
223 General (Table K22)
224 Vassalage. Peers (Table K22)
Including individuals, towns, and villages, and regions
226 Fief (Table K22)
228 Feudal capacity (Table K22)
230 Feudal succession (Table K22)
Rural (peasant) land tenure. Peasantry
232 General (Table K22)
Manorial estates. Lordships. Seigniories
234 General (Table K22)
236.A-Z Special topics, A-Z

History of law
By period
Medieval and early modern (to second half of 19th century)
Rural (peasant) land tenure. Peasantry -- Continued
Leasehold for years and inheritance
238 General (Table K22)
240.A-Z Special topics, A-Z
240.E46 Emphyteusis
Succession to rural holdings
242 General (Table K22)
244 Entail (Table K22)
The crown. Princes and rulers. Chieftains
246 General (Table K22)
248.A-Z Special topics, A-Z
Crown goods and dynastic estates see KL-KWX4 263
248.D95 Dynastic house rules
248.E43 Election
248.I45 Imperium
Legal status, juristic personality of ruling dynasty see KL-KWX4 248.D95
Prerogatives see KL-KWX4 248.R53
248.R53 Rights and prerogatives
248.S93 Succession and designation
250 The court. Court officials and councils (Table K22)
252.A-Z Particular, A-Z
254 Diet. Generale parlamentum. State and crown councils. Legislature (Table K22)
256 Military organization and administration (Table K22)
Finance. Revenue and expenditure
259 General (Table K22)
260 Camera. Organization and administration (Table K22)
263 Crown goods and dynastic house goods (Table K22)
Regalia. Taxes
268 General (Table K22)
269.A-Z Particular taxes, A-Z
Administration. Public order and safety
Class here works on subjects not represented elsewhere in the schedule
For works on the history of subjects, see the subject
270 General (Table K22)
Administrative organization. Bureaucracy. Hierarchy
272 General (Table K22)
274 Administrative divisions (not A-Z)
275 Organs of government. Civil service. Officials (Table K22)
276.A-Z Special topics, A-Z

History of law
By period
Medieval and early modern (to second half of 19th century) -- Continued
State and religion. State and church
Class here historical works on the relationship of the state and church (e.g. Eastern Orthodox), and on state and practice of religion in general
280 General (Table K22)
281 Sources
282.A-Z Private law. Special topics, A-Z
Class here works on subjects not represented elsewhere in the schedule
For works on the history of other subjects, see the subject
Judiciary. Court organization
283 General (Table K22)
284 Administration of justice. Officials (Table K22)
285.A-Z Particular courts, tribunals, etc., A-Z
285.E22 Ecclesiastical courts
285.H65 Courts of honor
285.L38 Courts of last resort
285.M36 Manorial courts
285.M86 Municipal courts
Procedure
287 General (Table K22)
288.A-Z Special topics, A-Z
Criminal law and procedure
Class here works on topics not represented elsewhere in the schedule
For works on the history of other subjects, see the subject
292 General (Table K22)
294.A-Z Particular crimes, A-Z
294.W58 Witchcraft
296.A-Z Particular procedures, A-Z
296.O74 Ordeal
Wages of battle see KL-KWX4 296.O74
298.A-Z Particular penalties, A-Z
298.A66 Amputation of limbs
298.B36 Banishment
298.B73 Branding
298.C37 Castration
298.F56 Flogging
298.L68 Lowering of civil status
298.M87 Mutilation
298.S87 Strangling

<350> Indigenous peoples. Ethnic groups
For works on the law of indigenous peoples regardless of whether identified with one or more countries in the region, see KM, KN, KNQ, KQ, or as directed
Philosophy, jurisprudence, and theory of law
Class here works on doctrines peculiar to legal institutions of a country
For works on the philosophy of a particular branch of the law (e.g., constitutional law or criminal law), see the branch
For works on the philosophy of law in general, see K237+
440 General works
The concept of law
Including the definition of law
442 General works
443 The object of law. Law and justice
444 Ethics. Morality of law. Public policy
445 Law and the state. Legal order. Respect for law
446 Rights and duties. Sanction
446.5 Effectiveness and validity of the law
447 Certainty of law
Including customary (indigenous) law
448.A-Z Other topics, A-Z
Sources of law
449 General works
449.3 Customs and observances. Indigenous law
449.5 Legislation
Methodology
Including unification, integration, and harmonization of both substantive law and conflict rules
For unification of the law on a particular subject, see the subject
450 General works
451 Reconciliation and integration of customary (indigenous) law and civil law, or multiple customary (indigenous) laws
452 Legal hermeneutics. Interpretation and construction
Including lacunae in law and judge-made law
Semantics see KL-KWX4 92
Schools of legal theory
455 General works
457 Natural law
463 Modern political theory of law
464 Socialist. Communist
465 Sociological jurisprudence
465.5 Law and public policy
465.6 Social psychology of law
466 Social pathology
468 Pluralism in law

469 Influence of other legal systems on the law. Superimposition of foreign rule on the customary (indigenous) law (Table K11)
Including reception of traditional, customary and religious law, and multiplicity of laws

470 Law reform and policies. Criticism (Table K11)
Including reform of administration of justice

471.A-Z Concepts applying to several branches of the law, A-Z
Bona fides see KL-KWX4 471.G66
471.D87 Duress
471.E88 Estoppel
471.F73 Freedom of conscience
471.G66 Good faith. Reliance
471.L44 Legal documents
471.L52 Liability
471.L63 Locus poenitentiae
471.T55 Time periods

471.5 Intertemporal law. Retroactive law

474 Regional divisions. Subregions
Class here general works on the law or the legal systems in force within a single subregion of the country (e.g. laws in force in Soviet Central Asia, KLA477)
For works on a particular subject, see the subject

479 Private law
Class here works on all aspects of private law

Private international law. Plurality of laws conflict. Legal polycentricity
Class here works on conflict of laws in a multicultural country with two or more coexisting legal systems (e.g. secular and religious law, civil law and one or more indigenous (tribal, customary) legal system
For regional unification of conflict rules, see the appropriate region, e.g. Middle East, KMC subdivided by Table KL-KWX2, 126-136
For conflict of laws between the United States and a particular jurisdiction, see KF416
For works on conflict rules of branches other than private law (e.g. tax law, criminal law, etc.), see the subject

480 General (Table K11)
481 Public order. Ordre Public (Table K11)
481.7 Jurisdiction (Table K11)
Choice of law
Including indigenous (tribal, customary) law and civil law
482 General (Table K11)
483 Connecting factors. Points of contact. Nationality and domicile (Table K11)
483.5 Interlocal (interstate) law (Table K11)
484 Party autonomy (Table K11)

Private international law. Plurality of laws conflict. Legal polycentricity

Choice of law -- Continued

484.5 Renvoi (Table K11)

485.A-Z Particular branches and subjects of the law, A-Z

Adoption see KL-KWX4 485.F35

Arbitration see KL-KWX4 485.P76

Bankruptcy see KL-KWX4 485.P76

Capacity see KL-KWX4 485.P47

Cartels see KL-KWX4 485.C67

485.C655 Commercial papers and negotiable instruments (Table K12)

485.C657 Commercial sales (Table K12)

485.C658 Contracts. Obligations. Debtor and creditor (Table K12)

485.C67 Corporations. Industrial trusts. Cartels (Table K12)

For procedure in antitrust cases see KL-KWX4 3244+

Criminal law see KL-KWX4 3835

Debtor and creditor see KL-KWX4 485.C658

Decedents' estate see KL-KWX4 485.I45

Divorce see KL-KWX4 485.M375

Execution see KL-KWX4 485.P76

485.F35 Family. Parent and child. Adoption (Table K12)

Foreign exchange see KL-KWX4 3539

Foreign judgments see KL-KWX4 1646

Illegality see KL-KWX4 485.T67

Incapacity see KL-KWX4 485.P47

Industrial property see KL-KWX4 485.I583

Industrial trusts see KL-KWX4 485.C67

485.I45 Inheritance and succession. Decedents' estates (Table K12)

485.I58 Insurance (Table K12)

485.I583 Intellectual and industrial property (Table K12)

Judicial assistance see KL-KWX4 1644

Justification see KL-KWX4 485.T67

485.L45 Limitation of action (Table K12)

485.L62 Loans (Table K12)

485.M37 Maritime (commercial) law (Table K12)

485.M375 Marriage. Matrimonial actions. Matrimonial property (Table K12)

Negotiable instruments see KL-KWX4 485.C655

Obligations see KL-KWX4 485.C658

Parent and child see KL-KWX4 485.F35

485.P47 Persons. Capacity. Incapacity (Table K12)

485.P76 Procedure. Arbitral awards. Execution and bankruptcy (Table K12)

485.R43 Refugees (Table K12)

Social insurance see KL-KWX4 1481

485.S8 Statelessness (Table K12)

Private international law. Plurality of laws conflict. Legal polycentricity
Particular branches and subjects of the law, A-Z -- Continued
485.T39 Taxation (Table K12)
485.T67 Torts. Illegality. Justification (Table K12)
485.T725 Transfer (Table K12)
485.T725 Transfer (Table K12)
Intertemporal law. Retroactive law see KL-KWX4 471.5
Civil law
491-500 General (Table K9c)
501 Applicability. Validity of the law (Table K11)
502 Interpretation. Analogy (Table K11)
Ethics (Morality of law). Public policy see KL-KWX4 444
502.3 Legal status (Table K11)
502.4 Rights (Table K11)
503 Immaterial rights (Table K11)
Acts and events
504 General (Table K11)
Illegal and unlawful acts see KL-KWX4 834+
Declaration of intention see KL-KWX4 860+
Agency. Power of attorney see KL-KWX4 861+
Mandate see KL-KWX4 864+
505 Conditions (Table K11)
505.5 Suspensive conditions amd resolutory conditions (Table K11)
506 Retroactivity (Table K11)
Time periods see KL-KWX4 471.T55
Limitation of actions
507 General (Table K11)
508 Delay (Table K11)
508.5.A-Z Special topics, A-Z
Subarrange each by Table K12
509 Exercise of rights. Protection of rights (Table K11)
509.5 Self-defense (Table K11)
Cf. KL-KWX4 3856 Criminal law
509.6 Necessity (Table K11)
510 Assistance in emergencies (Table K11)
Persons
511 General (Table K11)
Natural persons
512 Personality (Table K11)
513 Birth (Table K11)
513.3 Unborn children. Nasciturus (Table K11)
Death
513.5 General (Table K11)
514 Missing persons. Presumption of death (Table K11)
514.5 Declaration and certification of death (Table K11)

Civil law
Persons
Natural persons
Personality
Death -- Continued
Civil register see KL-KWX4 1854+
Capacity and incapacity
Including liability
For civil disability see KL-KWX4 4004
515 General (Table K11)
Minors. Children
Including human rights of the chld
515.5 General (Table K11)
516 Majority. Declaration of majority (Table K11)
517 Limited capacity (Table K11)
517.2.A-Z Special topics, A-Z
517.5 Women (Table K11)
Class here works on legal status under all aspects of law (e.g. religious, customary, private, and public)
For status of married women see KL-KWX4 550+
518 Insane persons. People with mental disabilities (Table K11)
For institutional care of the mentally ill see KL-KWX4 3113; KL-KWX4 3113
Interdiction see KL-KWX4 628+
518.5 Domicile (Table K11)
518.6.A-Z Other, A-Z
518.6.E93 Ex-convicts (Table K12)
518.6.P49 Physical disabilities, People with (Table K12)
518.7 Citizenship (Table K11)
For acquisition of citizenship and nationality see KL-KWX4 2430+
For aliens see KL-KWX4 3025+
Personality rights
519 General (Table K11)
519.5 Life. Body. Health (Table K11)
Freedom see KL-KWX4 842
520 Name (Table K11)
Including title of nobility and coat of arms
Dignity, honor, and reputation see KL-KWX4 842.7
Privacy see KL-KWX4 843+
Intellectual property see KL-KWX4 1160+
Protection of personality rights see KL-KWX4 835
Juristic persons of private law
For business corporations see KL-KWX4 1050+
For juristic persons of public law see KL-KWX4 2875+

Civil law
Persons
Juristic persons of private law -- Continued
521 General (Table K11)
521.3 Personality (Table K11)
521.4 Capacity. Ultra vires (Table K11)
521.5 Personality rights (Table K11)
For protection of personality rights see KL-KWX4 835
Associations
522 General (Table K11)
523 Incorporated society (Table K11)
Including profit and nonprofit corporations
523.3 Constitution. Dissolution
523.5 Registration (Table K11)
Liability see KL-KWX4 522+
524.A-Z Other, A-Z
Subarrange each by Table K12
Unincorporated society
525 General (Table K11)
Liability see KL-KWX4 525+
526 Foundations. Charitable trusts and uses. Endowments (Table K11)
526.5.A-Z Individual foundations. By name, A-Z
Subarrange each by Table K12
527.A-Z Particular kinds of foundations, A-Z
Subarrange each by Table K12
Domestic relations. Family law. Multiplicity of laws
Including one or more religious legal systems, customary law and civil law
531-540 General (Table K9c)
541 Constitutional guaranties (Table K11)
Marriage
542 General (Table K11)
Constitutional guaranties see KL-KWX4 541
543 Betrothal (Table K11)
544.A-Z Marriage impediments, A-Z
544.A43 Affinity (Table K12)
544.C65 Consanguinity (Table K12)
545 Premarital examinations. Marriage licenses (Table K11)
Performance of marriage. Civil marriage and religious ceremonies
546 General (Table K11)
Certificates. Registration see KL-KWX4 1860
546.2 Intermarriage (Table K11)
Including interracial, interethnic, and interfaith marriage
546.4 Multiple marriages. Polygamy. Polyandry (Table K11)

Civil law
Domestic relations. Family law. Multiplicity of laws
Marriage -- Continued
Husband and wife. Rights and duties
547 General (Table K11)
548 Domicile. Household (Table K11)
549 Family name (Table K11)
Legal status of married women
550 General (Table K11)
551 Equal rights. Emancipation and decision-making (Table K11)
Cf. KL-KWX4 2465+ Constitutional law
553.A-Z Special topics, A-Z
Subarrange each by Table K12
554.A-Z Special topics, A-Z
Subarrrange each by Table K12
Matrimonial actions. Dissolution of marriage
555 General (Table K11)
556 Defective marriage (Table K11)
Divorce
558 General (Table K11)
559.A-Z Individual grounds for divorce,. A-Z
Subarrange each by Table K12
560 Reconciliation (Condonation) (Table K11)
562 Procedure. Divorce suits (Table K11)
565 Separation (Table K11)
567 Settlement of claims from defective or dissolved marriages (Table K11)
Including alimony and dowry
568 Quasi-matrimonial relationships. Unmarried cohabitation (Table K11)
Marital property and regime
569 General (Table K11)
570 Statutory regimes (Table K11)
572 Contractual regimes. Antenuptial contracts. Marriage settlements (Table K11)
573 Separation of property (Table K11)
574 Community of property (Table K11)
578 Property questions arising from unmarried cohabitation (Table K11)
Matrimonial property register see KL-KWX4 1867
Consanguinity and affinity. Kinship
583 General (Table K11)
584 Support
Parent and child
587 General (Table K11)

Civil law
Domestic relations. Family law. Multiplicity of laws
Consanguinity and affinity. Kinship
Parent and child -- Continued
588 Constitutional rights and guaranties (Table K11)
Including human rights
Legitimate children
Including children from defective marriages, divorced marriages, legitimized children from subsequent marriages, etc.
590 General (Table K11)
(592) Human rights of the child
see KL-KWX4 515.5+
593 Citizenship of children (Table K11)
595 Legitimation of children (Table K11)
Including declaration of legitimacy and legitimation by subsequent marriage
Parental power
For illegitimate children see KL-KWX4 616
598 General (Table K11)
600 Equal rights of parents. Mutual agreements (Table K11)
602 Custody. Access to children (Table K11)
Including parental kidnapping
Education see KL-KWX4 3138+
606 Property management (Table K11)
607 Parental power of mother (Table K11)
Guardianship court see KL-KWX4 624.2
608 Stepchildren (Table K11)
Adoption
609 General (Table K11)
610 Consent of natural parents (Table K11)
For procedure see KL-KWX4 1872
611.A-Z Special topics, A-Z
Subarrange each by Table K12
Inter-country adoption of children see KL-KWX4 485.F35
Illegitimate children
612 General (Table K11)
Human rights of the child see KL-KWX4 515.5+
Citizenship of children see KL-KWX4 593
613 Legal status (Table K11)
614 Right of name (Table K11)
615 Inheritance and succession (Table K11)
616 Parental power. Custody (Table K11)
Affiliation (patrilineal and matrilineal)

Civil law
Domestic relations. Family law. Multiplicity of laws
Consanguinity and affinity. Kinship
Parent and child
Affiliation (patrilineal and matrilineal) -- Continued
616.5 General works
617 Illegitimate children (Table K11)
619.A-Z Special topics, A-Z
619.A77 Artificial insemination (Table K12)
Cf. KL-KWX4 3117 Public health
Cf. KL-KWX4 4108 Criminal law
619.P38 Paternity (Table K12)
Guardian and ward
622 General (Table K11)
623 Care for ward. Agency (Table K11)
624 Property management (Table K11)
624.2 Guardianship courts and procedure
Government guardianship see KL-KWX4 1548
Guardianship over minors
625 General (Table K11)
625.5.A-Z Special topics, A-Z
625.5.P75 Property management (Table K12)
Guardianship over adults
627 General (Table K11)
Interdiction
628 General (Table K11)
628.5.A-Z Special topics, A-Z
628.5.A45 Alcoholics (Table K12)
628.5.M45 Mentally ill (Table K12)
Curatorship
629 General (Table K11)
630 Curatorship for helpless (frail) adults (Table K11)
Property. Law of things
631-640 General (Table K9c)
641 Right of property. Constitutional guaranty (Table K11)
642 Socialist property. Doctrine (Table K11)
644.A-Z Types of private property, A-Z
Subarrange each by Table K12
Possession
646 General (Table K11)
647.A-Z Types of possession, A-Z
647.A28 Actual (immediate) possession (Table K12)
647.D47 Derivative possession (Table K12)
647.J64 Joint possession (Table K12)
647.P67 Possession of rights (Table K12)
Acquisition and transfer of possession

Civil law
Property. Law of things
Possession
Acquisition and transfer of possession -- Continued
648 General (Table K11)
650 Intent to possess (Table K11)
651 Dispossession (Table K11)
652 Possessory actions (Table K11)
Ownership
654 General (Table K11)
Right of ownership see KL-KWX4 641
Acquisition and loss of ownership
655 General (Table K11)
656 Occupation (Table K11)
657 Lost property (Table K11)
658 Treasure troves (Table K11)
659 Accessions (Table K11)
Including annexation (incorporation), confusion, and specification
663 Acquisition of fruits and parts of things (Table K11)
664 Prescription (Table K11)
665 Succession (Table K11)
Contractual acquisition
666 General (Table K11)
667 Conditions (Table K11)
For fiduciary transfer of ownership see KL-KWX4 733+
For retention of ownership, expectancies see KL-KWX4 877.2
Tradition
670 General (Table K11)
671 Assignment of chose in possession (Table K11)
672 Acquisition bona fide (Table K11)
673 Loss of ownership (Table K11)
Including abandonment and dereliction
For expropriation see KL-KWX4 2823+
674 Co-ownership (Table K11)
For co-ownership of land see KL-KWX4 694
For condominium and horizontal property see KL-KWX4 702+
Claims and actions resulting from ownership
675 General (Table K11)
675.5 Rei vindicatio (Table K11)

Civil law
Property. Law of things
Ownership
Claims and actions resulting from ownership -- Continued
676 Actio negatoria. Nuisances (Table K11)
For particular nuisances see KL-KWX4 701.N84
For ecological aspects of regional planning see KL-KWX4 3060
678 Liability of possessor (Table K11)
Including bona fide and mala fide possessor
Rights and defenses of possessor
Including bona fide and mala fide possessor
680 General (Table K11)
681 Payment for improvements (Table K11)
Real property. Land law
683 General (Table K11)
Land registration law see KL-KWX4 737+
684 Public and private restraint on real property (Table K11)
Eminent domain see KL-KWX4 2823+
Public policy. Land reform and land policy legislation see KL-KWX4 3056
Zoning laws see KL-KWX4 3064
Homestead law see KL-KWX4 3060
Concepts of customary (native) land rights
For new land system legislation (e.g. in African countries see KL-KWX4 3056+
685 General (Table K11)
685.5 National collective patrimony. Area of operation of customary land law, exercised collectively or individually (Table K11)
For co-operatives see KL-KWX4 3316+
Cf. KL-KWX4 3059+ Rural planning
686 Group lands. Terres communes. Terres collectives. Land possessed in common by ethnic groups (juristic persons) for use, but without shares in ownership (Table K11)
Constatation. Adjudication of customary land rights see KL-KWX4 735
Ownership
687 General (Table K11)
Acquisition and loss of ownership
687.5 General (Table K11)
687.6 Occupation of land by cultivator (Table K11)
687.7 Restoration of alienated land to customary ownership (Table K11)
Contractual acquisition

Civil law
Property. Law of things
Real property
Ownership
Acquisition and loss of ownership
Contractual acquisition -- Continued
688 General (Table K11)
689 Conditions (Table K11)
Registration see KL-KWX4 737+
Loss of ownership
Abandonment see KL-KWX4 673
692 Judicial decree (Table K11)
693 Expropriation (Table K11)
For procedure see KL-KWX4 2824+
694 Co-ownership of land. Customary co-ownership (Table K11)
For communal property (terres collectives) see KL-KWX4 686
Rights incident to ownership of land
695 General (Table K11)
696 Air and space above ground. Aeronautics (Table K11)
697 Underground. Minerals, metals, and other resources (Table K11)
Cf. KL-KWX4 3350+ Mining law
698 Riparian rights. Water rights. Underground water (Table K11)
699 Hunting and fishing rights (Table K11)
Cf. KL-KWX4 3337+ Game laws
Cf. KL-KWX4 3340+ Fishery laws
Commonage and pasture see KL-KWX4 708
Law of adjoining landowners
700 General (Table K11)
701.A-Z Special topics, A-Z
701.B68 Boundaries. Building across boundaries. Party walls (Table K12)
Building across boundaries see KL-KWX4 701.B68
701.E29 Eaves-drip (Table K12)
701.L54 Light or window rights (Table K12)
Mining rights see KL-KWX4 3350+
701.N84 Nuisances (Table K12)
Including fumes, heat, noise, smoke, and odor
Overfall see KL-KWX4 701.O83
701.O83 Overhang. Overfall (Table K12)
Party walls see KL-KWX4 701.B68
Transit of livestock see KL-KWX4 701.W39
701.W38 Water laws (Table K12)

Civil law
Property. Law of things
Real property
Ownership
Rights incident to ownership of land
Law of adjoining landowners
Special topics, A-Z -- Continued
701.W39 Way by necessity (Table K12)
Window rights see KL-KWX4 701.L54
Types of real property
Condominium. Horizontal property
702 General (Table K11)
702.5 Timesharing (Real estate) (Table K11)
703 Ships (Table K11)
Ship registers see KL-KWX4 984.3
Rights as to the use and profits of another's land. Droits d'usage
706 General (Table K11)
Fief see KL-KWX4 226
708 Commonage and pasture. Grazing rights (Table K11)
Servitudes
709 General (Table K11)
Real servitudes
710 General (Table K11)
711.A-Z Special types, A-Z
711.R54 Right of way (Table K12)
Way by necessity see KL-KWX4 701.W39
713 Personal servitudes
Including right of habitation
Usufruct
715 General (Table K11)
715.5.A-Z Particular, A-Z
Subarrange each by Table K12
716 Right of pre-emption (Table K11)
Hypothecation
717 General (Table K11)
Mortgage. Land charges
718 General (Table K11)
720.A-Z Special topics, A-Z
720.C48 Chattel (Table K12)
724 Rent charge (Table K11)
Pledges
726 General (Table K11)
Contractual pledges
727 General (Table K11)

Civil law
Property. Law of things
Pledges
Contractual pledges -- Continued
Pledges of personal property
Including possessory and nonpossessory pledges
728 General (Table K11)
729.A-Z Special topics, A-Z
729.A32 Accessority (Table K12)
729.P74 Priority (Table K12)
Pledges of rights
730 General (Table K11)
730.5.A-Z Special topics, A-Z
730.5.C46 Choses in action (Table K12)
730.5.E86 Expectancies (Table K12)
731 Lien or statutory pledge (Table K11)
Register of pledges
732 General (Table K11)
Aircraft mortgage see KL-KWX4 935.2
Ship mortgages see KL-KWX4 983
Transfer of ownership as security. Fiduciary transactions. Expectancies
733 General (Table K11)
734.A-Z Special topics, A-Z
Subarrange each by Table K12
735 Constatation. Adjudication of customary land rights
Including individual or collective holders of land
Land register and registration. Immatriculation
737 General (Table K11)
738 Publicity (Table K11)
739 Registration of proprietorship in common (Table K11)
742 Form requirements (Table K11)
743.A-Z Special topics, A-Z
743.P74 Priority of rights (Table K12)
745 Effect of registration (Table K11)
746 Remedies (Table K11)
758 Cadastral surveys. Cadaster (Table K11)
Class here general works on surveying agencies
For an individual surveying agency of a state or locality, see the state or locality
Inheritance. Succession upon death
761-770 General (Table K9c)
771 Right of inheritance. Constitutional guaranty (Table K11)
775 Inheritance. Estate (Table K11)
Intestate succession
777 General (Table K11)

Civil law
Inheritance. Succession upon death
Intestate succession -- Continued
Classes of heirs. Order of succession
778 General (Table K11)
779 Matrilineal and patrilineal descendants (Table K11)
Including monogamous and polygamous households
780 Surviving spouses. Surviving wives with or without children (Table K11)
781 Natural parents (Table K11)
782 Community of heirs (Table K11)
783.A-Z Special topics, A-Z
783.P76 Primogeniture
784 Liability. Debts of estate (Table K11)
Wills. Testamentary succession
785 General (Table K11)
785.7.A-Z Types of wills, A-Z
785.7.J64 Joint will (Table K12)
785.7.M88 Mutual will (Table K12)
785.7.R44 Religious wills (Table K12)
786 Appointment of heir (Table K11)
786.6 Form requirements (Table K11)
787 Legacy. Testamentary burden. Bequest. Distribution of estate (Table K11)
788 Revocation (Table K11)
789 Executors and administrators (Table K11)
Contract of inheritance
790 General (Table K11)
791 Statutory portion (Table K11)
791.5 Renunciation of inheritance (Table K11)
791.7 Unworthiness of heirs. Disinheritance (Table K11)
792 Purchase of inheritance (Table K11)
793 Certificate of inheritance. Proof of heirship (Table K11)
794 Gift causa mortis (Table K11)
Inheritance tax see KL-KWX4 3662
Land settlement systems and succession
795 General (Table K11)
796.A-Z Particular, A-Z
Subarrange each by Table K12
Obligations
801-810 General (Table K9c)
Debtor and creditor. Chose in action and obligation
811 General (Table K11)
Plurality of debtors and creditors. Joint obligations
812 General (Table K11)
Correality and solidarity

Civil law
Obligations
Debtor and creditor. Chose in action and obligation
Plurality of debtors and creditors. Joint obligations
Correality and solidarity -- Continued
813 General (Table K11)
813.5 Solidary obligation. Joint and several obligation (Table K11)
Types of obligations
814 Civil and natural obligations (Table K11)
Cf. KL-KWX4 899+ Aleatory contracts
814.5 Obligations to give (Table K11)
Including obligation in kind
For money obligations see KL-KWX4 820
815 Obligations to do or to refrain from doing (Table K11)
Transfer and assumption of obligations
816 General (Table K11)
816.5 Assignment of chose in action (Table K11)
Including future claims
816.7 Assumption of debts (Table K11)
Extinction of obligation
817 General (Table K11)
Performance. Payment
818 General (Table K11)
818.2 Due date of payment. Time of performance
For default (mora) see KL-KWX4 827.6
819 Consignation (Table K11)
Including emergency sale of perishables
820 Special rules as to payment of money debts
820.3 Gold clause. Valuta clause. Foreign currency debts (Table K11)
Cf. KL-KWX4 3538+ Foreign exchange control
820.5 Escalator clause (Table K11)
821 Revalorization of debts (Table K11)
Cf. KL-KWX4 3537.5 Public finance
821.5 Noncash payments (Table K11)
822 Compensation for maintenance and improvement (Table K11)

822.5 Enforcement (Table K11)
822.7 Liens (Table K11)
For liens of landlord see KL-KWX4 881.3
For commercial liens see KL-KWX4 936
822.9 Compensation. Set-off (Table K11)
823 Confusion of rights (Table K11)
823.5.A-Z Other, A-Z
823.5.A34 Achievement of purpose (Table K12)

Civil law
Obligations
Other, A-Z -- Continued
Cancellation see KL-KWX4 823.5.W58
823.5.C65 Contractual discharge (Table K12)
823.5.E85 Expiration and termination (Table K12)
823.5.N68 Novation (Table K12)
823.5.R45 Remission of debt (Table K12)
823.5.R47 Rescission (Table K12)
For Rebus sic stantibus clause see KL-KWX4 870.3
Termination see KL-KWX4 823.5.E85
823.5.W58 Withdrawal. Cancellation (Table K12)
Nonperformance
824 General (Table K11)
Culpa
824.5 General (Table K11)
824.6 Dolus (Table K11)
825 Negligence. Gross negligence (Table K11)
Respondeat superior doctrine see KL-KWX4 839.7
825.5 Culpa in contrahendo (Table K11)
826 Breach of contract (Table K11)
827 Impossibility of performance (Table K11)
Including original impossibility and supervening impossibility
827.6 Default (Table K11)
Damages
828 General (Table K11)
828.5 Liability (Table K11)
Class here general works including works comparing various sources of liability
For contractual liability see KL-KWX4 814
For tort liability see KL-KWX4 839+
For strict liability see KL-KWX4 841
Causation
829 General (Table K11)
829.3 Remote and proximate cause (Table K11)
830 Lost profits (Table K11)
Damages for pain and suffering
831 General (Table K11)
831.5.A-Z Specific damages, A-Z
Subarrange each by Table K12
832 Adjustment of claims
Including contributory and comparative negligence
832.7 Damages as counterplea (Table K11)
833.A-Z Special topics, A-Z
833.V34 Valuation (Table K12)
Delicts. Torts

Civil law
Obligations
Delicts. Torts -- Continued
834 General (Table K11)
Protected rights
834.5 General (Table K11)
835 Personality rights (Table K11)
Freedom see KL-KWX4 842
Life, body, and health see KL-KWX4 519.5
Name see KL-KWX4 520
Integrity see KL-KWX4 842.7
Privacy see KL-KWX4 843+
836 Privacy of communication (Table K11)
Parties to action in torts
837 General (Table K11)
837.5 Principal. Accessories (Table K11)
837.6 Joint tortfeasors (Table K11)
837.7.A-Z Other, A-Z
Illegality
838 General (Table K11)
838.5.A-Z Justification grounds, A-Z
838.5.C65 Consent of the injured party (Table K12)
838.5.P74 Privilege (Table K12)
838.5.S8 Standard of conduct (Table K12)
Liability
839 General (Table K11)
839.3 Dolus (Table K11)
839.5 Negligence. Aggravated negligence. Foresight (Table K11)
839.7 Liability for the torts of others (Table K11)
Including Respondeat superior doctrine
840 Exclusion of liability (Table K11)
Including contractual agreement, assumption of risk by injured part, and tacit (implied) agreement
841 Strict liability (Table K11)
For strict liability related to particular dangers or risks, see the topic
Individual torts
842 Violation of freedom (Table K11)
Physical injuries
842.2 General (Table K11)
842.3 Accidents (Table K11)
For particular types of accidents see KL-KWX4 848+
(842.5) Malpractice (Medical)
see KL-KWX4 3100.5

Civil law
Obligations
Delicts. Torts
Individual torts
Physical injuries -- Continued
842.6 Death by wrongful act (Table K11)
842.7 Violation of integrity (Table K11)
Including honor, dignity, and reputation
Violation of privacy
843 General (Table K11)
843.3 Confidential disclosure. Secrets (Table K11)
Including works on both civil and criminal aspects
843.4 Right in one's own picture (Table K11)
844 Public opinion polls (Table K11)
844.5 Personal data in information retrieval systems (Table K11)
Including public and private records, registers, statistics, etc.
Cf. KL-KWX4 843.3 Confidential disclosure
Immoral transactions and acts. Abuse of rights
845 General (Table K11)
845.5 Exceptio doli (Table K11)
846 Deceit. Misrepresentations. Forgery (Table K11)
Breach of contract. Interference with contractual relations see KL-KWX4 826
Enticement see KL-KWX4 1257.E58
Industrial espionage see KL-KWX4 1257.E86
846.5 Products liability (Table K11)
Ultrahazardous activities and occupations
847 General (Table K11)
847.5 Nuclear reactors. Nuclear damages (Table K11)
Sports. Sport fields or installations
848 General (Table K11)
848.5.A-Z Particular, A-Z
Liability for safe traffic conditions and accidents
849 General (Table K11)
849.3 Railroads and streetcars (Table K11)
850 Aviation (Table K11)
Automotive transportation and road traffic
850.3 General (Table K11)
850.5 Liability for accidents of owner and/or driver (Table K11)
Cf. KL-KWX4 1031+ Liability insurance (Automobiles)
Liability for safe conditions of streets, highways, public places, etc.

Civil law
Obligations
Delicts. Torts
Individual torts
Liability for safe conditions of streets, highways, public places, etc. -- Continued
851 General (Table K11)
851.3 Traffic signs (Table K11)
Violation of official duties
Cf. KL-KWX4 2840+ Government liability
852 General (Table K11)
852.3.A-Z Special topics, A-Z
Subarrange each by Table K12
852.4 Liability for environmental damages (Table K11)
For environmental crimes see KL-KWX4 4351.5+
853.A-Z Other liabilities, A-Z
853.A54 Animals (Table K12)
853.B84 Buildings, Liability for (Table K12)
Including public buildings
853.C65 Construction sites, Liability for (Table K12)
853.N84 Nuisance (Table K12)
Playground accidents see KL-KWX4 853.S34
Public buildings see KL-KWX4 853.B84
853.S34 School and playground accidents, Liability for (Table K12)
Unjust enrichment
854 General (Table K11)
854.7 Restitution (Table K11)
Contracts and transactions
For commercial contracts see KL-KWX4 911+
858 General (Table K11)
858.3 Liberty of contract. Party autonomy (Table K11)
858.5.A-Z Types of contracts, A-Z
858.5.A88 Atypical or mixed contracts (Table K12)
858.5.C65 Consensual and real contracts (Table K12)
858.5.O53 Onerous and gratuitous contracts (Table K12)
858.5.O67 Option (Table K12)
858.5.P32 Pactum de contrahendo. Preliminary contracts (Table K12)
859 Secured transactions. Security (Table K11)
Class here general works
For particular secured transactions, see the transaction, e.g. KL-KWX4 726 Pledge; KL-KWX4 733 Fiduciary transactions; KL-KWX4 900 Suretyship, etc.
Fiduciary transactions see KL-KWX4 733+
Declaration of intention

Civil law
Obligations
Contracts and transactions
Declaration of intention -- Continued
860 General (Table K11)
860.2 Reliance theory. Will theory (Table K11)
860.3 Mental reservation. Simulation (Table K11)
Agency
Including statutory agency
861 General (Table K11)
Authorized representation
861.3 General (Table K11)
861.6 To whom it may concern (Table K11)
862 Unauthorized representation. Falsus procurator (Table K11)
862.5 Agent for both contracting parties (Table K11)
Power of attorney
Including general discretionary power of attorney
862.7 General (Table K11)
863 Form requirements. Forms (Table K11)
863.3 Expiration and termination. Cancellation (Table K11)
Mandate
864 General (Table K11)
Negotiorum gestio
864.3 General (Table K11)
864.5.A-Z Particular, A-Z
864.5.A73 Architects (Table K12)
864.5.A88 Attorneys (Table K12)
Negotiorum gestio without mandate
865 General (Table K11)
865.5.A-Z Special topics, A-Z
Subarrange each by Table K12
866 Form requirements. Notice. Time of effectiveness (Table K11)
Void and voidable contracts and transactions
867 General (Table K11)
867.3 Error (Table K11)
867.5 Fraud. Duress (Table K11)
Cf. KL-KWX4 4258+ Criminal law
Immoral transactions. Unconscionable transactions
Including mortis causa
868 General (Table K11)
868.3.A-Z Special topics, A-Z
868.3.R47 Requirement contracts and other contracts limiting contractual freedom (Table K12)

Civil law
Obligations
Contracts and transactions -- Continued
Formation of contract
Including preliminary contract
869 General (Table K11)
Offer and acceptance
869.3 General (Table K11)
869.4 Contracts through correspondence, telephone, teletype, wire, etc. (Table K11)
869.5 Unordered merchandise by mail (Table K11)
Cf. KL-KWX4 1246 Unfair competition
869.55 Contracts by adhesion
869.6 Implied consent. De facto contract (Table K11)
Clauses
870 General (Table K11)
870.3 Clausula rebus sic stantibus (Table K11)
870.5 Contractual penalties (Table K11)
870.7.A-Z Other, A-Z
Subarrange each by Table K12
871 Earnest (Table K11)
871.3 Pactum de non petendo. Release. Covenant not to sue (Table K11)
872 Stipulation (Table K11)
872.5 Formalities (Table K11)
Parties to contract
873 General (Table K11)
873.3 Third parties (Table K11)
873.5 Effect of retroactive legislation on contract (Table K11)
873.7 Effect of market orders and price controls on contracts (Table K11)
Individual contracts and transactions
Sale
Cf. KL-KWX4 926+ Commercial law
874 General (Table K11)
874.3 Impossibility (Table K11)
Including supervening impossibility
874.5 Default (Table K11)
Including mora accipiendi
Warranty
875 General (Table K11)
875.3 Existence of right or chose in action (Table K11)
876 Defects in goods sold
Including bettering damages, and rescission
Producer liability see KL-KWX4 846.5
Modes of sale

Civil law
Obligations
Contracts and transactions
Individual contracts and transactions
Sale
Modes of sale -- Continued
Conditional sale
877 General (Table K11)
877.2 Retention of ownership and expectancies (Table K11)
Cf. KL-KWX4 667 Ownership
877.3 Installment plans (Table K11)
Including installment payments through commercial finance companies
878.A-Z Other, A-Z
878.P73 Preemption (Table K12)
878.R48 Retractive sale (Table K12)
878.S24 Sale after approval (Table K12)
878.S25 Sale in kind (species) (Table K12)
878.S26 Sale on approval (Table K12)
878.S44 Self-service (Table K12)
Commodities (goods) for sale see KL-KWX4 926.5.A+
Atypical or mixed contracts see KL-KWX4 858.5.A88
879 Exchange. Barter (Table K11)
879.3 Donations. Gifts inter vivos (Table K11)
For dispositions mortis causa see KL-KWX4 794
879.4 Aestimatum (Table K11)
Consignment see KL-KWX4 928
Lease. Landlord and tenant
880 General (Table K11)
880.5 Parties to contract (Table K11)
Including landlord and tenant, subtenants, third parties, etc.
Rights and claims from lease contract
Including subtenant
880.8 Rent (Table K11)
For rent subsidies see KL-KWX4 1524.R45
881 Compensation for improvements by tenant (Table K11)
881.3 Liens of landlord (Table K11)
882 Termination of lease (Table K11)
Including expiration, rescission, and notice
882.3 Protection of the tenant (Table K11)
883 Lease litigation and execution (eviction) (Table K11)
Including procedure at regular civil courts and special tribunals, and including remedies

Civil law
Obligations
Contracts and transactions
Individual contracts and transactions
Lease. Landlord and tenant -- Continued
884.A-Z Types of property
884.B85 Buildings. Rooms. Apartments (Table K12)
For social housing see KL-KWX4 885+
884.C66 Commercial space (Table K12)
884.R43 Real property (Table K12)
Social housing measures. State policy and planning
885 General (Table K11)
885.5 Public subsidies (Table K11)
Including subsidies and tax exemptions and deductions for home building and restoration
886 Rationing and distribution of housing (Table K11)
886.3 Rent control (Table K11)
Including subtenant
887 Publicly subsidized housing (Table K11)
Rent subsidies see KL-KWX4 1524.R45
887.4.A-Z Housing provided for particular groups, A-Z
887.4.V47 Veterans (Table K12)
888 Commercial and industrial property (Table K11)
Including operating leasing, producer leasing, etc.
Atypical or mixed contracts
888.3 General (Table K11)
888.5.A-Z Particular, A-Z
Commercial and industrial leasing see KL-KWX4 888
Farm and farm equipment leasing see KL-KWX4 3311
888.5.I58 Investment leasing (Table K12)
Including sale-and-lease-back
888.5.P47 Perpetual delivery and sale (Table K12)
Fiduciary transactions. Trust and trustee
889 General (Table K11)
Transfer of ownership see KL-KWX4 733+
Charitable trusts see KL-KWX4 526
890 Loan for use. Commodatum (Table K11)
891 Personal loans. Mutuum (Table K11)
Including secured loans
Cf. KL-KWX4 955+ Commercial law
Contracts of service and labor. Master and servant
892 General (Table K11)
Independent work. Professions
892.3 General (Table K11)

Civil law
Obligations
Contracts and transactions
Individual contracts and transactions
Contracts of service and labor. Master and servant
Independent work. Professions -- Continued
892.4.A-Z Particular professions and services, A-Z
Architects see KL-KWX4 864.5.A73
Attorneys see KL-KWX4 864.5.A88
892.4.P49 Physicians (Table K12)
Dependent work
892.5 General (Table K11)
892.6 Servants. Domestics (Table K11)
Employees. Labor contract see KL-KWX4 1279+
892.7.A-Z Particular groups, A-Z
Subarrange each by Table K12
Contract for work and labor
893 General (Table K11)
893.3.A-Z Particular contracts, A-Z
893.3.B84 Building construction. Engineering (Table K12)
893.3.C65 Computer contracts (Table K12)
893.3.T72 Transportation contracts (Table K12)
Including package tours
894 Security. Liens (Table K11)
Brokerage see KL-KWX4 929+
895 Reward. Award (Table K11)
Mandate see KL-KWX4 864+
896 Deposit (Table K11)
Including depositum irregulare
Cf. KL-KWX4 956+ Banking
Civil companies
For associations see KL-KWX4 522+
For personal companies and stock companies see KL-KWX4 1043+
897 General (Table K11)
898 De facto company (Table K11)
898.3 Termination. Liquidation (Table K11)
898.5 Life annuity (Table K11)
Aleatory contracts. Natural obligations
899 General (Table K11)
899.3 Gambling. Betting (Table K11)
899.5 Lotteries (Table K11)
Marriage brokers' fees see KL-KWX4 929.3.M37
900 Suretyship (Table K11)
901 Compromise (Table K11)
902 Promise of debt. Promissory note (Table K11)

Civil law
Obligations
Contracts and transactions
Individual contracts and transactions -- Continued

903 Acknowledgment of debt (Table K11)
904 Discovery (Disclosure) (Table K11)

Commercial law. Commercial transactions

911-920 General (Table K9c)

Merchant and business enterprise

921 General (Table K11)
922 Business names. Firma (Table K11)
Including goodwill
922.5 Domicile (Table K11)
923 Accounting (Table K11)
Including inventory
For tax accounting see KL-KWX4 3562+
924 Agency and prokura (Table K11)
Including commercial employees, traveling salespeople, etc.
For commercial agents (Independent) see KL-KWX4 927
925 Commercial registers (Table K11)
For publicity see KL-KWX4 1852

Commercial sale

926 General (Table K11)
926.2.A-Z Particular, A-Z
926.2.C65 Consignation (Table K12)
926.2.D43 Default of buyer (Table K12)
926.2.F87 Futures (Table K12)
926.3.A-Z Special modes of selling, A-Z
926.3.F72 Franchises (Table K12)
926.3.T73 Traveling salesmen (Table K12)
Vending machines see KL-KWX4 3420.V45
926.5.A-Z Particular products or goods, A-Z
926.5.A88 Automobilies (new or used) (Table K12)
926.5.C65 Computers (Table K12)
Used automobiles see KL-KWX4 926.5.A88
927 Commercial agents (Table K11)
928 Consignment. Commission merchants (Table K11)

Brokerage

929 General (Table K11)
929.3.A-Z Types of brokers, A-Z
929.3.M37 Marriage brokers (Table K12)
929.3.R42 Real estate agents (Table K12)
930 Auctioneers (Table K11)
930.3 Warehousing (Table K11)

Freight forwarders and carriers. Carriage of passengers and goods

Commercial law. Commercial transactions
Freight forwarders and carriers. Carriage of passengers and goods -- Continued
931 General (Table K11)
931.3 Bill of lading (Table K11)
932 Liens (Table K11)
932.3.A-Z Other, A-Z
932.3.D44 Delivery (Table K12)
Types of carriers
For regulatory (administrative) aspects see KL-KWX4 3440+
933 Railroads (Table K11)
933.5 Passenger carriers. Bus lines (Table K11)
934 Trucklines
Airlines
935 General (Table K11)
935.2 Airline creditors. Aircraft mortgages (Table K11)
935.4 Aircraft registration (Table K11)
Carriage by sea see KL-KWX4 971+
Commercial instruments see KL-KWX4 937+
936 Commercial liens (Table K11)
For freight forwarder liens see KL-KWX4 932
Negotiable instruments. Titles of credit
937 General (Table K11)
937.3 Possession, ownership, and transfer (Table K11)
Including legitimation and identification
Bills of exchange
938 General (Table K11)
938.3 Special topics, A-Z
938.3.A22 Acceptance (Table K12)
938.3.B52 Blanks (Table K12)
938.3.C52 Clauses (Table K12)
Contango see KL-KWX4 938.3.P76
938.3.E53 Endorsement (Table K12)
938.3.L52 Liability (Table K12)
Including drawer, acceptor, and endorser
938.3.P39 Payment and return of instrument (Table K12)
938.3.P76 Prolongation. Contango (Table K12)
938.3.P765 Protest (Table K12)
Return of instrument see KL-KWX4 938.3.P39
Stamp duties see KL-KWX4 3643
Checks
939 General (Table K11)
939.3.A-Z Special topics, A-Z
Subarrange each by Table K12
Letters of credit see KL-KWX4 955+

Commercial law. Commercial transactions
Negotiable instruments. Titles of credit -- Continued
Stock certificates and bonds see KL-KWX4 1064+
Trust investments see KL-KWX4 965
Bills of lading (Land transportation) see KL-KWX4 931.3
Maritime bills of lading see KL-KWX4 973
Promissory notes see KL-KWX4 902
Criminal provisions see KL-KWX4 4350
Banking. Stock exchange
940 General (Table K11)
940.3 State supervision (Table K11)
940.4 Accounting. Auditing (Table K11)
Types of banks and credit institutions
Banks of issue
941 General (Table K11)
941.3.A-Z Particular. By name, A-Z
Subarrange each by Table K12
942.A-Z Special topics, A-Z
942.D56 Discount policy (Table K12)
942.D57 Discount rate (Table K12)
Money see KL-KWX4 3534+
942.5 Foreign banks (Table K11)
943 Mortgage banks (Table K11)
944 Savings banks (Table K11)
Including public and private banks, and state supervision
945 Types of savings programs (Table K11)
For investment savings see KL-KWX4 961.5+
945.3.A-Z Special topics, A-Z
Identification see KL-KWX4 945.3.L44
945.3.L44 Legitimation. Identification (Table K12)
945.3.S39 Savings bonds (Table K12)
946 Criminal provisions (Table K11)
947 Building and loan associations (Table K11)
948 Cooperative societies (Table K11)
949 Clearinghouses (Table K11)
950 Warehouses (Table K11)
Banking transactions
951 General (Table K11)
952 Security of deposits. Insurance (Table K11)
953 Banking secret. Confidential communication (Table K11)
Contract see KL-KWX4 951
Deposits see KL-KWX4 956+
Loans. Credit
955 General (Table K11)
955.4 Interest rate (Table K11)
For usury see KL-KWX4 4268; KL-KWX4 4268

Commercial law. Commercial transactions
Banking. Stock exchange
Banking transactions
Loans. Credit -- Continued
955.5.A-Z Special types of loans, A-Z
955.5.C65 Consumer credit. Small loans (Table K12)
Small loans see KL-KWX4 955.5.C65
955.6 Letters of credit
Deposit banking. Custodianship accounts
956 General (Table K11)
957 Trading of securities (Table K11)
Including electronic data processing
958 Criminal provisions
959 Discount (Table K11)
960 Account current (Table K11)
960.3 Collecting of accounts (Table K11)
961 Noncash funds transfer (Table K11)
Including electronic funds transfer, and bill paying services
Investments
For tax measures see KL-KWX4 3553.3
961.5 General (Table K11)
Foreign investments see KL-KWX4 3202+
Stock exchange transactions. Securities
962 General (Table K11)
962.12.A-Z Particular types of securities, A-Z
962.12.M67 Mortgage-backed securities (Table K12)
962.5 Stockbrokers (Table K11)
962.7.A-Z Particular stock exchanges. By place, A-Z
Subarrange each by Table K12
Commodity exchanges. Produce exchanges
962.8 General (Table K11)
962.9.A-Z Particular commodity exchanges. By place, A-Z
Subarrange each by Table K12
Investment trust
963 General (Table K11)
964 Real estate investment trust (Table K11)
965 Trust investments (Table K11)
966 Criminal provisions (Table K11)
Including money laundering
967 Foreign exchange (Table K11)
Taxation of banking transactions see KL-KWX4 3640.B35
Taxation of stock exchange transactions see KL-KWX4 3640.S76
Maritime law
For regulatory aspects of water transportation, navigation, and pilotage see KL-KWX4 3470+

Commercial law. Commercial transactions
Maritime law -- Continued
970 General (Table K11)
970.3 Shipowners. Ship operators. Shipmasters (Table K11)
Affreightment. Carriage of goods at sea and inland waters
971 General (Table K11)
972 Freight forwarders
Including liability
973 Ocean bills of lading
974 Charter parties
975 Act of God. War. Act of government
976 Carriage of passengers at sea and inland waters
Including carriage of passengers' luggage
Average
978 General (Table K11)
979 Havarie grosse (Table K11)
Special average. Collision at sea
Cf. KL-KWX4 3470+ Water transportation
980 General (Table K11)
980.3 Criminal provisions (Table K11)
Insurance see KL-KWX4 985+
Salvage. Shipwreck
981 General (Table K11)
981.3 Criminal provisions (Table K11)
Ship creditors
982 General (Table K11)
983 Bottomry and respondentia. Ship mortgages. Maritime liens (Table K11)
984 Shipbrokers (Table K11)
984.3 Ship registers (Table K11)
984.5 Maritime courts (Table K11)
Prize courts
see KZ6640+
Marine insurance
985 General (Table K11)
Contract see KL-KWX4 985
986 Accidents. Average (Table K11)
986.3 Seaworthiness (Table K11)
Maritime social legislation
Including legislation for merchant mariners for inland navigation
987 General (Table K11)
Labor law for merchant mariners
987.5 General (Table K11)
988 Collective labor agreements. Maritime unions (Table K11)

Commercial law. Commercial transactions
Maritime law
Maritime social legislation
Labor law for merchant mariners -- Continued
991 Labor standards (Table K11)
Including hours of labor, wages, nonwage benefits, and vacations
993 Discipline (Table K11)
Social insurance for merchant mariners
Including all branches of social insurance
995 General (Table K11)
996 Organization and administration (Table K11)
Insurance law
Including regulation of insurance business
998 General (Table K11)
999 Insurance carriers. Private insurance associations (Table K11)
Including cooperatives, mutual companies, etc.
1001 State supervision (Table K11)
Including control of restraint of trade
Contract see KL-KWX4 998
1002 Limitation of risk (Table K11)
1004 Group insurance (Table K11)
1005 Adjustment of claims (Table K11)
1006 Agents. Brokers (Table K11)
Life insurance
1008 General (Table K11)
Contract. Parties to contract see KL-KWX4 1008
1009 Group insurance (Table K11)
1010 Old age pensions (Table K11)
1011 Survivors' benefits (Table K11)
1013 Health insurance. Medical care insurance (Table K11)
Accident insurance
1015 General (Table K11)
Contract. Parties to contract see KL-KWX4 1015
1016.A-Z Special topics, A-Z
1016.T72 Traveler's insurance (Table K12)
Property insurance
1018 General (Table K11)
1019 Multiple line insurance (Table K11)
Including home owners insurance
1020.A-Z Particular hazards, A-Z
Burglary see KL-KWX4 1020.T43
1020.F57 Fire (Table K12)
1020.T43 Theft. Burglary. Robbery (Table K12)
1020.W38 Water damage (Table K12)

Commercial law. Commercial transactions
Insurance law
Property insurance -- Continued
1022.A-Z Types of property and business, A-Z
Subarrange each by Table K12
Suretyship. Guaranty. Title insurance
1024 General (Table K11)
1025 Credit insurance (Table K11)
Pension trust insurance see KL-KWX4 1340
1025.5 Litigation insurance (Table K11)
1026 Mortgage insurance (Table K11)
Liability insurance
Including both statutory and private insurance
1027 General (Table K11)
Contract. Parties to contract see KL-KWX4 1027
1027.5 Limitation of risk (Table K11)
1028 Adjustment of claims (Table K11)
Other risks and damages
Traffic
1030 General (Table K11)
Automobiles
1031 General (Table K11)
Contract. Parties to contract see KL-KWX4 1031
1032.3 Adjustment of claims (Table K11)
1034 Automotive transportation (General) (Table K11)
Including trucking, bus lines, etc.
1035 Aviation (Table K11)
1036.A-Z Other special, A-Z
1036.N83 Nuclear hazards and damages (Table K12)
1036.P64 Pollution liability (Table K12)
1038 Reinsurance (Table K11)
Business associations
1040 General (Table K11)
1041 Constitutional aspects. Interdiction of private business associations (Table K11)
1042 Expropriation and nationalization of business associations (Table K11)
Personal companies. Unincorporated business associations
For civil companies see KL-KWX4 897+
1043 General (Table K11)
Contract. Articles of partnership
Including liberty of contract
1043.13 General (Table K11)
1043.14 Void and voidable contracts. Partnerhip de facto (Table K11)
1043.2 Registration (Table K11)

Commercial law. Commercial transactions
Business associations
Personal companies. Unincorporated business associations -- Continued
Partners
Including natural persons and juristic persons
1043.3 General (Table K11)
1043.35 Management (Table K11)
Including voting, resolutions, and objections
Entering, leaving, and exclusion of partners see KL-KWX4 1043.3
1043.4 Capital and profits (Table K11)
1043.5 Accounting. Financial statements. Auditing (Table K11)
Agency and prokura see KL-KWX4 924
1043.6 Liability (Table K11)
Including debtor and creditor and limitation of actions
Termination. Dissolution. Liquidation
1043.7 General (Table K11)
1043.8 Division and separation (Table K11)
1043.9 Inheritance and succession (Table K11)
Including executors and administrators
1045 Partnership (Table K11)
1047 Limited partnership (Table K11)
1049 Silent partners (Table K11)
Stock companies. Incorporated business associations
1050 General (Table K11)
1051 Foreign corporations (Table K11)
Stock corporations
1052 General (Table K11)
Incorporation and promoters
1053 General (Table K11)
Capital see KL-KWX4 1062
1053.3 Liability before registration (Table K11)
1053.4 Defective incorporation (Table K11)
1053.5 Domicile (Table K11)
1054 State supervision (Table K11)
1055 Registration and publicity (Table K11)
Organization and management
1056 General (Table K11)
Director or executive board
1057 General (Table K11)
1058.A-Z Special topics, A-Z
1058.D57 Dismissal (Table K12)
1058.E43 Election (Table K12)
1058.L33 Liability (Table K12)

Commercial law. Commercial transactions
Business associations
Stock companies. Incorporated business associations
Stock corporations
Organization and management -- Continued
1059 Board of controller and supervisors (Table K11)
For employees' representation in management see KL-KWX4 1370+
1059.5 Corporate legal departments (Table K11)
Stockholders' meetings see KL-KWX4 1078
Auditors see KL-KWX4 1075.5
1060 Liability. Relationship to third parties (Table K11)
Corporate finance
1061 General (Table K11)
1062 Capital stock (Table K11)
Including increase of capital
1063 Corporation ownership of its own stock or stock of other corporations (Table K11)
Securities
1064 General (Table K11)
1065 Stocks (Table K11)
Including bearer stock, common stock (with or without par value), and preferred stock
1067 Dividends and profits (Table K11)
Bonds
1068 General (Table K11)
1069 Bearer bonds (Table K11)
Including personal bonds (Inscribed bonds)
1070.A-Z Other, A-Z
1070.C54 Convertible bonds (Table K12)
1070.J68 Jouissance share (Table K12)
1070.M67 Mortgage bonds (Table K12)
1071 Trust investments (Table K11)
Accounting. Financial statements. Auditing
Cf. KL-KWX4 3562+ Tax accounting
1072 General (Table K11)
1073 Valuation (Table K11)
1074 Corporation reserves (Table K11)
1075 Pension trusts (Table K11)
Cf. KL-KWX4 1340 Labor law
1075.5 Auditors (Table K11)
Stocks and stockholders' rights. Stock transfer
1077 General (Table K11)
1078 Stockholders' meetings (Table K11)
Including voting, resolutions, confidential communications, etc.

Commercial law. Commercial transactions
Business associations
Stock companies. Incorporated business associations
Stock corporations
Stocks and stockholders' rights. Stock transfer -- Continued
1079 Minority stockholders (Table K11)
1080 Business report. Rendering of account (Table K11)
1081 Stockholders' pre-emption rights (Table K11)
1082 Loss of stockholders' rights (Table K11)
Including exclusion or leaving of shareholders and recall of stocks
1083.A-Z Types of corporations
1083.F36 Family corporations (Table K12)
1083.O64 One-person companies (Table K12)
Subsidiary and parent companies see KL-KWX4 1145
1085 Termination. Dissolution. Liquidation (Table K11)
Corporate reorganization see KL-KWX4 1147+
Consolidation and merger see KL-KWX4 1148
1086 Criminal provisions
1087 Partnership partly limited by shares (Table K11)
Private company
1090 General (Table K11)
Incorporation
1092 General (Table K11)
Capital see KL-KWX4 1102; KL-KWX4 1102
1093 Liability before registration (Table K11)
1093.3 Defective incorporation (Table K11)
1094 Domicile (Table K11)
1095 Registration and publicity (Table K11)
Organization and management
1096 General (Table K11)
Directors
1097 General (Table K11)
1098.A-Z Special topics, A-Z
Dismissal see KL-KWX4 1098.E43
1098.E43 Election. Dismissal (Table K12)
1098.L43 Legal status. Liability (Table K12)
1099 Board of controllers and supervisors (Table K11)
Stockholders' meetings see KL-KWX4 1106; KL-KWX4 1106
Liability see KL-KWX4 1090+
Company finance
1101 General (Table K11)

Commercial law. Commercial transactions
Business associations
Stock companies. Incorporated business associations
Private company
Company finance -- Continued
1102 Capital stock (Table K11)
Including increase and decrease
1102 Capital stock (Table K11)
Including increase and decrease
1103 Accounting. Financial statements. Auditing (Table K11)
Stock and stockholders' rights. Stock transfer
1104 General (Table K11)
1104 General (Table K11)
Stocks see KL-KWX4 1104; KL-KWX4 1104
1106 Stockholders' meetings (Table K11)
Including voting and resolutions
1106 Stockholders' meetings (Table K11)
Including voting and resolutions
1108 Succession. Inheritance (Table K11)
1109 Loss of stockholders' rights (Table K11)
Including exclusion or leaving of stockholders
Types of private companies
1112 Family corporations (Table K11)
1113 One-person companies (Table K11)
1114 Close corporations (Table K11)
1116 Multi-national corporation (Table K11)
1117 Colonial companies (History) (Table K11)
Cooperative societies
1120 General (Table K11)
1120 General (Table K11)
1121 Incorporation and promoters (Table K11)
1122 Registration and publicity (Table K11)
Organization and management
1123 General (Table K11)
1124 Executive board (Table K11)
1125 Board of controllers and supervisors (Table K11)
Membership meetings see KL-KWX4 1132; KL-KWX4 1132
Liability. Limited liability see KL-KWX4 1120; KL-KWX4 1120
Cooperatives' finance
1127 General (Table K11)
1128 Depositors' fund (Table K11)
1129 Accounting. Financial statements. Auditing (Table K11)
Membership

Commercial law. Commercial transactions
Business associations
Cooperative societies
Membership -- Continued
1131 General (Table K11)
1131 General (Table K11)
1132 Membership meetings (Table K11)
Including voting and resolutions
1132 Membership meetings (Table K11)
Including voting and resolutions
Leaving and entering of members see KL-KWX4 1131; KL-KWX4 1131
1133.A-Z Types of cooperative societies, A-Z
1133.C65 Consumer cooperatives (Table K12)
1134 Termination. Dissolution. Liquidation (Table K11)
Consolidation and merger see KL-KWX4 1148
Combinations. Industrial trusts
For government control see KL-KWX4 3223+
1137 General (Table K11)
1138 Consortium (Table K11)
1139 Joint ventures (Table K11)
Business concerns
1140 General (Table K11)
1141 Organization and management (Table K11)
1142 Accounting. Financial statements. Auditing (Table K11)
Liability see KL-KWX4 1140
1144 Holding company (Table K11)
1145 Subsidiary and parent company (Table K11)
Corporate reorganization
1147 General (Table K11)
1148 Consolidation and merger (Table K11)
For government control see KL-KWX4 3224
1150 Corporations and companies as partners and shareholders (Table K11)
1152.A-Z Special topics, A-Z
Subarrange each by Table K12
1153 Criminal provisions (Table K11)
Insolvency see KL-KWX4 1885+
Bankruptcy see KL-KWX4 1942+
Intellectual and industrial property
1155 General (Table K11)
Principles
1156 Intangible property (Table K11)
1157 Personality rights. Moral rights (Table K11)
Cf. KL-KWX4 521.5 Civil law
1158 Territoriality (Table K11)

Intellectual and industrial property -- Continued
Copyright
1160 General (Table K11)
1160.2 Authorship (Table K11)
Including multiple authorship and author cooperatives, and anonyms and pseudonyms
1160.23 Intangible property (Table K11)
1160.3 Plagiarism (Table K11)
1160.4 Procedures. Formalities (Table K11)
Including registration of claim, transfer, licenses, deposit, and notice
1160.5 Protected works (Table K11)
Including original works, subsequent rights, idea and title
Scope of protection
1160.6 General (Table K11)
1160.62 Personality rights (Table K11)
1160.63 Mechanical reproduction
Including documentation and dissemination, and fair use
1160.65 Exhibition rights (Table K11)
1160.7 Performing rights (Table K11)
Including societies and industrial trusts
Cf. KL-KWX4 1184 Quasi copyright
1160.73 Broadcasting rights (Table K11)
1160.75 Recording rights (Table K11)
Including phonographs, magnetic recorders, and jukeboxes
1160.76 Filming and photographing (Table K11)
1160.78 Translation (Table K11)
1160.8 Employees' copyright
1160.82 Duration and renewal (Table K11)
1160.9 Delicts. Torts (Table K11)
Branches of copyright
1165 Literary copyright (Table K11)
1170 Musical copyright (Table K11)
Fine art and photography
1175 General (Table K11)
Violation of rights in one's own picture see KL-KWX4 843.4
Motion pictures see KL-KWX4 1180+
1177 Designs and models (Table K11)
1179 Prints and labels (Table K11)
Including works of commercial art, catalogs, sample books, etc.
Motion pictures and television programs
1180 General (Table K11)
1182.A-Z Special topics, A-Z
1183 Computer programs (Table K11)

KL-KWX4–KL-KWX5

Intellectual and industrial property
Copyright
Branches of copyright -- Continued
1184 Quasi copyright and neighboring rights (Table K11)
Author and publisher
Including the publishing contract
1185 General (Table K11)
1186 Plays and stage productions (Table K11)
1187 Motion pictures (Table K11)
1188 Music (Table K11)
1189 Scientific literature (Table K11)
1190.A-Z Special topics, A-Z
1192 Litigation and execution (Table K11)
International copyright
see K1414+
Patent law and trademarks
1194 General (Table K11)
1195 Scope of protection (Table K11)
1197 Relation to antitrust laws (Table K11)
1200 Patent office (Table K11)
Patent practice and procedure
1202 General (Table K11)
Invention
Including priority and novelty
1203 General (Table K11)
1204 Legal status of inventors. Community of inventors (Table K11)
1205 Employees' invention and technological innovation (Table K11)
1206 Claim drafting (Table K11)
Including collision of patents
1207 Res judicata (Table K11)
1207.3 Fees (Table K11)
1208 Duration and renewal (Table K11)
1209.A-Z Types of patents, A-Z
Subarrange each by Table K12
1210.A-Z Patented products, processes, and engineering methods, A-Z
Subarrange each by Table K12
1210.P55 Plants (Table K12)
1212 Designs and utility models (Table K11)
Licenses
Including compulsory licenses and fees
1213 General (Table K11)
1214 Foreign licensing agreements (Table K11)
Including know-how

Intellectual and industrial property
Patent law and trademarks -- Continued
Patent litigation and infringements
1215 General (Table K11)
1216.A-Z Special topics, A-Z
Subarrange each by Table K12
1218 Patent attorneys (Table K11)
International uniform law on patents and trademarks
see K1501+
Trademarks
1220 General (Table K11)
1221.A-Z Types of trademarks, A-Z
1221.A25 Accompanying marks (Table K12)
1221.B7 Brand names and numerals (Table K12)
1221.C67 Marks of corporations (Table K12)
1221.F35 Famous and notorious marks (Table K12)
Notorious marks see KL-KWX4 1221.F35
1221.O74 Marks of origin (certificates) (Table K12)
1221.Q34 Quality marks (Table K12)
1221.S47 Service marks (Table K12)
1223 Scope of protection (Table K11)
1224 Relationship to antitrust law (Table K11)
Practice and procedure
1225 General (Table K11)
1226 Claim drafting and registration (Table K11)
Including collision of trademarks, use and compelled use of trademarks, and unused marks
1229 Transfer of trademarks (Table K11)
1230 Licenses. Foreign licensing agreements (Table K11)
1232 Litigation (Table K11)
Unfair competition
For restraint of trade see KL-KWX4 3220+
1234 General (Table K11)
1235 Public policy (Table K11)
Advertising
1237 General (Table K11)
1238 Disparagement of goods (Table K11)
Including comparative advertising
1240 Misleading representation. False claims (Table K11)
Including superlative advertising
1242 Testing of commercial products (Table K11)
1245 Imitation (Table K11)
Cf. KL-KWX4 1160.3 Plagiarism
1246 Pushing for sales (Table K11)
Including unordered merchandise by mail
Cf. KL-KWX4 869.5 Contracts

Intellectual and industrial property
Unfair competition -- Continued
1248 Special sales (Table K11)
1250 Rebates and premiums (Table K11)
1252 Price cutting (Table K11)
1253.A-Z By industry or occupation, A-Z
Delicts. Torts
Cf. KL-KWX4 834+ Civil law
1255 General (Table K11)
1256.A-Z Protected rights, A-Z
1256.T72 Trade and industrial secrets (Table K12)
1257.A-Z Torts, A-Z
Subarrange each by Table K12
1257.B69 Boycott (Table K12)
1257.B73 Breach of contract. Evasion (Table K12)
1257.B74 Bribery (Table K12)
1257.E58 Enticement (Table K12)
1257.E86 Espionage, Industrial (Table K12)
Evasion see KL-KWX4 1257.B73
Industrial espionage see KL-KWX4 1257.E86
1258 Practice and procedure (Table K11)
Including arbitration and award
Labor law
Including works on both labor law and social insurance, and private labor law as it applies to the labor contract and to the labor-management relationship
Criticism and reform see KL-KWX4 1468
1261-1270 General (Table K9c)
1272 Right and duty to work. Constitutional aspects (Table K11)
1273 Ideology and labor law (Table K11)
1274 Politics and labor (Table K11)
1275 Labor policies. Competition and incentives for high performance (Table K11)
Organization and administration
Class here works on national departments and boards of labor, national, state and local departments and boards, or departments and boards of several states or administrative districts
For departments or boards (several or individual) of an individual state or administrative district, see the state or district
1276 General (Table K11)
1277.A-Z Particular, A-Z
Subarrange each by Table K12
1278 Conflict of laws (Table K4)
Labor contract and employment
1279 General (Table K11)

Labor law
Labor contract and employment -- Continued
1280.A-Z Types of employment
1280.D68 Double employment (Table K12)
1280.P37 Part-time employment (Table K12)
1280.P47 Permanent employment (Table K12)
1280.P76 Probationary employment (Table K12)
1280.S83 Subcontracting (Table K12)
1280.S86 Supplementary employment (Table K12)
1280.T46 Temporary employment (Table K12)
Including seasonal work
Individual labor contract and collective agreements. Liberty of contract
1287 General (Table K11)
Working standards see KL-KWX4 1382
Works agreements see KL-KWX4 1355; KL-KWX4 1355
Principle of most favorable wage rate see KL-KWX4 1381
Freedom of employment and restraint on freedom of employment
1290 General (Table K11)
1292 Preferential employment (Table K11)
Including people with severe disabilities, veterans, sheltered workshops, etc.
Formation of contract
1295 General (Table K11)
1296 State and labor contract (Table K11)
1297.A-Z Clauses and terms, A-Z
1297.A34 Age limit (Table K12)
Operational changes. Relocation of enterprises see KL-KWX4 1311
Standardized labor conditions see KL-KWX4 1379+
1299 Formalities (Table K11)
Including hiring practices and selection
Parties to contract
1300 General (Table K11)
Parties to collective bargaining see KL-KWX4 1384+
Prohibition of discrimination in employment see KL-KWX4 1326+
1302 Void and voidable contracts. Immoral contracts (Table K11)
Extinction of employment
Cf. KL-KWX4 817+ Obligation
1303 General (Table K11)
1304 Dismissal and resignation of employees (Table K11)
Including economic crisis dismissal, layoff, short hours, suspension, reinstatement, dismissal wage, etc.

Labor law
Labor contract and employment
Extinction of employment -- Continued
1308.A-Z Other special topics, A-Z
Subarrange each by Table K12
Job security
1310 General (Table K11)
1311 Special provisions (Table K11)
Including changes of conditions, operational changes, automation, relocation of enterprise, etc.
1312 Procedure (Table K11)
1313.A-Z Protected groups, A-Z
Subarrange each by Table K12
Nonperformance
Cf. KL-KWX4 824+ Civil law
1315 General (Table K11)
1316 Breach of contract (Table K11)
Cf. KL-KWX4 1257.B73 Unfair competition
1318 Impossibility of performance (Table K11)
Including seasonal employment (weather conditions and seasonal industry), plant shutdown, automation, etc.
Liability
Including liability of employer, employee, and liability toward co-worker and third parties
1322 General (Table K11)
1323 Hazardous occupations (Table K11)
1324 Accidents (Table K11)
Cf. KL-KWX4 1430+ Labor hygiene and industrial safety
Cf. KL-KWX4 3015+ Police and public safety
Prohibition of discrimination in employment. Equal opportunity
1326 General (Table K11)
1327 Wage discrimination. Equal pay for equal work (Table K11)
1328.A-Z Groups discriminated against, A-Z
1328.A33 Aged. Older people (Table K12)
1328.A44 Alien laborers (Table K12)
1328.D58 Disabilities, People with (Table K12)
1328.H58 HIV-positive persons (Table K12)
Older people see KL-KWX4 1328.A33
People with disabilities see KL-KWX4 1328.D58
1328.W58 Women (Table K12)
Including sexual harassment of women
Wages
1330 General (Table K11)
Principle of most favored wage rate see KL-KWX4 1381
Types of wages and modes of remuneration

Labor law
Wages
Types of wages and modes of remuneration -- Continued
1332 Daywork. Piecework (Table K11)
1333 Incentive wages (Table K11)
Including bonus system, profit sharing, etc.
1334 Collective wages (Table K11)
1335 Adjustments. Cost-of-living adjustments (Table K11)
1336 Overtime payments (Table K11)
Including night differentials
1337 Time, place, and mode of payment (Table K11)
Nonwage payments and fringe benefits
1338 General (Table K11)
Pension and retirement plans
1339 General (Table K11)
1340 Pension trusts (Table K11)
Including insolvency insurance
1341.A-Z Other, A-Z
Subarrange each by Table K12
1343.A-Z Groups of employees or industries, A-Z
Subarrange each by Table K12
1343.T43 Teachers (Table K12)
1345 Employees' references (Table K11)
Labor-management relations
1347 General (Table K11)
1348 Constitutional aspects. Private autonomy. Property rights (Table K11)
1349 Political activities. Limitations (Table K11)
Works councils
Including election, organization, parliamentary practice, etc.
1350 General (Table K11)
1352 Works assembly (Table K11)
Works councils of business concerns see KL-KWX4 1370+
1353 Union participation (Table K11)
Employee participation in management and planning
1354 General (Table K11)
Constitutional aspects. Property rights see KL-KWX4 1348
1355 Works agreements (Table K11)
1355 Works agreements (Table K11)
Standardized labor conditions see KL-KWX4 1379+
Production tasks
1357 General (Table K11)
1358 Maximum increase of labor productivity (Table K11)
1359 Technological improvements of enterprise. Innovations (Table K11)
1360 Rationalization (Table K11)

Labor law
Labor-management relations
Employee participation in management and planning -- Continued
Labor standards and protection of labor
1362 General (Table K11)
1362.5 Profit sharing. Employee ownership (Table K11)
1363 Working hours (Table K11)
1364 Social (welfare) provisions (Table K11)
Including pension trusts, health insurance, housing, cafeterias, etc.
1365 Employee rules and discipline (Table K11)
Including procedure and penalties
Personnel management
1366 General (Table K11)
1367 Hiring. Dismissal. Transfer (Table K11)
Including occupational training or retraining, apprenticeship, etc.
For personnel questionnaires and tests see KL-KWX4 1299
1369 Economic policies (Table K11)
Including control of operational changes
Employee representation on board of controllers and supervisors
Including unincorporated and incorporated business associations, cooperative societies, industrial trusts, etc.
1370 General (Table K11)
1372.A-Z Industries, A-Z
Subarrange each by Table K12
1373 Youth representatives (Table K11)
1374.A-Z Industries and trades, A-Z
Subarrange each by Table K12
1375 Criminal provisions (Table K11)
Collective bargaining and labor agreements
1376 General (Table K11)
1377 Constitutional aspects (Table K11)
1378 Standards for conclusion of labor contracts (Table K11)
Standardized labor conditions
1379 General (Table K11)
1380.A-Z By industry, A-Z
Subarrange each by Table K12
1381 Most favorable wage (Table K11)
1382 Working standards (Table K11)
1383 Formation of contract (Table K11)
Parties to contract
1384 General (Table K11)

Labor law
Collective bargaining and labor agreements
Parties to contract -- Continued
Unions see KL-KWX4 1402+
Employers' associations see KL-KWX4 1406
1386 Validity, applicability, and effectiveness (Table K11)
Including planning periods
1387.A-Z By industry or occupation, A-Z
1387.C66 Construction industry (Table K12)
1387.E48 Educational personnel. School personnel (Table K12)
1387.E57 Entertainers (Table K12)
1387.H67 Hospital and medical personnel (Table K12)
1387.J68 Journalists (Table K12)
Medical personnel see KL-KWX4 1387.H67
School personnel see KL-KWX4 1387.E48
1387.T73 Transport workers (Table K12)
Collective labor disputes
1388 General (Table K11)
Constitutional aspects see KL-KWX4 1348
1389 Arbitration. Conciliation (Table K11)
Strikes and lockouts. Boycott
1390 General (Table K11)
1392 Picketing (Table K11)
Wildcat strikes. Sympathy strikes. Political strikes
1393 General (Table K11)
1394 Damages (Table K11)
1395 Criminal provisions (Table K11)
1396 Nonparticipants. Strike breakers (Table K11)
Corporate representation
1399 General (Table K11)
1400 Constitutional aspects. Freedom of coalition (Table K11)
Unions
1402 General (Table K11)
1403 Personality and capacity (Table K11)
1404 Union organization (Table K11)
Including election, legal status, etc. of officers
1406 Employers' associations (Table K11)
Protection of labor
1408 General (Table K11)
1409 Protection of human resources (Table K11)
Hours of labor
Including night work and Sunday labor
1410 General (Table K11)
1412 Overtime (Table K11)
Part-time employment see KL-KWX4 1280.P37
1413 Shifts (Table K11)

Labor law
Protection of labor
Hours of labor -- Continued
1414.A-Z By industry or type of employment, A-Z
Subarrange each by Table K12
Vacations
1415 General (Table K11)
1416 Constitutional aspects. Right to recreation (Table K11)
1417 Leave of absence (Table K11)
1418 Sick leave (Table K11)
1419 Holidays (Table K11)
1420 Cash compensation and holiday pay (Table K11)
1421.A-Z By industry or type of labor, A-Z
Subarrange each by Table K12
1422 Child and youth labor (Table K11)
Including hours of labor
Women's labor
Including hours of labor
1424 General (Table K11)
1426 Maternal welfare (Table K11)
1428 Home labor (Table K11)
Labor hygiene and industrial safety
Including safety regulations for equipment
1430 General (Table K11)
1432 Factory inspection (Table K11)
1433.A-Z By industry or type of labor, A-Z
1433.B84 Building and construction industry (Table K12)
1433.C48 Chemical industry (Table K12)
1433.M43 Medical personnel (Table K12)
1433.P35 Paper products industry (Table K12)
1433.P48 Petroleum industry (Table K12)
1433.P75 Printing industry (Table K12)
1434.A-Z By machinery, equipment, etc. A-Z
Subarrange each by Table K12
1435.A-Z Labor law for particular industries or occupations, A-Z
1435.A37 Agricultural laborers (Table K12)
1435.D66 Domestics (Table K12)
1435.E93 Executives (Table K12)
1435.T73 Transportation (Table K12)
Labor supply. Manpower control. Manpower planning
1437 General (Table K11)
1438.A-Z Particular agencies, A-Z
Subarrange each by Table K12
1439 Criminal provisions (Table K11)

Labor law -- Continued
Labor courts and procedure
Class here works on courts of several jurisdictions
For courts (several or individual) of an individual jurisdiction, see the jurisdiction
1440 General (Table K11)
1442.A-Z Particular courts, A-Z
Subarrange each by Table K12
Procedural principles
1443 General (Table K11)
1444 Due process of law (Table K11)
Including frivolous suits
1445 Parties to action (Table K11)
Pretrial procedures
1446 General (Table K11)
1447 Dispute commissions. Grievance boards (Table K11)
Procedure at first instance
1448 General (Table K11)
1450 Jurisdiction (Table K11)
Including competence in subject matter and venue
Actions and defense
1452 General (Table K11)
1454 Judicial review of grievance procedures (Table K11)
1455 Settlement (Table K11)
1457 Evidence. Burden of proof (Table K11)
Judgments. Judicial decisions
1458 General (Table K11)
1459 Res judicata (Table K11)
1460 Remedies. Appellate procedures (Table K11)
1462 Execution (Table K11)
1463 Costs (Table K11)
Arbitration
1464 General (Table K11)
1465.A-Z By trade or profession, A-Z
Subarrange each by Table K12
Competence conflicts between labor and social courts see KL-KWX4 2810

Social legislation
1468 Social reform and policies (Table K11)
Including all branches of social legislation and labor
1469 General (Table K11)
Social insurance. Social security
For works on both labor law and social insurance see KL-KWX4 1260.2+
Criticism and reform see KL-KWX4 1468+

Social legislation
Social insurance. Social security -- Continued
Information retrieval and electronic data processing see KL-KWX4 47.5
1472 General (Table K11)
1473 Constitutional aspects. Private autonomy and compulsory insurance (Table K11)
Organization and administration
Including insurance carriers
For national departments and boards of labor and social insurance see KL-KWX4 1276+
1474 General (Table K11)
1474.2 Corporate rights and personality (Table K11)
1474.3 Autonomy. Self-government (Table K11)
1474.4 Officials and employees (Table K11)
Including labor-management relations
1474.5 Finance
Including accounting and auditing, dues (employers' and employees' contribution), etc.
1474.8 State supervision (Table K11)
Coverage and benefits
1476 General (Table K11)
1478.A-Z Groups of beneficiaries, A-Z
Merchant mariners see KL-KWX4 995+
Miners see KL-KWX4 3365
1479.A-Z Special subjects applying to all branches of social insurance, A-Z
1480 Criminal provisions (Table K11)
1481 Conflict of laws (Table K11)
Health insurance (Compulsory)
For private health insurance see KL-KWX4 1013
For health insurance plans see KL-KWX4 1364
1483 General (Table K11)
1485 Right to insurance
1486 Organization and administration
1487.A-Z Coverage and benefits, A-Z
Subarrange each by Table K12
For public employees and officials see KL-KWX4 2978.4
1488.A-Z Groups of beneficiaries, A-Z
Subarrange each by Table K12
The medical profession and health insurance
1489 General (Table K11)
1490 Physicians employed by the health administration (Table K11)

Social legislation
Social insurance. Social security
Health insurance
The medical profession and health insurance -- Continued
1492 Hospitals and pharmacies under contract with the sickness fund (Table K11)
1493 Criminal provisions (Table K11)
Workers' compensation
Including occupational diseases
For merchant mariners see KL-KWX4 995+
1495 General (Table K11)
1498 Organization and administration (Table K11)
1498.5.A-Z Special topics, A-Z
1498.5.D56 Disability evaluation (Table K12)
1500.A-Z Coverage and benefits, A-Z
1501.A-Z Groups of beneficiaries, A-Z
1502 Criminal provisions (Table K11)
Old age, survivors and disability insurance (Compulsory)
For pensions and retirement plans of private enterprise see KL-KWX4 1339+
Social reform see KL-KWX4 1468+
1504 General (Table K11)
1506 Organization and administration
For merchant mariners see KL-KWX4 995+
For miners see KL-KWX4 3365
Social security taxes see KL-KWX4 3585
1508.A-Z Coverage and benefits, A-Z
1508.M43 Medical benefits
1508.O35 Occupational disability pensions
1508.O43 Old age pensions
1510.A-Z Groups of beneficiaries, A-Z
1510.C66 Construction workers (Table K12)
1510.L34 Laborers abroad
1510.P48 Petroleum industry workers
Unemployment insurance (Compulsory)
For pension trusts see KL-KWX4 1340
For civil service pensions see KL-KWX4 2978.4
1512 General (Table K11)
1514 Organization and administration
1516.A-Z Coverage and benefits, A-Z
1516.U53 Unemployment cash benefits
1518.A-Z Groups of beneficiaries, A-Z
Social services. Public welfare
Criticism and reform see KL-KWX4 1468
1520 General (Table K11)
Organization and administration

Social legislation
Social services. Public welfare
Organization and administration -- Continued
1522 General (Table K11)
1523 Practice and procedure (Table K11)
Including domicile
1524.A-Z Coverage and benefits, A-Z
Family planning. Family counseling see KL-KWX4 3124+
Infant welfare see KL-KWX4 1524.M38
1524.I57 Institutional care
For old age homes and nursing homes see KL-KWX4 3114.O42; KL-KWX4 3114.O42
1524.M38 Maternal and infant welfare
1524.R45 Rent subsidies
1525 Social work and social workers (Table K11)
Including rural social services
Social service beneficiaries
1528 The poor and destitute (Table K11)
1529 Older people (Table K11)
1530 Pensioners (Table K11)
1531 Large families (Table K11)
People with disabilities
Including people with physical, mental, and emotional disabilities
1532 General (Table K11)
1533.A-Z Coverage and benefits, A-Z
1533.R43 Rehabilitation (Table K12)
Cf. KL-KWX4 1292 Sheltered workshops
1534.A-Z Beneficiaries, A-Z
1534.B54 Blind (Table K12)
1534.D42 Deaf-mute (Table K12)
1534.S38 People with severe disabilities (Table K12)
1535 Asocial types (Table K11)
1536 Evacuated and homeless persons (Table K11)
War-related groups of beneficiaries
1537 General (Table K11)
1538 Refugees. Expelled or forcefully repatriated persons (Table K11)
1539 Prisoners of war and political prisoners. Veterans (Table K11)
1540 Services for war victims and war invalids (Table K11)
Children. Youth
1542 General (Table K11)
1543 Constitutional aspects (Table K11)
1544 Organization and administration (Table K11)
Including supervision of juvenile detention homes

Social legislation
Social services. Public welfare
Social service beneficiaries
Children. Youth -- Continued
Measures and provisions
1545 General (Table K11)
1546 Protection of children in public (Table K11)
Including restaurants, taverns, theaters, gambling, etc.
1547 Protection of children against obscenity (Table K11)
1548 Government guardianship (Table K11)
Custodial education. Collective education
1549 General (Table K11)
1550.A-Z Particular, A-Z
1550.O75 Orphanages (Table K12)
Disaster relief see KL-KWX4 3037
Social courts and procedure
Class here works on courts of several jurisdictions
For courts (several or individual) of an individual jurisdiction, see the jurisdiction
1552 General (Table K11)
1554.A-Z Particular courts, A-Z
Subarrange each by Table K12
1556 Procedural principles (Table K11)
1557 Parties to action (Table K11)
Pretrial procedures
1558 General (Table K11)
1559 Administrative remedies (Table K11)
Procedure at first instance
1560 General (Table K11)
1562 Jurisdiction (Table K11)
Including competence in subject matter and venue
1564 Judicial decisions and judgments (Table K11)
1565 Remedies. Appellate procedures (Table K11)
1567 Execution (Table K11)
1568 Costs (Table K11)
Competence conflicts between administrative, labor, and social courts see KL-KWX4 2810
Courts and procedure
The administration of justice. The organization of the judiciary
Including the administration of criminal justice
Criticism. Reform see KL-KWX4 470
1572 General (Table K11)
1574 The judiciary and foreign relations

Courts and procedure
The administration of justice. The organization of the judiciary -- Continued
1576 Organization and administration (Table K11)
Class here works on national and state departments of justice or departments of justice of several states
For the departments of justice of an individual state, see the state
Judicial statistics see KL-KWX4 30+
Judicial assistance see KL-KWX4 1642+
Criminal policy see KL-KWX4 3950+
Courts
Including courts of both criminal and civil jurisdiction
1580 General (Table K11)
Regular courts
Class here works on national (federal) courts and on courts of several jurisdictions
For courts (several or individual) of an individual jurisdiction, see the jurisdiction
1582 General (Table K11)
1583 Local courts. Municipal courts. Magistrate courts. Justice of the peace (Lowest courts). People's courts (Table K11)
Juvenile courts see KL-KWX4 4720+
1584 Regional courts. Provincial courts. District courts. District people's courts (Table K11)
1585 Courts of assizes. Juries (Table K11)
Including jury room proceedings
1586 Supreme courts of states or republics (Table K11)
National (Federal) supreme courts. Supreme courts of cassation
1587 General (Table K11)
Labor courts see KL-KWX4 1440+
Constitutional courts see KL-KWX4 2620+
Finance courts see KL-KWX4 3682+
Courts of special jurisdiction. Special tribunals
1588 General (Table K11)
Religious courts and councils
1588.4 General (Table K11)
1588.5 Sharia courts. Kadi courts (Table K11)
1588.6 Rabbinical courts (Table K11)
1588.8 Customary (native) courts of law (Table K11)
1589 Consular courts (Table K11)
1589.5 Mixed courts (Table K11)

Courts and procedure
Courts
Courts of special jurisdiction. Special tribunals
1590 Competence conflict courts (Table K11)
For competence conflicts between administrative, labor, and social courts see KL-KWX4 2810
1591 Courts of honor (Table K11)
Class here general works
For individual courts (Business) see KL-KWX4 3439
For individual courts (Professions) see KL-KWX4 3522
Other courts of special jurisdiction
see the subject, e.g. KL-KWX4 1440+ Labor courts; KL-KWX4 3770 Military courts; etc.
1591.5 Supreme judicial councils (Table K11)
1592 Special tribunal within a court (Table K11)
1593.A-Z Other public bodies with judicial functions, A-Z
1593.C65 Comrade's courts (Table K12)
1593.M85 Municipal arbitral boards (Table K12)
1594 Deliberating and voting. Secrecy (Table K11)
For jury room procedure see KL-KWX4 1585
1595 Court decorum and discipline. Conduct of court proceedings. Mass media (Table K11)
1596 Terms of court (Table K11)
1597 Judicial opinions. Advisory opinions (Table K11)
The legal profession
Including judicial officers and personnel, and including salaries, allowances, pensions, etc.
1600 General (Table K11)
Law school education see KL-KWX4 50+
1602 Post-law school education (Table K11)
1604 Judicial personnel other than lawyers (Table K11)
1605 Nationality and citizenship (Table K11)
1606.A-Z Minorities, A-Z
Subarrange each by Table K12
Judges
1610 General (Table K11)
Women judges see KL-KWX4 1606.A+
1612 Independence of judges (Table K11)
1613 Political activity of judges (Table K11)
1614 Ethics and discipline (Table K11)
Office of the public prosecutor. Procuracy
1615 General (Table K11)
1617 Supervision. Procuratorial supervision (Table K11)
1618 Jurisdiction (Table K11)
Notaries see KL-KWX4 1846+
Auxiliary personnel. Clerk's office

Courts and procedure
The legal profession
Auxiliary personnel. Clerk's office -- Continued
1620 General (Table K11)
Clerks to the court
1621 General (Table K11)
1623 Business administration. Court records (Table K11)
For personal data protection in information retrieval systems see KL-KWX4 844.5
1624 Bailiffs (Table K11)
Experts and expert witnesses
1626 General (Table K11)
1627 Medical examiners (Table K11)
For forensic medicine, see RA1001+
Practice of law
1629 General (Table K11)
Attorneys
1630 General (Table K11)
Admission to the bar see KL-KWX4 54+
1631 Legal ethics and etiquette (Table K11)
1632 Attorney and client (Table K11)
For violation of confidential disclosures see KL-KWX4 843.3; KL-KWX4 4164
1633 Law office management (Table K11)
Including secretaries' and clerks' handbooks, manuals, etc.
1634 Costs (Table K11)
For in forma pauperis see KL-KWX4 1639
Courts of honor. Disbarment see KL-KWX4 54+
1635.A-Z Special topics, A-Z
Subarrange each by Table K12
1636 Legal consultants (Table K11)
Procurators see KL-KWX4 1615+
1639 Legal aid. Legal services to the poor. Community legal services (Table K11)
For public defender see KL-KWX4 4630.D43
Professional associations see KL-KWX4 54+
Judicial assistance
Including judicial assistance in criminal matters
1642 General (Table K11)
1644 International judicial assistance (Table K11)
1646 Foreign judgments (Conflicts of laws) (Table K11)
Procedure in general
Class here works on civil and criminal procedure and works on civil, commercial, and labor procedure combined
1650 General (Table K11)
Procedural principles

Courts and procedure
Procedure in general
Procedural principles -- Continued
1651 Due process of law (Table K11)
1652 Uniformity of law application. Stare decisis (Table K11)
1653 Publicity and oral procedure (Table K11)
1654 Speedy trial. Court congestion and delay (Table K11)
Parties to action
1655 General (Table K11)
1656 Privileged parties (Table K11)
1657 Litigant. Plaintiff. Defendant (Table K11)
1658 Citizen suits (Table K11)
Pretrial procedures
1660 General (Table K11)
1662.A-Z Particular, A-Z
Subarrange each by Table K12
Procedure at first instance. Trial
1663 General (Table K11)
1664 Jurisdiction (Table K11)
Actions and defenses
1666 General (Table K11)
1667.A-Z Particular, A-Z
Subarrange each by Table K12
1668 Particular proceedings (Table K11)
Evidence. Burden of proof
1672 General (Table K11)
1673 Admission of evidence (Table K11)
Witnesses
1675 General (Table K11)
1676 Privileged witnesses (Confidential communication). Expert testimony (Table K11)
1676.7 Documentary evidence (Table K11)
1677.A-Z Special topics, A-Z
Subarrange each by Table K12
Judicial decisions
1679 General (Table K11)
1680.A-Z Particular decisions, A-Z
Subarrange each by Table K12
Remedies
1686 General (Table K11)
1687 Appellate procedures (Table K11)
1689 New trial. Reopening of a case (Table K11)
1690 Execution (Table K11)
1692 Costs. Fees (Table K11)
Civil procedure
1695 Criticism. Reform (Table K11)

Courts and procedure
Civil procedure -- Continued
1701-1710 General (Table K9c)
1712 Civil procedure law relating to other branches of the law (Table K11)
Procedural principles
1714 Due process of law (Table K11)
Including frivolous suits
1715 Stare decisis (Table K11)
1716 Publicity and oral procedure (Table K11)
Principles of evidence see KL-KWX4 1772
1718 Speedy trial (Table K11)
1719 Truthfulness and falsehood. Discovery (disclosure) (Table K11)
1720 Prejudicial actions (Table K11)
Parties to action
1722 General (Table K11)
1723 Juristic persons (Table K11)
1724 Privileged parties (Table K11)
Litigant. Plaintiff. Defendant
1725 General (Table K11)
Change of parties see KL-KWX4 1758.C53
1726 Judges (Table K11)
State prosecutor see KL-KWX4 1615+
Pretrial procedures
1728 General (Table K11)
1729 Summons, service of process, subpoena, etc. (Table K11)
1730 Time periods. Deadlines (Table K11)
Including default and restitution
1732 Suspension of procedure (Table K11)
Procedure at first instance
1734 General (Table K11)
Jurisdiction. Competence in subject matter and venue
1737 General (Table K11)
1738 Forum rei sitae (Table K11)
1739 Domicile or place of business (Table K11)
1740 Prorogation (Table K11)
1742 Venue for corporate bodies (Table K11)
1743 Capacity to sue and to be sued (Table K11)
1744 Right to litigate (Table K11)
1746 Representation. Power of attorney (Table K11)
Lis pendens see KL-KWX4 1756.L58
Res judicata see KL-KWX4 1756.R48
1748 Object at issue (Table K11)
Time periods. Deadlines see KL-KWX4 1730
Actions and defenses

Courts and procedure
Civil procedure
Procedure at first instance
Actions and defenses -- Continued
1749 General (Table K11)
Classification of actions see KL-KWX4 1789+
1750 Form requirements (Table K11)
1752 Joinder of actions. Compounded claims (Table K11)
1753 Amendment. Withdrawal (Table K11)
Defenses and exceptions
1755 General (Table K11)
1756.A-Z Defenses, A-Z
Counterclaim see KL-KWX4 1756.S48
1756.L55 Limitation of actions (Table K12)
1756.L58 Lis pendens (Table K12)
1756.R48 Res judicata (Table K12)
1756.S48 Set-off. Counterclaim (Cross section) (Table K12)
1758.A-Z Particular proceedings, A-Z
1758.C53 Change of parties (Table K12)
Including death of party
1758.C57 Class action. Citizen suits (Table K12)
1758.C66 Compromise (Table K12)
1758.C68 Contumacy (Table K12)
1758.D44 Decision without trial (Table K12)
1758.D46 Default judgments (Table K12)
1758.D57 Dismissal and nonsuit (Table K12)
1758.I62 Intervention (Table K12)
1758.I67 Interpleader (Table K12)
1758.S47 Settlement before trial (Table K12)
Evidence
1771 General (Table K11)
1772 Principles of evidence. Free evaluation of evidence (Table K11)
1773 Burden of proof (Table K11)
1774 Prima facie (Table K11)
Admission of evidence
1775 General (Table K11)
1776 Physical examinations. Blood tests (Table K11)
Cf. RA1001+, Forensic medicine
Witnesses
1777 General (Table K11)
1778 Privileged witnesses (Confidential communication) (Table K11)
Expert testimony
1779 General (Table K11)
1779.5.A-Z Particular groups of expert witnesses, A-Z

Courts and procedure
Civil procedure
Procedure at first instance
Evidence
Expert testimony
Particular groups of expert witnesses, A-Z -- Continued
1779.5.A35 Accountants. Auditors (Table K12)
Architects see KL-KWX4 1779.5.E63
1779.5.E63 Engineers. Architects (Table K12)
1780 Documentary evidence (Table K11)
1781 Circumstantial evidence (Table K11)
1782 Testimony of party (Table K11)
1783 Presumptions (Table K11)
1784 Oath (Table K11)
Including oath of witnesses and parties
Judicial decisions
1785 General (Table K11)
Judgment
1787 General (Table K11)
1788 Judicial discretion (Table K11)
Including equity
Types of judgment
1789 Judgments to do, to tolerate, to refrain from doing (Table K11)
1790 Declaratory judgment (Table K11)
1791 Motion to dismiss, and judgment in rem (Table K11)
1793 Agreed judgment (Table K11)
Judgment by default see KL-KWX4 1758.D46
Decision without trial see KL-KWX4 1758.D44
Dismissal and nonsuit see KL-KWX4 1758.D57
1795 Interlocutory decisions (Table K11)
1796 Void judgments and nonjudgments (Table K11)
1798 Mistakes (error) (Table K11)
Including correction or withdrawal of faulty decision
1799 Res judicata (Table K11)
1800 Court records. Minutes of evidence (Table K11)
Including clerks' mistakes and corrections
1802 Advisory opinions (Table K11)
Particular procedures
1804 General (Table K11)
Matrimonial actions see KL-KWX4 562
1807 Procedures in parent and child cases (Table K11)
For procedure in guardianship cases see KL-KWX4 624.2
1809 Interdiction. Mental competency procedure (Table K11)
1810 Public summons (Table K11)

Courts and procedure
Civil procedure
Special procedures -- Continued
Settlement before trial see KL-KWX4 1758.S47
1812 Hortatory procedures (Table K11)
1814 Small claims. Procedures before the justice of the peace or magistrate (Table K11)
Remedies
1816 General (Table K11)
1817 Injunctions. Arrest (Table K11)
1818 Reformatio in peius (Table K11)
1819 Recourse (Table K11)
Appellate procedure
1822 General (Table K11)
1824 Revision (Table K11)
1825 Cassation (Table K11)
1826 New trial. Reopening of a case (Table K11)
1828 Waiver of appeal (Table K11)
1829 Arbitration (Table K11)
Including commercial arbitration
1830 Costs
Including in forma pauperis
Noncontentious (ex parte) jurisdiction
1834 General (Table K11)
1835 Parties to action (Table K11)
1838 Evidence (Table K11)
1839 Decisions (Table K11)
1840 Remedies and special procedures (Table K11)
1842 Res judicata (Table K11)
Notaries. Notarial practice and procedure
Class here works on notaries of several jurisdictions
For notaries (several or individual) of an individual state, administrative district, or municipality, see the state, district, or municipality
1846 General (Table K11)
1847 Legal instruments. Certification (Table K11)
1848 Costs (Table K11)
Registration. Recording
Class here works on registers of several jurisdictions
For registers (several or individual) of an individual state, administrative district, or municipality, see the state, district or municipality
1850 General (Table K11)
1852 Publicity (Table K11)
Civil register
1854 General (Table K11)

Courts and procedure
Noncontentious (ex parte) jurisdiction
Registration. Recording
Civil register -- Continued
Registration of civil status
1856 General (Table K11)
1857 Family names (Table K11)
1860 Marriage (Table K11)
1862 Birth (Table K11)
1864 Death (Table K11)
For absence and presumption of death see KL-KWX4 514
1865 Aliens. Stateless foreigners (Table K11)
1866 Costs (Table K11)
1867 Register of matrimonial property (Table K11)
Land registers see KL-KWX4 737+
Ship registers see KL-KWX4 984.3
Commercial registers see KL-KWX4 925
Business associations (Personal companies) see KL-KWX4 1043.2
Business associations (Stock corporations) see KL-KWX4 1055
Domestic relations procedure
1870 General (Table K11)
1872 Adoption procedures (Table K11)
Guardianship court see KL-KWX4 624.2
Government guardianship see KL-KWX4 1548
Interdiction see KL-KWX4 628+
1880 Inheritance (Probate court) procedure (Table K11)
1882 Costs (Table K11)
Class here general works
For costs of a particular branch of noncontentious jurisdiction, see the branch
Insolvency
1885 General (Table K11)
1886 State of insolvency (Table K11)
Execution
1888 General (Table K11)
1890 Parties to execution (Table K11)
Including executors and administration, and succession during execution
Bailiffs see KL-KWX4 1624
1894 Titles for execution (Table K11)
Including judgments (res judicata), documents of title, etc., and provisional enforcement
Procedure in execution

Courts and procedure
Insolvency
Execution
Procedure in execution -- Continued
1896 General (Table K11)
1897 Discovery proceedings. Poor debtors oath (Table K11)
Including inventory
1900 Judicial decisions (Res judicata) (Table K11)
Execution for payment due
1902 General (Table K11)
Hortatory procedures see KL-KWX4 1812
1904 Attachment and garnishment of personal property (Table K11)
Attachment and garnishment of rights and choses in action
1906 General (Table K11)
1907 Pledges. Expectancies (Table K11)
Other, A-Z
Subarrange each by Table K12
1909 Judicial sale (Table K11)
Including transfer of ownership
1912 Distribution (Table K11)
1913 Detention of debtor (Table K11)
Poor debtors oath see KL-KWX4 1897
Remedies see KL-KWX4 1926+
1915 Execution in real property (Table K11)
Including foreclosure sale, judicial sale, and receivership
Exemptions and restrictions see KL-KWX4 1934+
1919 Enforcement of surrender of goods or documents (Table K11)
1920 Enforcement of acts (commissions or omissions) (Table K11)
1922 Executions against associations, personal companies, and corporations (Table K11)
Including execution against juristic persons of public law
1924 Injunction. Arrest. Seizure (Table K11)
1925 Astreinte (Fine for debtor's delay) (Table K11)
Remedies
1926 General (Table K11)
1927 Objections of third party claiming ownership and seeking release (Table K11)
1928 Costs (Table K11)
Protection against abuse of claims enforcement
1930 General (Table K11)
Moratorium see KL-KWX4 1975
1932 Suspension. Accord and satisfaction (Table K11)

Courts and procedure
Insolvency
Execution
Protection against abuse of claims enforcement -- Continued
1933 Compromise (Table K11)
Restriction of execution
1934 General (Table K11)
1935 Salaries. Wages. Pensions (Table K11)
1936 Support (Domestic relations) (Table K11)
1937 Minimum income. Beneficium competentiae (Table K11)
1938 Damages. Compensation for unjustified execution (Table K11)
1939.A-Z Special topics, A-Z
Subarrange each by Table K12
Bankruptcy
1942 General (Table K11)
1943 Court (Table K11)
Parties to action
1944 General (Table K11)
1945 Referee (Judge) (Table K11)
1946 Debtor and creditor (Table K11)
Including legal status, liability, etc.
1947 Trustees in bankruptcy. Receivers. Syndics (Table K11)
1948 Third parties (Table K11)
Including spouses (Matrimonial property)
1950 Insolvent estate (Table K11)
Including avoidance of transfers, and property not included in the bankrupt estate (exempted property)
Procedure in bankruptcy
1952 General (Table K11)
Priority of credits
1954 General (Table K11)
1956 Privileged and secured credits (Table K11)
1957.A-Z Particular secured or privileged credits, A-Z
1958 Distribution (Table K11)
1959 Composition to end bankruptcy (Table K11)
1961 Judicial review of voidable transactions
For fraudulent conveyances see KL-KWX4 4276
1963 Effect of bankruptcy on obligations and rights (Table K11)
1965 Costs (Table K11)
Debtors' relief
For wartime debtor's relief see KL-KWX4 3717
1970 General (Table K11)

Courts and procedure
Insolvency
Debtor's relief -- Continued
1972 Composition to avoid bankruptcy. Deferment of execution
Including receivership
1974 Corporate reorganization (Table K11)
1975 Moratorium (Table K11)
Costs
Including bookkeeping and accounting
1976 General (Table K11)
1978 Courts (Table K11)
Including witnesses and expert witnesses
Costs in special proceedings or special courts
see the subject, e.g. KL-KWX4 1634 Attorneys; KL-KWX4 1830 Civil procedure; KL-KWX4 1866 Civil registers; KL-KWX4 4850 Criminal courts
1979 Execution. Enforcement (Table K11)
Public law
Class here works on all aspects of public law, including early works
For civics see KL-KWX4 72
2000 General (Table K11)
The State
Including philosophy and theory of the state
For non-legal works on political theory, see JC
2010 General (Table K11)
2015 Sovereignty. Potestas (Table K11)
Federalism see KL-KWX4 2373
Centralization of powers see KL-KWX4 2260
Rule of law
2020 General (Table K11)
Socialist state
2025 General (Table K11)
2030 Democratic centralism (Table K11)
2035 Theocratic state (Table K11)
Including philosophy and theory of the theocratic state
Cf. BL65.S8 Religion in relation to the state
Constitutional law
For works on the constitutional aspects of a subject, see the subject
History see KL-KWX4 2101+
2050 Constitutional reform. Criticism. Polemic
For works on a particular constitution, see the constitution
2061 Bibliography
Including bibliography of constitutional history
2061.2 Periodicals
2062 Monographic series

Constitutional law -- Continued
Sources
Including early constitutions and related materials
2064 Collections. Compilations. By date
2064.5<date> Individual constitutions
Arrange chronologically by appending the date of adoption to this number and deleting any trailing zeros. Subarrange each by Table K17
2064.6<date> Individual sources other than constitutions
Arrange chronologically by appending the date of adoption or issuance to this number and deleting any trailing zeros. Subarrange by main entry
Court decisions
2066 Indexes and tables
2066.3 Serials
2066.5 Monographs. By date
2066.7 Digests. Analytical abstracts
Decisions of regulatory agencies. Orders. Rulings
2066.8 Serials
2066.9 Monographs. By date
2067 Collections of summaries of cases decided by courts or regulatory agencies
2067.3 Dictionaries. Encyclopedias
2067.4 Form books. Graphic materials
Yearbooks see KL-KWX4 2061.2
2069 Conferences. Symposia
Including papers devoted to the scholarly exploration of the subject of constitutional law
Collected works (nonserial) see KL-KWX4 2070
2070 General works. Treatises
Compends. Outlines. Examination aids. Popular works see KL-KWX4 2070
Addresses, essays, lectures see KL-KWX4 2070
Constitutional history
For individual constitutions see KL-KWX4 2064.5<date>
2090 General (Table K11)
By period
Ancient/Early to ca. 1800 see KL-KWX4 202+
From ca. 1800 to most recent constitution
Including periods of European colonization
2101 General (Table K11)
Constitutional principles
2110 General
2112 Legitimacy (Table K11)
2114 Legality (Table K11)
Rule of law see KL-KWX4 2020+

Constitutional law
Constitutional history
By period
From ca. 1800 to most recent constitution
Constitutional principles
2120 Sovereignty of parliament (Table K11)
2130 Rulers, princes, dynasties (Table K11)
Including dynastic rules and works on legal status and juristic personality of ruling houses
2140 Privileges of classes and particular groups. Rights of peerage (Table K11)
2150 Privileges, prerogatives, and immunities of rulers of states (Table K11)
2160 Sources and relationships of law (Table K11)
Intergovernmental relations. Jurisdiction
2170 General
2180 Federal-state (republic), national-provincial controversies. State-state or interprovincial disputes
Privileges, prerogatives, and immunities of particular states or estates see KL-KWX4 2150
2190 Distribution of legislative power. Exclusive and concurrent legislative power. Reservation of provincial legislation (Table K11)
2200.A-Z Special topics, A-Z
Class here works on topics not provided for elsewhere
For the history of a particular subject, see the subject
2200.S55 Slavery (Table K12)
2220 Interpretation and construction (Table K11)
Modern constitutional principles
2240 Legitimacy (Table K11)
2250 Legality. Socialist legality (Table K11)
Rule of law see KL-KWX4 2020+
2260 Centralization of powers (Table K11)
Separation and delegation of powers
2270 General (Table K11)
2275 Conflict of interests. Incompatibility of offices. Ethics in government (Table K11)
Executive privilege see KL-KWX4 2300
2280 Judicial review of legislative acts (Table K11)
2290 Privileges of classes (estates) and particular groups. Rights of peerage (Table K11)
2300 Privileges, prerogatives, and immunities of rulers of states (Table K11)
Sources and relationships of the law
2320 Preconstitutional and constitutional law (Table K11)

Constitutional law
Sources and relationships of the law -- Continued
2325 International law and municipal law (Table K11)
Statutory law and delegated legislation
2330 General (Table K11)
2335 Retroactivity (Table K11)
2340 Customary law and observances (Table K11)
2350 Socialist plans (Table K11)
2360 Decrees (individual) (Table K11)
Intergovernmental relations. Jurisdiction
2370 General (Table K11)
2373 Federalism (Table K11)
2375 Federal-state (republic), national-provincial controversies. Interstate (Interprovincial, etc.) disputes (Table K11)
2380 Cooperation of states, republics, provinces, etc. (Table K11)
2385 Exclusive and concurring jurisdiction (Table K11)
Including national (federal) and state (republic, province, etc.) jurisdiction
2390 National (Federal) territory (Table K11)
Including boundary disputes
Foreign relations
2400 General (Table K11)
Foreign service see KL-KWX4 2608
2410 Executive agreements (Table K11)
Foreign assistance programs see KL-KWX4 3205
2415 Neutrality (Table K11)
2420.A-Z Other, A-Z
Subarrange each by Table K12
Individual and state
Nationality and citizenship
For rights and status of citizens see KL-KWX4 518.7
2430 General (Table K11)
2432 Indigenous ancestry (Table K11)
2440 Immigration. Naturalization (Table K11)
For procedure see KL-KWX4 3023
2445 Expatriation (Table K11)
Emigration see KL-KWX4 3024
Statelessness see KL-KWX4 485.S8
2450.A-Z Particular groups, A-Z
2450.O84 Overseas communities. Descendants of émigrés (Table K12)
Human rights. Civil and political rights. Civic (socialist) duties
2460 General (Table K11)
Equality before the law. Antidiscrimination in general
2465 General (Table K11)

Constitutional law
Individual and state
Human rights. Civil and political rights. Civic (socialist) duties
Equality before the law. Antidiscrimination in general -- Continued
2467.A-Z Groups discriminated against, A-Z
2467.G39 Gay men. Lesbians (Table K12)
Jews see KL-KWX4 2467.M56
Lesbians see KL-KWX4 2467.G39
2467.M56 Minorities (Ethnic, religious, racial, and national) (Table K12)
2467.W65 Women (Table K12)
2468.A-Z Special subjects, A-Z
Culture see KL-KWX4 2468.L36
2468.L36 Language and culture (Table K12)
For language regulation in general see KL-KWX4 3137.9
Freedom
2469 General (Table K11)
2470 Freedom of expression (Table K11)
2472 Freedom of religion and conscience (Table K11)
Freedom of thought and speech
2474 General (Table K11)
2476 Freedom of information (Table K11)
2478 Prohibition of censorship (Table K11)
2480 Right of opposition to government (Table K11)
2482 Freedom of movement (Table K11)
2483 Freedom of assembly, association, and demonstration (Table K11)
2484 Due process of law (Table K11)
2484.5 Right to life (Table K11)
2484.7 Privacy of communication. Official and private secrets (Table K11)
2485 Right to petition (Table K11)
2486 Right to resistance against government (Table K11)
2488 Political parties and mass organizations (Table K11)
Including subordinate or connected organizations, and pressure groups, etc.
2490 Internal security (Table K11)
Including control of subversive activities or groups
Organs of national government. Supreme organs of state power and state administration
Including federal and state government
2500 General (Table K11)
The people

Constitutional law
Organs of national government. Supreme organs of state power and state administration
The people -- Continued
2504 General (Table K11)
2505 Initiative and referendum. Plebiscite (Table K11)
Political parties see KL-KWX4 2488
2506 Election law (Table K11)
The legislature. Legislative power
2510 General (Table K11)
2512 Control of government (Table K11)
2514 Legislative bodies. People's assemblies (Table K11)
Including legislative bodies with one or two chambers, and including their presidium and other organs
Legislative process
Including parliamentary practice
2516 General (Table K11)
2518 Interpellation (Table K11)
2520 Bill drafting (Table K11)
Committees and councils
2522 General (Table K11)
2524 Economic councils (Table K11)
2525 Parliamentary minorities (Table K11)
2526 Lobbying (Table K11)
2528 Legislators (Table K11)
Including immunity, indemnity, incompatibility, etc.
Heads of state
2530 General (Table K11)
Kings, princes, and rulers. Traditional leaders
2532 General (Table K11)
2535.A-Z Special topics, A-Z
2535.A23 Abdication (Table K12)
2535.D9 Dynastic rules. Legal status of dynasty (Table K12)
2535.E43 Election (Table K12)
Legal status of dynasty see KL-KWX4 2535.D9
2535.S92 Succession to the throne (Table K12)
Presidents. Governors. Governors-General
2540 General (Table K11)
2544.A-Z Special topics, A-Z
2544.I58 Impeachment (Table K12)
2544.S83 Succession (Table K12)
2548 Collective heads of state. State councils. Presidential councils (Socialist) (Table K11)
Prerogatives and powers of the head of state
2550 General (Table K11)
2554 Crown privilege (Table K11)

Constitutional law
Organs of national government. Supreme organs of state power and state administration
Heads of state
Prerogatives and powers of the head of state -- Continued
2558 Treatymaking power (Table K11)
2562 Veto power (Table K11)
2564 War and emergency power (Table K11)
Other supreme organs
2570 Central People's Committee (Socialist) (Table K11)
2575 National (Federal) Executive Council (Socialist) (Table K11)
The executive branch. Government
National (Federal) Executive Councils (Socialist) see KL-KWX4 2575
Presidium. Presidential councils see KL-KWX4 2548
2580 The Prime Minister and the Cabinet (Table K11)
2585 Council of Ministers and other Supreme Councils of Control (Socialist) (Table K11)
Including presidium and other organs
Government departments, ministries, and other organizations of government
2600 General (Table K11)
Departments. Ministries
Class here works on several departments not related to a particular branch of law or subject
Including subordinate administrative divisions, councils, etc.
For works on several departments related to a branch of law or subject, as well as individual departments and their regulatory agencies, see the branch of law or subject
2602 General (Table K11)
Department of State. Foreign office
2604 General (Table K11)
2608 The foreign service (Table K11)
2610 Subordinate regulatory agencies (Table K11)
Class here works on several agencies
For an individual agency, see the branch of law or the subject
2612.A-Z Special boards, commissions, bureaus, task forces, etc. By name, A-Z
Subarrange each by Table K12
2613 The judiciary. Judicial power (Table K11)
2614.A-Z Special topics, A-Z
Subarrange each by Table K12
Constitutional courts (tribunals) and procedure

Constitutional law
Constitutional courts (tribunals) and procedure -- Continued
2620 General (Table K11)
2630 Court organization (Table K11)
2640 Procedural principles (Table K11)
2650 Jurisdiction (Table K11)
2660.A-Z Special topics, A-Z
Subarrange each by Table K12
2660.C65 Constitutional torts (Table K12)
2670 National emblem. Flag. Seal. Seat of government. National anthem (Table K11)
2672 Political oath (Table K11)
2674 Patriotic customs and observances (Table K11)
2676 Decorations of honor. Awards. Dignities (Table K11)
2677 Commemorative medals (Table K11)
Economic constitution see KL-KWX4 3191+
Colonial law
2680 General (Table K11)
2684.A-Z Particular, A-Z
Subarrange each by Table K12
State and religion
Class here works on the relationship of state and religion, regardless of denomination
For works on the internal law and government of religious corporations, sects, etc., see KB
For works on a particular subject, see the subject
Sources
Including constitutions, articles, injunctions, ordinances, enactments of the Parliament or the legislature affecting the religious order and life
Collections. Compilations
2685 Serials
2686 Monographs
2687.A-Z Individual sources, A-Z
2688 General (Table K11)
Constitutional aspects
Human rights. Fundamental rights and constitutional guaranties
(2689) General
see Table KL-KWX4 2460+
(2690) Freedom of religion. Freedom of worship
see Table KL-KWX4 2472
2692 Separation of religion and state. Independence of church (Table K11)

State and religion -- Continued
2693 Religious corporations, institutions, organizations, etc. (Table K11)
Including membership
2696 Autonomy of religious corporations, organizations, institutions, etc., and state control (Table K11)
Legal schools
2698 General (Table K11)
2699.A-Z Particular schools, A-Z
Subarrange each by Table K12
2700 Lands of religious corporations, sects, etc. (Table K11)
Including taxation and tax assessment, etc.
2702 Religious trusts. Charities. Endowments (Waqf), etc. (Table K11)
2707.A-Z Offenses against religion, A-Z
Subarrange each by Table K12
Class here works that can not be classed elsewhere
Religious courts see KL-KWX4 1588+
Administrative law
2711-2720 General (Table K9c)
Administrative principles
2722 Rule of the law (Table K11)
2724 Autonomy. Rulemaking power (Table K11)
2726 Limitation and freedom of administration (Table K11)
For abuse of administrative power. Ombudsman see KL-KWX4 2760
2728 People's participation in administration (Table K11)
Administrative process
2730 General (Table K11)
2732 Acts of government (Table K11)
Administrative acts
2735 General (Table K11)
2737 Classification of acts (Table K11)
2739 Defective acts (Table K11)
Judicial review of administrative acts see KL-KWX4 2790
2740 Recognition of foreign administrative acts (Table K11)
Legal transactions
2750 General (Table K11)
2754 Public contracts. Procurement (Table K11)
2757 Enforcement. Administrative sanctions (Table K11)
2760 Ombudsman. Control over abuse of administrative power (Table K11)
Administrative courts and procedure
2764 General (Table K11)
2770 Court organization (Table K11)
2780 Procedural principles (Table K11)

Administrative law
Administrative courts and procedure -- Continued
2785 Pretrial procedures. Administrative remedies (Table K11)
Including remonstration, administrative appeals, etc.
2790 Procedure. Judicial decisions. Remedies (Table K11)
Including judicial review of administrative acts
2795 Execution (Table K11)
2800 Arbitration (Table K11)
2810 Competence conflicts (Table K11)
Indemnification for acts performed by government
2820 General (Table K11)
Eminent domain. Nationalization. Public restraint on private property
Including procedure
Expropriation, or land appropriation by the state for regional land resettlement and land development plans
Cf. KL-KWX4 3056+ Public land law
2824 General (Table K11)
2825 Expropriation of land owned by virtue of customary right of an individual or community (collectivité) for public utility's sake (Table K11)
2827 Declaration of land to state property and incorporation into state's private domain for public utility (Table K11)
Including unpopulated, under populated, derelict and underdeveloped (unexploited) land
2829 Categories of land (Table K11)
Including agricultural, grazing, hunting, and forest land
2833 Indemnity and compensation (Table K11)
Government liability
2840 General (Table K11)
2845 Acts of government (Table K11)
2850 Administrative and judicial acts (Table K11)
2852.A-Z Other, A-Z
Reparation see KL-KWX4 2852.V52
2852.V52 Victims of crimes, Compensation to. Reparation (Table K12)
Administrative organization
2860 Centralization and decentralization in government (Table K11)
2864 State supervision and enforcement (Table K11)
2866 State apparatus. Interagency relations (Table K11)
2868 Collegial structure (Table K11)
Juristic persons of public law
2875 General (Table K11)
Public corporations

Administrative law
Administrative organization
Juristic persons of public law
Public corporations -- Continued
2877 General (Table K11)
2880 Regional corporations (Table K11)
Class here general works
For local government see KL-KWX4 2920+
For municipal government see KL-KWX4 2937+
For special districts see KL-KWX4 2964+
2885 Cooperative societies of public law (Table K11)
Class here general works
For particular cooperative societies, see the subject, e.g. Agricultural cooperative societies
2888 Public institutions (Table K11)
2890 Public foundations (Table K11)
Cf. KL-KWX4 526 Foundations in civil law
2893 Government business enterprises (Table K11)
Including government controlled business enterprises
For particular enterprises, see the subject
Administrative departments of national government
Including federal and central government
2898 Department of the Interior (Table K11)
2905 Subordinate regulatory agencies (Table K11)
For particular agencies, see the subject
Special councils, commissions, etc.
2910 General (Table K11)
Ombudsman see KL-KWX4 2760
Administrative departments of the states, republics, etc.
2915 General (Table K11)
2917 Department of the Interior (Table K11)
Administrative and political divisions. Local government other than municipal
Including those of centralized national governments or federal governments
2920 General (Table K11)
2923 Self-government and state supervision (Table K11)
2928 Councils, boards, standing commissions (Table K11)
2935.A-Z Particular administrative districts, counties, regions, etc., A-Z
Including official gazettes, bylaws, statutory orders, regulations, and general works, as well as works on specific legal topics
Municipal government
2937 General (Table K11)
2938 Autonomy and rulemaking power (Table K11)

Administrative law
Administrative organization
Municipal government -- Continued
2939 Self-government and state supervision (Table K11)
2940 Municipal territory (Table K11)
Including boundaries and incorporation
2940.5 Name. Flags. Insignia. Seals (Table K11)
Constitution and organization of municipal government
2942 General (Table K11)
2943 Legislative branch. Councils and civic associations (Table K11)
Executive branch. Officers and employees
Including elected and honorary offices
For works on the executive branch of an individual municipality, see the municipality
2945 General (Table K11)
2946 Mayor. City director (Table K11)
Municipal civil service see KL-KWX4 2989
2948.A-Z Special topics, A-Z
Subarrange each by Table K12
Municipal finance and economy
2950 General (Table K11)
2952 Property (Table K11)
Budget see KL-KWX4 3656
Municipal public services
2954 General (Table K11)
Public utilities
For regulation of energy industry see KL-KWX4 3431+
2955 General (Table K11)
Electricity. Gas see KL-KWX4 3432+
2956 Water. Sewage (Table K11)
For ecological aspects see KL-KWX4 3131
2958 Trash collection (Table K11)
2960 Public transportation (Table K11)
Supramunicipal corporation and cooperation
2962 General (Table K11)
Special districts
For special districts within a particular state (Land, canton, etc.), see the state, republic, etc.
2964 General (Table K11)
2965.A-Z Particular types of districts, A-Z
Subarrange each by Table K12
For water districts see KL-KWX4 3052.A+
2967 Federation of municipal corporations (Table K11)
Civil service. Public officials and functionaries

Civil service. Public officials and functionaries -- Continued
2970 General (Table K11)
2972 Tenure (Table K11)
2973 Official (superior) order (Table K11)
2974 Incompatibility of offices (Table K11)
2975 Appointment and election (Table K11)
2977 Conditions of employment
Including discipline and illicit political activities
2978.4 Remuneration. Allowances. Retirement. Pensions, etc. (Table K11)
2979 Dismissal (Table K11)
Labor law and collective labor law
2980 General (Table K11)
Management-labor relations
2982 General (Table K11)
2983 Work councils (Table K11)
2984 Participation of employees in management (Table K11)
2984.5 Collective bargaining and labor agreement (Table K11)
2985 Collective labor disputes. Strikes (Table K11)
2986 Corporate representation (Table K11)
2987 State civil service (Table K11)
For works on the civil service of an individual state, republic, etc., see the state, republic, etc.
2989 Municipal civil service (Table K11)
For works on the civil service of an individual municipality, see the municipality
2990 Civil service of public corporations other than state or municipal (Table K11)
2992 Public officials and functionaries of the economic administration (Socialist) (Table K11)
Police and public safety
3000 General (Table K11)
Organization and administration
3001 General (Table K11)
3002 Licenses, concessions, permits (Table K11)
Police magistrates
Including procedure and penalties
3003 General (Table K11)
3005.A-Z Particular violations, A-Z
Begging see KL-KWX4 3005.V35
3005.V35 Vagrancy. Begging
3006 Police measures (Table K11)
Police force
3007 General (Table K11)
3008.A-Z Police forces, A-Z
3008.B67 Border patrols (Table K12)

Police and public safety
Police force
Police forces, A-Z -- Continued
3008.P74 Private police (Table K12)
3008.T73 Traffic police (Table K12)
Public safety
3009 General (Table K11)
3010 Weapons. Explosives (Table K11)
Including manufacturing, import, and trade of firearms and ammunition
Hazardous articles and processes
Including transportation by land
For product safety see KL-KWX4 846.5
For transportation by sea see KL-KWX4 3472+
3011 General (Table K11)
3012 Nuclear power. Reactors (Table K11)
Including protection from radiation, and including nuclear waste disposal
Cf. KL-KWX4 847.5 Torts
3013 Flammable materials (Table K11)
3014.A-Z Poisons and toxic substances, A-Z
3014.A83 Asbestos (Table K12)
3014.P34 Paint (Table K12)
Accident control
3015 General (Table K11)
3015.5.A-Z Particular, A-Z
Electric engineering see KL-KWX4 3015.5.E43
3015.5.E43 Electric installations. Electric engineering (Table K12)
Fire prevention and control
3016 General (Table K11)
3018 Theaters. Auditoriums (Table K11)
Including motion picture theaters and safety films
Flood control see KL-KWX4 3050
Weather bureaus. Meteorological stations see KL-KWX4 3513
Control of individuals
3022 General (Table K11)
Identification and registration
Including registration of residence
3022.2 General (Table K11)
Registration of birth, marriage, and death see KL-KWX4 1854+
3022.5 Identity cards (Table K11)
3022.7 Passports (Table K11)
3022.9.A-Z Other, A-Z
Subarrange each by Table K12

Police and public safety
Control of individuals -- Continued
3023 Immigration and naturalization. Procedure (Table K11)
For citizenship see KL-KWX4 2430+
3024 Emigration (Table K11)
For freedom of movement see KL-KWX4 2482
Particular groups
Aliens
Including homeless aliens and refugees
3025 General (Table K11)
3026 Temporary admission and residence (Table K11)
3026.5 Identification. Registration (Table K11)
3027 Restriction in political activities (Table K11)
3028 Employment. Business enterprise (Table K11)
Naturalization see KL-KWX4 3023
3029 Deportation (Table K11)
Minorities (Ethnic, religious, racial)
3031 General (Table K11)
3032.A-Z Particular groups, A-Z
3032.G96 Gypsies. Romanies
3032.K67 Koreans
3032.R88 Russians
3033 Traveling and transit traffic. Tourism (Table K11)
Including road traffic and traffic on inland waterways
Control of social activities
3034 General (Table K11)
3034.5 Vacationing (Table K11)
Including campgrounds, hostels, outdoor swimming facilities, etc.
Sport activities
Including corporate representation
3035 General (Table K11)
3035.5 Mass events (Table K11)
3036.A-Z Particular sports, A-Z
3036.A65 Aquatic sports (Table K12)
3036.S65 Soccer (Table K12)
3036.5.A-Z Other, A-Z
3036.5.D45 Demonstrations. Processions (Table K12)
3036.5.G35 Gambling (Table K12)
Including lotteries, games of chance, etc.
Processions see KL-KWX4 3036.5.D45
3036.5.T7 Traveling shows (Table K12)
Including circuses, puppet theaters, air shows, open-air shows, etc.
3037 Disaster control. Disaster relief (Table K11)
Public property

Public property. Public restraint on private property -- Continued
3040 General (Table K11)
Government property
3040.5 General (Table K11)
3041 Constitutional aspects. Interdiction of private ownership. Socialist theory of government property (Table K11)
Administration. Powers and control
3041.5 General (Table K11)
3042 Records management. Access to public records (Table K11)
Including data bases and general data protection
3043 Expropriation. Nationalization (Table K11)
For indemnification see KL-KWX4 2820+
For government-owned business enterprises see KL-KWX4 3217+
3043.5 Res communes omnium. Things in common use (Table K11)
Environmental planning. Conservation of natural resources see KL-KWX4 3129
Roads and highways
3043.7 General (Table K11)
3044 Interstate and state highways (Table K11)
3044.5.A-Z Other, A-Z
Subarrange each by Table K12
3044.7 Common use. Toll (Table K11)
3044.9 Construction and maintenance (Table K11)
Including regional planning
Safety see KL-KWX4 851+
Water resources
Including rivers, lakes, watercourses, etc.
3046 General (Table K11)
3046.5 Common use (Table K11)
3046.7 Water rights (Table K11)
Cf. KL-KWX4 698 Riparian rights in civil law
3047 Abutting property (Table K11)
Protection against pollution see KL-KWX4 3131
Development and conservation of water resources
3049 General (Table K11)
3050 Flood control (Table K11)
Including dams and dikes
Particular inland waterways and channels see KL-KWX4 3480.A+
3052.A-Z Particular bodies and districts. By name, A-Z
Subarrange each by Table K12
3053 Shore protection. Coastal zone management (Table K11)
Land reclamation. Irrigation. Drainage see KL-KWX4 3058

Public property. Public restraint on private property
3054 National preserves. Forests. Savannas (Table K11)
For wildlife conservation and wilderness preservation see KL-KWX4 3134+
Architectural landmarks and historic monuments see KL-KWX4 3183
Continental shelf and its resources see KL-KWX4 3347
Natural resources and mines see KL-KWX4 3350+
3055.5.A-Z Other, A-Z
Subarrange each by Table K12
Public land law
3056 Land reform and land policy. Legislation on new land systems (Table K11)
Including agrarian land policy legislation
Regional planning. Land development
Including resettlement and redistribution of population
3057 General (Table K11)
3057.3 Public land acquisition legislation (Table K11)
For incorporation of derelict, undeveloped (unexploited), and unoccupied (terres vacantes et sans maitre) land see KL-KWX4 2827
3057.5 Organization and administration (Table K11)
Class here works on task forces, land settlement authorities and commissions, development associations and trusteeship councils in restructuring the system of land holding, land settlement, and land use
3058 Public irrigation zones
Rural planning and development zones
3059 General (Table K11)
3060 Land settlement. Government constituted homesteads. Village settlement (Table K11)
National collective patrimony see KL-KWX4 685.5
Group lands. Terres collectives see KL-KWX4 686
Restoration of alienated land to customary ownership see KL-KWX4 687.7
3061 Consolidation of land holdings and reallocation (Table K11)
City planning and redevelopment
3062 General (Table K11)
3063 Consolidation of urban land holdings (Table K11)
Including procedure
3064 Zoning (Table K11)
Including procedure
3065 Assessment of utilities (Table K11)
Including sanitation

Public property
Public land law
Regional planning
Building and construction
Including administrative control and procedure
Cf. KL-KWX4 3402+ Building and construction industry
3067 General (Table K11)
3069 Adjoining landowners (Table K11)
3071 Building safety and control (Table K11)
3072.A-Z Special topics, A-Z
3072.B37 Barrier-free design (Table K12)
3072.E45 Elevators (Table K12)
Housing see KL-KWX4 885+
3073 Public works (Table K11)
Including public works contracts
Public health
3075 General (Table K11)
3076 Organization and administration (Table K11)
Class here works on national departments and boards, national, state, and local departments and boards, or departments and boards of several states or administrative districts
For departments and boards (several or individual) of an individual state or administrative district, see the state or district
3078 Burial and cemetery laws. Disposal of the dead (Table K11)
Including cremation
Contagious, infectious, and other diseases
3080 General (Table K11)
3082.A-Z Particular diseases, A-Z
3082.A53 AIDS (Table K12)
3082.C35 Cancer (Table K12)
3082.S27 SARS (Disease) (Table K12)
3082.T82 Tuberculosis (Table K12)
3082.V45 Venereal diseases (Table K12)
Public health measures
Including compulsory measures
3084 General (Table K11)
Immunization. Vaccination
3085 General (Table K11)
3086.A-Z Diseases, A-Z
3086.P65 Poliomyelitis (Table K12)
3086.S62 Smallpox (Table K12)
3087 Quarantine (Table K11)
Eugenics see KL-KWX4 3121+
Environmental pollution see KL-KWX4 3130+
3088.A-Z Other public health hazards and measures, A-Z

Public health
Other public health hazards and measures, A-Z -- Continued
3088.R43 Refuse disposal (Table K12)
3088.S77 Street cleaning (Table K12)
3089 Drinking water standards. Fluoridation (Table K11)
Food laws see KL-KWX4 3377+
Drug laws
3090 General (Table K11)
3091 Pharmaceutical procedures (Table K11)
3092 Narcotics. Opium legislation (Table K11)
Including psychopharmaca
3093 Poisons (Table K11)
3094 Pharmacists and pharmacies (Table K11)
3096 Trade regulation. Advertising (Table K11)
Including consumer protection
3097 Alcohol. Alcoholic beverages. Liquor laws (Table K11)
3097.5 Cosmetics (Table K11)
Medical legislation
3098 General (Table K11)
3098.5 Medical ethics
3099.A-Z Public institutions, agencies, and special bureaus. By name, A-Z
Subarrange each by Table K12
The health professions
Class here works on education, licensing, professional representation, fees, and liability
For malpractice, see individual professions
For medical ethics see 3098.5
General see KL-KWX4 3100
Physicians
Including works on medical personnel in general
3100 General (Table K11)
3100.5 Malpractice
Cf. KL-KWX4 4100 Offenses against the person
3101 Dentists. Dental hygienists (Table K11)
3103.A-Z Other, A-Z
3103.G96 Gynecologists. Obstetricians (Table K12)
3103.H42 Healers (Table K12)
Including herbalists, homeopathic physicians, naturopaths, etc.
3103.N87 Nutritionists (Table K12)
Obstetricians see KL-KWX4 3103.G96
3103.P79 Psychologists. Psychotherapists (Table K12)
3103.R33 Radiologists (Table K12)
Auxiliary medical professions. Paramedical professions
3104 General (Table K11)

Medical legislation
The health professions
Auxiliary medical professions. Paramedical professions -- Continued
3105 Nurses and nursing (Table K11)
3106 Midwives (Table K11)
3107 Physical therapists (Table K11)
3108.A-Z Health organizations. By name, A-Z
3108.R43 Red Cross (Table K12)
Cf. KL-KWX4 3037 Disaster relief
Hospitals and other medical institutions or health services
3110 General (Table K11)
3111 Health resorts and spas (Table K11)
3112 Blood banks (Table K11)
Including blood donations
3113 Institutions for the mentally ill (Table K11)
3113 Institutions for the mentally ill (Table K11)
3114.A-Z Other health organizations, institutions, or services, A-Z
Abortion clinics see KL-KWX4 3124+
3114.D39 Day care centers for infants and children
3114.E43 Emergency medical services
3114.L32 Laboratories, Medical
Nursing homes see KL-KWX4 3114.O42; KL-KWX4 3114.O42
3114.O42 Old age homes. Nursing homes
Including invalid adults
3114.O42 Old age homes. Nursing homes
Including invalid adults
3114.S35 School health services
Biomedical engineering. Medical technology
Including human experimentation in medicine
Cf. KL-KWX4 4096+ Criminal aspects of medicine
3115 General (Table K11)
3115.5 Genetic engineering (Table K11)
For artificial insemination (Human reproductive technology) see KL-KWX4 3117
3116 Transplantation of organs, tissues, etc. (Table K11)
Including donation of organs, tissues, etc.
3117 Human reproductive technology
Including artificial insemination, fertilization in vitro, etc.
Cf. KL-KWX4 619.A77 Family law
3119.A-Z Special topics, A-Z
3119.C65 Confidential communications (Table K12)
For data protection see KL-KWX4 844.5
3119.F45 Female circumcision (Table K12)
3119.I54 Informed consent (Table K12)

Medical legislation
Special topics, A-Z -- Continued
3119.M43 Medical instruments and apparatus. Medical devices (Table K12)
Disorders of character, behavior, and intelligence
3120 Alcoholism (Table K4)
Including works on treatment and rehabilitation
Eugenics. Sterilization and castration
3121 General (Table K11)
3121.5.A-Z Special topics, A-Z
3121.5.R46 Reproduction bans (mentally retarded)
Euthanasia see KL-KWX4 4058
3122 Veterinary medicine and hygiene. Veterinary public health (Table K11)
Animal protection. Animal welfare. Animal rights
Including prevention of cruelty to animals
For animal rights as a social issue see HV4701+
3123 General works (Table K11)
3123.2 Animal experimentation and research (Table K11)
Including vivisection and dissection
3123.3 Slaughtering of animals (Table K11)
3123.4.A-Z Other special topics, A-Z
3123.4.M86 Mutilation
Birth control. Family planning. Population control
Cf. KL-KWX4 4070 Illegal abortion (Criminal law)
3124 General (Table K11)
3125.A-Z Special topics, A-Z
3125.A36 Abortion, Forced, for population control
Environmental law
For civil liability see KL-KWX4 852.4
3127 General (Table K11)
3128 Organization and administration (Table K11)
3129 Environmental planning. Conservation of environmental resources (Table K11)
Environmental pollution
3130 General (Table K11)
3130.5 Air pollution (Table K11)
Including noxious gases, automobile emissions, tobacco smoking, etc.
3131 Water and groundwater pollution (Table K11)
Including pollutants and sewage control
Pollutants
3131.5 General (Table K11)
3132 Radioactive substances (Table K11)

Environmental law
Environmental pollution
Pollutants -- Continued
3132.5 Noise (Table K11)
Including traffic noise, and noise control
Cf. KL-KWX4 701.N84 Property
3133 Recycling of refuse (Table K11)
Wilderness preservation
Including natural monuments, parks, and forests
3134 General (Table K11)
3134.5 Constitutional right to recreation (Table K11)
3134.6 Plant protection (Table K11)
Wildlife conservation
Including game, birds, and fish
3135 General (Table K11)
Game laws and hunting see KL-KWX4 3337+
Fishery laws see KL-KWX4 3340+
Land reclamation in mining see KL-KWX4 3369.A+
Criminal provisions see KL-KWX4 4351.5+
Cultural affairs
3137 General (Table K11)
3137.5 Constitutional aspects. Freedom of science and the arts. Academic freedom (Table K11)
3137.7 Cultural policy. State encouragement of science and the arts (Table K11)
3137.8 Organization and administration (Table K11)
Class here works on national, state and/or local departments, boards, commissions, etc., of cultural affairs
For the department of cultural affairs of an individual state or district, see the state or district
3137.9 National language (Table K11)
Including regulation of use, purity, etc.
Education
3138 General (Table K11)
3138.3 Constitutional safeguards (Table K11)
3138.4 Boards and commissions (Table K11)
School government. School districts
Including curriculum and participation in school government in general
3138.55 General (Table K11)
3138.6 School discipline (Table K11)
Religious instruction see KL-KWX4 3158
Students
3139 General (Table K11)
3139.3 Constitutional aspects (Table K11)
Including right and duty to education

Cultural affairs
Education
Students -- Continued
3139.4 Compulsory education (Table K11)
Teachers. School functionaries (General)
For particular teachers, see the level of instruction, e.g. KL-KWX4 3152 University teachers
3140 General (Table K11)
3140.4 Constitutional aspects (Table K11)
Including freedom of speech
3140.5 Education and training (Table K11)
Including religious education
3140.7 Disciplinary power (Table K11)
3140.9 Preschool education (Table K11)
Elementary education
Including teachers
3141 General (Table K11)
3142 Rural schools (Table K11)
Education of children with disabilities
3143 General (Table K11)
3143.4 Children with social disabilities (Table K11)
Including orphans, outcasts, paupers, etc.
3143.6 Children with physical and mental disabilities (Table K11)
3144 Vocational education (Table K11)
Including teachers
Secondary education
3146 General (Table K11)
3146.6.A-Z Special topics, A-Z
Subarrange each by Table K12
3146.7.A-Z Schools and other institutions of secondary education. By place, A-Z
3146.8.A-Z Teaching methods and media, A-Z
Subarrange each by Table K12
Higher education. Universities
For legal education see KL-KWX4 50+
For research policies in higher education see KL-KWX4 3160
3147 General (Table K11)
3147.3 Constitutional aspects. Numerus clausus (Table K11)
3147.4 Intelligentsia (General) (Table K11)
Administration. Institutional management in higher education
3148 General (Table K11)
3148.3 Self-government and autonomy (Table K11)
3149 Disciplinary power and tribunals (Table K11)
3150.A-Z Special topics, A-Z

Cultural affairs
Education
Higher education. Universities
Administration. Institutional management in higher education
Special topics, A-Z -- Continued
3150.D45 Degrees (Table K12)
3152 Teachers (Table K11)
Including professors (ordinarii, extraordinarii, and emeriti), magisters, etc.
Students
3153 General (Table K11)
3153.7 Fellowships. Grants (Table K11)
3153.8 Selection for higher education (Table K11)
3154 Political activities (Table K11)
Including strikes
3154.3 Student societies (Table K11)
3155.A-Z Universities. By place, A-Z
3156.A-Z Other schools or institutions of higher education. By place, A-Z
Including colleges or institutes of technology, schools of music, art, drama, etc.
For academies see KL-KWX4 3162.A+
3157 Private schools (Table K11)
3158 Religious schools (e.g. Quran schools) (Table K11)
3158.5 Adult education (Table K11)
3159 Physical education. Sports (Table K11)
For liability for sports accidents see KL-KWX4 848+
Cf. KL-KWX4 3035+ Sports activities
Science and the arts
For constitutional guaranties see KL-KWX4 3137.5
3160 Public policies in research (Table K11)
Including research in higher education
Public institutions
3161 General (Table K11)
3162.A-Z Academies and institutes. By name, A-Z
Subarrange each by Table K12
3165.A-Z Branches and subjects, A-Z
3165.A35 Agricultural research (Table K12)
3165.A68 Antarctic research (Table K12)
3165.A72 Archaeology (Table K12)
3165.A75 Asia and Middle East studies (Table K12)
3165.C37 Cartography (Table K12)
Language see KL-KWX4 3137.9
Meteorology see KL-KWX4 3513
Oceanography see KL-KWX4 3470+

Cultural affairs
Science and the arts
Branches and subjects
3165.S73 Statistical services (Table K12)
For data protection see KL-KWX4 3042
The arts
3168 General (Table K11)
3169 Fine arts (Table K11)
Performing arts
3170 General (Table K11)
3171 Music. Musicians (Table K11)
Theater
Including managerial, performing, and technical staff
For copyright see KL-KWX4 1186
For labor contracts and collective labor agreement of stagehands see KL-KWX4 1387.A+
3172 General (Table K11)
3172.7 Playwrights. Contracts (Table K11)
Motion pictures
3173 General (Table K11)
3173.5 Regulation of industry (Table K11)
Including trade practice and censorship
3174 Screenwriters. Contracts (Table K11)
Public collections
3176 General (Table K11)
3177 Archives. Historic documents (Table K11)
Libraries
3179 General (Table K11)
3180.A-Z Types of libraries, A-Z
Subarrange each by Table K12
3180.3 Librarians and other library personnel (Table K11)
3180.5 Legal deposit of books (Table K11)
3182.2 Criminal provisions (Table K11)
Cf. KL-KWX4 1547 Protection of children against obscenity
3182.5 Museums and galleries (Table K11)
3183 Historic buildings and monuments. Architectural landmarks (Table K11)
Including vessels, battleships, archaeological sites, etc.
3184 Educational, scientific, and cultural exchanges (Table K11)
Economic law
3190 General (Table K11)
Economic constitution
3191 General (Table K11)

Economic law
Economic constitution -- Continued
3192 Theories and concepts (Table K11)
Including liberalism, national planning (planification), socialist theory of government ownership of resources, industries, distribution systems, etc.
3193 Organization and administration
Class here works on national departments and boards of commerce, national, state, and local departments and boards, or departments and boards of several states or administrative districts
For departments and boards (several or individual) of an individual state or administrative district, see the state or district
Government control and policy
3195 General (Table K11)
National planning
3197 General (Table K11)
3198 Planning agencies and bureaus (Table K11)
3199 Planning periods (Table K11)
Including Five-Year Plans, Two-Year Plans, etc., and including techniques and methods of planning
3200 Contract systems. Systems of cooperation (Table K11)
3201 Expansion control (Table K11)
Including business cycles
Investments. Investment control
Including foreign investments
3202 General (Table K11)
3203 Funds (Table K11)
3204.A-Z By industry or project, A-Z
Subarrange each by Table K12
3205 Assistance to developing countries (Table K11)
For tax measures see KL-KWX4 3553.5
Economic assistance
3206 General (Table K11)
Subsidies
3207 General (Table K11)
3207.3 Investment credits (Table K11)
Agricultural credits see KL-KWX4 3322
3208 Marketing orders (Table K11)
Class here general works
For particular marketing orders, see the subject, e.g. Agriculture
Prices and price control
3210 General (Table K11)
3211.A-Z Industries, services, or products, A-Z
Subarrange each by Table K12

Economic law
Government control and policy
Prices and price control -- Continued
Price delicts see KL-KWX4 4290
3212 Distribution (Table K11)
Money see KL-KWX4 3534+
Foreign exchange control see KL-KWX4 3538+
Industrial priorities, allocations, and circulation
Including organizations
For industrial priorities and allocations in wartime see KL-KWX4 3720
3213 General (Table K11)
3214.A-Z Raw materials, A-Z
Subarrange each by Table K12
3215.A-Z Industries or products, A-Z
3215.D44 Defense industries (Table K12)
Rationing see KL-KWX4 3724
Government business enterprises
3217 General (Table K11)
3218 Central administration (Table K11)
Including local administration
3219.A-Z By industry, A-Z
Subarrange each by Table K12
Control of contracts and combinations in restraint of trade. Competition rules
For unfair competition see KL-KWX4 1234+
3220 General (Table K11)
3220.3 Constitutional aspects (Table K11)
3222 Antidiscrimination (Table K11)
Horizontal and vertical combinations
3223 General (Table K11)
3224 Corporate consolidation, merger, etc. (Table K11)
Cartels
3225 General (Table K11)
3227.A-Z Types of cartels, A-Z
Subarrange each by Table K12
3228.A-Z Industries, occupations, etc., A-Z
Subarrange each by Table K12
For works relating to an individual company see KL-KWX4 3248.A+
Combines (Socialist)
3229 General (Table K11)
3230.A-Z By industry, A-Z
Subarrange each by Table K12
3231 Exclusive dealing or use arrangements. Requirement contracts (Table K11)

Economic law
Government control and policy
Control of contracts and combinations in restraint of trade. Competition rules
Horizontal and vertical combinations -- Continued
3232 Restraint-of-competition clause in labor relations (Table K11)
Including collective labor agreement clauses
3233 Restraint-of-competition clause in business concern contracts and in articles of incorporation and partnership (Table K11)
Price maintenance and open price system
3235 General (Table K11)
3236.A-Z Industries, products, etc., A-Z
Subarrange each by Table K12
3237 Licensing contracts (Table K11)
3238 DIN-norms (Table K11)
3239 Standardized forms of contract (Table K11)
Monopolies. Oligopolies. Antitrust law
For government monopolies see KL-KWX4 3639
3242 General (Table K11)
3243 Market dominance (Table K11)
Cartel agencies and procedure
Including procedures
3244 General (Table K11)
3246 Cartel register (Table K11)
Including procedure
3247 Damages (Private law) and indemnification (Public law) (Table K11)
Criminal provisions see KL-KWX4 4286+
3248.A-Z Mergers, cartels, combinations, business concerns, etc., A-Z
Subarrange each by Table K12
3249 Small business (Table K11)
Cooperative societies
3250 General (Table K11)
3251.A-Z By industry, A-Z
Subarrange each by Table K12
3253 Chambers of commerce (Table K11)
Boards of trade see KL-KWX4 3429.7
Money, currency, and foreign exchange control see KL-KWX4 3534+
Standards. Norms
For standards, grading, and quality control of agricultural or consumer products, see the product
3254 General (Table K11)

Economic law
Standards. Norms -- Continued
3255 Quality control (Table K11)
Weights and measures. Containers
3257 General (Table K11)
3258.A-Z By instrument, A-Z
Subarrange each by Table K12
Standardization
3259 General (Table K11)
Engineering standards
3260 General (Table K11)
3262.A-Z By material, A-Z
Subarrange each by Table K12
3263.A-Z By instrument, A-Z
Subarrange each by Table K12
Norms and standards for conservation of raw or scarce materials
Including recycling of refuse (Metal, glass, paper, wood, etc.)
3264 General (Table K11)
3265 Prohibition of industrial use of scarce materials (Table K11)
3266.A-Z By industry or product, A-Z
Subarrange each by Table K12
Price norms see KL-KWX4 3210+
3268 Labeling
Class here general works
For the labeling of particular goods or products, see the good or product
Regulation of industry, trade and commerce
3272 General (Table K11)
3272.5 Constitutional aspects (Table K11)
Including freedom of trade and commerce
For freedom of choice of occupation or profession see KL-KWX4 3515.5
3273 Licensing (Table K11)
3274 State supervision of installations (Table K11)
3276 Consumer protection (Table K11)
Advertising
3280 General (Table K11)
3282 Trade fairs and expositions (Table K11)
Including national and international fairs and expositions
3283.A-Z By industry or product, A-Z
Subarrange each by Table K12
3284.A-Z By medium, A-Z
Subarrange each by Table K12
Testing of commercial products see KL-KWX4 1242

Economic law
Regulation of industry, trade and commerce
Primary production. Extractive industries
Agriculture. Forestry. Rural law
Land reform and agrarian land policy see KL-KWX4 3056
3295 General (Table K11)
Organization and administration
3296 General (Table K11)
3297.A-Z Particular organizations, agricultural science and research institutions, etc. A-Z
Subarrange each by Table K12
3299 Conservation of agricultural and forestry lands (Table K11)
Including soil conservation, field irrigation, erosion control
Cf. KL-KWX4 3369.A+ Land reclamation
3300 Control of agricultural pests, plant diseases, predatory animals (Table K11)
Including weed control, plant import, and quarantine
Rural housing see KL-KWX4 3313
Rural schools see KL-KWX4 3142
3306 Agricultural contracts
Leasing of rural property. Farm tenancy (individual)
Class here civil law provisions as well as legislation aimed at protection and stability for land settlement
3310 General (Table K11)
3311 Farm equipment leasing (Table K11)
3313 Rural housing (Table K11)
3314 Collective farming (Table K11)
Agricultural cooperatives
3316 General (Table K11)
3317 Producers and marketing cooperatives (Table K11)
Including grazing associations
Including administration, management, membership, etc.
Cf. KL-KWX4 3059+ Rural planning and development
3318 Government agricultural enterprises (Table K11)
Including central and local government
Marketing orders
3320 General (Table K11)
3320.5.A-Z By commodity, A-Z
3320.5.G7 Grain
Economic assistance
3321 General (Table K11)
3322 Agricultural credits, loans, mortgages, etc. (Table K11)

Economic law
Regulation of industry, trade and commerce
Primary production. Extractive industries
Agriculture. Forestry. Rural law
Marketing orders
Economic assistance -- Continued
3323 Production control and quotas. Price support and regulations (Table K11)
3324 Distribution of seed grain, fertilizer, pesticides, etc. (Table K11)
Priorities, allocations, and distribution
3325 General (Table K11)
3325.5.A-Z By product, commodity,. etc., A-Z
Subarrange each by Table K12
3325.8 Standards and grading (Table K11)
Importing and stockpiling
3326 General (Table K11)
Rationing see KL-KWX4 3724
3326.5.A-Z Field crops, A-Z
3326.5.C63 Coffee
3326.5.S93 Sugar
Livestock industry and trade
3327 General (Table K11)
3328.A-Z Particular, A-Z
Subarrange each by Table K12
Milk production. Dairy farming
3329 General (Table K11)
3329.5.A-Z Products, A-Z
Subarrange each by Table K12
3330 Agricultural courts and procedure (Table K11)
3332 Criminal provisions (Table K11)
3333 Viticulture (Table K11)
3334 Apiculture. Beekeeping (Table K11)
3335 Horticulture (Table K11)
Forestry
Including timber laws
3336 General (Table K11)
Game laws
3337 General (Table K11)
3338 Game leases and licenses (Table K11)
Fishery
For conservation and ecological aspects see KL-KWX4 3135+
3340 General (Table K11)
3342.A-Z Particular fish or marine fauna, A-Z
Subarrange each by Table K12

Economic law
Regulation of industry, trade, and commerce
Primary production. Extractive industries
Fishery
Sport fishing see KL-KWX4 3036.A+
Mining and quarrying
Including metallurgy
3344 General (Table K11)
3345 Constitutional aspects. Government ownership or rights to mines and mineral resources (Table K11)
3346 Organization and administration (Table K11)
Class here works on national departments and boards, national, state, and local departments and boards, or departments and boards of several states or administrative districts
For departments and boards (several or individual) of an individual state or administrative district, see the state or district
3347 Continental shelf and its resources (Table K11)
Rights to mines and mineral resources
Including procedure and registration
3350 General (Table K11)
Public restraint on property rights and positions. Government rights see KL-KWX4 3345
3352 Adjoining landowners (Table K11)
Mining industry and finance
3353 General (Table K11)
3354 Economic assistance (Table K11)
3355 Corporations and cooperatives (Table K11)
3357 Planning and planning periods (Table K11)
Including calculation of reserves
Social legislation
3359 General (Table K11)
Labor law for miners
3360 General (Table K11)
3363 Unions (Table K11)
3364 Mine safety regulations. Rescue work (Table K11)
Including equipment
3365 Social insurance for miners (Table K11)
Including all branches of social insurance
Resources
Petroleum. Oil. Gas
3366 General (Table K11)
3366.3 Conservation (Table K11)
3366.5 Regulation of industry (Table K11)
Including concessions, trade practices, etc.

Economic law
Regulation of industry, trade and commerce
Primary production. Extractive industries
Mining and quarrying
Resources
Petroleum. Oil. Gas -- Continued
3367 Oil and gas leases (Table K11)
3367.3.A-Z Particular oil fields, reserves, etc., A-Z
Subarrange each by Table K12
3368.A-Z Particular companies, A-Z
Subarrange each by Table K12
3369.A-Z Other resources, A-Z
3369.C63 Coal (Table K12)
3369.C66 Copper (Table K12)
3369.D53 Diamonds. Gems (Table K12)
Gems see KL-KWX4 3369.D53
3369.S34 Salt (Table K12)
3369.T46 Tin (Table K12)
3370 Environmental laws. Land reclamation (Table K11)
Manufacturing industries
Including heavy and light industries
3372 General (Table K11)
3373.A-Z Types of manufacture, A-Z
3373.B56 Biotechnology industries (Table K12)
Energy industry see KL-KWX4 3431+
3373.F47 Fertilizer industry (Table K12)
3373.F87 Fur industry (Table K12)
3373.H68 Household appliances industry (Table K12)
3373.M34 Machinery industry (Table K12)
3373.R37 Rattan (Table K12)
3373.T48 Textiles (Table K12)
3373.T62 Tobacco products (Table K12)
3373.T68 Toy industry (Table K12)
3375 Recycling industries (Table K11)
Food processing industries. Food products
Class here works on trade practices, economic assistance, labeling, sanitation and quality inspection
Including regulation of adulteration and additives

3377 General (Table K11)
3378 Labeling (Table K11)
3379 Purity (Table K11)
Including regulation of adulteration and food additives
3380 Cereal products (Table K11)
3381 Fruits and vegetables (Table K11)
3382 Confectionary industry (Table K11)
3383 Meat (Table K11)

Economic law
Regulation of industry, trade and commerce
Food processing industries. Food products -- Continued
3384 Poultry products (Table K11)
3386 Egg products (Table K11)
Dairy products
3388 General (Table K11)
3390 Cheese (Table K11)
3392 Fishery products. Seafood (Table K11)
3393 Oils and fats (Table K11)
Beverages
3395 Brewing (Table K11)
3397 Winemaking (Table K11)
3398 Distilling (Table K11)
For taxation see KL-KWX4 3640.D58
3399 Mineral waters (Table K11)
3400.A-Z Related industries, A-Z
Subarrange each by Table K12
Building and construction industry
For building laws see KL-KWX4 3067+
3402 General (Table K11)
3403 Contracts and specifications (Table K11)
International trade
3405 General (Table K11)
3406 Organization and administration (Table K11)
Export and import controls
Including foreign trade practice and procedure
3407 General (Table K11)
Foreign exchange control see KL-KWX4 3538+
Trade agreements see KL-KWX4 3646+
3410 Export trade (Table K11)
3411 Commercial agents for foreign corporations (Table K11)
3413.A-Z By region or country, A-Z
3413.E87 European Economic Community countries (Table K12)
Domestic trade
For consumer protection see KL-KWX4 3276
3415 General (Table K11)
3415.5 Organization and administration (Table K11)
3415.6 Planning and planning periods (Table K11)
3416 Wholesale trade. Government wholesale trade (Table K11)
Retail trade. Government retail trade
Cf. KL-KWX4 3429+ Artisans
3418 General (Table K11)
3419 Conditions of trading (Table K11)
Including licensing and Sunday legislation

Economic law
Regulation of industry, trade and commerce
Domestic trade
Retail trade. Government retail trade -- Continued
3420.A-Z Modes of trading, A-Z
Chain stores see KL-KWX4 3420.D46
3420.D46 Department stores. Chain stores (Table K12)
3420.D57 Direct selling (Table K12)
Fairs see KL-KWX4 3420.M37
3420.M34 Mail-order business (Table K12)
3420.M37 Markets. Fairs (Table K12)
For trade fairs and expositions see KL-KWX4 3282
3420.P43 Peddling (Table K12)
3420.V45 Vending machines (Table K12)
3421 Cooperative retail trade (Table K11)
3422.A-Z Products, A-Z
3422.A88 Automobiles (Table K12)
3422.M48 Metals (Table K12)
Metals, Precious see KL-KWX4 3422.P73
3422.P46 Petroleum. Petroleum products (Table K12)
3422.P73 Precious metals (Table K12)
3422.R83 Rubber (Table K12)
Second-hand trade
3423 General (Table K11)
3423.5.A-Z Types of trade, A-Z
3423.5.A82 Auction houses (Table K12)
3423.5.P38 Pawnbrokers (Table K12)
Including charitable pawnbrokers
Service trades
3424 General (Table K11)
Old age homes see KL-KWX4 3114.A+
3424.5 Hotels, taverns, and restaurants (Table K11)
For railroad dining and sleeping cars see KL-KWX4 3461.3.A+
3425 Travel agencies. Tourist trade (Table K11)
3425.5.A-Z Other service trades, A-Z
3425.5.U53 Undertakers (Table K12)
Artisans
3426 General (Table K11)
3427 Apprentices (Table K11)
3428 Licensing and registration (Table K11)
Including examinations and examination boards, diplomas, etc.
Corporate representation
3429 General (Table K11)
3429.3 Cooperative societies (Table K11)

Economic law
Regulation of industry, trade and commerce
Artisans
Corporate representation -- Continued
3429.5 Trade associations (Table K11)
3429.7 Boards of trade (Table K11)
3430.A-Z Crafts, A-Z
Subarrange each by Table K12
Energy policy. Power supply
Including publicly and privately owned utilities
3431 General (Table K11)
3431.15 National, state, and local jurisdiction and supervision (Table K11)
3431.2 Planning and conservation (Table K11)
3431.25 Licensing (Table K11)
3431.3 Ratemaking (Table K11)
3431.4 Corporate structure (Table K11)
3431.5 Monopolies and freedom of contract (Table K11)
3431.6 Accounting. Taxation (Table K11)
3431.7 Engineering (Table K11)
Particular sources of power
3432 Electricity (Table K11)
3433 Gas. Natural gas (Table K11)
Water see KL-KWX4 2956
3435 Heat. Steam distributed by central plants (Table K11)
3436 Atomic energy (Table K11)
For protection from radiation see KL-KWX4 3012
For ecological aspects see KL-KWX4 3132
3437.A-Z Other sources of power, A-Z
3437.G46 Geothermal resources (Table K12)
3438 Industrial arbitral courts and procedure (Table K11)
3439 Business ethics. Courts of honor (Table K11)
Criminal provisions see KL-KWX4 4286+
Transportation
3440 General (Table K11)
3441 Organization and administration (Table K11)
Class here works on national departments and boards of transportation, national, state, and local departments and boards, or departments and boards of several states or administrative districts
For departments and boards (several or individual) of an individual state or administrative district, see the state or district
Road traffic. Automotive transportation
3442 General (Table K11)
Motor vehicles

Transportation
Road traffic. Automotive transportation
Motor vehicles -- Continued
3443 General (Table K11)
3443.5 Registration (Table K11)
3444 Safety equipment (Table K11)
3445 Drivers' licenses (Table K11)
Including driving schools and instructors
3446 Compulsory insurance (Table K11)
3447.A-Z Vehicles, A-Z
Traffic regulations and enforcement
3448 General (Table K11)
Traffic violations
For criminal interference with street traffic see KL-KWX4 4384+
3450 General (Table K11)
Driving while intoxicated see KL-KWX4 4386
Hit-and-run drivers see KL-KWX4 4390
3452 Traffic courts and procedure (Table K11)
Including fines
Highway safety
3453 General (Table K11)
3454.A-Z Particular provisions, A-Z
3454.C75 Crossings (Table K12)
3454.T7 Traffic signs (Table K12)
Carriage of passengers and goods
3455 General (Table K11)
3455.5 Passenger carriers. Bus lines. Taxicabs (Table K11)
Goods carriers
3456 General (Table K11)
3457 Ratemaking (Table K11)
3458 Sunday and holiday legislation (Table K11)
Railroads
3459 General (Table K11)
Operation of railroads
3460 General (Table K11)
3461 Railroad land. Right-of-way (Table K11)
3461.3.A-Z Rolling stock and equipment, A-Z
3461.3.D55 Dining cars (Table K12)
3461.3.S43 Sleeping cars (Table K12)
3462 Railroad safety (Table K11)
Including railroad crossings, etc. and liability
3464 Ratemaking (Table K11)
3464.3 Carriage of passengers and goods (Table K11)
3465.A-Z Kinds of railroads or railways, A-Z
3465.C32 Cable railways (Table K12)

Transportation
Railroads
Kinds of railroads or railways, A-Z -- Continued
Private-track railroads see KL-KWX4 3465.S42
3465.S42 Secondary railroads. Private-track railroads (Table K12)
3465.S98 Suspended railways (Table K12)
Criminal provisions see KL-KWX4 4382
Postal services see KL-KWX4 3485+
3466 Pipelines (Table K11)
Aviation. Air law
3467 General (Table K11)
3467.5 Aircraft. Nationality (Table K11)
For registration see KL-KWX4 935.4
3468 Air traffic rules (Table K11)
Including air safety and airworthiness
3468.3 Airports (Table K11)
3468.4 Pilots. Flight crew (Table K11)
Including licensing, wages, etc.
Liability see KL-KWX4 850
Crimes aboard aircraft see KL-KWX4 4396
3469 Space law (Table K11)
Water transportation
3470 General (Table K11)
Ships
3471 General (Table K11)
3471.3 Ship's papers (Table K11)
For registration see KL-KWX4 984.3
Safety regulations
3472 General (Table K11)
3472.3 Fire prevention (Table K11)
3472.4 Ship crews (Table K11)
3472.5.A-Z Types of cargo, A-Z
3472.5.D35 Dangerous articles (Table K12)
Navigation and pilotage
3473 General (Table K11)
3474 Rule of the road at sea (Table K11)
3475 Coastwise and inland navigation (Table K11)
Harbors and ports of entry
3476 General (Table K11)
3476.3.A-Z By name, A-Z
Subarrange each by Table K12
Coastwise and inland shipping
Including rafting
3478 General (Table K11)
3479 Carriage of passengers and goods (Table K11)
Cf. KL-KWX4 971+ Affreightment (Commercial law)

Transportation
Water transportation -- Continued
3480.A-Z Individual waterways and channels, A-Z
Subarrange each by Table K12
Marine labor law see KL-KWX4 987+
Marine insurance see KL-KWX4 985+
3480.5 Combined transportation (Table K11)
Communication. Mass media
3482 General (Table K11)
3483 Constitutional aspects. Freedom of communication. Censorship (Table K11)
3483.3 Policy. Competition between media (Table K11)
Postal services. Telecommunications
3485 General (Table K11)
Privacy of mail and telecommunication see KL-KWX4 3483
3485.5 Organization and administration (Table K11)
Class here works on national departments, national, state and local departments and boards of several states or administrative districts
For departments and boards (several or individual) of an individual state or administrative district, see the state or district
3485.7 Government monopoly (Table K11)
3485.8.A-Z Services other than mail, A-Z
Money orders see KL-KWX4 3485.8.P68
3485.8.P68 Postal notes. Money orders (Table K12)
3486 Rates. Postage. Modes of collection (Table K11)
Including postage stamps
Telecommunication
3487 General (Table K11)
3487.3 Installation and interference (Table K11)
3488 Telegraph (Table K11)
3489 Teletype and data transmission systems (Table K11)
Telephone
3490 General (Table K11)
3490.3 Rates (Table K11)
Including local and long distance rates
3490.5 Telephone lines (Table K11)
Including extensions
Radio communications
Including radio and television broadcasting
3491 General (Table K11)
Freedom of radio communication see KL-KWX4 3483
Competition between different media see KL-KWX4 3483.3
Organization and administration
Including national and state jurisdiction

Communication. Mass media
Radio communications
Organization and administration -- Continued
3492 General (Table K11)
3492.3 Private and public institutions. State supervision (Table K11)
Stations. Networks
Including frequency allocations and licensing
3494 General (Table K11)
3494.3 Post monopoly (Table K11)
3494.5 Amateur stations (Table K11)
Broadcasting
3495 General (Table K11)
Programming. Censorship
3496 General (Table K11)
3496.5.A-Z Programs, A-Z
Subarrange each by Table K12
3497 Labor law (Table K11)
Including collective labor law
3497.5.A-Z Stations, A-Z
Subarrange each by Table K12
Criminal provisions
3498 General (Table K11)
3498.3 Pirate stations (Table K11)
3499 Illegal operation of a station (Table K11)
Press law
3500 General (Table K11)
Freedom of the press and censorship see KL-KWX4 3483
3500.3 Right to information (Table K11)
3500.5 Organization and information. Institutions (Table K11)
Planning and planning periods
3502 General (Table K11)
3502.3.A-Z Types of literature, A-Z
3502.3.P47 Periodicals (Table K12)
3502.3.S34 Schoolbooks (Table K12)
Including all levels of education
Publishers and publishing
3503 General (Table K11)
3504 Government publishing enterprises (Table K11)
Including central administration
3504.3 Journalists. Domestic and foreign correspondents (Table K11)
Including liability
Bookdealers
3504.5 General (Table K11)
3505 Government enterprises (Table K11)

Communication. Mass media
Press law
Publishers and publishing -- Continued
3506 Right to obtain retraction or restatement of facts by offender (or an opportunity to reply) (Table K11)
3506.3.A-Z Special topics, A-Z
3506.3.P37 Party press (Table K12)
3506.3.P65 Political advertising (Table K12)
3506.3.R48 Resistance. Underground press (Table K12)
3506.3.U54 University press (Table K12)
Underground press see KL-KWX4 3506.3.R48
3506.3.Y68 Youth press (Table K12)
Press and criminal justice
3507 General (Table K11)
3507.3 Newspaper court reporting (Table K11)
Press delicts
Including works on both press delicts and particular procedures
For criminal procedure in general see KL-KWX4 4614
3508 General (Table K11)
3510 Liability (Table K11)
Libel and slander
3510.5 General (Table K11)
3510.6 Privileged comment (Table K11)
Right to obtain retraction or restatement of facts (or an opportunity to reply) see KL-KWX4 3506
3510.7 Treason by publishing official secrets (Table K11)
Cf. KL-KWX4 4442 Treasonable espionage
3511 Contempt of court (Table K11)
3512 Information services. Databases (Table K11)
3513 Weather bureau. Meteorological stations (Table K11)
Professions. Intelligentsia
3515 General (Table K11)
3515.5 Constitutional aspects (Table K11)
Including freedom of choice of occupation
Violation of confidential communication see KL-KWX4 4164
3516 Professional associations (Table K11)
For particular professional associations, see the profession
Individual professions
Including technical intelligentsia of government industrial enterprises; and including education, licensing, liability, etc.
Health professions see KL-KWX4 3098+
Pharmacists see KL-KWX4 3094
Veterinarians see KL-KWX4 3122
Attorneys see KL-KWX4 1630+
Economic and financial advisors

Professions. Intelligentsia (Socialist)
Individual professions
Economic and financial advisors -- Continued
3517 Accountants (Table K11)
3518 Auditors (Table K11)
Tax consultants see KL-KWX4 3562.5
Engineering and construction
3519 Architects (Table K11)
3520 Engineers (Table K11)
3521.A-Z Other professions, A-Z
3521.A67 Appraisers (Table K12)
Graphic artists see KL-KWX4 3521.P74
Journalists see KL-KWX4 3504.3
Librarians see KL-KWX4 3180.3
Performing artists see KL-KWX4 3170+
3521.P74 Printers. Graphic artists (Table K12)
3521.R4 Real estate agents (Table K12)
Social workers see KL-KWX4 1525
Teachers see KL-KWX4 3140+
3522 Professional ethics. Courts of honor (Table K11)
For a particular court of honor, see the profession
Public finance
Finance reform and policies
Cf. KL-KWX4 3195+ Government control and policy
3525 General (Table K11)
Monetary policies see KL-KWX4 3534+
3526 General (Table K11)
3526.3 Constitutional aspects (Table K11)
Organization and administration
Class here works on national departments or agencies of finance, national, state, and local departments or agencies, or departments and agencies of several states or administrative districts
For departments and agencies (several or individual) of an individual state or administrative district, see the state or administrative district
For financial courts see KL-KWX4 3682+
3527 General (Table K11)
3527.3.A-Z Particular national departments and agencies, A-Z
Subarrange each by Table K12
3527.5 Officers and personnel. Functionaries (Table K11)
Including tenure, salaries, pensions, etc., and discipline
Budget. Government expenditures
3528 General (Table K11)
Constitutional aspects see KL-KWX4 3526.3

Public finance
Organization and administration
Budget. Government expenditures -- Continued
3528.3 Accounting (Table K11)
Including central or local organs of national government
Expenditure control. Auditing
3529 General (Table K11)
3530 National courts of audit (Table K11)
Public debts. Loans. Bond issues
3531 General (Table K11)
3532 External debts. International loan agreements (Table K11)
Revenue see KL-KWX4 3540+
3533 Intergovernmental fiscal relations (Table K11)
Including revenue sharing
Money
Including control of circulation
3534 General (Table K11)
3535 Coinage. Mint regulations (Table K11)
3536 Bank notes. Banks of issue (Table K11)
Class here public law aspects of banks of issue
For banking law see KL-KWX4 940+
3537 Gold trading and gold standard (Table K11)
3537.5 Currency reforms. Revalorization of debts (Table K11)
Foreign exchange control
3538 General (Table K11)
Valuta clause and gold clause see KL-KWX4 820.3
Criminal provisions see KL-KWX4 4292
3539 Conflict of laws (Table K11)
National revenue
3540 General (Table K11)
3540.3 Fees. Fines (Table K11)
Taxation
Criticism and reform see KL-KWX4 3525+
3541-3550 General (Table K9c)
3551 Constitutional aspects (Table K11)
Including equality
Double taxation
3552 General (Table K11)
3552.3 Domicile (Table K11)
3552.4.A-Z Special topics, A-Z
3552.4.F67 Foreign corporations and foreign stockholders (Table K12)
3552.4.M85 Multi-national corporations (Table K12)
Taxation and tax exemption as a measure of social and economic policy
3553 General (Table K11)

Public finance
National revenue
Taxation
Taxation and tax exemption as a measure of social and economic policy -- Continued
3553.3 Investments (Table K11)
Including foreign investments
3553.5 Assistance to developing countries (Table K11)
3554 Export sales (Table K11)
3555.A-Z Classes of taxpayers or lines of businesses, A-Z
Subarrange each by Table K12
3556.A-Z Taxation of particular activities, A-Z
Subarrange each by Table K12
3557 Tax saving (Table K11)
For tax planning relating to a particular tax, see the tax
For tax avoidance see KL-KWX4 3695
Tax administration. Revenue service
3558 General (Table K11)
National departments and agencies see KL-KWX4 3527.3.A+
Financial courts see KL-KWX4 3682+
Officers and personnel. Functionaries see KL-KWX4 3527.5
3559 Jurisdiction for tax allocation (Table K11)
Including concurrent taxing powers of national and state government
Double taxation see KL-KWX4 3552+
Collection and enforcement
3560 General (Table K11)
Tax accounting. Financial statements
Including personal companies and stock companies, etc.
For a particular tax, see the tax
3562 General (Table K11)
3562.5 Tax consultants (Table K11)
3563 Tax returns (Table K11)
3564.A-Z Special topics, A-Z
Subarrange each by Table K12
Administrative acts
3565 General (Table K11)
3566 Assessment (Table K11)
3567 Tax remission. Delay granted for payment (Table K11)
Administrative remedies see KL-KWX4 3683+
Judicial review see KL-KWX4 3685+
3568 Tax auditing (Table K11)
Cf. KL-KWX4 3701 Tax and customs investigation

Public finance
National revenue
Taxation
Tax administration. Revenue service
Collection and enforcement -- Continued
3569 Default (Table K11)
Including penalties
Tax avoidance see KL-KWX4 3700
3569.3 Tax credit and refunds (Table K11)
3570 Execution (Table K11)
3572.A-Z Classes of taxpayers or lines of business, A-Z
3572.A37 Agriculture. Horticulture (Table K12)
Horticulture see KL-KWX4 3572.A37
3572.P83 Publishing houses (Table K12)
Income tax
3573 General (Table K11)
3574 Tax planning. Estate planning (Table K11)
3575 Accounting and financial statements (Table K11)
3576 Assessment (Table K11)
3577 Tax returns (Table K11)
Taxable income. Exemptions
3578 General (Table K11)
3578.5.A-Z Particular, A-Z
Capital gains see KL-KWX4 3578.5.P75
3578.5.D48 Deferred compensation (Table K12)
3578.5.P75 Profits. Capital gains (Table K12)
3578.5.T38 Tax-exempt securities (Table K12)
Deductions
3579 General (Table K11)
3579.3 Amortization. Depreciation allowances (Table K11)
3580 Charitable or educational gifts and contributions (Table K11)
3580.5 Church tax (Table K11)
Expenses and losses
3582 General (Table K11)
3582.3.A-Z Kinds of expenses, A-Z
3582.3.B88 Business expenses (Table K12)
3582.3.E38 Educational expenses (Table K12)
3582.3.E58 Entertainment expenses (Table K12)
Surtaxes see KL-KWX4 3624+
Salaries and wages
Including fringe benefits, nonwage payments, etc.
3584 General (Table K11)
3585 Social security tax (Table K11)
3586.A-Z Classes of taxpayers, A-Z
Subarrange each by Table K12

Public finance
National revenue
Taxation
Income tax -- Continued
3588 Capital investment (Table K11)
Including foreign investment
Cf. KL-KWX4 3553+ Taxation as a measure of economic policy
3589 Pensions and annuities (Table K11)
3589.3.A-Z Other sources of income, A-Z
Subarrange each by Table K12
Payment at source of income
Payroll deduction. Withholding tax
3590 General (Table K11)
Social security tax see KL-KWX4 3585
3591.A-Z Classes of taxpayers or lines of business, A-Z
3591.A44 Aliens (Table K12)
3591.A87 Artisans (Table K12)
3591.A88 Artists (Table K12)
Casinos see KL-KWX4 3591.G36
3591.E83 Executives (Table K12)
3591.G36 Gambling. Casinos (Table K12)
3591.M37 Married couples (Table K12)
Including persons in polygamous marriages
3591.M47 Merchant mariners (Table K12)
3591.P75 Professions (Table K12)
3591.T42 Teachers (Table K12)
Corporation tax
3592 General (Table K11)
Nonprofit associations, nonprofit corporations, foundations (endowments), and pension trust funds
3593 General (Table K11)
3593.5.A-Z Special topics, A-Z
3593.5.T39 Tax avoidance (Table K12)
Personal companies (Unincorporated business associations)
3594 General (Table K11)
3594.5.A-Z Special topics, A-Z
Subarrange each by Table K12
Cooperatives
3595 General (Table K11)
3595.5.A-Z Special topics, A-Z
Subarrange each by Table K12
Stock companies (Incorporated business associations
3596 General (Table K11)
3597 Tax accounting. Financial statements (Table K11)

Public finance
National revenue
Taxation
Income tax
Corporation tax
Stock companies (Incorporated business associations -- Continued
3597.3 Assessment (Table K11)
3598 Tax returns (Table K11)
Taxable income. Exemptions
3599 General (Table K11)
3600.A-Z Particular, A-Z
3600.C35 Capital stock (Table K12)
3600.D58 Dividends (Table K12)
3600.I58 Inventories (Table K12)
3600.P75 Profits (Table K12)
3600.R48 Reserves (Table K12)
Deductions
3602 General (Table K11)
3603 Depreciation of property, plant, and equipment (Table K11)
3604 Pension reserves (Table K11)
Cf. KL-KWX4 3593+ Pension trust funds
3605.A-Z Expenses and losses, A-Z
Subarrange each by Table K12
Surtaxes see KL-KWX4 3624+
Corporate reorganization
3606 General (Table K11)
3607 Conversions (Table K11)
3608 Merger, fusion, and consolidation (Table K11)
3609 Liquidation (Table K11)
3610 Limited partnership (Table K11)
3611 Stock corporation (Table K11)
3612.A-Z Other, A-Z
3612.B87 Business concern, holding company, and industrial trusts (Table K12)
3612.G68 Government business corporations (Table K12)

3613.A-Z Lines of corporate business, A-Z
3613.A55 Animal industry (Table K12)
3613.B35 Banks. Credit institutions (Table K12)
3613.C65 Construction industry (Table K12)
Credit institutions see KL-KWX4 3613.B35
3613.H4 Health facilities (Table K12)
3613.M54 Mining. Extractive industries (Table K12)
Including severance tax
3613.P48 Petroleum industry (Table K12)

Public finance
National revenue
Taxation
Income tax
Corporation tax -- Continued
Foreign corporations and stockholders
3614 General (Table K11)
Double taxation see KL-KWX4 3552+
Multi-national corporations
3615 General (Table K11)
Double taxation see KL-KWX4 3552+
Property tax. Taxation of capital
For real property tax see KL-KWX4 3670+
Cf. KL-KWX4 3663+ Property tax (State and local finance)
3616 General (Table K11)
3617 Tax valuation (Table K11)
3618 Accounting. Financial statements (Table K11)
3619 Assessment (Table K11)
3620 Taxable property. Exemptions (Table K11)
3621 Estate, inheritance, and gift taxes (Table K11)
3623 Capital gain tax (Table K11)
Development gains tax see KL-KWX4 3672
Surtaxes
3624 General (Table K11)
3625 Excess profits tax (Table K11)
Including war profits tax
Poll tax see KL-KWX4 3680.P65
Indirect taxation. Excise taxes. Taxes on transactions
*Indirect taxation*
3627 General (Table K11)
Sales tax
3628 General (Table K11)
3629 Accounting (Table K11)
3630 Assessment (Table K11)
3631 Tax returns (Table K11)
3633 Turnover tax
Including value-added tax and import and export sales
Personal companies and stock companies
3637 General (Table K11)
3638 Municipal corporations (Table K11)
Particular commodities, services, and transactions see KL-KWX4 3640.A+
3639 Government monopolies (Table K11)
Including monopolies delegated by the state to others
3640.A-Z Commodities, services, and transactions, A-Z

Public finance
National revenue
Taxation
Indirect taxation. Excise taxes. Taxes on transactions
Commodities, services, and transactions, A-Z -- Continued
3640.A42 Alcoholic beverages (General) (Table K12)
3640.B35 Banking transactions (Table K12)
3640.B37 Bars and taverns (Table K12)
3640.B38 Betting (Bookmaking) (Table K12)
3640.B55 Bills of exchange tax (Table K12)
Bonds see KL-KWX4 3640.S42
Brandy see KL-KWX4 3640.L57
Champagne see KL-KWX4 3640.W55
3640.D58 Distilleries (Table K12)
3640.E96 Export-import sales (Table K12)
Gambling see KL-KWX4 3669
3640.H68 Hotels and motels (Table K12)
Import sales see KL-KWX4 3640.E96
3640.L57 Liquors (Table K12)
3640.M38 Matches (Table K12)
Motels see KL-KWX4 3640.H68
3640.M68 Motor fuels (Table K12)
3640.P48 Petroleum (Table K12)
3640.P82 Public utilities (Table K12)
3640.R47 Restaurants (Table K12)
3640.R48 Retail trade (Table K12)
3640.S42 Securities and bonds (Table K12)
3640.S76 Stock exchange transactions (Table K12)
Taverns see KL-KWX4 3640.B37
3640.T62 Tobacco (Table K12)
3640.T72 Transportation of persons or goods (Table K12)
3640.W46 Wholesale trade (Table K12)
3640.W55 Wine (Table K12)
Methods of assessment and collection
For assessment and collection of a particular tax, see the tax
3642 General (Table K11)
3643 Stamp duties (Table K11)
For bills of exchange see KL-KWX4 3640.B55
Customs. Tariff
For foreign trade regulations see KL-KWX4 3407+
3645 General (Table K11)
Tables see KL-KWX4 3645+
Trade agreements
3646 General (Table K11)

Public finance
National revenue
Customs. Tariff
Trade agreements -- Continued
3647 Favored nation clause (Table K11)
3648 Customs organization and administration (Table K11)
Including officers and personnel
3650 Jurisdiction. Custom territory (Table K11)
Practice and procedure
Including remedies and enforcement
3651 General (Table K11)
3651.3 Duty by weight (Table K11)
3652 Custom appraisal (Table K11)
3652.5 Dumping. Antidumping duties (Table K11)
3653.A-Z Commodities and services, A-Z
3653.A87 Automobiles
3654 Costs. Fees (Table K11)
3654.5 Free ports and zones (Table K11)
Criminal provisions see KL-KWX4 3693+
State and local finance
For the public finance of an individual state, administrative district, or municipality, see the state or municipality
Finance reform see KL-KWX4 3525+
3655 General (Table K11)
3656 Budget. Expenditure control (Table K11)
Including accounting and auditing
3657 Public debts. Loans (Table K11)
3658 Intergovernmental fiscal relations (Table K11)
Class here works on local taxes shared by state and locality
For state taxes shared by state and national government see KL-KWX4 3533
3659 Fees. Fines (Table K11)
Including license fees
Taxation
3660 General (Table K11)
3661 Jurisdiction for tax allocation (Table K11)
For concurrent taxing powers of national government and states see KL-KWX4 3559
Tax administration see KL-KWX4 3558+
Income tax see KL-KWX4 3573+
Sales taxes see KL-KWX4 3628+
3662 Estate, inheritance, and gift taxes (Table K11)
Property tax. Taxation of capital
Including juristic persons and business enterprises
For real property tax see KL-KWX4 3670+
3663 General (Table K11)

Public finance
State and local finance
Taxation
Property tax. Taxation of capital -- Continued
3664 Tax valuation
Including industries or industrial properties
3665 Accounting. Financial statements (Table K11)
3665.5 Assessment (Table K11)
3665.7 Tax returns (Table K11)
3666 Taxable property (Table K11)
3667 Deductions (Table K11)
3668 Motor vehicles tax (Table K11)
3669 Taxes from gambling tables. Casinos (Table K11)
Real property tax
3670 General (Table K11)
3671 Valuation of real property. Assessment (Table K11)
3672 Capital gains tax (Table K11)
Including development gains
Business tax
3674 General (Table K11)
3675 Assessment (Table K11)
3676 Tax returns (Table K11)
3677 Taxable income (Table K11)
3678 Deductions (Table K11)
3679.A-Z Classes of taxpayers or lines of business, A-Z
Subarrange each by Table K12
Other taxes, A-Z
Gasoline see KL-KWX4 3680.M68
3680.M68 Motor fuels. Gasoline (Table K12)
3680.P65 Poll tax (Table K12)
Tax and customs courts and procedure
Class here works on national courts, national, state and district courts and boards, or courts and boards of several states or administrative districts
For courts and boards (several or individual) of an individual state or administrative district, see the state or district
3682 General (Table K11)
Pretrial procedures. Administrative remedies
3683 General (Table K11)
3684 Tax protest (Table K11)
Procedure at first instance. Judicial review
3685 General (Table K11)
3686 Actions. Defenses (Table K11)
3687 Evidence (Table K11)
3688 Judicial decisions. Judgments (Table K11)
Including court records

Public finance
Tax and customs courts and procedure -- Continued
Remedies. Means of review
3689 General (Table K11)
3690 Appellate procedures (Table K11)
3691 Special procedures (Table K11)
Refunds and tax credit see KL-KWX4 3569.3
Tax and customs crimes and delinquency. Procedure
3693 General (Table K11)
Individual offenses
3695 Tax evasion and tax avoidance (Table K11)
3696 Receiving bootleg merchandise (Table K11)
3697 Violation of confidential disclosure (Table K11)
Including denunciation
Smuggling of contraband see KL-KWX4 3695
3698 Organized smuggling (Table K11)
3699 Forgery of seals, stamps, etc. (Table K11)
3700 Delinquency (Table K11)
Including faulty accounting and bookkeeping, etc.
Procedure
For criminal procedure in general see KL-KWX4 4600.9+
General see KL-KWX4 3693
3701 Tax and customs investigation (Table K11)
3703 Evidence (Table K11)
3704 Special procedures in criminal tax cases (Table K11)
3705 Amnesty. Pardon (Table K11)
Government measures in time of war, national emergency, or economic crisis
3709 General (Table K11)
Particular measures
3710 Military requisitions from civilians. Requisitioned land (Table K11)
For damages and compensation see KL-KWX4 3727+
3712 Control of property. Confiscations (Table K11)
Including enemy and alien property
For damages and compensation see KL-KWX4 3727+
Control of unemployment. Manpower control
3714 General (Table K11)
3715 Compulsory and forced labor (Table K11)
3717 Insolvent debtors. Wartime and crisis relief (Table K11)
For composition and deferment of execution see KL-KWX4 1972
For moratorium see KL-KWX4 1975
For agricultural credits see KL-KWX4 3322

Government measures in time of war, national emergency, or economic crisis
Particular measures -- Continued
3719 Finances (Table K11)
For special levies, war taxes, etc. see KL-KWX4 3625
For procurement and defense contracts see KL-KWX4 3730
3720 Industrial priorities and allocations. Economic recovery measures. Nationalization
3722 Strategic material. Stockpiling
3724 Rationing. Price control
3726 Criminal provisions (Table K11)
War damage compensation
Including foreign claims settlement
3727 General (Table K11)
3728.A-Z Particular claims, A-Z
Confiscations see KL-KWX4 3728.R47
Demontage see KL-KWX4 3728.R46
Military occupation damages see KL-KWX4 3728.R47
3728.P47 Personal damages. Property loss or damages (Table K12)
Property loss or damages see KL-KWX4 3728.P47
3728.R46 Reparations. Demontage (Table K12)
3728.R47 Requisitions. Confiscations. Military occupation damages (Table K12)
3729.A-Z Particular victims, A-Z
Subarrange each by Table K12
3730 Military occupation. Procurement
For military occupation damages see KL-KWX4 3728.R47
National defense. Military law
For emergency and wartime legislation see KL-KWX4 3709+
3735 General (Table K11)
3737 Organization and administration. Command (Table K11)
The armed forces
3738 General (Table K11)
Compulsory service
Including draft and selective service
3739 General (Table K11)
3740.A-Z Special topics, A-Z
3740.A44 Aliens
3740.C65 Conscientious objection
3740.E38 Education and training
Training see KL-KWX4 3740.E38
3742 Discharge (Table K11)

National defense. Military law
The armed forces
3744 Tenure, pay, and benefits (Table K11)
Including disability pensions and rehabilitation
For war invalids, war victims, and prisoners of war see KL-KWX4 1539
3745 Equipment (Table K11)
Including weapons, plants, and installations
3746 Hospitals (Table K11)
3748.A-Z Particular branches of service, A-Z
Subarrange each by Table K12
3749 Auxiliary services during war or emergency (Table K11)
3750 Civil status and rights of military personnel (Table K11)
Civil defense
3752 General (Table K11)
3753 Air defense. Air raid shelters (Table K11)
3754 Evacuation (Table K11)
Military criminal law and procedure
Cf. KL-KWX4 4470+ Crimes against national defense
3758 General (Table K11)
3758.5 Illegality and justification. Superior orders (Table K11)
Individual offenses
3760 Desertion (Table K11)
3761 Incitement. Mutiny (Table K11)
3762 Insubordination (Table K11)
3763 Self-mutilation. Malingering (Table K11)
3764 Calumny. Assault on subordinates (Table K11)
3765 Sabotaging weapons, equipment or means of defense (Table K11)
3767.A-Z Other, A-Z
3767.D7 Draft evasion (Table K12)
Firearms, Illegal use of see KL-KWX4 3767.I45
3767.G38 Guard duty offenses (Table K12)
3767.I45 Illegal use of firearms (Table K12)
3770 Courts and procedure
Including procedure in honor cases
3775 Punishment. Execution (Table K11)
3777 Probation and parole (Table K11)
Trials. Courts martial
Including trials of civilians by military courts
3778 Collections
3779 Particular trials. By defendant, A-Z
Military discipline. Law enforcement. Procedure
Including all branches of the armed forces
3780 General (Table K11)
3782 Superior orders. Enforcement of orders (Table K11)

National defense. Military law -- Continued
3785.A-Z Other, A-Z
3785.M55 Military maneuvers (Table K12)
Criminal law
3790 Reform of criminal law, procedure, and execution (Table K11)
For works limited to a particular subject, see the subject. For works pertaining exclusively to the codes, see the code
Administration of criminal justice see KL-KWX4 1571.2+
3791-3800 General (Table K9c)
3810 Constitutional aspects (Table K11)
Philosophy of criminal law
3812 General (Table K11)
Theories of punishment. Criminal policy see KL-KWX4 3950+
3813 Ideological theories of criminal law (Table K11)
3816.A-Z Special topics, A-Z
Subarrange each by Table K12
Relationship of criminal law to other disciplines, subjects or phenomena
3817 General (Table K11)
3818 Criminal law and society
Cf. HV6115+, Social pathology
3819 Criminal law and psychology
Cf. HV6080+, Criminal psychology
3821 Interpretation and construction. Legal hermeneutics
3823.A-Z Terms and phrases, A-Z
3823.D35 Danger (Table K12)
Drugs see KL-KWX4 3823.F67
3823.F67 Force (Table K12)
Including drugs and hypnosis
Hypnosis see KL-KWX4 3823.F67
Concepts and principles
3824 General (Table K11)
Applicability and validity of the law
3825 General (Table K11)
3826 Nulla poena sine lege. Nullum crimen sine lege (Table K11)
3827 Retroactivity. Ex post facto laws (Table K11)
3829 Customary law (Table K11)
Territorial applicability
3830 General (Table K11)
3831 Place of commission of crime (Table K11)
For press delicts see KL-KWX4 3508+
For crimes aboard aircraft see KL-KWX4 4396
3835 Conflict of laws (Table K11)

Criminal law
Concepts and principles
Applicability and validity of the law -- Continued
3836 Temporal applicability
Including intertemporal law
3838 Personal applicability. Immunities (Table K11)
Criminal offense
Including felony, misdemeanor, and transgression
3840 General (Table K11)
3842 Crimes by commission or omission (Table K11)
3844 Crimes aggravated by personal characteristics (Table K11)
Criminal act
3845 General (Table K11)
3847 Corpus delicti. Fact-pattern conformity (Table K11)
3851 Causation. Proximate cause
Form of criminal act
3852 General (Table K11)
3853 Omission (Table K11)
3854 Attempt. Preparation. Preliminary crimes. Inchoate offenses (Table K11)
For accessory to attempted crime see KL-KWX4 3931
Illegality. Justification of otherwise illegal acts
3855 General (Table K11)
3856 Self-defense or defense of another (Table K11)
3857 Necessity (Table K11)
Superior orders see KL-KWX4 3900
Medical treatment see KL-KWX4 4096+
3859 Duty to act (Legal authority or duty) (Table K11)
Consent of the injured party
3861 General (Table K11)
3862 Assumption of risk (Table K11)
3863 Presumed consent (Table K11)
3865.A-Z Other grounds for justification, A-Z
Subarrange each by Table K12
3867 Criminal intent. Mens rea (Table K11)
Including purpose and scienter, dolus eventualis, etc.
3874 Negligence and wantonness (Table K11)
Including foresight and standard of conduct
Criminal liability. Guilt
3878 General (Table K11)
Capacity
3880 General (Table K11)
Incapacity and limited capacity
3882 General (Table K11)

Criminal law
Concepts and principles
Criminal offense
Criminal liability. Guilt
Capacity
Incapacity and limited capacity -- Continued
3884 Insane persons. People with mental or emotional disbilities (Table K11)
Cf. HV6133, Psychopathology and crime
3886 Minors (Table K11)
Including infants, juveniles, and young adults
3892.A-Z Special topics, A-Z
3892.D58 Distemper (Table K12)
3892.I58 Intoxication (Table K12)
3892.L58 Litigious paranoia (Table K12)
Passion see KL-KWX4 3892.D58
3895 Criminal liability of juristic persons (Table K11)
3896 Ignorance or mistake of law (Table K11)
3897 Exculpating circumstances (Table K11)
3900 Superior orders and justification or excusation (Table K11)
Cf. KL-KWX4 3758.5 Military criminal law
3902 Error
Including error about fact, error about grounds for justification or excusation, and other error about extenuating circumstances, error in persona, etc.
Forms of the criminal act
Omission see KL-KWX4 3852+
Attempt see KL-KWX4 3852+
Perpetrators
3920 General (Table K11)
Principals and accessories
3922 General (Table K11)
3925 Co-principals (Table K11)
3927 Accessory before the fact (Table K11)
Including abettor
3929 Accessory after the fact (Table K11)
3931 Accessory at attempted crime (Table K11)
3933 Complicity (Table K11)
3934 Agent provocateur (Table K11)
Aggravating and extenuating circumstances see KL-KWX4 4022+
3940 Compound offenses and compound punishment (Table K11)
Punishment
3946 General (Table K11)
3948 Constitutional aspects (Table K11)

Criminal law
Punishment -- Continued
Theory and policy of punishment
3950 General (Table K11)
3952 Retaliation. Retribution (Table K11)
3954 Safeguarding the social and political system (Table K11)
3956 General and special prevention (Table K11)
Including education, rehabilitation, and resocialization of perpetrator
Criminal anthropology
see HV6030+
3960 Criminal sociology (Table K11)
For non-legal works, see HV6030+
Penalties and measures of rehabilitation and safety
For juveniles and young adults see KL-KWX4 4726+
For execution of sentence see KL-KWX4 4794.2+
3962 General (Table K11)
3964 Capital punishment (Table K11)
Imprisonment
Including maximum and minimum terms
3970 General (Table K11)
Prisons and jails see KL-KWX4 4824
Reformatories see KL-KWX4 4732
3972 Short-term sentence (Table K11)
3974 Sentencing to probation (Punishment without imprisonment). Conditional sentencing (Table K11)
Including terms of probation, e.g. education and resocialization through labor
3976 Fines (Table K11)
3978 Reprimand (Table K11)
3980.A-Z Other penalties, A-Z
3980.B43 Beating. Flogging (Table K12)
3980.D43 Death by fire (Table K12)
Flogging see KL-KWX4 3980.B43
3980.M87 Mutilation (Table K12)
3980.W58 Witch-execution (Table K12)
Measures entailing deprivation of liberty
3982 General (Table K11)
3984 Commitment to medical or psychiatric treatment (Table K11)
3986 Commitment to medical, nursing, or socio-therapeutic institutions (Table K11)
3990 Commitment of addicts to institutions for withdrawal treatment (Table K11)
3992 Protective custody (Table K11)
Including dangerous or habitual criminals

Criminal law
Punishment
Penalties and measures of rehabilitation and safety -- Continued
Other measures
3995 Protective surveillance (Table K11)
3997 Expulsion (Table K11)
4002 Prohibition against practicing a profession (Table K11)
4004 Loss of civil rights. Infamy. Disfranchisement (Table K11)
4006 Property confiscation (Table K11)
4010 Forfeiture (Table K11)
Sentencing and determining the measure of punishment
4012 General (Table K11)
4016 Fixed and indeterminate sentence (Table K11)
Juvenile delinquents see KL-KWX4 4722
Circumstances influencing measures of penalty
4020 General (Table K11)
Aggravating and extenuating circumstances
Including principals and accessories
4022 General (Table K11)
4024 Recidivism (Table K11)
4026 Detention pending investigation (Table K11)
Causes barring prosecution or execution of sentence
4030 General (Table K11)
4034 Pardon and amnesty. Clemency (Table K11)
For suspension of punishment see KL-KWX4 4828
For probation and parole see KL-KWX4 4830+
Limitation of actions
4038 General (Table K11)
4040.A-Z Crimes exempt from limitation of action, A-Z
4040.C74 Crimes against humanity and human rights (Table K12)
4040.T73 Treasonable endangering of the peace (Table K12)
4040.W37 War crimes (Table K12)
Criminal registers see KL-KWX4 4845
Criminal statistics see KL-KWX4 31
Individual offenses
4048 General (Table K11)
Offenses against the person
Including aggravating circumstances
4049 General (Table K11)
Homicide
4050 General (Table K11)
4052 Murder (Table K11)
4054 Manslaughter (Table K11)
4056 Killing on request (Table K11)

Criminal law
Individual offenses
Offenses against the person
Homicide -- Continued
4058 Euthanasia (Table K11)
4062 Parricide (Table K11)
4064 Infanticide (Table K11)
4065 Negligent homicide (Table K11)
4067 Desertion. Exposing persons to mortal danger (Table K11)
4070 Crimes against inchoate life. Illegal abortion
Including ethical, social, medical, and eugenic aspects
For birth control and family planning see KL-KWX4 3124+
Crimes against physical inviolability
4074 General (Table K11)
4076 Battery (Table K11)
4076.5 Stalking (Table K11)
4077 Conjugal violence. Wife abuse. Husband abuse
4078 Communicating venereal disease (Table K11)
4082 Abuse of defenseless persons or dependents. Abuse of older people (Table K11)
For child abuse see KL-KWX4 4190
4084 Consent. Justified assault (Table K11)
For sports injuries see KL-KWX4 848+
For medical treatment and operations see KL-KWX4 4096+
Cf. KL-KWX4 3861+ Criminal law concepts
4088 Compound offenses (Table K11)
4090 Poisoning (Table K11)
Criminal aspects of surgical and other medical treatment
Including biomedical engineering and medical technology
4096 General (Table K11)
4100 Malpractice (Table K11)
Cf. KL-KWX4 3100.5 Torts
4102 Treatment without consent (Table K11)
Euthanasia see KL-KWX4 4058
4103 Genetic engineering (Table K11)
4108 Human reproductive technology (Table K11)
Including artificial insemination, fertilization in vitro, etc.
4110 Transplantation of organs, tissues, etc. (Table K11)
Including donation of organs, tissues, etc.
4112 Sterilization (Table K11)
Confidential communication see KL-KWX4 4696.A+
Psychopharmaca damages see KL-KWX4 4100
Crimes against personal freedom

Criminal law
Individual offenses
Offenses against the person
Crimes against personal freedom -- Continued
4116 General (Table K11)
4118 False imprisonment (Table K11)
4120 Extortionate kidnapping (Table K11)
Abduction
Cf. KL-KWX4 602 Parental kidnapping
4125 General (Table K11)
4127 Political abduction (Table K11)
4130 Abduction of a woman without her consent (Table K11)
4132 Abduction of a female minor (Table K11)
4136 Threats of a felonious injury (Table K11)
4138 Duress (Table K11)
4140 Unlawful entry (Table K11)
Crimes against dignity and honor
Including juristic persons and families
4143 General (Table K11)
4145 Insult (Table K11)
4147 Defamation (Table K11)
4149 Calumny (Table K11)
4152 Disparagement of memory of the dead (Table K11)
4154 Defamatory statement and truth (Table K11)
4156 Privileged comment (Table K11)
Including criticism of scientific, artistic, or professional accomplishments
For press delicts see KL-KWX4 3510.6
Violation of personal privacy and secrets
4160 General (Table K11)
4162 Constitutional aspects (Table K11)
4164 Violation of confidential disclosures by professional persons (Table K11)
4166 Opening of letters (Table K11)
4168 Eavesdropping. Wiretapping (Table K11)
Offenses against religious tranquility and the peace of the dead
4170 General (Table K11)
4172 Blasphemy (Table K11)
4174 Disturbing a religious observance (Table K11)
4176 Disturbing the peace of the dead (Table K11)
Including cemeteries and funerals
Offenses against marriage, family, and family status
4180 General (Table K11)
4182 Incest (Table K11)
4184 Adultery (Table K11)

Criminal law
Individual offenses
Offenses against marriage, family, and family status -- Continued
4186 Bigamy (Table K11)
(4188) Abduction of a minor from legal custodian. Parental kidnapping
see KL-KWX4 602
4190 Abandonment, neglect, or abuse of a child (Table K11)
4192 Breach of duty of support (Table K11)
4194 Breach of duty of assistance to a pregnant woman (Table K11)
Abortion see KL-KWX4 4070
Artificial insemination see KL-KWX4 4108
Offenses against sexual integrity
4200 General (Table K11)
4202 Rape (Table K11)
4204 Lewd acts with persons incapable of resistance (Table K11)
4206 Abduction for lewd acts (Table K11)
4208 Lewd acts with children or charges. Seduction (Table K11)
4210 Lewd acts by persons taking advantage of official position (Table K11)
4220 Obscenity (Table K11)
Including production, exhibition, performance, advertising, etc.
4224 Pandering and pimping. Slave traffic
Offenses against private and public property
4230 General (Table K11)
Larceny and embezzlement
4234 General (Table K11)
4236 Burglary (Table K11)
4238 Armed theft and theft by gangs (Table K11)
4250 Embezzlement (Table K11)
Including embezzlement in office
4254 Robbery and rapacious theft (Table K11)
4256 Destruction of property and conversion (Table K11)
Fraud
4258 General (Table K11)
4260 Fraudulent insurance claims (Table K11)
4262 Fraud by litigation (Table K11)
4263 Credit card fraud (Table K11)
Fraudulent bankruptcy see KL-KWX4 4276
4264 Extortion (Table K11)
4265 Organized crime. Racketeering (Table K11)
4266 Breach of trust (Table K11)

Criminal law
Individual offenses
Offenses against private and public property -- Continued
4268 Usury (Table K11)
4268 Usury (Table K11)
Defeating rights of creditors
4270 General (Table K11)
4276 Fraudulent bankruptcy (Table K11)
4280 Game and fish poaching (Table K11)
4282 Aiding criminals in securing benefits (Table K11)
Including the receiving of stolen goods
Offenses against the national economy
4286 General (Table K11)
4290 Violation of price regulations (Table K11)
Including price fixing, hoarding, discrimination, overselling and underselling prices established by government etc.
4292 Foreign exchange violations (Table K11)
4294 Economic and industrial secrets. Unauthorized possession or disclosure (Table K11)
Cf. KL-KWX4 1257.E86 Industrial espionage
4298 False statements concerning national planning (Table K11)
Counterfeiting money and stamps see KL-KWX4 4346+
Offenses against public property see KL-KWX4 4230+
4300.A-Z Other, A-Z
4300.A58 Antitrust violations (Table K12)
Tax and customs crimes see KL-KWX4 3693+
Offenses against public order and convenience
Including aggravating circumstances
4305 General (Table K11)
4307 Inciting insubordination (Table K11)
4309 Rowdyism. Vandalism (Table K11)
4310 Inciting crime (Table K11)
4314 Criminal societies (Table K11)
4316 Parasitism (Table K11)
Disrupting the peace of the community
4320 Demonstrations and failure to disperse (Table K11)
4322 Inciting acts against minorities (Table K11)
Threatening the community. Terrorist activities see KL-KWX4 4351.5+
Crimes against security of legal and monetary transactions and documents
4330 General (Table K11)
4334 Forgery and suppression of evidence and documents (Table K11)

Criminal law
Individual offenses
Offenses against public order and convenience
Crimes against security of legal and monetary transactions and documents -- Continued
4338 Forgery and suppression of mechanical records (Table K11)
Including forgery of sound recordings and electronic data bases
4340 Physical and identifying marks
Counterfeiting money and stamps
Including postage stamps
4346 General (Table K11)
4348 Passing counterfeit money (Table K11)
4350 Counterfeiting securities (Table K11)
Including checks, bills of exchange, etc.
Customs crimes see KL-KWX4 3693+
Tax evasion see KL-KWX4 3695
4351.A-Z Other, A-Z
4351.D57 Displacing boundaries (Table K12)
4351.F34 False certification (Table K12)
4351.F67 Forgery of art works (Table K12)
4351.M57 Misuse of credentials (Table K12)
Crimes involving danger to the community. Crimes against the environment. Terrorism
4351.5 General (Table K11)
4352 Common danger (Table K11)
4354 Arson (Table K11)
4356 Causing explosion (Table K11)
Including explosives and nuclear energy
4358 Misuse of ionizing radiation (Table K11)
4360 Releasing natural forces (Table K11)
Including flood, avalanche, rockfall, etc.
4362 Dangerous use of poisonous substances (Table K11)
4364 Poisoning wells or soil (Table K11)
4366 Poisoning food, medicine, etc. (Table K11)
4368 Spreading communicable diseases, morbific agents, or parasites (Table K11)
4370 Damaging water and power installations (Table K11)
4372 Impairing industrial safety appliances (Table K11)
4374 Sabotage of essential services, utilities, warning systems, etc. (Table K11)
4376 Causing danger in construction (Table K11)
Including collapse, faulty gas or electric installation, etc.
4378 Human trafficking. Human smuggling (Table K11)
Crimes affecting traffic

Criminal law
Individual offenses
Offenses against public order and convenience
Crimes affecting traffic -- Continued
4380 Dangerous interference with rail, ship, or air traffic
4382 Unsafe operation of a rail vehicle, ship, or aircraft (Table K11)
Dangerous interference with street traffic
For minor traffic violations resulting in fines see KL-KWX4 3450+
4384 General (Table K11)
4386 Driving while intoxicated (Table K11)
4388 Duress. Constraint (Table K11)
4390 Leaving the scene of an accident. Hit-and-run driving (Table K11)
Predatory assault on motorists
4392 General (Table K11)
4394 Assault on taxicab drivers (Table K11)
4396 Crimes aboard aircraft. Air piracy (Table K11)
4398 Riots (Table K11)
Crimes against public health
4400 General (Table K11)
4402 Intoxication (Table K11)
4404 Illicit use of, possession of, and traffic in narcotics (Table K11)
Communicating venereal diseases see KL-KWX4 4078
4406 Gambling (Table K11)
Including illegal operation of a lottery or games of chance, and participation
Cf. KL-KWX4 3036.5.G35 Police and public safety
Offenses against the government. Political offenses.
Offenses against the peace
4415 General (Table K11)
High treason and treason
4417 General (Table K11)
High treason against the state
Including national and state (republic, etc.)
4420 General (Table K11)
4422 Preparation of treasonable acts (Table K11)
4424 Treason against the constitution (Table K11)
4426 Assault on the head of state (Table K11)
4428 Inciting treason (Table K11)
4432 Sabotage endangering the state (Table K11)
4434 Undermining the state apparatus (Table K11)
4438 Lese majesty (Table K11)

Criminal law
Individual offenses
Offenses against the government. Political offenses.
Offenses against the peace
High treason against the state -- Continued
4440 Disparagement of the state and its symbols. Disparaging constitutional organs (Table K11)
4442 Treasonable espionage (Table K11)
For publication of official secrets by the press see KL-KWX4 3510.7
4444 Subversive activities (Table K11)
4446 Intelligence activities (Table K11)
4448 Propaganda endangering the state (Table K11)
4455 Treasonable endangering of the peace or of international relations (Table K11)
Including propaganda, planning, preparation, or participation in an aggressive war
Crimes in connection with election and voting
4458 General (Table K11)
4460 Bribery. Corrupt practices (Table K11)
4466 Falsifying votes and voting results (Table K11)
4468 Obstructing voting (Table K11)
Crimes against national defense
4470 General (Table K11)
4473 Sabotaging and depicting means of defense (Table K11)
4475 Violation of secrecy regulations (Table K11)
Opposition to power of the state
4476 General (Table K11)
4478 Constraining official action or inaction (Table K11)
4480 Prison escape. Mutiny. Freeing prisoners (Table K11)
4482.A-Z Other forms of opposition, A-Z
4482.D35 Damaging official announcements (Table K12)
Endangering the administration of justice. Obstruction of justice
4483 General (Table K11)
False testimony
4484 General
4486 False unsworn testimony (Table K11)
4490 Perjury (Table K11)
4492 False affirmation (Table K11)
4494 Causing false testimony (Table K11)
4496 False accusation (Table K11)
4498 Bringing false complaint (Table K11)
4500 Thwarting criminal justice (Table K11)
4502 Failure to report felony. Misprision (Table K11)
4504 Coercion of testimony (Table K11)

Criminal law
Individual offenses
Offenses against the government. Political offenses.
Offenses against the peace
Endangering the administration of justice. Obstruction of justice -- Continued
4506 Intentional misconstruction by law officers (Table K11)
4507 Prosecuting innocent persons (Table K11)
Including execution
4508 Repressing conflicting interests. Prevarication (Table K11)
4510 Contempt of court (Table K11)
For contempt of court by the press see KL-KWX4 3511
Assisting in securing benefits see KL-KWX4 4282
Crimes against the civil service
4514 General (Table K11)
Corruption
Including omission of official acts
4516 General (Table K11)
4520 Bribery. Granting benefits to civil servants (Table K11)
4522 Illegal compensation to arbitrators (Table K11)
Bribery in connection with election see KL-KWX4 4460
Embezzlement see KL-KWX4 4250
Violating official secrecy
4526 General (Table K11)
4528 Disclosing official secrets (Table K11)
4532.A-Z Other, A-Z
4532.M35 Mail and telecommunication (Table K12)
Crimes against humanity
4538 General (Table K11)
4540 Genocide (Table K11)
4543 Crimes against foreign states, supranational institutions, or international institutions (Table K11)
4545 War crimes (Table K11)
4548 Offenses commited through the mail (Table K11)
For threats, extortion, and blackmail see KL-KWX4 4264
Business associations criminal provisions see KL-KWX4 1153
Labor law criminal provisions see KL-KWX4 1375
Social insurance criminal provisions see KL-KWX4 1502
Radio communication criminal provisions see KL-KWX4 3498+
Press law criminal provisions see KL-KWX4 3507+
Tax and customs crimes see KL-KWX4 3693+
Military criminal law see KL-KWX4 3758+

Criminal procedure

For works on both criminal and civil procedure, including codes of both criminal and civil procedure see KL-KWX4 1650+

For works on both criminal law and criminal procedure, including codes of both criminal law and criminal procedure see KL-KWX4 3790+

Criticism and reform see KL-KWX4 3790

4601-4610 General (Table K9c)

4612 Constitutional aspects (Table K11)

4614 Criminal procedure and public opinion (Table K11)

Including trial by newspaper

4616 Sociology of criminal procedure (Table K11)

Including scandals

Administration of criminal justice see KL-KWX4 1571.2+

Court organization see KL-KWX4 1580+

Procedural principles

4620 Due process of law (Table K11)

4622 Uniformity of law application. Stare decisis (Table K11)

4624 Accusation principle (Table K11)

4625 Principles of defense. Equality (Table K11)

4626 Publicity and oral procedure (Table K11)

4628 Prejudicial actions (Table K11)

Including all branches of the law

4630.A-Z Parties to action, A-Z

4630.A25 Accused. Person charged. Defendant (Table K12)

4630.C74 Criminal judge (Table K12)

Defendant see KL-KWX4 4630.A25

4630.D43 Defense attorney. Public defender (Table K12)

Person charged see KL-KWX4 4630.A25

Procurator see KL-KWX4 4630.S73

Public defender see KL-KWX4 4630.D43

4630.S73 State prosecutor. Procurator (Table K12)

Class here works on the legal status of the prosecutor in criminal procedure

For general works on the office of the public prosecutor see KL-KWX4 1615+

4630.S93 Suspect (Table K12)

4630.V52 Victim (Table K12)

Pretrial procedures

4632 General (Table K11)

4634 Penal report. Charges brought against a person (Table K11)

Investigation

For techniques of criminal investigation, see HV8073

Cf. KL-KWX4 4679+ Admission of evidence

4636 General (Table K11)

Criminal procedure
Pretrial procedures
Investigation -- Continued
4638 Examination of the accused (Table K11)
Public charges by prosecutor
4642 General (Table K11)
4644 Stare decisis (Table K11)
4646 Summonses, service of process, and subpoena. Wanted notice (Table K11)
4648 Time periods. Deadlines (Table K11)
Compulsory measures against the accused. Securing of evidence
4650 General (Table K11)
4652 Search and seizure (Table K11)
Including search of persons, buildings, institution's records, etc.
4654 Provisional apprehension (Table K11)
4655 Torture (Table K11)
4657 Detention pending investigation (Table K11)
Including bail
Cf. KL-KWX4 4798+ Execution of sentence
4660 Extradition (Table K11)
Including constitutional aspects
Procedure at first instance
4664 General (Table K11)
4666 Jurisdiction (Table K11)
Including competence in subject matter and venue
4668 Action. Complaint (Table K11)
4670 Exclusion and challenge of court members (Table K11)
Time period and deadlines see KL-KWX4 4648
Limitation of action see KL-KWX4 4038+
4672 Plea bargaining (Table K11)
Trial
4673 General (Table K11)
Evidence. Burden of proof
4675 General (Table K11)
4677 Presumption of innocence (Table K11)
Admission of evidence
4679 General (Table K11)
4681 Confession. Self-incrimination. Entrapment (Table K11)
4683 Informers. Official secrets (Table K11)
4685 Narcoanalysis, lie detectors, etc. (Table K11)
4687 Physical examination (Table K11)
Including blood tests, urine tests, etc.
For forensic medicine, see RA1001+

Criminal procedure
Procedure at first instance
Trial
Evidence. Burden of proof
Admission of evidence -- Continued
4689 Electronic listening and recording devices (Table K11)
Including wiretapping
4690 Previous testimony, police records, etc. (Table K11)
Witnesses
4692 General (Table K11)
4696.A-Z Privileged witnesses (confidential communication), A-Z
4698.A-Z Other witnesses, A-Z
4698.C46 Child witnesses (Table K12)
4700 Expert testimony (Table K11)
For forensic medicine, chemistry, psychology, psychiatry, toxicology, etc. see RA1001+
4702 Testimony of accused (Table K11)
4704 Documentary evidence (Table K11)
4705 Circumstantial evidence (Table K11)
4706 Alibi (Table K11)
4709.A-Z Other, A-Z
4709.T72 Trace evidence (Table K12)
Particular proceedings
4711 Summary proceedings (Table K11)
4713 Proceedings against absentee and fugitives (Table K11)
4717 Recourse against decisions of grievance boards (Table K11)
Procedure for juvenile delinquency
4720 General (Table K11)
4722 The juvenile delinquent. The young adult perpetrator (Table K11)
4724 Juvenile crime (Table K11)
Criminal liability and guilt see KL-KWX4 3878+
Punishment. Correctional or disciplinary measures
Including measures of rehabilitation and safety
4726 General (Table K11)
4730 Custodial education (Table K11)
4732 Detention homes. Reformatories (Table K11)
Cf. KL-KWX4 4824 Execution of sentence
Execution of sentence see KL-KWX4 4794.2+
Judicial decisions
4736 General (Table K11)
4738 Judgment (Table K11)
For sentencing and determination of punishment see KL-KWX4 4012+

Criminal procedure
Procedure at first instance
Trial
Judicial decisions -- Continued
4740 Judicial discretion (Table K11)
Including opportunity and equity
4744 Acquittal (Table K11)
4746 Conviction (Table K11)
Including measures of rehabilitation and safety
4750 Dismissal (Table K11)
Probation see KL-KWX4 4830+
4753 Correction or withdrawal of faulty decisions (errors) (Table K11)
4754 Res judicata (Table K11)
For waiver of appeal see KL-KWX4 4788
4760 Court records. Minutes of evidence (Table K11)
Including clerks, translators, and correction of records
Participation of injured party in criminal procedure
4762 General (Table K11)
4764 Private charge (Table K11)
Including public interest
4766 Intervention (Table K11)
4767 Civil suits of victims in connection with criminal proceedings (Table K11)
Including reparation (Compensation to victims of crimes)
Special procedures
4768 Procedure before justice of the peace (Table K11)
Commitment of insane criminals see KL-KWX4 3986
Other procedures
see the subject, e.g. KL-KWX4 3700.2+ Tax and customs criminal procedures; KL-KWX4 3758+ Military criminal procedure; etc.
Remedies
4770 General (Table K11)
Appellate procedure
4780 General (Table K11)
4786 Cassation (Table K11)
4788 Waiver of appeal (Table K11)
Post-conviction remedies
4790 General (Table K11)
4792 Reopening a case. New trial (Table K11)
For procedure before constitutional court see KL-KWX4 2620+
Execution of sentence
Including execution of sentence of juvenile courts
Criticism and reform see KL-KWX4 3790

Criminal procedure
Execution of sentence -- Continued
4795 General (Table K11)
Capital punishment see KL-KWX4 3964
Imprisonment
Including regulation of detention pending investigation and short-term sentence
For penalties in general, including imprisonment see KL-KWX4 3962+
4798 General (Table K11)
4800 Administration of penal or correctional institutions (Table K11)
Including discipline, hygiene, etc.
The prisoner
4810 General (Table K11)
4812.A-Z Particular, A-Z
Dangerous criminals see KL-KWX4 3992
4812.E38 Education of prisoners. Education through labor (Table K12)
Insane criminals see KL-KWX4 3986
4812.J88 Juvenile prisoners (Table K12)
4812.P64 Political prisoners (Table K12)
4820 Labor and industries in correctional institutions (Table K11)
Including wages
Rehabilitation and resocialization see KL-KWX4 3956
4824 Penal or correctional institutions (Table K11)
Including prisons, jails, penal colonies, reformatories, juvenile detention homes, etc.
Exile. Banishment. Punitive deportation
4826 General (Table K11)
Deportation of aliens see KL-KWX4 3029
Pardon, amnesty, and clemency see KL-KWX4 4034
4828 Suspension of punishment (Table K11)
4829 Restitution. Reparation (Table K11)
Probation. Parole
Including conditions
4830 General (Table K11)
4834 Probation and parole for juvenile delinquents (Table K11)
4840 Remission (Table K11)
4845 Criminal registers (Table K11)
Judicial error and compensation see KL-KWX4 2850
Extradition see KL-KWX4 4660
4850 Costs (Table K11)
Victimology
4855 General (Table K11)
4857 Children and sexual crimes (Table K11)

Criminal procedure
Victimology -- Continued
Compensation to victims of crimes see KL-KWX4 2852.A+
Criminology and penology
see HV6001+

Bibliography
For bibliography of special topics, see the topic
For manuals on legal bibliography, legal research and the use of law books see KL-KWX5 4.2+
1 General bibliography
1.2 Indexes to periodical literature, society publications, and collections
For indexes to a particular publication, see the publication
Indexes to Festschriften see KL-KWX5 6.7
<1.3> Periodicals
For periodicals consisting predominantly of legal articles, regardless of subject matter and jurisdiction, see K1+
For periodicals consisting primarily of informative material (newsletters, bulletins, etc.) relating to a special subject, see the subject and form division tables for periodicals
For law reports, official bulletins or circulars intended chiefly for the publication of laws and regulations, see appropriate entries in the text or form division tables
1.4 Monographic series
Official gazettes
1.5 General
State or city gazettes
see the issuing state or city
Departmental gazettes
see the issuing department or agency
1.6 Indexes (General)
Legislative documents
see class J
1.7 Other materials relating to legislative histroy
Including recommended legislation; legislation passed and vetoed
Legislation
For statutes, statutory orders, regulations, etc. on a particular subject, see the subject
Indexes and tables
Including indexes to statutes of several states
For indexes to a particular publication, see the publication; for indexes limited to one state, see the state
General
1.75.A-Z Serials
1.8 Monographs. By date
1.83 Chronological indexes. By date
Statutes
Including statutory orders and regulations, and decree law
Collections and compilations
Including official and private editions
1.85 Serials

Legislation
Statutes
Collections and compilations -- Continued
1.9 Monographs. By date
Including unannotated and annotated editions
1.94 Collected codes
Class here works consisting of private and public law codes, and customary law codes
For codes on a particular branch of law, see the branch of law
For works consisting of the civil and commercial codes see KL-KWX5 48.2
For collected public law codes see KL-KWX5 200+
Administrative and executive publications
Including statutory orders and regulations, orders in council, proclamations, etc.
For regulations on a particular subject, see the subject
1.95 Serials
2 Monographs. By date
Presidential proclamations, etc.
see class J
Treaties
For treaties on international public law, see class KZ
For treaties on international uniform law not limited to a region, see class K
For treaties on international uniform law of a particular region, see the region
Court decisions and related materials. Reports
Including decisions of national (federal) courts and decisions of two or more states, and national (federal) and state decisions combined. Class decisions of an individual state with the law of the respective jurisdiction
For decisions on a particular subject, see the subject
National (Federal) courts
Constitutional courts see KL-KWX5 262+
2.2 Highest courts of appeal. Supreme courts. Courts of Cassation (Table K19)
Lower courts
2.23 Various courts (Table K19)
Including highest court and lower courts, or national (federal) courts of two or more states combined
Intermediate appellate courts. National (Federal) courts of appeal
2.24 Collective (Table K19)
2.25.A-Z Particular courts, A-Z
Courts of first instance. District courts
2.26 Collective (Table K19)

Court decisions and related materials. Reports
National (Federal) courts
Lower courts
Intermediate appellate courts. National (Federal) courts of appeal
Courts of first instance. District courts -- Continued
2.27.A-Z Particular courts, A-Z
State courts
2.3 Collections (Reports) covering all states or selected states (Table K19)
2.33 Collections (Reports) covering national (federal) decisions and decisions of the courts of two or more states (Table K19)
Decisions (Reports) of an individual state
see the state
2.4 Decisions of national (federal) administrative agencies
For decisions of particular agencies, see the subject
2.5 Encyclopedias
2.6 Dictionaries. Words and phrases
For bilingual and multilingual dictionaries, see K52+
For dictionaries on a particular subject, see the subject
2.7 Maxims. Quotations
2.8 Form books (General)
For form books on a particular subject, see the subject
Judicial statistics
3 General
3.2 Criminal statistics
3.23 Juvenile crime
3.3.A-Z Other. By subject, A-Z
3.3.L34 Labor law
Directories
3.32 National and regional
3.33.A-Z By specialization, A-Z
Trials
3.4 General collections
Criminal trials and judicial investigations
3.5 Collections. Compilations
3.6.A-Z Particular offenses, A-Z
3.6.A78 Arson
3.6.F73 Fraud
3.6.P64 Political crimes
3.6.R56 Riots
War crimes see KL-KWX5 3.82+
Individual trials
Including records, briefs, commentaries, and stories on a particular trial

Trials
Criminal trials and judicial investigations
Individual trials -- Continued
3.7.A-Z By defendant, A-Z
3.8.A-Z By best known (popular) name, A-Z
War crime trials
Trials by international military tribunals
see class KZ
3.9 Collections
Other trials
4 Collections. Compilations
4.15.A-Z Individual trials. By plaintiff, defendant, or best known (popular) name, A-Z
Including records, briefs, commentaries, and stories on a particular trial
Legal research. Legal bibliography
Including methods of bibliographic research and how to find the law
4.2 General
4.3 Electronic data processing. Information retrieval
4.4.A-Z By subject, A-Z
4.5 Systems of citation. Legal abbreviations
4.6 Legal composition and draftsmanship
Legal education
5 General works
Law schools
5.3 General works
5.4.A-Z Particular law schools. By name, A-Z
Including constitution and bylaws, statutes, regulations, degrees, and general works (history)
The legal profession see KL-KWX5 160+
5.5 Bar associations. Law societies. Law institutes
Class here works on, and journals by, individual societies and their activities, e.g., annual reports, proceedings, incorporating statutes, bylaws, handbooks, and works (history) about the society
Including courts of honor and disbarment
For journals devoted to legal subjects, either wholly or in part, see K1+
For publications of associations on special subjects, see the subject
For membership directories see KL-KWX5 3.33.A+
For biography (Collective) see KL-KWX5 10.5
For Biography (Individual) see KL-KWX5 11.A+
Notarial law. Public instruments see KL-KWX5 184.6+
Public registers. Registration
5.53 General (Table K11)
Civil registry see KL-KWX5 185.4+

Public registers. Registration
Commercial registers see KL-KWX5 97.3
5.6 Property registration. Registration of pledges (Table K11)
5.8.A-Z Congresses. Conferences. By name of congress or conference, A-Z
5.9.A-Z Academies. By name of academy, A-Z
6.3 General works. Treatises
6.4 Compends, outlines, examination aids, etc.
Forms, graphic materials, blanks, atlases see KL-KWX5 2.8
6.5 Popular works. Civics
6.7 Addresses, essays, lectures
Including single essays, collected essays of several authors, festschriften, indexes to festschriften, etc.
7.3.A-Z Manuals and other works for particular groups of users. By user, A-Z
7.3.A75 Armed Forces personnel
7.3.B87 Businesspeople. Foreign investors
7.3.F37 Farmers
Foreign investors see KL-KWX5 7.3.B87
7.3.W65 Women
Semantics and language see KL-KWX5 9.2
Legal symbolism see KL-KWX5 9.4+
Legal anecdotes, wit and humor
see K184.4
Law and lawyers in literature
see classes PB-PH
Law and art
see K487.C8
Law and history
see K487.C8
7.8.A-Z Works on diverse aspects of a particular subject and falling within several branches of the law. By subject, A-Z
7.8.C65 Computers (Table K12)
7.8.P83 Public interest law (Table K12)
7.8.P85 Public relations (Table K12)
Women see KL-KWX5 52.3
History of law
8.5 Bibliography
8.6 Periodicals
Auxiliary sciences
8.7 General works
9 Paleography
9.2 Linguistics. Semantics
Archaeology. Folklife studies. Symbolism
9.4 General works
9.6.A-Z Special topics, A-Z

History of law
Auxiliary sciences
Archaeology. Folklife studies. Symbolism
Special topics, A-Z -- Continued
9.6.S76 Stool, Ancestral
10 Heraldry. Seals. Flags. Insignia. Armory
Biography of lawyers
10.5 Collective
10.7 Collections of portraits
11.A-Z Individual, A-Z
Subarrange each by Table KL-KWX11
12 General works. Treatises
By period
Ancient and early, including ancient people in the region
see KL, KQ, or particular jurisdiction, as specified (e.g. Russia, Japan)
Medieval and early modern (to second half of 19th century)
Including precolonial and early colonial periods
Sources
For sources of a territory or town, see the appropriate territory or town
12.5 Studies on sources
Including history and methodology, e.g. epigraphy, papyrology, etc.
For philological studies, see classes P, PJ, PK, and PL
12.9 Collections. Compilations. Selections
Class here comprehensive collections of legal sources in various (native) scripts
Individual sources or groups of sources
National (imperial) laws and legislation
Including constitutional laws (leges fundamentales)
14 Collections. Compilations
14.2<date> Individual
Arrange chronologically by appending the date of the source to this number and deleting any trailing zeros. Subarrange each by Table K20b
Royal (imperial) privileges
Including privileges for particular classes, ecclesiastical rulers, religious groups, courts of justice, etc.
14.4 Collections. Compilations
14.6<date> Individual
Arrange chronologically by appending the date of the source to this number and deleting any trailing zeros. Subarrange each by Table K20b
Royal (imperial) edicts, etc. of princes and rulers. Decrees. Mandates

History of law
By period
Medieval and early modern (to second half of 19th century)
Sources
Individual sources or groups of sources
Royal (imperial) edicts, etc. of princes and rulers. Decrees. Mandates -- Continued
14.8 Collections. Compilations
15.2<date> Individual
Arrange chronologically by appending the date of the source to this number and deleting any trailing zeros. Subarrange each by Table K20b
Treaties
Treaties on international public law
see KZ118+
Treaties on international uniform law
see K524+ , KJC38+ , KMC , KNC , KQC and KVC
Court decisions. Cases. Precedents. Advisory opinions. Dooms. Digests
16 Several courts
16.4.A-Z Particular courts, A-Z
Law faculties
16.6 Several faculties
16.8.A-Z Individual faculties. By place, A-Z
Trials
Criminal trials and judicial investigations
17 Collections. Compilations
17.2.A-Z Particular offenses, A-Z
17.2.W58 Witchcraft
17.4.A-Z Individual trials. By defendant, or best known (popular) name, A-Z
Including records, briefs, commentaries, and stories on a particular trial
Other trials
17.6 Collections. Compilations
17.8 Individual trials. By plaintiff, defendant, or best known (popular) name, A-Z
Contemporary legal literature
18.2 Compends. Digests. Indexes
Formularies
Including notarial art
18.4 Collections. Compilations
18.5 Particular clauses and formulae
18.7 Encyclopedic works. Dictionaries
19.2 General works
19.5 Addresses, essays, lectures

| | |
|---|---|
| | History of law |
| | By period |
| | Medieval and early modern (to second half of 19th century) -- Continued |
| | The State and its constitution |
| 20.2 | General works (Table K22) |
| | Estates. Classes. Castes |
| 20.4 | General (Table K22) |
| 20.5.A-Z | Particular classes, A-Z |
| 20.7.A-Z | Special topics, A-Z |
| 20.7.B57 | Birth rights |
| 20.7.D94 | Dynastic rules |
| | Feudal capacity see KL-KWX5 22.8 |
| 20.7.P44 | Peerage, Rights of |
| | State and religion see KL-KWX5 28 |
| 20.9 | Territory (Table K22) |
| 21.2 | Foreign relations (Table K22) |
| | Feudal law |
| | Class here works on feudal law beginning ca. 12th century |
| 21.3 | General works (Table K22) |
| | Sources |
| 21.4 | Collections. Compilations |
| 22.2<date> | Individual sources, A-Z |
| | Arrange chronologically by appending the date of the source to this number and deleting any trailing zeros. Subarrange each by Table K20b |
| | Feudal institutes |
| | Feudal lords. Provincial (regional) lords |
| 22.3 | General (Table K22) |
| 22.4 | Vassalage. Peers (Table K22) |
| | Including individuals, towns, and villages, and regions |
| 22.6 | Fief (Table K22) |
| 22.8 | Feudal capacity (Table K22) |
| 23 | Feudal succession (Table K22) |
| | Rural (peasant) land tenure. Peasantry |
| 23.2 | General (Table K22) |
| 23.4 | Manorial estates. Lordships. Seigniories (Table K22) |
| 23.8 | Leasehold for years and inheritance (Table K22) |
| | Succession to rural holdings |
| 24.2 | General (Table K22) |
| 24.4 | Entail (Table K22) |
| 24.6 | The crown. Princes and rulers. Chieftains (Table K22) |
| 25 | The court. Court officials and councils (Table K22) |
| 25.6 | Military organization and administration (Table K22) |
| | Finance. Revenue and expenditure |
| 26 | Camera. Organization and administration (Table K22) |

History of law
By period
Medieval and early modern (to second half of 19th century)
Finance. Revenue and expenditure -- Continued
26.3 Crown goods and dynastic house goods (Table K22)
Regalia. Taxes
26.8 General (Table K22)
26.9.A-Z Particular taxes, A-Z
Administration. Public order and safety
Class here works on subjects not represented elsewhere in the schedule
For works on the history of subjects, see the subject
27 General (Table K22)
Administrative organization. Bureaucracy. Hierarchy
27.2 General (Table K22)
27.4 Administrative divisions (not A-Z)
27.5 Organs of government. Civil service. Officials (Table K22)
27.6.A-Z Special topics, A-Z
28 State and religion. State and church
Class here historical works on the relationship of the state and church (e.g. Eastern Orthodox), and on state and practice of religion in general
28.2.A-Z Private law. Special topics, A-Z
Class here works on subjects not represented elsewhere in the schedule
For works on the history of other subjects, see the subject
Judiciary. Court organization
28.3 General (Table K22)
28.7 Procedure (Table K22)
29.2 Criminal law and procedure (Table K22)
<35> Indigenous peoples Ethnic groups
For works on the law of indigenous peoples regardless of whether identified with one or more countries in the region, see KM, KN, KNQ, KQ, or as directed
Philosophy, jurisprudence, and theory of law
Class here works on doctrines peculiar to legal institutions of a country
For works on the philosophy of a particular branch of the law (e.g., constitutional law or criminal law), see the branch
For works on the philosophy of law in general, see K237+
44 General works
The concept of law
Including the definition of law
44.2 General works
44.3 The object of law. Law and justice

Philosophy, jurisprudence, and theory of law
The concept of law -- Continued
44.4 Ethics. Morality of law. Public policy
44.5 Law and the state. Legal order. Respect for law
44.6.A-Z Other topics, A-Z
Sources of law
44.9 General works
44.93 Customs and observance. Indigenous law
44.95 Legislation
Methodology
Including unification, integration, and harmonization of both substantive law and conflict rules
For unification of the law on a particular subject, see the subject
45 Reconciliation and integration of customary (indigenous) law and civil law, or multiple customary (indigenous) laws
45.2 Legal hermeneutics. Interpretation and construction
Including lacunae in law and judge-made law
Semantics see KL-KWX5 9.2
Schools of legal theory
45.5 General works
45.7 Natural law
46.3 Modern political theory of law
46.4 Socialist. Communist
46.5 Sociological jurisprudence
46.7 Influence of other legal systems on the law. Superimposition of foreign rule on the customary (indigenous) law (Table K11)
Including reception of traditional, customary and religious law, and multiplicity of laws
46.8 Law reform and policies. Criticism (Table K11)
Including reform of administration of justice
47.A-Z Concepts applying to several branches of the law, A-Z
Bona fides see KL-KWX5 47.G66
47.D87 Duress
47.E88 Estoppel
47.F73 Freedom of conscience
47.G66 Good faith. Reliance
47.L44 Legal documents
47.L52 Liability
47.L63 Locus poenitentiae
47.T55 Time periods
47.5 Intertemporal law. Retroactive law (Table K11)
48 Regional divisions. Subregions
Class here general works on the law or the legal systems in force within a single subregion of the country (e.g. laws in force in Soviet Central Asia, KLA477)
For works on a particular subject see KL-KWX5 48.2

48.2 Private law

Class here works on all aspects of private law

Private international law. Plurality of laws conflict. Legal polycentricity

Class here works on conflict of laws in a multicultural country with two or more coexisting legal systems (e.g. secular and religious law, civil law and one or more indigenous (tribal, customary) legal system

For regional unification of conflict rules, see the appropriate region, e.g. Middle East, KMC, subdivided by Table KL-KWX2, 126-136

For conflict of laws between the United States and a particular jurisdiction, see KF416

For works on conflict rules of branches other than private law (e.g. tax law, criminal law, etc.), see the subject

48.3 General (Table K11)

48.35 Public order. Ordre Public (Table K11)

48.37 Jurisdiction (Table K11)

48.4 Choice of law

Including indigenous (tribal, customary) law and civil law

48.5.A-Z Particular branches and subjects of the law, A-Z

Adoption see KL-KWX5 48.5.F35

Arbitration see KL-KWX5 48.5.P76

Bankruptcy see KL-KWX5 48.5.P76

Capacity see KL-KWX5 48.5.P47

Cartels see KL-KWX5 48.5.C67

48.5.C655 Commercial papers and negotiable instruments (Table K12)

48.5.C657 Commercial sales (Table K12)

48.5.C658 Contracts. Obligations. Debtor and creditor (Table K12)

48.5.C67 Corporations. Industrial trusts. Cartels (Table K12)

For procedure in antitrust cases see KL-KWX5 324.4+

Criminal law see KL-KWX5 383

Debtor and creditor see KL-KWX5 48.5.C658

Decedents' estate see KL-KWX5 48.5.I45

Divorce see KL-KWX5 48.5.M375

Execution see KL-KWX5 48.5.P76

48.5.F35 Family. Parent and child. Adoption (Table K12)

Foreign judgments see KL-KWX5 164.6

Illegality see KL-KWX5 48.5.T67

Incapacity see KL-KWX5 48.5.P47

Industrial property see KL-KWX5 48.5.I583

Industrial trusts see KL-KWX5 48.5.C67

48.5.I45 Inheritance and succession. Decedents' estates (Table K12)

48.5.I58 Insurance (Table K12)

48.5.I583 Intellectual and industrial property (Table K12)

Judicial assistance see KL-KWX5 164.4

Justification see KL-KWX5 48.5.T67

| | |
|---|---|
| | Private international law. Plurality of laws conflict. Legal polycentricity |
| | Particular branches and subjects of the law, A-Z -- Continued |
| 48.5.L45 | Limitation of action (Table K12) |
| 48.5.L62 | Loans (Table K12) |
| 48.5.M37 | Maritime (commercial) law (Table K12) |
| 48.5.M375 | Marriage. Matrimonial actions. Matrimonial property (Table K12) |
| | Negotiable instruments see KL-KWX5 48.5.C655 |
| | Obligations see KL-KWX5 48.5.C658 |
| | Parent and child see KL-KWX5 48.5.F35 |
| 48.5.P47 | Persons. Capacity. Incapacity (Table K12) |
| 48.5.P76 | Procedure. Arbitral awards. Execution and bankruptcy (Table K12) |
| 48.5.R43 | Refugees (Table K12) |
| 48.5.S8 | Statelessness (Table K12) |
| 48.5.T67 | Torts. Illegality. Justification (Table K12) |
| 48.5.T725 | Transfer (Table K12) |
| | Intertemporal law. Retroactive law see KL-KWX5 47.5 |
| | Civil law |
| 49 | General (Table K11) |
| 50 | Applicability. Validity of the law (Table K11) |
| | Ethics (Morality of law). Public policy see KL-KWX5 44.4 |
| 50.3 | Legal status (Table K11) |
| 50.4 | Rights (Table K11) |
| 50.5 | Immaterial rights (Table K11) |
| | Acts and events |
| 50.55 | General (Table K11) |
| | Illegal and unlawful acts see KL-KWX5 83.5+ |
| 50.6 | Conditions (Table K11) |
| | Time periods see KL-KWX5 47.T55 |
| | Limitation of actions |
| 50.7 | General (Table K11) |
| 50.8 | Exercise of rights. Protection of rights (Table K11) |
| | Persons |
| 51 | General (Table K11) |
| | Natural persons |
| 51.2 | Personality (Table K11) |
| 51.3 | Birth (Table K11) |
| | Death |
| 51.5 | General (Table K11) |
| 51.7 | Missing persons. Presumption of death (Table K11) |
| 51.9 | Capacity and incapacity (Table K11)<br>Including liability<br>For civil disability see KL-KWX5 400.4 |

Civil law
Persons
Natural persons
Capacity and incapacity -- Continued
Minors
Including human rights of the child
51.95 General (Table K11)
52 Majority. Declaration of majority (Table K11)
52.3 Women (Table K11)
Class here works on legal status under all aspects of law (e.g. religious, customary, private, and public)
For status of married women see KL-KWX5 55.4
52.5 Insane persons. People with mental disabilities (Table K11)
For institutional care of the mentally ill see KL-KWX5 312.3
52.55 Domicile (Table K11)
52.56.A-Z Other, A-Z
52.56.E93 Ex-convicts (Table K12)
52.56.P49 Physical disabilities, People with (Table K12)
52.6 Citizenship (Table K11)
For acquisition of citizenship and nationality see KL-KWX5 243+
For aliens see KL-KWX5 302.9
Personality rights
52.7 General (Table K11)
Freedom see KL-KWX5 85
52.9 Name (Table K11)
Including title of nobility and coat of arms
Dignity, honor, and reputation see KL-KWX5 85.7
Privacy see KL-KWX5 85.9+
Intellectual property see KL-KWX5 115.2+
Protection of personality rights see KL-KWX5 83.7
Juristic persons of private law
For business corporations see KL-KWX5 108.9+
For juristic persons of public law see KL-KWX5 287+
53 General (Table K11)
Associations
53.3 General (Table K11)
53.5 Incorporated society (Table K11)
Including profit and nonprofit corporations
Unincorporated society
53.7 General (Table K11)
Liability see KL-KWX5 53.7+
53.8 Foundations. Charitable trusts and uses. Endowments

Civil law -- Continued
Domestic relations. Family law. Multiplicity of laws
Including one or more religious legal systems, customary law and civil law
54 General (Table K11)
Marriage
54.2 General (Table K11)
54.3 Betrothal (Table K11)
54.4.A-Z Marriage impediments, A-Z
54.4.A43 Affinity (Table K12)
54.4.C65 Consanguinity (Table K12)
54.6 Premarital examinations. Marriage licenses (Table K11)
Performance of marriage. Civil marriage and religious ceremonies
54.7 General (Table K11)
Certificates. Registration see KL-KWX5 186
55 Intermarriage (Table K11)
Including interracial, interethnic, and interfaith marriage
55.2 Multiple marriages. Polygamy. Polyandry (Table K11)
Husband and wife. Rights and duties
55.3 General (Table K11)
55.4 Legal status of married women (Table K11)
Matrimonial actions. Dissolution of marriage
55.5 General (Table K11)
Divorce
55.8 General (Table K11)
56 Procedure. Divorce suits (Table K11)
56.5 Separation (Table K11)
56.7 Settlement of claims from defective or dissolved marriages (Table K11)
Including alimony and dowry
56.8 Quasi-matrimonial relationships. Unmarried cohabitation (Table K11)
Marital property and regime
56.9 General (Table K11)
57 Statutory regimes (Table K11)
57.2 Contractual regimes. Antenuptial contracts. Marriage settlements (Table K11)
57.3 Separation of property (Table K11)
57.4 Community of property (Table K11)
58 Property questions arising from unmarried cohabitation (Table K11)
Matrimonial property register see KL-KWX5 186.7
Consanguinity and affinity. Kinship
58.3 General (Table K11)
58.4 Support (Table K11)

Civil law
Domestic relations. Family law. Multiplicity of laws
Consanguinity and affinity. Kinship -- Continued
Parent and child
Legitimate children
Including children from defective marriages, divorced marriages, legitimized children from subsequent marriages, etc.
59 General (Table K11)
(59.2) Human rights of the child (Table K11)
see KL-KWX5 51.98+
59.5 Legitimation of children (Table K11)
Including declaration of legitimacy kand legitimation by subsequent marriage
Parental power
For illegitimate children see KL-KWX5 61.9
59.8 General (Table K11)
60 Custody. Access to children (Table K11)
Including parental kidnapping
60.3 Stepchildren (Table K11)
Adoption
61 General (Table K11)
61.5.A-Z Special topics, A-Z
Subarrange each by Table K12
Inter-country adoption of children see KL-KWX5 48.5.F35
Illegitimate children
61.8 General (Table K11)
Human rights of the child see KL-KWX5 51.95+
61.9 Parental power. Custody (Table K11)
Affiliation (patrilineal and matrilineal)
62 General works
62.2 Illegitimate children (Table K11)
62.3.A-Z Special topics, A-Z
62.3.A77 Artificial insemination (Table K12)
Cf. KL-KWX5 312.8 Public health
Cf. KL-KWX5 410.8 Criminal law
62.3.P38 Paternity (Table K12)
Guardian and ward
62.4 General (Table K11)
62.5 Guardianship courts and procedure
Government guardianship see KL-KWX5 154.8
Guardianship over minors
62.58 General (Table K11)
62.6.A-Z Special topics, A-Z
62.6.P75 Property management (Table K12)

Civil law
Domestic relations. Family law. Multiplicity of laws
Guardian and ward -- Continued
62.8 Guardianship over adults (Table K11)
Property. Law of things
63 General (Table K11)
64 Right of property. Constitutional guaranty (Table K11)
64.5 Socialist property. Doctrine (Table K11)
64.8.A-Z Types of private property, A-Z
Subarrange each by Table K12
Possession
65 General (Table K11)
65.3 Acquisition and transfer of possession (Table K11)
Ownership
65.7 General (Table K11)
Acquisition and loss of ownership
65.8 General (Table K11)
65.9 Accessions (Table K11)
Including annexation (incorporation), confusion, and specification
66 Acquisition of fruits and parts of things (Table K11)
66.3 Prescription (Table K11)
66.4 Succession (Table K11)
Contractual acquisition
66.5 General (Table K11)
66.8 Conditions (Table K11)
For fiduciary transfer of ownership see KL-KWX5 74.3
67 Tradition (Table K11)
67.2 Acquisition bona fide (Table K11)
67.3 Loss of ownership
Including abandonment and dereliction
For expropriation see KL-KWX5 282.4
67.4 Co-ownership (Table K11)
For condominium and horizontal property see KL-KWX5 70.4
Claims and actions resulting from ownership
67.5 General (Table K11)
67.6 Actio negatoria. Nuisances (Table K11)
For particular nuisances see KL-KWX5 70.3.N84
For ecological aspects of regional planning see KL-KWX5 307.4
67.8 Liability of possessor (Table K11)
Including bona fide and mala fide possessor, and damages
68 Rights and defenses of possessor (Table K11)
Including bona fide and mala fide possessor

Civil law
Property. Law of things -- Continued
Real property. Land law
68.3 General (Table K11)
Land registration law see KL-KWX5 74.4+
Public and private restraint on real property
68.4 General (Table K11)
Public policy. Land reform and land policy legislation see KL-KWX5 306.5
Zoning laws see KL-KWX5 307.8
Homestead law see KL-KWX5 307.4
68.6 Concepts of customary (native) land rights (Table K11)
Ownership
Acquisition and loss of ownership
68.8 Contractual acquisition (Table K11)
Rights incident to ownership of land
69 General (Table K11)
69.3 Air and space above ground. Aeronautics (Table K11)
69.4 Underground. Minerals, metals, and other resources (Table K11)
Cf. KL-KWX5 335 Mining law
69.5 Riparian rights. Water rights. Underground water (Table K11)
69.7 Hunting and fishing rights (Table K11)
Cf. KL-KWX5 333.7+ Game laws
Cf. KL-KWX5 334+ Fishery laws
Commonage and pasture see KL-KWX5 70.8
Law of adjoining landowners
70 General (Table K11)
70.3.A-Z Special topics, A-Z
70.3.B68 Boundaries. Building across boundaries. Party walls (Table K12)
Building across boundaries see KL-KWX5 70.3.B68
70.3.E29 Eaves-drip (Table K12)
70.3.L54 Light or window rights (Table K12)
Mining rights see KL-KWX5 335
70.3.N84 Nuisances (Table K12)
Including fumes, heat, noise, smoke, and odor
Overfall see KL-KWX5 70.3.O83
70.3.O83 Overhang. Overfall (Table K12)
Party walls see KL-KWX5 70.3.B68
Transit of livestock see KL-KWX5 70.3.W39
70.3.W38 Water laws (Table K12)
70.3.W39 Way by necessity (Table K12)
Window rights see KL-KWX5 70.3.L54
Types of real property

Civil law
Property. Law of things
Real property
Types of real property -- Continued
70.4 Condominium. Horizontal property (Table K11)
Rights as to the use and profits of another's land. Droits d'usage
70.6 General (Table K11)
Fief see KL-KWX5 22.6
70.8 Commonage and pasture. Grazing rights (Table K11)
Servitudes
71 General (Table K11)
71.3 Real servitudes (Table K11)
71.5 Personal servitudes (Table K11)
Including right of habitation
71.6 Usufruct (Table K11)
71.7 Right of pre-emption (Table K11)
Hypothecation
72 General (Table K11)
72.3 Mortgage. Land charges (Table K11)
72.9 Rent charge (Table K11)
Pledges
73 General (Table K11)
Contractual pledges
Pledges of personal property
Including possessory and nonpossessory pledges
73.3 General (Table K11)
73.5.A-Z Special topics, A-Z
73.5.A32 Accessority (Table K12)
73.5.P74 Priority (Table K12)
73.7 Pledges of rights (Table K11)
73.9 Lien or statutory pledge (Table K11)
74 Register of pledges (Table K11)
74.3 Transfer of ownership as security. Fiduciary transactions. Expectancies (Table K11)
Land register and registration. Immatriculation
74.4 General (Table K11)
74.5 Registration of proprietorship in common (Table K11)
75 Cadastral surveys. Cadaster (Table K11)
Class here general works on surveying agencies
For an individual surveying agency of a state or locality, see the state or locality
Inheritance. Succession upon death
76 General (Table K11)
76.5 Inheritance. Estate (Table K11)
Intestate succession

Civil law
Inheritance. Succession upon death
Intestate succession -- Continued
76.7 General (Table K11)
Classes of heirs. Order of succession
77 Matrilineal and patrilineal descendants (Table K11)
Including monogamous and polygamous households
77.2 Surviving spouses. Surviving wives with or without children (Table K11)
77.3 Natural parents (Table K11)
78 Community of heirs (Table K11)
78.3.A-Z Special topics, A-Z
78.3.P76 Primogeniture (Table K12)
Wills. Testamentary succession
78.5 General (Table K11)
78.6 Appointment of heir (Table K11)
78.7 Legacy. Testamentary burden. Bequest. Distribution of estate (Table K11)
78.8 Executors and administrators (Table K11)
79 Contract of inheritance (Table K11)
79.2 Purchase of inheritance (Table K11)
79.3 Certificate of inheritance. Proof of heirship (Table K11)
Obligations
80 General (Table K11)
Debtor and creditor. Chose in action and obligation
80.2 General (Table K11)
Plurality of debtors and creditors. Joint obligations
80.3 General (Table K11)
80.4 Correality and solidarity (Table K11)
Types of obligations
81 Obligations to give (Table K11)
Including obligation in kind
For money obligations see KL-KWX5 82
81.3 Transfer and assumption of obligations (Table K11)
Extinction of obligation
81.5 General (Table K11)
Performance. Payment
81.7 General (Table K11)
81.8 Due date of payment. Time of performance
For default (mora) see KL-KWX5 82.7
81.9 Consignation (Table K11)
Including emergency sale of perishables
82 Special rules as to payment of money debts
82.3 Compensation. Set-off (Table K11)
Nonperformance
Including liability and exclusion from liability

Civil law
Obligations
Nonperformance -- Continued
82.4 General (Table K11)
82.5 Impossibility of performance (Table K11)
Including original impossibility and supervening impossibility
82.7 Default (Table K11)
Damages
82.8 General (Table K11)
83 Causation (Table K11)
83.2 Damages for pain and suffering (Table K11)
Delicts. Torts
83.5 General (Table K11)
Protected rights
83.6 General (Table K11)
Personality rights
Freedom see KL-KWX5 85
Name see KL-KWX5 52.9
Integrity see KL-KWX5 85.7
Privacy see KL-KWX5 85.9+
Parties to action in torts
84 General (Table K11)
84.3 Principal. Accessories (Table K11)
84.4 Joint tortfeasors (Table K11)
84.6 Illegality (Table K11)
Liability
84.7 General (Table K11)
84.8 Exclusion of liability (Table K11)
Including contractual agreement, assumption of risk by injured part, and tacit (implied) agreement
84.9 Strict liability (Table K11)
For strict liability related to particular dangers, risks, or damages, see the topic under particular torts
Individual torts
85 Violation of freedom (Table K11)
Physical injuries
85.2 General (Table K11)
85.3 Accidents (Table K11)
For particular types of accidents see KL-KWX5 86.9
(85.5) Malpractice (Medical)
see KL-KWX5 310.95
85.6 Death by wrongful act (Table K11)
85.7 Violation of integrity (Table K11)
Including honor, dignity, and reputation
Violation of privacy
85.9 General (Table K11)

Civil law
Obligations
Delicts. Torts
Individual torts
Violation of privacy -- Continued
86 Right in one's own picture (Table K11)
86.3 Public opinion polls (Table K11)
86.5 Personal data in information retrieval systems (Table K11)
Including public and private records, registers, statistics, etc.
86.6 Immoral transactions and acts. Abuse or rights (Table K11)
86.7 Deceit. Misrepresentations. Forgery (Table K11)
86.72 Products liability (Table K11)
86.8 Ultrahazardous activities and occupations (Table K11)
86.9 Sports. Sport fields or installations (Table K11)
87 Liability for safe traffic conditions and accidents (Table K11)
Liability for safe conditions of streets, highways, public places, etc.
87.2 General (Table K11)
87.3 Traffic signs (Table K11)
87.4 Violation of official duties (Table K11)
Cf. KL-KWX5 283+ Government liability
87.45 Liability for environmental damages (Table K11)
For environmental crimes see KL-KWX5 435.2+
87.5 Unjust enrichment (Table K11)
Contracts and transactions
For commercial contracts see KL-KWX5 97+
87.6 General (Table K11)
87.7 Liberty of contract (Table K11)
87.8 Secured transactions. Security (Table K11)
Class here general works
For particular secured transactions, see the transaction, e.g. KL-KWX5 73+ Pledge; KL-KWX5 95.8 Suretyship, etc.
Declaration of intention
87.9 General (Table K11)
Agency
Including statutory agency
88 General (Table K11)
88.3 Power of attorney (Table K11)
Including general discretionary power of attorney
Mandate
88.5 General (Table K11)
88.7 Negotiorum gestio (Table K11)

Civil law
Obligations
Contracts and transactions
Mandate -- Continued
88.8 Negotiorum gestio without mandate (Table K11)
Void and voidable contracts and transactions
88.9 General (Table K11)
89 Error (Table K11)
89.3 Immoral transactions. Unconscionable transactions (Table K11)
Including mortis causa
Formation of contract
Including preliminary contract
89.5 General (Table K11)
Offer and acceptance
89.55 Contracts by adhesion (Table K11)
Clauses
89.6 General (Table K11)
89.66 Clausula rebus sic stantibus (Table K11)
89.7 Stipulation (Table K11)
Individual contracts and transactions
Sale
Cf. KL-KWX5 97.5+ Commercial law
89.75 General (Table K11)
89.77 Default (Table K11)
Including mora accipiendi
89.8 Warranty
Modes of sale
Conditional sale
89.85 General (Table K11)
89.87 Installment plans (Table K11)
Including installment payments through commercial finance companies
89.9.A-Z Other, A-Z
89.9.P73 Preemption (Table K12)
89.9.R48 Retractive sale (Table K12)
89.9.S24 Sale after approval (Table K12)
89.9.S25 Sale in kind (species) (Table K12)
89.9.S26 Sale on approval (Table K12)
89.9.S44 Self-service (Table K12)
90 Exchange. Barter (Table K11)
90.3 Donations. Gifts (Table K11)
90.4 Aestimatum (Table K11)
Consignment see KL-KWX5 97.7
Lease. Landlord and tenant
90.5 General (Table K11)

Civil law
Obligations
Contracts and transactions
Individual contracts and transactions
Lease. Landlord and tenant -- Continued
90.6 Parties to contract (Table K11)
Rights and claims from lease contract
Including subtenant
90.7 Liens of landlord (Table K11)
90.9 Lease litigation and execution (eviction) (Table K11)
Including procedure at regular civil courts and special tribunals, and including remedies
91.A-Z Types of property, A-Z
91.B85 Buildings. Rooms. Apartments (Table K12)
For social housing see KL-KWX5 91.3+
91.C66 Commercial space (Table K12)
91.R43 Real property (Table K12)
Social housing measures. State policy and planning
91.3 General (Table K11)
91.6 Public subsidies
Including subsidies and tax exemptions and deductions for home building and restoration
91.7 Rationing and distribution of housing (Table K11)
91.8 Rent control (Table K11)
Including subtenant
92 Publicly subsidized housing
92.3 Commercial and industrial property (Table K11)
Including operating leasing, producer leasing, etc.
92.4 Atypical or mixed contracts (Table K11)
Including operating leasing, producer leasing, etc.
Fiduciary transactions. Trust and trustee
92.5 General (Table K11)
Transfer of ownership see KL-KWX5 74.3
Charitable trusts see KL-KWX5 53.8
92.6 Loan for use. Commodatum (Table K11)
92.7 Personal loans. Mutuum (Table K11)
Including secured loans
Cf. KL-KWX5 100.5 Commercial law
Contracts of service and labor. Master and servant
93 General (Table K11)
93.3 Independent work. Professions (Table K11)
93.5 Dependent work (Table K11)
93.6 Contract for work and labor (Table K11)
Brokerage see KL-KWX5 97.8
93.7 Reward. Award (Table K11)
Mandate see KL-KWX5 88.5+

Civil law
Obligations
Contracts and transactions
Individual contracts and transactions -- Continued
93.8 Deposit (Table K11)
Including depositum irregulare
Cf. KL-KWX5 100.6 Banking
Civil companies
For associations see KL-KWX5 53.3+
For personal companies and stock companies see KL-KWX5 108+
93.9 General (Table K11)
94 De facto company (Table K11)
94.2 Termination. Liquidation (Table K11)
94.3 Life annuity (Table K11)
Aleatory contracts
95 General (Table K11)
95.3 Gambling. Betting (Table K11)
95.5 Lotteries (Table K11)
95.8 Suretyship (Table K11)
Including accessority
96 Compromise (Table K11)
96.3 Promise of debt. Promissory note (Table K11)
96.4 Acknowledgment of debt (Table K11)
96.5 Discovery (Disclosure) (Table K11)
Commercial law. Commercial transactions
97 General (Table K11)
Merchant and business enterprise
97.2 General (Table K11)
97.25 Accounting (Table K11)
Including inventory
For tax accounting see KL-KWX5 355.4
97.3 Commercial registers (Table K11)
For publicity see KL-KWX5 185.2
Commercial sale
97.5 General (Table K11)
97.52.A-Z Particular, A-Z
97.52.F87 Futures (Table K12)
97.6 Commercial agents (Table K11)
97.7 Consignment. Commission merchant (Table K11)
97.8 Brokerage (Table K11)
97.9 Auctioneers. Auctions (Table K11)
98 Warehousing (Table K11)
Freight forwarders and carriers. Carriage of passengers and goods
98.2 General (Table K11)

Commercial law. Commercial transactions
Freight forwarders and carriers. Carriage of passengers and goods -- Continued
98.3 Bill of lading (Table K11)
98.5 Liens (Table K11)
98.53.A-Z Other, A-Z
98.53.D44 Delivery (Table K12)
Types of carriers
For regulatory (administrative) aspects see KL-KWX5 344+
98.6 Railroads (Table K11)
98.62 Passenger carriers. Bus lines (Table K11)
98.7 Trucklines (Table K11)
98.8 Airlines (Table K11)
Carriage by sea see KL-KWX5 101.9+
Commercial instruments see KL-KWX5 99+
98.9 Commercial liens
For freight forwarder liens see KL-KWX5 98.5
Negotiable instruments. Titles of credit
99 General (Table K11)
99.3 Bills of exchange (Table K11)
Stamp duties see KL-KWX5 363.3
99.4 Checks (Table K11)
Letters of credit see KL-KWX5 100.5
Stock certificates and bonds see KL-KWX5 109.9+
Trust investments see KL-KWX5 101.4
Bills of lading (Land transportation) see KL-KWX5 98.3
Promissory notes see KL-KWX5 96.3
Criminal provisions see KL-KWX5 435
Banking. Stock exchange
99.5 General (Table K11)
Types of banks and credit institutions
99.6 Banks of issue (Table K11)
99.7 Mortgage banks (Table K11)
99.8 Savings banks (Table K11)
Including public and private banks, and state supervision
99.9 Building and loan associations (Table K11)
100 Cooperative societies (Table K11)
100.2 Clearinghouses (Table K11)
100.3 Warehouses (Table K11)
Banking transactions
100.4 General (Table K11)
Contract see KL-KWX5 100.4
Deposits see KL-KWX5 100.6
100.5 Loans. Credit (Table K11)
100.55 Letters of credit (Table K11)

Commercial law. Commercial transactions
Banking. Stock exchange
Banking transactions -- Continued
100.6 Deposit banking. Custodianship accounts (Table K11)
100.7 Account current (Table K11)
100.8 Noncash funds transfer (Table K11)
Including electronic funds transfer, and bilkl paying services
Investments
100.9 General (Table K11)
Foreign investments see KL-KWX5 321.3
101 Stock exchange transactions. Securities (Table K11)
101.15 Commodity exchanges. Produce exchanges (Table K11)
Investment trust
101.2 General (Table K11)
101.3 Real estate investment trust (Table K11)
101.4 Trust investments (Table K11)
101.5 Criminal provisions (Table K11)
Including money laundering
Taxation of banking and stock exchange transactions see KL-KWX5 362.4.B35
Maritime law
For regulatory aspcets of water transportation, navigation, and pilotage see KL-KWX5 347+
101.6 General (Table K11)
101.7 Shipowners. Ship operators. Shipmasters (Table K11)
Affreightment. Carriage of goods at sea and inland waters
101.9 General (Table K11)
102 Freight forwarders (Table K11)
Including liability
102.4 Carriage of passengers at sea and inland waters
Including carriage of passengers' luggage
Average
102.6 General (Table K11)
102.7 Havarie grosse (Table K11)
Special average. Collision at sea
102.8 General (Table K11)
Insurance see KL-KWX5 103.5
102.9 Salvage. Shipwreck (Table K11)
Ship creditors
103 General (Table K11)
103.2 Bottomry and respondentia. Ship mortgages. Maritime liens (Table K11)
103.3 Ship registers (Table K11)
103.4 Maritime courts (Table K11)
103.5 Marine insurance (Table K11)

Commercial law. Commercial transactions
Maritime law -- Continued
Maritime social legislation
Including legislation for merchant mariners for inland navigation
103.6 General (Table K11)
Labor law for merchant mariners
103.7 General (Table K11)
103.8 Labor standards (Table K11)
Including hours of labor, wages, nonwage benefits, and vacations
103.9 Discipline (Table K11)
104 Social insurance for merchant mariners (Table K11)
Including all branches of social insurance
Insurance law
Including regulation of insurance business
104.3 General (Table K11)
Life insurance
104.6 General (Table K11)
104.7 Group insurance (Table K11)
104.8 Old age pensions (Table K11)
104.9 Survivors' benefits (Table K11)
105 Health insurance. Medical care insurance (Table K11)
105.3 Accident insurance (Table K11)
Property insurance
105.5 General (Table K11)
105.6 Multiple line insurance (Table K11)
Including home owners insurance
105.7.A-Z Particular hazards, A-Z
Burglary see KL-KWX5 105.7.T43
105.7.F57 Fire (Table K12)
Robbery see KL-KWX5 105.7.T43
105.7.T43 Theft. Burglary. Robbery (Table K12)
105.7.W38 Water damage (Table K12)
105.8.A-Z Types of property and business, A-Z
Subarrange each by Table K12
Suretyship. Guaranty. Title insurance
106 General (Table K11)
106.3 Credit insurance (Table K11)
106.35 Litigation insurance (Table K11)
106.4 Mortgage insurance (Table K11)
106.5 Liability insurance (Table K11)
Including both statutory and private insurance
Other risks and damages
Traffic
106.7 General (Table K11)
106.8 Automobiles

Commercial law. Commercial transactions
Insurance law
Other risks and damages
Traffic -- Continued
106.9 Automotive transportation (General) (Table K11)
Including trucking, bus lines, etc.
107 Aviation (Table K11)
107.3 Reinsurance (Table K11)
Business associations
107.5 General (Table K11)
107.6 Constitutional aspects. Interdiction of private business associations (Table K11)
107.7 Expropriation and nationalization of business associations (Table K11)
Personal companies. Unincorporated business associations
For civil companies see KL-KWX5 93.9+
108 General (Table K11)
108.3 Partners (Table K11)
Including natural persons and juristic persons
108.4 Accounting. Financial statements. Auditing (Table K11)
108.5 Termination. Dissolution. Liquidation (Table K11)
108.6 Partnership (Table K11)
108.7 Limited partnership (Table K11)
108.8 Silent partners (Table K11)
Stock companies. Incorporated business associations
108.9 General (Table K11)
Stock corporations
109 General (Table K11)
109.3 Incorporation and promoters (Table K11)
109.7 Organization and management (Table K11)
Corporate finance
109.8 General (Table K11)
Securities
109.9 Stocks (Table K11)
Including bearer stock, common stock (with or without par value), and preferred stock
110 Bonds (Table K11)
110.3 Stocks and stockholders' rights. Stock transfer (Table K11)
110.4.A-Z Types of corporations, A-Z
110.4.F36 Family corporations (Table K12)
110.4.O64 One-person companies (Table K12)
110.6 Termination. Dissolution. Liquidation (Table K11)
Corporate reorganization see KL-KWX5 113.6+
Consolidation and merger see KL-KWX5 113.7
110.65 Criminal provisions

Commercial law. Commercial transactions
Business associations
Stock companies. Incorporated business associations -- Continued
110.7 Partnership partly limited by shares (Table K11)
Private company
110.9 General (Table K11)
Liability see KL-KWX5 110.9
111 Stock and stockholders' rights. Stock transfer (Table K11)
Types of private companies
111.4 Family corporations (Table K11)
111.5 One-person companies (Table K11)
111.6 Multi-national corporations (Table K11)
111.7 Colonial companies (History) (Table K11)
Cooperative societies
112 General (Table K11)
112.3 Membership (Table K11)
112.5.A-Z Types of cooperative societies, A-Z
112.5.C65 Consumer cooperatives (Table K12)
Consolidation and merger see KL-KWX5 113.7
Combinations. Industrial trusts
For government control see KL-KWX5 322.2+
113 General (Table K11)
113.3 Consortium (Table K11)
113.4 Joint ventures (Table K11)
Business concerns
113.5 General (Table K11)
Liability see KL-KWX5 113.5
Corporate reorganization
113.6 General (Table K11)
113.7 Consolidation and merger (Table K11)
For government control see KL-KWX5 322.3
113.8.A-Z Special topics, A-Z
Subarrange each by Table K12
Insolvency and bankruptcy see KL-KWX5 194+
Intellectual and industrial property
115 General (Table K11)
Copyright
115.2 General (Table K11)
115.3 Authorship (Table K11)
Including multiple authorship and author cooperatives, and anonyms and pseudonyms
115.4 Intangible property (Table K11)

Intellectual and industrial property
Copyright -- Continued
115.5 Procedures. Formalities (Table K11)
Including registration of claim, transfer, licenses, deposit, and notice
115.6 Protected works (Table K11)
Including original works, subsequent rights, idea and title
115.7 Scope of protection (Table K11)
115.8 Employees' copyright (Table K11)
115.9 Delicts. Torts (Table K11)
Branches of copyright
116 Literary copyright (Table K11)
117 Musical copyright (Table K11)
Fine art and photography
117.5 General (Table K11)
Violation of rights in one's own picture see KL-KWX5 86
Motion pictures see KL-KWX5 118
117.7 Designs and models (Table K11)
117.9 Prints and labels (Table K11)
Including works of commercial art, catalogs, sample books, etc.
118 Motion pictures and television programs (Table K11)
118.3 Computer programs (Table K11)
118.4 Quasi copyright and neighboring rights (Table K11)
Author and publisher
Including the publishing contract
118.5 General (Table K11)
118.6 Plays and stage productions (Table K11)
118.7 Motion pictures (Table K11)
118.8 Music (Table K11)
118.9 Scientific literature (Table K11)
Patent law and trademarks
119 General (Table K11)
120 Patent office (Table K11)
Patent practice and procedure
120.2 General (Table K11)
Invention
Including priority and novelty
120.3 General (Table K11)
120.5 Employees' invention and technological innovation (Table K11)
120.6 Designs and utility models (Table K11)
Licenses
Including compulsory licenses and fees
120.7 General (Table K11)

Intellectual and industrial property
Patent law and trademarks
Licenses -- Continued
120.8 Foreign licensing agreements (Table K11)
Including know-how
121 Patent litigation and infringements (Table K11)
Trademarks
122 General (Table K11)
122.5 Practice and procedure (Table K11)
Unfair competition
For restraint of trade see KL-KWX5 322+
123 General (Table K11)
Advertising
123.3 General (Table K11)
123.5 Disparagement of goods (Table K11)
Including comparative advertising
123.7 Testing of commercial products (Table K11)
124 Pushing for sales (Table K11)
Including unordered merchandise by mail
124.3 Rebates and premiums (Table K11)
125 Delicts. Torts (Table K11)
Cf. KL-KWX5 83.5+ Civil law
125.5 Practice and procedure (Table K11)
Including arbitration and award
Labor law
Including works on both labor law and social insurance, and private labor law as it applies to the labor contract and to the labor-management relationship
Criticism and reform see KL-KWX5 146
126 General (Table K11)
126.3 Labor policies. Competition and incentives for high performance (Table K11)
126.4 Organization and administration (Table K11)
Class here works on national departments and boards of labor, national, state and local departments and boards, or departments and boards of several states or administrative districts
For departments or boards (several or individual) of an individual state or administrative district, see the state or district
Labor contract and employment
127 General (Table K11)
127.3 Individual labor contract and collective agreements. Liberty of contract (Table K11)
Freedom of employment and restraint on freedom of employment
128 General (Table K11)

Labor law
Labor contract and employment
Freedom of employment and restraint on freedom of employment -- Continued
128.3 Preferential employment (Table K11)
Including people with severe disabilities, veterans, etc.
128.5 Formation of contract (Table K11)
128.7 Parties to contract (Table K11)
Prohibition of discrimination in employment see KL-KWX5 131+
Extinction of employment
Cf. KL-KWX5 81.5+ Obligation
129 General (Table K11)
129.3 Dismissal and resignation of employees (Table K11)
Including economic crisis dismissal, layoff, short hours, suspension, reinstatement, dismissal wage, etc.
130 Job security (Table K11)
130.3 Nonperformance (Table K11)
Cf. KL-KWX5 82.4+ Civil law
130.4 Liability (Table K11)
Including liability of employer, employee, and liability toward co-worker and third parties
Prohibition of discrimination in employment. Equal opportunity
131 General (Table K11)
131.3 Wage discrimination. Equal pay for equal work (Table K11)
131.4.A-Z Groups discriminated against, A-Z
131.4.A33 Aged. Older people (Table K12)
131.4.A44 Alien laborers (Table K12)
131.4.D58 Disabilities, People with (Table K12)
Older people see KL-KWX5 131.4.A33
People with disabilities see KL-KWX5 131.4.D58
131.4.W58 Women (Table K12)
Wages
132 General (Table K11)
Types of wages and modes of remuneration
132.3 Incentive wages (Table K11)
Including bonus system, profit sharing, etc.
132.4 Collective wages (Table K11)
132.5 Adjustments. Cost-of-living adjustments (Table K11)
133 Nonwage payments and fringe benefits (Table K11)
133.4.A-Z Groups of employees or industries, A-Z
Subarrange each by Table K12
Labor-management relations
134 General (Table K11)
Works councils
Including election, organization, parliamentary practice, etc.

Labor law
Labor-management relations
Works councils -- Continued
134.3 General (Table K11)
134.4 Works assembly (Table K11)
Works councils of business concerns see KL-KWX5 137
134.5 Union participation (Table K11)
Employee participation in management and planning
135 General (Table K11)
136 Labor standards and protection of labor (Table K11)
136.6 Personnel management (Table K11)
137 Employee representation on board of controllers and supervisors (Table K11)
Including unincorporated and incorporated business associations, cooperative societies, industrial trusts, etc.
Collective bargaining and labor agreements
137.5 General (Table K11)
137.7 Standardized labor conditions (Table K11)
Collective labor disputes
138 General (Table K11)
Strikes and lockouts. Boycott
138.3 General (Table K11)
138.5 Wildcat strikes. Sympathy strikes. Political strikes (Table K11)
Corporate representation
139 General (Table K11)
139.3 Unions (Table K11)
139.5 Employers' associations (Table K11)
Protection of labor
140 General (Table K11)
140.3 Hours of labor (Table K11)
Including night work and Sunday labor
Vacations
141 Sick leave (Table K11)
141.3 Holidays (Table K11)
141.5 Child and youth labor (Table K11)
Including hours of labor
141.7 Women's labor (Table K11)
Including hours of labor
142 Home labor (Table K11)
142.3 Labor hygiene and industrial safety (Table K11)
Including safety regulations for equipment
142.5.A-Z By industry or type of labor, A-Z
142.5.B84 Building and construction industry (Table K12)
142.5.C48 Chemical industry (Table K12)
142.5.N82 Nuclear industry (Table K12)

Labor law
Protection of labor
By industry or type of labor, A-Z -- Continued
142.5.P35 Paper products industry (Table K12)
142.5.P48 Petroleum industry (Table K12)
142.5.P75 Printing industry (Table K12)
142.8.A-Z Labor law for particular industries or occupations, etc., A-Z
142.8.A37 Agricultural laborers (Table K12)
142.8.E93 Executives (Table K12)
143 Labor supply. Manpower control. Manpower planning (Table K11)
Labor courts and procedure
Class here works on courts of several jurisdictions
For courts (several or individual) of an individual jurisdiction, see the jurisdiction
144 General (Table K11)
144.3 Procedural principles (Table K11)
Procedure at first instance
144.5 General (Table K11)
Actions and defenses
144.6 Judicial review of grievance procedures (Table K11)
145 Evidence. Burden of proof (Table K11)
145.2 Remedies. Appellate procedures (Table K11)
145.3 Arbitration (Table K11)
Competence conflicts between labor, and social courts see KL-KWX5 281
Social legislation
146 Social reform and policies (Table K11)
Including all branches of social legislation and labor
146.3 General (Table K11)
Social insurance. Social security
For works on both labor law and social insurance see KL-KWX5 125.92+
Criticism and reform see KL-KWX5 146+
Information retrieval and electronic data processing see KL-KWX5 4.3
146.5 General (Table K11)
147 Organization and administration (Table K11)
Including insurance carriers
For national departments and boards of labor and social insurance see KL-KWX5 126.4
147.6 Coverage and benefits (Table K11)
Health insurance
For private health insurance see KL-KWX5 105
148 General (Table K11)
148.4 Organization and administration

Social legislation
Social insurance
Health insurance -- Continued
148.5.A-Z Coverage and benefits, A-Z
Subarrange each by Table K12
For public employees and officials see KL-KWX5 297.8
148.8.A-Z Groups of beneficiaries, A-Z
Subarrange each by Table K12
149 Workers' compensation (Table K11)
Including occupational diseases
For merchant mariners see KL-KWX5 104
150.4 Old age, survivors and disability insurance (Compulsory) (Table K11)
151 Unemployment insurance (Compulsory) (Table K11)
For civil service pensions see KL-KWX5 297.8
Social services. Public welfare
Criticism and reform see KL-KWX5 146
152 General (Table K11)
152.3 Organization and administration (Table K11)
152.5 Social work and social workers (Table K11)
Including rural social services
Social service beneficiaries
152.6 The poor and destitute (Table K11)
152.7 Older people (Table K11)
152.8 Pensioners (Table K11)
152.9 Large families (Table K11)
People with disabilities
Including people with physical, mental, and emotional disabilities
153 General (Table K11)
153.4.A-Z Beneficiaries, A-Z
153.4.B54 Blind (Table K12)
153.4.D42 Deaf-mute (Table K12)
153.4.S38 Severe disabilities, People with (Table K12)
153.5 Asocial types (Table K11)
153.6 Evacuated and homeless persons (Table K11)
War-related groups of beneficiaries
153.7 General (Table K11)
153.8 Refugees. Expelled or forcefully repatriated persons (Table K11)
153.9 Prisoners of war and political prisoners. Veterans (Table K11)
154 Services for war victims and war invalids (Table K11)
Children. Youth
154.2 General (Table K11)
Measures and provisions

Social legislation
Social services. Public welfare
Social service beneficiaries
Children. Youth
Measures and provisions -- Continued
154.5 General (Table K11)
154.6 Protection of children in public (Table K11)
Including restaurants, taverns, theaters, gambling, etc.
154.8 Government guardianship (Table K11)
154.9 Custodial education. Collective education (Table K11)
Social courts and procedure
Class here works on courts of several jurisdictions
For courts (several or individual) of an individual jurisdiction, see the jurisdiction
155 General (Table K11)
155.4.A-Z Particular courts, A-Z
Subarrange each by Table K12
155.5 Parties to action
Pretrial procedures
156 Procedure at first instance (Table K11)
156.4 Judicial decisions and judgments (Table K11)
156.7 Execution (Table K11)
156.8 Costs (Table K11)
Competence conflicts between administrative, labor, and social courts see KL-KWX5 281
Courts and procedure
The administration of justice. The organization of the judiciary
Including the administration of criminal justice
Criticism. Reform see KL-KWX5 46.8
157 General (Table K11)
157.6 Organization and administration (Table K11)
Class here works on national and state departments of justice or departments of justice of several states
For the departments of justice of an individual state, see the state
Judicial statistics see KL-KWX5 3+
Judicial assistance see KL-KWX5 164+
Criminal policy see KL-KWX5 395+
Courts
Including courts of both criminal and civil jurisdiction
158 General (Table K11)
Regular courts
Class here works on national (federal) courts and on courts of several jurisdictions
For courts (several or individual) of an individual jurisdiction, see the jurisdiction

Courts and procedure
Courts
Regular courts -- Continued
158.2 General (Table K11)
158.3 Local courts. Municipal courts. Magistrate courts. Justice of the peace (Lowest courts) (Table K11)
Juvenile courts see KL-KWX5 472+
158.4 Regional courts. Provincial courts. District courts. District people's courts (Table K11)
158.6 Supreme courts of state or republics (Table K11)
National (Federal) supreme courts. Supreme courts of cassation
158.65 General (Table K11)
Labor courts see KL-KWX5 144+
Constitutional courts see KL-KWX5 262+
Finance courts see KL-KWX5 368+
Courts of special jurisdiction. Special tribunals
158.7 General (Table K11)
Religious courts and councils
158.74 General (Table K11)
158.75 Sharia courts. Kadi courts (Table K11)
158.76 Rabbinical courts (Table K11)
158.78 Customary (native) courts of law (Table K11)
158.8 Consular courts (Table K11)
158.9 Courts of honor (Table K11)
Class here general works
For individual courts (Business) see KL-KWX5 343.9
For individual courts (Professions) see KL-KWX5 352.7
Other courts of special jurisdiction
see the subject, e.g. KL-KWX5 144+ Labor courts; KL-KWX5 376.7 Military courts; etc.
158.92 Supreme judicial councils (Table K11)
159 Special tribunal within a court (Table K11)
159.3.A-Z Other public bodies with judicial functions, A-Z
159.3.C65 Comrade's courts (Table K12)
159.3.M85 Municipal arbitral boards (Table K12)
159.7 Judicial opinions. Advisory opinions (Table K11)
The legal profession
Including judicial officers and personnel, and including salaries, allowances, pensions, etc.
160 General (Table K11)
Law school education see KL-KWX5 5+
160.4 Judicial personnel other than lawyers (Table K11)
160.5 Nationality and citizenship (Table K11)
160.6.A-Z Minorities, A-Z
Subarrange each by Table K12

Courts and procedure
The legal profession -- Continued
Judges
160.7 General (Table K11)
Women judges see KL-KWX5 160.6.A+
160.75 Ethics and discipline (Table K11)
Office of the public prosecutor. Procuracy
160.8 General (Table K11)
160.9 Supervision. Procuratorial supervision (Table K11)
Notaries see KL-KWX5 184.6+
Auxiliary personnel. Clerk's office
162 General (Table K11)
Clerks to the court
162.3 Business administration. Court records (Table K11)
For personal data protection in information retrieval systems see KL-KWX5 86.5
162.4 Bailiffs (Table K11)
162.6 Experts and expert witnesses (Table K11)
Practice of law
162.9 General (Table K11)
Attorneys
163 General (Table K11)
Admission to the bar see KL-KWX5 5.5
Courts of honor. Disbarment see KL-KWX5 5.5
163.3 Legal consultants (Table K11)
Procurators see KL-KWX5 160.8+
163.9 Legal aid. Legal services to the poor. Community legal services
Judicial assistance
Including judicial assistance in criminal matters
164 General (Table K11)
164.4 International judicial assistance (Table K11)
164.6 Foreign judgments (Conflicts of laws) (Table K11)
Procedure in general
Class here works on civil and criminal procedure and works on civil, commercial, and labor procedure combined
165 General (Table K11)
Procedural principles
165.15 Due process of law (Table K11)
165.5 Parties to action (Table K11)
166 Pretrial procedures (Table K11)
Procedure at first instance. Trial
166.3 General (Table K11)
166.6 Actions and defenses (Table K11)
166.8 Particular proceedings (Table K11)
Evidence. Burden of proof

Courts and procedure
Procedure in general
Procedure at first instance. Trial
Evidence. Burden of proof -- Continued
167 General (Table K11)
167.5 Witnesses (Table K11)
167.7 Documentary evidence (Table K11)
167.9 Judicial decisions (Table K11)
168.6 Remedies (Table K11)
169 Execution (Table K11)
169.2 Costs. Fees (Table K11)
Civil procedure
169.5 Criticism. Reform (Table K11)
170 General (Table K11)
170.2 Civil procedure law relating to other branches of the law (Table K11)
Procedural principles
170.4 Due process of law (Table K11)
Including frivolous suits
170.6 Publicity and oral procedure (Table K11)
Parties to action
171 General (Table K11)
Litigant. Plaintiff. Defendant
171.5 General (Table K11)
Change of parties see KL-KWX5 176.C53
State prosecutor see KL-KWX5 160.8+
Pretrial procedures
172 General (Table K11)
172.3 Time periods. Deadlines (Table K11)
Including default and restitution
172.5 Suspension of procedure (Table K11)
Procedure at first instance
173 General (Table K11)
173.7 Jurisdiction. Competence in subject matter and venue (Table K11)
174 Representation. Power of attorney (Table K11)
Lis pendens see KL-KWX5 175.6.L58
Res judicata see KL-KWX5 175.6.R48
Time periods. Deadlines see KL-KWX5 172.3
Actions and defenses
174.5 General (Table K11)
Classification of actions see KL-KWX5 178.5+
Defenses and exceptions
175 General (Table K11)
175.6.A-Z Defenses, A-Z
Counterclaim see KL-KWX5 175.6.S48

| | |
|---|---|
| | Courts and procedure |
| | Civil procedure |
| | Procedure at first instance |
| | Actions and defenses |
| | Defenses and exceptions |
| | Defenses, A-Z -- Continued |
| 175.6.L55 | Limitation of actions (Table K12) |
| 175.6.L58 | Lis pendens (Table K12) |
| 175.6.R48 | Res judicata (Table K12) |
| 175.6.S48 | Set-off. Counterclaim (Cross section) (Table K12) |
| 176.A-Z | Particular proceedings, A-Z |
| 176.C53 | Change of parties (Table K12)<br>Including death of party |
| 176.C57 | Class action. Citizen suits (Table K12) |
| 176.C66 | Compromise (Table K12) |
| 176.D44 | Decision without trial (Table K12) |
| 176.D46 | Default judgments (Table K12) |
| 176.D57 | Dismissal and nonsuit (Table K12) |
| 176.I67 | Interpleader (Table K12) |
| 176.I68 | Intervention (Table K12) |
| 176.S47 | Settlement before trial (Table K12) |
| | Evidence |
| 177 | General (Table K11) |
| 177.3 | Burden of proof (Table K11) |
| 177.5 | Admission of evidence (Table K11) |
| | Witnesses |
| 177.7 | General (Table K11) |
| 177.8 | Privileged witnesses (Confidential communication) (Table K11) |
| 177.9 | Expert testimony (Table K11) |
| | Judicial decisions |
| 178 | General (Table K11) |
| | Judgment |
| 178.3 | General (Table K11) |
| | Types of judgment |
| 178.5 | Judgments to do, to tolerate, to refrain from doing (Table K11) |
| 178.7 | Agreed judgment (Table K11) |
| | Judgment by default see KL-KWX5 176.D46 |
| | Decision without trial see KL-KWX5 176.D44 |
| | Dismissal and nonsuit see KL-KWX5 176.D57 |
| 179 | Interlocutory decisions (Table K11) |
| 179.3 | Res judicata (Table K11) |
| 179.4 | Court records. Minutes of evidence (Table K11)<br>Including clerks' mistakes and corrections |
| 180 | Advisory opinions (Table K11) |

Courts and procedure
Civil procedure -- Continued
Particular procedures
180.4 General (Table K11)
180.7 Procedures in parent and child cases (Table K11)
For procedures in guardianship cases see KL-KWX5 62.5
180.9 Interdiction. Mental competency procedure (Table K11)
181 Public summons (Table K11)
Settlement before trial see KL-KWX5 176.S47
181.2 Hortatory procedures (Table K11)
181.4 Small claims. Procedures before the justice of the peace or magistrate (Table K11)
Remedies
181.6 General (Table K11)
Appellate procedure
182 General (Table K11)
182.4 Revision (Table K11)
182.5 Cassation (Table K11)
182.6 New trial. Reopening of a case (Table K11)
182.9 Arbitration (Table K11)
Including commercial arbitration
183 Costs (Table K11)
Including in forma pauperis
Noncontentious (ex parte) jurisdiction
183.4 General (Table K11)
183.5 Parties to action (Table K11)
183.8 Evidence (Table K11)
184 Remedies and special procedures (Table K11)
Notaries. Notarial practice and procedure
Class here works on notaries of several jurisdictions
For notaries (several or individual) of an individual state, administrative district, or municipality, see the state, district, or municipality
184.6 General (Table K11)
184.7 Legal instruments. Certification (Table K11)
184.8 Costs (Table K11)
Registration. Recording
Class here works on registers of several jurisdictions
For registers (several or individual) of an individual state, administrative district, or municipality, see the state, district or municipality
185 General (Table K11)
185.2 Publicity (Table K11)
Civil register
185.4 General (Table K11)

Courts and procedure
Noncontentious (ex parte) jurisdiction
Registration. Recording
Civil register -- Continued
Registration of civil status
185.6 General (Table K11)
185.7 Family names (Table K11)
186 Marriage (Table K11)
186.2 Birth (Table K11)
186.4 Death (Table K11)
For absence and presumption of death see KL-KWX5 51.7
186.5 Aliens. Stateless foreigners (Table K11)
186.6 Costs (Table K11)
186.7 Register of matrimonial property (Table K11)
Land registers see KL-KWX5 74.4+
Ship registers see KL-KWX5 103.3
Commercial registers see KL-KWX5 97.3
Domestic relations procedure
187 General (Table K11)
187.2 Adoption procedures (Table K11)
Guardianship court see KL-KWX5 62.5
Government guardianship see KL-KWX5 154.8
188 Inheritance (Probate court) procedure (Table K11)
188.2 Costs (Table K11)
Class here general works
For costs of a particular branch of noncontentious jurisdiction, see the branch
Insolvency
188.5 General (Table K11)
Execution
188.8 General (Table K11)
189 Parties to execution (Table K11)
Including executors and administration, and succession during execution
Bailiffs see KL-KWX5 162.4
189.4 Titles for execution (Table K11)
Including judgments (res judicata), documents of title, etc., and provisional enforcement
Procedure in execution
189.6 General (Table K11)
189.7 Discovery proceedings. Poor debtors oath (Table K11)
Including inventory
190 Judicial decisions (Res judicata) (Table K11)
Execution for payment due
190.2 General (Table K11)

Courts and procedure
Insolvency
Execution
Procedure in execution
Execution for payment due -- Continued
Hortatory procedures see KL-KWX5 181.2
190.4 Attachment and garnishment of personal property (Table K11)
Attachment and garnishment of rights and choses in action
190.6 General (Table K11)
190.8.A-Z Other, A-Z
Subarrange each by Table K12
190.9 Judicial sale (Table K11)
Including transfer of ownership
Poor debtors oath see KL-KWX5 189.7
Remedies see KL-KWX5 192.7
191 Execution in real property (Table K11)
Including foreclosure sale, judicial sale, and receivership
Exemptions and restrictions see KL-KWX5 193.4
192 Enforcement of surrender of goods or documents (Table K11)
192.5 Executions against associations, personal companies, and corporations (Table K11)
Including execution against juristic persons of public law
192.6 Injunction. Arrest. Seizure (Table K11)
192.7 Remedies (Table K11)
192.9 Costs (Table K11)
Protection against abuse of claims enforcement
193 General (Table K11)
Moratorium see KL-KWX5 197.5
193.2 Suspension. Accord and satisfaction (Table K11)
193.3 Compromise (Table K11)
193.4 Restriction of execution (Table K11)
Bankruptcy
194 General (Table K11)
194.4 Parties to action (Table K11)
195 Insolvent estate (Table K11)
Including avoidance of transfers, and property not included in the bankrupt estate (exempted property)
Procedure in bankruptcy
195.2 General (Table K11)
Priority of credits
195.4 General (Table K11)
195.7.A-Z Particular secured or privileged credits, A-Z
Subarrange each by Table K12

Courts and procedure
Insolvency
Bankruptcy
Procedure -- Continued
195.8 Distribution (Table K11)
195.9 Composition to end bankruptcy (Table K11)
196 Judicial review of voidable transactions
For fraudulent conveyances see KL-KWX5 427.6
196.3 Effect of bankruptcy on obligations and rights (Table K11)
196.5 Costs (Table K11)
Debtors' relief
For wartime debtors' relief see KL-KWX5 371.7
197 General (Table K11)
197.2 Composition to avoid bankruptcy. Deferment of execution
Including receivership
197.5 Moratorium (Table K11)
197.6 Costs (Table K11)
Including bookkeeping and accounting
Public law
Class here works on all aspects of public law, including early works
For civics see KL-KWX5 6.5
200 General (Table K11)
The State
Including philosophy and theory of the state
For non-legal works on political theory, see JC
201 General (Table K11)
201.5 Sovereignty. Potestas (Table K11)
Federalism see KL-KWX5 237.3
Centralization of powers see KL-KWX5 226
Rule of law
202 General (Table K11)
Socialist state
202.5 General (Table K11)
203 Democratic centralism (Table K11)
Constitutional law
For works on the constitutional aspects of a subject, see the subject
History see KL-KWX5 208.2+
205 Constitutional reform. Criticism. Polemic (Table K11)
For works on a particular constitution, see the constitution
207.A12 Bibliography
Including bibliography of constitutional history
207.A15 Periodicals
Including gazettes, yearbooks, bulletins, etc.
Monographic series see KL-KWX5 207.A15
Sources
Including early constitutions and related materials

Constitutional law

Sources -- Continued

207.A28 Collections. Compilations. By date

207.A31<date> Individual constitutions

Arrange chronologically by appending the date of adoption to this number and deleting any trailing zeros. Subarrange each by main entry

207.A32<date> Individual sources other than constitutions

Arrange chronologically by appending the date of adoption or issuance to this number and deleting any trailing zeros. Subarrange each by main entry

Court decisions and related materials. Reports

Including decisions of quasi-judicial (regulatory) agencies

207.A473 Indexes and tables. Digests

207.A48 Serials

207.A49 Monographs. By date

Decisions of regulatory agencies. Orders. Rulings see KL-KWX5 207.A473+

Dictionaries. Encyclopedias see KL-KWX5 207.A9+

Form books see KL-KWX5 207.A9+

Yearbooks see KL-KWX5 207.A15

Collected works (nonserial) see KL-KWX5 207.A9+

207.A67 Conferences. Symposia

Including papers devoted to the scholarly exploration of the subject of constitutional law

207.A9-.Z9 General works. Treatises

Constitutional history

For individual constitutions see KL-KWX5 207.A31<date>

209 General (Table K11)

By period

Ancient/Early to ca. 1800 see KL-KWX5 20.2+

From ca. 1800 to most recent constitution

210 General (Table K11)

Constitutional principles

212 Sovereignty of parliament (Table K11)

213 Rulers, princes, dynasties (Table K11)

Including dynastic rules and works on legal status and juristic personality of ruling houses

214 Privileges of classes and particular groups. Rights of peerage (Table K11)

215 Privileges, prerogatives, and immunities of rulers of states (Table K11)

216 Sources and relationships of law (Table K11)

Intergovernmental relations. Jurisdiction

217 General (Table K11)

Constitutional law
Constitutional history
By period
From ca. 1800 to most recent constitution
Intergovernmental relations. Jurisdiction -- Continued
218 Federal-state (republic), national-provincial controversies. State-state or interprovincial disputes (Table K11)
Privileges, prerogatives, and immunities of particular states or estates see KL-KWX5 230
219 Distribution of legislative power. Exclusive and concurrent legislative power. Reservation of provincial legislation (Table K11)
220.A-Z Special topics, A-Z
Subarrange each by Table K12
Class here works on topics not provided for elsewhere
For the history of a particular subject, see the subject
222 Interpretation and construction (Table K11)
Modern constitutional principles
224 Legitimacy (Table K11)
225 Legality. Socialist legality (Table K11)
Rule of law see KL-KWX5 202+
226 Centralization of powers (Table K11)
Separation and delegation of powers
227 General (Table K11)
227.5 Conflict of interests. Incompatibility of offices. Ethics in government (Table K11)
Executive privilege see KL-KWX5 230
228 Judicial review of legislative acts (Table K11)
229 Privileges of classes (estates) and particular groups. Rights of peerage (Table K11)
230 Privileges, prerogatives, and immunities of rulers of states (Table K11)
Sources and relationships of the law
232 Preconstitutional and constitutional law (Table K11)
232.5 International law and municipal law (Table K11)
233 Statutory law and delegated legislation (Table K11)
234 Customary law and observances (Table K11)
236 Decrees (individual) (Table K11)
Intergovernmental relations. Jurisdiction
237 General (Table K11)
237.3 Federalism (Table K11)
237.5 Federal-state (republic), national-provincial controversies. Interstate (Interprovincial, etc.) disputes (Table K11)
238 Cooperation of states, republics, provinces, etc. (Table K11)

Constitutional law
Intergovernmental relations. Jurisdiction -- Continued
238.5 Exclusive and concurring jurisdiction (Table K11)
Including national (federal) and state (republic, province, etc.) jurisdiction
239 National (Federal) territory (Table K11)
Including boundary disputes
Foreign relations
240 General (Table K11)
Foreign service see KL-KWX5 260.8
241 Executive agreements (Table K11)
Foreign assistance programs see KL-KWX5 321.4
241.3 Neutrality (Table K11)
242.A-Z Other, A-Z
Subarrange each by Table K12
Individual and state
Nationality and citizenship
For rights and status of citizens see KL-KWX5 52.6
243 General (Table K11)
244 Immigration. Naturalization (Table K11)
For procedure see KL-KWX5 302.5
244.5 Expatriation (Table K11)
Emigration see KL-KWX5 302.7
Statelessness see KL-KWX5 48.5.S8
245.A-Z Particular groups, A-Z
245.O84 Overseas communities. Descendants of émigrés (Table K12)
Human rights. Civil and political rights. Civic (socialist) duties
246 General (Table K11)
Equality before the law. Antidiscrimination in general
246.5 General (Table K11)
246.7.A-Z Groups discriminated against, A-Z
246.7.G39 Gay men. Lesbians (Table K12)
Jews see KL-KWX5 246.7.M56
Lesbians see KL-KWX5 246.7.G39
246.7.M56 Minorities (ethnic, religious, racial, and national) (Table K12)
246.7.W65 Women (Table K12)
246.8.A-Z Special subjects, A-Z
Culture see KL-KWX5 246.8.L36
246.8.L36 Language and culture (Table K12)
Freedom
246.9 General (Table K11)
247 Freedom of expression (Table K11)
247.2 Freedom of religion and conscience (Table K11)

Constitutional law
Individual and state
Human rights. Civil and political rights. Civic (socialist) duties
Freedom -- Continued
Freedom of thought and speech
247.4 General (Table K11)
247.6 Freedom of information (Table K11)
247.8 Prohibition of censorship (Table K11)
248 Right of opposition to government (Table K11)
248.2 Freedom of movement (Table K11)
248.3 Freedom of assembly, association, and demonstration (Table K11)
248.4 Due process of law (Table K11)
248.6 Right to resistance against government (Table K11)
248.8 Political parties and mass organizations
Including subordinate or connected organizations, and pressure groups, etc.
249 Internal security (Table K11)
Including control of subversive activities or groups
Organs of national government. Supreme organs of state power and state administration
Including federal and state government
250 General (Table K11)
The people
250.4 General (Table K11)
Political parties see KL-KWX5 248.8
250.5 Initiative and referendum. Plebiscite (Table K11)
250.6 Election law (Table K11)
The legislature. Legislative power
251 General (Table K11)
251.2 Control of government (Table K11)
251.4 Legislative bodies. People's assemblies. People's councils (Table K11)
Including legislative bodies with one or two chambers, and including their presidium and other organs
Legislative process
Including parliamentary practice
251.6 General (Table K11)
251.8 Interpellation (Table K11)
252 Bill drafting (Table K11)
252.2 Committees and councils (Table K11)
252.5 Parliamentary minorities (Table K11)
252.8 Legislators (Table K11)
Including immunity, indemnity, incompatibility, etc.
Heads of state

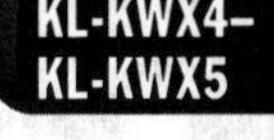

Constitutional law
Organs of national government. Supreme organs of state power and state administration
Heads of state -- Continued
253 General (Table K11)
Kings, princes, and rulers. Traditional leaders
253.2 General (Table K11)
253.5.A-Z Special topics, A-Z
253.5.A23 Abdication (Table K12)
253.5.D9 Dynastic rules. Legal status of dynasty (Table K12)
253.5.E43 Election (Table K12)
Legal status of dynasty see KL-KWX5 253.5.D9
253.5.S92 Succession to the throne (Table K12)
Presidents
254 General (Table K11)
254.4.A-Z Special topics, A-Z
254.4.I58 Impeachment (Table K12)
254.4.S83 Succession (Table K12)
254.8 Collective heads of state. State councils. Presidential councils (Socialist) (Table K11)
Prerogatives and powers of the head of state
255 General (Table K11)
255.4 Crown privilege (Table K11)
255.8 Treatymaking power (Table K11)
256 Veto power (Table K11)
256.4 War and emergency power (Table K11)
Other supreme organs
257 Central People's Committee (Socialist) (Table K11)
257.5 Federal Executive Council (Socialist) (Table K11)
The executive branch. Government
Federal Exectutive Councils see KL-KWX5 257.5
Presidium. Presidential councils see KL-KWX5 254.8
258 The Prime Minister and the Cabinet (Table K11)
258.5 Council of Ministers and other Supreme Councils of Control (Socialist) (Table K11)
Including presidium and other organs
Government departments, ministries, and other organizations of government
260 General (Table K11)

Constitutional law
Organs of national government. Supreme organs of state power and state administration
The executive branch. Government
Government departments, ministries, and other organizations of government -- Continued
Departments. Ministries
Class here works on several departments not related to a particular branch of law or subject
Including subordinate administrative divisions, councils, etc.
For works on several departments related to a branch of law or subject, as well as individual departments and their regulatory agencies, see the branch of law or subject
260.2 General (Table K11)
Department of State
260.4 General (Table K11)
260.8 The foreign service (Table K11)
261 Subordinate regulatory agencies (Table K11)
Class here works on several agencies
For an individual agency, see the branch of law or the subject
261.2.A-Z Special boards, commissions, bureaus, task forces, etc. By name, A-Z
Subarrange each by Table K12
261.3 The judiciary. Judicial power (Table K11)
261.4.A-Z Special topics, A-Z
Subarrange each by Table K12
Constitutional courts (tribunals) and procedure
262 General (Table K11)
263 Court organization (Table K11)
264 Procedural principles (Table K11)
265 Jurisdiction (Table K11)
266.A-Z Special topics, A-Z
Subarrange each by Table K12
267 National emblem. Flag. Seal. Seat of government. National anthem (Table K11)
267.2 Political oath (Table K11)
267.4 Patriotic customs and observances (Table K11)
267.6 Decorations of honor. Awards. Dignities (Table K11)
267.7 Commemorative medals (Table K11)
Colonial law
268 General (Table K11)
268.5.A-Z Particular, A-Z
Subarrange each by Table K12

State and religion
Class here works on the relationship of state and religion, regardless of denomination
For works on the internal law and government of religious corporations, sects, etc., see KB
For works on a particular subject, see the subject
Sources
Including constitutions, articles, injunctions, ordinances, enactments of the Parliament or the legislature affecting the religious order and life
Collections. Compilations
268.7 Serials
268.8 Monographs
268.9.A-Z Individual sources, A-Z
270 General (Table K11)
Constitutional aspects
Human rights. Fundamental rights and constitutional guaranties
(270.2) General
see Table KL-KWX5 246+
(270.3) Freedom of religion. Freedom of worship
see Table KL-KWX5 247.2
270.4 Separation of religion and state. Independence of church (Table K11)
270.5 Religious corporations, institutions, organizations, etc. (Table K11)
Including membership
270.6 Autonomy of religious corporations, organizations, institutions, etc. and state control (Table K11)
Legal schools
271 General (Table K11)
271.2.A-Z Particular schools, A-Z
Subarrange each by Table K12
271.3 Lands of religious corporations, sects, etc. (Table K11)
Including taxation and tax assessment, etc.
271.35 Religious trusts. Charities. Endowments (Waqf), etc. (Table K11)
271.4.A-Z Offenses against religion, A-Z
Subarrange each by Table K12
Class here works that can not be classed elsewhere
Religious courts see KL-KWX5 158.74+
Administrative law
272 General (Table K11)
272.2 Administrative principles (Table K11)
Administrative process
273 General (Table K11)

Administrative law
Administrative process -- Continued
273.2 Acts of government (Table K11)
274 Administrative acts (Table K11)
Legal transactions
275 General (Table K11)
275.4 Public contracts. Procurement (Table K11)
275.7 Enforcement. Administrative sanctions (Table K11)
276 Ombudsman. Control over abuse of administrative power (Table K11)
Administrative courts and procedure
276.4 General (Table K11)
278 Pretrial procedures. Administrative remedies (Table K11)
Including remonstration, administrative appeals, etc.
279 Procedure. Judicial decisions. Remedies (Table K11)
Including judicial review of administrative acts
280 Arbitration (Table K11)
281 Competence conflicts (Table K11)
Indemnification for acts performed by government
282 General (Table K11)
Eminent domain. Nationalization. Public restraint on private property
Including procedure
282.4 Expropriation, or land appropriation by the state for regional land resettlement and land development plans (Table K11)
Cf. KL-KWX5 306.5 Public land law
Government liability
283 General (Table K11)
283.5 Acts of government (Table K11)
284 Administrative and judicial acts (Table K11)
Administrative organization
285 Centralization and decentralization in government (Table K11)
Juristic persons of public law
287 General (Table K11)
Public corporations
287.7 General (Table K11)
288 Regional corporations (Table K11)
Class here general works
For local government see KL-KWX5 292+
For municipal government see KL-KWX5 293.7+
For special districts see KL-KWX5 297+

Administrative law
Administrative organization
Juristic persons of public law
Public corporations -- Continued
288.5 Cooperative societies of public law (Table K11)
Class here general works
For particular cooperative societies, see the subject, e.g. Agricultural cooperative societies
289 Public foundations (Table K11)
Cf. KL-KWX5 53.8 Foundations in civil law
289.3 Government business enterprises (Table K11)
Including government controlled business enterprises
For particular enterprises, see the subject
Administrative departments of national government
Including federal and central government
289.8 Department of the Interior (Table K11)
290 Subordinate regulatory agencies
For particular agencies, see the subject
Special councils, commissions, etc.
291 General (Table K11)
Ombudsman see KL-KWX5 276
Administrative departments of the states, republics, etc.
291.5 General (Table K11)
291.7 Department of the Interior (Table K11)
Administrative and political divisions. Local government other than municipal
Including those of centralized national governments or federal governments
292 General (Table K11)
292.8 Councils, boards, standing commissions (Table K11)
293.5.A-Z Particular administrative districts, counties, regions, etc., A-Z
Including official gazettes, bylaws, statutory orders, regulations, and general works, as well as works on specific legal topics
Municipal government
293.7 General (Table K11)
293.8 Name. Flags. Insignia. Seals (Table K11)
294 Constitution and organization of municipal government (Table K11)
295 Municipal finance and economy (Table K11)
Municipal public services
295.6 General (Table K11)
Public utilities
For regulation of the energy industry see KL-KWX5 343.2+

Administrative law
Administrative organization
Municipal government
Municipal public services
Public utilities -- Continued
295.8 General (Table K11)
Electricity see KL-KWX5 343.3
296 Water. Sewage (Table K11)
For ecological aspects see KL-KWX5 314
296.2 Trash collection (Table K11)
296.5 Public transportation (Table K11)
Supramunicipal corporation and cooperation
296.8 General (Table K11)
Special districts
For special districts within a particular state, republic, etc., see the state, republic, etc.
297 General (Table K11)
297.2.A-Z Particular types of districts, A-Z
Subarrange each by Table K12
For water districts see KL-KWX5 305.8.A+
Civil service. Public officials and functionaries
297.4 General (Table K11)
297.7 Conditions of employment (Table K11)
Including discipline and illicit political activities
297.8 Remuneration. Allowances. Retirement. Pensions, etc. (Table K11)
Labor law and collective labor law
298 General (Table K11)
Management-labor relations
298.2 General (Table K11)
298.3 Work councils (Table K11)
298.5 Collective labor disputes. Strikes (Table K11)
298.7 State civil service (Table K11)
For works on the civil service of an individual state, see the state
298.9 Municipal civil service (Table K11)
For works on the civil service of an individual municipality, see the municipality
299 Civil service of public corporations other than state or municipal (Table K11)
299.2 Public officials and functionaries of the economic administration (Socialist) (Table K11)
Police and public safety
300 General (Table K11)
Police magistrates
Including procedure and penalties
300.3 General (Table K11)

Police and public safety
Police magistrates -- Continued
300.5.A-Z Particular violations, A-Z
Begging see KL-KWX5 300.5.V34
300.5.V34 Vagrancy. Begging (Table K12)
Police forces
300.7 General (Table K11)
300.9.A-Z Particular forces, A-Z
300.9.B67 Border patrols (Table K12)
Public safety
301 Weapons. Explosives (Table K11)
Including manufacturing, import, and trade of firearms and ammunition
Hazardous articles and processes
Including transportation by land
For product safety see KL-KWX5 86.72
For transportation by sea see KL-KWX5 347.3
301.2 Nuclear power. Reactors (Table K11)
Including protection from radiation, and including nuclear waste disposal
301.3 Flammable materials (Table K11)
301.4.A-Z Poisons and toxic substances, A-Z
301.4.P34 Paint (Table K12)
Accident control
301.5 General (Table K11)
301.6.A-Z Particular, A-Z
Electric engineering see KL-KWX5 301.6.E43
301.6.E43 Electric installations. Electric engineering (Table K12)
Fire prevention and control
301.7 General (Table K11)
301.8 Theaters. Auditoriums (Table K11)
Including motion picture theaters and safety films
Flood control see KL-KWX5 305+
Weather bureaus. Meteorological stations see KL-KWX5 351.8
Control of individuals
302 General (Table K11)
Identification and registration
Including registration of residence
302.2 General (Table K11)
Registration of birth, marriage, and death see KL-KWX5 185.4+
302.3.A-Z Other, A-Z
Subarrange each by Table K12
302.5 Immigration and naturalization. Procedure (Table K11)
For citizenship see KL-KWX5 243+

Police and public safety
Control of individuals -- Continued
302.7 Emigration (Table K11)
For freedom of movement see KL-KWX5 248.2
Particular groups
302.9 Aliens (Table K11)
Including homeless aliens and refugees
303 Minorities (ethnic, religious, racial) (Table K11)
Control of social activities
303.3 General (Table K11)
303.4 Vacationing (Table K11)
Including campgrounds, hostels, outdoor swimming facilities, etc.
Sport activities
Including corporate representation
303.5 General (Table K11)
303.6 Mass events (Table K11)
303.7.A-Z Particular sports, A-Z
303.7.S65 Soccer (Table K12)
303.8.A-Z Other, A-Z
303.8.D45 Demonstrations. Processions (Table K12)
303.8.G35 Gambling (Table K12)
Including lotteries, games of chance, etc.
Processions see KL-KWX5 303.8.D45
303.8.T7 Traveling shows (Table K12)
Including circuses, puppet theaters, air shows, open-air shows, etc.
Public property
304 General (Table K11)
Government property
304.2 Constitutional aspects. Interdiction of private ownership. Socialist theory of government property (Table K11)
Administration. Powers and control
304.3 General (Table K11)
304.5 Records management. Access to public records (Table K11)
Including data bases and general data protection
304.6 Expropriation. Nationalization (Table K11)
Roads and highways
304.7 General (Table K11)
304.8 Interstate and state highways (Table K11)
Water resources
Including rivers, lakes, watercourses, etc.
305 General (Table K11)
305.3 Water rights (Table K11)
Cf. KL-KWX5 69.5 Riparian rights in civil law

Public property. Public restraint on private property
Water resources -- Continued
Protection against pollution see KL-KWX5 314
Development and conservation of water resources
305.5 General (Table K11)
305.7 Flood control (Table K11)
Including dams and dikes
305.8.A-Z Particular bodies and districts. By name, A-Z
Subarrange each by Table K12
306 Shore protection. Coastal zone management (Table K11)
Land reclamation. Irrigation. Drainage see KL-KWX5 307
306.3 National preserves. Forests. Savannas (Table K11)
Architectural landmarks and historic monuments see KL-KWX5 320.4
Continental shelf and its resources see KL-KWX5 334.7
Natural resources and mines see KL-KWX5 335
Public land law
306.5 Land reform and land policy. Legislation on new land systems (Table K11)
Including agrarian land policy legislation
Regional planning. Land development
Including resettlement and redistribution of population
306.6 General (Table K11)
306.7 Organization and administration (Table K11)
Class here works on task forces, land settlement authorities and commissions, development associations and trusteeship councils in restructuring the system of land holding, land settlement, and land use
307 Public irrigation zones
Rural planning and development zones
307.2 General (Table K11)
307.4 Land settlement. Government constituted homesteads. Village settlement (Table K11)
307.5 Consolidation of land holdings and reallocation (Table K11)
City planning and redevelopment
307.7 General (Table K11)
307.8 Zoning (Table K11)
Including procedure
Building and construction
Including administrative control and procedure
Cf. KL-KWX5 340.2+ Building and construction industry
308 General (Table K11)
308.2 Adjoining landowners (Table K11)
308.3 Building safety and control (Table K11)
308.35.A-Z Special topics, A-Z

Public property. Public restraint on private property
Public land law
Regional planning
Building and construction
Special topics, A-Z -- Continued
308.35.B37 Barrier-free design (Table K12)
308.35.E45 Elevators (Table K12)
308.4 Public works (Table K11)
Including public works contracts
Public health
308.5 General (Table K11)
308.8 Burial and cemetery laws. Disposal of the dead
Including cremation
Contagious and infectious diseases. Parasitic diseases
308.9 General (Table K11)
309.A-Z Diseases. Agents. Parasites, A-Z
309.A53 AIDS (Table K12)
309.T82 Tuberculosis (Table K12)
309.V45 Venereal diseases (Table K12)
Public health measures
Including compulsory measures
309.2 General (Table K11)
Immunization. Vaccination
309.3 General (Table K11)
309.4.A-Z Diseases, A-Z
309.4.P65 Poliomyelitis (Table K12)
309.4.S62 Small pox (Table K12)
309.5 Quarantine (Table K11)
Eugenics see KL-KWX5 313
Environmental pollution see KL-KWX5 313.8+
309.7.A-Z Other public health hazards and measures, A-Z
309.7.R43 Refuse disposal (Table K12)
309.7.S77 Street cleaning (Table K12)
Food laws see KL-KWX5 337.7+
Drug laws
310 General (Table K11)
310.2 Pharmaceutical procedures (Table K11)
310.3 Narcotics. Opium legislation (Table K11)
Including psychopharmaca
310.4 Poisons (Table K11)
310.5 Pharmacists and pharmacies (Table K11)
310.6 Trade regulation. Advertising (Table K11)
Including consumer protection
Medical legislation
310.8 General (Table K11)

Medical legislation -- Continued
The health professions
Class here works on education, licensing, professional representation, ethics, fees, and liability
For malpractice, see individual professions
Physicians
Including works on medical personnel in general
310.9 General (Table K11)
310.95 Malpractice
Cf. KL-KWX5 410 Offenses against the person
311 Dentists. Dental hygienists (Table K11)
311.2.A-Z Other, A-Z
311.2.G95 Gynecologists. Obstetricians (Table K12)
311.2.H42 Healers (Table K12)
Including herbalists, homeopathic physicians, naturopaths, etc.
311.2.N87 Nutritionists (Table K12)
Obstetricians see KL-KWX5 311.2.G95
311.2.P79 Psychologists. Psychotherapists (Table K12)
311.2.R33 Radiologists (Table K12)
Auxiliary medical professions. Paramedical professions
311.4 General (Table K11)
311.5 Nurses and nursing (Table K11)
311.6 Midwives (Table K11)
311.7 Physical therapists (Table K11)
Hospitals and other medical institutions or health services
312 General (Table K11)
312.2 Blood banks (Table K11)
Including blood donations
312.3 Institutions for the mentally ill (Table K11)
312.4.A-Z Other health organizations, institutions, or services, A-Z
Abortion clinics see KL-KWX5 313.4+
312.4.D39 Day care centers for infants and children (Table K12)
312.4.E43 Emergency medical services (Table K12)
Nursing homes see KL-KWX5 312.4.O42
312.4.O42 Old age homes. Nursing homes (Table K12)
Including invalid adults
Biomedical engineering. Medical technology
Including human experimentation in medicine
Cf. KL-KWX5 409.6+ Criminal aspects of medicine
312.5 General (Table K11)
312.6 Genetic engineering (Table K11)
For artificial insemination (Human reproductive technology) see KL-KWX5 312.8
312.7 Transplantation of organs, tissues, etc. (Table K11)
Including donation of organs, tissues, etc.

Medical legislation
Biomedical engineering
312.8 Human reproductive technology (Table K11)
Including artificial insemination, fertilization in vitro
Cf. KL-KWX5 62.3.A77 Family law
312.9.A-Z Special topics, A-Z
312.9.C65 Confidential communications (Table K12)
For data protection see KL-KWX5 86.5
312.9.F45 Female circumcision (Table K12)
312.9.I54 Informed consent (Table K12)
313 Eugenics. Sterilization and castration (Table K11)
Euthanasia see KL-KWX5 405.8
313.2 Veterinary medicine and hygiene. Veterinary public health (Table K11)
313.3 Animal protection. Animal welfare. Animal rights (Table K11)
Including prevention of cruelty to animals
For animal rights as a social issue see HV4701+
Birth control. Family planning. Population control
Cf. KL-KWX5 407 Illegal abortion (Criminal law)
313.4 General (Table K11)
313.5.A-Z Special topics, A-Z
313.5.A36 Abortion, Forced, for population control
Environmental law
313.7 General (Table K11)
313.75 Environmental planning. Conservation of environmental resources (Table K11)
Environmental pollution
313.8 General (Table K11)
313.9 Air pollution (Table K11)
Including noxious gases, automobile emissions, etc.
314 Water and groundwater pollution (Table K11)
Including pollutants and sewage control
Pollutants
314.2 General (Table K11)
314.3 Radioactive substances (Table K11)
314.5 Noise (Table K11)
Including traffic noise, and noise control
Cf. KL-KWX5 70.3.N84 Property
314.6 Recycling of refuse (Table K11)
Wilderness preservation
Including natural monuments, parks, and forests
314.7 General (Table K11)
314.75 Plant protection (Table K11)
Wildlife conservation
Including game, birds, and fish
314.8 General (Table K11)

Environmental law
Wilderness preservation
Wildlife conservation -- Continued
Game laws and hunting see KL-KWX5 333.7+
Fishery laws see KL-KWX5 334+
Land reclamation in mining see KL-KWX5 337.3.A+
Criminal provisions see KL-KWX5 435.2+
Cultural affairs
315 General (Table K11)
315.2 Cultural policy. State encouragement of science and the arts (Table K11)
315.29 National language (Table K11)
Including regulation of use, purity, etc.
Education
315.3 General (Table K11)
School government. School districts
Including curriculum and participation in school government in general
315.5 General (Table K11)
315.6 School discipline (Table K11)
Students
315.7 General (Table K11)
315.8 Compulsory education (Table K11)
316 Teachers. School functionaries (Table K11)
For particular teachers, see the level of instruction, e.g. KL-KWX5 317.5 University teachers
316.3 Elementary education (Table K11)
Including teachers
316.4 Education of children with disabilities (Table K11)
316.5 Vocational education (Table K11)
Including teachers
316.6 Secondary education (Table K11)
Higher education. Universities
For legal education see KL-KWX5 5+
For research policies in higher education see KL-KWX5 318.8
316.8 General (Table K11)
316.9 Intelligentsia (General) (Table K11)
Administration. Institutional management in higher education
317 General (Table K11)
317.3.A-Z Special topics, A-Z
317.3.D45 Degrees (Table K12)
317.5 Teachers (Table K11)
Including professors (ordinarii, extraordinarii, and emeriti), magisters, etc.

Cultural affairs
Education
Higher education. Universities -- Continued
Students
317.7 General (Table K11)
317.9 Selection for higher education (Table K11)
318 Political activities (Table K11)
Including strikes
318.2.A-Z Universities. By place, A-Z
Subarrange each by Table K12
318.3.A-Z Other schools or institutions of higher education. By place, A-Z
Subarrange each by Table K12
Including colleges or schools of religion, technology, music, art, drama, etc.
318.5 Private schools (Table K11)
318.6 Adult education (Table K11)
318.7 Physical education. Sports (Table K11)
For liability for sports accidents see KL-KWX5 86.9
Cf. KL-KWX5 303.5+ Sports activities
Science and the arts
318.8 Public policies in research (Table K11)
Including research in higher education
318.9 Public institutions (Table K11)
319.A-Z Branches and subjects, A-Z
319.A68 Antarctic research (Table K12)
319.A72 Archaeology (Table K12)
319.A75 Asia and Middle East studies (Table K12)
319.C37 Cartography (Table K12)
Language see KL-KWX5 315.29
Meteorology see KL-KWX5 351.8
Oceanography see KL-KWX5 347+
319.S73 Statistical services (Table K12)
For data protection see KL-KWX5 304.5
The arts
319.2 General (Table K11)
319.3 Fine arts (Table K11)
Performing arts
319.4 General (Table K11)
319.5 Music. Musicians (Table K11)
Theater
Including managerial, performing, and technical staff
For copyright see KL-KWX5 118.6
319.6 General (Table K11)
319.7 Playwrights. Contracts (Table K11)
319.8 Motion pictures (Table K11)

Cultural affairs
Science and the arts -- Continued
Public collections
319.9 General (Table K11)
320 Archives. Historic documents (Table K11)
320.2 Libraries (Table K11)
320.3 Museums and galleries (Table K11)
320.4 Historic buildings and monuments. Architectural landmarks (Table K11)
Including vessels, battleships, archaeological sites, etc.
320.6 Educational, scientific, and cultural exchanges (Table K11)
Economic law
320.7 General (Table K11)
Economic constitution
320.8 General (Table K11)
320.9 Organization and administration (Table K11)
Class here works on national departments and boards of commerce, national, state, and local departments and boards, or departments and boards of several states or administrative districts
For departments and boards (several or individual) of an individual state or administrative district, see the state or district
Government control and policy
321 General (Table K11)
321.2 National planning (Table K11)
321.3 Investments. Investment control (Table K11)
Including foreign investments
321.4 Assistance to developing countries (Table K11)
321.5 Economic assistance (Table K11)
321.6 Marketing orders
Class here general works
For particular marketing orders, see the subject, e.g. Agriculture
321.7 Prices and price control (Table K11)
321.8 Industrial priorities, allocations, and circulation (Table K11)
Including organizations
For industrial priorities and allocations in wartime see KL-KWX5 372
Rationing see KL-KWX5 372.5
321.9 Government business enterprises (Table K11)
Control of contracts and combinations in restraint of trade. Competition rules
For unfair competition see KL-KWX5 123+
322 General (Table K11)
Horizontal and vertical combinations
322.2 General (Table K11)

Economic law
Government control and policy
Control of contracts and combinations in restraint of trade.
Competition rules
Horizontal and vertical combinations -- Continued
322.3 Corporate consolidation, merger, etc. (Table K11)
Cartels
322.5 General (Table K11)
322.7.A-Z Types of cartels, A-Z
Subarrange each by Table K12
322.8.A-Z Industries, occupations, etc., A-Z
Subarrange each by Table K12
For works relating to an individual company see KL-KWX5 324.8.A+
Combines (Socialist)
323 General (Table K11)
323.3.A-Z By industry, A-Z
Subarrange each by Table K12
323.5 Restraint-of-competition clause in business concern contracts and in articles of incorporation and partnership (Table K11)
323.7 Price maintenance and open price system (Table K11)
324 Monopolies. Oligopolies. Antitrust law (Table K11)
For government monopolies see KL-KWX5 362.2
Cartel agencies and procedure
Including procedures
324.4 General (Table K11)
324.6 Cartel register (Table K11)
Including procedure
324.7 Damages (Private law) and indemnification (Public law)
Criminal provisions see KL-KWX5 428.6+
324.8.A-Z Mergers, cartels, combinations, business concerns, etc. By name, A-Z
Subarrange each by Table K12
324.9 Small business (Table K11)
325 Cooperative societies (Table K11)
325.3 Chambers of commerce (Table K11)
Money, currency, and foreign exchange control see KL-KWX5 353.55+
Standards. Norms
For standards, grading, and quality control of agricultural or consumer products, see the product
325.4 General (Table K11)
325.5 Quality control (Table K11)
Weights and measures. Containers
325.7 General (Table K11)

Economic law
Government control and policy
Standards. Norms
Weights and measures. Containers -- Continued
325.8.A-Z By instrument, A-Z
Subarrange each by Table K12
Standardization
325.9 General (Table K11)
Engineering standards
326 General (Table K11)
326.2.A-Z By material, A-Z
Subarrange each by Table K12
326.3.A-Z By instrument, A-Z
Subarrange each by Table K12
Norms and standards for conservation of raw or scarce materials
Including recycling of refuse (Metal, glass, paper, wood, etc.)
326.5 General (Table K11)
326.6 Prohibition of industrial use of scarce materials (Table K11)
Price norms see KL-KWX5 321.7
326.8 Labeling
Class here general works
For the labeling of particular goods or products, see the good or product
Regulation of industry, trade and commerce
327 General (Table K11)
327.6 Consumer protection (Table K11)
Advertising
328 General (Table K11)
328.2 Trade fairs and expositions (Table K11)
Including national and international fairs and expositions
Testing of commercial products see KL-KWX5 123.7
Primary production. Extractive industries
Agriculture. Forestry. Rural law
Land reform and agrarian land policy legislation see KL-KWX5 306.5
328.5 General (Table K11)
Organization and administration
328.6 General (Table K11)
328.7.A-Z Particular organizations, agricultural science and research institutions, etc. A-Z
Subarrange each by Table K12
329.6 Agricultural contracts (Table K11)

Economic law
Regulation of industry, trade and commerce
Primary production. Extractive industries
Agriculture
Agricultural contracts
Leasing of rural property. Farm tenancy (individual)
Class here civil law provisions as well as legislation aimed at protection and stability for tenancy
331 General (Table K11)
331.2 Farm equipment leasing (Table K11)
Agricultural cooperatives
331.6 General (Table K11)
331.7 Producers and marketing cooperatives (Table K11)
Including administration, management, membership, etc.
Including grazing associations
Cf. KL-KWX5 307.2+ Rural planning and development
331.8 Government agricultural enterprises (Table K11)
Including central and local administration
Marketing orders
332 General (Table K11)
Economic assistance
332.2 General (Table K11)
332.5 Priorities, allocations, and distribution (Table K11)
332.6 Importing and stockpiling (Table K11)
332.7 Livestock industry and trade (Table K11)
332.9 Milk production. Dairy farming (Table K11)
333 Agricultural courts and procedure (Table K11)
333.2 Criminal provisions (Table K11)
333.3 Viticulture (Table K11)
333.4 Apiculture. Beekeeping (Table K11)
333.5 Horticulture (Table K11)
Forestry
Including timber laws
333.6 General (Table K11)
Game laws
333.7 General (Table K11)
333.8 Game leases and licenses (Table K11)
Fishery
For conservation and ecological aspects see KL-KWX5 314.8+
334 General (Table K11)
334.2.A-Z Particular fish or marine fauna, A-Z
Subarrange each by Table K12
Sport fishing see KL-KWX5 303.7.A+

Economic law
Regulation of industry, trade and commerce
Primary production. Extractive industries -- Continued
Mining and quarrying
Including metallurgy
334.4 General (Table K11)
334.6 Organization and administration (Table K11)
Class here works on national departments and boards, national, state, and local departments and boards, or departments and boards of several states or administrative districts
For departments and boards (several or individual) of an individual state or administrative district, see the state or district
334.7 Continental shelf and its resources (Table K11)
335 Rights to mines and mineral resources (Table K11)
Including procedure and registration
Mining industry and finance
335.3 General (Table K11)
335.4 Economic assistance (Table K11)
335.5 Corporations and cooperatives (Table K11)
335.7 Planning and planning periods (Table K11)
Including calculation of reserves
Social legislation
335.9 General (Table K11)
Labor law for miners
336 General (Table K11)
336.3 Unions (Table K11)
336.4 Mine safety regulations. Rescue work (Table K11)
Including equipment
336.5 Social insurance for miners (Table K11)
Including all branches of social insurance
Resources
Petroleum. Oil. Gas
336.6 General (Table K11)
336.8 Oil and gas leases (Table K11)
336.9.A-Z Particular oil fields, reserves, etc., A-Z
Subarrange each by Table K12
337.A-Z Particular companies, A-Z
Subarrange each by Table K12
337.3.A-Z Other resources, A-Z
337.3.C63 Coal (Table K12)
337.3.C66 Copper (Table K12)
337.3.D53 Diamonds. Gems (Table K12)
Gems see KL-KWX5 337.3.D53
337.3.S34 Salt (Table K12)

Economic law
Regulation of industry, trade and commerce
Primary production. Extractive industries
Mining and quarrying
Resources
Other resources, A-Z -- Continued
337.3.T56 Tin (Table K12)
337.4 Environmental laws. Land reclamation (Table K11)
Manufacturing industries
Including heavy and light industries
337.45 General (Table K11)
337.5 Recycling industries (Table K11)
Food processing industries. Food products
Class here works on trade practices, economic assistance, labeling, sanitation and quality inspection
Including regulation of adulteration and additives
337.7 General (Table K11)
337.8 Labeling (Table K11)
337.9 Purity (Table K11)
Including regulation of adulteration and food additives
338 Cereal products (Table K11)
338.2 Fruits and vegetables (Table K11)
338.3 Confectionary industry (Table K11)
338.4 Meat (Table K11)
338.5 Poultry products (Table K11)
338.6 Egg products (Table K11)
Dairy products
338.8 General (Table K11)
339 Cheese (Table K11)
339.2 Fishery products. Seafood (Table K11)
339.3 Oils and fats (Table K11)
Beverages
339.5 Brewing (Table K11)
339.7 Winemaking (Table K11)
339.8 Distilling (Table K11)
For taxation see KL-KWX5 362.4.D58
339.9 Mineral waters (Table K11)
340.A-Z Related industries, A-Z
Subarrange each by Table K12
Building and construction industry
For building laws see KL-KWX5 308+
340.2 General (Table K11)
340.3 Contracts and specifications (Table K11)
International trade
340.5 General (Table K11)

Economic law
Regulation of industry, trade and commerce
International trade -- Continued
Export and import controls
Including foreign trade practice and procedure
340.7 General (Table K11)
Foreign exchange control see KL-KWX5 353.8+
Trade agreements see KL-KWX5 364.3
341 Export trade (Table K11)
341.3.A-Z By region or country, A-Z
341.3.E87 European Economic Community countries (Table K12)
Domestic trade
For consumer protection see KL-KWX5 327.6
341.5 General (Table K11)
341.6 Planning and planning periods (Table K11)
341.7 Wholesale trade. Government wholesale trade (Table K11)
Retail trade. Government retail trade
Cf. KL-KWX5 342.9+ Artisans
341.8 General (Table K11)
341.9 Conditions of trading (Table K11)
Including licensing and Sunday legislation
342.A-Z Modes of trading, A-Z
Chain stores see KL-KWX5 342.D46
342.D46 Department stores. Chain stores (Table K12)
342.D57 Direct selling (Table K12)
Fairs see KL-KWX5 342.M37
342.M34 Mail-order business (Table K12)
342.M37 Markets. Fairs (Table K12)
For trade fairs and expositions see KL-KWX5 328.2
342.P43 Peddling (Table K12)
342.V45 Vending machines (Table K12)
342.2 Cooperative retail trade (Table K11)
342.25.A-Z Products, A-Z
342.25.M48 Metals (Table K12)
Metals, Precious see KL-KWX5 342.25.P73
342.25.P73 Precious metals (Table K12)
Second-hand trade
342.3 General (Table K11)
342.35.A-Z Types of trade, A-Z
342.35.P38 Pawnbrokers (Table K12)
Including charitable pawnbrokers
Service trades
342.4 General (Table K11)
Old age homes see KL-KWX5 312.4.O42
342.5 Travel agencies. Tourist trade (Table K11)

Economic law
Regulation of industry, trade and commerce -- Continued
Artisans
342.6 General (Table K11)
342.7 Apprentices (Table K11)
Corporate representation
342.9 General (Table K11)
343.A-Z Crafts, A-Z
Subarrange each by Table K12
Energy policy. Power supply
Including publicly and privately owned utilities
343.2 General (Table K11)
Particular sources of power
343.3 Electricity (Table K11)
343.4 Gas. Natural gas (Table K11)
Water see KL-KWX5 296
343.6 Heat. Steam distributed by central plant (Table K11)
343.62 Atomic energy (Table K11)
For protection from radiation see KL-KWX5 301.2
For ecological aspects see KL-KWX5 314.3
343.7.A-Z Other sources of power, A-Z
343.8 Industrial arbitral courts and procedure (Table K11)
343.9 Business ethics. Courts of honor (Table K11)
Criminal provisions see KL-KWX5 428.6+
Transportation
344 General (Table K11)
Road traffic. Automotive transportation
344.2 General (Table K11)
Motor vehicles
344.3 General (Table K11)
344.4 Registration (Table K11)
344.6 Safety equipment (Table K11)
344.7 Drivers' licenses (Table K11)
Including driving schools and instructors
344.8 Compulsory insurance (Table K11)
Traffic regulations and enforcement
344.9 General (Table K11)
Traffic violations
For criminal interference with street traffic see KL-KWX5 438.4+
345 General (Table K11)
Driving while intoxicated see KL-KWX5 438.6
Hit-and-run drivers see KL-KWX5 439
345.2 Traffic courts and procedure (Table K11)
345.3 Highway safety (Table K11)
Carriage of passengers and goods

Transportation
Road traffic. Automotive transportation
Traffic regulations and enforcement
Carriage of passengers and goods -- Continued
345.5 General (Table K11)
345.6 Goods carriers (Table K11)
Railroads
346 General (Table K11)
Operation of railroads
346.2 General (Table K11)
346.3 Railroad safety (Table K11)
Including railroad crossings, etc. and liability
346.4 Carriage of passengers and goods (Table K11)
346.5.A-Z Kinds of railroads or railways, A-Z
346.5.C32 Cable railways (Table K12)
Private-track railroads see KL-KWX5 346.5.S42
346.5.S42 Secondary railroads. Private-track railroads (Table K12)
346.5.S98 Suspended railways (Table K12)
Criminal provisions see KL-KWX5 348.5+
Postal services see KL-KWX5 348.5+
346.6 Pipelines (Table K11)
Aviation. Air law
346.7 General (Table K11)
346.8 Air traffic rules (Table K11)
Including air safety and airworthiness
Water transportation
347 General (Table K11)
Ships
347.2 General (Table K11)
347.3 Safety regulations (Table K11)
Navigation and pilotage
347.4 General (Table K11)
347.5 Rule of the road at sea (Table K11)
347.6 Coastwise and inland navigation (Table K11)
347.7 Harbors and ports of entry (Table K11)
Coastwise and inland shipping
Including rafting
347.8 General (Table K11)
347.9 Carriage of passengers and goods (Table K11)
Cf. KL-KWX5 101.9+ Affreightment (Commercial law)
348.A-Z Individual waterways and channels, A-Z
Subarrange each by Table K12
Marine labor law see KL-KWX5 103.6+
Marine insurance see KL-KWX5 103.5
Communication. Mass media
348.2 General (Table K11)

Communication. Mass media -- Continued

348.3 Constitutional aspects. Freedom of communication. Censorship (Table K11)

Postal services. Telecommunications

348.5 General (Table K11)

Privacy of mail and telecommunication see KL-KWX5 348.3

348.6 Rates. Postage. Modes of collection (Table K11)

Including postage stamps

Telecommunication

348.7 General (Table K11)

348.8 Telegraph (Table K11)

348.9 Teletype and data transmission systems (Table K11)

349 Telephone (Table K11)

Radio communication

Including radio and television broadcasting

349.2 General (Table K11)

Freedom of radio communication see KL-KWX5 348.3

349.3 Organization and administration (Table K11)

Including national and state jurisdiction

349.5 Stations. Networks (Table K11)

Including frequency allocations and licensing

Broadcasting

349.6 General (Table K11)

349.7 Programming. Censorship (Table K11)

349.8 Labor law (Table K11)

Including collective labor law

349.9 Criminal provisions (Table K11)

Press law

350 General (Table K11)

Freedom of the press and censorship see KL-KWX5 348.3

350.2 Right to information (Table K11)

Planning and planning periods

350.3.A-Z Types of literature, A-Z

350.3.P47 Periodicals (Table K12)

350.3.S34 Schoolbooks (Table K12)

Including all levels of education

Publishers and publishing

350.4 General (Table K11)

350.5 Journalists. Domestic and foreign correspondents (Table K11)

Including liability

350.6 Bookdealers (Table K11)

350.7.A-Z Special topics, A-Z

350.7.P37 Party press (Table K12)

350.7.P65 Political advertising (Table K12)

350.7.R48 Resistance. Underground press (Table K12)

Communication. Mass media
Press law
Special topics, A-Z -- Continued
Underground press see KL-KWX5 350.7.R48
350.7.U54 University press (Table K12)
350.7.Y68 Youth press (Table K12)
Press and criminal justice
350.8 General (Table K11)
Press delicts
Including works on both press delicts and particular procedures
351 General (Table K11)
Libel and slander
351.2 General (Table K11)
351.3 Treason by publishing official secrets (Table K11)
Cf. KL-KWX5 444.2 Treasonable espionage
351.5 Contempt of court (Table K11)
351.8 Weather bureau. Meteorological stations (Table K11)
Professions. Intelligentsia
352 General (Table K11)
Violation of confidential communication see KL-KWX5 416.4
352.2 Professional associations (Table K11)
For particular professional associations, see the profession
Individual professions
Including technical intelligentsia of government industrial enterprises, and including education, licensing, liability, etc.
Health professions see KL-KWX5 310.8+
Pharmacists see KL-KWX5 310.5
Veterinarians see KL-KWX5 313.2
Attorneys see KL-KWX5 163+
Economic and financial advisors
352.3 Accountants (Table K11)
352.4 Auditors (Table K11)
Engineering and construction
352.5 Architects (Table K11)
352.6 Engineers (Table K11)
352.65 Real estate agents (Table K11)
352.7 Professional ethics. Courts of honor (Table K11)
For a particular court of honor, see the profession
Public finance
Finance reform and policies
Cf. KL-KWX5 321+ Government control and policy
352.8 General (Table K11)
Monetary policies see KL-KWX5 353.55+
352.9 General (Table K11)

Public finance -- Continued
Organization and administration
Class here works on national departments or agencies of finance, national, state, and local departments or agencies, or departments and agencies of several states or administrative districts
For departments and agencies (several or individual) of an individual state or administrative district, see the state or administrative district
For financial courts see KL-KWX5 368+
353 General (Table K11)
Budget. Government expenditures
353.2 General (Table K11)
353.3 Accounting (Table K11)
Including central or local organs of national government
353.4 Expenditure control. Auditing (Table K11)
353.45 Public debts. Loans. Bond issues (Table K11)
Revenue see KL-KWX5 353.9+
353.5 Intergovernmental fiscal relations (Table K11)
Including revenue sharing
Money
Including control of circulation
353.55 General (Table K11)
353.58 Coinage. Mint regulations (Table K11)
353.6 Bank notes. Banks of issue (Table K11)
Class here public law aspects of banks of issue
For banking law see KL-KWX5 99.5+
353.7 Gold trading and gold standard (Table K11)
Foreign exchange control
353.8 General (Table K11)
Criminal provisions see KL-KWX5 429.2
National revenue
353.9 General (Table K11)
Taxation
Criticism and reform see KL-KWX5 352.8+
354 General (Table K11)
354.2 Double taxation (Table K11)
Taxation and tax exemption as a measure of social and economic policy
354.3 General (Table K11)
354.5 Export sales (Table K11)
354.6.A-Z Classes of taxpayers or lines of businesses, A-Z
Subarrange each by Table K12
354.7.A-Z Taxation of particular activities, A-Z
Subarrange each by Table K12

Public finance
National revenue
Taxation -- Continued
354.8 Tax saving. Tax avoidance (Table K11)
For tax planning relating to a particular tax, see the tax
Tax administration. Revenue service
355 General (Table K11)
Financial courts see KL-KWX5 368+
Double taxation see KL-KWX5 354.2
Collection and enforcement
355.3 General (Table K11)
355.4 Tax accounting. Financial statements (Table K11)
Including personal companies and stock companies, etc.
For a particular tax, see the tax
355.6.A-Z Special topics, A-Z
Subarrange each by Table K12
Administrative acts
355.7 General (Table K11)
Administrative remedies see KL-KWX5 368.3
Judicial review see KL-KWX5 368.5+
356 Tax auditing (Table K11)
Cf. KL-KWX5 370.3 Tax and customs investigation
356.3 Execution (Table K11)
Cf. KL-KWX5 370.3 Tax and customs investigation
356.5.A-Z Classes of taxpayers or lines of business, A-Z
Subarrange each by Table K12
Income tax
356.6 General (Table K11)
357 Taxable income. Exemptions (Table K11)
Deductions
357.3 General (Table K11)
357.4 Expenses and losses (Table K11)
Surtaxes see KL-KWX5 361.2
357.5 Salaries and wages (Table K11)
Including fringe benefits, nonwage payments, etc.
357.6 Capital investment (Table K11)
Including foreign investment
Cf. KL-KWX5 354.3+ Taxation as a measure of economic policy
357.7 Pensions and annuities (Table K11)
Payment at source of income
358 Payroll deduction. Withholding tax (Table K11)
358.2.A-Z Classes of taxpayers or lines of business, A-Z
358.2.A44 Aliens (Table K12)
358.2.A87 Artisans (Table K12)
358.2.A88 Artists (Table K12)

Public finance
National revenue
Taxation
Income tax
Classes of taxpayers or lines of business, A-Z -- Continued
358.2.E83 Executives (Table K12)
358.2.M37 Married couples (Table K12)
Including persons in polygamous marriages
358.2.M47 Merchant mariners (Table K12)
358.2.P75 Professions (Table K12)
358.2.T42 Teachers (Table K12)
Corporation tax
358.3 General (Table K11)
358.4 Nonprofit associations, nonprofit corporations, foundations (endowments), and pension trust funds (Table K11)
358.5 Personal companies (Unincorporated business associations) (Table K11)
358.6 Cooperatives (Table K11)
Stock companies (Incorporated business associations
358.7 General (Table K11)
359 Taxable income. Exemptions (Table K11)
359.2 Deductions (Table K11)
359.3 Corporate reorganization (Table K11)
359.4 Limited partnership (Table K11)
359.5 Stock corporation (Table K11)
360.A-Z Lines of corporate business, A-Z
360.C65 Construction industry (Table K12)
360.M54 Mining (Table K12)
Foreign corporations and stockholders
360.2 General (Table K11)
Double taxation see KL-KWX5 354.2
Multi-national corporations
360.3 General (Table K11)
Double taxation see KL-KWX5 354.2
360.4 Property tax. Taxation of capital (Table K11)
For real property tax see KL-KWX5 367+
Cf. KL-KWX5 366.2 Property tax (State and local finance)

360.5 Estate, inheritance, and gift taxes (Table K11)
361 Capital gain tax (Table K11)
Development gains tax see KL-KWX5 367.3
361.2 Surtaxes (Table K11)
Poll tax see KL-KWX5 367.7.P65
Excise taxes. Taxes on transactions

Public finance
National revenue
Taxation
Excise taxes. Taxes on transactions -- Continued
361.25 General (Table K11)
Sales tax
361.3 General (Table K11)
361.5 Turnover tax (Table K11)
Including value-added tax and import and export sales
362 Personal companies and stock companies (Table K11)
Particular commodities, services, and transactions see KL-KWX5 362.4.A+
362.2 Government monopolies (Table K11)
Including monopolies delegated by the state to others
362.4.A-Z Commodities, services, and transactions, A-Z
362.4.A42 Alcoholic beverages (General) (Table K12)
362.4.B35 Banking transactions (Table K12)
362.4.B37 Bars and taverns (Table K12)
362.4.B38 Betting (Bookmaking) (Table K12)
362.4.B55 Bills of exchange tax (Table K12)
Bonds see KL-KWX5 362.4.S42
Brandy see KL-KWX5 362.4.L57
Champagne see KL-KWX5 362.4.W55
362.4.D58 Distilleries (Table K12)
362.4.E96 Export-import sales (Table K12)
Gambling see KL-KWX5 366.5
362.4.H68 Hotels and motels (Table K12)
Import sales see KL-KWX5 362.4.E96
362.4.L57 Liquors (Table K12)
362.4.M38 Matches (Table K12)
Motels see KL-KWX5 362.4.H68
362.4.M68 Motor fuels (Table K12)
362.4.P48 Petroleum (Table K12)
362.4.P82 Public utilities (Table K12)
362.4.R47 Restaurants (Table K12)
362.4.R48 Retail trade (Table K12)
362.4.S42 Securities and bonds (Table K12)
362.4.S76 Stock exchange transactions (Table K12)
Taverns see KL-KWX5 362.4.B37
362.4.T62 Tobacco (Table K12)
362.4.T72 Transportation of persons or goods (Table K12)
362.4.W36 Waste products. Recycled products (Table K12)
362.4.W46 Wholesale trade (Table K12)
362.4.W55 Wine (Table K12)

Public finance
National revenue
Taxation
Excise taxes. Taxes on transactions -- Continued
Methods of assessment and collection
For assessment and collection of a particular tax, see the tax
363 General (Table K11)
363.3 Stamp duties (Table K11)
For bills of exchange see KL-KWX5 362.4.B55
Customs. Tariff
For foreign trade regulations see KL-KWX5 340.7+
364 General (Table K11)
Tables see KL-KWX5 364
364.3 Trade agreements (Table K11)
364.4 Customs organization and administration (Table K11)
Including officers and personnel
364.5.A-Z Commodities and services, A-Z
364.5.A87 Automobiles (Table K12)
364.7 Free ports and zones (Table K11)
Criminal provisions see KL-KWX5 370+
State and local finance
For the public finance of an individual state, administrative district, or municipality, see the state or municipality
Finance reforms see KL-KWX5 352.8+
365 General (Table K11)
365.3 Fees. Fines (Table K11)
Including license fees
Taxation
365.5 General (Table K11)
Tax administration see KL-KWX5 355+
Income tax see KL-KWX5 356.6+
Sales taxes see KL-KWX5 361.3+
366 Estate, inheritance, and gift taxes (Table K11)
366.2 Property tax. Taxation of capital (Table K11)
Including juristic persons and business enterprises
For real property tax see KL-KWX5 367+
366.3 Motor vehicles tax (Table K11)
366.5 Taxes from gambling tables. Casinos (Table K12)
Real property tax
367 General (Table K11)
367.3 Capital gains tax (Table K11)
Including development gains
367.5 Business tax (Table K11)
Other taxes, A-Z
367.7.P65 Poll tax (Table K12)

Public finance -- Continued
Tax and customs courts and procedure
Class here works on national courts, national, state and district courts and boards, or courts and boards of several states or administrative districts
For courts and boards (several or individual) of an individual state or administrative district, see the state or district
368 General (Table K11)
368.3 Pretrial procedures. Administrative remedies (Table K11)
Procedure at first instance. Judicial review
368.5 General (Table K11)
368.6 Actions. Defenses (Table K11)
369 Evidence (Table K11)
369.3 Judicial decisions. Judgments (Table K11)
Including court records
Remedies. Means of review
369.4 General (Table K11)
369.5 Appellate procedures (Table K11)
Tax and customs crimes and delinquency. Procedure
370 General (Table K11)
Individual offenses
370.2 Tax evasion and tax avoidance (Table K11)
Smuggling of contraband see KL-KWX5 370.2
370.25 Organized smuggling (Table K11)
Procedure
For criminal procedure in general see KL-KWX5 459.9+
370.3 Tax and customs investigation (Table K11)
370.5 Evidence (Table K11)
370.6 Amnesty. Pardon (Table K11)
Government measures in time of war, national emergency, or economic crisis
370.9 General (Table K11)
Particular measures
371 Military requisitions from civilians. Requisitioned land (Table K11)
For damages and compensation see KL-KWX5 373+
371.2 Control of property. Confiscations (Table K11)
Including enemy and alien property
For damages and compensation see KL-KWX5 373+
Control of unemployment. Manpower control
371.4 General (Table K11)
371.5 Compulsory and forced labor (Table K11)
371.7 Insolvent debtors. Wartime and crisis relief (Table K11)
For composition and deferment of execution see KL-KWX5 197.2
For moratorium see KL-KWX5 197.5

Government measures in time of war, national emergency, or economic crisis
Particular measures -- Continued
371.8 Finances (Table K11)
For procurement and defense contracts see KL-KWX5 373.5
372 Industrial priorities and allocations. Economic recovery measures. Nationalization (Table K11)
372.3 Strategic material. Stockpiling (Table K11)
372.5 Rationing. Price control (Table K11)
372.7 Criminal provisions (Table K11)
War damage compensation
Including foreign claims settlement
373 General (Table K11)
373.3.A-Z Particular claims, A-Z
Confiscations see KL-KWX5 373.3.R47
Demontage see KL-KWX5 373.3.R46
Military occupation damages see KL-KWX5 373.3.R47
373.3.P47 Personal damages. Property loss or damages (Table K12)
Property loss or damages see KL-KWX5 373.3.P47
373.3.R46 Reparations. Demontage (Table K12)
373.3.R47 Requisitions. Confiscations. Military occupation damages (Table K12)
373.4.A-Z Particular victims, A-Z
Subarrange each by Table K12
373.5 Military occupation. Procurement (Table K11)
For military occupation damages see KL-KWX5 373.3.R47
National defense. Military law
For emergency and wartime legislation see KL-KWX5 370.9+
374 General (Table K11)
374.3 Organization and administration. Command (Table K11)
The armed forces
374.5 General (Table K11)
Compulsory service
Including draft and selective service
374.6 General (Table K11)
374.7.A-Z Special topics, A-Z
374.7.A44 Aliens (Table K12)
374.7.C65 Conscientious objection (Table K12)
375.A-Z Particular branches of service, A-Z
Subarrange each by Table K12
375.15 Foreign armed forces. Status of forces agreements (Table K11)
Including damages
Civil defense
375.2 General (Table K11)

National defense. Military law
Civil defense -- Continued
375.3 Air defense. Air raid shelters (Table K11)
Military criminal law and procedure
Cf. KL-KWX5 447+ Crimes against national defense
375.8 General (Table K11)
Individual offenses
376 Desertion (Table K11)
376.7 Courts and procedure (Table K11)
Including procedure in honor cases
377 Punishment. Execution (Table K11)
377.5 Probation and parole (Table K11)
Military discipline. Law enforcement
Including all branches of the armed forces
378 General (Table K11)
378.2 Superior orders. Enforcement of orders (Table K11)
378.5.A-Z Other, A-Z
378.5.M55 Military maneuvers (Table K12)
Criminal law
379 Reform of criminal law, procedure, and execution (Table K11)
For works limited to a particular subject, see the subject
For works pertaining exclusively to the codes, see the code
Administration of criminal justice see KL-KWX5 156.92+
379.5 General (Table K11)
380 Constitutional aspects (Table K11)
380.2 Philosophy of criminal law (Table K11)
380.6 Relationship of criminal law to other disciplines, subjects or phenomena (Table K11)
381 Interpretation and construction. Legal hermeneutics (Table K11)
Concepts and principles
381.15 General (Table K11)
Applicability and validity of the law
381.2 General (Table K11)
381.3 Nulla poena sine lege. Nullum crimen sine lege (Table K11)
Territorial applicability
382 General (Table K11)
383 Conflict of laws (Table K11)
383.2 Temporal applicability (Table K11)
Including intertemporal law
383.3 Personal applicability. Immunities (Table K11)
Criminal offense
Including felony, misdemeanor, and transgression
384 General (Table K11)
384.3 Crimes by commission or omission (Table K11)

Criminal law
Concepts and principles
Criminal offense -- Continued
384.4 Crimes aggravated by personal characteristics (Table K11)
Criminal act
384.5 General (Table K11)
384.6 Corpus delicti. Fact-pattern conformity (Table K11)
Form of criminal act
384.7 General (Table K11)
385 Omission (Table K11)
385.2 Attempt. Preparation (Table K11)
For accessory to attempted crime see KL-KWX5 393
Illegality. Justification of otherwise illegal acts
385.5 General (Table K11)
385.6 Self-defense or defense of another (Table K11)
Superior orders see KL-KWX5 390
Medical treatment see KL-KWX5 409.6+
Consent of the injured party
386 General (Table K11)
386.2 Presumed consent (Table K11)
386.5.A-Z Other grounds for justification, A-Z
Subarrange each by Table K12
386.7 Criminal intent. Mens rea (Table K11)
Including purpose and scienter, dolus, eventualis, etc.
387 Negligence and wantonness (Table K11)
Including foresight and standard of conduct
Criminal liability. Guilt
387.5 General (Table K11)
Capacity
387.7 General (Table K11)
Incapacity and limited capacity
388 General (Table K11)
388.2 Insane persons. People with mental or emotional disabilities (Table K11)
Cf. HV6133, Psychopathology and crime
388.3 Minors (Table K11)
Including infants, juveniles, and young adults
388.5.A-Z Special topics, A-Z
388.5.D58 Distemper (Table K12)
388.5.I58 Intoxication (Table K12)
388.5.L58 Litigious paranoia (Table K12)
Passion see KL-KWX5 388.5.D58
388.7 Criminal liability of juristic persons (Table K11)
390 Superior orders and justification or excusation (Table K11)

Criminal law
Concepts and principles
Criminal offense -- Continued
390.3 Error
Including error about fact, error about grounds for justification or excusation, and other error about extenuating circumstances, error in persona, etc.
Forms of the criminal act
Omission see KL-KWX5 385
Attempt see KL-KWX5 385.2
Perpetrators
392 General (Table K11)
Principals and accessories
392.2 General (Table K11)
392.5 Co-principals (Table K11)
392.7 Accessory before the fact (Table K11)
Including abettor
393 Accessory at attempted crime (Table K11)
393.3 Complicity (Table K11)
393.4 Agent provocateur (Table K11)
Aggravating and extenuating circumstances see KL-KWX5 402.2+
394 Compound offenses and compound punishment (Table K11)
Punishment
394.6 General (Table K11)
394.8 Constitutional aspects (Table K11)
Theory and policy of punishment
395 General (Table K11)
395.2 Retaliation. Retribution (Table K11)
395.4 Safeguarding the social and political system (Table K11)
395.6 General and special prevention (Table K11)
Including education, rehabilitation, and resocialization of perpetrator
Criminal anthropology
see HV6030+
396 Criminal sociology (Table K11)
For non-legal works, see HV6030+
Penalties and measures of rehabilitation and safety
For juveniles and young adults see KL-KWX5 472.6+
For execution of sentence see KL-KWX5 479.42+
396.2 General (Table K11)
396.4 Capital punishment (Table K11)
Imprisonment
Including maximum and minimum terms
397 General (Table K11)

Criminal law
Punishment
Penalties and measures of rehabilitation and safety
Imprisonment -- Continued
Prisons and jails see KL-KWX5 482.4
Reformatories see KL-KWX5 473.2
397.2 Short-term sentence (Table K11)
397.4 Sentencing to probation (Punishment without imprisonment). Conditional sentencing (Table K11)
Including terms of probation, e.g. education and resocialization through labor
397.8 Fines (Table K11)
398 Reprimand (Table K11)
398.2.A-Z Other penalties, A-Z
398.2.B43 Beating. Flogging (Table K12)
398.2.D43 Death by fire (Table K12)
Flogging see KL-KWX5 398.2.B43
398.2.M87 Mutilation (Table K12)
398.2.W58 Witch-execution (Table K12)
Measures entailing deprivation of liberty
398.3 General (Table K11)
398.4 Commitment to medical or psychiatric treatment (Table K11)
398.6 Commitment to medical, nursing, or socio-therapeutic institutions (Table K11)
399 Commitment of addicts to institutions for withdrawal treatment (Table K11)
399.2 Protective custody (Table K11)
Including dangerous or habitual criminals
Other measures
399.5 Protective surveillance (Table K11)
399.7 Expulsion (Table K11)
400 Prohibition against practicing a profession (Table K11)
400.4 Loss of civil rights. Infamy. Disfranchisement (Table K11)
400.6 Property confiscation (Table K11)
401 Forfeiture (Table K11)
Sentencing and determining the measure of punishment
401.2 General (Table K11)
401.6 Fixed and indeterminate sentence (Table K11)
Juvenile delinquents see KL-KWX5 472.2
Circumstances influencing measures of penalty
402 General (Table K11)
Aggravating and extenuating circumstances
Including principals and accessories
402.2 General (Table K11)

Criminal law
Punishment
Sentencing and determining the measure of punishment
Circumstances influencing measures of penalty
Aggravating and extenuating circumstances -- Continued
402.4 Recidivism (Table K11)
402.6 Detention pending investigation (Table K11)
Causes barring prosecution or execution of sentence
403 General (Table K11)
403.4 Pardon and amnesty. Clemency (Table K11)
For suspension of punishment see KL-KWX5 482.8
For probation and parole see KL-KWX5 483+
Limitation of actions
403.8 General (Table K11)
404.A-Z Crimes exempt from limitation of action, A-Z
404.C74 Crimes against humanity and human rights (Table K12)
404.T73 Treasonable endangering of the peace (Table K12)
404.W37 War crimes (Table K12)
Criminal registers see KL-KWX5 485
Criminal statistics see KL-KWX5 3.2
Individual offenses
404.5 General (Table K11)
Offenses against the person
Including aggravating circumstances
Homicide
405 General (Table K11)
405.2 Murder (Table K11)
405.4 Manslaughter (Table K11)
405.6 Killing on request (Table K11)
405.8 Euthanasia (Table K11)
406.2 Parricide (Table K11)
406.4 Infanticide (Table K11)
406.5 Negligent homicide (Table K11)
406.7 Desertion. Exposing persons to mortal danger (Table K11)
407 Crimes against inchoate life. Illegal abortion
Including ethical, social, medical, and eugenic aspects
For birth control and family planning see KL-KWX5 313.4+
Crimes against physical inviolability
407.4 General (Table K11)
407.6 Battery (Table K11)
407.8 Conjugal violence. Wife abuse. Husband abuse (Table K11)
408 Communicating venereal disease (Table K11)

Criminal law

Individual offenses

Offenses against the person

Crimes against physical inviolability -- Continued

408.2 Abuse of defenseless persons or dependents. Abuse of older people (Table K11)

For child abuse see KL-KWX5 419

408.4 Consent. Justified assault (Table K11)

For sports injuries see KL-KWX5 86.9

For medical treatment and operations see KL-KWX5 409.6+

Cf. KL-KWX5 386+ Criminal law concepts

408.8 Compound offenses (Table K11)

409 Poisoning (Table K11)

Criminal aspects of surgical and other medical treatment

Including biomedical engineering and medical technology

409.6 General (Table K11)

410 Malpractice (Table K11)

Cf. KL-KWX5 310.95 Torts

410.2 Treatment without consent (Table K11)

Euthanasia see KL-KWX5 405.8

410.3 Genetic engineering (Table K11)

410.8 Human reproductive technology (Table K11)

Including artificial insemination, fertilization in vitro, etc.

411 Transplantation of organs, tissues, etc. (Table K11)

Including donation of organs, tissues, etc.

411.2 Sterilization (Table K11)

Confidential communication see KL-KWX5 469.6.A+

Psychopharmaca damages see KL-KWX5 410

Crimes against personal freedom

411.6 General (Table K11)

411.8 False imprisonment (Table K11)

412 Extortionate kidnapping (Table K11)

Abduction

Cf. KL-KWX5 60 Parental kidnapping

412.5 General (Table K11)

412.7 Political abduction (Table K11)

413 Abduction of a woman without her consent (Table K11)

413.2 Abduction of a female minor (Table K11)

413.6 Threats of a felonious injury (Table K11)

413.8 Duress (Table K11)

414 Unlawful entry (Table K11)

Crimes against dignity and honor

Including juristic persons and families

414.3 General (Table K11)

414.5 Insult (Table K11)

Criminal law
Individual offenses
Offenses against the person
Crimes against dignity and honor -- Continued
414.7 Defamation (Table K11)
414.9 Calumny (Table K11)
415 Disparagement of memory of the dead (Table K11)
415.4 Defamatory statement and truth (Table K11)
415.6 Privileged comment (Table K11)
Including criticism of scientific, artistic, or professional accomplishments
For press delicts see KL-KWX5 351+
Violation of personal privacy and secrets
416 General (Table K11)
416.2 Constitutional aspects (Table K11)
416.4 Violation of confidential disclosures by professional persons (Table K11)
416.6 Opening of letters (Table K11)
416.8 Eavesdropping. Wiretapping (Table K11)
Offenses against religious tranquility and the peace of the dead
417 General (Table K11)
417.2 Blasphemy (Table K11)
417.4 Disturbing a religious observance (Table K11)
417.6 Disturbing the peace of the dead (Table K11)
Including cemeteries and funerals
Offenses against marriage, family, and family status
418 General (Table K11)
418.2 Incest (Table K11)
418.4 Adultery (Table K11)
418.6 Bigamy (Table K11)
(418.8) Abduction of a minor from legal custodian. Parental kidnapping
see KL-KWX5 60
419 Abandonment, neglect, or abuse of a child (Table K11)
419.2 Breach of duty of support (Table K11)
419.4 Breach of duty of assistance to a pregnant woman (Table K11)
Abortion see KL-KWX5 407
Artificial insemination see KL-KWX5 410.8
Offenses against sexual integrity
420 General (Table K11)
420.2 Rape (Table K11)
420.4 Lewd acts with persons incapable of resistance (Table K11)
420.6 Abduction for lewd acts (Table K11)

Criminal law
Individual offenses
Offenses against sexual integrity -- Continued
420.8 Lewd acts with children or charges. Seduction (Table K11)
421 Lewd acts by persons taking advantage of official position (Table K11)
421.4 Pandering and pimping. Slave traffic (Table K11)
Offenses against private and public property
423 General (Table K11)
Larceny and embezzlement
423.4 General (Table K11)
423.6 Burglary (Table K11)
424 Armed theft and theft by gangs (Table K11)
425 Embezzlement (Table K11)
Including embezzlement in office
425.4 Robbery and rapacious theft (Table K11)
425.6 Destruction of property and conversion (Table K11)
Fraud
426 General (Table K11)
426.2 Fraud by litigation (Table K11)
Fraudulent bankruptcy see KL-KWX5 427.6
426.4 Extortion (Table K11)
426.6 Breach of trust (Table K11)
426.8 Usury (Table K11)
Defeating rights of creditors
427 General (Table K11)
427.6 Fraudulent bankruptcy (Table K11)
428 Game and fish poaching (Table K11)
428.2 Aiding criminals in securing benefits (Table K11)
Including the receiving of stolen goods
Offenses against the national economy
428.6 General (Table K11)
429 Violation of price regulations (Table K11)
Including price fixing, hoarding, discrimination, overselling and underselling prices established by government etc.
429.2 Foreign exchange violations (Table K11)
429.4 Economic and industrial secrets. Unauthorized possession or disclosure (Table K11)
429.8 False statements concerning national planning (Table K11)
Counterfeiting money and stamps see KL-KWX5 434.6+
Offenses against public property see KL-KWX5 423+
430.A-Z Other, A-Z
Subarrange each by Table K12
Tax and customs crimes see KL-KWX5 370+
Offenses against public order and convenience
Including aggravating circumstances

KL-KWX4-KL-KWX5

Criminal law
Individual offenses
Offenses against public order and convenience -- Continued
430.5 General (Table K11)
430.7 Inciting insubordination (Table K11)
430.9 Rowdyism. Vandalism (Table K11)
431 Inciting crime (Table K11)
431.4 Parasitism (Table K11)
Disrupting the peace of the community
432 Demonstrations and failure to disperse (Table K11)
432.2 Inciting acts against minorities (Table K11)
Threatening the community. Terrorist activities see KL-KWX5 435.2+
Crimes against security of legal and monetary transactions and documents
433 General (Table K11)
433.4 Forgery and suppression of documents (Table K11)
433.8 Forgery and suppression of mechanical records (Table K11)
Including forgery of sound recordings and electronic data bases
434 Physical and identifying marks (Table K11)
Counterfeiting money and stamps
Including postage stamps
434.6 General (Table K11)
434.8 Passing counterfeit money (Table K11)
435 Counterfeiting securities (Table K11)
Including checks, bills of exchange, etc.
Customs crimes see KL-KWX5 370+
Tax evasion see KL-KWX5 370.2
435.15.A-Z Other, A-Z
435.15.D57 Displacing boundaries (Table K12)
435.15.F34 False certification (Table K12)
435.15.F67 Forgery of art works (Table K12)
435.15.M57 Misuse of credentials (Table K12)
Crimes involving danger to the community. Crimes against the environment. Terrorism
435.2 Common danger (Table K11)
435.4 Arson (Table K11)
435.6 Causing explosion (Table K11)
Including explosives and nuclear energy
435.8 Misuse of ionizing radiation (Table K11)
436 Releasing natural forces (Table K11)
Including flood, avalanche, rockfall, etc.
436.2 Dangerous use of poisonous substances (Table K11)
436.4 Poisoning wells or soil (Table K11)

Criminal law
Individual offenses
Offenses against public order and convenience
Crimes involving danger to the community. Crimes against the environment. Terrorism -- Continued
436.6 Poisoning food, medicine, etc. (Table K11)
436.8 Spreading communicable diseases, morbific agents, or parasites. Biological terrorism (Table K11)
437 Damaging water and power installations (Table K11)
437.2 Impairing industrial safety appliances (Table K11)
437.4 Sabotage of essential services, utilities, warning systems, etc. (Table K11)
437.6 Causing danger in construction (Table K11)
Including collapse, faulty gas or electric installation, etc.
Crimes affecting traffic
438 Dangerous interference with rail, ship, or air traffic (Table K11)
438.2 Unsafe operation of a rail vehicle, ship, or aircraft (Table K11)
Dangerous interference with street traffic
For minor traffic violations resulting in fines see KL-KWX5 345+
438.4 General (Table K11)
438.6 Driving while intoxicated (Table K11)
438.8 Duress. Constraint (Table K11)
439 Leaving the scene of an accident. Hit-and-run driving (Table K11)
Predatory assault on motorists. Highway robbery
439.2 General (Table K11)
439.4 Assault on taxicab drivers (Table K11)
439.6 Crimes aboard aircraft. Air piracy (Table K11)
439.8 Riots (Table K11)
Crimes against public health
440 General (Table K11)
440.4 Illicit use of, possession of, and traffic in narcotics (Table K11)
Communicating venereal diseases see KL-KWX5 408
440.6 Gambling (Table K11)
Including illegal operation of a lottery or games of chance, and participation
Cf. KL-KWX5 303.8.G35 Police and public safety
Offenses against the government. Political offenses.
Offenses against the peace
440.7 General (Table K11)
High treason and treason
440.8 General (Table K11)

Criminal law
Individual offenses
Offenses against the government. Political offenses.
Offenses against the peace
High treason and treason -- Continued
High treason against the state
Including national and state (republic, etc.)
442 General (Table K11)
442.2 Preparation of treasonable acts (Table K11)
442.4 Treason against the constitution (Table K11)
442.6 Assault on the head of state' (Table K11)
442.8 Inciting treason (Table K11)
443.2 Sabotage endangering the state (Table K11)
443.4 Undermining the state apparatus (Table K11)
443.8 Lese majesty (Table K11)
444 Disparagement of the state and its symbols. Disparaging constitutional organs (Table K11)
444.2 Treasonable espionage (Table K11)
For publication of official secrets by the press see KL-KWX5 351.3
444.4 Subversive activities (Table K11)
444.6 Intelligence activities (Table K11)
444.8 Propaganda endangering the state (Table K11)
445.5 Treasonable endangering of the peace or of international relations (Table K11)
Including propaganda, planning, preparation, or participation in an aggressive war
Crimes in connection with election and voting
445.8 General (Table K11)
446 Bribery. Corrupt practices (Table K11)
446.3 Falsifying votes and voting results (Table K11)
446.5 Obstructing voting (Table K11)
Crimes against national defense
447 General (Table K11)
447.3 Sabotaging and depicting means of defense (Table K11)
447.45 Violation of secrecy regulations (Table K11)
Opposition to power of the state
447.6 General (Table K11)
447.8 Constraining official action or inaction (Table K11)
448 Prison escape. Mutiny. Freeing prisoners (Table K11)
448.2.A-Z Other forms of opposition, A-Z
448.2.D35 Damaging official announcements (Table K12)
Endangering the administration of justice. Obstruction of justice
448.3 General (Table K11)
False testimony

Criminal law
Individual offenses
Offenses against the government. Political offenses.
Offenses against the peace
Endangering the administration of justice. Obstruction of justice
False testimony -- Continued
448.4 General (Table K11)
448.6 False unsworn testimony (Table K11)
449 Perjury (Table K11)
449.2 False affirmation (Table K11)
449.4 Causing false testimony (Table K11)
449.6 False accusation (Table K11)
449.8 Bringing false complaint (Table K11)
450 Thwarting criminal justice (Table K11)
450.2 Failure to report felony. Misprision (Table K11)
450.4 Coercion of testimony (Table K11)
450.6 Intentional misconstruction by law officers (Table K11)
450.7 Prosecuting innocent persons (Table K11)
Including execution
450.8 Repressing conflicting interests. Prevarication (Table K11)
451 Contempt of court (Table K11)
For contempt of court by the press see KL-KWX5 351.5
Assisting in securing benefits see KL-KWX5 428.2
Crimes against the civil service
451.4 General (Table K11)
Corruption
Including omission of official acts
451.6 General (Table K11)
452 Bribery. Granting benefits to civil servants (Table K11)
452.2 Illegal compensation to arbitrators (Table K11)
Bribery in connection with election see KL-KWX5 446
Embezzlement see KL-KWX5 425
Violating official secrecy
452.6 General (Table K11)
452.8 Disclosing official secrets (Table K11)
453.A-Z Other, A-Z
453.M35 Mail and telecommunication (Table K12)
Crimes against humanity
453.8 General (Table K11)
454 Genocide (Table K11)
454.3 Crimes against foreign states, supranational institutions, or international institutions (Table K11)
454.5 War crimes (Table K11)

Criminal law
Individual offenses -- Continued
454.8 Offenses commited through the mail (Table K11)
For threats, extortion, and blackmail see KL-KWX5 426.4
Radio communication criminal provisions see KL-KWX5 349.9
Press law criminal provisions see KL-KWX5 350.8+
Tax and customs crimes see KL-KWX5 370+
Military criminal law see KL-KWX5 375.8+
Criminal procedure
For works on both criminal and civil procedure, including codes of both criminal and civil procedure see KL-KWX5 165+
For works on both criminal law and criminal procedure, including codes of both criminal law and criminal procedure see KL-KWX5 379+
Criticism and reform see KL-KWX5 379
460 General (Table K11)
460.2 Constitutional aspects (Table K11)
460.4 Criminal procedure and public opinion (Table K11)
Including trial by newspaper
Administration of criminal justice see KL-KWX5 156.92+
Court organization see KL-KWX5 158+
Procedural principles
462 Due process of law (Table K11)
462.2 Uniformity of law application. Stare decisis (Table K11)
462.4 Accusation principle (Table K11)
462.6 Publicity and oral procedure (Table K11)
462.8 Prejudicial actions (Table K11)
Including all branches of the law
463.A-Z Parties to action, A-Z
463.A25 Accused. Person charged. Defendant (Table K12)
463.C74 Criminal judge (Table K12)
Defendant see KL-KWX5 463.A25
463.D43 Defense attorney. Public defender (Table K12)
Person charged see KL-KWX5 463.A25
Procurator see KL-KWX5 463.S73
Public defender see KL-KWX5 463.D43
463.S73 State prosecutor. Procurator (Table K12)
Class here works on the legal status of the prosecutor in criminal procedure
For general works on the office of the public prosecutor see KL-KWX5 160.8+
463.S93 Suspect (Table K12)
463.V52 Victim (Table K12)
Pretrial procedures

Criminal procedure
Pretrial procedures -- Continued
463.2 General (Table K11)
463.4 Penal report. Charges brought against a person (Table K11)
Investigation
For techniques of criminal investigation, see HV8073
Cf. KL-KWX5 467.9+ Admission of evidence
464 General (Table K11)
464.12 Examination of the accused (Table K11)
Public charges by prosecutor
464.2 General (Table K11)
464.4 Stare decisis (Table K11)
464.6 Summonses, service of process, and subpoena. Wanted notice (Table K11)
464.8 Time periods. Deadlines (Table K11)
Compulsory measures against the accused. Securing of evidence
465 General (Table K11)
465.2 Search and seizure (Table K11)
Including search of persons, buildings, institution's records, etc.
465.4 Provisional apprehension (Table K11)
465.5 Torture (Table K11)
465.7 Detention pending investigation (Table K11)
Including bail
Cf. KL-KWX5 479.8+ Execution of sentence
466 Extradition (Table K11)
Including constitutional aspects
Procedure at first instance
466.4 General (Table K11)
466.6 Jurisdiction (Table K11)
Including competence in subject matter and venue
466.8 Action. Complaint (Table K11)
467 Exclusion and challenge of court members (Table K11)
Time period and deadlines see KL-KWX5 464.8
Limitation of action see KL-KWX5 403.8+
Trial
467.3 General (Table K11)
Evidence. Burden of proof
467.5 General (Table K11)
Admission of evidence
467.9 General (Table K11)
468 Confession. Self-incrimination. Entrapment (Table K11)
468.3 Informers. Official secrets (Table K11)
468.5 Narcoanalysis, lie detectors, etc. (Table K11)

Criminal procedure
Procedure at first instance
Trial
Evidence. Burden of proof
Admission of evidence -- Continued
468.7 Physical examination (Table K11)
Including blood tests, urine tests, etc.
For forensic medicine, see RA1001+
468.9 Electronic listening and recording devices (Table K11)
Including wiretapping
469 Previous testimony, police records, etc. (Table K11)
Witnesses
469.2 General (Table K11)
469.6.A-Z Privileged witnesses (confidential communication), A-Z
469.8.A-Z Other witnesses, A-Z
469.8.C46 Child witnesses (Table K12)
470 Expert testimony (Table K11)
For forensic medicine, chemistry, psychology, psychiatry, toxicology, etc. see RA1001+
470.2 Testimony of accused (Table K11)
470.4 Documentary evidence (Table K11)
470.5 Circumstantial evidence (Table K11)
470.6 Alibi (Table K11)
470.9.A-Z Other, A-Z
Particular proceedings
471 Summary proceedings (Table K11)
471.3 Proceedings against absentee and fugitives (Table K11)
471.7 Recourse against decisions of grievance boards (Table K11)
Procedure for juvenile delinquency
472 General (Table K11)
472.2 The juvenile delinquent. The young adult perpetrator (Table K11)
472.4 Juvenile crime (Table K11)
Criminal liability and guilt see KL-KWX5 387.5+
Punishment. Correctional or disciplinary measures
Including measures of rehabilitation and safety
472.6 General (Table K11)
472.8 Custodial education (Table K11)
473.2 Detention homes. Reformatories (Table K11)
Cf. KL-KWX5 482.4 Execution of sentence
Execution of sentence see KL-KWX5 479.42+
Judicial decisions
473.6 General (Table K11)

Criminal procedure
Procedure at first instance
Trial
Judicial decisions -- Continued
473.8 Judgment (Table K11)
For sentencing and determination of punishment see KL-KWX5 401.2+
474 Judicial discretion (Table K11)
Including opportunity and equity
474.4 Acquittal (Table K11)
474.6 Conviction (Table K11)
Including measures of rehabilitation and safety
475 Dismissal. Decision ab instantia (Table K11)
Probation see KL-KWX5 483+
475.3 Correction or withdrawal of faulty decisions (errors) (Table K11)
475.4 Res judicata
For waiver of appeal see KL-KWX5 478.8
476 Court records. Minutes of evidence (Table K11)
Including clerks, translators, and correction of records
Participation of injured party in criminal procedure
476.2 General (Table K11)
476.4 Private charge (Table K11)
Including public interest
476.6 Intervention (Table K11)
476.7 Civil suits of victims in connection with criminal proceedings (Table K11)
Including reparation (Compensation to victims of crimes)
Special procedures
476.8 Procedure before the justice of the peace (Table K11)
Commitment of insane criminals see KL-KWX5 398.6
Other procedures
see the subject, e.g. KL-KWX5 370.3+ Tax and customs criminal procedure; KL-KWX5 375.8+ Military criminal procedure; etc.
Remedies
477 General (Table K11)
Appellate procedure
478 General (Table K11)
478.6 Cassation (Table K11)
478.8 Waiver of appeal (Table K11)
Post-conviction remedies
479 General (Table K11)
479.2 Reopening a case. New trial (Table K11)
For procedure before constitutional court see KL-KWX5 262+

Criminal procedure -- Continued
Execution of sentence
Including execution of sentence of juvenile courts
Criticism and reform see KL-KWX5 379
479.5 General (Table K11)
Imprisonment
Including regulation of detention pending investigation and short-term sentence
For penalties in general, including imprisonment see KL-KWX5 396.2+
479.8 General (Table K11)
480 Administration of penal or correctional institutions (Table K11)
Including discipline, hygiene, etc.
The prisoner
481 General (Table K11)
481.2.A-Z Particular, A-Z
Dangerous criminals see KL-KWX5 399.2
481.2.E38 Education of prisoners. Education through labor (Table K12)
Insane criminals see KL-KWX5 398.6
481.2.J88 Juvenile prisoners (Table K12)
481.2.P64 Political prisoners (Table K12)
482 Labor and industries in correctional institutions (Table K11)
Including wages
Rehabilitation and resocialization see KL-KWX5 395.6
482.4 Penal or correctional institutions (Table K11)
Including prisons, jails, penal colonies, reformatories, juvenile detention homes, etc.
482.6 Exile. Banishment. Punitive deportation (Table K11)
Pardon, amnesty, and clemency see KL-KWX5 403.4
482.8 Suspension of punishment (Table K11)
482.9 Restitution. Reparation (Table K11)
Probation. Parole
Including conditions
483 General (Table K11)
483.4 Probation and parole for juvenile delinquents (Table K11)
484 Remission (Table K11)
485 Criminal registers (Table K11)
Judicial error and compensation see KL-KWX5 284
Extradition see KL-KWX5 466
486 Costs (Table K11)
Victimology
487 General (Table K11)
487.4 Children and sexual crimes (Table K11)

Criminal procedure -- Continued
Criminology and penology
see HV6001+

Bibliography
For bibliography of special topics, see the topic
For manuals on legal bibliography, legal research and the use of law books see KL-KWX6 47+
2 Bibliography of bibliography
3 General bibliography
4 Library catalogs
4.5 Sales catalogs
5 Indexes to periodical literature, society publications, and collections
For indexes to a particular publication, see the publication
Indexes to festschriften see KL-KWX6 74
<6> Periodicals
For periodicals consisting predominantly of legal articles, regardless of subject matter and jurisdiction, see K1+
For periodicals consisting primarily of informative material (newsletters, bulletins, etc.) relating to a special subject, see the subject and form division tables for periodicals
For law reports, official bulletins or circulars intended chiefly for the publication of laws and regulations, see appropriate entries in the text or form division tables
6.5 Monographic series
Official gazettes
7 General
State or city gazettes
see the issuing state or city
Departmental gazettes
see the issuing department or agency
8 Indexes (General)
Legislative documents
see class J
9 Other materials relating to legislative history
Including recommended legislation; legislation passed and vetoed
Legislation
For statutes, statutory orders, regulations, etc. on a particular subject, see the subject
Indexes and tables
Including indexes to statutes of several states
For indexes to a particular publication, see the publication
For indexes limited to one state, see the state
10 General
10.5 Chronological indexes. By date
10.6 Indexes to publisher editions (unannotated and annotated). By date
10.7 Other bibliographical aids
11 Abridgements and digests

Legislation -- Continued

12 Citators to statutes and/or administrative regulations

For citators to both reports and statutes, see the citators to reports

Statutes

Including statutory orders and regulations, comparative state legislation

Collections and compilations

Including official and private editions

13 Serials

14 Monographs. By date

Including unannotated and annotated editions

Administrative and executive publications

Including statutory orders and regulations, orders in council, proclamations, etc.

For regulations on a particular subject, see the subject

17 Serials

17.5 Monographs. By date

17.6 Digests

17.7 Indexes. By date

Presidential proclamations, etc.

see class J

Treaties

For treaties on international public law, see class KZ

For treaties on international uniform law not limited to a region, see class K

For treaties on international uniform law of a particular region, see the region

Law reports and related materials

Including national (federal) and regional reports

For reports of an individual state or territory, including reports of the older courts, see the appropriate jurisdiction

For reports relating to a particular subject, and for reports of courts of limited jurisdiction other than those listed below, see the appropriate subject

National (Federal) courts

18 Highest courts of appeal. Supreme courts. Courts of Cassation (Table K18)

Lower courts

19 Various courts (Table K18)

Including highest court and lower courts, or national (federal) courts of two or more state combined; or regional (provincial) courts

Intermediate appellate courts. Circuit courts of appeal

20 Collective (Table K18)

21.A-Z Particular courts, A-Z

Law reports and related materials
National (Federal) courts -- Continued
(22) Digests and indexes to federal decisions
see KL-KWX6 18 ; KL-KWX6 19 ; etc.
State courts
For reports of an individual state, see the state
23 Reports covering all states or selected states (Table K18)
24 Reports covering national (federal) decisions and decisions of the courts of two or more states (Table K18)
25.A-Z Decisions of supreme (federal) courts in, or of cases before federal courts arising in particular states. By state, A-Z
25.4 Decisions of national (federal) administrative agencies
For decisions of particular agencies, see the subject
25.5 Encyclopedias
26 Dictionaries. Words and phrases
For bilingual and multilingual dictionaries, see K52.A+
For dictionaries on a particular subject, see the subject
27 Maxims. Quotations
28 Form books
Class here general works
For form books on a particular subject, see the subject
Judicial statistics
30 General
Criminal statistics
31 General
31.3 Juvenile crime
32.A-Z Other. By subject, A-Z
32.D65 Domestic relations. Family law
Family law see KL-KWX6 32.D65
Directories
33 National and regional
34.A-Z By state, A-Z
35.A-Z Local. By administrative district or city, A-Z
36.A-Z By specialization, A-Z
Trials
Class all trials, including those occurring in national, state (provincial, etc.), or local courts, in the numbers provided for trials at the national level
38 General collections
Criminal trials and judicial investigations
For military trials see KL-KWX6 3395
Collections. Compilations
39 General
40.A-Z Particular offenses, A-Z
40.A78 Arson
40.A87 Assassination

Trials
Criminal trials and judicial investigations
Collections. Compilations
Particular offenses, A-Z -- Continued
40.F73 Fraud
40.M87 Murder
40.P64 Political crimes
War crimes see KL-KWX6 42.2+
41.A-Z Individual trials. By defendant or best known (popular name), A-Z
Including records, briefs, commentaries, and stories on a particular trial
War crime trials
Trials by international military tribunals
see class KZ
43 Collections
44.A-Z Individual trials. By defendant or best known (popular) name, A-Z
Including records, briefs, commentaries, and stories on a particular trial
Other trials
45 Collections. Compilations
46.A-Z Individual trials. By plaintiff, defendant, or best known (popular) name, A-Z
Including records, briefs, commentaries, and stories on a particular trial
Legal research. Legal bibliography
Including methods of bibliographic research and how to find the law
47 General
Electronic data processing. Information retrieval
47.5 General works
47.7.A-Z By subject, A-Z
Litigation see KL-KWX6 47.7.P76
47.7.P76 Procedure. Litigation
48 Systems of citation. Legal abbreviations
48.5 Surveys of legal research
48.7 Legal composition and draftsmanship. Legal drafting. Officers. Parliamentary counsels
Legal education
50 General works
Study and teaching
General works see KL-KWX6 50
50.3 Teaching methods
Including clinical method, case method, etc.
51.A-Z By subject, A-Z

Legal education
Study and teaching -- Continued
51.7 Students' guides
For introductory surveys of the law see KL-KWX6 50
51.8 Teachers' manuals
52 Pre-law school education
52.3 Law teachers
52.4 Law students
Including sociology and psychology of law students
Law schools
52.5 General works
53.A-Z Particular law schools. By name, A-Z
Including constitution and bylaws, statutes, regulations, degrees, and general works (history)
Post-law school education
53.2 General works
53.25 Judicial education (Table K11)
The legal profession
53.3 General works
53.35.A-Z Particular classes of lawyers and types of careers, A-Z
Practice of law
53.4 General works
Attorneys
53.5 General works
53.55 Admission to the bar. Bar examinations
53.6 Attorney and client
For violation of confidential disclosure see KL-KWX6 4164
53.8 Legal ethics and etiquette. Courts of honor. Disbarment
Economics of law practice
53.84 General works
53.85 Fees (Table K11)
53.9 Legal consultants. Procurators
53.92 Legal aid. Legal services to the poor. People's lawyer. Community legal services. Public solicitors
For public defender see KL-KWX6 4630.D43
Bar associations. Law societies. Law institutes
Class here works on, and journals by, individual societies and their activities, e.g., annual reports, proceedings, incorporation statutes, bylaws, handbooks, and works (history) about the society
Including courts of honor and disbarment
For publications of associations on special subjects, see the subject
For journals devoted to legal subjects, either wholly or in part, see K1+
For membership directories see KL-KWX6 36.A+

Bar associations. Law societies -- Continued
54 General works
54.3.A-Z National associations. By name, A-Z
For biography (collective) see KL-KWX6 105+
For biography (individual) see KL-KWX6 110.A+
54.5.A-Z State associations. By state, A-Z
Class here works on, and journals by, individual societies and their activities, e.g. annual reports, proceedings, incorporation statutes, bylaws, handbooks, and works (history) about the society
For biography (collective) see KL-KWX6 105+
For biography (Individual) see KL-KWX6 110.A+
54.7.A-Z Local associations, lawyers' clubs, etc. By county or city, A-Z
Class here works on, and journals by, individual societies and their activities, e.g. annual reports, proceedings, incorporation statutes, bylaws, handbooks, and works (history) about the society
For biography (collective) see KL-KWX6 105+
For biography (Individual) see KL-KWX6 110.A+
Notaries. Notarial practice and procedure
Class here works on notaries of several jurisdictions
For notaries (several or individual) of an individual state, administrative district, or municipality, see the state, district, or municipality
55 General works
55.2 Legal instruments. Certification
Public registers. Registration
56 General works
Civil registry see KL-KWX6 522
Registration of juristic persons. Incorporated associations see KL-KWX6 954.3
57 Registration of miscellaneous titles and documents
Property registration. Registration of pledges
58 General works
Land registers see KL-KWX6 715
Aircraft registers see KL-KWX6 1050.5
Ship registers see KL-KWX6 1056.4
62 Congresses. Conferences
63.A-Z Collected works (nonserial). By author, A-Z
Including collected opinions
64.A-Z Academies. Institutes. By name, A-Z
68 General works. Treatises
70 Compends, outlines, examination aids, etc.
Forms, graphic materials, blanks, atlases see KL-KWX6 28
72 Popular works. Civics

74 Addresses, essays, lectures
Including single essays, collected essays of several authors, festschriften, and indexes to festschriften
78.A-Z Manuals and other works for particular groups of users. By user, A-Z
78.A34 Accountants. Auditors
78.A77 Artists
Auditors see KL-KWX6 78.A34
78.A85 Authors
78.B87 Businesspeople. Foreign investors
78.E53 Engineers
78.F37 Farmers
Foreign investors see KL-KWX6 78.B87
78.M87 Musicians
78.S63 Social workers
Semantics and language see KL-KWX6 92
Legal symbolism see KL-KWX6 94+
Legal anecdotes, wit and humor
see K184.4
Law and lawyers in literature
see classes PB-PH
Law and art
see K487.C8
Law and history
see K487.C8
80.A-Z Works on diverse aspects of a particular subject and falling within several branches of the law. By subject, A-Z
80.C65 Computers
80.H67 Horses
Legal advertising see KL-KWX6 80.N68
80.M4 Meetings
80.N68 Notice. Legal advertising
80.P78 Public interest law
80.P8 Public relations
History of law
85 Bibliography
86 Periodicals
86.2 Encyclopedias
86.3 Law dictionaries. Vocabularies. Terms and phrases
Auxiliary sciences
87 General works
92 Linguistics. Semantics
Archaeology. Folklife studies. Symbolism
94 General works
96.A-Z Special topics, A-Z
96.S76 Stool, Ancestral

History of law
Auxiliary sciences -- Continued
98 Inscriptions
100 Heraldry. Seals. Flags. Insignia. Armory
Law and lawyers in literature
see classes PB-PH
Biography of lawyers
Collective
105 General
107 Collections of portraits
110.A-Z Individual, A-Z
Subarrange each by Table KL-KWX11
120 General works. Treatises
By period
<122> Ancient and early, including ancient people in the region
see KL, KQ, or particular jurisdiction, as specified (e.g. India)
Medieval and early modern (to second half of the 19th century)
Including precolonial and early colonial periods
132 General works
Sources
For sources of a territory or town, see the appropriate territory or town
Studies on sources
Including history and methodology (e.g. epigraphy, papyrology, etc.)
For philological studies, see classes P, PJ, PK, and PL
133 General works
133.5 Classification of sources
134 Collections. Compilations. Selections
Class here comprehensive collections of legal sources in various native (vernacular) scripts
Individual sources or groups of sources
National (imperial) laws and legislation
Including constitutional laws
140 Collections. Compilations
142 Individual. By date
Subarrange each by Table K20b
Royal (imperial) privileges
Including privileges for particular classes, groups, communities, courts of justice, etc.
144 Collections. Compilations
146 Individual. By date
Subarrange each by Table K20b
Royal (imperial) mandates. Decrees, orders, etc.. of princes and rulers

History of law
By period
Medieval and early modern (to second half of the 19th century)
Sources
Individual sources or groups of sources
Royal (imperial) edicts, etc. of princes and rulers. Decrees. Mandates -- Continued
148 Collections. Compilations
150 Individual. By date
Subarrange each by Table K20b
Treaties
Treaties on international public law
see KZ
Treaties on international uniform law
see K524+ KJC38+ KMC, KNC, KQC, and KVC
Court decisions. Cases. Advisory opinions. Reports. Digests
160 Several courts
164.A-Z Particular courts. By place, A-Z
Trials
Criminal trials and judicial investigations
Collections. Compilations
170 General
172.A-Z Particular offenses, A-Z
172.W58 Witchcraft
174.A-Z Individual trials. By defendant, or best known (popular) name, A-Z
Including records, briefs, commentaries, and stories on a particular trial
Other trials
176 Collections. Compilations
178.A-Z Individual trials. By plaintiff, defendant, or best known (popular) name, A-Z
180 Contemporary legal literature. Documents. Public and private records
Class here general collections
For collections or individual documents on a topic, see the topic
The State and its constitution
202 General (Table K22)
Classes. Castes, etc.
204 General works
205.A-Z Special topics, A-Z
205.B57 Birth rights
205.D94 Dynastic rules

History of law
By period
Medieval and early modern (to second half of the 19th century)
The State and its constitution
Estates. Classes. Castes
Special topics, A-Z -- Continued
205.E62 Equality of birth
Feudal capacity see KL-KWX6 228
205.O87 Outlawry. Outcasts
209 Territory (Table K22)
212 Foreign relations (Table K22)
Feudal law
213 General (Table K22)
Sources
214 Collections. Compilations
220.2<date> Individual sources
Arrange chronologically by appending the date of the source to this number and deleting any trailing zeros. Subarrange each by Table K20b
Feudal institutes
221 General (Table K22)
Feudal lords and vassalage
222 General (Table K22)
223 Peers (Table K22)
Fief
224 General (Table K22)
226.A-Z Special topics, A-Z
226.C65 Commendation. Hommage
Hommage see KL-KWX6 226.C65
226.L3 Land
226.V5 Villages. Towns
228 Feudal capacity (Table K22)
230 Feudal succession (Table K22)
Rural (peasant) land tenure and peasantry
232 General (Table K22)
Leasehold for years and inheritance
238 General (Table K22)
240.A-Z Special topics, A-Z
242 Succession to rural holdings (Table K22)
Kings. Princes and rulers. Chiefs
246 General (Table K22)
248.A-Z Special topics, A-Z
Crown goods and dynastic estates see KL-KWX6 263
248.E43 Election
Prerogatives see KL-KWX6 248.R53

History of law
By period
Medieval and early modern (to second half of the 19th century)
The state and its constitution
Kings. Princes and rulers. Chieftains
Special topics, A-Z -- Continued
248.R53 Rights and prerogatives
248.S93 Succession and designation
250 The court. Court officials and councils (Table K22)
254 Legislature. Diet (Table K22)
256 Military organization (Table K22)
Finance
Class here works on topics not represented elsewhere in the schedule
For works on the history of particular subjects, see the subject
259 General (Table K22)
263 Crown goods and dynastic house goods (Table K22)
268.A-Z Special topics, A-Z
Judiciary. Court organization and procedure
Class here comprehensive works on the development of the judiciary, and on a defunct court or court system
For the history of a particular court system or court, see KL-KWX6 3441+ or the jurisdiction
For reports see KL-KWX6 17.8+
283 General (Table K22)
288.A-Z Special topics, A-Z
Criminal law and procedure
Class here works on topics not represented elsewhere in the schedule
For works on the history of other subjects, see the subject
292 General (Table K22)
294.A-Z Particular crimes, A-Z
296.A-Z Particular procedures, A-Z
298.A-Z Particular penalties, A-Z
<350> Indigenous peoples. Ethnic groups
For works on the law of indigenous peoples regardless of whether identified with one or more countries in the region, see KM, KN, KQ, or as indicated
Philosophy, jurisprudence, and theory of law
Class here works on doctrines peculiar to legal institutions of a country
For works on the philosophy of a particular branch of the law (e.g., constitutional law or criminal law), see the branch
For works on the philosophy of law in general, see K201+

Philosophy, jurisprudence, and theory of law -- Continued
440 General works
The concept of law
Including the definition of law
442 General works
443 The object of law. Law and justice
Ethics. Morality of law. Public policy
444 General works
444.5 Repugnancy clause (British)
444.7 Chicanery. Abuse of rights
445 Law and the state. Legal order. Respect for law
446 Rights and duties. Sanction
447 Effectiveness and validity of the law
448.A-Z Other topics, A-Z
Determinism see KL-KWX6 448.F73
448.F73 Free will and determinism
Sources of law
449 General works
449.3 Customs and observances. Indigenous law
449.5 Legislation
Judge-made law see KL-KWX6 451
Rule of law see KL-KWX6 1726
Law reform. Criticism see KL-KWX6 470
451 Methodology. Interpretation and construction
Including judge-made law
Modern political theory of law
463 General works
464 Socialist. Communist
Schools of legal theory
Sociological jurisprudence
465 General works
465.5 Law and public policy
465.6 Social psychology of law
466 Social pathology
467 Natural law
469 Pluralism in law
469.5 Influence of other legal systems on the law. Superimposition of foreign rule on the customary (indigenous) law
Including reception of traditional, customary and religious law, and multiplicity of law
470 Law reform and policies. Criticism
Including reform of administration of justice
471.A-Z Concepts applying to several branches of the law, A-Z
471.E88 Estoppel
471.G65 Good faith. Reliance

Concepts applying to several branches of the law, A-Z -- Continued
471.L55 Limitation of actions
Cf. KL-KWX6 3591 Civil procedure
471.L63 Locus poenitentiae
471.5 Intertemporal law. Retroactive law
474 Regional divisions. Subregions
Class here general works on the law or the legal systems in force within a single subregion of the country
For works on a particular subject, see the subject
479 Private law (Table K11)
Class here works on all aspects of private and civil law in force within a country with mixed legal systems
Conflict of laws
For conflict of laws between the United States and a particular jurisdiction, see KF416
For works on conflict rules of branches other than private law and law of procedure (e.g. tax law, criminal law, etc.), see the subject
480 General (Table K11)
481 Plurality of laws conflict. Two or more different legal systems in force in the same country (Table K11)
Class here works on conflict of laws in a multicultural country with two or more coexisting legal systems (e.g. secular and religious law, common law, indigenous law (tribal, customary), and religious law, etc.)
481.3 Public order (Table K11)
Choice of law
Including indigenous (tribal, customary) law and civil law
482 General (Table K11)
483 Connecting factors. Points of contact. Nationality and domicile (Table K11)
483.5 Interlocal (interstate) law (Table K11)
483.7 Repugnancy clause (British (Table K11)
484 Party autonomy (Table K11)
485 Renvoi (Table K11)
486.A-Z Particular branches and subjects of the law, A-Z
486.A55 Aliens (Table K12)
Arbitral awards see KL-KWX6 486.P75
486.A83 Arbitration (Table K12)
Class here works on arbitration courts, commissions, and proceedings
For comparative works on arbitration, see the region
Bankruptcy see KL-KWX6 486.P75
486.C38 Caste. Personal status (Table K12)
Divorce see KL-KWX6 486.M37

Conflict of laws
Particular branches and subjects of the law, A-Z -- Continued
Execution see KL-KWX6 486.P75
486.M37 Marriage. Matrimonial actions. Matrimonial property (Table K12)
Matrimonial actions see KL-KWX6 486.M37
Matrimonial property see KL-KWX6 486.M37
Personal status see KL-KWX6 486.C38
486.P75 Procedure. Arbitral awards. Execution and bankruptcy (Table K12)
486.S8 Statelessness (Table K12)
Retroactive law. Intertemporal law see KL-KWX6 471.5
490 Equity (Table K11)
Persons
511 General (Table K11)
Natural persons
511.2 General (Table K11)
Civil status
511.3 General (Table K11)
512 Domicile (Table K11)
513 Name (Table K11)
513.3 Caste (Table K11)
Cf. KL-KWX6 583+
514 Absence. Missing persons. Presumption of death (Table K11)
Capacity and disability
515 General (Table K11)
516 Women (Table K11)
Class here works on legal status under all aspects of law (e.g. religious, customary, private, and public law)
For married women see KL-KWX6 550
516.5 Men (Table K11)
517 Minors. Infants (Table K11)
Including liability
Persons of unsound mind. Mentally ill persons. People with mental disabilities
For guardianship and curatorship see KL-KWX6 622
For care of the mentally ill see KL-KWX6 1523
518 General (Table K11)
518.5.A-Z Particular diseases or impairments, A-Z
Subarrange each by Table K12
519.A-Z Other, A-Z
Aborigines see KL-KWX6 519.I64
519.A54 Aliens (Table K12)
Cf. KL-KWX6 2155.A43 Control of individuals
519.E93 Ex-convicts (Table K12)

Persons
Natural persons
Capacity and disability
Other, A-Z -- Continued
519.I64 Indigenous people. Aborigines (Table K12)
519.P48 Physical disabilities, People with (Table K12)
519.U53 Unborn children. Nasciturus (Table K12)
522 Recording and registration. Civil registry. Registers of births, marriages, and deaths. Birth and death certificates. Census. Vital statistics
Juristic persons, corporate persons, associations, etc. see KL-KWX6 954+
Domestic relations. Family law. Multiplicity of laws
Including one or more religious legal systems, customary law and common law
531-540 General (Table K9c)
541 Domestic relations courts and procedure (Table K11)
Including civil courts, Rabbinical courts, Islamic (Shariah) courts, etc.
542 Domicile with regard to domestic relations (Table K11)
Marriage. Husband and wife
543 General (Table K11)
543.5 Betrothal (Table K11)
Including breach of promise
544.A-Z Marriage impediments, A-Z
544.C37 Caste (Table K12)
544.W54 Widowhood (Table K12)
545 Certificates. Premarital examinations (Table K11)
546 Performance of marriage. Civil and religious ceremonies (Table K11)
546.2 Intermarriage (Table K11)
Including interracial, interethnic, and interfaith marriage
546.4 Multiple marriages. Polygamy. Polyandry (Table K11)
546.5 Head of the family (Table K11)
Rights and duties of husband and wife
547 General (Table K11)
548 Domicile. (Table K11)
549 Family name (Table K11)
550 Legal status of married women
For family name see KL-KWX6 513
Marital property relationships
552 General (Table K11)
554 Separation of property (Table K11)
558 Community property (Table K11)
560 Marriage settlements. Antenuptial contracts (Table K11)
564.A-Z Other, A-Z

Persons
Domestic relations. Family law. Multiplicity of laws
Marriage. Husband and wife
Marital property relationships
Other, A-Z -- Continued
564.D68 Dowry (Table K12)
Cf. KL-KWX6 4053 Dowry killing
568 Quasi-matrimonial relationships (Table K11)
Including common law marriages (unmarried cohabitation), concubinage, etc., and including property relationships of such marriages
Matrimonial actions. Dissolution of marriage
For courts and procedures see KL-KWX6 3689
570 General (Table K11)
Void and voidable marriages. Annulment
Including non-marriages
572 General (Table K11)
574.A-Z Special topics, A-Z
Subarrange each by Table K12
Divorce
577 General (Table K11)
578.A-Z Grounds for divorce, A-Z
578.A48 Adultery (Table K12)
578.B37 Barren wife (Table K12)
578.D47 Desertion (Table K12)
578.D68 Dower, Non-payment of (Table K12)
580 Separation (Table K11)
581 Settlement of claims from defective or dissolved marriages (Table K11)
Including alimony and dowry
For dowry killing see KL-KWX6 4053
Consanguinity and affinity. Kinship
Including works on caste system
583 General (Table K11)
584 Support (Table K11)
Parent and child
587 General (Table K11)
590 Legitimacy
594 Illegitimacy (Table K11)
598 Affiliation (patrilineal and matrilineal) (Table K11)
600 Adoption (Table K11)
Parental rights and duties. Property of minors. Custody
Access to children
Including parental kidnapping
For procedure see KL-KWX6 3690
610 General (Table K11)

Persons
Domestic relations. Family law. Multiplicity of laws
Consanguinity and affinity. Kinship
Parent and child
Parental rights and duties. Property of minors. Custody -- Continued
611 Support. Desertion and non-support (Table K11)
612.A-Z Special topics, A-Z
612.A78 Artificial insemination (Table K12)
612.S87 Surrogate motherhood (Table K12)
622 Guardianship (Table K11)
Including procedure and including also guardianship over minors and adults
629 Curatorship (Table K11)
Including procedure
Property
631-640 General (Table K9c)
641 Right of property (Table K11)
Possession and ownership
642 General (Table K11)
646 Acquisition and loss (Table K11)
647 Possessory actions (Table K11)
Particular kinds of property
648 General (Table K11)
650 Enemy property (Table K11)
Matrimonial property see KL-KWX6 552+
Public property. Government property see KL-KWX6 2500+
655 Socialist property (Table K11)
Real property. Land law
658 General (Table K11)
658.5 Alien ownership (Table K11)
Public policy. Customary land policy legislation see KL-KWX6 2550+
Land tenure
659 General (Table K11)
Feudal tenure
660 General (Table K11)
Free tenure
662 General (Table K11)
663.A-Z Particular types, A-Z
Subarrange each by Table K12
Unfree tenure
664 General (Table K11)
665.A-Z Particular types, A-Z
Subarrange each by Table K12
667 Inquisitiones post mortem

Property
Real property. Land law
Land tenure -- Continued
Estates and interests. Ownership
671 General (Table K11)
Particular estates and interests (legal or equitable)
672 General (Table K11)
Freehold estates
673 General (Table K11)
Fee simple
674 General (Table K11)
675 Extent of ownership above and below surface (Table K11)
Including airspace, minerals, metals, etc.
Particular kinds
677 Flats. Horizontal property. Housing condominium, etc. (Table K11)
678 Fee tail. Entailed interests (Table K11)
Life interests. Possessory estates
Fixtures. Improvements see KL-KWX6 696
Rights of user. Waste. Dilapidations. Repairs see KL-KWX6 697
679 Dower. Curtesy (Table K11)
Estates less than freehold
680 General (Table K11)
Leasehold interests. Landlord and tenant see KL-KWX6 689+
681 Equitable ownership. Equitable conversion (Table K11)
682 Uses and trusts. Statute of uses (Table K11)
682.5 Settlements and trusts for sale (Table K11)
Future estates and interests
Including works on future interests in both real and personal property
683 General (Table K11)
684 Power of appointment (Table K11)
684.5 Reversions. Reversionary interests (Table K11)
684.6 Remainders. Contingent remainders. Executory devices (Table K11)
Concurrent ownership. Co-ownership
Including works on concurrent ownership in both real and personal property
685 General (Table K11)
Joint tenancy. Tenancy in common
686 General (Table K11)
687 Joint family property (Table K11)
687.3 Partition (Table K11)

Property
Real property. Land law
Land tenure
Estates and interests. Ownership
Particular estates and interests
Concurrent ownership. Co-ownership
Joint tenancy. Tenancy in common
Housing cooperatives see KL-KWX6 677
687.5 Estates and interests arising from marriage (Table K11)
Tenancy. Leaseholds. Landlord and tenant
689 General (Table K11)
690 Rent (Table K11)
Including rent control
692.A-Z Particular kinds of tenancy and leaseholds, A-Z
Building leases see KL-KWX6 692.G75
692.C65 Commercial leases (Table K12)
Farm tenancy see KL-KWX6 989.3+
692.G75 Ground leases. Building leases (Table K12)
Oil and gas leases see KL-KWX6 1012.2
Gratuitous tenancy see KL-KWX6 710.5
Rights and interests incident to ownership and possession. Interests less than estates
695 General (Table K11)
696 Fixtures. Improvements (Table K11)
697 Rights of user. Waste. Dilapidations. Repair (Table K11)
698 Boundaries. Fences (Table K11)
699 Riparian rights. Water rights of individuals (Table K11)
For fishing rights see KL-KWX6 1004+
700 Grazing rights. Hunting rights (Table K11)
701 Action to recover the possession of land. Ejectment (Table K11)
For trespass to land see KL-KWX6 943.6
Right to dispose of land. Public and private restraints of alienation
702 General (Table K11)
703 Ancestral property. Family property. Property of kinship groups (Table K11)
For return of alientated land to customary ownership see KL-KWX6 716.7
703.5 Prohibition of sale to non-indigenous persons and other alienations affecting customary title to land (Table K11)
Rights to use and profits of another's land. Incorporeal hereditaments
704 General (Table K11)

Property
Real property. Land law
Land tenure
Estates and interests. Ownership
Rights and interests incident to ownership and possession. Interests less than estates
Rights to use and profits of another's land. Incorporeal hereditaments -- Continued

705.A-Z Easements, A-Z
705.L55 Light and air (Table K12)
705.P37 Party walls. Support of land (Table K12)
705.R55 Right of way (Table K12)
708 Commons and enclosures (Table K11)
709 Restrictive covenants. Prohibition of indefinite use rights (Table K11)
710 Rent charges (Table K11)
Annuities see KL-KWX6 736
710.5 Gratuitous tenancy (Table K11)
711.A-Z Special topics, A-Z
711.P73 Prescription (Table K12)
711.S68 Squatting (Table K12)
Transfer of rights in land
712 General (Table K11)
Government land grants see KL-KWX6 2553.6
Transfer inter vivos. Vendor and purchaser
712.5 General (Table K11)
Conveyances. Title investigation. Abstracts
713 General (Table K11)
713.5 Adjudication of existing rights (Table K11)
714 Deeds (Table K11)
715 Registration. Land title system (Table K11)
Including Torrens system
716 Description of land. Surveying (Table K11)
716.5.A-Z Other modes of transfer, A-Z
Subarrange each by Table K12
Prescription see KL-KWX6 711.P73
716.7 Restoration of alienated land to customary ownership (Table K11)
716.8 Right of pre-emption (Table K11)
Mortgages. Liens. Land charges
717 General (Table K11)
719.A-Z Special topics, A-Z
Subarrange each by Table K12
720 Real estate management (Table K11)
Including estate management and urban estate management
Personal property

Property
Personal property -- Continued
722 General (Table K11)
Ownership and possession
723 General (Table K11)
724 Interests. Future interests. Concurrent ownership (Table K11)
Fixtures see KL-KWX6 696
Acquisition of property
725 General (Table K11)
Original acquisition
726 General (Table K11)
727.A-Z Particular modes of acquisition, A-Z
727.A33 Accession and confusion (Table K12)
Transfer
728 General (Table K11)
Choses in possession
729 General (Table K11)
Auction sale see KL-KWX6 865.5
Bill of sale see KL-KWX6 879
Sale see KL-KWX6 863+
Bailment see KL-KWX6 876+
Gifts
730 General (Table K11)
Transfers as security see KL-KWX6 904
732 Actions to recover personal property. Replevin (Table K11)
Particular kinds of personal property
734 General (Table K11)
Tangible. Choses in possession see KL-KWX6 729+
Intangible. Choses in action
735 General (Table K11)
736 Annuities (Table K11)
Debts see KL-KWX6 903+
Intellectual property see KL-KWX6 1100+
Negotiable instruments see KL-KWX6 880+
Shares, stocks, and debentures see KL-KWX6 957+
Trusts and trustees
740 General (Table K11)
Particular kinds of trusts
741 Private trusts. General trusts (Table K11)
Constructive trusts see KL-KWX6 939.7
742 Resulting trusts (Table K11)
Charitable trusts. Endowments. Foundations see KL-KWX6 955.F68
Trusts for sale see KL-KWX6 682.5
Trustees

Trusts and trustees
Trustees -- Continued
746 General (Table K11)
748 Trust companies (Table K11)
Public trustees see KL-KWX6 797+
750 Liability. Breach of trust (Table K11)
753 Accounting (Table K11)
Legal investments. Trust investments see KL-KWX6 912+
755 Estate planning (Table K11)
Succession upon death
761-770 General (Table K9c)
Capacity and disability to inherit
Cf. KL-KWX6 515+ Capacity
771 General (Table K11)
772 Unworthiness (Table K11)
773.A-Z Particular types of persons, A-Z
773.A64 Aliens (Table K12)
773.M56 Minors (Table K12)
773.5 Family provisions
Testamentary succession. Wills
774 General (Table K11)
774.5 Capacity to make a will. Freedom of testation (Table K11)
775.A-Z Forms of wills, A-Z
775.H64 Holographic wills (Table K12)
Military wills see KL-KWX6 775.P74
Notarial wills see KL-KWX6 775.P74
775.P74 Privileged wills (Table K12)
Including military wills and notarial wills
Testamentary dispositions. Legacies
776 General (Table K11)
777 Charitable bequests. Request for the benefit of the poor (Table K11)
779 Disinheritance (Table K11)
Probate law. Probate courts and procedure
780 General (Table K11)
781.A-Z Special topics, A-Z
Subarrange each by Table K12
783 Contracts of inheritance (Table K11)
Intestate succession
785 General (Table K11)
Classes of heirs. Order of succession
786 General (Table K11)
Descendants and ascendants
787 General (Table K11)
788 Legitimate descendants. Legitimate children (Table K11)

Succession upon death
Intestate succession
Classes of heirs. Order of succession
Descendants and ascendants -- Continued
790 Illegitimate descendants. Illegitimate children (Table K11)
791 Adopted children (Table K11)
792 Surviving spouses. Several surviving wives with or without children (Table K11)
793 Natural parents (Table K11)
795 The state (Table K11)
796 Succession to rights and duties in relation to persons. Guardianship (Table K11)
Including rights and duties exercised by a husband over his wife; and including guardianship over children and illegitimate children
Trustees
797 General (Table K11)
797.5.A-Z Special topics, A-Z
Subarrange each by Table K12
The distributable estate. Distribution of property. Traditional property
Including land, livestock, crops, weapons and ornaments, etc.
798 General (Table K11)
799 Estate of married person with one or more spouses (Table K11)
800 Estate of widowed person (Table K11)
Contracts
801-810 General (Table K9c)
Classification of contracts
812 General (Table K11)
812.2 Consensual, formal, and real contracts (Table K11)
Including verbal contracts
812.3 Synallagmatic and unilateral contracts (Table K11)
Including imperfect synallagmatic contracts
813 Standardized terms of contracts (Table K11)
For a particular type of standardized contract, see the type, e.g., KL-KWX6 868 Bills of lading
813.3 Contracts imposed by the law (Table K11)
813.4 Individual contracts and collective agreements (Table K11)
814 Commutative and aleatory contracts (Table K11)
814.3 Nominate and innominate contracts (Table K11)
815 Contracts of unspecified duration (Table K11)
Formation of contracts
817 General (Table K11)
Precontractual obligations

Contracts
Formation of contracts
Precontractual obligations -- Continued
818 General (Table K11)
Promise of contract
Including preliminary contract
818.3 General (Table K11)
818.4 Option (Table K11)
Offer and acceptance. Consent
819 General (Table K11)
819.5 Invitation to offers (Table K11)
Including contract to keep the offer open
819.7 Contracts by mail (Table K11)
Including contracts by telegram, teletype, telephone, etc.
Faults of consent see KL-KWX6 833+
820 Contracts by adhesion (Table K11)
821 Earnest (Table K11)
822 Form of contract. Formalities (Table K11)
Including written contracts, contracts under seal, etc.
823.A-Z Collateral provisions. Clauses, A-Z
823.A72 Arbitration clause (Table K12)
823.C65 Contractual penalty (Table K12)
Hold harmless agreements see KL-KWX6 823.I53
823.I53 Indemnity against liability. Hold harmless agreements (Table K12)
Monetary terms see KL-KWX6 839+
Time and place of performance see KL-KWX6 839.3
Parties to contract
825 General (Table K11)
Agency see KL-KWX6 951+
826 Contract with oneself (Table K11)
827 Assignment of contracts (Table K11)
Third party beneficiary see KL-KWX6 844
Void and voidable contracts
Including pertinent actions
830 General (Table K11)
832.A-Z Immoral and unlawful contracts, A-Z
Subarrange each by Table K12
Lack of genuine consent
833 General (Table K11)
834 Mistake (Table K11)
834.3 Duress. Undue influence (Table K11)
834.4 Misrepresentation. Fraud (Table K11)
834.5 Simulation (Table K11)
Discharge of contract
835 General (Table K11)

Contracts
Discharge of contract -- Continued
837 Accord and satisfaction (Table K11)
Performance
838 General (Table K11)
Payment. Tender
839 General (Table K11)
839.3 Time and place of performance (Table K11)
Including days of grace, moratorium, etc.
839.4 Gold clause. Valuta clause (Table K11)
840 Escalator clause (Table K11)
842 Payment in goods other than money (Table K11)
843 Subrogation. Substituted performance (Table K11)
Including contractual and statutory subrogation
844 Third parties (Table K11)
Including third-party beneficiary and promise of a third party's performance
845 Enforced performance (Table K11)
846 Impossibility of performance (Table K11)
Breach of contract. Remedies
848 General (Table K11)
849 Damages (Table K11)
849.5 Rescission and restitution (Table K11)
Contractual penalty see KL-KWX6 823.C65
Public contracts. Government contracts. Procurement
850 General (Table K11)
851 Municipal contracts (Table K11)
852 Defense contracts. Military procurement (Table K11)
853 Research and development contracts (Table K11)
855 Building and construction contracts. Public works contracts (Table K11)
Individual contracts and transactions. Commercial transactions
Including commercial law in general
856 General (Table K11)
Contract of service. Master and servant
857 General (Table K11)
Civil service see KL-KWX6 2400+
Contract for work and labor. Independent contractors
858 General (Table K11)
860 Mechanics' liens. Workers' liens. Contractors' liens (Table K11)
861.A-Z Particular types of contracts, A-Z
861.B84 Building and construction. Engineering (Table K12)
861.C65 Computer contracts (Table K12)
Engineering see KL-KWX6 861.B84

Contracts
Individual contracts and transactions. Commercial transactions -- Continued
Sale of goods
863 General (Table K11)
Transfer of property and title
865 General (Table K11)
865.5 Auction sales (Table K11)
Conditional sale see KL-KWX6 905
Documents of title
867 General (Table K11)
868 Bills of lading (Table K11)
Ocean bills of lading see KL-KWX6 923.3
869 Warehouse receipts (Table K11)
Performance
Including conditions, clauses, and warranties
870 General (Table K11)
872 Overseas sales. C.I.F. clause. F.O.B. clause (Table K11)
Right of unpaid seller
873 General (Table K11)
Liens see KL-KWX6 906+
874.A-Z Particular goods and chattels, A-Z
Contracts involving bailments
876 General (Table K11)
877 Deposit of goods. Warehouses (Table K11)
For warehouse receipts see KL-KWX6 869
878 Bailment of securities (Table K11)
879 Bill of sale (Table K11)
879.5 Innkeeper and guest (Table K11)
For hotel and restaurant trade see KL-KWX6 1030.3.H66
Negotiable instruments
880 General (Table K11)
Bills of exchange
881 General (Table K11)
881.5.A-Z Special topics, A-Z
881.5.L55 Limitation of actions (Table K12)
881.5.P75 Protest (Table K12)
882 Checks (Table K11)
Securities see KL-KWX6 956.5
883 Promissory note (Table K11)
Warehouse receipts see KL-KWX6 869
Banking
885 General (Table K11)
885.5 State control (Table K11)

Contracts
Individual contracts and transactions. Commercial transactions
Banking -- Continued
886 National banks. Central banks. Banks of issue (Table K11)
Cf. KL-KWX6 2766 Bank notes
Monetary policy see KL-KWX6 2760+
887 Foreign banks (Table K11)
887.3 Mortgage banks (Table K11)
889 Savings banks (Table K11)
889.3 Investment banks (Table K11)
891 Cooperative societies. Credit unions (Table K11)
892 Building and loan associations (Table K11)
Trust companies see KL-KWX6 960.3
Agricultural banks see KL-KWX6 997.5
Mining banks see KL-KWX6 1009.5
893 Deposit banking and accounts (Table K11)
Investments
894 General (Table K11)
Stock exchange transactions
894.3 General (Table K11)
894.4.A-Z Particular transactions, A-Z
894.4.I57 Insider trading in corporate securities (Table K12)
894.5.A-Z Particular exchanges. By place, A-Z
Subarrange each by Table K12
896 Collecting of accounts. Collection laws (Table K11)
897 Discount. Discount rate. Rediscount (Table K11)
898 Escrow business (Table K11)
Bank credit. Bank loan
900 General (Table K11)
900.5 Discount. Discount rate. Rediscount (Table K11)
902 Documentary credit. Letters of credit. Advances on commercial documents (Table K11)
Foreign exchange regulations see KL-KWX6 2772+
902.5.A-Z Other, A-Z
Bank secrets see KL-KWX6 902.5.R43
902.5.E4 Electronic funds transfer (Table K12)
Money laundering see KL-KWX6 902.5.R43
902.5.R43 Record keeping (Table K12)
Including bank secrets, money laundering
Loan of money. Debtor and creditor
903 General (Table K11)
903.5 Interest. Usury (Table K11)
903.6.A-Z Other, A-Z
903.6.C65 Consumer credit (Table K12)

Contracts
Individual contracts and transactions. Commercial transactions -- Continued
903.8 Suretyship. Guaranty (Table K11)
Secured transactions
904 General (Table K11)
Chattel mortgages
904.5 General (Table K11)
904.7.A-Z Particular kinds of personal property, A-Z
Subarrange each by Table K12
905 Conditional sale. Installment sale. Lease purchase (Table K11)
Liens
906 General (Table K11)
906.5.A-Z Particular kinds, A-Z
Maritime liens see KL-KWX6 924.5.L5
Mechanics' liens see KL-KWX6 860
906.5.P68 Possessory liens (Table K12)
907 Pledge (Table K11)
For pawnbrokers see KL-KWX6 1029.3.P37
Suretyship and guaranty see KL-KWX6 903.8
907.5 Trust receipts (Table K11)
908.A-Z Other, A-Z
Subarrange each by Table K12
Marketing of securities. Investments. Stock exchange transactions
909 General (Table K11)
910 Stockbrokers (Table K11)
910.5 Investment advisers (Table K11)
911.A-Z Particular transactions, A-Z
Subarrange each by Table K12
911.2.A-Z Particular stock exchanges, A-Z
Subarrange each by Table K12
911.3 Over-the-counter markets (Table K11)
Investment trusts. Investment companies. Mutual funds
912 General (Table K11)
913 Real estate investment companies (Table K11)
913.5 Small business investment companies (Table K11)
Particular securities
914 General (Table K11)
914.3 Legal investments. Trust investments (Table K11)
Stocks see KL-KWX6 957+
Mortgages see KL-KWX6 717+
914.5.A-Z Special topics, A-Z
Subarrange each by Table K12
Commodity exchanges. Produce exchanges

Contracts
Individual contracts and transactions. Commercial transactions
Commodity exchanges. Produce exchanges -- Continued
915 General (Table K11)
915.3.A-Z Particular commodities, A-Z
Subarrange each by Table K12
915.5.A-Z Particular commodity exchanges, A-Z
Subarrange each by Table K12
Carriage of goods and passengers. Carriers
Cf. KL-KWX6 1039+ Transportation
916 General (Table K11)
Carriage by land
916.5 General (Table K11)
Motor carriers see KL-KWX6 1042+
Railroads see KL-KWX6 1044+
917 Carriage by air (Table K11)
Cf. KL-KWX6 1050+ Commercial aviation
Combined transportation see KL-KWX6 1061.7
Carriage by sea. Maritime commercial law. Admiralty
919 General (Table K11)
919.3 Shipowners and their agents (Table K11)
Including officers and mariners, rights and responsibilities
920 Maritime torts. Collision at sea (Table K11)
921 Liability of operators of nuclear-powered ships (Table K11)
921.3 Average (Table K11)
Admiralty courts and proceedings
922 General (Table K11)
Prize law
see KZ6590+
Carriage of goods. Affreightment
923 General (Table K11)
923.3 Ocean bills of lading (Table K11)
923.5 Charter parties (Table K11)
923.7 Demurrage. Lay days (Table K11)
924 Carriage of passengers (Table K11)
Including passengers' luggage
924.5.A-Z Special topics, A-Z
924.5.A88 Assistance and salvage at sea (Table K12)
Including assistance and salvage of or by aircraft at sea
924.5.B68 Bottomry and respondentia (Table K12)
924.5.I55 Immunity of state-owned ships (Table K12)
924.5.L5 Liens, Maritime (Table K12)
Salvage at sea see KL-KWX6 924.5.A88
924.5.S86 Stowage (Table K12)

Contracts
Individual contracts and transactions. Commercial transactions
Carriage of goods and passengers. Carriers
Carriage by sea. Maritime commercial law. Admiralty -- Continued
Maritime social legislation
925 General (Table K11)
Maritime labor law. Merchant mariners
925.3 General (Table K11)
925.5 Qualification and certification (Table K11)
925.7 Maritime unions. Collective labor agreements (Table K11)
926 Labor disputes and arbitration (Table K11)
Labor standards
926.3 General (Table K11)
926.5.A-Z Special topics, A-Z
Subarrange each by Table K12
927 Protection of labor. Labor hygiene and safety (Table K11)
Social insurance
928 General (Table K11)
928.3 Health insurance (Table K11)
928.4 Workers' compensation (Table K11)
928.5 Unemployment compensation (Table K11)
928.7.A-Z Other, A-Z
Subarrange each by Table K12
Coastwise and inland navigation see KL-KWX6 1057.5+
Inland water transportation see KL-KWX6 1061
Fisheries see KL-KWX6 1004+
Marine insurance
929 General (Table K11)
930.A-Z Particular risks, A-Z
930.W37 War risks (Table K12)
Insurance
Including regulation of insurance carriers, etc.
For social insurance see KL-KWX6 1410+
931 General (Table K11)
931.3 Insurance carriers. State supervision (Table K11)
931.5 Mutual insurance. Cooperative insurance (Table K11)
Including fraternal insurance and friendly societies
931.7 Insurance business. Brokers. Agents (Table K11)
Particular lines of insurance
932 Life (Table K11)
933 Health (Table K11)
934 Accident (Table K11)

Contracts
Individual contracts and transactions. Commercial transactions
Insurance
Particular lines of insurance -- Continued
935 Property (Table K11)
935.3 Multiple line insurance (Table K11)
935.4.A-Z Particular hazards, A-Z
Burglary see KL-KWX6 935.4.T43
935.4.F57 Fire (Table K12)
Robbery see KL-KWX6 935.4.T43
935.4.T43 Theft. Burglary. Robbery (Table K12)
935.4.W38 Water damage (Table K12)
935.5.A-Z Types of property and business, A-Z
Subarrange each by Table K12
936 Suretyship insurance. Guaranty. Title insurance (Table K11)
936.3 Litigation insurance (Table K11)
Liability insurance
937 General (Table K11)
937.4.A-Z Particular risks, A-Z
937.4.A87 Automobiles (Table K12)
937.4.A88 Automotive transportation (General) (Table K12)
Including trucking, bus lines, etc.
937.4.A94 Aviation (Table K12)
937.4.P76 Products liability (Table K12)
937.6 Reinsurance (Table K11)
Aleatory contracts. Wagering contracts
938 General (Table K11)
938.3 Betting and gambling (Table K11)
Quasi-contracts. Restitution
939 General (Table K11)
939.3 Unjust enrichment. Recovery of undue payment (Table K11)
939.5 Negotiorum gestio (Table K11)
939.7 Remedies. Constructive trust (Table K11)
Torts. Extracontractual liability (Delicts and quasi-delicts)
940 General (Table K11)
941 Damages (Table K11)
Respondeat superior doctrine see KL-KWX6 949.3
Torts in respect to persons
942 General (Table K11)
942.5 Personal injuries. Death by wrongful act (Table K11)
942.55 Wrongful life (Table K11)
Violation of privacy
942.6 General (Table K11)

Torts. Extracontractual liability (Delicts and quasi-delicts)
Torts in respect to persons
Violation of privacy -- Continued
942.7.A-Z Special aspects, A-Z
942.7.C65 Computers and privacy. Data protection (Table K12)
Privacy and computers see KL-KWX6 942.7.C65
943 Torts in respect to reputation. Libel and slander (Table K11)
For disparagement (Unfair competition) see KL-KWX6 1178
943.3 Abuse of legal process (Table K11)
943.4 Malicious prosecution (Table K11)
943.5 Deceit. Fraud (Table K11)
Unfair competition see KL-KWX6 1174+
943.6 Trespass to land. Squatting (Table K11)
For ejectment see KL-KWX6 701
944 Nuisance (Table K11)
Particular torts
945 Torts affecting chattels. Trespass to goods. Conversion. Trover (Table K11)
Negligence
945.3 General (Table K11)
945.4 Contributory negligence (Table K11)
945.5 Liability for condition and use of land. Premises liability (Table K11)
946 Malpractice (Table K11)
For malpractice and tort liability of particular professions, see the profession
946.3.A-Z Particular types of accidents, A-Z
946.3.A85 Automobile accidents (Table K12)
946.3.A88 Aviation accidents (Table K12)
946.3.B84 Building accidents (Table K12)
Liability of common air carriers see KL-KWX6 1053.4
Marine accidents see KL-KWX6 920
Railroad accidents see KL-KWX6 1047.2
Strict liability. Liability without fault
947 General (Table K11)
947.2.A-Z Ultrahazardous activities and occupations, A-Z
Subarrange each by Table K12
947.3 Damage caused by animals (Table K11)
Products liability
For products liability insurance see KL-KWX6 937.4.P76
947.5 General (Table K11)
947.7.A-Z By product, A-Z
947.7.D78 Drugs (Table K12)
947.7.M42 Medical instruments and apparatus (Table K12)

Torts. Extracontractual liability (Delicts and quasi-delicts) -- Continued

948 Environmental damages (Table K11)

For environmental crimes see KL-KWX6 4352+

Parties to actions in torts

948.2 General (Table K11)

948.3 Corporations (Table K11)

Minors. Infants see KL-KWX6 517

948.5 Municipal corporations (Table K11)

948.6 Public officers and government employees (Table K11)

948.7 Labor unions (Table K11)

948.8 Joint tortfeasors (Table K11)

Liability for torts of others. Vicarious liability

949 General (Table K11)

949.3 Master and servant (Table K11)

Including respondeat superior doctrine

949.4 Employers' liability. Fellow servant rule (Table K11)

Government torts

949.5 General (Table K11)

949.6.A-Z Particular, A-Z

Subarrange each by Table K12

950 Compensation to victims of crimes. Reparation (Table K11)

Including injuries to both person and property and compensation by government

Agency

951 General (Table K11)

951.3 Power of attorney (Table K11)

951.5.A-Z Particular types of agency, A-Z

951.5.B75 Brokers. Commission merchants. Factors (Table K12)

Commission merchants see KL-KWX6 951.5.B75

Factors see KL-KWX6 951.5.B75

951.5.S45 Ship brokers (Table K12)

Associations

Including business enterprises in general, regardless of form of organization

952 General (Table K11)

952.3 Accounting law. Auditing. Financial statements (Table K11)

For corporation accounting see KL-KWX6 956.5

952.4 Business records. Record keeping and retention (Table K11)

Unincorporated associations

953 General (Table K11)

953.3.A-Z Particular types of associations, A-Z

953.3.C58 Clubs (Table K12)

Labor unions see KL-KWX6 1362+

Business associations. Partnerships

953.5 General (Table K11)

Associations
Unincorporated associations
Business associations. Partnerships -- Continued
953.6 Limited partnerships (Table K11)
953.7 Joint ventures (Table K11)
Incorporated associations. Corporations. Juristic persons
954 General (Table K11)
954.3 Registration (Table K11)
954.5 Ultra vires doctrine (Table K11)
Nonprofit corporations
954.7 General (Table K11)
955.A-Z Particular types, A-Z
955.F68 Foundations. Endowments (Table K12)
Waqf see KL-KWX6 2168.5
Business corporations. Companies
956 General (Table K11)
956.2 Government regulation and control (Table K11)
956.22 Incorporation. Corporate charters and bylaws (Table K11)
Including promoters and prospectus
956.3 Management (Table K11)
Including boards of directors and officers
956.35 Corporate legal departments (Table K11)
Corporate finance. Capital. Dividends
956.4 General (Table K11)
956.5 Securities. Issuance of securities (Table K11)
For security exchanges see KL-KWX6 894.3+
956.6 Accounting. Auditing. Financial statements (Table K11)
Stock and stockholders' rights. Stock transfers
957 General (Table K11)
957.3 Stockholders' meetings (Table K11)
Including voting, proxy rules, etc.
958 Debentures. Bonds. Preferred stocks (Table K11)
Including receivers for debenture holders
Particular types of corporations or companies
959 General (Table K11)
960 Subsidiary and parent companies. Holding companies (Table K11)
960.3 Combines. Industrial trusts. Business concerns (Table K11)
960.5 Private companies. Family companies. Close companies (Table K11)

960.6 Publicly chartered corporations. Chartered companies (Table K11)
Government companies see KL-KWX6 975.3+
Cooperative societies
961 General (Table K11)

Associations
Incorporated associations. Corporations. Juristic persons
Business corporations. Companies
Particular types of corporations or companies
Cooperative societies -- Continued
961.3.A-Z Particular, A-Z
Subarrange each by Table K12
962 Dissolution. Liquidation (Table K11)
962.3 Consolidation and merger (Table K11)
Insolvency and bankruptcy. Creditor's rights
963 General (Table K11)
Bankruptcy
964 General (Table K11)
Bankruptcy court and procedure
965 General (Table K11)
965.3.A-Z Special topics, A-Z
965.3.C68 Costs (Table K12)
Liquidators see KL-KWX6 965.3.C68
965.3.R42 Receivers in bankruptcy. Trustees. Liquidators (Table K12)
Trustees see KL-KWX6 965.3.R42
965.5 Priority of claims (Table K11)
965.6 Fraudulent conveyances (Table K11)
965.7.A-Z Other topics, A-Z
Subarrange each by Table K12
Debtors' relief
966 General (Table K11)
967 Wartime relief (Table K11)
For general moratorium see KL-KWX6 2666
968 Composition. Receivership to avoid bankruptcy. Deeds of arrangement (Table K11)
969.A-Z Other forms of debtors' relief, A-Z
969.A77 Assignment for the benefit of creditors (Table K12)
969.C67 Corporate reorganization (Table K12)
Economic constitution. Economic legislation
970 General (Table K11)
970.2 Economic policy (Table K11)
Organization and administration
Including public, semi-private, and private organs of economic intervention and councils
970.5 General (Table K11)
970.7.A-Z Particular, A-Z
Subarrange each by Table K12
971 National planning (Table K11)
971.3 Distribution (Table K11)

Economic constitution. Economic legislation -- Continued

971.5 Investments (Table K11)

Including foreign investments

Foreign exchange control see KL-KWX6 2772+

State control of banks and coordination of credits see KL-KWX6 885.5

Economic assistance

Including industrial promotion

972 General (Table K11)

972.3 Finance. Subsidies (Table K11)

Including national (federal) subsidies to states, local government, and private enterprise

For economic assistance to a particular industry, trade, etc., see the subject, e.g., KL-KWX6 996.3+

972.5.A-Z Economic assistance to particular regions. By region, A-Z

Subarrange each by Table K12

Economic assistance to a particular state

see the state or municipality

Prices and price control

973 General (Table K11)

973.3 Price fixing (Table K11)

974 Forced price boost (Table K11)

974.3 Price delicts and sanctions (Table K11)

Government-owned industry. Government business enterprises

Including semi-public enterprises

For a particular type of industry or business, see the business or industry

975 General (Table K11)

Government companies. Companies partly owned by government

975.3 General (Table K11)

976 Nationalized enterprises (Table K11)

Cf. KL-KWX6 2544+ Public property

Public utilities see KL-KWX6 1032+

Competition rules. Restraint of trade control

977 General (Table K11)

Horizontal and vertical combinations

977.3 General (Table K11)

978 Corporate consolidation, merger, etc. (Table K11)

Cartels

978.3 General (Table K11)

978.4.A-Z Types of cartels, A-Z

Subarrange each by Table K12

978.5.A-Z By industry, occupation, etc., A-Z

Subarrange each by Table K12

Economic constitution. Economic legislation
Competition rules. Restraint of trade control -- Continued
979 Monopolies. Oligopolies. Antitrust law (Table K11)
979.5 Small business (Table K11)
980 Corporate representation. Trade associations (Table K11)
Money, currency, and foreign exchange control see KL-KWX6 2760+
Standards. Norms. Quality control
For standards, grading, and quality control of agricultural products or consumer products, see the product
981 General (Table K11)
981.3 Weights and measures. Containers (Table K11)
Standardization
981.4 General (Table K11)
981.5 Engineering standards (Table K11)
981.6 Standard time (Table K11)
Including regulation of calendar
981.7 Labeling (Table K11)
For labeling of a particular product, see the product
Regulation of industry, trade, and commerce
982 General (Table K11)
Boards of trade see KL-KWX6 980
982.3 Consumer protection (Table K11)
Advertising
For works limited to a particular industrial or trade line, see the industrial or trade line
982.4 General (Table K11)
983 Bill posting (Table K11)
983.2.A-Z By industry or product, A-Z
Subarrange each by Table K12
983.3.A-Z By medium, A-Z
Subarrange each by Table K12
State control of banks and coordination of credits see KL-KWX6 885.5
Primary production. Extractive industries
Agriculture. Forestry. Rural law
Organization and administration
985 General (Table K11)
985.3 Department of Agriculture
985.5 Other organs
Including councils, boards, societies, etc.
985.7 Agricultural courts and procedure (Table K11)
Large estates. Feudal land grants see KL-KWX6 660+
Common lands. Stool land (chiefdom land) see KL-KWX6 2563+
Family (ancestral) land see KL-KWX6 703

Regulation of industry, trade, and commerce
Primary production. Extractive industries
Agriculture. Forestry. Rural law -- Continued
Government constituted homesteads see KL-KWX6 2553
Land use. Agrarian land policy legislation
For public land law and policy see KL-KWX6 2550+
986 General (Table K11)
986.3 Colonization. Agrarian colonies (Table K11)
Transformation of the agricultural structure
Including nationalization or purchase of agricultural land holdings and their redistribution by the state
For land grants, government constituted homesteads, etc., see KL-KWX6 2553+
988 General (Table K11)
988.6 Protection of tenants. Elimination of precarious tenancies (Table K11)
988.7.A-Z Special topics, A-Z
Subarrange each by Table K12
Agricultural contracts
989 General (Table K11)
Farm tenancy. Rural partnerships
Class here works on provision of both civil law and other legislation ensuring stability for tenants and the land they cultivate
Cf. KL-KWX6 988+ Agrarian land policy
989.3 General (Table K11)
989.5 Lease of pastures (Table K11)
990 Sharecropping contracts. Tenancies for consideration (Table K11)
991 Livestock share-partnership contracts (Table K11)
992.A-Z Special topics, A-Z
992.R87 Rural housing (Table K12)
Agricultural pledges and liens see KL-KWX6 998
Agricultural labor in general see KL-KWX6 1395.A34
Rural housing see KL-KWX6 992.R87
Rural schools see KL-KWX6 1631.3
994 Conservation of agricultural and forestry lands (Table K11)
Including soil conservation, field irrigation, erosion control
Cf. KL-KWX6 2554 Land reclamation
Control of agricultural pests, plant diseases, predatory animals
Including weed control, plant import, and quarantine
994.3 General (Table K11)
994.5.A-Z Particular diseases, pests, etc., A-Z
Subarrange each by Table K12
995 Farm corporations (Table K11)

Regulation of industry, trade, and commerce
Primary production. Extractive industries
Agriculture. Forestry. Rural law -- Continued
995.2 Collective farming (Table K11)
995.3 Farm producers' and marketing cooperatives (Table K11)
996 Farmers' associations (Table K11)
Economic assistance
996.3 General (Table K11)
996.5 Distribution of seed grain, fertilizer, pesticides, etc. (Table K11)
Price supports
997 General (Table K11)
997.3.A-Z By field crops or commodity, A-Z
Subarrange each by Table K12
997.5 Agricultural credit. Farm loans (Table K11)
Including agricultural banks and agricultural cooperative credit associations
998 Agricultural pledges and liens (Table K11)
Agricultural production
Including marketing, standards, and grading
998.3 General (Table K11)
998.5 Seeds (Table K11)
Cf. KL-KWX6 996.5 Distribution of seed grain
999.A-Z Field crops, A-Z
999.C6 Coconut (Table K12)
999.C63 Coffee (Table K12)
Cf. KL-KWX6 1025.7.C63 Export trade
999.C65 Corn (Table K12)
999.C66 Cotton (Table K12)
Seeds see KL-KWX6 998.5
999.S93 Sugar (Table K12)
999.T43 Tea (Table K12)
Livestock industry and trade
1000 General (Table K11)
Meat industry see KL-KWX6 1023
1001.A-Z Particular kinds of livestock, A-Z
Subarrange each by Table K12
Dairy industry see KL-KWX6 1023.3
1002 Forestry. Timber laws. Game laws (Table K11)
1003 Viticulture (Table K11)
For wine and wine making see KL-KWX6 1544.W54
Game laws see KL-KWX6 1002
Fishing industry
Including regulation of ownership, native fishing rights, exploration, and exploitation
1004 General (Table K11)

Regulation of industry, trade, and commerce
Primary production. Extractive industries
Fishing industry -- Continued
1004.3 Conservation and management. Administration. Maritime authorities (Table K11)
1004.5.A-Z Coastal and inland fisheries. By area, A-Z
Subarrange each by Table K12
Including fishing in the marine space beyond twelve miles from the island baselines (e.g. Pacific island jurisdictions)
For high seas fisheries, see K3898
For particular species see KL-KWX6 1005.A+
1005.A-Z Particular fish and marine fauna, A-Z
1005.T84 Tuna (Table K12)
Mining. Quarrying
1006 General (Table K11)
1006.3 Conservation of mineral resources (Table K11)
1006.5 Mining rights (Table K11)
Including rights vested in state or crown, and including prospecting and exploration permits; concessions for exploration, and royalties to landowners
1006.8 Continental shelf (Table K11)
1007 Strip mining. Land reclamation (Table K11)
Ownership of mines and mineral resources
1007.2 General (Table K11)
Cf. KL-KWX6 675 Extent of land ownership above and below surface
1007.3 Expropriation. Nationalization. State ownership (Table K11)
Cf. KL-KWX6 2544+ Eminent domain
1007.4 Mine servitudes (Table K11)
Mining corporations and partnerships
1008 General (Table K11)
1008.3.A-Z Particular corporations, A-Z
Subarrange each by Table K12
1008.4 Mining contracts. Mining leases (Table K11)
1009 Mining social legislation (Table K11)
For mine safety regulations see KL-KWX6 1393.M56
1009.5 Mining banks (Table K11)
Resources
1010 General (Table K11)
Petroleum. Oil and gas
1010.5 General (Table K11)
1011 Conservation (Table K11)
1012 Regulation of industry (Table K11)
Including concessions, trade practices, etc.
1012.2 Oil and gas leases (Table K11)

Regulation of industry, trade, and commerce
Primary production. Extractive industries
Mining. Quarrying
Resources
Petroleum. Oil and gas -- Continued
1012.3.A-Z Particular oil fields, reserves, etc., A-Z
Subarrange each by Table K12
1013 Natural gas (Table K11)
1014.A-Z Other resources
1014.C63 Coal (Table K12)
1014.C66 Copper (Table K12)
1014.D53 Diamonds. Gems (Table K12)
Gems see KL-KWX6 1014.D53
1014.G64 Gold (Table K12)
1014.P56 Phosphate (Table K12)
1014.T56 Tin (Table K12)
1014.U73 Uranium (Table K12)
Manufacturing industries
1016 General (Table K11)
Chemical industries
1016.3 General (Table K11)
1016.4.A-Z Particular products, A-Z
1016.4.F45 Fertilizers (Table K12)
1016.5 Drug and pharmaceutical industries (Table K11)
Cf. KL-KWX6 1536+ Drug laws
Cf. KL-KWX6 1537 Retail trade
Textile industries
1016.6 General (Table K11)
1017.A-Z Particular products, A-Z
1017.S56 Silks (Table K12)
1018.A-Z Major and heavy industries, A-Z
1018.A95 Automobile industry (Table K12)
1018.B56 Biotechnology industries (Table K12)
1018.E43 Electric industries (Table K12)
1018.H54 High technology industries (Table K12)
1018.I76 Iron and steel industries (Table K12)
1018.P34 Paper industry (Table K12)
1018.R83 Rubber industry (Table K12)
Steel industry see KL-KWX6 1018.I76
1019.A-Z Consumer products. Light industries, A-Z
1019.B66 Book industries and trade (Table K12)
1019.L4 Leather industry (Table K12)
1019.T62 Tobacco products (Table K12)

Regulation of industry, trade, and commerce -- Continued
Food processing industries
Class here works on trade practices and antitrust measures, economic assistance, sanitation, standards (grading) and quality inspection
Including regulation of adulteration and additives
1020 General (Table K11)
1021 Sugar refining (Table K11)
Fruit and vegetables
1022 General (Table K11)
1022.5.A-Z Particular products, A-Z
1022.5.B34 Banana (Table K12)
1022.5.C57 Citrus fruit (Table K12)
1022.5.O55 Olives (Table K12)
Wine and wine making see KL-KWX6 1544.W54
1023 Meat industry (Table K11)
Including slaughtering and slaughterhouses
1023.3 Dairy industry (Table K11)
Including distribution
1023.35 Spices. Herbs (Table K11)
1023.4 Beverages (Table K11)
Cf. KL-KWX6 1543+ Alcoholic beverages
1023.5 Construction and building industry. Contractors (Table K11)
Cf. KL-KWX6 2590+ Building laws
Trade
1024 General (Table K11)
1024.3.A-Z Particular commodities, A-Z
1024.3.C66 Cotton (Table K12)
1024.3.G73 Grain (Table K12)
1024.3.T62 Tobacco (Table K12)
International trade. Foreign trade
1025 General (Table K11)
1025.3.A-Z Particular commodities, A-Z
Subarrange each by Table K12
Export trade
Including export controls, regulations, and promotion
1025.5 General (Table K11)
1025.7.A-1025.Z Particular commodities, A-Z
1025.7.B64 Books (Table K12)
1025.7.C63 Coffee (Table K12)
1025.7.C66 Cotton (Table K12)
1025.7.S93 Sugar (Table K12)
Import trade
Including import controls and regulations
For tariff see KL-KWX6 3190+
1026 General (Table K11)

Regulation of industry, trade, and commerce
Trade
International trade. Foreign trade
Import trade -- Continued
1026.3.A-Z Particular commodities, A-Z
Subarrange each by Table K12
1026.5 Wholesale trade (Table K11)
Retail trade
1026.7 General (Table K11)
Conditions of trading
1027 General (Table K11)
1027.3 Sunday legislation (Table K11)
Special modes of trading
1027.5 General (Table K11)
1027.7 Markets. Fairs (Table K11)
1027.8 Peddling. Canvassing (Table K11)
1028.A-Z Particular products, A-Z
1028.A88 Automobiles. Motor vehicles (Table K12)
Motor vehicles see KL-KWX6 1028.A88
Secondhand trade
1029 General (Table K11)
1029.3.A-Z Particular types, A-Z
1029.3.A92 Auction houses. Auctioneers (Table K12)
Cf. KL-KWX6 865.5 Auction sales
1029.3.P37 Pawnbrokers (Table K12)
Including charitable pawnshops
Service trades
Including licensing
1030 General (Table K11)
1030.3.A-Z Particular service trades, A-Z
Auctioneers see KL-KWX6 1029.3.A92
Caravan parks see KL-KWX6 1030.3.T7
1030.3.E46 Employment agencies (Table K12)
1030.3.H66 Hotels. Restaurants (Table K12)
Cf. KL-KWX6 879.5 Innkeeper and guest
Insurance agents and brokers see KL-KWX6 931.7
1030.3.P74 Private investigators (Table K12)
Restaurants see KL-KWX6 1030.3.H66
1030.3.R47 Retirement communities (Table K12)
1030.3.T67 Tourist trade (Table K12)
1030.3.T7 Trailer camps. Caravan parks (Table K12)
1031 Warehouses. Storage (Table K11)
For warehouse contracts see KL-KWX6 876+
Public utilities
Including private, publicly owned, and public-private (mixed) utility companies

Regulation of industry, trade, and commerce
Public utilities -- Continued
1032 General (Table K11)
1033 Public service commissions (Table K11)
1033.3 National (Federal), state, and local jurisdiction (Table K11)
1033.4 Concessions (Table K11)
1033.5 Valuation (Table K11)
1033.6 Finance (Table K11)
1033.7 Ratemaking (Table K11)
1033.8 Expropriation or nationalization of public utilities (General) (Table K11)
For expropriation or nationalization of a particular type of utility, see the utility
Energy policy. Power supply
Including energy resources and development in general
1034 General (Table K11)
Electricity
1035 General (Table K11)
1035.3 Concessions (Table K11)
For particular concessions see KL-KWX6 1035.6.A+
1035.4 Rural electrification (Table K11)
1035.5 Expropriation. Nationalization. Purchase by the public (Table K11)
Including national, state, and municipal utilities
1035.6.A-Z Particular companies, A-Z
Subarrange each by Table K12
Including concessions, litigation, decisions, awards, rulings, etc.
1036 Gas (Table K11)
1037 Water (Table K11)
Including water supply
For water power development see KL-KWX6 2532+
Atomic power
1038 General (Table K11)
1038.3 Atomic energy commissions (Table K11)
1038.4 Liability (Table K11)
1038.5.A-Z Other sources of power, A-Z
1038.5.G45 Geothermal power (Table K12)
1038.5.S65 Solar energy (Table K12)
1038.5.W56 Wind power (Table K12)
Transportation and communication
1039 General (Table K11)
1039.3 Transportation commissions, directorates, etc. (Table K11)
Offenses against means of tranportation and communication see KL-KWX6 4380+
Road traffic. Automotive transportation

Regulation of industry, trade, and commerce
Transportation and communication
Road traffic. Automotive transportation -- Continued
1040 General (Table K11)
(1040.3) Safety responsibility laws. Financial responsibility laws. Compulsory insurance
see KL-KWX6 937.4.A87
1040.4.A-Z Particular vehicles, A-Z
Subarrange each by Table K12
Traffic regulation and enforcement
1040.5 General (Table K11)
Traffic violations
1041 General (Table K11)
Drunk driving see KL-KWX6 4386
Passenger carriers
1042 General (Table K11)
1042.3.A-Z Particular types of passenger carriers, A-Z
1042.3.B86 Bus lines (Table K12)
1042.3.T37 Taxicabs (Table K12)
1043 Carriers of goods. Truck lines (Table K11)
Railroads
Including corporate structure and regulation of industry
1044 General (Table K11)
1044.3 Railroad commissions and boards, etc. (Table K11)
Including practice and procedure
1044.4 National and state jurisdiction (Table K11)
1045 Concessions for railroad construction and operation (Table K11)
Including public works contracts for railroad construction
For particular concessions see KL-KWX6 1035.6.A+
1045.3 Consolidation and merger (Table K11)
1045.4 Government ownership (Table K11)
Operation of railroads. Finance. Rates
1045.5 General (Table K11)
Freight. Freight classification
1046 General (Table K11)
1046.3 Demurrage (Table K11)
1046.4.A-Z Particular commodities, A-Z
Subarrange each by Table K12
1047 Passenger fares (Table K11)
1047.2 Liability for personal injuries and damage to property (Table K11)
1048.A-Z Special railroads and railroad companies, A-Z
Subarrange each by Table K12
Including concessions, litigation, decisions, awards, rulings, etc.

Regulation of industry, trade, and commerce
Transportation and communication -- Continued
1048.3 Local transit (Table K11)
1049 Pipe lines (Table K11)
Aviation
1050 General (Table K11)
1050.3 Air safety (Table K11)
Including air traffic rules and airworthiness; aeronautical telecommunication and radio aids to air navigation
Aircraft
1050.4 General (Table K11)
1050.5 Nationality. Registration. Transfer (Table K11)
1050.6.A-Z Particular types of aircraft, A-Z
1050.6.H45 Helicopters (Table K12)
1051 Airports (Table K11)
1051.3 Pilots. Crews. Ground personnel (Table K11)
Commercial aviation. Airlines
1052 General (Table K11)
1052.3 Regulatory agencies (Table K11)
1052.4 Finance. Accounting. Auditing (Table K11)
1052.5 Rates (Table K11)
Including ratemaking, rate agreements, and passenger fares
1053 Air charters (Table K11)
1053.3 Cargo. Air freight (Table K11)
1053.4 Liability for personal injuries and property damage (Table K11)
For general tort liability for aviation see KL-KWX6 946.3.A88
1054.A-Z Particular airlines, A-Z
Subarrange each by Table K12
1055 Space law (Table K11)
Water transportation. Navigation and shipping
1056 General (Table K11)
Merchant mariners see KL-KWX6 925.3+
Ships
1056.3 General (Table K11)
1056.4 Registration (Table K11)
1056.5 Safety regulations (Table K11)
Including inspection and manning requirements
1057.A-Z Particular types of vessels, A-Z
Subarrange each by Table K12
1057.3.A-Z Particular types of cargo, A-Z
1057.3.D35 Dangerous articles and materials (Table K12)

Regulation of industry, trade, and commerce
Transportation and communication
Water transportation. Navigation and shipping
Ships -- Continued
Navigation and pilotage
Including coastwise navigation
Cf. K4184, International rules of the road at sea
1057.5 General (Table K11)
Particular waterways see KL-KWX6 2540.A+
Harbors and ports
Including port charges and tonnage fees
1058 General (Table K11)
1058.3.A-Z Particular ports, A-Z
Subarrange each by Table K12
1059 Lighthouses (Table K11)
1059.3 Regulation of the shipping industry (Table K11)
Merchant marine
1060 General (Table K11)
1060.3 Ratemaking and rate agreements (Table K11)
Merchant fleet
1060.5 General (Table K11)
1060.6 Finance. Shipping bounties and subsidies (Table K11)
Merchant mariners. Officers see KL-KWX6 919.3
1061 Domestic shipping. Coastwise shipping (Table K11)
Including inland water carriers
1061.5 Ocean freight forwarders (Table K11)
1061.7 Combined transportation (Table K11)
Postal service
Including works on all postal services, telegraph, and telephone combined
1062 General (Table K11)
1062.4 Organization and administration. Officers and personnel (Table K11)
Including salaries, wages, and pensions
1063 Classification of mails. Rates (Table K11)
1063.3 Postal money orders. Postal notes (Table K11)
Crimes committed through the mail see KL-KWX6 4548+
Violation of the privacy of letters see KL-KWX6 4166
1064 Forwarding agents. Freight forwarders (Table K11)
For ocean freight forwarders see KL-KWX6 1061.5
Communication. Mass media
1064.5 General (Table K11)
Press law
Including legal status of journalists
For works on the freedom of the press see KL-KWX6 2119

Regulation of industry, trade, and commerce
Transportation and communication
Communication. Mass media
Press law -- Continued
1065 General (Table K11)
Press censorship see KL-KWX6 2120
Criminal provisions
Including procedural aspects
1065.3 General (Table K11)
1065.5 Publication of official secrets by the press (Table K11)
1065.7.A-Z Other, A-Z
1065.7.C66 Contempt of court (Table K12)
Telecommunication
1066 General (Table K11)
1066.2 Artificial satellites in telecommunication (Table K11)
Telegraph. Teletype. Fax
Including telegraph and telephone combined
1066.3 General (Table K11)
1066.4 Ratemaking (Table K11)
Telephone
Including radio telephone
1066.5 General (Table K11)
Particular companies see KL-KWX6 1068.6.A+
Radio and television communication
1067 General (Table K11)
1067.3 Radio and television stations. Concessions. Licensing (Table K11)
Including frequency allocations
Radio broadcasting
1068 General (Table K11)
Radio aids to air navigation see KL-KWX6 1050.3
1068.5 Television broadcasting (Table K11)
1068.6.A-Z Particular companies, A-Z
Subarrange each by Table K12
1068.8 Electronic mail (Table K11)
Including spam
1069 Weather bureau. Metereological stations (Table K11)
Professions. Intelligentsia
1070 General (Table K11)
Violation of confidential communication see KL-KWX6 4164
1072 Professional associations (Table K11)
For particular professional associations, see the profession

Professions. Intelligentsia -- Continued
Individual professions
Class here works on education, licensing, professional representation, ethics, and liability
Including technical intelligentsia of government industrial enterprises
The health professions
General see KL-KWX6 1074+
Physicians
Including works on medical personnel in general
1074 General (Table K11)
1074.5 Malpractice (Table K11)
Cf. KL-KWX6 4100 Offenses against the person
1075 Dentists. Dental hygienists (Table K11)
1076.A-Z Other, A-Z
1076.G94 Gynecologists. Obstetricians (Table K12)
1076.H42 Healers (Table K12)
Including herbalists, homeopathic physicians, naturopaths, etc.
Obstetricians see KL-KWX6 1076.G94
1076.O65 Optometrists (Table K12)
1076.R33 Radiologists (Table K12)
Auxiliary medical professions. Paramedical professions
1078 General (Table K11)
1079 Nurses and nursing (Table K11)
1080 Midwives (Table K11)
1081 Physical therapists (Table K11)
Pharmacists see KL-KWX6 1540
Veterinarians see KL-KWX6 1532
Attorneys see KL-KWX6 53.5+
Economic and financial advisers
1082 General (Table K11)
1083 Accountants (Table K11)
1084 Auditors (Table K11)
Tax consultants see KL-KWX6 2818
Engineering and construction
1084.5 General (Table K11)
1085 Architects (Table K11)
1086 Engineers (Table K11)
Graphic artists see KL-KWX6 1090
Journalists see KL-KWX6 1065+
Librarians see KL-KWX6 1695.6
Performing artists see KL-KWX6 1680+
1090 Printers. Graphic artists (Table K11)
1092 Real estate agents (Table K11)
Social workers see KL-KWX6 1475+

Professions. Intelligentsia
Individual professions -- Continued
School functionaries see KL-KWX6 1624+
1092.5 Surveyors (Table K11)
Teachers see KL-KWX6 1624+
1094 Professional ethics. Courts of honor (Table K11)
For a particular court of honor, see the profession
Intellectual and industrial property
1100 General (Table K11)
Principles
1101 Intangible property (Table K11)
1102 Moral rights (Table K11)
1102.5 Traditional ecological knowledge (Table K11)
1103 Territoriality (Table K11)
Copyright
1104 General (Table K11)
International Union for the Protection of Literary and Artistic works (Bern Union)
see K1412+
Universal Copyright Convention
see K1414+
Authorship
Including multiple authorship and author cooperatives
1104.2 General (Table K11)
1104.22 Acronyms and synonyms (Table K11)
1104.23 Intangible property (Table K11)
1104.3 Plagiarism (Table K11)
1104.4 Procedures. Formalities (Table K11)
Including registration of claim, transfer, licenses, deposit, and notice
1104.5 Protected works (Table K11)
Including original works, subsequent rights, idea and title
Scope of protection
1104.6 General (Table K11)
1104.62 Personality rights (Table K11)
Mechanical reproduction
1104.63 General (Table K11)
1104.64 Documentation and dissemination (Table K11)
Including fair use
1104.65 Exhibition rights (Table K11)
Performing rights
Cf. KL-KWX6 1124 Quasi copyright
1104.7 General (Table K11)
1104.72 Societies and industrial trusts (Table K11)
1104.73 Broadcasting rights (Table K11)

Intellectual and industrial property
Copyright
Scope of protection -- Continued
1104.75 Recording rights (Table K11)
Including phonographs, magnetic recorders, and jukeboxes
1104.76 Filming and photographing (Table K11)
1104.78 Translation (Table K11)
1104.8 Employees' copyright (Table K11)
1104.82 Duration and renewal (Table K11)
1104.9 Delicts. Torts (Table K11)
1105-1124 Branches of copyright
1105 Literary copyright (Table K11)
1110 Musical copyright (Table K11)
Fine art and photography
1115 General (Table K11)
Violation of rights in one's own picture see KL-KWX6 942+
Motion pictures see KL-KWX6 1120+
1117 Designs and models (Table K11)
1119 Prints and labels (Table K11)
Including works of commercial art, catalogs, sample books, etc.
Motion pictures and television programs
1120 General (Table K11)
1122.A-Z Special topics, A-Z
Subarrange each by Table K12
1123 Computer programs. Computer software (Table K11)
1124 Quasi copyright and neighboring rights (Table K11)
Author and publisher
Including the publishing contract
1125 General (Table K11)
1126 Plays and stage productions (Table K11)
1127 Motion pictures (Table K11)
1128 Music (Table K11)
1129 Scientific literature (Table K11)
1130.A-Z Special topics, A-Z
Subarrange each by Table K12
1132 Litigation and execution (Table K11)
International copyright
see K1411+
Patent law and trademarks
1134 General (Table K11)
1135 Scope of protection (Table K11)
1137 Relation to antitrust laws (Table K11)
1140 Patent office (Table K11)
Patent practice and procedure

Intellectual and industrial property
Patent law and trademarks
Patent practice and procedure -- Continued
1142 General (Table K11)
Invention
Including priority and novelty
1143 General (Table K11)
1144 Legal status of inventors. Community of inventors (Table K11)
1145 Employees' invention and technological innovation (Table K11)
1146 Claim drafting (Table K11)
Including collision of patents
1147 Res judicata (Table K11)
1148 Duration and renewal (Table K11)
1149.A-Z Types of patents, A-Z
Subarrange each by Table K12
1150.A-Z Patented products, processes, and engineering methods, A-Z
Drugs see KL-KWX6 1150.M44
1150.M44 Medicines. Drugs (Table K12)
1150.P55 Plants (Table K12)
1152 Designs and utility models (Table K11)
Licenses
Including compulsory licenses and fees
1153 General (Table K11)
1154 Foreign licensing agreements (Table K11)
Including know-how
Patent litigation and infringements
1155 General (Table K11)
1156.A-Z Special topics, A-Z
Subarrange each by Table K12
1158 Patent attorneys (Table K11)
International uniform law on patents and trademarks see K1501+
Trademarks
1160 General (Table K11)
1160.5.A-Z Types of trademarks, A-Z
1160.5.A25 Accompanying marks (Table K12)
1160.5.B7 Brand names and numerals (Table K12)
1160.5.C67 Marks of corporations (Table K12)
1160.5.F35 Famous and notorious marks (Table K12)
Notorious marks see KL-KWX6 1160.5.F35
1160.5.O74 Marks of origin (certificates) (Table K12)
1160.5.Q34 Quality marks (Table K12)
1160.5.S47 Service marks (Table K12)

Intellectual and industrial property
Patent law and trademarks
Trademarks -- Continued
1162.A-Z Others, A-Z
Subarrange each by Table K12
1163 Scope of protection (Table K11)
1164 Relationship to antitrust law (Table K11)
Practice and procedure
1165 General (Table K11)
Claims drafting and registration
1166 General (Table K11)
1167 Collision of trademarks (Table K11)
1168 Use and compelled use of trademarks. Unused marks (Table K11)
1169 Transfer of trademarks (Table K11)
1170 Licenses. Foreign licensing agreements (Table K11)
1172 Litigation (Table K11)
Unfair competition
For restraint of trade see KL-KWX6 977+
1174 General (Table K11)
1175 Public policy (Table K11)
Advertising
1177 General (Table K11)
1178 Disparagement of goods (Table K11)
Including comparative advertising
1180 Misleading representation. False claims (Table K11)
Including superlative advertising
1182 Testing of commercial products (Table K11)
1185 Imitation (Table K11)
Cf. KL-KWX6 1104.3 Plagiarism
Pushing for sales
1186 General (Table K11)
1187 Unordered merchandise for mail (Table K11)
1188 Special sales (Table K11)
Rebates and premiums
1190 General
1191.A-Z Special topics, A-Z
Subarrange each by Table K12
1192 Price cutting (Table K11)
1193.A-Z By industry or occupation, A-Z
Torts
Cf. KL-KWX6 940+ Civil law
1195 General (Table K11)
1196.A-Z Protected rights, A-Z
1196.T72 Trade and industrial secrets (Table K12)
1197.A-Z Torts, A-Z

Intellectual and industrial property
Unfair competition
Delicts. Torts
Torts, A-Z -- Continued
1197.B69 Boycott (Table K12)
1197.B73 Breach of contract. Evasion (Table K12)
1197.B74 Bribery (Table K12)
1197.E58 Enticement (Table K12)
1197.E86 Espionage, Industrial (Table K12)
Evasion see KL-KWX6 1197.B73
Industrial espionage see KL-KWX6 1197.E86
1200 Practice and procedure (Table K11)
Including arbitration and award
Social legislation
Including works on both labor law, social insurance, social services, and private labor law as it applies to the labor contract and to the labor-management relationship
1205 General (Table K11)
1208 Social reform and policies (Table K11)
Including all branches of social legislation and labor
Labor law
Criticism and reform see KL-KWX6 1208
1211-1220 General (Table K9c)
1222 Right and duty to work. Constitutional aspects (Table K11)
1223 Ideology and labor law (Table K11)
1224 Politics and labor (Table K11)
1225 Labor policies. Competition and incentives for high performance (Table K11)
Organization and administration
Class here works on national departments and boards of labor, national, state and local departments and boards, or departments and boards of several states or administrative districts
For departments or boards (several or individual) of an individual state or administrative district, see the state or district
1226 General (Table K11)
1227.A-Z Particular, A-Z
Labor contract and employment
1229 General (Table K11)
Types of employment
1230 Permanent employment (Table K11)
1231 Temporary employment (Table K11)
Including seasonal work
1232 Double employment (Table K11)
1233 Part-time employment (Table K11)
1234 Supplementary employment (Table K11)

Labor law
Labor contract and employment
Types of employment -- Continued
1235 Subcontracting (Table K11)
1236 Constitutional rights in employment (Table K11)
Individual labor contract and collective agreements. Liberty of contract
1237 General (Table K11)
Working standards see KL-KWX6 1342
Principle of most favorable wage rate see KL-KWX6 1341
Freedom of employment and restraint on freedom of employment
For slavery, peonage and bonded labor see KL-KWX6 2112
1240 General (Table K11)
1242 Preferential employment (Table K11)
Including people with severe disabilities, veterans, sheltered workshops, etc.
Formation of contract
1245 General (Table K11)
1246 State and labor contract (Table K11)
1247.A-Z Clauses and terms, A-Z
1247.A34 Age limit (Table K12)
Operational changes. Relocation of enterprises see KL-KWX6 1261.A+
Standardized labor conditions see KL-KWX6 1339+
1249 Formalities (Table K11)
Including hiring practices and selection
Parties to contract
1250 General (Table K11)
Parties to collective bargaining see KL-KWX6 1344+
Prohibition of discrimination in employment see KL-KWX6 1276+
1252 Void and voidable contracts. Immoral contracts (Table K11)
Extinction of employment
Cf. KL-KWX6 835+ Contracts
1253 General (Table K11)
1254 Dismissal and resignation of employees (Table K11)
Including economic crisis dismissal, layoff, short hours, suspension, reinstatement, dismissal wage, etc.
1257 Mandatory retirement (Table K11)
1258.A-Z Other special topics, A-Z
Subarrange each by Table K12
Job security
1260 General (Table K11)

Labor law
Labor contract and employment
Extinction of employment
Job security -- Continued
1261.A-Z Special provisions
Including changes of conditions, operational changes, automation, relocation of enterprise, etc.
1262 Procedure (Table K11)
1263.A-Z Protected groups, A-Z
Subarrange each by Table K12
Nonperformance
1265 General (Table K11)
1266 Breach of contract (Table K11)
Cf. KL-KWX6 1197.B73 Unfair competition
Impossibility of performance
1268 General (Table K11)
Automation see KL-KWX6 1261.A+
1269 Seasonal unemployment (Table K11)
Including weather conditions and seasonal industry
1270 Plant shutdown (Table K11)
Liability
Including liability of employer, employee, and liability toward co-worker and third parties
1272 General (Table K11)
1273 Hazardous occupations (Table K11)
1274 Accidents (Table K11)
Cf. KL-KWX6 1390+ Labor hygiene and industrial safety
Cf. KL-KWX6 1550+ Police and public safety
Prohibition of discrimination in employment. Equal opportunity
1276 General (Table K11)
1277 Wage discrimination. Equal pay for equal work (Table K11)
1278.A-Z Groups discriminated against, A-Z
1278.A33 Aged. Older people (Table K12)
1278.A44 Alien laborers (Table K12)
1278.D58 Disabilities, People with (Table K12)
Older people see KL-KWX6 1278.A33
People with disabilities see KL-KWX6 1278.D58
1278.W58 Women (Table K12)
Wages
1280 General (Table K11)
Principle of most favored wage rate see KL-KWX6 1341
Types of wages and modes of remuneration
1282 Daywork. Piecework (Table K11)
1283 Incentive wages (Table K11)
Including bonus system, profit sharing, etc.

Labor law
Wages
Types of wages and modes of remuneration -- Continued
1283.5 Employee stock options (Table K11)
1284 Collective wages (Table K11)
1285 Adjustments. Cost-of-living adjustments (Table K11)
1286 Overtime payments (Table K11)
Including night differentials
1287 Time, place, and mode of payment (Table K11)
Nonwage payments and fringe benefits
1288 General (Table K11)
Pension and retirement plans
1289 General (Table K11)
1290 Pension trusts (Table K11)
Including insolvency insurance
1291.A-Z Other, A-Z
Subarrange each by Table K12
1293.A-Z Groups of employees or industries, A-Z
Subarrange each by Table K12
1295 Employees' references (Table K11)
Labor-management relations
1297 General (Table K11)
1298 Constitutional aspects. Private autonomy. Property rights (Table K11)
1300 Political activities. Limitations (Table K11)
Works councils
Including election, organization, parliamentary practice, etc.
1301 General (Table K11)
1302 Works assembly (Table K11)
Works councils of business concerns see KL-KWX6 1327+
1303 Union participation (Table K11)
Employee participation in management and planning
1304 General (Table K11)
Constitutional aspects. Property rights see KL-KWX6 1298
1305 Works agreements (Table K11)
Standardized labor conditions see KL-KWX6 1339+
Production tasks
1307 General (Table K11)
1308 Maximum increase of labor productivity (Table K11)
1309 Technological improvements of enterprise. Innovations (Table K11)
1310 Rationalization (Table K11)
Labor standards and protection of labor
1312 General (Table K11)
1313 Working hours (Table K11)

Labor law
Labor-management relations
Employee participation in management and planning
Labor standards and protection of labor
1314 Social (welfare) provisions (Table K11)
Including pension trusts, health insurance, housing, cafeterias, etc.
1315 Employee rules and discipline (Table K11)
Including procedure and penalties
Personnel management
1320 General (Table K11)
1322 Hiring. Dismissal. Transfer (Table K11)
For personnel questionnaires and tests see KL-KWX6 1249
1324 Occupational training or retraining (Table K11)
Including apprenticeship
1325 Economic policies (Table K11)
Including control of operational changes
Employee representation on board of controllers and supervisors
Including unincorporated and incorporated business associations, cooperative societies, industrial trusts, etc.
1327 General (Table K11)
1330.A-Z Industries, A-Z
Subarrange each by Table K12
1333 Youth representatives (Table K11)
1334.A-Z Industries and trades, A-Z
Subarrange each by Table K12
1335 Criminal provisions (Table K11)
Collective bargaining and labor agreements
1336 General (Table K11)
1337 Constitutional aspects (Table K11)
1338 Standards for conclusion of labor contracts (Table K11)
Standardized labor conditions
1339 General (Table K11)
1340.A-Z By industry, A-Z
Subarrange each by Table K12
1341 Most favorable wage (Table K11)
1342 Working standards (Table K11)
1343 Formation of contract (Table K11)
Parties to contract
1344 General (Table K11)
Unions see KL-KWX6 1362+
Employers' associations see KL-KWX6 1366
Validity, applicability, and effectiveness
Including planning periods

Labor law
Collective bargaining and labor agreements
Validity, applicability, and effectiveness -- Continued
1346 General (Table K11)
1347.A-Z By industry or occupation, A-Z
Subarrange each by Table K12
Collective labor disputes
1348 General (Table K11)
1349 Arbitration. Conciliation (Table K11)
Strikes and lockouts. Boycott
1350 General (Table K11)
1352 Picketing (Table K11)
Wildcat strikes. Sympathy strikes. Political strikes
1353 General (Table K11)
1354 Damages (Table K11)
1355 Criminal provisions (Table K11)
1356 Nonparticipants. Strike breakers (Table K11)
Corporate representation
1359 General (Table K11)
1360 Constitutional aspects. Freedom of coalition (Table K11)
Unions
Including personality and capacity
1362 General (Table K11)
1364 Union organization (Table K11)
Including election, legal status, etc. of officers
1366 Employers' associations (Table K11)
Protection of labor
1368 General (Table K11)
1369 Protection of human resource (Table K11)
Hours of labor
Including night work and Sunday labor
1370 General (Table K11)
1372 Overtime (Table K11)
Part-time employment see KL-KWX6 1233
1373 Shifts (Table K11)
1374.A-Z By industry or type of employment, A-Z
Subarrange each by Table K12
Vacations
1375 General (Table K11)
1376 Constitutional aspects. Right to recreation (Table K11)
1377 Leave of absence (Table K11)
1378 Sick leave (Table K11)
1379 Holidays (Table K11)
1380 Cash compensation and holiday pay (Table K11)
1381.A-Z By industry or type of labor, A-Z
Subarrange each by Table K12

Labor law
Protection of labor -- Continued
1382 Child and youth labor (Table K11)
Including hours of labor
Women's labor
Including hours of labor
1384 General (Table K11)
1386 Maternal welfare (Table K11)
1388 Home labor (Table K11)
Labor hygiene and industrial safety
Including safety regulations for equipment
1390 General (Table K11)
1392 Factory inspection (Table K11)
1393.A-Z By industry or type of labor, A-Z
1393.C65 Construction industry (Table K12)
1393.M56 Mining industry (Table K12)
1394.A-Z By machinery, equipment, etc. A-Z
Subarrange each by Table K12
1395.A-Z Labor law for particular industries or occupations, A-Z
1395.A34 Agricultural labor (Table K12)
1395.C54 Clerks (Table K12)
1395.C65 Construction industry (Table K12)
1395.M56 Mining industry (Table K12)
1395.P37 Petroleum industry (or workers) (Table K12)
1395.R35 Railroads (Table K12)
Labor supply. Manpower control. Manpower planning
1397 General (Table K11)
1398.A-Z Particular agencies, A-Z
Subarrange each by Table K12
Practice and procedure. Courts
1400 General (Table K11)
1402 Judicial review of grievance procedures. Judicial decisions (Table K11)
1404 Remedies. Appellate procedures (Table K11)
Arbitration
1405 General (Table K11)
1406.A-Z By trade or profession, A-Z
Subarrange each by Table K12
1408 Criminal provisions (Table K11)
Social insurance. Social security
For works on both labor law and social insurance see KL-KWX6 1205+
1410 General (Table K11)
Criticism and reform see KL-KWX6 1208
Information retrieval and electronic data processing see KL-KWX6 47.5+

Social insurance. Social security -- Continued
Organization and administration
Including insurance carriers
For national departments and boards of labor and social insurance see KL-KWX6 1226+
Finance
1417 General (Table K11)
1419 Dues. Employers' and employees' contribution (Table K11)
1420 State supervision (Table K11)
Coverage and benefits
1422 General (Table K11)
1423.A-Z Groups of beneficiaries, A-Z
Subarrange each by Table K12
Merchant mariners see KL-KWX6 925.3+
Miners see KL-KWX6 1009
1425.A-Z Special subjects applying to all branches of social insurance, A-Z
Subarrange each by Table K12
Criminal provisions see KL-KWX6 1455
1429 Conflict of laws (Table K11)
Health insurance
For private health insurance see KL-KWX6 933
For health insurance plans see KL-KWX6 1314
1430 General (Table K11)
1432 Compulsory insurance (Table K11)
Including exemptions
1435.A-Z Coverage and benefits, A-Z
Subarrange each by Table K12
Public employees and officials see KL-KWX6 2414
1437.A-Z Groups of beneficiaries, A-Z
Subarrange each by Table K12
1439 The medical profession and health insurance (Table K11)
Workers' compensation
Including occupational diseases
For merchant mariners see KL-KWX6 928.4
1440 General (Table K11)
1442.A-Z Coverage and benefits, A-Z
Subarrange each by Table K12
1443.A-Z Groups of beneficiaries, A-Z
Subarrange each by Table K12
Old age, survivors and disability insurance
For pensions and retirement plans of private enterprise see KL-KWX6 1289+
1446 General (Table K11)
Social reform see KL-KWX6 1208

Social insurance. Social security
Old age, survivors and disability insurance (Compulsory)
1447 Compulsory insurance. Exemptions (Table K11)
For merchant mariners see KL-KWX6 928+
1448.A-Z Coverage and benefits, A-Z
1448.M43 Medical benefits (Table K12)
1448.O35 Occupational disability pensions (Table K12)
1448.O43 Old age pensions (Table K12)
1449.A-Z Groups of beneficiaries, A-Z
1449.M55 Miners (Table K12)
Unemployment insurance
For pension trusts see KL-KWX6 1290
For civil service pensions see KL-KWX6 2414
1451 General (Table K11)
1452 Compulsory insurance (Table K11)
Including exemptions
1453.A-Z Coverage and benefits, A-Z
Subarrange each by Table K12
1454.A-Z Groups of beneficiaries, A-Z
1454.A34 Agricultural laborers (Table K12)
1455 Criminal provisions (Table K11)
Social services. Public welfare
1456 General (Table K11)
Criticism and reform see KL-KWX6 1208
1457 Practice and procedure (Table K11)
Including domicile
1458.A-Z Coverage and benefits, A-Z
Family planning. Family counseling see KL-KWX6 1482+
Infant welfare see KL-KWX6 1458.M38
1458.I57 Institutional care (Table K12)
For old age homes and nursing homes see KL-KWX6 1524.O42
1458.M38 Maternal and infant welfare (Table K12)
1458.R45 Rent subsidies (Table K12)
Social work and social workers
1459 General (Table K11)
1460 Rural social services (Table K11)
Social service beneficiaries
1462 General (Table K11)
1463 The poor and destitute (Table K11)
1464 Older people (Table K11)
1465 Large families (Table K11)
People with disabilities
Including people with physical, mental, and emotional disabilities
1466 General (Table K11)

Social services. Public welfare
Social service beneficiaries
People with disabilities -- Continued
1467.A-Z Coverage and benefits, A-Z
1467.R43 Rehabilitation (Table K12)
Cf. KL-KWX6 1242 Preferential employment
1468.A-Z Beneficiaries, A-Z
1468.B54 Blind (Table K12)
1468.D42 Deaf-mute (Table K12)
1468.S38 Severe disabilities, People with (Table K12)
1469 Asocial types (Table K11)
1470 Evacuated and homeless persons (Table K11)
War-related groups of beneficiaries
1471 General (Table K11)
1472 Refugees. Expelled or forcefully repatriated persons (Table K11)
1473 Prisoners of war and political prisoners. Veterans (Table K11)
1474 Services for war victims and war invalids (Table K11)
Children. Youth
1475 General (Table K11)
1476 Organization and administration (Table K11)
Including supervision of juvenile detention homes
Measures and provisions
1478 General (Table K11)
1479 Protection of children in public, and against obscenity (Table K11)
Including taverns, theaters, gambling, and literature
Custodial education. Collective education
1480 General (Table K11)
1481.A-Z Particular, A-Z
1481.O75 Orphanages (Table K12)
Disaster relief see KL-KWX6 1589
Human reproduction
1482 General (Table K11)
1483 Birth control (Table K11)
1483.4 Abortion (Table K11)
1485.A-Z Special topics, A-Z
1485.A36 Abortion clinics
Public health
1488 General (Table K11)

Public health -- Continued
1490 Organization and administration (Table K11)
Class here works on national departments and boards, national, state, and local departments and boards, or departments and boards of several states or administrative districts
For departments and boards (several or individual) of an individual state or administrative district, see the state or district
1492 Burial and cemetery laws (Table K11)
Contagious and infectious diseases. Parasitic diseases
1493 General (Table K11)
1494.A-Z Diseases. Agents. Parasites, A-Z
1494.A53 AIDS (Table K12)
1494.T82 Tuberculosis (Table K12)
1494.V45 Venereal diseases (Table K12)
Public health measures
Including compulsory measures
1495 General (Table K11)
Immunization. Vaccination
1496 General (Table K11)
1496.5.A-Z Diseases, A-Z
1496.5.P65 Poliomyelitis (Table K12)
1496.5.S62 Smallpox (Table K12)
1497 Quarantine (Table K11)
Eugenics see KL-KWX6 1530
Environmental pollution see KL-KWX6 1510+
1498.A-Z Other public health hazards and measures, A-Z
1498.R43 Refuse disposal (Table K12)
1498.S77 Street cleaning (Table K12)
1500 Drinking water standards. Fluoridation (Table K11)
Food laws see KL-KWX6 1020+
Mental health
1502 General (Table K11)
1503 The mentally ill (Table K11)
For institutions for the mentally ill see KL-KWX6 1523
1504 Drug addiction (Table K11)
Including works on narcotics and toxic substances and including works on social legislation relating to drug addiction
1505 Alcoholism (Table K11)
Narcotics see KL-KWX6 1538+
Poisons. Toxic substances see KL-KWX6 1564.9+
Environmental law. Environmental policy
For civil liability see KL-KWX6 948
1507 General (Table K11)
1508 Organization and administration (Table K11)

Environmental law. Environmental policy -- Continued

1509 Environmental planning. Conservation of environmental resources (Table K11)

For ecological aspects of regional planning see KL-KWX6 2574

Environmental pollution

1510 General (Table K11)

1510.5 Air pollution (Table K11)

Including noxious gases, automobile emissions, etc.

1511 Water and groundwater pollution (Table K11)

Including pollutants and sewage control

Pollutants

1512 General (Table K11)

1513 Radioactive substances (Table K11)

1513.5 Noise (Table K11)

Including traffic noise, and noise control

Cf. KL-KWX6 944 Nuisance

1514 Recycling of refuse (Table K11)

Wilderness preservation

Including natural monuments, parks, and forests

1515 General (Table K11)

1515.5 Constitutional right to recreation (Table K11)

1516.6 Plant protection (Table K11)

Wildlife conservation

Including game, birds

1517 General (Table K11)

Game laws and hunting see KL-KWX6 1002

Fishery laws see KL-KWX6 1004.3

Land reclamation in mining see KL-KWX6 1007

Environmental crimes see KL-KWX6 4352+

Environmental damages (Civil liability) see KL-KWX6 948

Medical legislation

1520 General (Table K11)

1520.5 Patients' rights (Table K11)

Medical institutions or health services. Hospitals

1521 General (Table K11)

1521.5 Health resorts and spas (Table K11)

1522 Blood banks (Table K11)

Including blood donation

1523 Institutions for the mentally ill (Table K11)

1524.A-Z Other medical institutions or services, A-Z

Abortion clinics see KL-KWX6 1485.A36

1524.D39 Day care centers for infants and children (Table K12)

1524.E43 Emergency medical services (Table K12)

Nursing homes see KL-KWX6 1524.O42

Medical legislation
Medical institutions or health services. Hospitals
Other medical institutions or services, A-Z -- Continued
1524.O42 Old age homes. Nursing homes (Table K12)
Including invalid adults
1524.5.A-Z Health organizations. By name, A-Z
1524.5.R43 Red Cross (Table K12)
Biomedical engineering. Medical technology
Including human experimentation in medicine
Cf. KL-KWX6 4096+ Criminal aspects of medicine
1525 General (Table K11)
1525.5 Genetic engineering (Table K11)
For artificial insemination (human reproductive technology) see KL-KWX6 1527
1526 Transplantation of organs, tissues, etc. (Table K11)
Including donation of organs, tissues, etc.
1527 Human reproductive technology (Table K11)
Including artificial insemination, fertilization in vitro, etc.
Cf. KL-KWX6 612.A78 Family law
1529.A-Z Special topics, A-Z
1529.A88 Autopsy. Postmortem examination (Table K12)
1529.C65 Confidential communications (Table K12)
For data protection see KL-KWX6 942.7.C65
Hospital records see KL-KWX6 1529.R42
1529.I64 Informed consent (Table K12)
Postmortem examination see KL-KWX6 1529.A88
1529.R42 Medical records. Hospital records (Table K12)
1530 Eugenics. Sterilization and castration (Table K11)
1531 Euthanasia. Right to die. Living wills (Table K11)
1532 Veterinary medicine and hygiene. Veterinary public health (Table K11)
Animal protection. Animal welfare. Animal rights
Including prevantion of cruelty to animals
For animal rights as a social issue see HV4701+
1533 General (Table K11)
1534.2 Animal experimentation and research (Table K11)
Including vivisection and dissection
1534.3 Slaghtering of animals (Table K11)
1534.4.A-Z Other special topics, A-Z
1534.4.M86 Mutilation
Drug laws. Liquor laws
Including laws on prohibition
For food laws see KL-KWX6 1020+
1536 General (Table K11)
1537 Pharmaceutical products (Table K11)

Drug laws -- Continued
Narcotics. Intoxicating drugs
Including psychopharmaca
1538 General (Table K11)
1538.5.A-Z Particular drugs, A-Z
1538.5.C35 Cannabis (Table K12)
Including hashish and marijuana
(1538.5.H37) Hashish
see KL-KWX6 1538.5.C35
1538.5.O65 Opium (Table K12)
Poisons see KL-KWX6 1564.9+
1540 Pharmacists and pharmacies (Table K11)
1541 Trade regulation. Advertising (Table K11)
Including consumer protection
Alcoholic beverages
1543 General (Table K11)
1544.A-Z Particular products, A-Z
1544.W54 Wine and wine making (Table K12)
Police and public safety
1550 General (Table K11)
Organization and administration
1551 General (Table K11)
1552 Licenses, concessions, permits (Table K11)
1553 Police magistrates. Lay magistrates. Village (tribal) arbitral tribunals (Table K11)
1556.A-Z Police forces, A-Z
1556.B67 Border patrols (Table K12)
1556.S43 Secret service (Table K12)
Including secret police
Public safety
1559 General (Table K11)
1560 Weapons. Explosives (Table K11)
Including manufacturing, import, and trade of firearms and ammunition
Hazardous articles and processes
Including transportation by land
For product safety see KL-KWX6 947.5+
For transportation by sea see KL-KWX6 1057.3.D35
1562 General (Table K11)
1563 Nuclear power. Reactors. Radioactive substances (Table K11)
Including protection from radiation, and including nuclear waste disposal
Cf. KL-KWX6 947.2.A+ Torts
1564 Flammable materials (Table K11)
Poisons and toxic substances

Police and public safety
Public safety
Hazardous articles and processes
Poisons and toxic substances -- Continued
1564.9 General (Table Table K11)
1565.A-Z Particular, A-Z
1565.P47 Pesticides (Table K12)
Accident control
1566 General (Table K11)
1566.5.A-Z Particular, A-Z
Subarrange each by Table K12
Fire prevention and control
1568 General (Table K11)
1569 Theaters. Auditoriums (Table K11)
Flood control see KL-KWX6 2535
Weather bureaus. Meteorological stations see KL-KWX6 1069
Control of individuals
1572 General (Table K11)
Identification and registration
Including registration of residence
1573 General (Table K11)
Registration of birth, marriage, and death see KL-KWX6 522
1574 Identity cards (Table K11)
1575 Passports (Table K11)
1576.A-Z Other, A-Z
Subarrange each by Table K12
Immigration and naturalization see KL-KWX6 2144
Emigration see KL-KWX6 2150
Particular groups
(1578) Aliens
see KL-KWX6 2155.A43
(1579-1580) Minorities (Ethnic, religious, racial)
see KL-KWX6 2155.A+
Control of social activities
1582 General (Table K11)
1583 Travel and transit traffic. Tourism (Table K11)
Including road traffic and traffic on inland waterways
1584 Vacationing (Table K11)
Including campgrounds, hostels, outdoor swimming facilities, etc.
Sports activities
1585 General (Table K11)
1586 Mass events (Table K11)

Police and public safety
Control of social activities
Sports activities -- Continued
1587.A-Z Particular sports, A-Z
Subarrange each by Table K12
1588.A-Z Other, A-Z
1588.D45 Demonstrations. Processions (Table K12)
Gambling
see KL-KWX6 4406
Processions see KL-KWX6 1588.D45
1588.T7 Traveling shows (Table K12)
Including circuses, puppet theaters, air shows, open-air shows, etc.
1589 Disaster control. Disaster relief (Table K11)
Including emergency management
Cultural affairs
1600 General (Table K11)
1602 Constitutional aspects. Freedom of science and the arts. Academic freedom (Table K11)
1604 Cultural policy. State encouragement of science and the arts (Table K11)
1606 Organization and administration (Table K11)
Class here works on national, state and/or local departments, boards, commissions, etc., of cultural affairs
For the department of cultural affairs of an individual state or district, see the state or district
1607 National language (Table K11)
Including regulation of use, purity, etc.
Education
1610 General (Table K11)
1611 Constitutional safeguards. Parental rights (Table K11)
1612 Boards and commissions (Table K11)
School government. School districts
Including curriculum and participation in school government in general
1615 General (Table K11)
1617 School discipline (Table K11)
1618 Religious instruction (Table K11)
Including public schools and denominations
For religious schools see KL-KWX6 1661
1619 Political science (Table K11)
Students
1620 General (Table K11)
1621 Constitutional aspects (Table K11)
Including right and duty to education, freedom of speech and expression, etc.

Cultural affairs
Education
Students -- Continued
1622 Compulsory education (Table K11)
Teachers. School functionaries (General)
For particular teachers, see the level of instruction, e.g. KL-KWX6 1652 Teachers in higher education
1624 General (Table K11)
1625 Constitutional aspects (Table K11)
Including freedom of speech
1626 Education and training (Table K11)
Including religious education
1627 Disciplinary power (Table K11)
1629 Preschool education (Table K11)
Elementary education
Including teachers
1631 General (Table K11)
1631.3 Rural schools (Table K11)
Education of children with disabilities
1633 General (Table K11)
1634 Children with social disabilities (Table K11)
Including orphans, outcasts, paupers, etc.
1635 Children with physical disabilities (Table K11)
1636 Children with mental disabilities (Table K11)
1638 Vocational education (Table K11)
Including teachers
Secondary education
Including teachers
1640 General (Table K11)
1641.A-Z Special topics, A-Z
1641.E93 Examinations (Table K12)
Including matriculation exams, school leaving exams, high school equivalency exams
High school equivalency exams see KL-KWX6 1641.E93
Matriculation exams see KL-KWX6 1641.E93
School leaving exams see KL-KWX6 1641.E93
1643.A-Z Teaching methods and media, A-Z
Subarrange each by Table K12
Higher education. Universities
For legal education see KL-KWX6 50+
For research policies in higher education see KL-KWX6 1672
1644 General (Table K11)
1645 Intelligentsia (General) (Table K11)
Administration. Institutional management in higher education

Cultural affairs
Education
Higher education. Universities
Administration. Institutional management -- Continued
1646 General (Table K11)
1647 Self-government and autonomy (Table K11)
1648 Disciplinary power and tribunals (Table K11)
1649 Degrees (Table K11)
1650.A-Z Special topics, A-Z
Subarrange each by Table K12
1652 Teachers (Table K11)
Including professors (ordinarii, extraordinarii, and emeriti), magisters, etc.
Students
1653 General (Table K11)
1654 Fellowships. Grants (Table K11)
1655 Selection for higher education (Table K11)
1656 Political activities (Table K11)
Including strikes
1657 Student societies (Table K11)
1658.A-Z Universities. By place, A-Z
Subarrange each by Table K12
1659.A-Z Other schools or institutions of higher education. By place, A-Z
Subarrange each by Table K12
Including colleges or institutes of technology, schools of music, art, drama, etc.
For academies see KL-KWX6 1674.A+
1660 Private schools (Table K11)
1661 Religious schools (Table K11)
Including Quran schools
1662 Adult education (Table K11)
1664 Physical education. Sports (Table K11)
Cf. KL-KWX6 1585+ Sports activities
Science and the arts
1670 General (Table K11)
1672 Public policies in research (Table K11)
Including research in higher education
Public institutions
1673 General (Table K11)
1674.A-Z Academies. Research institutes. By name, A-Z
Subarrange each by Table K12
1676.A-Z Branches and subjects, A-Z
1676.A72 Archaeology (Table K12)
1676.C37 Cartography (Table K12)
1676.I53 Industrial research (Table K12)

Cultural affairs
Science and the arts
Branches and subjects -- Continued
1676.L32 Laboratories (Table K12)
Language see KL-KWX6 1607
Meteorology see KL-KWX6 1069
1676.O34 Oceanography (Table K12)
1676.S73 Statistical services (Table K12)
For data protection see KL-KWX6 942.7.C65
The arts
1677 General (Table K11)
1679 Fine arts (Table K11)
Performing arts
1680 General (Table K11)
1682 Music. Musicians (Table K11)
Theater
Including managerial, performing, and technical personnel
For copyright see KL-KWX6 1125+
1684 General (Table K11)
1686 Playwrights. Contracts (Table K11)
Motion pictures
1687 General (Table K11)
1689 Regulation of industry (Table K11)
Including trade practice and censorship
For copyright see KL-KWX6 1120+
1690 Screenwriters. Contracts (Table K11)
Public collections
1692 General (Table K11)
1694 Archives. Historic documents (Table K11)
Libraries
1695 General (Table K11)
1695.5.A-Z Types of libraries, A-Z
1695.5.P82 Public (Table K12)
1695.6 Librarians and other library personnel (Table K11)
1697 Interlibrary loan
Including national and international loan
1698 Museums and galleries (Table K11)
1699 Criminal provisions (Table K11)
Historic buildings and monuments
1700 General (Table K11)
1700.5 Architectural landmarks (Table K11)
Including vessels, battleships, archaeological sites, etc.
1702 Educational, scientific, and cultural exchanges (Table K11)
Public law
Class here works on all aspects of public law, including early works
For civics see KL-KWX6 72

Public law -- Continued
1710 General (Table K11)
The state
Including philosophy and theory of the state
For non-legal works on political theory, see class J
1720 General (Table K11)
1724 Sovereignty. Potestas (Table K11)
Federalism see KL-KWX6 2035
1726 Rule of law (Table K11)
Socialist state
1728 General (Table K11)
1729 Democratic centralism (Table K11)
1730 Theocratic state (Table K11)
Including religious philosophies and theories of the state
Cf. BL65.S8, Religion in relation to the state
Constitutional law
For works on the constitutional aspects of a subject, see the subject
History see KL-KWX6 1760+
1734 Constitutional reform. Criticism. Polemic
For works on a particular constitution, see the constitution
1741 Bibliography
Including bibliography of constitutional history
1741.2 Periodicals
1742 Monographic series
Sources
Including early constitutions and related materials
1744 Collections. Compilations. By date
Class here national constitutions
For state constitutions and related materials see KL-KWX6 1745
1744.5<date> Individual constitutions
Arrange chronologically by appending the date of adoption to this number and deleting any trailing zeros. Subarrange each by Table K17
1744.6<date> Individual sources other than constitutions
Arrange chronologically by appending the date of adoption or issuance to this number and deleting any trailing zeros. Subarrange by main entry
1745 Collections of state, provincial, departmental, etc., constitutions. By date
Court decisions
1746 Indexes and tables
1746.3 Serials
1746.5 Monographs. By date
1746.7 Digests. Analytical abstracts
Decisions of regulatory agencies. Orders. Rulings

Constitutional law
Decisions of regulatory agencies. Orders. Rulings -- Continued
1746.8 Serials
1746.9 Monographs. By date
1747 Collections of summaries of cases decided by courts or regulatory agencies
1747.3 Dictionaries. Encyclopedias
1747.4 Form books. Graphic materials
Yearbooks see KL-KWX6 1741.2
1749 Conferences. Symposia
Including papers devoted to the scholarly exploration of the subject of constitutional law
Collected works (nonserial) see KL-KWX6 1750
1750 General works. Treatises
Compends. Outlines. Examination aids. Popular works see KL-KWX6 1750
Addresses, essays, lectures see KL-KWX6 1750
1753 Comparative works on state, provincial, departmental, etc., constitutional law
Constitutional history
For constitutional sources see KL-KWX6 1744+
By period
Medieval and early modern (to second half of the 19th century), including precolonial and early colonial periods see KL-KWX6 132+
Mid-19th century to most recent constitution
Including colonial periods to independence
1760 General (Table K11)
Constitutional principles
Rule of law see KL-KWX6 1726
1780 Sovereignty of parliament (Table K11)
1800 Rulers. Kings, princes, viceroys, chieftains (Table K11)
Including dynastic/tribal rules and works on legal status
1820 Privileges of classes and particular groups (Table K11)
1830 Sources and relationships of law (Table K11)
Intergovernmental relations. Jurisdiction
1840 General (Table K11)
1850 Federal-state (republic), national-provincial controversies. State-state or interprovincial disputes (Table K11)
1860 Distribution of legislative power. Exclusive and concurrent legislative power. Reservation of provincial legislation (Table K11)

Constitutional law
Constitutional history
By period
Mid-19th century to most recent constitution -- Continued
1870.A-Z Special topics, A-Z
Class here works on topics not provided for elsewhere
For the history of a particular subject, see the subject
Celebrations see KL-KWX6 1870.C45
1870.C45 Centennials. Celebrations (Table K12)
1890 Interpretation and construction (Table K11)
1892 Amending process (Table K11)
For a particular amendment, see the appropriate constitution
Modern constitutional principles
1895 General (Table K11)
1910 Legitimacy (Table K11)
1920 Legality. Socialist legality (Table K11)
Rule of law see KL-KWX6 1726
1930 Centralization of powers. Statism (Table K11)
1932 Decolonization. Decentralization (Table K11)
1934 Independence. Association or integration of states (Table K11)
Separation and delegation of powers
1940 General (Table K11)
1950 Judicial review of legislative acts (Table K11)
1960 Privileges of classes and particular groups (Table K11)
Sources and relationships of the law
1980 Preconstitutional and constitutional law (Table K11)
1985 International law and municipal law (Table K11)
Statutory law and delegated legislation
1990 General (Table K11)
1995 Retroactivity (Table K11)
2000 Customary (indigenous) and religious law and observances (Table K11)
2010 Socialist plans (Table K11)
2020 Decrees (individual) (Table K11)
Intergovernmental relations. Jurisdiction
2030 General (Table K11)
2035 Federalism (Table K11)
2040 Federal-state (republic), national-provincial controversies. Interstate (interprovincial, etc.) disputes (Table K11)
2050 Exclusive and concurring jurisdiction (Table K11)
Including national (federal) and state (republic, province, etc.) jurisdiction

Constitutional law -- Continued
2055 National (Federal) territory. Archipelagic territorial regimes (e.g. Pacific Area jurisdictions) (Table K11)
Including territorial integrity (fragmentation and boundary questions, politically and ethnically) at independence
Foreign relations
2060 General (Table K11)
Foreign service see KL-KWX6 2284
2070 Executive agreements (Table K11)
Foreign assistance programs see KL-KWX6 2803
2075 Neutrality (Table K11)
2080.A-Z Other, A-Z
Subarrange each by Table K12
Individual and state
General
Human rights. Civil and political rights. Civic (socialist) duties
2095 General (Table K11)
2097 Dignity. Respect for persons (Table K11)
Equality before the law. Antidiscrimination in general
2100 General (Table K11)
2107.A-Z Groups discriminated against, A-Z
2107.C37 Caste (Table K12)
2107.G38 Gays (Table K12)
Indigenous people. Aborigines see KL-KWX6 2107.M56
Jews see KL-KWX6 2107.M56
2107.M56 Minorities (ethnic, religious, racial, and national) (Table K12)
(2107.W65) Women
see KL-KWX6 2108
2108 Sex discrimination (Table K11)
2109.A-Z Special subjects, A-Z
Culture see KL-KWX6 2109.L36
Dialects see KL-KWX6 2109.L36
2109.L36 Language and culture (Table K12)
For language regulation in general see KL-KWX6 1607
Script see KL-KWX6 2109.L36
Freedom
2110 General (Table K11)
2111 Personal freedom (Table K11)
Including protection of life and health
2112 Prohibition of slavery (Table K11)
Including peonage and bonded labor
2113 Protection against forced labor (Table K11)

Constitutional law
Individual and state
Human rights. Civil and political rights. Civic (socialist) duties
Freedom -- Continued
2114 Free choice of employment (Table K11)
2115 Freedom of expression (Table K11)
2116 Freedom of religion and conscience (Table K11)
Freedom of thought and speech
2118 General (Table K11)
2119 Freedom of information (Table K11)
2120 Prohibition of censorship (Table K11)
2122 Right of opposition to government (Table K11)
2124 Freedom of movement (Table K11)
Including emigration
2125 Freedom of assembly, association, and demonstration (Table K11)
2126 Due process of law (Table K11)
2128 Right to resistance against government (Table K11)
2130 Political parties and mass organizations (Table K11)
Including subordinate or connected organizations, and pressure groups, etc.
Control of individuals see KL-KWX6 1572+
Nationality and citizenship
2140 General (Table K11)
2141 Rule of indigenous ancestry (Table K11)
2144 Immigration. Naturalization of aliens (Table K11)
2146 Expatriation (Table K11)
2150 Emigration (Table K11)
2155.A-Z Particular groups, A-Z
2155.A43 Aliens (Table K12)
Including stateless persons
2155.G96 Gypsies. Romanies (Table K12)
2155.M56 Minorities (Table K12)
Including ethnic, religious, racial, and minorities in general
2155.R43 Refugees (Table K12)
Including asylum seekers
Romanies see KL-KWX6 2155.G96
2160 Internal security (Table K11)
Including control of subversive activities or groups
Religion and state
For works on the internal law and government of religious corporations, sects, etc., see class KB
For works on particular subjects, see the subject (e.g. marriage and divorce, succession, guardianship, etc.)
2162 General (Table K11)

Constitutional law
State and religion -- Continued
Sources
Including constitutions, articles, injunctions, ordinances, enactments of the Parliament or the legislature affecting the religious order and life
For sources in general, see classes BL-BQ and KB
Collections. Compilations
2163 Serials
2164 Monographs
2165.A-Z Individual sources, A-Z
2166 Religious corporations. Institutions. Organization (Table K11)
Priesthood. Founders. Sainthood. Holymen
see class KB
Education and training of the leadership
see class KB
2167 Membership (Table K11)
2168 Lands of religious corporations, sects, etc. (Table K11)
2168.5 Religious trusts. Charities. Endowments (Waqf), etc. (Table K11)
2169.A-Z Offenses against religion, A-Z
Class here works that can not be classed elsewhere
Religious courts see KL-KWX6 3472+
Organs of national government. Supreme organs of state power and state administration
Including federal and state government
2172 General (Table K11)
The people
2174 General (Table K11)
Political parties see KL-KWX6 2130
Election law
2176 General (Table K11)
2177 Contested elections
The legislature. Legislative power
2180 General (Table K11)
2182 Control of government (Table K11)
Legislative bodies. People's assembly. Peoples' congress
Including bicameral and unicameral systems
2183 General (Table K11)
2184 Upper house (Table K11)
Including Senates, Councils of State
2185 Lower house (Table K11)
Including House of Representatives, Legislative Assemblies

Constitutional law
Organs of national government. Supreme organs of state power and state administration
The legislature. Legislative power -- Continued
Legislative process
Including parliamentary practice
2186 General (Table K11)
2188 Interpellation (Table K11)
2190 Bill drafting (Table K11)
Committees. Advisory and consultative councils
2192 General (Table K11)
2193 Houses of Chiefs (customary law) (Table K11)
2194 Economic councils (Table K11)
2195 Parliamentary minorities (Table K11)
2196 Lobbying (Table K11)
2198 Legislators (Table K11)
Including immunity, indemnity, incompatibility, etc.
Heads of state
2200 General (Table K11)
Monarchs, princes, chiefs, and other rulers
2202 General (Table K11)
2208.A-Z Special topics, A-Z
2208.A23 Abdication (Table K12)
2208.D9 Dynastic rules. Legal status of dynasty (Table K12)
2208.E43 Election (Table K12)
Legal status of dynasty see KL-KWX6 2208.D9
2208.S92 Succession to the crown (Table K12)
Presidents. Governor-General. Governors
2210 General (Table K11)
2214.A-Z Special topics, A-Z
Subarrange each by Table K12
2214.E43 Election
2214.I58 Impeachment (Table K12)
2218 Collective heads of state. Councils of state. Presidential councils (Table K11)
Prerogatives and powers of the head of state. Executive privilege
2220 General (Table K11)
2224 Treatymaking power (Table K11)
2228 Veto power (Table K11)
2232 War and emergency power (Table K11)
Other supreme organs
2234 General (Table K11)
2235 Central People's Committee (Table K11)

Constitutional law

Organs of national government. Supreme organs of state power and state administration -- Continued

2244 The Judiciary. Judicial power (Table K11)

Class here constitutional status only

For judicial review see KL-KWX6 2461

Cf. KL-KWX6 3409+ Courts, administration of justice, and organization of the judiciary

The executive branch. Government

2250 General (Table K11)

National Executive Councils see KL-KWX6 2218

Presidium. Presidential councils see KL-KWX6 2218

House of Chiefs see KL-KWX6 2193

2260 The Prime Minister and the Cabinet. Premiers (Table K11)

2265 Council of Ministers (Table K11)

2270 Supreme Councils of Control (Table K11)

Government departments, ministries, and other organizations of national (federal) government

2275 General (Table K11)

Departments. Ministries

Class here works on several departments not related to a particular branch of law or subject

Including subordinate administrative divisions, councils, etc.

For works on several departments related to a branch of law or subject, as well as individual departments and its regulatory agencies, see the branch of law or subject

2278 General (Table K11)

2280 Department of State. Foreign office (Table K11)

2284 The foreign service (Table K11)

2288 Department of the Interior. Home Affairs (Table K11)

2290 Subordinate regulatory agencies (Table K11)

Class here works on several agencies

For an individual agency, see the branch of law or the subject

Special boards, commissions, bureaus, councils, task forces, etc.

2292 General (Table K11)

2293.A-Z By name, A-Z

Subarrange each by Table K12

Administrative departments of federal states, provinces, etc.

2295 General (Table K11)

2297 Department of the Interior (Table K11)

Administrative and political divisions. Local government other than municipal

2300 General (Table K11)

2303 Self-government and state supervision (Table K11)

Administrative and political divisions. Local government other than municipal -- Continued

2308 Councils, boards, standing commissions, etc. (Table K11)

2315.A-Z Particular (1st order) administrative districts, counties, regions, etc., A-Z

Including official gazettes, bylaws, statutory orders, regulations, and general works, as well as works on specific legal topics

Municipal government

Including village and town government

2320 General (Table K11)

2325 Autonomy and rulemaking power (Table K11)

2328 Self-government and state supervision (Table K11)

2332 Municipal territory (Table K11)

Including boundaries and incorporation

2338 Name. Flags. Insignia. Seals (Table K11)

Constitution and organization of municipal government

2340 General (Table K11)

2343 Legislative branch. Councils. Elders (Table K11)

Executive branch. Officers and employees

Including elected and honorary offices

For works on the executive branch of an individual municipality, see the municipality

2345 General (Table K11)

2346 Mayor. City director. Chief (Table K11)

Municipal civil service see KL-KWX6 2424

2348.A-Z Special topics, A-Z

Subarrange each by Table K12

Municipal finance and economy

2350 General (Table K11)

2352 Property (Table K11)

Budget see KL-KWX6 3224

Municipal public services

2354 General (Table K11)

2355 Public utilities (Table K11)

For regulation of the energy industry see KL-KWX6 1032+

Electricity see KL-KWX6 1035+

2356 Water. Sewage (Table K11)

For ecological aspects see KL-KWX6 1511

2358 Trash collection (Table K11)

2360 Public transportation (Table K11)

Supramunicipal corporations and cooperation

2362 General (Table K11)

Special districts

For special districts within a particular state, etc., see the state

2364 General (Table K11)

Supramunicipal corporations and cooperation
Special districts -- Continued
2365.A-Z Particular types of districts, A-Z
Subarrange each by Table K12
For water districts see KL-KWX6 2542.A+
2370 Public foundations (Table K11)
Cf. KL-KWX6 955.F68 Foundations in civil law
(2380) Government business enterprises
see KL-KWX6 975+
2390 Constitutional courts (tribunals) and procedure (Table K11)
2392 National emblem. Flag. Seal. Seat of government. National anthem (Table K11)
2394 Political oath (Table K11)
2396 Patriotic customs and observances (Table K11)
2398 Decorations of honor. Awards. Dignities (Table K11)
2399 Commemorative medals (Table K11)
Civil service. Public officials and functionaries
2400 General (Table K11)
2402 Tenure (Table K11)
2403 Official (superior) order (Table K11)
2404 Incompatibility of offices (Table K11)
2405 Appointment and election (Table K11)
2408 Discipline (Table K11)
2410 Illicit political activities (Table K11)
2414 Remuneration. Retirement. Pensions (Table K11)
Including health benefits
2419 Dismissal (Table K11)
2420 Labor law (Table K11)
2422 State civil service (Table K11)
For works on the civil service of an individual state, see the state
2424 Municipal civil service (Table K11)
For works on the civil service of an individual municipality, see the municipality
2430 Civil service of public corporations other than state or municipal (Table K11)
2434 Public officials and functionaries of the economic administration (Socialist) (Table K11)
Administrative law. Administrative process and procedure
2450 General (Table K11)
Regulatory agencies
Including rulemaking power and regulations
2454 General (Table K11)
2456 Admission of attorneys and rules of practice (Table K11)
2458 Citizen (people) participation (Table K11)
Administrative tribunals
2460 General (Table K11)

Administrative law. Administrative process and procedure
Administrative tribunals -- Continued
2461 Judicial review. Appeals (Table K11)
2465 Enforcement. Administrative sanctions (Table K11)
2468 Ombudsman. Control of abuse of administrative power (Table K11)
Tort liability of the government and of public officers see KL-KWX6 949.6.A+
Public property. Public restraint on private property
2500 General (Table K11)
Environmental planning. Conservation of natural resources see KL-KWX6 1509
Recycling of waste see KL-KWX6 1514
Roads and highways
2510 General (Table K11)
2513 Interstate and state highways (Table K11)
2514.A-Z Other, A-Z
Subarrange each by Table K12
2516 Common use. Toll (Table K11)
2518 Construction and maintenance (Table K11)
Including regional planning
Water resources
Including rivers, lakes, watercourses, etc.
2522 General (Table K11)
2525 Common use (Table K11)
2527 Water rights (Table K11)
Cf. KL-KWX6 699 Riparian rights in civil law
2529 Abutting property (Table K11)
Protection against pollution see KL-KWX6 1511
Development and conservation of water resources
2532 General (Table K11)
2535 Flood control (Table K11)
Including dams and dikes
2540.A-Z Particular inland waterways and channels, A-Z
Subarrange each by Table K12
2542.A-Z Particular bodies of water and districts. By name, A-Z
Subarrange each by Table K12
Architectural landmarks and historic monuments see KL-KWX6 1700+
Eminent domain. Expropriation. Nationalization
Including works on protection from compulsory acquisitions by the state (crown)
For works on land expropriated and redistributed to customary owners see KL-KWX6 2553.6
2544 General (Table K11)
2544.2 Court (Supreme Court) rulings (Table K11)

Public property
Eminent domain. Expropriation. Nationalization -- Continued
2544.3 Compensation. Indemnification (Table K11)
Public land law
2550 General (Table K11)
Land policy legislation
For agricultural land law, including land reform see KL-KWX6 988+
2552 General (Table K11)
2553 Government constituted homesteads. Land settlement (Table K11)
2553.6 Government land grants. Land redistribution (Table K11)
Cf. KL-KWX6 2544+ Eminent domain
2554 Reclamation. Irrigation. Drainage (Table K11)
Including arid lands, swamp lands, etc.
2556 Shore protection. Coastal zone management (Table K11)
National preserves. Forests. Savannas
2560 General (Table K11)
Wildlife protection and wilderness preservation see KL-KWX6 1515+
Continental shelf and its resources see KL-KWX6 1006.8
Natural resources and mines see KL-KWX6 1006+
Native (customary) land
2562 General (Table K11)
Common lands. Stool land (chiefdom land)
2563 General (Table K11)
2564.A-Z Particular lands. By chiefdom, tribe, community, etc., A-Z
Native (customary) land legislation, trust acts, treaties, etc.
Including works on prohibition of indefinite use rights (perpetual leasing), and/or administration of trust lands by government
2565 General (Table K11)
2566 Administration. Trust and land boards, land advisory committees and commissions, etc. (Table K11)
e.g. Maori Land Board, New Zealand
2567 Native reserves (Table K11)
Land claims
2568 General (Table K11)
2569 Tribunals, land courts, etc. for claims adjudication (Table K11)
Restoration of land to customary (native) ownership see KL-KWX6 716.7
Regional planning. Land development
2570 General (Table K11)
2574 Ecological aspects (Table K11)
City planning and redevelopment

Public property, Public restraint on private property
Regional planning. Land development
City planning and redevelopment -- Continued
2578 General (Table K11)
2580 Consolidation of urban land holdings (Table K11)
2582 Zoning (Table K11)
2584 Assessment of utilities (Table K11)
Including sanitation
2588 Housing (Table K11)
Building and construction laws
Including administrative control and procedure
2590 General (Table K11)
2592 Design development (Table K11)
2594 Adjoining landowners (Table K11)
2596 Building materials (Table K11)
2598 Building safety and control (Table K11)
Government property
2600 General (Table K11)
Constitutional aspects
2603 General (Table K11)
2604 Interdiction of private ownership (Table K11)
Including socialist theory of government ownership
2605 State or crown (chief's) rights and interests protected against customary claims
Including land, mines and minerals, seabed rights, etc.
Administration. Powers and control
2608 General (Table K11)
2610 Records management. Access to public records (Table K11)
Including data bases and general data protection
Expropriation. Nationalization. Eminent domain see KL-KWX6 2544+
Particular properties
2619 Government buildings (Table K11)
Embassies. Consulates
2620 General (Table K11)
2622.A-Z By place, A-Z
Subarrange each by Table K12
2624 Military installations (Table K11)
2626 Cemeteries (National) (Table K11)
2628 Public works (Table K11)
Government measures in time of war, national emergency, or economic crisis
2650 General (Table K11)
Particular measures

Government measures in time of war, national emergency, or economic crisis
Particular measures -- Continued
2654 Military requisitions from civilians. Requisitioned land (Table K11)
For damages and compensation see KL-KWX6 2690.A+
2660 Control of property. Confiscations (Table K11)
Including enemy and alien property
For damages and compensation see KL-KWX6 2686+
Control of unemployment. Manpower control
2662 General (Table K11)
2664 Compulsory and forced labor (Table K11)
2666 Insolvent debtors. Wartime and crisis relief. General moratorium (Table K11)
2668 Finances (Table K11)
For procurement and defense contracts see KL-KWX6 2700+
For special levies, war taxes, etc. see KL-KWX6 3140+
Industrial priorities and allocations. Economic recovery measures. Nationalization
2670 General (Table K11)
2672.A-Z By industry or commodity, A-Z
Subarrange each by Table K12
Strategic material. Stockpiling
2675 General (Table K11)
2677.A-Z By commodity, A-Z
Subarrange each by Table K12
Rationing. Price control
2679 General (Table K11)
2682.A-Z By commodity, A-Z
Subarrange each by Table K12
2684 Criminal provisions (Table K11)
War damage compensation
Including foreign claims settlement
2686 General (Table K11)
2690.A-Z Particular claims, A-Z
Confiscations see KL-KWX6 2690.R47
Demontage see KL-KWX6 2690.R46
Military occupation damages see KL-KWX6 2690.R47
2690.P47 Personal damages. Property loss or damages (Table K12)
Property loss or damages see KL-KWX6 2690.P47
2690.R46 Reparations. Demontage (Table K12)
2690.R47 Requisitions. Confiscations. Military occupation damages (Table K12)
2695.A-Z Particular victims, A-Z
Subarrange each by Table K12

Government measures in time of war, national emergency, or economic crisis -- Continued
Military occupation. Procurement
2700 General (Table K11)
2704.A-Z Particular, A-Z
Military occupation damages see KL-KWX6 2690.R47
Public finance
Finance reform and policies
Cf. KL-KWX6 972.3 Government control and policy
2715 General (Table K11)
Monetary policies see KL-KWX6 2760+
2721 General (Table K11)
Organization and administration
Class here works on national departments or agencies of finance, national, state, and local departments or agencies, or departments and agencies of several states or administrative districts
For departments and agencies (several or individual) of an individual state or administrative district, see the state or administrative district
2732 General (Table K11)
2735 Particular national departments and agencies (Table K11)
Including officers, personnel, and functionaries
Budget. Government expenditures
2740 General (Table K11)
2742 Accounting (Table K11)
Expenditure control. Auditing. Public accounting
Including central or local organs of national government
2744 General (Table K11)
2746 Investment of public funds (Table K11)
Public debts. Loans. Bond issues
2748 General (Table K11)
2750 External debts. International loan agreements (Table K11)
2753 Intergovernmental fiscal relations (Table K11)
Including revenue sharing
Money. Monetary policy
Including control of circulation
2760 General (Table K11)
2762 Currency reforms (Table K11)
2764 Coinage. Mint regulations (Table K11)
2766 Bank notes. Banks of issue (Table K11)
Class here public law aspects of banks of issue
For banking law see KL-KWX6 885+
2768 Gold trading and gold standard (Table K11)
2770 Silver regulation (Table K11)
Foreign exchange control

Public finance
Money
Foreign exchange control -- Continued
2772 General (Table K11)
Valuta clause and gold clause see KL-KWX6 839.4
Criminal provisions see KL-KWX6 4292
2774 Conflict of laws (Table K11)
National revenue
2778 Fees. Fines. Other charges (Table K11)
Taxation
Criticism and reform see KL-KWX6 2715+
2781-2790 General (Table K9c)
2792 Constitutional aspects (Table K11)
Including equality
Double taxation
2794 General (Table K11)
2796 Domicile (Table K11)
2798.A-Z Special topics, A-Z
2798.F67 Foreign corporations and foreign stockholders (Table K12)
2798.M85 Multi-national corporations (Table K12)
Taxation and tax exemption as a measure of social and economic policy
2800 General (Table K11)
2802 Investments (Table K11)
Including foreign investments
2803 Assistance to developing countries (Table K11)
2805 Export sales (Table K11)
2806.A-Z Classes of taxpayers or lines of businesses, A-Z
Subarrange each by Table K12
2807.A-Z Taxation of particular activities, A-Z
Subarrange each by Table K12
2808 Tax saving. Tax avoidance (Table K11)
For tax planning relating to a particular tax, see the tax
Tax administration. Revenue service
2810 General (Table K11)
National departments and agencies see KL-KWX6 2735
2812 Jurisdiction for tax allocation (Table K11)
Including concurrent taxing powers of national and state government
Double taxation see KL-KWX6 2794+
Collection and enforcement
2814 General (Table K11)
Tax accounting. Financial statements
Including personal companies and stock companies, etc.
For a particular tax, see the tax

Public finance
National revenue
Taxation
Tax administration. Revenue service
Collection and enforcement
Tax accounting. Financial statements -- Continued
2816 General (Table K11)
2818 Tax consultants (Table K11)
2820.A-Z Special topics, A-Z
2820.A77 Assessment (Table K12)
2820.E94 Execution (Table K12)
Cf. KL-KWX6 3330+ Tax and customs investigation
2820.R46 Remedies (Table K12)
2820.T39 Tax auditing (Table K12)
Cf. KL-KWX6 3330+ Tax and customs investigation
2820.T42 Tax courts (Table K12)
2820.T44 Taxpayer advocates (Table K12)
2825.A-Z Classes of taxpayers or lines of business, A-Z
2825.N65 Non-residents (Table K12)
2830 Particular taxes (several, collective) (Table K11)
Income tax
2832 General (Table K11)
2834 Tax planning. Estate planning (Table K11)
2836 Accounting and financial statements (Table K11)
2837 Assessment (Table K11)
Taxable income. Exemptions
2840 General (Table K11)
2842.A-Z Particular, A-Z
Capital gains see KL-KWX6 2842.P75
2842.P75 Profits. Capital gains (Table K12)
2842.T38 Tax-exempt securities (Table K12)
Deductions
2844 General (Table K11)
2845 Amortization. Depreciation allowances (Table K11)
2846 Charitable or educational gifts and contributions (Table K11)
Expenses and losses
2848 General (Table K11)
2850.A-Z Kinds of expenses, A-Z
2850.B88 Business expenses (Table K12)
2850.E38 Educational expenses (Table K12)
2850.E58 Entertainment expenses (Table K12)
Surtaxes see KL-KWX6 3140+
Particular sources of income

Public finance
National revenue
Taxation
Income tax
Particular sources of income -- Continued
Salaries and wages
Including fringe benefits, nonwage payments, etc.
2854 General (Table K11)
2856.A-Z Classes of taxpayers, A-Z
Subarrange each by Table K12
2858 Capital investment (Table K11)
Including foreign investment
Cf. KL-KWX6 971.5 Taxation as a measure of economic policy
2859 Pensions and annuities (Table K11)
2860.A-Z Other sources of income, A-Z
2860.L43 Leases (Table K12)
2862.A-Z Classes of taxpayers or lines of business, A-Z
2862.A44 Aliens (Table K12)
2862.F37 Farmers (Table K12)
2862.T78 Trusts (Table K12)
Corporation tax
2866 General (Table K11)
Nonprofit associations, nonprofit corporations, foundations (endowments), and pension trust funds
2868 General (Table K11)
2870.A-Z Special topics, A-Z
2870.T39 Tax avoidance (Table K12)
Personal companies (Unincorporated business associations)
2880 General (Table K11)
2889.A-Z Special topics, A-Z
Subarrange each by Table K12
Cooperatives
2890 General (Table K11)
2892.A-Z Special topics, A-Z
Subarrange each by Table K12
Stock companies (Incorporated business associations
3000 General (Table K11)
3002 Tax accounting. Financial statements (Table K11)
3003 Assessment (Table K11)
Taxable income. Exemptions
3005 General (Table K11)
3007.A-Z Particular, A-Z
3007.C35 Capital stock (Table K12)
3007.D58 Dividends (Table K12)

Public finance
National revenue
Taxation
Income tax
Corporation tax
Stock companies (Incorporated business associations
Taxable income. Exemptions
Particular, A-Z -- Continued
3007.I58 Inventories (Table K12)
3007.P75 Profits (Table K12)
3007.R48 Reserves (Table K12)
Deductions
3010 General (Table K11)
3012 Depreciation of property, plant, and equipment (Table K11)
3014 Pension reserves (Table K11)
3016 Charitable, religious, or educational gifts and contributions (Table K11)
3018.A-Z Expenses and losses, A-Z
Subarrange each by Table K12
Surtaxes see KL-KWX6 3140+
Corporate reorganization
3020 General (Table K11)
3022 Conversions (Table K11)
3024 Merger, fusion, and consolidation (Table K11)
3026 Liquidation (Table K11)
3030 Limited partnership (Table K11)
3040 Stock corporation (Table K11)
3050 Business concern, holding company, and industrial trusts (Table K11)
3060 Government business corporations (Table K11)
3070.A-Z Lines of corporate business, A-Z
3070.E44 Electronic commerce (Table K12)
3070.P48 Petroleum industry (Table K12)
Foreign corporations and stockholders
3080 General (Table K11)
Double taxation see KL-KWX6 2794+
Multi-national corporations
3090 General (Table K11)
Double taxation see KL-KWX6 2794+
Property tax. Taxation of capital
Including real property tax
For state and local property taxes see KL-KWX6 3250+
For state and local real property tax see KL-KWX6 3290+
3100 General (Table K11)

Public finance
National revenue
Taxation
Property tax. Taxation of capital -- Continued
3102 Taxation valuation (Table K11)
3104 Accounting. Financial statements (Table K11)
3106 Assessment (Table K11)
3107 Taxable property. Exemptions (Table K11)
3110 Estate, inheritance, and gift taxes (Table K11)
3120 Taxation of religious institutions or corporations
3130 Capital gain tax (Table K11)
Surtaxes
3140 General (Table K11)
3142 Excess profits tax (Table K11)
Including war profits tax
Poll tax see KL-KWX6 3310.P65
Excise taxes. Taxes on transactions
3145 General (Table K11)
Sales tax
Including value-added tax
3147 General (Table K11)
Turnover tax
3150 General (Table K11)
3152 Private use. Expenses (Table K11)
3154 Import sales and export sales (Table K11)
Personal companies and stock companies
3166 General (Table K11)
3168 Municipal corporations (Table K11)
Particular commodities, services, and transactions see KL-KWX6 3174.A+
3170 Government monopolies (Table K11)
Including monopolies delegated by the state to others
3174.A-Z Commodities, services, and transactions, A-Z
3174.A3 Admissions. Amusements
Methods of assessment and collection
For assessment and collection of a particular tax, see the tax
3180 General (Table K11)
3184 Stamp duties (Table K11)
Criminal provisions see KL-KWX6 3315+
Customs. Tariff
For foreign trade regulations see KL-KWX6 1025+
3190 General (Table K11)
Trade agreements
3194 General (Table K11)
3196 Favored nation clause (Table K11)

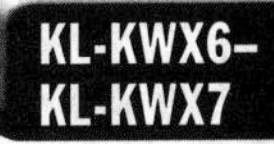

Public finance
National revenue
Customs. Tariff -- Continued
Customs organization and administration
Including officers and personnel
3200 General (Table K11)
3201 Origin of goods. Certificates of origin (Table K11)
3202 Jurisdiction. Custom territory (Table K11)
Practice and procedure
Including remedies and enforcement
3204 General (Table K11)
3206 Duty by weight (Table K11)
3207 Custom appraisal (Table K11)
3208 Dumping. Antidumping duties (Table K11)
3208.5 Drawbacks (Table K11)
3209.A-Z Commodities and services, A-Z
Subarrange each by Table K12
3211 Free ports and zones (Table K11)
3212 Customs courts. Court of customs appeal (Table K11)
Including court rules
Criminal provisions see KL-KWX6 3315+
State and local finance
For the public finance of an individual state, administrative district, or municipality, see the state or municipality
3220 General (Table K11)
Finance reform see KL-KWX6 2715+
3224 Budget. Expenditure control (Table K11)
Including accounting and auditing
3226 Public debts. Loans (Table K11)
3228 Intergovernmental fiscal relations (Table K11)
Class here works on local taxes shared by state and locality
For state taxes shared by state and national government see KL-KWX6 2753
Taxation
3230 General (Table K11)
Tax administration see KL-KWX6 2810+
Income tax see KL-KWX6 2832+
Sales, turnover, and value-added taxes see KL-KWX6 3147+
3240 Estate, inheritance, and gift taxes (Table K11)
Property tax. Taxation of capital
Including juristic persons and business enterprises
For real property tax see KL-KWX6 3290+
3250 General (Table K11)
3255.A-Z Particular industries or industrial properties, A-Z
Subarrange each by Table K12

Public finance
State and local finance
Taxation
Property tax. Taxation of capital -- Continued
3257 Accounting. Financial statements (Table K11)
3259 Assessment (Table K11)
3262.A-Z Taxable property, A-Z
Subarrange each by Table K12
3264 Deductions (Table K11)
3270 Motor vehicles tax (Table K11)
3280 Taxes from gambling tables. Casinos (Table K11)
Real property tax
3290 General (Table K11)
3292 Valuation of real property. Assessment (Table K11)
3294 Capital gains tax (Table K11)
Including development gains
3296.A-Z Properties, A-Z
Subarrange each by Table K12
Business tax
3300 General (Table K11)
3302 Assessment (Table K11)
3304 Taxable income (Table K11)
3306 Deductions (Table K11)
3308.A-Z Classes of taxpayers or lines of business, A-Z
Subarrange each by Table K12
Other taxes, A-Z
3310.I55 Impact fees (Table K12)
3310.P65 Poll tax (Table K12)
Tax and customs crimes and delinquency. Procedure
3315 General (Table K11)
Individual offenses
3319 Tax evasion and tax avoidance (Table K11)
3320 Receiving bootleg merchandise (Table K11)
3322 Violation of confidential disclosure (Table K11)
Including denunciation
Smuggling of contraband see KL-KWX6 3319
3324 Organized smuggling (Table K11)
3326 Forgery of seals, stamps, etc. (Table K11)
Procedure
For criminal procedure in general see KL-KWX6 4600.9+
3330 General (Table K11)
3332 Evidence (Table K11)
3335 Special procedures in criminal tax cases (Table K11)
3340 Amnesty. Pardon (Table K11)
National defense. Military law
For emergency and wartime legislation see KL-KWX6 2650+

National defense. Military law -- Continued
3350 General (Table K11)
3352 Organization and administration. Department of Defense (Table K11)
The armed forces
3354 General (Table K11)
Compulsory service
Including draft and selective service
3356 General (Table K11)
Deferment
Including disqualification
3357 General (Table K11)
3358.A-Z Particular groups, A-Z
3358.A44 Aliens (Table K12)
3358.C65 Conscientious objectors (Table K12)
3359 Discharge (Table K11)
3360 Disability pensions. Rehabilitation (Table K11)
For war invalids, war victims, and prisoners of war see KL-KWX6 1471+
3362 Equipment (Table K11)
Including weapons, plants, and installations
3364 Hospitals (Table K11)
3365 Postal services (Table K11)
3366.A-Z Particular branches of service, A-Z
Subarrange each by Table K12
3368 Auxiliary services during war or emergency (Table K11)
3369 Civil status and rights of military personnel (Table K11)
3370 Foreign armed forces. Status of forces agreements (Table K11)
Including damages
3372 Civil defense (Table K11)
Military criminal law and procedure
Cf. KL-KWX6 4470+ Crimes against national defense
3380 General (Table K11)
3382 Illegality and justification. Superior orders (Table K11)
Individual offenses
3385 Desertion (Table K11)
3386 Incitement. Mutiny (Table K11)
3387 Insubordination (Table K11)
3388 Self-mutilation. Malingering (Table K11)
3389 Calumny. Assault on subordinates (Table K11)
3390 Sabotaging weapons, equipment or means of defense (Table K11)
3392.A-Z Other, A-Z
Subarrange each by Table K12

National defense. Military law
Military criminal law and procedure -- Continued
3395 Courts and procedure. Courts-martial (Table K11)
Including procedure in honor cases
3397 Punishment. Execution (Table K11)
3399 Probation and parole (Table K11)
Trials. Courts martial
Including trials of civilians by military courts
3399.5 Collections
3399.6 Particular trials. By defendant, A-Z
Military discipline. Law enforcement. Procedure
Including all branches of the armed forces
3400 General (Table K11)
3402 Superior orders. Enforcement of orders (Table K11)
3405.A-Z Special topics, A-Z
3405.M55 Military maneuvers (Table K12)
Courts and procedure
3407 General (Table K11)
The administration of justice. The organization of the judiciary
Including the administration of criminal justice
3409 Reform and criticism
Including the reform of criminal justice
3411 General (Table K11)
Organization and administration
Class here works on national and state departments of justice or departments of justice of several states
For the department of justice of an individual state, see the state
3426 General (Table K11)
3428 National department of justice. Office of the Attorney General (Table K11)
Including legal opinions, e. g. Attorneys General's opinions
For legal opinions on a specific subject, see the subject
Judicial statistics see KL-KWX6 30+
Judicial assistance
Including judicial assistance in criminal matters
3430 General (Table K11)
3432 International judicial assistance (Table K11)
3433 Foreign judgments (Conflict of laws) (Table K11)
Courts
Class here works on courts of several jurisdictions
Including courts of both criminal and civil jurisdiction
For courts (several or individual) of an individual jurisdiction, see the jurisdiction
3441 General (Table K11)
3450.5 State and federal jurisdiction (Table K11)

Courts and procedure
Courts -- Continued
Lowest courts. Local courts
Including law courts
3451 General (Table K11)
3453 Municipal courts. Village courts (Native courts) (Table K11)
3455 Magistrate courts (Table K11)
3457 Neighborhood courts. Peoples' courts. Comrades' courts (Table K11)
3459 Justice of the peace (Table K11)
3462 Regional courts. Provincial courts. District courts. District peoples' courts (Table K11)
3464 High courts of the states or republics. Superior state courts (Table K11)
3465 National (Federal) appeals courts (Table K11)
3466 National (Federal) supreme courts. Supreme Peoples' courts. Courts of Cassation (Table K11)
Courts of special jurisdiction
3468 General (Table K11)
3470 Special tribunals (Table K11)
For tribunals for native land claims adjudication see KL-KWX6 2569
Religious courts and councils
3472 General (Table K11)
3474 Sharia courts. Kadi courts. Islamic courts. (Table K11)
3476 Rabbinical courts (Table K11)
Customary (native) courts of law
3478 General (Table K11)
3480 Houses of chiefs. Traditional councils (native or regional) (Table K11)
3481 Village or family arbitral tribunals. Village (tribal) elders (Table K11)
3482 Consular courts (Table K11)
3483 Peasant association tribunals (Table K11)
3484 Competence conflict courts (Table K11)
Other courts of special jurisdiction
see the subject, e.g. KL-KWX6 3395 Military courts
3485 Supreme judicial councils (Table K11)
3486 Special tribunals within a court (Table K11)
3487 Deliberating and voting. Secrecy (Table K11)
3488 Court decorum and discipline. Conduct of court proceedings (Table K11)
3488.5 Congestion and delay (Table K11)
3489 Terms of court (Table K11)
3490 Judicial opinions. Advisory opinions (Table K11)

Courts and procedure -- Continued
Judicial officers. Court employees
3492 General (Table K11)
Law school education and post-law school education see KL-KWX6 50+
3493 Nationality and citizenship (Table K11)
3494.A-Z Minorities, A-Z
Subarrange each by Table K12
3495 Salaries, allowances, pensions, etc. (Table K11)
Judges
3497 General (Table K11)
3497.5 Rating (Table K11)
Women judges see KL-KWX6 3494.A+
3498 Independence of judges (Table K11)
3499 Political activity of judges (Table K11)
3500 Ethics and discipline (Table K11)
Office of the public prosecutor. Director of prosecution
3502 General (Table K11)
3503 Jurisdiction (Table K11)
Notaries see KL-KWX6 55+
Auxiliary personnel. Clerk's (Registrar's) office
3504 General (Table K11)
Clerks to the court
3505 General (Table K11)
3506 Business administration. Court records (Table K11)
For personal data protection in information retrieval systems see KL-KWX6 942.7.C65
3508 Bailiffs (Table K11)
3510 Medical examiners. Coroners (Table K11)
For forensic medicine, see RA1001+
Procedure in general
Class here works on civil and criminal procedure and works on civil, commercial, and labor procedure combined
3520 General (Table K11)
Procedural principles
3522 General (Table K11)
3523 Due process of law (Table K11)
3524 Uniformity of law application. Stare decisis (Table K11)
3525 Publicity and oral procedure (Table K11)
3525.8 Standing. Locus standi (Table K11)
Parties to action
3526 General (Table K11)
3527 Privileged parties (Table K11)
3528 Litigant. Plaintiff. Defendant (Table K11)
Pretrial procedures
3530 General (Table K11)

Courts and procedure
Procedure in general
Pretrial procedures -- Continued
3532.A-Z Particular, A-Z
Subarrange each by Table K12
Procedure at first instance. Trial
3534 General (Table K11)
3535 Trial practice. Trial tactics (Table K11)
3536 Cross examination (Table K11)
3537 Actions and defenses (Table K11)
3538 Summation. Closing argument (Table K11)
3539 Particular proceedings (Table K11)
Evidence. Burden of proof
3542 General (Table K11)
3543 Presumption. Prima-facie evidence (Table K11)
Admission of evidence
3544 General (Table K11)
3544.5 Hearsay (Table K11)
Witnesses
3545 General (Table K11)
3546 Privileged witnesses (Confidential communication). Expert testimony (Table K11)
3547.A-Z Special topics, A-Z
Subarrange each by Table K12
Judicial decisions
3548 General (Table K11)
3549.A-Z Particular decisions, A-Z
Subarrange each by Table K12
Remedies
3552 General (Table K11)
3553 Appellate procedure (Table K11)
3554 New trial. Reopening of a case (Table K11)
3555 Execution (Table K11)
Civil procedure
3557 Criticism. Reform (Table K11)
3561-3570 General (Table K9c)
Procedural principles
3572 General (Table K11)
3573 Due process of law (Table K11)
Including frivolous suits
3574 Stare decisis (Table K11)
3574.5 Prohibition of abuse of legal procedure and chicanery (Table K11)
3575 Publicity and oral procedure (Table K11)
Principles of evidence see KL-KWX6 3649
3576 Speedy trial (Table K11)

Courts and procedure
Civil procedure
Procedural principles -- Continued
3577 Truthfulness and falsehood. Discovery (disclosure) (Table K11)
3578 Prejudicial actions (Table K11)
3579 Nisi prius procedure (Table K11)
Equity practice and procedure
3580 General (Table K11)
3581 Legislative documents (Table K11)
3582 Court rules (Table K11)
Jurisdiction. Venue
3583 General (Table K11)
3584 Removal of causes (Table K11)
3585 Disqualification of judges (Table K11)
Action
3586 General (Table K11)
3587 Process and service (Table K11)
Pleading and motions
3587.5 General (Table K11)
3588 Motions (Table K11)
3589 Special pleadings (Table K11)
Defenses and objections (Exceptions)
3590 General (Table K11)
3591 Limitation of actions (Table K11)
3592 Lis pendens (Table K11)
3595 Set-off. Counterclaim and cross claim (Table K11)
3596 Confession of judgment (Table K11)
Parties to action
3598 General (Table K11)
3599 Juristic persons (Table K11)
3600 Privileged parties (Table K11)
3602 Litigant. Plaintiff. Defendant (Table K11)
3603 Joinder of claims and remedies (Table K11)
3604 Joinder of parties (Table K11)
3605 Interpleader (Table K11)
3606 Class action (Table K11)
Pretrial procedures
3610 General (Table K11)
3611 Deposition and discovery. Interrogatories (Table K11)
3612 Summons, service of process, subpoena, etc. (Table K11)
Time periods. Deadlines
3613 General (Table K11)
3614 Default and restitution (Table K11)
3615 Suspension of procedure (Table K11)
Procedure at first instance

Courts and procedure
Civil procedure
Procedure at first instance -- Continued
3617 General (Table K11)
Jurisdiction. Competence in subject matter and venue
3618 General (Table K11)
3619 Forum rei sitae (Table K11)
3620 Domicile or place of business (Table K11)
3621 Prorogation (Table K11)
3622 Venue for corporate bodies (Table K11)
3623 Right to litigate (Table K11)
3624 Representation. Power of attorney (Table K11)
Lis pendens see KL-KWX6 3631.L58
Res judicata see KL-KWX6 3631.R48
3625 Object at issue (Table K11)
Time periods. Deadlines see KL-KWX6 3613+
Actions and defenses
3627 General (Table K11)
3629 Joinder of actions. Compounded claims (Table K11)
3630 Amendment. Withdrawal (Table K11)
3631.A-Z Defenses and exceptions, A-Z
3631.L55 Limitation of actions (Table K12)
3631.L58 Lis pendens (Table K12)
3631.R48 Res judicata (Table K12)
Particular proceedings
3635 Joinder of parties (Table K11)
3637 Intervention (Table K11)
3639 Interpleader (Table K11)
3640 Change of parties (Table K11)
Including death of party
3641 Default judgments (Table K11)
3642 Decision without trial (Table K11)
3643 Dismissal and nonsuit (Table K11)
3644 Settlement out of court (Table K11)
3645 Compromise (Table K11)
Evidence
3647 General (Table K11)
3649 Principles of evidence. Free evaluation of evidence (Table K11)
3650 Burden of proof (Table K11)
3651 Prima facie (Table K11)
Admissibility and exclusion of evidence
3652 General (Table K11)
3653 Physical examinations. Blood tests (Table K11)
Cf. RA1001+ Forensic medicine
Witnesses

Courts and procedure
Civil procedure
Procedure at first instance
Evidence
Witnesses -- Continued
3654 General (Table K11)
3655 Privileged witnesses (Confidential communication) (Table K11)
3656 Expert testimony (Table K11)
3657 Documentary evidence (Table K11)
3658 Circumstantial evidence (Table K11)
3659 Testimony of party (Table K11)
3660 Presumptions (Table K11)
3661 Oath (Table K11)
Including oath of witnesses and parties
Jury and jurors
3665 General (Table K11)
3666 Jury trial of right (Table K11)
3667 Selection. Jury commissions (Table K11)
3668 Special verdicts and findings (Table K11)
3669 Instructions to juries (Table K11)
3670 Special masters. Referees. Auditors. Examiners (Table K11)
Judicial decisions
3671 General (Table K11)
Judgment (General)
3672 General (Table K11)
3673 Judicial discretion (Table K11)
Including equity
3675 Summary judgment (Table K11)
3677 Declaratory judgment (Table K11)
3678 Agreed judgment (Table K11)
Judgment by default see KL-KWX6 3641
Decision with trial see KL-KWX6 3642
Dismissal and nonsuit see KL-KWX6 3643
3679 Interlocutory decisions (Table K11)
3680 Void judgments and nonjudgments (Table K11)
3681 New trial. Reopening a case (Table K11)
3682 Mistakes (error) (Table K11)
Including correction, recall, or withdrawal of faulty decision
3683 Res judicata. Estoppel by judgment (Table K11)
3684 Court records. Minutes of evidence (Table K11)
Including clerks' mistakes and corrections
3685 Advisory opinions (Table K11)
Particular procedures
3689 Matrimonial actions (Table K11)

Courts and procedure
Civil procedure
Particular procedures -- Continued
3690 Procedures in parent and child chases (Table K11)
For procedures in guardianship and curatorship cases see KL-KWX6 622
3692 Interdiction. Mental competency procedure (Table K11)
3693 Public summons (Table K11)
Settlement see KL-KWX6 3755
3695 Hortatory procedures (Table K11)
3697 Small claims. Procedures before the justice of the peace or magistrate (Table K11)
Procedures before particular courts (e.g., native courts, comrade's courts, etc.) see KL-KWX6 3451+
Remedies and special proceedings
3700 General (Table K11)
3701 Summary proceedings (Table K11)
3702 Habeas corpus (Table K11)
3704 Injunctions. Provisional remedies (Table K11)
Interpleader see KL-KWX6 3639
3706 Receivers in equity (Table K11)
Receivers in bankruptcy see KL-KWX6 965.3.R42
Possessory actions see KL-KWX6 647
Extraordinary remedies
Including older remedies
3710 General (Table K11)
Particular remedies
3714 Quo warranto (Table K11)
3716 Mandamus (Table K11)
Habeas corpus see KL-KWX6 3702
3718 Coram nobis (Table K11)
3720 Imprisonment for debt (Table K11)
3740 Appellate procedure (Table K11)
Execution of judgment
3745 General (Table K11)
3747 Attachment. Garnishment (Table K11)
3750.A-Z Exemptions, A-Z
Subarrange each by Table K12
3755 Negotiated settlement. Compromise (Table K11)
3760 Arbitration (Table K11)
Including commercial arbitration
Costs
3765 General (Table K11)
3767 In forma pauperis (Table K11)
Criminal law

Criminal law -- Continued

3790 Reform of criminal law, procedure, and execution

For works limited to a particular subject, see the subject

For works pertaining exclusively to the codes, see the code

For reform of criminal justice, administration see KL-KWX6 3409

Administration of criminal justice see KL-KWX6 3409+

3791-3800 General (Table K9c)

3810 Constitutional aspects (Table K11)

Philosophy of criminal law

3812 General (Table K11)

Theories of punishment. Criminal policy see KL-KWX6 3950+

3813 Ideological theories of criminal law (Table K11)

3816.A-Z Special topics, A-Z

Subarrange each by Table K12

Relationship of criminal law to other disciplines, subjects or phenomena

3817 General (Table K11)

3818 Criminal law and society (Table K11)

Cf. HV6115+ Social pathology

3819 Criminal law and psychology (Table K11)

Cf. HV6080+ Criminal psychology

3821 Interpretation and construction. Legal hermeneutics (Table K11)

3823.A-Z Terms and phrases, A-Z

Drugs see KL-KWX6 3823.F67

3823.F67 Force (Table K12)

Including force by use of drugs and hypnosis

3823.H66 Honor (Table K12)

Hypnosis see KL-KWX6 3823.F67

Applicability and validity of the law

3827 Retroactivity. Ex post facto laws (Table K11)

3828 Interpretation. Analogy (Table K11)

3829 Customary law. Indigenous law. Repugnancy clause (Table K11)

Territorial applicability

3830 General (Table K11)

Place of commission of crime

3831 General (Table K11)

3832 Press delicts (Table K11)

3833 Crimes aboard aircraft (Table K11)

3835 Conflict of laws (Table K11)

Temporal applicability

3836 General (Table K11)

3837 Intertemporal law (Table K11)

Criminal law
Applicability and validity of the law -- Continued
3838 Personal applicability. Immunities (Table K11)
Criminal offense
3840 General (Table K11)
3844 Crimes aggravated by personal characteristics (Table K11)
Criminal act
3845 General (Table K11)
3847 Corpus delicti (Table K11)
3849 Omission (Table K11)
Causation
3851 General (Table K11)
3853 Proximate cause (Table K11)
Forms of the act see KL-KWX6 3912+
Illegality. Justification of otherwise illegal acts
3855 General (Table K11)
3856 Self-defense or defense of another (Table K11)
3857 Necessity (Table K11)
Superior orders see KL-KWX6 3900
Medical treatment see KL-KWX6 4096+
3861 Consent of the injured party. Assumption of risk (Table K11)
3865.A-Z Other grounds for justification, A-Z
Subarrange each by Table K12
3867 Criminal intent. Mens rea (Table K11)
Including purpose and scienter
Negligence and wantonness
3874 General (Table K11)
3876 Foresight. Standard of conduct (Table K11)
Criminal liability. Guilt. Culpability
3878 General (Table K11)
Capacity. Incapacity and limited capacity
3880 General (Table K11)
3884 Insane persons. People with mental or emotional disabilities (Table K11)
Cf. HV6133, Psychopathology and crime
Minors
3886 General (Table K11)
3888 Infants (Table K11)
3890 Juveniles. Young adults (Table K11)
3892.A-Z Special topics, A-Z
3892.D58 Distemper (Table K12)
3892.I58 Intoxication (Table K12)
Passion see KL-KWX6 3892.D58
3895 Criminal liability of juristic persons (Table K11)
3897 Exculpating circumstances (Table K11)

Criminal law
Criminal offense -- Continued
3900 Superior orders and justification or excusation (Table K11)
Cf. KL-KWX6 3402 Military criminal law
Error
3902 General (Table K11)
3904 Error about fact (Table K11)
3906 Error about grounds for justification or excusation (Table K11)
3908 Other (Table K11)
Including error about extenuating circumstances, error in persona, error in objecto, aberratio ictus, etc.
Forms of the criminal act
3912 General (Table K11)
Omission see KL-KWX6 3849
3913 Attempt (Table K11)
Including intent and preparation, and active repentance
Perpetrators
3920 General (Table K11)
Principals and accessories
3922 General (Table K11)
3924 Liability of each participant (Table K11)
3925 Co-principals (Table K11)
3927 Accessory before the fact (Table K11)
Including after the fact
3933 Complicity (Table K11)
3934 Agent provocateur (Table K11)
Aggravating and extenuating circumstances see KL-KWX6 4020+
3940 Compound offenses and compound punishment (Table K11)
Punishment
3946 General (Table K11)
Theory and policy of punishment
3950 General (Table K11)
3952 Retaliation. Retribution. Vendetta (Table K11)
3954 Safeguarding the social and political system (Table K11)
3956 General and special prevention (Table K11)
Including education, rehabilitation, and resocialization of perpetrator
Criminal anthropology
see HV6035+
3960 Criminal sociology (Table K11)
For non-legal works, see HV6001+

Criminal law
Punishment -- Continued
Penalties and measures of rehabilitation and safety
For juveniles and young adults see KL-KWX6 4726+
For execution of sentence see KL-KWX6 4795+
3962 General (Table K11)
3964 Capital punishment (Table K11)
Imprisonment
Including maximum and minimum terms
3970 General (Table K11)
Prisons and jails see KL-KWX6 4824
3972 Short-term sentence (Table K11)
3974 Sentencing to probation (Punishment without imprisonment). Conditional sentencing (Table K11)
Including terms of probation, e.g. education and resocialization through labor
3978 Fines (Table K11)
3980 Reprimand (Table K11)
Measures entailing deprivation of liberty, A-Z
3982.C64 Commitment of addicts to institutions for withdrawal treatment (Table K12)
3982.C65 Commitment to medical, nursing, or socio-therapeutic institutions (Table K12)
3982.C66 Commitment to medical or psychiatric treatment (Table K12)
3982.C67 Confiscation and destruction of corpus delicti (Table K12)
Disenfranchisment see KL-KWX6 3982.L67
3982.D75 Driver's license revocation (Table K12)
3982.E96 Expulsion (Table K12)
3982.F68 Forfeiture (Table K12)
Infamy see KL-KWX6 3982.L67
3982.L67 Loss of civil rights. Infamy. Disfranchisement (Table K12)
3982.P76 Prohibition against practicing a profession (Table K12)
3982.P765 Property confiscation (Table K12)
3982.P77 Protective custody (Table K12)
Including dangerous or habitual criminals
3982.P78 Protective surveillance (Table K12)
Sentencing and determining the measure of punishment
4012 General (Table K11)
4016 Fixed and indeterminate sentence (Table K11)
Juvenile delinquents see KL-KWX6 4722
Aggravating and extenuating circumstances
Including principals and accessories
4020 General (Table K11)
4024 Recidivism (Table K11)

Criminal law
Punishment
Sentencing and determining the measure of punishment -- Continued
4026 Detention pending investigation (Table K11)
Causes barring prosecution or execution of sentence
4030 General (Table K11)
4032 Active repentance (Table K11)
Pardon and amnesty. Clemency
4034 General (Table K11)
Suspension of punishment see KL-KWX6 4828
Probation and parole see KL-KWX6 4830
4038 Limitation of actions (Table K11)
Criminal registers see KL-KWX6 4845
Criminal statistics see KL-KWX6 31+
Individual offenses
Including national (federal) statutory law and common law offenses in general, including comparative state (provincial) law
For criminal law of a particular state (province), see the jurisdiction
Offenses against the person
Including aggravating circumstances
4049 General (Table K11)
4049.5.A-Z Crimes against special classes of persons, A-Z
4049.5.W65 Women (Table K12)
Homicide
4050 General (Table K11)
Murder
4052 General (Table K11)
4053 Dowry killing (Table K11)
4054 Manslaughter (Table K11)
4056 Killing on request (Table K11)
4058 Euthanasia (Table K11)
4060 Suicide. Aiding and abetting suicide (Table K11)
4062 Parricide (Table K11)
4064 Infanticide (Table K11)
4065 Negligent homicide (Table K11)
4067 Desertion. Exposing persons to mortal danger (Table K11)
Illegal abortion
4070 General (Table K11)
4072 Justification of abortion. Legal abortion (Table K11)
For birth control and family planning see KL-KWX6 1482+
Crimes against physical inviolability

Criminal law
Individual offenses
Offenses against the person
Crimes against physical inviolability -- Continued
4074 General (Table K11)
4076 Battery (Table K11)
4077 Conjugal violence. Wife abuse. Husband abuse (Table K11)
4078 Communicating disease (Table K11)
4080 Failure to render assistance (Table K11)
4082 Abuse of defenseless persons or dependents. Abuse of older people (Table K11)
For child abuse see KL-KWX6 4190
4084 Consent. Justified assault (Table K11)
Including sports injuries
For medical treatment and operations see KL-KWX6 4096+
4090 Poisoning (Table K11)
4092 Dueling (Table K11)
4094 Brawling (Table K11)
Criminal aspects of surgical and other medical treatment
Including biomedical engineering and medical technology
4096 General (Table K11)
4100 Malpractice (Table K11)
Cf. KL-KWX6 1074.5 Civil liability
4102 Treatment without consent (Table K11)
Euthanasia see KL-KWX6 4058
4103 Genetic engineering (Table K11)
4108 Human reproductive technology (Table K11)
Including artificial insemination, fertilization in vitro, etc.
4110 Transplantation of organs, tissues, etc. (Table K11)
Including donation of organs, tissues, etc.
4112 Sterilization (Table K11)
Confidential communication see KL-KWX6 4696.A+
Psychopharmaca damages see KL-KWX6 4100
Crimes against personal freedom
4116 General (Table K11)
4118 False imprisonment (Table K11)
4120 Extortionate kidnapping (Table K11)
Abduction
Cf. KL-KWX6 610+ Parental kidnapping
4125 General (Table K11)
4127 Political abduction (Table K11)
4130 Abduction of a woman without her consent (Table K11)
4132 Abduction of a female minor (Table K11)
4134 Political accusation (Table K11)

Criminal law
Individual offenses
Offenses against the person
Crimes against personal freedom -- Continued
4136 Threats of a felonious injury (Table K11)
4138 Duress (Table K11)
Crimes against dignity and honor
Including juristic persons and families
4143 General (Table K11)
Honor see KL-KWX6 3823.H66
4145 Insult (Table K11)
4147 Defamation. Calumny (Table K11)
4152 Disparagement of memory of the dead (Table K11)
4156 Privileged comment (Table K11)
Including criticism of scientific, artistic, or professional accomplishments
For press law see KL-KWX6 1065+
Violation of personal privacy and secrets
4160 General (Table K11)
4164 Violation of confidential disclosures by professional persons (Table K11)
4166 Opening of letters (Table K11)
4168 Eavesdropping. Wiretapping (Table K11)
Offenses against religious tranquility and the peace of the dead
4170 General works (Table K11)
4172 Blasphemy (Table K11)
Offenses against marriage, family, and family status
4180 General (Table K11)
4182 Incest (Table K11)
4184 Adultery (Table K11)
4186 Bigamy (Table K11)
(4188) Parental kidnapping
see KL-KWX6 610
4190 Abandonment, neglect, or abuse of a child (Table K11)
4192 Breach of duty of support (Table K11)
4194 Breach of duty of assistance to a pregnant woman (Table K11)
Abortion see KL-KWX6 4070+
4196 Falsification of civil status (Table K11)
Offenses against sexual integrity
4200 General (Table K11)
4202 Rape (Table K11)
Child molesting see KL-KWX6 4190
4216 Sodomy. Homosexual acts (Table K11)
4218 Bestiality (Table K11)

KL-KWX6-KL-KWX7

Criminal law
Individual offenses
Offenses against sexual integrity -- Continued
4220 Obscenity (Table K11)
Including production, exhibition, performance, advertising, etc.
Prostitution. Procuring
4224 General works (Table K11)
4225 Pandering and pimping. White slave traffic (Table K11)
Offenses against private and public property
Offenses against private and public property
Including works on white collar crime and offenses against the economic order in general
4230 General (Table K11)
Larceny and embezzlement
4234 General (Table K11)
4236 Burglary (Table K11)
4238 Armed theft and theft by gangs (Table K11)
4242 Domestic and family theft (Table K11)
4250 Embezzlement (Table K11)
4254 Robbery and rapacious theft (Table K11)
4256 Destruction of property and conversion (Table K11)
Fraud
4258 General (Table K11)
Fraudulent bankruptcy see KL-KWX6 4276
4264 Extortion (Table K11)
4266 Breach of trust (Table K11)
4268 Usury (Table K11)
4276 Defeating rights of creditors. Fraudulent bankruptcy (Table K11)
4280 Game and fish poaching (Table K11)
4282 Aiding criminals in securing benefits. Receiving stolen goods (Table K11)
Offenses against the national economy
4286 General (Table K11)
4290 Violation of price regulations (Table K11)
Including price fixing, hoarding, discrimination, overselling and underselling prices established by government etc.
4292 Foreign exchange violations (Table K11)
4294 Economic and industrial secrets. Unauthorized possession or disclosure (Table K11)
Cf. KL-KWX6 1197.E86 Industrial espionage
4298 False statements concerning national planning (Table K11)
Counterfeiting money and stamps see KL-KWX6 4346
Offenses against public property see KL-KWX6 4230+; KL-KWX6 4230+

Criminal law
Individual offenses
Offenses against private and public property
4300.A-Z Other, A-Z
Subarrange each by Table K12
Money laundering see KL-KWX6 902.5.R43
Offenses against public order and convenience
Including aggravating circumstances
4305 General (Table K11)
4307 Inciting insubordination (Table K11)
4309 Rowdyism. Vandalism (Table K11)
4310 Inciting crime (Table K11)
4316 Parasitism (Table K11)
4320 Demonstrations and failure to disperse (Table K11)
4322 Inciting acts against minorities (Table K11)
Threatening the community. Terrorist activities see KL-KWX6 4352+
4324 Misuse of titles, uniforms, and insignia (Table K11)
Crimes against security of legal and monetary transactions and documents
4330 General (Table K11)
4332 Evidence (Table K11)
4334 Forgery of documents and of mechanical records (Table K11)
Including forgery of electronic data bases
4340 Physical and identifying marks (Table K11)
4346 Counterfeiting money and stamps (Table K11)
Including postage stamps, checks, bills of exchange, etc.
Customs crimes see KL-KWX6 3315+
Tax evasion see KL-KWX6 3319
4351.A-Z Other, A-Z
4351.D57 Displacing boundaries (Table K12)
4351.F34 False certification (Table K12)
Crimes involving danger to the community. Crimes against the environment. Terrorism
4352 General (Table K11)
4354 Arson (Table K11)
4356 Causing explosion (Table K11)
Including explosives and nuclear energy
4358 Misuse of ionizing radiation (Table K11)
4360 Releasing natural forces (Table K11)
Including flood, avalanche, rockfall, etc.
4362 Dangerous use of poisonous substances (Table K11)
4364 Poisoning wells or soil (Table K11)
4366 Poisoning food, medicine, etc. (Table K11)

Criminal law
Individual offenses
Offenses against public order and convenience
Crimes involving danger to the community. Crimes against the environment. Terrorism -- Continued
4368 Spreading communicable diseases, morbific agents, or parasites. Biological terrorism (Table K11)
4370 Damaging water and power installations (Table K11)
4372 Impairing industrial safety appliances (Table K11)
4374 Sabotage of essential services, utilities, warning systems, etc. (Table K11)
4376 Causing danger in construction (Table K11)
Including collapse, faulty gas or electric installation, etc.
4378 Human trafficking. Human smuggling (Table K11)
Crimes affecting traffic. Dangerous interference with rail, ship, or aircraft
Including unsafe operation of a rail vehicle, ship, or aircraft
4380 General (Table K11)
Dangerous interference with street traffic
For minor traffic violations resulting in fines see KL-KWX6 1041+
4384 General (Table K11)
4386 Driving while intoxicated (Table K11)
4388 Duress. Constraint (Table K11)
4390 Leaving the scene of an accident. Hit-and-run driving (Table K11)
4392 Predatory assault on motorists (Table K11)
4396 Crimes aboard aircraft. Air piracy (Table K11)
4398 Riots (Table K11)
Crimes against public health
4400 General (Table K11)
4402 Intoxication (Table K11)
4404 Illicit use of, possession of, and traffic in narcotics (Table K11)
Communicating venereal diseases see KL-KWX6 4078
4406 Gambling (Table K11)
Including illegal operation of a lottery or games of chance, and participation
4407 Vagrancy. Begging (Table K11)
Offenses against the government. Political offenses. Offenses against the people
4410 General (Table K11)
High treason and treason
4415 General (Table K11)

Criminal law
Individual offenses
Offenses against the government. Political offenses.
Offenses against the peace
High treason and treason -- Continued
4417 High treason against the state (Table K11)
Including national and state (republic, etc.), and including preparation of treasonable acts
4424 Treason against the constitution (Table K11)
4426 Assault on the head of state (Table K11)
4428 Inciting treason (Table K11)
4430 Preparation of a despotism (Table K11)
4432 Sabotage endangering the state (Table K11)
4434 Undermining the state apparatus (Table K11)
4438 Lese majesty (Table K11)
4440 Disparagement of the state and its symbols. Disparaging constitutional organs (Table K11)
4442 Treasonable espionage (Table K11)
For publication of official secrets by the press see KL-KWX6 1065.5
4444 Subversive activities (Table K11)
4446 Intelligence activities (Table K11)
4448 Propaganda endangering the state (Table K11)
4455 Treasonable endangering of the peace or of international relations (Table K11)
Including propaganda, planning, preparation, or participation in an aggressive war
Crimes in connection with election and voting
4458 General (Table K11)
4460 Bribery. Corrupt practices (Table K11)
4464 Deceiving voters (Table K11)
4466 Falsifying votes and voting results (Table K11)
4468 Obstructing voting (Table K11)
Crimes against national defense
4470 General (Table K11)
4473 Sabotaging and depicting means of defense (Table K11)
Opposition to power of the state
4476 General (Table K11)
4478 Constraining official action or inaction (Table K11)
4480 Prison escape. Mutiny. Freeing prisoners (Table K11)
4482.A-Z Other forms of opposition, A-Z
Subarrange each by Table K12
Endangering the administration of justice. Obstruction of justice
4484 General (Table K11)

Criminal law
Individual offenses
Offenses against the government. Political offenses.
Offenses against the peace
Endangering the administration of justice. Obstruction of justice -- Continued
4490 False testimony
Including false unsworn testimony and perjury
4496 False accusation (Table K11)
4498 Bringing false complaint (Table K11)
4500 Thwarting criminal justice (Table K11)
4502 Failure to report felony. Misprision (Table K11)
4504 Coercion of testimony (Table K11)
4506 Intentional misconstruction by law officers (Table K11)
4507 Prosecuting innocent persons (Table K11)
Including execution
4507.5 Chicanery and abuse of legal process (Table K11)
4508 Repressing conflicting interests. Prevarication (Table K11)
4510 Contempt of court (Table K11)
For contempt or court by the press see KL-KWX6 1065.7.C66
Crimes against the civil service
4514 General (Table K11)
4516 Bribery. Corrupt practices (Table K11)
4526 Violating official secrecy. Disclosure (Table K11)
Crimes against humanity
4538 General (Table K11)
4540 Genocide (Table K11)
4543 Crimes against foreign states, supranational institutions, or international institutions (Table K11)
4545 War crimes (Table K11)
Offenses commited through the mail
4548 General (Table K11)
Obscenity see KL-KWX6 4220
Threats, extortion, and blackmail see KL-KWX6 4264
Labor law criminal provisions see KL-KWX6 1408
Social insurance criminal provisions see KL-KWX6 1455
Press law criminal provisions see KL-KWX6 1065.3+
Tax and customs crimes see KL-KWX6 3315+
Military criminal law see KL-KWX6 3380+

Criminal procedure
For works on both criminal and civil procedure, including codes of both criminal and civil procedure see KL-KWX6 3520+
For works on both criminal law and criminal procedure, including codes of both criminal law and criminal procedure see KL-KWX6 3790+
Criticism and reform see KL-KWX6 3790
4601-4610 General (Table K9c)
4616 Sociology of criminal procedure (Table K11)
Including scandals
Administration of criminal justice see KL-KWX6 3409+
Court organization see KL-KWX6 3441+
Procedural principles
4619 General (Table K11)
4620 Due process of law (Table K11)
4622 Uniformity of law application. Stare decisis (Table K11)
Prohibition of abuse of legal process. Chicanery see KL-KWX6 3574.5
4624 Accusation principle (Table K11)
4626 Publicity and oral procedure (Table K11)
4628 Prejudicial actions (Table K11)
Including all branches of the law
4630.A-Z Parties to action, A-Z
4630.A25 Accused. Person charged. Defendant (Table K12)
Defendant see KL-KWX6 4630.A25
4630.D43 Defense attorney. Public defender (Table K12)
Person charged see KL-KWX6 4630.A25
Public defender see KL-KWX6 4630.D43
4630.S73 State prosecutor (Table K12)
Class here works on the legal status of the prosecutor in criminal procedure
For general works on the office of the public prosecutor see KL-KWX6 3502+
4630.S93 Suspect (Table K12)
4630.V52 Victim (Table K12)
Pretrial procedures
4632 General (Table K11)
4634 Penal report. Charges brought against a person (Table K11)
Investigation
4636 General (Table K11)
Techniques of criminal investigation see HV8073+
4638 Examination of the accused (Table K11)
Cf. KL-KWX6 4679+ Admissibility of evidence
4640 Preliminary judicial investigation (Table K11)

Criminal procedure
Pretrial procedures -- Continued
4642 Public charges by prosecutor (Table K11)
4646 Summonses, service of process, and subpoena. Wanted notice (Table K11)
4648 Time periods. Deadlines (Table K11)
Compulsory measures against the accused. Securing of evidence
4650 General (Table K11)
4652 Search and seizure (Table K11)
Including search of persons, buildings, institution's records, etc.
4654 Arrest. Provisional apprehension (Table K11)
Detention pending investigation
Cf. KL-KWX6 4798+ Execution of sentence
4657 General (Table K11)
4659 Bail (Table K11)
4660 Extradition (Table K11)
Procedure at first instance
4664 General (Table K11)
4666 Jurisdiction (Table K11)
Including competence in subject matter and venue
4668 Action. Complaint (Table K11)
4670 Exclusion and challenge of court members (Table K11)
Time periods and deadlines see KL-KWX6 4648
Limitation of action see KL-KWX6 4038
Trial
4673 General (Table K11)
Evidence. Burden of proof
4675 General (Table K11)
4677 Presumption of innocence (Table K11)
Admissibility of evidence
4679 General (Table K11)
4681 Confession. Self-incrimination. Entrapment (Table K11)
4683 Informers. Official secrets (Table K11)
4685 Narcoanalysis, lie detectors, etc. (Table K11)
4687 Physical examination (Table K11)
Including blood tests, urine tests, etc.
For forensic medicine, see RA1001+
4689 Electronic listening and recording devices (Table K11)
Including wiretapping
4690 Previous testimony, police records, etc. (Table K11)
Witnesses
4692 General (Table K11)
4696.A-Z Privileged witnesses (confidential communication), A-Z
Subarrange each by Table K12

Criminal procedure
Procedure at first instance
Trial
Evidence
Witnesses
4698.A-Z Other witnesses, A-Z
Subarrange each by Table K12
4700 Expert testimony (Table K11)
For forensic medicine, chemistry, psychology, psychiatry, toxicology, etc. see RA1001+
4702 Testimony of accused (Table K11)
4704 Documentary evidence (Table K11)
4705 Circumstantial evidence (Table K11)
4706 Alibi (Table K11)
4709.A-Z Other, A-Z
Subarrange each by Table K12
4710 Jury and jurors (Table K11)
Including instructions to jury
Particular proceedings
4711 General (Table K11)
4713 Summary proceedings (Table K11)
4715 Proceedings against absentee and fugitives (Table K11)
4717 Recourse against decisions of grievance boards (Table K11)
Procedure for juvenile delinquency
4720 General (Table K11)
4722 The juvenile delinquent. The young adult perpetrator (Table K11)
4724 Juvenile crime (Table K11)
Criminal liability and guilt see KL-KWX6 3886+
Punishment. Correctional or disciplinary measures
Including measures of rehabilitation and safety
4726 General (Table K11)
4728 Custodial education. Detention homes. Reformatories (Table K11)
4734 Punishment without imprisonment (Table K11)
Execution of sentence see KL-KWX6 4795+
Judicial decisions
4736 General (Table K11)
Judgment
4738 General (Table K11)
Sentencing and determination of punishment see KL-KWX6 4012+
4740 Judicial discretion (Table K11)
Including opportunity and equity
4744 Acquittal (Table K11)

Criminal procedure
Procedure at first instance
Trial
Judicial decisions -- Continued
4746 Conviction (Table K11)
Including measures of rehabilitation and safety
4750 Dismissal. Decision ab instantia (Table K11)
Probation see KL-KWX6 4830
4752 Void judgments (Table K11)
4753 Correction or withdrawal of faulty decisions (errors) (Table K11)
Res judicata
4754 General (Table K11)
Waiver of appeal see KL-KWX6 4788
4760 Court records. Minutes of evidence (Table K11)
Including clerks, translators, and correction of records
4762 Participation of injured party in criminal procedure. Private charge
Including public interest
Special procedures
4768 Procedure before justice of the peace (Table K11)
Commitment of insane criminals see KL-KWX6 3982.A+
Procedure in confiscation of corpus delicti see KL-KWX6 3982.C67
Other procedures
see the subject, e.g., KL-KWX6 3315+ Tax and customs criminal procedures; KL-KWX6 3380+ Military criminal procedure; etc.
Remedies
4770 General (Table K11)
4780 Appellate procedure. Cassation
4788 Waiver of appeal (Table K11)
4790 Post-conviction remedies (Table K11)
4792 Reopening a case. New trial (Table K11)
For procedure before the constitutional court see KL-KWX6 2390
Execution of sentence
Including execution of sentence of juvenile courts
4795 General (Table K11)
Law reform. Criticism see KL-KWX6 3790
Imprisonment
Including regulations of detention pending investigation and short-term sentences
4798 General (Table K11)

Criminal procedure
Execution of sentence
Imprisonment -- Continued
4800 Administration of penal or correctional institutions (Table K11)
Including discipline, hygiene, etc.
The prisoner
4810 General (Table K11)
4812.A-Z Particular, A-Z
Dangerous criminals see KL-KWX6 3982.P77
4812.E38 Education of prisoners. Education through labor (Table K12)
Insane criminals see KL-KWX6 3982.P77
4812.J88 Juvenile prisoners (Table K12)
4812.P64 Political prisoners (Table K12)
4820 Labor and industries in correctional institutions (Table K11)
Including wages
Rehabilitation and resocialization see KL-KWX6 3956
4824 Penal or correctional institutions (Table K11)
Including prisons, jails, penal colonies, reformatories, juvenile detention homes, etc.
Pardon, amnesty, and clemency see KL-KWX6 4034+
4828 Suspension of punishment (Table K11)
4830 Probation. Parole (Table K11)
Including conditions and probation and parole for juvenile delinquents
4845 Criminal registers (Table K11)
4847 Judicial error and compensation (Table K11)
Extradition see KL-KWX6 4660
4850 Costs (Table K11)
Victimology
4855 General (Table K11)
4857 Children and sexual crimes (Table K11)
Compensation to victims of crimes see KL-KWX6 950
Criminology and penology
see HV6001+

Bibliography

For bibliography of special topics, see the topic

For manuals on legal bibliography, legal research and the use of law books see KL-KWX7 4.2+

1 General bibliography

1.2 Indexes to periodical literature, society publications, and collections

For indexes to a particular publication, see the publication

1.2 Indexes to periodical literature, society publications, and collections

For indexes to a particular publication, see the publication

Indexes to Festschriften see KL-KWX7 6.7

<1.3> Periodicals

For periodicals consisting predominantly of legal articles, regardless of subject matter and jurisdiction, see K1+

For periodicals consisting primarily of informative material (newsletters, bulletins, etc.) relating to a special subject, see the subject and form division tables for periodicals

For law reports, official bulletins or circulars intended chiefly for the publication of laws and regulations, see appropriate entries in the text or form division tables

1.4 Monographic series

Official gazettes

1.5 General

State or city gazettes

see the issuing state or city

Departmental gazettes

see the issuing department or agency

1.6 Indexes (General)

Legislative documents

see class J

1.7 Other materials relating to legislative history

Including recommended legislation; legislation passed and vetoed

Legislation

For statutes, statutory orders, regulations, etc. on a particular subject, see the subject

1.8 Indexes and tables

Including indexes to statutes of several states

For indexes to a particular publication, see the publication

For indexes limited to one state, see the state

Statutes

Including statutory orders and regulations; comparative state legislation

Collections and compilations

Including official and private editions

1.85 Serials

Legislation
Statutes
Collections and compilations -- Continued
1.9 Monographs. By date
Including unannotated and annotated editions
Administrative and executive publications
Including statutory orders and regulations, orders in council, proclamations, etc.
For regulations on a particular subject, see the subject
1.95 Serials
2 Monographs. By date
Presidential proclamations, etc.
see class J
Treaties
For treaties on international public law, see class KZ
For treaties on international uniform law not limited to a region, see class K
For treaties on international uniform law of a particular region, see the region
National (Federal) courts
Law reports and related materials
Including national (federal) and regional reports
For reports of an individual state or territory, including reports of the older courts, see the appropriate jurisdiction
For reports relating to a particular subject, and for reports of courts of limited jurisdiction other than those listed below, see the appropriate subject
National (Federal) courts
2.2 Highest courts of appeal. Supreme courts. Courts of Cassation (Table K18)
Lower courts
2.23 Various courts (Table K18)
Including highest court and lower courts, or national (federal) courts of two or more states combined; or regional (provincial) courts
Intermediate appellate courts. Circuit courts of appeal
2.24 Collective (Table K18)
2.25.A-Z Particular courts, A-Z
(2.27) Digests and indexes to federal decisions
see KL-KWX7 2.2 ; KL-KWX7 2.23 ; etc.
State courts
For reports of an individual state, see the state
2.3 Reports covering all states or selected states (Table K18)
2.4 Decisions of national (federal) administrative agencies
For decisions of particular agencies, see the subject
2.5 Encyclopedias

2.6 Dictionaries. Words and phrases
For bilingual and multilingual dictionaries, see K52.A+
For dictionaries on a particular subject, see the subject
2.7 Maxims. Quotations
2.8 Form books (General)
Class here general works
For form books on a particular subject, see the subject
Judicial statistics
3 General
3.2 Criminal statistics
3.23.A-Z Other. By subject, A-Z
3.23.D65 Domestic relations. Family law
Family law see KL-KWX7 3.23.D65
Directories
3.3 National and regional
3.33.A-Z By specialization, A-Z
Trials
Class all trials, including those occurring in national, state (provincial, etc.), or local courts, in the numbers provided for trials at the national level
3.4 General collections
Criminal trials and judicial investigations
For military trials see KL-KWX7 324+
Collections. Compilations
3.5 General
3.6.A-Z Particular offenses, A-Z
3.6.A78 Arson
3.6.F73 Fraud
3.6.P64 Political crimes
War crimes see KL-KWX7 3.9
3.7.A-Z Individual trials. By defendant or best known (popular) name, A-Z
Including records, briefs, commentaries, and stories on a particular trial
3.9 War crime trials
Trials by international military tribunals see class KZ
4.A-Z Other trials. By defendant or best known (popular) name, A-Z
Legal research. Legal bibliography
Including methods of bibliographic research and how to find the law
4.2 General
Electronic data processing. Information retrieval
4.3 General works
4.4.A-Z By subject, A-Z
Litigation see KL-KWX7 4.4.P76
4.4.P76 Procedure. Litigation

Legal research. Legal bibliography -- Continued
4.5 Systems of citation. Legal abbreviations
4.6 Legal composition and draftsmanship. Legal drafting. Officers. Parliamentary counsels
Legal education
5 General works
Law schools
5.3 General works
5.4.A-Z Particular law schools. By name, A-Z
Including constitution and bylaws, statutes and regulations, degrees, and general works (history)
5.42 Post-law school education
The legal profession
5.43 General works
Practice of law
5.44 General works
Attorneys
5.45 General works
5.455 Admission to the bar. Bar examinations
5.46 Attorney and client
For violation of confidential disclosures see KL-KWX7 416.4
5.48 Legal ethics and etiquette. Courts of honor. Disbarment
Economics of law practice
5.484 General works
5.485 Fees (Table K11)
5.49 Legal consultants. Procurators
5.492 Legal aid. Legal services to the poor. People's lawyer. Community legal services. Public solicitors
5.5 Bar associations. Law societies. Law institutes
Class here works on and journals by, individual societies and their activities, e.g. annual reports, proceedings, incorporation statutes, bylaws, handbooks, and works (history) about the society
Including courts of honor and disbarment
For publications of associations on special subjects, see the subject
For journals devoted to legal subjects, either wholly or in part, see K1+
For membership directories see KL-KWX7 3.33.A+
5.52 Notaries. Notarial practice and procedure
Class here works on notaries of several jurisdictions
For notaries (several or individual) of an individual state, administrative district, or municipality, see the state, district, or municipality
Public registers. Registration
5.53 General works

Public registers. Registration -- Continued
Civil registry see KL-KWX7 52.6
5.6 Property registration. Registration of pledges
5.8 Congresses. Conferences
5.9.A-Z Academies. Institutes. By name, A-Z
6.3 General works. Treatises
6.4 Compends, outlines, examination aids, etc.
Forms, graphic materials, blanks, atlases see KL-KWX7 2.8
6.5 Popular works. Civics
6.7 Addresses, essays, lectures
Including single essays, collected essays of several authors, festschriften, and indexes to festschriften
7.3.A-Z Manuals and other works for particular groups of users. By user, A-Z
7.3.A34 Accountants. Auditors
7.3.A77 Artists
Auditors see KL-KWX7 7.3.A34
7.3.A85 Authors
7.3.B87 Businesspeople. Foreign investors
7.3.E53 Engineers
7.3.F37 Farmers
Foreign investors see KL-KWX7 7.3.B87
7.3.M87 Musicians
7.3.S63 Social workers
Semantics and language see KL-KWX7 9.2
Legal symbolism see KL-KWX7 9.4+
Legal anecdotes, wit and humor
see K184.4
Law and lawyers in literature
see classes PB-PH
Law and art
see K487.C8
Law and history
see K487.C8
7.8.A-Z Works on diverse aspects of a particular subject and falling within several branches of the law. By subject, A-Z
7.8.C65 Computers
7.8.H67 Horses
Legal advertising see KL-KWX7 7.8.N68
7.8.N68 Notice. Legal advertising
7.8.P78 Public interest law
7.8.P8 Public relations
History of law
8.5 Bibliography
8.52 Periodicals
8.6 Encyclopedias

History of law -- Continued
Auxiliary sciences
8.7 General works
9 Paleography
9.2 Linguistics. Semantics
Archaeology. Folklife studies. Symbolism
9.4 General works
9.6.A-Z Special topics, A-Z
9.6.S76 Stool, Ancestral
9.8 Inscriptions
10 Heraldry. Seals. Flags. Insignia. Armory
Law and lawyers in literature
see classes PB-PH
Biography of lawyers
Class biography of lawyers from specific states in the numbers for biography at the national level.
Collective
10.5 General
10.7 Collections of portraits
11.A-Z Individual, A-Z
Subarrange each by Table KL-KWX11
12 General works. Treatises
By period
<12.2> Ancient and early, including ancient people in the region
see KL, KQ, or particular jurisdiction, as specified (e.g. India)
Medieval and early modern (to second half of the 19th century)
Including precolonial and early colonial periods
12.3 General works
Sources
For sources of a territory or town, see the appropriate territory or town
12.5 Studies on sources
Including history and methodology, e.g. epigraphy, papyrology, etc.
For philological studies, see classes P, PJ, PK, and PL
12.9 Collections. Compilations. Selections
Class here comprehensive collections of legal sources in various native (vernacular) scripts
Individual sources or groups of sources
National (imperial) laws and legislation
Including constitutional laws
14 Collections. Compilations
14.2 Individual. By date
Subarrange each by Table K20b

History of law
By period
Medieval and early modern (to second half of the 19th century)
Sources
Individual sources or groups of sources -- Continued
Royal (imperial) privileges
Including privileges for particular classes, groups, communities, courts of justice, etc.
14.4 Collections. Compilations
14.6 Individual. By date
Subarrange each by Table K20b
Royal (imperial) mandates. Decrees, orders, etc. of princes and rulers
14.8 Collections. Compilations
15 Individual. By date
Subarrange each by Table K20b
Treaties
Treaties on international public law
see KZ
Treaties on international uniform law
see K524+ KJC38+ KMC, KNC, KQC, and KVC
Court decisions. Cases. Advisory opinions. Reports. Digests
16 Several courts
16.4.A-Z Particular courts. By place, A-Z
Trials
Criminal trials and judicial investigations
Collections. Compilations
17 General
17.2.A-Z Particular offenses, A-Z
17.2.W58 Witchcraft
17.4.A-Z Individual trials. By defendant, or best known (popular) name, A-Z
Including records, briefs, commentaries, and stories on a particular trial
Other trials
17.6 Collections. Compilations
17.8.A-Z Individual trials. By plaintiff, defendant, or best known (popular) name, A-Z
18 Contemporary legal literature
18.2 Documents. Public and private records
Class here general collections
For collections or individual documents on a topic, see the topic
The State and its constitution

History of law
By period
Medieval and early modern (to second half of the 19th century)
The State and its constitution -- Continued
20.2 General (Table K22)
Classes. Castes, etc.
20.4 General works
20.5.A-Z Special topics, A-Z
20.5.B57 Birth rights
20.5.D94 Dynastic rules
20.5.E62 Equality of birth
Feudal capacity see KL-KWX7 22.8
20.5.O87 Outlawry. Outcasts
20.9 Territory (Table K22)
21.2 Foreign relations (Table K22)
Feudal law
21.3 General (Table K22)
Sources
21.4 Collections. Compilations
22.2<date> Individual sources
Arrange chronologically by appending the date of the source to this number and deleting any trailing zeros. Subarrange each by Table K20b
Feudal institutes
22.3 Feudal lords and vassalage (Table K22)
Fief
22.4 General (Table K22)
22.6.A-Z Special topics, A-Z
22.6.C65 Commendation. Hommage
22.6.L3 Land
22.6.V5 Villages. Towns
22.8 Feudal capacity (Table K22)
23 Feudal succession (Table K22)
Rural (peasant) land tenure. Peasantry
23.2 General (Table K22)
23.8 Leasehold for years and inheritance (Table K22)
24.2 Succession to rural holdings (Table K22)
24.6 Kings. Princes and rulers. Chiefs (Table K22)
25 The court. Court officials and councils (Table K22)
25.4 Legislature. Diet (Table K22)
25.6 Military organization (Table K22)

History of law
By period
Medieval and early modern (to second half of the 19th century) -- Continued
Finance
Class here works on topics not represented elsewhere in the schedule
For works on the history of particular subjects, see the subject
25.8 General (Table K22)
26 Crown goods and dynastic house goods (Table K22)
26.8.A-Z Special topics, A-Z
29 Judiciary. Court organization
Class here comprehensive works on the development of the judiciary, and on a defunct court or court system
For the history of a particular court system or court, see KL-KWX7 332+ or the jurisdiction
For reports see KL-KWX7 2.2+
<35> Indigenous peoples Ethnic groups
For works on the law of indigenous peoples regardless of whether identified with one or more countries in the region, see KM, KN, KQ, or as indicated
Philosophy, jurisprudence, and theory of law
Class here works on doctrines peculiar to legal institutions of a country
For works on the philosophy of law in general, see K201+
For works on the philosophy of a particular branch of the law (e.g., constitutional law or criminal law), see the branch
44 General works
The concept of law
Including the definition of law
44.2 General works
44.3 The object of law. Law and justice
44.4 Ethics. Morality of law. Public policy
44.5 Law and the state. Legal order. Respect for law
44.6 Rights and duties. Sanctions
Sources of law
44.9 General works
44.93 Customs and observance. Indigenous law
Judge-made law see KL-KWX7 45
45 Methodology. Interpretation and construction
Including judge-made law
Schools of legal theory
46.5 Sociological jurisprudence

46.7 Influence of other legal systems on the law. Superimposition of foreign rule on the customary (indigenous) law
Including reception of traditional, customary and religious law, and multiplicity of law
46.8 Law reform and policies. Criticism
Including reform of administration of justice
47.A-Z Concepts applying to several branches of the law, A-Z
47.E88 Estoppel
47.G65 Good faith. Reliance
47.L55 Limitation of actions
Cf. KL-KWX7 357.5 Civil procedure
47.L63 Locus poenitentiae
47.5 Intertemporal law. Retroactive law
47.8 Regional divisions. Subregions
Class here general works on the law or the legal systems in force within a single subregion of the country
For works on a particular subject, see the subject
47.9 Private law (Table K11)
Class here works on all aspects of private and civil law in force within a country with mixed legal systems
Conflict of laws
For conflict of laws between the United States and a particular jurisdiction, see KF416
For works on conflict rules of branches other than private law and law of procedure (e.g. tax law, criminal law, etc.), see the subject
48 General (Table K11)
48.2 Plurality of laws conflict. Two or more different legal systems in force in the same country (Table K11)
Class here works on conflict of laws in a multicultural country with two or more coexisting legal systems (e.g., secular and religious law, common law, indigenous (tribal, customary), and religious law, etc.)
Choice of law
Including indigenous (tribal, customary) law and civil law
48.3 General (Table K11)
48.32 Connecting factors. Points of contact. Nationality and domicile (Table K11)
48.6.A-Z Particular branches and subjects of the law, A-Z
48.6.A55 Aliens (Table K12)
48.6.A83 Arbitration (Table K12)
Class here works on arbitration courts, commissions, and proceedings
For comparative works on arbitration, see the region
48.6.C38 Caste. Personal status (Table K12)
Divorce see KL-KWX7 48.6.M37

Conflict of laws
Particular branches and subjects of the law, A-Z -- Continued
48.6.M37 Marriage. Matrimonial actions. Matrimonial property (Table K12)
Matrimonial actions see KL-KWX7 48.6.M37
Matrimonial property see KL-KWX7 48.6.M37
Personal status see KL-KWX7 48.6.C38
48.6.S8 Statelessness (Table K12)
Retroactive law. Intertemporal law see KL-KWX7 47.5
49 Equity (Table K11)
Persons
51 General (Table K11)
Natural persons
51.2 General (Table K11)
Civil status
51.3 General (Table K11)
51.5 Absence. Missing persons. Presumption of death (Table K11)
Capacity and disability
51.8 General (Table K11)
51.9 Women (Table K11)
Class here works on legal status under all aspects of law (e.g. religious, customary, private, and public)
For married women see KL-KWX7 55.7
52 Minors. Infants (Table K11)
Including liability
Persons of unsound mind. Mentally ill persons. People with mental disabilities
For guardianship and curatorship see KL-KWX7 61
For care of the mentally ill see KL-KWX7 157.7
52.3 General (Table K11)
52.5.A-Z Particular diseases or impairments, A-Z
Subarrange each by Table K12
52.55.A-Z Other, A-Z
Aborigines see KL-KWX7 52.55.I64
52.55.A54 Aliens (Table K12)
Cf. KL-KWX7 215.5.A43 Control of individuals
52.55.E93 Ex-convicts (Table K12)
52.55.I64 Indigenous people. Aborigines (Table K12)
52.55.P48 Physical disabilities, People with (Table K12)
52.55.U53 Unborn children. Nasciturus (Table K12)
52.6 Recording and registration. Civil registry. Registers of births, marriages, and deaths. Birth and death certificates. Census. Vital statistics
Juristic persons, corporate persons, associations, etc. see KL-KWX7 97.85+

Persons -- Continued
Domestic relations. Family law. Multiplicity of laws
Including one or more religious legal systems, customary law and common law
54 General (Table K11)
54.2 Domestic relations courts and procedure (Table K11)
Including civil courts, Rabbinical courts, Islamic (Shariah) courts, etc.
54.3 Domicile with regard to domestic relations (Table K11)
Marriage. Husband and wife
54.4 General (Table K11)
54.5.A-Z Marriage impediments, A-Z
54.5.C37 Caste (Table K12)
54.5.W54 Widowhood (Table K12)
54.8 Certificates. Premarital examinations (Table K11)
55 Performance of marriage. Civil marriage and religious ceremonies (Table K11)
55.2 Intermarriage (Table K11)
Including interracial, interethnic, and interfaith marriage
55.3 Multiple marriages. Polygamy. Polyandry (Table K11)
55.4 Head of family (Table K11)
Rights and duties of husband and wife
55.5 General (Table K11)
55.6 Family name (Table K11)
55.7 Legal status of married women (Table K11)
Marital property relationships
56 General (Table K11)
56.2 Separation of property (Table K11)
56.4 Community property (Table K11)
56.6 Marriage settlements. Antenuptial contracts (Table K11)
57.A-Z Other, A-Z
57.D68 Dowry (Table K12)
Cf. KL-KWX7 404.3 Dowry killing
57.2 Quasi-matrimonial relationships (Table K11)
Including common law marriages (unmarried cohabitation), concubinage, etc., and including property relations of such marriages
Matrimonial actions. Dissolution of marriage
For courts and procedures see KL-KWX7 369
57.3 General (Table K11)
57.4 Void and voidable marriages. Annulment (Table K11)
Including non-marriages
57.6 Divorce (Table K11)
58 Separation (Table K11)

Persons
Domestic relations. Family law. Multiplicity of laws
Marriage. Husband and wife
Matrimonial actions. Dissolution of marriage -- Continued
58.2 Settlement of claims from defective or divorced marriages (Table K11)
Including alimony and dowry
For dowry killing see KL-KWX7 404.3
Consanguinity and affinity. Kinship
Including works on caste systems
58.4 General (Table K11)
58.6 Support (Table K11)
Parent and child
58.8 General (Table K11)
59 Legitimacy (Table K11)
59.4 Illegitimacy (Table K11)
59.8 Affiliation (patrilineal and matrilineal) (Table K11)
60 Adoption (Table K11)
Parental rights and duties. Property of minors. Custody. Access to children
Including parental kidnapping
For procedure see KL-KWX7 369.3
60.2 General (Table K11)
60.4 Support. Desertion and non-support (Table K11)
61 Guardianship (Table K11)
Including procedure and including also guardianship over minors and adults
62 Curatorship (Table K11)
Including procedure
Agency. Legal representation see KL-KWX7 97.75
Property
63 General (Table K11)
64 Right of property (Table K11)
Possession and ownership
64.5 General (Table K11)
64.6 Acquisition and loss (Table K11)
Particular kinds of property
64.7 General (Table K11)
Matrimonial property see KL-KWX7 56+
Public property. Government property see KL-KWX7 250+
65 Socialist property (Table K11)
Real property. Land law
66 General (Table K11)
66.2 Alien ownership (Table K11)
Public policy. Customary land policy legislation see KL-KWX7 253+

| | |
|---|---|
| | Property |
| | Real property. Land law -- Continued |
| | Land tenure |
| 66.3 | General (Table K11) |
| 66.4 | Feudal tenure |
| | Estates and interests. Ownership |
| 67 | General (Table K11) |
| | Particular estates and interests (legal or equitable) |
| 67.2 | General (Table K11) |
| | Freehold estates |
| 67.3 | General (Table K11) |
| 67.6 | Fee tail. Entailed interests (Table K11) |
| 68 | Estates less than freehold (Table K11) |
| 68.2 | Equitable ownership. Equitable conversion (Table K11) |
| 68.3 | Uses and trusts. Statute of uses (Table K11) |
| 68.4 | Future estates and interests (Table K11)<br>Including works on future interests in both real and personal property |
| 68.7 | Estates and interests arising from marriage (Table K11) |
| | Tenancy. Leaseholds. Landlord and tenant |
| 68.8 | General (Table K11) |
| 68.9 | Rent (Table K11)<br>Including rent control |
| 68.92.A-Z | Particular kinds of tenancy and leaseholds, A-Z |
| | Building leases see KL-KWX7 68.92.G75 |
| 68.92.C65 | Commercial leases (Table K12) |
| 68.92.G75 | Ground leases. Building leases (Table K12) |
| | Oil and gas leases see KL-KWX7 102.3 |
| | Rights and interests incident to ownership and possession. Interests less than estates |
| 69 | General (Table K11) |
| 69.2 | Boundaries. Fences (Table K11) |
| 69.3 | Riparian rights. Water rights of individuals (Table K11)<br>For fishing rights see KL-KWX7 101.4+ |
| 69.4 | Grazing rights. Hunting rights (Table K11) |
| 69.5 | Action to recover the possession of land. Ejectment (Table K11) |
| | Right to dispose of land. Public and private restraints of alienation |
| 69.6 | General (Table K11) |
| 70 | Ancestral property. Family property. Property of kinship groups (Table K11) |
| | Rights to use and profits of another's land. Incorporeal hereditaments |
| 70.6 | General (Table K11) |
| 70.7 | Commons and enclosures (Table K11) |

Property
Real property. Land law
Land tenure
Estates and interests. Ownership
Rights and interests incident to ownership and possession. Interests less than estates
Rights to use and profits of another's land. Incorporeal hereditaments -- Continued
70.8 Rent charges (Table K11)
Annuities see KL-KWX7 73.6
Transfer of rights in land
71 General (Table K11)
Transfer inter vivos. Vendor and purchaser
Conveyances. Title investigation. Abstracts
71.3 General (Table K11)
71.35 Registration. Land title system (Table K11)
Including Torrens system
Mortgages. Liens. Land charges
71.4 General (Table K11)
71.6.A-Z Special topics, A-Z
Subarrange each by Table K12
71.8 Real estate management (Table K11)
Including estate management and urban estate management
Personal property
72 General (Table K11)
Ownership and possession
72.3 General (Table K11)
72.4 Interests. Future interests. Concurrent ownership (Table K11)
Acquisition of property
72.5 General (Table K11)
Original acquisition
72.6 General (Table K11)
72.7.A-Z Particular modes of acquisition, A-Z
72.7.A33 Accession and confusion (Table K12)
Transfer
72.8 General (Table K11)
Choses in possession
72.9 General (Table K11)
Sale see KL-KWX7 86+
Bailment see KL-KWX7 87.7
Gifts
73 General (Table K11)
Transfers as security see KL-KWX7 90.4+
73.2 Actions to recover personal property. Replevin (Table K11)
Particular kinds of personal property

Property
Personal property
Particular kinds of personal property -- Continued
73.4 General (Table K11)
Tangible. Choses in possession see KL-KWX7 72.9+
Intangible. Choses in action
73.5 General (Table K11)
73.6 Annuities (Table K11)
Debts see KL-KWX7 90.2
Intellectual property see KL-KWX7 112+
Negotiable instruments see KL-KWX7 88+
Trusts and trustees
73.8 General (Table K11)
Particular kinds of trusts
74 Resulting trusts (Table K11)
Trustees
74.3 General (Table K11)
Public trustees see KL-KWX7 79.7
Legal investments. Trust investments see KL-KWX7 91.7
75 Estate planning (Table K11)
Succession upon death
76 General (Table K11)
Capacity and disability to inherit
Cf. KL-KWX7 51.8+ Capacity
76.4 Unworthiness (Table K11)
76.5.A-Z Particular types of persons, A-Z
76.5.A64 Aliens (Table K12)
76.5.M56 Minors (Table K12)
76.7 Family provisions
Testamentary succession. Wills
77 General (Table K11)
77.5.A-Z Forms of wills, A-Z
77.5.H64 Holographic wills (Table K12)
Military wills see KL-KWX7 77.5.P74
Notarial wills see KL-KWX7 77.5.P74
77.5.P74 Privileged wills (Table K12)
Including military wills and notarial wills
Testamentary dispositions. Legacies
77.6 General (Table K11)
77.7 Charitable bequests. Request for the benefit of the poor (Table K11)
77.8 Disinheritance (Table K11)
78 Probate law. Probate courts and procedure (Table K11)
78.2 Contracts of inheritance (Table K11)
Intestate succession
78.3 General (Table K11)

Succession upon death
Intestate succession -- Continued
Classes of heirs. Order of succession
Descendants and ascendants
78.4 Legitimate descendants. Legitimate children (Table K11)
78.5 Illegitimate descendants. Illegitimate children (Table K11)
79 Surviving spouses. Several surviving wives with or without children (Table K11)
79.2 Natural parents (Table K11)
79.6 Succession to rights and duties in relation to persons. Guardianship (Table K11)
Including rights and duties exercised by a husband over his wife; and including guardianship over children and illegitimate children
79.7 Trustees
The distributable estate. Distribution of property. Traditional property
Including land, livestock, crops, weapons and ornaments, etc.
79.8 General (Table K11)
79.9 Estate of married person with one or more spouses (Table K11)
Contracts
81 General (Table K11)
Classification of contracts
81.2 General (Table K11)
81.3 Standardized terms of contracts (Table K11)
For a particular type of standardized contract, see the type, e.g., KL-KWX7 86.9 Bills of lading
81.4 Commutative and aleatory contracts (Table K11)
81.5 Contracts of unspecified duration (Table K11)
Formation of contracts
81.7 General (Table K11)
Precontractual obligations
81.8 Promise of contract (Table K11)
Including preliminary contract
82 Offer and acceptance. Consent (Table K11)
82.2 Form of contract. Formalities (Table K11)
Including written contracts, contracts under seal, etc.
82.3.A-Z Collateral provisions. Clauses, A-Z
82.3.A72 Arbitration clause (Table K12)
82.3.C65 Contractual penalty (Table K12)
Hold harmless agreements see KL-KWX7 82.3.I53
82.3.I53 Indemnity against liability. Hold harmless agreements (Table K12)
Monetary terms see KL-KWX7 83.5+

Contracts -- Continued
Parties to contract
82.5 General (Table K11)
Agency see KL-KWX7 97.75
Third-party beneficiary see KL-KWX7 84
Void and voidable contracts
Including pertinent actions
83 General (Table K11)
83.2.A-Z Immoral and unlawful contracts, A-Z
Subarrange each by Table K12
Lack of genuine consent
83.3 Mistake (Table K11)
Discharge of contract
83.4 General (Table K11)
Performance
Payment. Tender
83.5 General (Table K11)
83.7 Payment in goods other than money (Table K11)
84 Third parties (Table K11)
Including third-party beneficiary and promise of a third party's performance
84.2 Enforced performance (Table K11)
84.3 Impossibility of performance (Table K11)
Breach of contract
84.4 General (Table K11)
84.5 Damages (Table K11)
Contractual penalty see KL-KWX7 82.3.C65
84.6 Public contracts. Government contracts. Procurement (Table K11)
Individual contracts and transactions. Commercial transactions
Including commercial law in general
85 General (Table K11)
Contract of service. Master and servant
85.2 General (Table K11)
Civil service see KL-KWX7 240+
Contract for work and labor. Independent contractors
85.4 General works (Table K11)
85.6.A-Z Particular types of contracts, A-Z (Table K11)
85.6.B84 Building and construction. Engineering (Table K12)
85.6.C65 Computer contracts (Table K12)
Engineering see KL-KWX7 85.6.B84
Sale of goods
86 General (Table K11)
Transfer of property and title
Conditional sale see KL-KWX7 90.6

Contracts
Individual contracts and transactions. Commercial transactions
Sale of goods -- Continued
Documents of title
86.7 General (Table K11)
86.9 Bills of lading (Table K11)
Performance
Including conditions, clauses, and warranties
87 General (Table K11)
87.3 Overseas sales. C.I.F. clause. F.O.B. clause (Table K11)
Right of unpaid seller
87.5 General (Table K11)
Liens see KL-KWX7 91
87.6.A-Z Particular goods and chattels, A-Z
Subarrange each by Table K12
87.7 Contracts involving bailments (Table K11)
Negotiable instruments
88 General (Table K11)
88.3 Bills of exchange (Table K11)
88.4 Checks (Table K11)
88.5 Promissory note (Table K11)
Banking
88.6 General (Table K11)
88.7 National banks. Central banks. Banks of issue (Table K11)
Cf. KL-KWX7 272.6 Bank notes
Monetary policy see KL-KWX7 272+
88.8 Savings banks (Table K11)
88.9 Investment banks (Table K11)
89 Cooperative societies. Credit unions (Table K11)
89.2 Deposit banking and accounts (Table K11)
89.4 Collecting of accounts. Collection laws (Table K11)
Bank credit. Bank loan
89.5 General (Table K11)
89.6 Discount. Discount rate. Rediscount (Table K11)
90 Documentary credit. Letters of credit. Advances on commercial documents (Table K11)
Foreign exchange regulations see KL-KWX7 273.4+
90.15.A-Z Other, A-Z
Bank secrets see KL-KWX7 90.15.R43
90.15.E4 Electronic funds transfer (Table K12)
Money laundering see KL-KWX7 90.15.R43
90.15.R43 Record keeping (Table K12)
Including bank secrets, money laundering

Contracts
Individual contracts and transactions. Commercial transactions -- Continued
90.2 Loan of money. Debtor and creditor (Table K11)
90.3 Suretyship. Guaranty (Table K11)
Secured transactions
90.4 General (Table K11)
90.6 Conditional sale. Installment sale. Lease purchase (Table K11)
91 Liens (Table K11)
91.2 Pledge (Table K11)
Suretyship and guaranty see KL-KWX7 90.3
Marketing of securities. Investments. Stock exchange transactions
91.4 General (Table K11)
91.5 Stockbrokers (Table K11)
91.7 Investment trusts. Investment companies. Mutual funds (Table K11)
Particular securities
91.8 General (Table K11)
91.9 Legal investments. Trust investments (Table K11)
Mortgages see KL-KWX7 71.4+
92 Commodity exchanges. Produce exchanges (Table K11)
Carriage of goods and passengers. Carriers
Cf. KL-KWX7 106.2+ Transportation
92.5 General (Table K11)
Carriage by land
92.6 General (Table K11)
Motor carriers see KL-KWX7 106.4
Railroads see KL-KWX7 106.6+
92.7 Carriage by air (Table K11)
Cf. KL-KWX7 107+ Commercial aviation
Carriage by sea. Maritime commercial law. Admiralty
93 General (Table K11)
93.2 Maritime torts. Collision at sea (Table K11)
93.3 Liability of operators of nuclear-powered ships (Table K11)
Admiralty courts and proceedings
93.5 General (Table K11)
Prize law
see KZ6590+
93.7 Carriage of goods. Affreightment (Table K11)
94 Carriage of passengers (Table K11)
Including passengers' luggage
Maritime social legislation
94.2 General (Table K11)

Contracts
Individual contracts and transactions. Commercial transactions
Carriage of goods and passengers. Carriers
Carriage by sea. Maritime commercial law. Admiralty
Maritime social legislation -- Continued
Maritime labor law. Merchant mariners
94.3 Maritime unions. Collective labor agreements (Table K11)
94.5 Protection of labor. Labor hygiene and safety (Table K11)
Social insurance
94.7 General (Table K11)
94.8 Health insurance (Table K11)
94.9 Workers' compensation (Table K11)
Inland water transportation see KL-KWX7 107.8
Fisheries see KL-KWX7 101.4+
95 Marine insurance (Table K11)
95.2 Insurance (Table K11)
Including regulation of insurance carriers, etc.
For social insurance see KL-KWX7 143.8+
95.5 Aleatory contracts. Wagering contracts (Table K11)
Quasi-contracts. Restitution
95.7 General (Table K11)
95.8 Unjust enrichment. Recovery of undue payment (Table K11)
Torts. Extracontractual liability (Delicts and quasi-delicts)
96 General (Table K11)
96.3 Damages (Table K11)
96.4 Torts in respect to persons (Table K11)
96.5 Torts in respect to reputation. Libel and slander (Table K11)
For disparagement (Unfair competition) see KL-KWX7 121.5
96.8 Nuisance (Table K11)
Particular torts
97 Torts affecting chattels. Trespass to goods. Conversion. Trover (Table K11)
Negligence
97.2 General (Table K11)
97.25.A-Z Particular types of accidents, A-Z
97.25.A85 Automobile accidents (Table K12)
97.25.A88 Aviation accidents (Table K12)
97.25.B84 Building accidents (Table K12)
Liability of common air carriers see KL-KWX7 107.4
Marine accidents see KL-KWX7 93.2
Strict liability. Liability without fault

Torts. Extracontractual liability (Delicts and quasi-delicts)
Strict liability. Liability without fault -- Continued
97.3 General (Table K11)
97.4 Products liability (Table K11)
97.5 Environmental damages (Table K11)
For environmental crimes see KL-KWX7 435.3+
Liability for torts of others. Vicarious liability
97.6 General (Table K11)
97.7 Government torts (Table K11)
97.74 Compensation to victims of crimes. Reparation (Table K11)
Including injuries to both person and property and compensation by government
97.75 Agency (Table K11)
Associations
Including business enterprises in general, regardless of form of organization
97.8 Unincorporated associations (Table K11)
Incorporated associations. Corporations. Juristic persons
97.85 General (Table K11)
Business corporations. Companies
97.9 General (Table K11)
Particular types of corporations or companies
98 General (Table K11)
98.2 Cooperative societies (Table K11)
Insolvency and bankruptcy. Creditor's rights
98.3 General (Table K11)
Bankruptcy
98.4 General (Table K11)
98.5 Bankruptcy court and procedure (Table K11)
Economic constitution. Economic legislation
99 General (Table K11)
99.2 Economic policy (Table K11)
99.3 Organization and administration
Including public, semi-private, and private organs of economic intervention and councils
99.5 National planning (Table K11)
99.55 Investments (Table K11)
Including foreign investments
Foreign exchange control see KL-KWX7 273.4+
Economic assistance
Including industrial promotion
99.6 General (Table K11)
Economic assistance to a particular state or municipality see the state or municipality
99.7 Prices and price control (Table K11)

Economic constitution. Economic legislation -- Continued
Government-owned industry. Government business enterprises
Including semi-public enterprises
For a particular type of industry or business, see the business or industry
99.8 General (Table K11)
Public utilities see KL-KWX7 105.4+
99.85 Competition rules. Restraint of trade control (Table K11)
Money, currency, and foreign exchange control see KL-KWX7 272+
99.9 Standards. Norms. Quality control (Table K11)
For standards, grading, and quality control of agricultural products or consumer products, see the product
Regulation of industry, trade, and commerce
100 General (Table K11)
100.13 Consumer protection (Table K11)
100.16 Advertising (Table K11)
For works limited to a particular industrial or trade line, see the industrial or trade line
Primary production. Extractive industries
Agriculture. Forestry. Rural law
100.2 Organization and administration (Table K11)
Large estates. Feudal land grants see KL-KWX7 66.4
Common lands. Stool land (chiefdom land) see KL-KWX7 254.15+
Family (ancestral) land see KL-KWX7 70
Land use. Agrarian land policy legislation
For public land law and policy see KL-KWX7 253+
100.5 General (Table K11)
100.6 Transformation of the agricultural structure
Including nationalization or purchase of agricultural land holdings and their redistribution by the state
100.7 Agricultural contracts (Table K11)
100.8 Conservation of agricultural and forestry lands (Table K11)
Including soil conservation, field irrigation, erosion control
Cf. KL-KWX7 253.4 Land reclamation
Economic assistance
100.9 Price supports (Table K11)
Agricultural production
Including marketing, standards, and grading
100.95.A-Z Field crops, A-Z
100.95.C68 Cotton (Table K12)
Livestock industry and trade
101 General (Table K11)
Meat industry see KL-KWX7 104

Regulation of industry, trade, and commerce
Primary production. Extractive industries
Agriculture. Forestry. Rural law
Agricultural production -- Continued
Dairy industry see KL-KWX7 104.2
101.2 Forestry. Timber laws. Game laws (Table K11)
101.3 Viticulture (Table K11)
Game laws see KL-KWX7 101.2
Fishing industry
Including regulation of ownership, native fishing rights, exploration, and exploitation
101.4 General (Table K11)
101.5.A-Z Particular fish and marine fauna, A-Z
101.5.T84 Tuna (Table K12)
Mining. Quarrying
101.6 General (Table K11)
101.7 Ownership of mines and mineral resources (Table K11)
Resources
101.8 General (Table K11)
Petroleum. Oil and gas
101.9 General (Table K11)
102 Conservation (Table K11)
102.2 Regulation of industry (Table K11)
Including concessions, trade practices, etc.
102.3 Oil and gas leases (Table K11)
102.4.A-Z Particular oil fields, reserves, etc., A-Z
Subarrange each by Table K12
102.6 Natural gas (Table K11)
102.7.A-Z Other resources
102.7.C63 Coal (Table K12)
102.7.C66 Copper (Table K12)
102.7.D53 Diamonds. Gems (Table K12)
Gems see KL-KWX7 102.7.D53
102.7.G64 Gold (Table K12)
102.7.P56 Phosphate (Table K12)
102.7.T56 Tin (Table K12)
102.7.U73 Uranium (Table K12)
Manufacturing industries
103 General (Table K11)
103.3 Chemical industries (Table K11)
103.4 Textile industries (Table K11)
103.5.A-Z Major and heavy industries, A-Z
103.5.A95 Automobile industry (Table K12)
103.5.E43 Electric industries (Table K12)
103.5.H54 High technology industries (Table K12)
103.5.I76 Iron and steel industries (Table K12)

Regulation of industry, trade, and commerce
Manufacturing industries
Major and heavy industries, A-Z -- Continued
103.5.P34 Paper industry (Table K12)
103.5.R83 Rubber industry (Table K12)
Steel industry see KL-KWX7 103.5.I76
103.6.A-Z Consumer products. Light industries, A-Z
103.6.B66 Book industries and trade (Table K12)
103.6.L4 Leather industry (Table K12)
103.6.T62 Tobacco products (Table K12)
Food processing industries
Class here works on trade practices and antitrust measures, economic assistance, sanitation, standards (grading) and quality inspection
Including regulation of adulteration and additives
103.7 General (Table K11)
103.8 Sugar refining (Table K11)
103.9 Fruit and vegetables (Table K11)
104 Meat industry (Table K11)
Including slaughtering and slaughterhouses
104.2 Dairy industry (Table K11)
Including distribution
104.3 Beverages (Table K11)
104.5 Construction and building industry. Contractors
Cf. KL-KWX7 255+ Building laws
Trade
104.7 General (Table K11)
104.8 International trade. Foreign trade (Table K11)
104.9 Wholesale trade (Table K11)
105 Secondhand trade (Table K11)
105.2 Service trades (Table K11)
Including licensing
105.3 Warehouses. Storage (Table K11)
Public utilities
Including private, publicly owned, and public-private (mixed) utility companies
105.4 General (Table K11)
105.5 Public service commissions (Table K11)
Energy policy. Power supply
Including energy resources and development in general
105.6 General (Table K11)
105.7 Electricity (Table K11)
105.8 Gas (Table K11)
105.9 Water (Table K11)
Including water supply
For water power development see KL-KWX7 251.5+

Regulation of industry, trade, and commerce
Public utilities
Power supply -- Continued
106 Atomic power (Table K11)
Transportation and communication
106.2 General (Table K11)
Offenses against means of transportation and communication see KL-KWX7 438+
Road traffic. Automotive transportation
106.3 General (Table K11)
106.4 Passenger carriers (Table K11)
106.5 Carriers of goods. Truck lines (Table K11)
Railroads
Including corporate structure and regulation of industry
106.6 General (Table K11)
106.7 Concessions for railroad construction and operation (Table K11)
Including public works contracts for railroad construction
106.8 Operation of railroads. Finance. Rates (Table K11)
106.9 Pipe lines (Table K11)
Aviation
107 General (Table K11)
107.2 Airports (Table K11)
Commercial aviation. Airlines
107.3 General (Table K11)
107.4 Liability for personal injuries and property damage (Table K11)
For general tort liability for aviation see KL-KWX7 97.25.A88
107.45 Space law (Table K11)
Water transportation. Navigation and shipping
107.5 General (Table K11)
Merchant mariners see KL-KWX7 94.3+
107.6 Harbors and ports (Table K11)
Including port charges and tonnage fees
107.7 Lighthouses (Table K11)
Merchant marine. Regulation of the shipping industry
107.8 Domestic shipping. Coastwise shipping (Table K11)
Including inland water carriers
Postal service
Including works on all postal services, telegraph, and telephone combined
108 General (Table K11)
108.2 Classification of mails. Rates (Table K11)
Crimes committed through the mail see KL-KWX7 456+
Violation of the privacy of letters see KL-KWX7 416.6

Regulation of industry, trade, and commerce
Transportation and communication -- Continued
108.3 Forwarding agents. Freight forwarders (Table K11)
Communication. Mass media
108.35 General (Table K11)
Press law
Including legal status of journalists
For works on freedom of the press see KL-KWX7 211.8
108.5 General (Table K11)
108.6 Criminal provisions (Table K11)
Including procedural aspects
Telecommunication
109 General (Table K11)
109.2 Artificial satellites in telecommunication (Table K11)
109.3 Telegraph. Teletype. Fax (Table K11)
Including telegraph and telephone combined
109.4 Telephone (Table K11)
Including radio telephone
109.5 Radio and television communication (Table K11)
110 Weather bureau. Metereological stations (Table K11)
Professions. Intelligentsia
110.2 General (Table K11)
Violation of confidential communication see KL-KWX7 416.4
Individual professions
Class here works on education, licensing, professional representation, ethics, and liability
Including technical intelligentsia of government industrial enterprises
The health professions
General see KL-KWX7 110.4+
Physicians
Including works on medical personnel in general
110.4 General (Table K11)
110.45 Malpractice (Table K11)
Cf. KL-KWX7 410 Offenses against the person
110.5 Dentists. Dental hygienists (Table K11)
111 Auxiliary medical professions. Paramedical professions (Table K11)
111.3 Economic and financial advisers (Table K11)
111.5 Engineering and construction (Table K11)
Graphic artists see KL-KWX7 111.7
Journalists see KL-KWX7 108.5+
Performing artists see KL-KWX7 167+
111.7 Printers. Graphic artists (Table K11)
111.8 Real estate agents (Table K11)

111.9 Professional ethics. Courts of honor (Table K11)
For a particular court of honor, see the profession
Intellectual and industrial property
112 General (Table K11)
Copyright
112.2 General (Table K11)
International Union for the Protection of Literary and Artistic Works (Bern Union)
see K1412+
Universal Copyright Convention
see K1414+
112.3 Authorship (Table K11)
Including multiple authorship and author cooperatives
112.4 Intangible property (Table K11)
112.5 Procedures. Formalities (Table K11)
Including registration of claim, transfer, licenses, deposit, and notice
112.6 Protected works (Table K11)
Including original works, subsequent rights, idea and title
112.7 Scope of protection (Table K11)
112.8 Employees' copyright (Table K11)
112.9 Delicts. Torts (Table K11)
Branches of copyright
113 Literary copyright (Table K11)
114 Musical copyright (Table K11)
Fine art and photography
114.5 General (Table K11)
Motion pictures see KL-KWX7 115
114.7 Designs and models (Table K11)
114.9 Prints and labels (Table K11)
Including works of commercial art, catalogs, sample books, etc.
115 Motion pictures and television programs (Table K11)
115.3 Computer programs. Computer software (Table K11)
115.4 Quasi copyright and neighboring rights (Table K11)
Author and publisher
Including the publishing contract
115.5 General (Table K11)
115.6 Plays and stage productions (Table K11)
115.7 Motion pictures (Table K11)
115.8 Music (Table K11)
115.9 Scientific literature (Table K11)
International copyright
see K1411+
Patent law and trademarks
116 General (Table K11)

Intellectual and industrial property
Patent law and trademarks -- Continued
117 Patent office (Table K11)
Patent practice and procedure
117.2 General (Table K11)
Invention
Including priority and novelty
117.3 General (Table K11)
118.5 Employees' invention and technological innovation (Table K11)
118.6 Designs and utility models (Table K11)
Licenses
Including compulsory licenses and fees
118.7 General (Table K11)
118.8 Foreign licensing agreements (Table K11)
Including know-how
119 Patent litigation and infringements (Table K11)
International uniform law on patents and trademarks
see K1501+
Trademarks
120 General (Table K11)
120.5 Practice and procedure (Table K11)
Unfair competition
For restraint of trade see KL-KWX7 99.85
121 General (Table K11)
Advertising
121.3 General (Table K11)
121.5 Disparagement of goods (Table K11)
Including comparative advertising
121.7 Testing of commercial products (Table K11)
Pushing for sales
121.8 Unordered merchandise by mail (Table K11)
122 Special sales (Table K11)
122.3 Rebates and premiums (Table K11)
122.4 Torts (Table K11)
Cf. KL-KWX7 96+ Civil law
122.5 Practice and procedure (Table K11)
Including arbitration and award
Social legislation
Including works on both labor law, social insurance, social services, and private labor law as it applies to the labor contract and to the labor-management relationship
123 General (Table K11)
124 Social reform and policies (Table K11)
Including all branches of social legislation and labor
Labor law

Labor law -- Continued
Criticism and reform see KL-KWX7 124
125 General (Table K11)
125.3 Labor policies. Competition and incentives for high performance (Table K11)
125.4 Organization and administration (Table K11)
Class here works on national departments and boards of labor, national, state and local departments and boards, or departments and boards of several states or administrative districts
For departments or boards (several or individual) of an individual state or administrative district, see the state or district
Labor contract and employment
125.5 General (Table K11)
126 Types of employment (Table K11)
126.3 Individual labor contract and collective agreements. Liberty of contract (Table K11)
Freedom of employment and restraint on freedom of employment
127 General (Table K11)
127.3 Preferential employment (Table K11)
Including people with severe disabilities, veterans, etc.
127.5 Formation of contract (Table K11)
127.7 Parties to contract (Table K11)
Prohibition of discrimination in employment see KL-KWX7 130+
Extinction of employment
Cf. KL-KWX7 83.4+ Contracts
128 General (Table K11)
128.3 Dismissal and resignation of employees (Table K11)
Including economic crisis dismissal, layoff, short hours, suspension, reinstatement, dismissal wage, etc.
129 Job security (Table K11)
129.3 Nonperformance (Table K11)
129.4 Liability (Table K11)
Including liability of employer, employee, and liability toward co-worker and third parties
Prohibition of discrimination in employment. Equal opportunity
130 General (Table K11)
130.3 Wage discrimination. Equal pay for equal work (Table K11)
130.4.A-Z Groups discriminated against, A-Z
130.4.A33 Aged. Older people (Table K12)
130.4.A44 Alien laborers (Table K12)
130.4.D58 Disabilities, People with (Table K12)
Older people see KL-KWX7 130.4.A33
People with disabilities see KL-KWX7 130.4.D58

Labor law
Prohibition of discrimination in employment. Equal opportunity
Groups discriminated against, A-Z -- Continued
130.4.W58 Women (Table K12)
Wages
131 General (Table K11)
Types of wages and modes of remuneration
131.3 Incentive wages (Table K11)
Including bonus system, profit sharing, etc.
131.4 Collective wages (Table K11)
131.5 Adjustments. Cost-of-living adjustments (Table K11)
132 Nonwage payments and fringe benefits (Table K11)
132.4.A-Z Groups of employees or industries, A-Z
132.4.T73 Transport workers (Table K12)
Labor-management relations
133 General (Table K11)
Works councils
Including election, organization, parliamentary practice, etc.
133.3 General (Table K11)
133.4 Works assembly (Table K11)
Works councils of business concerns see KL-KWX7 136
133.5 Union participation (Table K11)
Employee participation in management and planning
134 General (Table K11)
Standardized labor conditions see KL-KWX7 137.5
135 Labor standards and protection of labor (Table K11)
135.6 Personnel management (Table K11)
136 Employee representation on board of controllers and supervisors (Table K11)
Including unincorporated and incorporated business associations, cooperative societies, industrial trusts, etc.
Collective bargaining and labor agreements
137 General (Table K11)
137.5 Standardized labor conditions (Table K11)
Collective labor disputes
138 General (Table K11)
138.3 Strikes and lockouts. Boycott (Table K11)
Corporate representation
139 General (Table K11)
139.3 Unions (Table K11)
Including personality and capacity
139.5 Employers' associations (Table K11)
Protection of labor
140 General (Table K11)
140.3 Hours of labor (Table K11)
Including night work and Sunday labor

Labor law
Protection of labor -- Continued
Vacations
140.5 General (Table K11)
141 Sick leave (Table K11)
141.3 Holidays (Table K11)
141.5 Child and youth labor (Table K11)
Including hours of labor
Women's labor
Including hours of labor
141.7 General (Table K11)
141.8 Maternal welfare (Table K11)
142 Home labor (Table K11)
142.3 Labor hygiene and industrial safety (Table K11)
Including safety regulations for equipment
143 Labor supply. Manpower control. Manpower planning (Table K11)
Practice and procedure. Courts
143.3 General (Table K11)
143.4 Judicial review of grievance procedures. Judicial decisions (Table K11)
143.5 Remedies. Appellate procedures (Table K11)
143.6 Arbitration (Table K11)
143.7 Criminal provisions (Table K11)
Social insurance. Social security
For works on both labor law and social insurance see KL-KWX7 123+
143.8 General (Table K11)
Criticism and reform see KL-KWX7 124
Information retrieval and electronic data processing see KL-KWX7 4.3+
Coverage and benefits
144.2 General (Table K11)
144.3.A-Z Groups of beneficiaries, A-Z
Subarrange each by Table K12
Merchant mariners see KL-KWX7 94.3+
144.5 Conflict of laws (Table K11)
Health insurance
145 General (Table K11)
145.3 Compulsory insurance (Table K11)
Including exemptions
145.5.A-Z Coverage and benefits, A-Z
Subarrange each by Table K12
Public employees and officials see KL-KWX7 241.4
145.8.A-Z Groups of beneficiaries, A-Z
Subarrange each by Table K12

Social insurance. Social security -- Continued
Workers' compensation
Including occupational diseases
For merchant mariners see KL-KWX7 94.9
146 General (Table K11)
147.A-Z Groups of beneficiaries, A-Z
Subarrange each by Table K12
Old age, survivors and disability insurance
148.4 General (Table K11)
Social reform see KL-KWX7 124
148.6 Compulsory insurance. Exemptions (Table K11)
For merchant mariners see KL-KWX7 94.7+
148.7 Unemployment insurance (Table K11)
For civil service pensions see KL-KWX7 241.4
Social services. Public welfare
149 General (Table K11)
Criticism and reform see KL-KWX7 124
149.5 Social work and social workers (Table K11)
Social service beneficiaries
149.6 General (Table K11)
149.7 The poor and destitute (Table K11)
149.8 Older people (Table K11)
149.9 Large families (Table K11)
People with disabilities
Including people with physical, mental, and emotional disabilities
150 General (Table K11)
150.4.A-Z Beneficiaries, A-Z
150.4.B54 Blind (Table K12)
150.4.D42 Deaf-mute (Table K12)
150.4.S38 Severe disabilities, People with (Table K12)
150.5 Asocial types (Table K11)
150.6 Evacuated and homeless persons (Table K11)
War-related groups of beneficiaries
150.7 General (Table K11)
150.8 Refugees. Expelled or forcefully repatriated persons (Table K11)
150.9 Prisoners of war and political prisoners. Veterans (Table K11)
151 Services for war victims and war invalids (Table K11)
Children. Youth
151.2 General (Table K11)
Measures and provisions
151.5 General (Table K11)

Social services. Public welfare
Social service beneficiaries
Children. Youth
Measures and provisions -- Continued
151.6 Protection of children in public, and against obscenity (Table K11)
Including taverns, theaters, gambling, and literature
151.9 Custodial education. Collective education (Table K11)
Human reproduction
152 General (Table K11)
152.3 Birth control (Table K11)
152.4 Abortion (Table K11)
Special topics, A-Z
152.5.A36 Abortion clinics (Table K12)
Public health
153 General (Table K11)
153.5 Burial and cemetery laws (Table K11)
Contagious and infectious diseases. Parasitic diseases
153.6 General (Table K11)
153.7.A-Z Diseases. Agents. Parasites, A-Z
153.7.A53 AIDS (Table K12)
153.7.S27 SARS (Table K12)
153.7.T82 Tuberculosis (Table K12)
153.7.V45 Venereal diseases (Table K12)
Public health measures
Including compulsory measures
154 General (Table K11)
154.2 Immunization. Vaccination (Table K11)
154.3 Quarantine (Table K11)
Environmental pollution see KL-KWX7 155.3+
154.4.A-Z Other public health hazards and measures, A-Z
154.4.R43 Refuse disposal (Table K12)
154.4.S77 Street cleaning (Table K12)
154.5 Drinking water standards. Fluoridation (Table K11)
Food laws see KL-KWX7 103.7+
154.7 Mental health (Table K11)
Narcotics see KL-KWX7 159.3
Poisons. Toxic substances see KL-KWX7 160.6.A+
Environmental law. Environmental policy
For civil liability see KL-KWX7 97.5
155 General (Table K11)
155.2 Environmental planning. Conservation of environmental resources (Table K11)
For ecological aspects of regional planning see KL-KWX7 254.3
Environmental pollution

Environmental law. Environmental policy
Environmental pollution -- Continued
155.3 General (Table K11)
155.35 Air pollution (Table K11)
Including noxious gases, automobile emissions, etc.
155.4 Water and groundwater pollution (Table K11)
Including pollutants and sewage control
Pollutants
156 Radioactive substances (Table K11)
156.2 Noise (Table K11)
Including traffic noise, and noise control
Cf. KL-KWX7 96.8 Nuisance
156.6 Recycling of refuse (Table K11)
Wilderness preservation
Including natural monuments, parks, and forests
157 General (Table K11)
Wildlife conservation
Including game, birds
157.2 General (Table K11)
Game laws and hunting see KL-KWX7 101.2
Fishery laws see KL-KWX7 101.4+
Environmental crimes see KL-KWX7 435.3+
Environmental damages (Civil liability) see KL-KWX7 97.5
Medical legislation
157.3 General (Table K11)
157.32 Patients' rights (Table K11)
Medical institutions or health services. Hospitals
157.4 General (Table K11)
157.6 Health resorts and spas (Table K11)
157.7 Institutions for the mentally ill (Table K11)
158.A-Z Other medical institutions or services, A-Z
Abortion clinics see KL-KWX7 152.5.A36
158.D39 Day care centers for infants and children (Table K12)
158.E43 Emergency medical services (Table K12)
Nursing homes see KL-KWX7 158.O42
158.O42 Old age homes. Nursing homes (Table K12)
Including invalid adults
158.3.A-Z Health organizations. By name, A-Z
158.3.R43 Red Cross (Table K12)
Biomedical engineering. Medical technology
Including human experimentation in medicine
Cf. KL-KWX7 409.6+ Criminal aspects of medicine
158.5 General (Table K11)
158.6 Genetic engineering (Table K11)
For artificial insemination (human reproductive technology) see KL-KWX7 158.8

Medical legislation
Biomedical engineering. Medical technology -- Continued
158.7 Transplantation of organs, tissues, etc. (Table K11)
Including donation of organs, tissues, etc.
158.8 Human reproductive technology (Table K11)
Including artificial insemination, fertilization in vitro, etc.
158.9.A-Z Special topics, A-Z
158.9.C65 Confidential communications (Table K12)
Hospital records see KL-KWX7 158.9.R42
158.9.I64 Informed consent (Table K12)
158.9.R42 Medical records. Hospital records (Table K12)
159 Veterinary medicine and hygiene. Veterinary public health (Table K11)
159.12 Animal protection. Animal welfare. Animal rights (Table K11)
Including prevention of cruelty to animals
For animal rights as a social issue see HV4701+
Drug laws. Liquor laws
Including laws on prohibition
For food laws see KL-KWX7 103.7+
159.2 General (Table K11)
159.3 Narcotics. Intoxicating drugs (Table K11)
Including psychopharmaca
Poisons see KL-KWX7 160.6.A+
Police and public safety
160 General (Table K11)
160.2 Police magistrates. Lay magistrates. Village (tribal) arbitral tribunals (Table K11)
Public safety
160.3 General (Table K11)
160.4 Weapons. Explosives (Table K11)
Including manufacturing, import, and trade of firearms and ammunition
Hazardous articles and processes
Including transportation by land
For product safety see KL-KWX7 97.4
160.5 Nuclear power. Reactors. Radioactive substances (Table K11)
Including protection from radiation, and including nuclear waste disposal
160.6.A-Z Poisons and toxic substances, A-Z
160.6.P47 Pesticides (Table K12)
160.7 Accident control (Table K11)
160.8 Fire prevention and control (Table K11)
Flood control see KL-KWX7 251.7
Weather bureaus. Meteorological stations see KL-KWX7 110

Police and public safety -- Continued
Control of individuals
160.9 General (Table K11)
Immigration and naturalization see KL-KWX7 214.4
Emigration see KL-KWX7 215
Particular groups
Aliens see KL-KWX7 215.5.A43
Control of social activities
161.2 General (Table K11)
161.3 Travel and transit traffic. Tourism (Table K11)
Including road traffic and traffic on inland waterways
161.4 Vacationing (Table K11)
Including campgrounds, hostels, outdoor swimming facilities, etc.
161.5 Sports activities (Table K11)
161.8.A-Z Other, A-Z
161.8.D45 Demonstrations. Processions (Table K12)
Gambling
see KL-KWX7 440.6
Processions see KL-KWX7 161.8.D45
161.8.T73 Traveling shows (Table K12)
Including circuses, puppet theaters, air shows, open-air shows, etc.
Cultural affairs
162 General (Table K11)
162.2 Cultural policy. State encouragement of science and the arts (Table K11)
162.3 National language (Table K11)
Including regulation of use, purity, etc.
Education
162.5 General (Table K11)
School government. School districts
Including curriculum and participation in school government in general
162.7 School discipline (Table K11)
Students
162.8 General (Table K11)
162.9 Compulsory education (Table K11)
163 Teachers. School functionaries (General)
For particular teachers, see the level of instruction, e.g. KL-KWX7 164 Teachers in higher education
163.2 Preschool education (Table K11)
163.3 Elementary education (Table K11)
Including teachers
163.4 Education of children with disabilities (Table K11)

Cultural affairs
Education -- Continued
163.5 Vocational education (Table K11)
Including teachers
163.6 Secondary education (Table K11)
Including teachers
Higher education. Universities
For legal education see KL-KWX7 5+
163.7 General (Table K11)
163.9 Administration. Institutional management in higher education (Table K11)
164 Teachers (Table K11)
Including professors (ordinarii, extraordinarii, and emeriti), magisters, etc.
Students
164.2 General (Table K11)
164.3 Political activities (Table K11)
Including strikes
164.4 Student societies (Table K11)
164.5.A-Z Universities. By place, A-Z
Subarrange each by Table K12
164.6.A-Z Other schools or institutions of higher education. By place, A-Z
Subarrange each by Table K12
Including colleges or institutes of technology, schools of music, art, drama, etc.
165 Private schools (Table K11)
165.2 Religious schools (Table K11)
Including Quran schools
165.3 Adult education (Table K11)
165.5 Physical education. Sports (Table K11)
Cf. KL-KWX7 161.5 Sports activities
Science and the arts
166 General (Table K11)
166.2 Public institutions (Table K11)
166.3.A-Z Branches and subjects, A-Z
166.3.A72 Archaeology (Table K12)
166.3.C37 Cartography (Table K12)
166.3.L32 Laboratories (Table K12)
Language see KL-KWX7 162.3
Meteorology see KL-KWX7 110
166.3.O34 Oceanography (Table K12)
166.3.S73 Statistical services (Table K12)
The arts
166.4 General (Table K11)
166.5 Fine arts (Table K11)

Cultural affairs
Science and the arts
The arts -- Continued
Performing arts
166.7 Music. Musicians (Table K11)
Theater
Including managerial, performing, and technical personnel
For copyright see KL-KWX7 115.6
167 General (Table K11)
167.2 Playwrights. Contracts (Table K11)
Motion pictures
168 General (Table K11)
168.4 Screenwriters. Contracts (Table K11)
Public collections
168.5 General (Table K11)
168.6 Archives. Historic documents (Table K11)
169 Libraries (Table K11)
169.2 Museums and galleries (Table K11)
169.3 Historic buildings and monuments (Table K11)
169.4 Educational, scientific, and cultural exchanges (Table K11)
Public law
Class here works on all aspects of public law, including early works
For civics see KL-KWX7 6.5
169.5 General (Table K11)
The state
Including philosophy and theory of the state
For non-legal works on political theory, see class J
169.7 Rule of law (Table K11)
Constitutional law
For works on the constitutional aspects of a subject, see the subject
History see KL-KWX7 171.92+
170 Constitutional reform. Criticism. Polemic
For works on a particular constitution, see the constitution
171.A12 Bibliography
Including bibliography of constitutional history
171.A15 Periodicals
Including gazettes, yearbooks, bulletins, etc.
Monographic series see KL-KWX7 171.A15
Sources
Including early constitutions and related materials
171.A2 Collections. Compilations. By date
171.A31<date> Individual constitutions
Arrange chronologically by appending the date of adoption to this number and deleting any trailing zeros. Subarrange each by main entry

Constitutional law
Sources -- Continued
171.A32<date> Individual sources other than constitutions
Arrange chronologically by appending the date of adoption or issuance to this number and deleting any trailing zeros. Subarrange by main entry
Court decisions and related materials. Reports
Including decisions of quasi-judicial (regulatory) agencies
171.A473 Indexes and tables. Digests
171.A48 Serials
171.A49 Monographs. By date
Decisions of regulatory agencies. Orders. Rulings see KL-KWX7 171.A473+
Dictionaries. Encyclopedias see KL-KWX7 171.A9+
Form books see KL-KWX7 171.A9+
Yearbooks see KL-KWX7 171.A15
Collected works (nonserial) see KL-KWX7 171.A9+
171.A67 Conferences. Symposia
Including papers devoted to the scholarly exploration of the subject of constitutional law
171.A9-.Z9 General works. Treatises
Constitutional history
For individual constitutions see KL-KWX7 171.A31<date>
By period
Medieval and early modern (to second half of the 19th century), including precolonial and early colonial periods see KL-KWX7 12.3+
Mid-19th century to most recent constitution
Including colonial periods to independence
172 General (Table K11)
Constitutional principles
Rule of law see KL-KWX7 169.7
174 Rulers. Kings, princes, viceroys, chieftains (Table K11)
Including dynastic/tribal rules and works on legal status
175 Privileges of classes and particular groups (Table K11)
176 Sources and relationships of law (Table K11)
Intergovernmental relations. Jurisdiction
177 Federal-state (republic), national-provincial controversies. State-state or interprovincial disputes (Table K11)
178 Distribution of legislative power. Exclusive and concurrent legislative power. Reservation of provincial legislation (Table K11)
179.A-Z Special topics, A-Z
Class here works on topics not provided for elsewhere
For the history of a particular subject, see the subject

Constitutional law
Constitutional history
By period
Mid-19th century to most recent constitution
Special topics, A-Z -- Continued
Celebrations see KL-KWX7 179.C45
179.C45 Centennials. Celebrations (Table K12)
180 Interpretation and construction (Table K11)
180.5 Amending process (Table K11)
Modern constitutional principles
181 General (Table K11)
182 Legitimacy (Table K11)
184 Legality. Socialist legality (Table K11)
Rule of law see KL-KWX7 169.7
186 Centralization of powers. Statism (Table K11)
187 Decolonization. Decentralization (Table K11)
Separation and delegation of powers
190 General (Table K11)
Executive privilege see KL-KWX7 202
195 Judicial review of legislative acts (Table K11)
196 Privileges of classes (estates) and particular groups (Table K11)
Sources and relationships of the law
198 Preconstitutional and constitutional law (Table K11)
199 International law and municipal law (Table K11)
200 Statutory law and delegated legislation (Table K11)
201 Socialist plans (Table K11)
202 Decrees (individual) (Table K11)
Intergovernmental relations. Jurisdiction
203 General (Table K11)
204 Federal-state (republic), national-provincial controversies. Interstate (Interprovincial, etc.) disputes (Table K11)
205 National (Federal) territory. Archipelagic territorial regimes (e.g. Pacific Area jurisdictions) (Table K11)
Including territorial integrity (fragmentation and boundary questions, politically and ethnically) at independence
Foreign relations
206 General (Table K11)
Foreign service see KL-KWX7 228.4
207 Executive agreements (Table K11)
208 Neutrality (Table K11)
Individual and state
209 General (Table K11)
Human rights. Civil and political rights. Civic (socialist) duties
209.5 General (Table K11)

Constitutional law
Individual and state
Human rights. Civil and political rights. Civic (socialist) duties -- Continued
Equality before the law. Antidiscrimination in general
210 General (Table K11)
210.7.A-Z Groups discriminated against, A-Z
210.7.C37 Caste (Table K12)
210.7.G38 Gays (Table K12)
Indigenous people. Aborigines see KL-KWX7 210.7.M56
Jews see KL-KWX7 210.7.M56
210.7.M56 Minorities (Ethnic, religious, racial, and national) (Table K12)
(210.7.W65) Women
see KL-KWX7 210.8
210.8 Sex discrimination (Table K11)
210.9.A-Z Special subjects, A-Z
Culture see KL-KWX7 210.9.L36
Dialects see KL-KWX7 210.9.L36
210.9.L36 Language and culture (Table K12)
For language regulation in general see KL-KWX7 162.3
Script see KL-KWX7 210.9.L36
Freedom
211 General (Table K11)
211.2 Personal freedom (Table K11)
Including protection of life and health
211.25 Free choice of employment (Table K11)
211.3 Freedom of expression (Table K11)
211.4 Freedom of religion and conscience (Table K11)
Freedom of thought and speech
211.6 General (Table K11)
211.8 Freedom of information (Table K11)
212 Prohibition of censorship (Table K11)
212.2 Right of opposition to government (Table K11)
212.4 Freedom of movement (Table K11)
Including emigration
212.5 Freedom of assembly, association, and demonstration (Table K11)
212.6 Due process of law (Table K11)
212.8 Right to resistance against government (Table K11)
213 Political parties and mass organizations
Including subordinate or connected organizations, and pressure groups, etc.
Control of individuals see KL-KWX7 160.9+

Constitutional law
Individual and state -- Continued
Nationality and citizenship
214 General (Table K11)
214.4 Immigration. Naturalization of aliens (Table K11)
214.6 Expatriation (Table K11)
215 Emigration (Table K11)
215.5.A-Z Particular groups, A-Z
215.5.A43 Aliens (Table K12)
Including stateless persons
215.5.R43 Refugees (Table K12)
Including asylum seekers
216 Internal security (Table K11)
Including control of subversive activities or groups
Religion and state
For works on the internal law and government of religious corporations, sects, etc., see class KB
For works on particular subjects, see the subject (e.g. marriage and divorce, succession, guardianship, etc.)
216.2 General (Table K11)
Sources
Including constitutions, articles, injunctions, ordinances, enactments of the Parliament or the legislature affecting the religious order and life
For sources in general, see classes BL-BQ and KB
216.3 Collections. Compilations
216.4 Religious corporations. Institutions. Organization (Table K11)
Priesthood. Founders. Sainthood. Holymen
see class KB
Education and training of the leadership
see class KB
216.5 Membership (Table K11)
216.6 Lands of religious corporations, sects, etc. (Table K11)
216.65 Religious trusts. Charities. Endowments (Waqf), etc. (Table K11)
216.7.A-Z Offenses against religion, A-Z
Class here works that can not be classed elsewhere
Religious courts see KL-KWX7 335.3+
Organs of national government. Supreme organs of state power and state administration
Including federal and state government
217 General (Table K11)
The people
217.4 General (Table K11)
Political parties see KL-KWX7 213

Constitutional law
Organs of national government. Supreme organs of state power and state administration
The people -- Continued
Election law
217.6 General (Table K11)
217.7 Contested elections
The legislature. Legislative power
218 General (Table K11)
218.2 Control of government (Table K11)
218.4 Legislative bodies. People's assembly. Peoples' congress (Table K11)
Including bicameral and unicameral systems
Legislative process
Including parliamentary practice
218.6 General (Table K11)
218.8 Interpellation (Table K11)
219 Bill drafting (Table K11)
219.2 Committees. Advisory and consultative councils (Table K11)
219.5 Parliamentary minorities (Table K11)
219.8 Legislators (Table K11)
Including immunity, indemnity, incompatibility, etc.
Heads of state
220 General (Table K11)
Monarchs, princes, chiefs, and other rulers
220.2 General (Table K11)
220.5.A-Z Special topics, A-Z
220.5.A23 Abdication (Table K12)
220.5.D9 Dynastic rules. Legal status of dynasty (Table K12)
220.5.E43 Election (Table K12)
Legal status of dynasty see KL-KWX7 220.5.D9
220.5.S92 Succession to the crown (Table K12)
Presidents. Governor-General. Governors
221 General (Table K11)
221.4.A-Z Special topics, A-Z
Subarrange each by Table K12
221.8 Collective heads of state. Councils of state. Presidential councils (Table K11)
Prerogatives and powers of the head of state. Executive privilege
222 General (Table K11)
222.8 Treatymaking power (Table K11)
223 Veto power (Table K11)
223.4 War and emergency power (Table K11)
224 Other supreme organs (Table K11)

Constitutional law
Organs of national government. Supreme organs of state power and state administration -- Continued
224.4 The Judiciary. Judicial power (Table K11)
Class here constitutional status only
Cf. KL-KWX7 329+ Courts, administration of justice, and organization of the judiciary
The executive branch. Government
225 General (Table K11)
National Executive Councils see KL-KWX7 221.8
Presidium. Presidential councils see KL-KWX7 221.8
226 The Prime Minister and the Cabinet. Premiers (Table K11)
226.5 Council of Ministers (Table K11)
227 Supreme Councils of Control (Table K11)
Government departments, ministries, and other organizations of national (federal) government
227.5 General (Table K11)
Departments. Ministries
Class here works on several departments not related to a particular branch of law of subject
Including subordinate administrative divisions, councils, etc.
For works on several departments related to a branch of law or subject, as well as individual departments and its regulatory agencies, see the branch of law or subject
227.8 General (Table K11)
228 Department of State. Foreign office (Table K11)
228.4 The foreign service (Table K11)
228.8 Department of the Interior. Home Affairs (Table K11)
229 Subordinate regulatory agencies (Table K11)
Class here works on several agencies
For an individual agency, see the branch of law or the subject
229.2 Special boards, commissions, bureaus, councils, task forces, etc. (Table K11)
Administrative departments of federal states, provinces, etc.
229.5 General (Table K11)
229.7 Department of the Interior (Table K11)
Administrative and political divisions. Local government other than municipal
230 General (Table K11)
230.3 Self-government and state supervision (Table K11)
230.5 Councils, boards, standing commissions, etc. (Table K11)
231.5.A-Z Particular (1st order) administrative districts, counties, regions, etc., A-Z
Including official gazettes, bylaws, statutory orders, regulations, and general works, as well as works on specific legal topics

Municipal government
Including village and town government
232 General (Table K11)
232.8 Autonomy and rulemaking power (Table K11)
233 Municipal territory (Table K11)
Including boundaries and incorporation
233.8 Name. Flags. Insignia. Seals (Table K11)
Constitution and organization of municipal government
234 General (Table K11)
234.3 Legislative branch. Councils. Elders (Table K11)
234.5 Executive branch. Officers and employees (Table K11)
Including elected and honorary offices
For works on the executive branch of an individual municipality, see the municipality
Municipal finance and economy
235 General (Table K11)
235.2 Property (Table K11)
Budget see KL-KWX7 308.2
Municipal public services
235.4 General (Table K11)
235.5 Public utilities (Table K11)
For regulation of the energy industry see KL-KWX7 105.4+
Electricity. Gas see KL-KWX7 105.7
236 Water. Sewage (Table K11)
For ecological aspects see KL-KWX7 155.4
236.2 Trash collection (Table K11)
236.5 Public transportation (Table K11)
Supramunicipal corporations and cooperation
236.8 General (Table K11)
Special districts
For special districts within a particular state, etc., see the state
237 General (Table K11)
237.2.A-Z Particular types of districts, A-Z
Subarrange each by Table K12
For water districts see KL-KWX7 252.2.A+
237.5 Public foundations (Table K11)
(238) Government business enterprises
see KL-KWX7 99.8+
239 Constitutional courts (tribunals) and procedure (Table K11)
239.2 National emblem. Flag. Seal. Seat of government. National anthem (Table K11)

239.4 Political oath (Table K11)
239.6 Patriotic customs and observances (Table K11)
239.8 Decorations of honor. Awards. Dignities (Table K11)
239.9 Commemorative medals (Table K11)

Civil service. Public officials and functionaries
240 General (Table K11)
240.2 Tenure (Table K11)
240.5 Appointment and election (Table K11)
240.8 Discipline (Table K11)
241 Illicit political activities (Table K11)
241.4 Remuneration. Retirement. Pensions (Table K11)
Including health benefits
241.9 Dismissal (Table K11)
242 State civil service (Table K11)
For works on the civil service of an individual state, see the state
242.4 Municipal civil service (Table K11)
For works on the civil service of an individual municipality, see the municipality
243 Civil service of public corporations other than state or municipal (Table K11)
243.4 Public officials and functionaries of the economic administration (Socialist) (Table K11)
Administrative law. Administrative process and procedure
245 General (Table K11)
Regulatory agencies
Including rulemaking power and regulations
245.4 General (Table K11)
245.6 Admission of attorneys and rules of practice (Table K11)
245.8 Citizen (people) participation (Table K11)
246 Administrative tribunals (Table K11)
246.8 Ombudsman. Control of abuse of administrative power (Table K11)
Tort liability of the government and of public officers see KL-KWX7 97.7
Public property. Public restraint on private property
250 General (Table K11)
Environmental planning. Conservation of natural resources see KL-KWX7 155.2
Recycling of waste see KL-KWX7 156.6
Roads and highways
250.2 General (Table K11)
250.4 Interstate and state highways (Table K11)
250.5.A-Z Other, A-Z
Subarrange each by Table K12
250.6 Common use. Toll (Table K11)
250.8 Construction and maintenance (Table K11)
Including regional planning
Water resources
Including rivers, lakes, watercourses, etc.
251 General (Table K11)

Public property. Public restraint on private property
Water resources -- Continued
251.2 Common use (Table K11)
251.4 Water rights (Table K11)
Cf. KL-KWX7 69.3 Riparian rights in civil law
Protection against pollution see KL-KWX7 155.4
Development and conservation of water resources
251.5 General (Table K11)
251.7 Flood control (Table K11)
Including dams and dikes
252.A-Z Particular inland waterways and channels, A-Z
Subarrange each by Table K12
252.2.A-Z Particular bodies of water and districts. By name, A-Z
Subarrange each by Table K12
Architectural landmarks and historic monuments see KL-KWX7 169.3
Eminent domain. Expropriation. Nationalization
Including works on protection from compulsory acquisitions by the state (crown)
252.4 General (Table K11)
252.6 Compensation. Indemnification (Table K11)
Public land law
253 General (Table K11)
253.2 Land policy legislation (Table K11)
For agricultural land law, including land reform see KL-KWX7 100.5+
253.4 Reclamation. Irrigation. Drainage (Table K11)
Including arid lands, swamp lands, etc.
253.6 Shore protection. Coastal zone management (Table K11)
National preserves. Forests. Savannas
253.8 General (Table K11)
Wildlife protection and wilderness preservation see KL-KWX7 157+
Natural resources and mines see KL-KWX7 101.6+
Native (customary) land
254 General (Table K11)
Common lands. Stool land (chiefdom land)
254.15 General (Table K11)
254.16.A-Z Particular lands. By chiefdom, tribe, community, etc., A-Z
Native (customary) land legislation, trust acts, treaties, etc.
Including works on prohibition of indefinite use rights (perpetual leasing), and/or administration of trust lands by government
254.17 General (Table K11)

Public property
Public land law
Native (customary) land
Native (customary) land legislation, trust acts, treaties, etc. -- Continued
254.18 Administration. Trust and land boards, land advisory committees and commissions, etc. (Table K11)
e.g. Maori Land Board, New Zealand
254.19 Native reserves (Table K11)
254.2 Land claims (Table K11)
Regional planning. Land development
254.23 General (Table K11)
254.3 Ecological aspects (Table K11)
City planning and redevelopment
254.4 General (Table K11)
254.5 Zoning (Table K11)
Building and construction laws
Including administrative control and procedure
255 General (Table K11)
255.2 Adjoining landowners (Table K11)
255.3 Building safety and control (Table K11)
Government property
256 General (Table K11)
257 Constitutional aspects (Table K11)
Administration. Powers and control
257.2 General (Table K11)
258 Records management. Access to public records (Table K11)
Including data bases and general data protection
Expropriation. Nationalization. Eminent domain see KL-KWX7 252.4+
Particular properties
259.15 Automobiles. Motor vehicles (Table K11)
259.3 Government buildings (Table K11)
260 Embassies. Consulates (Table K11)
260.2 Military installations (Table K11)
260.4 Cemeteries (National) (Table K11)
260.5 Public works (Table K11)
Government measures in time of war, national emergency, or economic crisis
262 General (Table K11)
Particular measures
262.4 Military requisitions from civilians. Requisitioned land (Table K11)
For damages and compensation see KL-KWX7 266+

Government measures in time of war, national emergency, or economic crisis
Particular measures -- Continued
263 Control of property. Confiscations (Table K11)
Including enemy and alien property
For damages and compensation see KL-KWX7 266+
Control of unemployment. Manpower control
263.2 General (Table K11)
263.4 Compulsory and forced labor (Table K11)
263.6 Insolvent debtors. Wartime and crisis relief. General moratorium (Table K11)
264 Finances (Table K11)
For procurement and defense contracts see KL-KWX7 267+
For special levies, war taxes, etc. see KL-KWX7 300
264.2 Industrial priorities and allocations. Economic recovery measures. Nationalization (Table K11)
Strategic material. Stockpiling
265 General (Table K11)
265.4.A-Z By commodity, A-Z
Subarrange each by Table K12
Rationing. Price control
265.5 General (Table K11)
265.6.A-Z By commodity, A-Z
Subarrange each by Table K12
265.7 Criminal provisions (Table K11)
War damage compensation
Including foreign claims settlement
266 General (Table K11)
266.2.A-Z Particular claims, A-Z
Confiscations see KL-KWX7 266.2.R47
Demontage see KL-KWX7 266.2.R46
Military occupation damages see KL-KWX7 266.2.R47
266.2.P47 Personal damages. Property loss or damages (Table K12)
Property loss or damages see KL-KWX7 266.2.P47
266.2.R46 Reparations. Demontage (Table K12)
266.2.R47 Requisitions. Confiscations. Military occupation damages (Table K12)
266.4.A-Z Particular victims, A-Z
Subarrange each by Table K12
Military occupation. Procurement
267 General (Table K11)
267.4.A-Z Particular, A-Z
Military occupation damages see KL-KWX7 266.2.R47
Public finance
Finance reform and policies

Public finance
Finance reform and policies -- Continued
268 General (Table K11)
Monetary policies see KL-KWX7 272+
269 General (Table K11)
Organization and administration
Class here works on national departments or agencies of finance, national, state, and local departments or agencies, or departments and agencies of several states or administrative districts
For departments and agencies (several or individual) of an individual state or administrative district, see the state or administrative district
269.2 General (Table K11)
269.3 Particular national departments and agencies (Table K11)
Including officers, personnel, and functionaries
Budget. Government expenditures
270 General (Table K11)
270.3 Accounting (Table K11)
270.4 Expenditure control. Auditing. Public accounting (Table K11)
Including central or local organs of national government
271 Intergovernmental fiscal relations (Table K11)
Including revenue sharing
Money. Monetary policy
Including control of circulation
272 General (Table K11)
272.2 Currency reforms (Table K11)
272.4 Coinage. Mint regulations (Table K11)
272.6 Bank notes. Banks of issue (Table K11)
Class here public law aspects of banks of issue
For banking law see KL-KWX7 88.6+
273 Gold trading and gold standard (Table K11)
273.2 Silver regulation (Table K11)
Foreign exchange control
273.4 General (Table K11)
Criminal provisions see KL-KWX7 429.2
273.6 Conflict of laws (Table K11)
National revenue
274 Fees. Fines. Other charges (Table K11)
Taxation
Criticism and reform see KL-KWX7 268+
275 General (Table K11)
275.2 Double taxation (Table K11)
Taxation and tax exemption as a measure of social and economic policy

Public finance
National revenue
Taxation
Taxation and tax exemption as a measure of social and economic policy -- Continued
276 General (Table K11)
276.2 Investments (Table K11)
Including foreign investments
276.5 Export sales (Table K11)
276.6.A-Z Classes of taxpayers or lines of businesses, A-Z
276.6.T45 Television industry (Table K12)
276.7.A-Z Taxation of particular activities, A-Z
Subarrange each by Table K12
276.8 Tax saving. Tax avoidance (Table K11)
For tax planning relating to a particular tax, see the tax
Tax administration. Revenue service
277 General (Table K11)
National departments and agencies see KL-KWX7 269.3
277.2 Jurisdiction for tax allocation (Table K11)
Including concurrent taxing powers of national and state government
Double taxation see KL-KWX7 275.2
Collection and enforcement
277.4 General (Table K11)
277.6 Tax accounting. Financial statements (Table K11)
Including personal companies and stock companies, etc.
For a particular tax, see the tax
278.A-Z Classes of taxpayers or lines of business, A-Z
278.N65 Non-residents (Table K12)
278.3 Particular taxes (several, collective) (Table K11)
Income tax
279 General (Table K11)
279.3 Assessment (Table K11)
280 Taxable income. Exemptions (Table K11)
Deductions
280.3 General (Table K11)
281 Expenses and losses (Table K11)
Surtaxes see KL-KWX7 300
Particular sources of income
281.4 Salaries and wages (Table K11)
Including fringe benefits, nonwage payments, etc.
281.6 Classes of taxpayers or lines of business, A-Z
281.6.A44 Aliens (Table K12)
281.6.F37 Farmers (Table K12)
281.6.T78 Trusts (Table K12)
Corporation tax

Public finance
National revenue
Taxation
Income tax
Corporation tax -- Continued
282 General (Table K11)
283 Nonprofit associations, nonprofit corporations, foundations (endowments), and pension trust funds (Table K11)
Personal companies (Unincorporated business associations)
284 General (Table K11)
284.2.A-Z Special topics, A-Z
Subarrrange each by Table K12
Cooperatives
285 General (Table K11)
285.2.A-Z Special topics, A-Z
Subarrange each by Table K12
Stock companies (Incorporated business associations)
286 General (Table K11)
286.2 Tax accounting. Financial statements (Table K11)
286.3 Assessment (Table K11)
286.5 Taxable income. Exemptions (Table K11)
289 Deductions (Table K11)
Surtaxes see KL-KWX7 300
Corporate reorganization
290 General (Table K11)
290.2 Conversions (Table K11)
290.4 Merger, fusion, and consolidation (Table K11)
290.6 Liquidation (Table K11)
291 Limited partnership (Table K11)
292 Stock corporation (Table K11)
293 Business concern, holding company, and industrial trusts (Table K11)
294 Government business corporations (Table K11)
295.A-Z Lines of corporate business, A-Z
295.P48 Petroleum industry (Table K12)
Foreign corporations and stockholders
296 General (Table K11)
Double taxation see KL-KWX7 275.2
Multi-national corporations
297 General (Table K11)
Double taxation see KL-KWX7 275.2

Public finance
National revenue
Taxation -- Continued
Property tax. Taxation of capital
Including real property tax
For state and local property taxes see KL-KWX7 311+
For state and local real property tax see KL-KWX7 313+
298 General (Table K11)
298.4 Tax valuation (Table K11)
298.5 Estate, inheritance, and gift taxes (Table K11)
299 Capital gain tax (Table K11)
300 Surtaxes (Table K11)
Poll tax see KL-KWX7 315.P65
Excise taxes. Taxes on transactions
301 General (Table K11)
Sales tax
Including value-added tax
301.2 General (Table K11)
Turnover tax
302 General (Table K11)
302.2 Import sales and export sales (Table K11)
Personal companies and stock companies
302.3 Municipal corporations (Table K11)
303 Government monopolies (Table K11)
Including monopolies delegated by the state to others
303.2.A-Z Commodities, services, and transactions, A-Z
Subarrange each by Table K12
Methods of assessment and collection
For assessment and collection of a particular tax, see the tax
304 General (Table K11)
304.4 Stamp duties (Table K11)
Criminal provisions see KL-KWX7 316+
Customs. Tariff
For foreign trade regulations see KL-KWX7 104.8
305 General (Table K11)
Trade agreements
305.2 General (Table K11)
305.3 Favored nation clause (Table K11)
Customs organization and administration
Including officers and personnel
306 General (Table K11)
306.2 Jurisdiction. Custom territory (Table K11)
Practice and procedure
Including remedies and enforcement

Public finance
National revenue
Customs. Tariff
Customs organization and administration
Practice and procedure -- Continued
307 Duty by weight (Table K11)
307.3 Free ports and zones (Table K11)
Criminal provisions see KL-KWX7 316+
State and local finance
For the public finance of an individual state, administrative district, or municipality, see the state or municipality
308 General (Table K11)
Finance reform see KL-KWX7 268+
308.2 Budget. Expenditure control (Table K11)
Including accounting and auditing
308.3 Public debts. Loans (Table K11)
Taxation
309 General (Table K11)
Tax administration see KL-KWX7 277+
Income tax see KL-KWX7 279+
Sales, turnover, and value-added taxes see KL-KWX7 301.2+
310 Estate, inheritance, and gift taxes (Table K11)
Property tax. Taxation of capital
Including juristic persons and business enterprises
For real property tax see KL-KWX7 313+
311 General (Table K11)
311.2.A-Z Particular industries or industrial properties, A-Z
Subarrange each by Table K12
312 Assessment (Table K11)
312.3 Motor vehicles tax (Table K11)
312.5 Taxes from gambling tables. Casinos (Table K11)
Real property tax
313 General (Table K11)
313.3 Capital gains tax (Table K11)
Including development gains
314 Business tax (Table K11)
Other taxes, A-Z
315.I55 Impact fees (Table K12)
315.P65 Poll tax (Table K12)
Tax and customs crimes and delinquency. Procedure
316 General (Table K11)
Individual offenses
316.3 Tax evasion and tax avoidance (Table K11)
Smuggling of contraband see KL-KWX7 316.3

Public finance
Tax and customs crimes and delinquency. Procedure -- Continued
317 Procedure (Table K11)
For criminal procedure in general see KL-KWX7 459.9+
318 Amnesty. Pardon (Table K11)
National defense. Military law
For emergency and wartime legislation see KL-KWX7 262+
319 General (Table K11)
319.2 Organization and administration. Department of Defense (Table K11)
The armed forces
320 General (Table K11)
Compulsory service
Including draft and selective service
320.2 General (Table K11)
320.3 Deferment (Table K11)
Including disqualification
321 Discharge (Table K11)
321.2 Disability pensions. Rehabilitation (Table K11)
For war invalids, war victims, and prisoners of war see KL-KWX7 150.9
321.4 Equipment (Table K11)
Including weapons, plants, and installations
322.A-Z Particular branches of service, A-Z
Subarrange each by Table K12
322.5 Auxiliary services during war or emergency (Table K11)
323 Civil defense (Table K11)
Military criminal law and procedure
Cf. KL-KWX7 447+ Crimes against national defense
324 General (Table K11)
324.2 Illegality and justification. Superior orders (Table K11)
Individual offenses
325 Incitement. Mutiny (Table K11)
325.2 Insubordination (Table K11)
325.3 Self-mutilation. Malingering (Table K11)
325.4 Calumny. Assault on subordinates (Table K11)
325.5 Sabotaging weapons, equipment or means of defense (Table K11)
326 Courts and procedure. Courts-martial (Table K11)
Including procedure in honor cases
326.3 Punishment. Execution (Table K11)
326.5 Probation and parole (Table K11)
Military discipline. Law enforcement
Including all branches of the armed forces
327 General (Table K11)

National defense. Military law
Military discipline. Law enforcement -- Continued
327.2 Superior orders. Enforcement of orders (Table K11)
327.5.A-Z Special topics, A-Z
327.5.M55 Military maneuvers (Table K12)
Courts and procedure
328 General (Table K11)
The administration of justice. The organization of the judiciary
Including the administration of criminal justice
329 General (Table K11)
Organization and administration
Class here works on national and state departments of justice or departments of justice of several states
For the department of justice of an individual state, see the state
329.2 General (Table K11)
329.3 National department of justice. Office of the Attorney General (Table K11)
Including legal opinions, e. g. Attorneys General's opinions
For legal opinions on a specific subject, see the subject
Judicial statistics see KL-KWX7 3+
Judicial assistance
Including judicial assistance in criminal matters
330 General (Table K11)
330.2 International judicial assistance (Table K11)
330.3 Foreign judgments (Conflict of laws) (Table K11)
Courts
Class here works on courts of several jurisdictions
Including courts of both criminal and civil jurisdiction
For courts (several or individual) of an individual jurisdiction, see the jurisdiction
332 General (Table K11)
332.5 State and federal jurisdiction (Table K11)
Lowest courts. Local courts
Including law courts
332.52 General (Table K11)
332.53 Municipal courts. Village courts (Native courts) (Table K11)
333 Magistrate courts (Table K11)
333.2 Neighborhood courts. Peoples' courts. Comrades' courts (Table K11)
333.3 Justice of the peace (Table K11)
334 Regional courts. Provincial courts. District courts. District peoples' courts (Table K11)
334.2 High courts of the states or republics. Superior state courts (Table K11)

Courts and procedure
Courts -- Continued
Courts of special jurisdiction
335 General (Table K11)
335.2 Special tribunals (Table K11)
Religious courts and councils
335.3 General (Table K11)
336 Sharia courts. Kadi courts (Table K11)
336.2 Rabbinical courts (Table K11)
Customary (native) courts of law
337 General (Table K11)
337.2 Houses of chiefs. Traditional councils (native or regional) (Table K11)
337.3 Village or family arbitral tribunals. Village (tribal) elders (Table K11)
338 Consular courts (Table K11)
338.2 Peasant association tribunals (Table K11)
Other courts of special jurisdiction
see the subject, e.g. KL-KWX7 326 Military courts
339 Supreme judicial councils (Table K11)
339.2 Special tribunals within a court (Table K11)
340 Deliberating and voting. Secrecy (Table K11)
340.2 Court decorum and discipline. Conduct of court proceedings (Table K11)
340.3 Judicial opinions. Advisory opinions (Table K11)
Judicial officers. Court employees
341 General (Table K11)
Law school education and post-law school education see KL-KWX7 5+
341.2 Nationality and citizenship (Table K11)
Judges
342 General (Table K11)
342.4 Independence of judges (Table K11)
343 Office of the public prosecutor. Director of prosecution (Table K11)
Notaries see KL-KWX7 5.52
Auxiliary personnel. Clerk's (Registrar's) office
343.2 Clerks to the court (Table K11)
344 Bailiffs (Table K11)
345 Medical examiners. Coroners (Table K11)
For forensic medicine, see RA1001+
Procedure in general
Class here works on civil and criminal procedure and works on civil, commercial, and labor procedure combined
346 General (Table K11)
Procedural principles

Courts and procedure
Procedure in general
Procedural principles -- Continued
346.2 General (Table K11)
346.3 Publicity and oral procedure (Table K11)
347 Parties to action (Table K11)
347.2 Pretrial procedures (Table K11)
Procedure at first instance. Trial
348 General (Table K11)
348.2 Cross examination (Table K11)
348.3 Summation. Closing argument (Table K11)
Evidence. Burden of proof
349 General (Table K11)
349.2 Presumption. Prima-facie evidence (Table K11)
349.3 Admission of evidence (Table K11)
349.4 Witnesses (Table K11)
350 Judicial decisions (Table K11)
Remedies
351 General (Table K11)
351.2 Appellate procedure (Table K11)
Civil procedure
352 Criticism. Reform (Table K11)
353 General (Table K11)
Procedural principles
353.2 General (Table K11)
353.3 Stare decisis (Table K11)
353.5 Publicity and oral procedure (Table K11)
Principles of evidence see KL-KWX7 364.2
354 Prejudicial actions (Table K11)
355 Equity practice and procedure (Table K11)
Jurisdiction. Venue
355.2 General (Table K11)
355.3 Removal of causes (Table K11)
355.4 Disqualification of judges (Table K11)
Action
356 General (Table K11)
357 Process and service (Table K11)
Pleading and motions
357.2 General (Table K11)
357.3 Motions (Table K11)
Defenses and objections (Exceptions)
357.4 General (Table K11)
357.5 Limitation of actions (Table K11)
357.6 Lis pendens (Table K11)
357.7 Set-off. Counterclaim and cross claim (Table K11)
358 Parties to action (Table K11)

Courts and procedure
Civil procedure -- Continued
Pretrial procedures
359 General (Table K11)
359.2 Deposition and discovery. Interrogatories (Table K11)
359.3 Summons, service of process, subpoena, etc. (Table K11)
Time periods. Deadlines
359.4 General (Table K11)
359.5 Default and restitution (Table K11)
Procedure at first instance
360 General (Table K11)
360.2 Jurisdiction. Competence in subject matter and venue (Table K11)
360.3 Right to litigate (Table K11)
Lis pendens see KL-KWX7 361.5.L58
Res judicata see KL-KWX7 361.5.R48
Time periods. Deadlines see KL-KWX7 359.4+
Actions and defenses
361 General (Table K11)
361.2 Joinder of actions. Compounded claims (Table K11)
361.3 Amendment. Withdrawal (Table K11)
361.5.A-Z Defenses and exceptions, A-Z
361.5.L55 Limitation of actions (Table K12)
361.5.L58 Lis pendens (Table K12)
361.5.R48 Res judicata (Table K12)
Particular proceedings
362 Joinder of parties (Table K11)
362.2 Intervention (Table K11)
362.3 Interpleader (Table K11)
363 Default judgments (Table K11)
363.3 Settlement out of court (Table K11)
363.4 Compromise (Table K11)
Evidence
364 General (Table K11)
364.2 Principles of evidence. Free evaluation of evidence (Table K11)
364.3 Burden of proof (Table K11)
364.4 Prima facie (Table K11)
Admissibility and exclusion of evidence
365 General (Table K11)
365.2 Physical examinations. Blood tests (Table K11)
Cf. RA1001+ Forensic medicine
Witnesses
365.3 General (Table K11)
365.4 Privileged witnesses (Confidential communication) (Table K11)

Courts and procedure
Civil procedure
Procedure at first instance
Evidence -- Continued
365.5 Expert testimony (Table K11)
366 Jury and jurors (Table K11)
366.2 Special masters. Referees. Auditors. Examiners (Table K11)
Judicial decisions
366.3 General (Table K11)
Judgment (General)
366.4 Declaratory judgment (Table K11)
367 Agreed judgment (Table K11)
Judgment by default see KL-KWX7 363
367.2 Interlocutory decisions (Table K11)
367.3 Void judgments and nonjudgments (Table K11)
367.4 New trial. Reopening a case (Table K11)
368 Mistakes (error) (Table K11)
Including correction, recall, or withdrawal of faulty decision
368.2 Res judicata. Estoppel by judgment (Table K11)
368.32 Court records. Minutes of evidence (Table K11)
Including clerks' mistakes and corrections
368.4 Advisory opinions (Table K11)
Particular procedures
369 Matrimonial actions (Table K11)
369.3 Procedures in parent and child cases (Table K11)
For procedures in guardianship and curatorship cases see KL-KWX7 61
369.4 Interdiction. Mental competency procedure (Table K11)
369.5 Public summons (Table K11)
Settlement see KL-KWX7 376
369.7 Small claims. Procedures before the justice of the peace or magistrate (Table K11)
Procedures before particular courts (e.g., native courts, comrade's courts, etc.) see KL-KWX7 332.52+
Remedies and special proceedings
370 General (Table K11)
370.1 Summary proceedings (Table K11)
370.2 Habeas corpus (Table K11)
370.3 Injunctions. Provisional remedies (Table K11)
Interpleader see KL-KWX7 362.3
370.4 Receivers in equity (Table K11)
Extraordinary remedies
Including older remedies
371 General (Table K11)
Particular remedies

Courts and procedure
Civil procedure
Remedies and special proceedings
Extraordinary remedies
Particular remedies -- Continued
372 Quo warranto (Table K11)
Habeas corpus see KL-KWX7 370.2
373 Appellate procedure (Table K11)
Execution of judgment
374 General (Table K11)
375 Attachment. Garnishment (Table K11)
376 Negotiated settlement. Compromise (Table K11)
377 Arbitration (Table K11)
Including commercial arbitration
378 Costs (Table K11)
Criminal law
379 Reform of criminal law, procedure, and execution
For works limited to a particular subject, see the subject
For works pertaining exclusively to the codes, see the code
Administration of criminal justice see KL-KWX7 329+
379.5 General (Table K11)
380 Constitutional aspects (Table K11)
Philosophy of criminal law
380.2 General (Table K11)
Theories of punishment. Criminal policy see KL-KWX7 395+
380.6 Relationship of criminal law to other disciplines, subjects or phenomena (Table K11)
381 Interpretation and construction. Legal hermeneutics (Table K11)
Applicability and validity of the law
381.2 Retroactivity. Ex post facto laws (Table K11)
381.4 Interpretation. Analogy (Table K11)
381.5 Customary law. Indigenous law. Repugnancy clause (Table K11)
Territorial applicability
382 General (Table K11)
Place of commission of crime
382.2 General (Table K11)
382.3 Press delicts (Table K11)
383 Crimes aboard aircraft (Table K11)
383.2 Conflict of laws (Table K11)
383.6 Temporal applicability (Table K11)
Including intertemporal law
Criminal offense
384 General (Table K11)
384.4 Crimes aggravated by personal characteristics (Table K11)

Criminal law
Criminal offense -- Continued
Criminal act
384.5 General (Table K11)
384.6 Corpus delicti (Table K11)
384.7 Omission (Table K11)
385 Causation (Table K11)
Forms of the act see KL-KWX7 391+
Illegality. Justification of otherwise illegal acts
385.5 General (Table K11)
385.6 Self-defense or defense of another (Table K11)
Superior orders see KL-KWX7 390
386 Consent of the injured party. Assumption of risk (Table K11)
386.5.A-Z Other grounds for justification, A-Z
Subarrange each by Table K12
386.7 Criminal intent. Mens rea (Table K11)
Including purpose and scienter
387 Negligence and wantonness (Table K11)
Criminal liability. Guilt. Culpability
387.5 General (Table K11)
Capacity. Incapacity and limited capacity
387.7 General (Table K11)
388.2 Insane persons. People with mental or emotional disabilities (Table K11)
Cf. HV6133 Psychopathology and crime
388.3 Minors (Table K11)
388.5.A-Z Special topics, A-Z
388.5.D58 Distemper (Table K12)
388.5.I58 Intoxication (Table K12)
Passion see KL-KWX7 388.5.D58
388.7 Criminal liability of juristic persons (Table K11)
390 Superior orders and justification or excusation (Table K11)
Cf. KL-KWX7 327.2 Military criminal law
390.3 Error (Table K11)
Forms of the criminal act
391 General (Table K11)
Omission see KL-KWX7 384.7
391.2 Attempt (Table K11)
Including intent and preparation, and active repentance
Perpetrators
392 General (Table K11)
Principals and accessories
392.2 General (Table K11)
392.5 Co-principals (Table K11)

Criminal law
Criminal offense
Forms of the criminal act
Perpetrators
Principals and accessories -- Continued
392.7 Accessory before the fact (Table K11)
Including after the fact
393 Complicity (Table K11)
393.4 Agent provocateur (Table K11)
Aggravating and extenuating circumstances see KL-KWX7 402.2+
394 Compound offenses and compound punishment (Table K11)
Punishment
394.6 General (Table K11)
Theory and policy of punishment
395 General (Table K11)
395.2 Retaliation. Retribution. Vendetta (Table K11)
395.4 Safeguarding the social and political system (Table K11)
395.6 General and special prevention (Table K11)
Including education, rehabilitation, and resocialization of perpetrator
Criminal anthropology
see HV6035+
396 Criminal sociology (Table K11)
For non-legal works, see HV6001+
Penalties and measures of rehabilitation and safety
For juveniles and young adults see KL-KWX7 472.6+
For execution of sentence see KL-KWX7 479.5+
396.2 General (Table K11)
Imprisonment
Including maximum and minimum terms
397 General (Table K11)
Prisons and jails see KL-KWX7 482.4
Reformatories see KL-KWX7 472.8
397.2 Short-term sentence (Table K11)
397.4 Sentencing to probation (Punishment without imprisonment). Conditional sentencing (Table K11)
Including terms of probation, e.g. education and resocialization through labor
397.8 Fines (Table K11)
398 Reprimand (Table K11)
398.2.A-Z Measures entailing deprivation of liberty, A-Z
398.2.C64 Commitment of addicts to institutions for withdrawal treatment (Table K12)
398.2.C65 Commitment to medical, nursing, or socio-therapeutic institutions (Table K12)

Criminal law
Punishment
Penalties and measures of rehabilitation and safety
Measures entailing deprivation of liberty, A-Z -- Continued
398.2.C66 Commitment to medical or psychiatric treatment (Table K12)
398.2.C67 Confiscation and destruction of corpus delicti (Table K12)
Disfranchisement see KL-KWX7 398.2.L67
398.2.D75 Driver's license revocation (Table K12)
398.2.E96 Expulsion (Table K12)
398.2.F68 Forfeiture (Table K12)
Infamy see KL-KWX7 398.2.L67
398.2.L67 Loss of civil rights. Infamy. Disfranchisement (Table K12)
398.2.P76 Prohibition against practicing a profession (Table K12)
398.2.P765 Property confiscation (Table K12)
398.2.P77 Protective custody (Table K12)
Including dangerous or habitual criminals
398.2.P78 Protective surveillance (Table K12)
Sentencing and determining the measure of punishment
398.3 General (Table K11)
398.6 Fixed and indeterminate sentence (Table K11)
Juvenile delinquents see KL-KWX7 472.2
Aggravating and extenuating circumstances
Including principals and accessories
402.2 General (Table K11)
402.4 Recidivism (Table K11)
402.6 Detention pending investigation (Table K11)
Causes barring prosecution or execution of sentence
403 General (Table K11)
403.2 Active repentance (Table K11)
Pardon and amnesty. Clemency
403.4 General (Table K11)
Suspension of punishment see KL-KWX7 482.8
Probation and parole see KL-KWX7 484
403.8 Limitation of actions (Table K11)
Criminal registers see KL-KWX7 485
Criminal statistics see KL-KWX7 3.2
Individual offenses
Including national (federal) statutory law and common law offenses in general, including comparative state (provincial) law
For criminal law of a particular state (province), see the jurisdiction
Offenses against the person
Including aggravating circumstances

Criminal law
Individual offenses
Offenses against the person -- Continued
403.9 General (Table K11)
Homicide
404 General (Table K11)
Murder
404.2 General (Table K11)
404.3 Dowry killing (Table K11)
405 Manslaughter (Table K11)
405.6 Killing on request (Table K11)
405.8 Euthanasia (Table K11)
406 Suicide. Aiding and abetting suicide (Table K11)
406.2 Parricide (Table K11)
406.4 Infanticide (Table K11)
406.5 Negligent homicide (Table K11)
406.7 Desertion. Exposing persons to mortal danger (Table K11)
Illegal abortion
407 General (Table K11)
407.2 Justification of abortion. Legal abortion (Table K11)
For birth control and family planning see KL-KWX7 152+
Crimes against physical inviolability
407.4 General (Table K11)
407.6 Battery (Table K11)
Child abuse see KL-KWX7 419
407.7 Conjugal violence. Wife abuse. Husband abuse (Table K11)
407.8 Communicating disease (Table K11)
408 Failure to render assistance (Table K11)
408.2 Abuse of defenseless persons or dependents. Abuse of older people (Table K11)
For child abuse see KL-KWX7 419
408.4 Consent. Justified assault (Table K11)
Including sports injuries
For medical treatment and operations see KL-KWX7 409.6+
409 Poisoning (Table K11)
409.2 Dueling (Table K11)
409.4 Brawling (Table K11)

Criminal aspects of surgical and other medical treatment
Including biomedical engineering and medical technology
409.6 General (Table K11)
410 Malpractice (Table K11)
Cf. KL-KWX7 110.45 Civil liability

Criminal law
Individual offenses
Offenses against the person
Criminal aspects of surgical and other medical treatment -- Continued
410.2 Treatment without consent (Table K11)
Euthanasia see KL-KWX7 405.8
410.3 Genetic engineering (Table K11)
410.8 Human reproductive technology (Table K11)
Including artificial insemination, fertilization in vitro, etc.
411 Transplantation of organs, tissues, etc. (Table K11)
Including donation of organs, tissues, etc.
411.2 Sterilization (Table K11)
Confidential communication see KL-KWX7 469.6.A+
Psychopharmaca damages see KL-KWX7 410
Crimes against personal freedom
411.6 General (Table K11)
411.8 False imprisonment (Table K11)
412 Extortionate kidnapping (Table K11)
Abduction
Cf. KL-KWX7 60.2+ Parental kidnapping
412.5 General (Table K11)
412.7 Political abduction (Table K11)
413 Abduction of a woman without her consent (Table K11)
413.2 Abduction of a female minor (Table K11)
413.4 Political accusation (Table K11)
413.8 Duress (Table K11)
Crimes against dignity and honor
Including juristic persons and families
414.3 General (Table K11)
414.5 Insult (Table K11)
414.7 Defamation. Calumny (Table K11)
415 Disparagement of memory of the dead (Table K11)
415.6 Privileged comment (Table K11)
Including criticism of scientific, artistic, or professional accomplishments
For press law see KL-KWX7 108.5+
Violation of personal privacy and secrets
416 General (Table K11)
416.4 Violation of confidential disclosures by professional persons (Table K11)
416.6 Opening of letters (Table K11)
416.8 Eavesdropping. Wiretapping (Table K11)
417 Offenses against religious observance and the peace of the dead (Table K11)
Offenses against marriage, family, and family status

Criminal law
Individual offenses
Offenses against marriage, family, and family status -- Continued
418 General (Table K11)
418.2 Incest (Table K11)
418.4 Adultery (Table K11)
418.6 Bigamy (Table K11)
(418.8) Parental kidnapping
see KL-KWX7 60.2
419 Abandonment, neglect, or abuse of a child (Table K11)
419.2 Breach of duty of support (Table K11)
419.4 Breach of duty of assistance to a pregnant woman (Table K11)
Abortion see KL-KWX7 407+
419.6 Falsification of civil status (Table K11)
Offenses against sexual integrity
420 General (Table K11)
420.2 Rape (Table K11)
Child molesting see KL-KWX7 419
420.6 Sodomy. Homosexual acts (Table K11)
420.8 Bestiality (Table K11)
422 Obscenity (Table K11)
Including production, exhibition, performance, advertising, etc.
Prostitution. Procuring
422.4 General works (Table K11)
422.45 Pandering and pimping. White slave traffic (Table K11)
Offenses against private and public property
423 General (Table K11)
Larceny and embezzlement
423.4 General (Table K11)
423.6 Burglary (Table K11)
424 Armed theft and theft by gangs (Table K11)
424.2 Domestic and family theft (Table K11)
425 Embezzlement (Table K11)
425.4 Robbery and rapacious theft (Table K11)
425.6 Destruction of property and conversion (Table K11)
Fraud
425.8 General (Table K11)
Fraudulent bankruptcy see KL-KWX7 427.6
426 Extortion (Table K11)
426.6 Breach of trust (Table K11)
426.8 Usury (Table K11)
427.6 Defeating rights of creditors. Fraudulent bankruptcy (Table K11)

Criminal law
Individual offenses
Offenses against private and public property -- Continued
428 Game and fish poaching (Table K11)
428.2 Aiding criminals in securing benefits. Receiving stolen goods (Table K11)
Offenses against the national economy
428.6 General (Table K11)
429 Violation of price regulations (Table K11)
Including price fixing, hoarding, discrimination, overselling and underselling prices established by government etc.
429.2 Foreign exchange violations (Table K11)
429.4 Economic and industrial secrets. Unauthorized possession or disclosure (Table K11)
429.8 False statements concerning national planning (Table K11)
Counterfeiting money and stamps see KL-KWX7 434.6
Offenses against public property see KL-KWX7 423+
430.A-Z Other, A-Z
Subarrange each by Table K12
Money laundering see KL-KWX7 90.15.R43
Offenses against public order and convenience
Including aggravating circumstances
430.5 General (Table K11)
430.7 Inciting insubordination (Table K11)
430.9 Rowdyism. Vandalism (Table K11)
431 Inciting crime (Table K11)
431.4 Parasitism (Table K11)
432 Demonstrations and failure to disperse (Table K11)
432.2 Inciting acts against minorities (Table K11)
Threatening the community. Terrorist activities see KL-KWX7 435.3+
432.4 Misuse of titles, uniforms, and insignia (Table K11)
Crimes against security of legal and monetary transactions and documents
433 General (Table K11)
433.2 Evidence (Table K11)
433.4 Forgery of documents and of mechanical records (Table K11)
Including forgery of electronic data bases
434 Physical and identifying marks (Table K11)
434.6 Counterfeiting money, stamps and securities (Table K11)
Including postage stamps, checks, bills of exchange, etc.
Customs crimes see KL-KWX7 316+
Tax evasion see KL-KWX7 316.3
435.12.A-Z Other, A-Z
435.12.D57 Displacing boundaries (Table K12)

Criminal law
Individual offenses
Offenses against public order and convenience
Crimes against security of legal and monetary transactions and documents
Other, A-Z
435.12.F34 False certification (Table K12)
Crimes involving danger to the community. Crimes against the environment. Terrorism
435.3 General (Table K11)
435.4 Arson (Table K11)
435.6 Causing explosion (Table K11)
Including explosives and nuclear energy
435.8 Misuse of ionizing radiation (Table K11)
436 Releasing natural forces (Table K11)
Including flood, avalanche, rockfall, etc.
436.2 Dangerous use of poisonous substances (Table K11)
436.4 Poisoning wells or soil (Table K11)
436.6 Poisoning food, medicine, etc. (Table K11)
436.8 Spreading communicable diseases, morbific agents, or parasites. Biological terrorism (Table K11)
437 Damaging water and power installations (Table K11)
437.2 Impairing industrial safety appliances (Table K11)
437.4 Sabotage of essential services, utilities, warning systems, etc. (Table K11)
437.6 Causing danger in construction (Table K11)
Including collapse, faulty gas or electric installation, etc.
Crimes affecting traffic. Dangerous interference with rail, ship, or air traffic
Including unsafe operation of a rail vehicle, ship, or aircraft
438 General (Table K11)
Dangerous interference with street traffic
438.4 General (Table K11)
438.6 Driving while intoxicated (Table K11)
438.8 Duress. Constraint (Table K11)
439 Leaving the scene of an accident. Hit-and-run driving (Table K11)
439.2 Predatory assault on motorists (Table K11)
439.6 Crimes aboard aircraft. Air piracy (Table K11)
439.8 Riots (Table K11)
Crimes against public health
440 General (Table K11)
440.2 Intoxication (Table K11)
440.4 Illicit use of, possession of, and traffic in narcotics (Table K11)
Communicating venereal disease see KL-KWX7 407.8

Criminal law
Individual offenses
Offenses against public order and convenience -- Continued
440.6 Gambling (Table K11)
Including illegal operation of a lottery or games of chance, and participation
440.7 Vagrancy. Begging (Table K11)
440.8 Loitering (Table K11)
Offenses against the government. Political offenses. Offenses against the people
441 General (Table K11)
High treason and treason
441.5 General (Table K11)
441.7 High treason against the state (Table K11)
Including national and state (republic, etc.), and including preparation of treasonable acts
442.4 Treason against the constitution (Table K11)
442.6 Assault on the head of state (Table K11)
442.8 Inciting treason (Table K11)
443.2 Sabotage endangering the state (Table K11)
443.4 Undermining the state apparatus (Table K11)
443.8 Lese majesty (Table K11)
444 Disparagement of the state and its symbols. Disparaging constitutional organs (Table K11)
444.2 Treasonable espionage (Table K11)
444.4 Subversive activities (Table K11)
444.6 Intelligence activities (Table K11)
444.8 Propaganda endangering the state (Table K11)
445.5 Treasonable endangering of the peace or of international relations (Table K11)
Including propaganda, planning, preparation, or participation in an aggressive war
Crimes in connection with election and voting
445.8 General (Table K11)
446 Bribery. Corrupt practices (Table K11)
446.4 Deceiving voters (Table K11)
446.6 Falsifying votes and voting results (Table K11)
Crimes against national defense
447 General (Table K11)
447.3 Sabotaging and depicting means of defense (Table K11)
Opposition to power of the state
447.6 General (Table K11)
447.8 Constraining official action or inaction (Table K11)
448 Prison escape. Mutiny. Freeing prisoners (Table K11)
448.2.A-Z Other forms of opposition, A-Z
Subarrange each by Table K12

Criminal law
Individual offenses
Offenses against the government. Political offenses.
Offenses against the peace -- Continued
Endangering the administration of justice. Obstruction of justice
448.4 General (Table K11)
448.5 False testimony (Table K11)
Including false unsworn testimony and perjury
448.6 False accusation (Table K11)
448.8 Bringing false complaint (Table K11)
450 Thwarting criminal justice (Table K11)
450.2 Failure to report felony. Misprision (Table K11)
450.4 Coercion of testimony (Table K11)
450.6 Intentional misconstruction by law officers (Table K11)
450.7 Prosecuting innocent persons (Table K11)
Including execution
450.8 Repressing conflicting interests. Prevarication (Table K11)
451 Contempt of court (Table K11)
Crimes against the civil service
451.4 General (Table K11)
452 Bribery. Corrupt practices (Table K11)
452.4 Violating official secrecy. Disclosure (Table K11)
Crimes against humanity
453.8 General (Table K11)
454 Genocide (Table K11)
454.3 Crimes against foreign states, supranational institutions, or international institutions (Table K11)
454.5 War crimes (Table K11)
Offenses committed through the mail
456 General (Table K11)
Obscenity see KL-KWX7 422
Threats, extortion, and blackmail see KL-KWX7 426
Labor law criminal provisions see KL-KWX7 143.7
Press law criminal provisions see KL-KWX7 108.6
Tax and customs crimes see KL-KWX7 316+
Military criminal law see KL-KWX7 324+
Criminal procedure
For works on both criminal and civil procedure, including codes of both criminal and civil procedure see KL-KWX7 352+
For works on both criminal law and criminal procedure, including codes of both criminal law and criminal procedure see KL-KWX7 379+
Criticism and reform see KL-KWX7 379

Criminal procedure -- Continued

460 General (Table K11)

Adminstration of criminal justice see KL-KWX7 329+

Court organization see KL-KWX7 332+

Procedural principles

461 General (Table K11)

462 Due process of law (Table K11)

462.2 Uniformity of law application. Stare decisis (Table K11)

462.4 Accusation principle (Table K11)

462.6 Publicity and oral procedure (Table K11)

462.8 Prejudicial actions (Table K11)

Including all branches of the law

463.A-Z Parties to action, A-Z

463.A25 Accused. Person charged. Defendant (Table K12)

Defendant see KL-KWX7 463.A25

463.D43 Defense attorney. Public defender (Table K12)

Person charged see KL-KWX7 463.A25

Public defender see KL-KWX7 463.D43

463.S73 State prosecutor (Table K12)

Class here works on the legal status of the prosecutor in criminal procedure

For general works on the office of the public prosecutor see KL-KWX7 343

463.S93 Suspect (Table K12)

463.V52 Victim (Table K12)

Pretrial procedures

463.2 General (Table K11)

463.4 Penal report. Charges brought against a person (Table K11)

Investigation

463.6 General (Table K11)

463.62 Techniques of criminal investigation

see HV8073+

463.8 Examination of the accused

Cf. KL-KWX7 467.9+ Admissability of evidence

464 Preliminary judicial investigation (Table K11)

464.2 Public charges by prosecutor (Table K11)

464.6 Summonses, service of process, and subpoena. Wanted notice (Table K11)

464.8 Time periods. Deadlines (Table K11)

Compulsory measures against the accused. Securing of evidence

465 General (Table K11)

465.2 Search and seizure (Table K11)

Including search of persons, buildings, institution's records, etc.

465.4 Arrest. Provisional apprehension (Table K11)

Criminal procedure
Compulsory measures against the accused. Securing of evidence -- Continued
Detention pending investigation
Cf. KL-KWX7 479.8+ Execution of sentence
465.7 General (Table K11)
465.9 Bail (Table K11)
466 Extradition (Table K11)
Procedure at first instance
466.4 General (Table K11)
466.6 Jurisdiction (Table K11)
Including competence in subject matter and venue
466.8 Action. Complaint (Table K11)
467 Exclusion and challenge of court members (Table K11)
Time period and deadlines see KL-KWX7 464.8
Limitation of action see KL-KWX7 403.8
Trial
467.3 General (Table K11)
Evidence. Burden of proof
467.5 General (Table K11)
Admissability of evidence
467.9 General (Table K11)
468 Confession. Self-incrimination. Entrapment (Table K11)
468.3 Informers. Official secrets (Table K11)
468.5 Narcoanalysis, lie detectors, etc. (Table K11)
468.7 Physical examination (Table K11)
Including blood tests, urine tests, etc.
For forensic medicine, see RA1001+
468.9 Electronic listening and recording devices (Table K11)
Including wiretapping
469 Previous testimony, police records, etc. (Table K11)
Witnesses
469.2 General (Table K11)
469.6.A-Z Privileged witnesses (confidential communication), A-Z
Subarrange each by Table K12
469.8.A-Z Other witnesses, A-Z
Subarrange each by Table K12
470 Expert testimony (Table K11)
For forensic medicine, chemistry, psychology, psychiatry, toxicology, etc. see RA1001+
470.2 Testimony of accused (Table K11)
470.4 Documentary evidence (Table K11)
470.5 Circumstantial evidence (Table K11)
470.6 Alibi (Table K11)

Criminal procedure
Procedure at first instance
Trial
Evidence -- Continued
470.9.A-Z Other, A-Z
Subarrange each by Table K12
Particular proceedings
471 General (Table K11)
471.3 Summary proceedings (Table K11)
471.5 Proceedings against absentee and fugitives (Table K11)
471.7 Recourse against decisions of grievance boards (Table K11)
Procedure for juvenile delinquency
472 General (Table K11)
472.2 The juvenile delinquent. The young adult perpetrator (Table K11)
472.4 Juvenile crime (Table K11)
Criminal liability and guilt see KL-KWX7 387.5+
Punishment. Correctional or disciplinary measures
Including measures of rehabilitation and safety
472.6 General (Table K11)
472.8 Custodial education. Detention homes. Reformatories (Table K11)
473.4 Punishment without imprisonment (Table K11)
Execution of sentence see KL-KWX7 479.5+
Judicial decisions
473.6 General (Table K11)
Judgment
473.8 General (Table K11)
Sentencing and determination of punishment see KL-KWX7 398.3+
474 Judicial discretion (Table K11)
Including opportunity and equity
474.4 Acquittal (Table K11)
474.6 Conviction (Table K11)
Including measures of rehabilitation and safety
475 Dismissal. Decision ab instantia (Table K11)
Probation see KL-KWX7 484
475.2 Void judgments (Table K11)
475.3 Correction or withdrawal of faulty decisions (errors) (Table K11)
Res judicata
475.4 General (Table K11)
Waiver of appeal see KL-KWX7 478.8
476 Court records. Minutes of evidence (Table K11)
Including clerks, translators, and correction of records

Criminal procedure -- Continued

476.2 Participation of injured party in criminal procedure. Private charge (Table K11)

Including public interest

Special procedures

476.5 Procedure before justice of the peace (Table K11)

Commitment of insane criminals see KL-KWX7 398.2.A+

Procedure in confiscation of corpus delicti see KL-KWX7 398.2.C67

Other procedures

see the subject, e.g. KL-KWX7 316+ Tax and customs criminal procedures; KL-KWX7 324+ Military criminal procedure; etc.

Remedies

477 General (Table K11)

478 Appellate procedure. Cassation

478.8 Waiver of appeal (Table K11)

479 Post-conviction remedies (Table K11)

479.2 Reopening a case. New trial (Table K11)

For procedure before the constitutional court see KL-KWX7 239

Execution of sentence

Including execution of sentence of juvenile courts

479.5 General (Table K11)

Law reform. Criticism see KL-KWX7 379

Imprisonment

Including regulations of detention pending investigation and short-term sentences

479.8 General (Table K11)

480 Administration of penal or correctional institutions (Table K11)

Including discipline, hygiene, etc.

The prisoner

481 General (Table K11)

481.2.A-Z Particular, A-Z

Dangerous criminals see KL-KWX7 398.2.P77

481.2.E38 Education of prisoners. Education through labor (Table K12)

Insane criminals see KL-KWX7 398.2.C65

481.2.J88 Juvenile prisoners (Table K12)

481.2.P64 Political prisoners (Table K12)

482 Labor and industries in correctional institutions (Table K11)

Including wages

Rehabilitation and resocialization see KL-KWX7 395.6

Criminal procedure
Execution of sentence
Imprisonment -- Continued
482.4 Penal or correctional institutions (Table K11)
Including prisons, jails, penal colonies, reformatories, juvenile detention homes, etc.
Pardon, amnesty, and clemency see KL-KWX7 403.4+
482.8 Suspension of punishment (Table K11)
484 Probation. Parole (Table K11)
Including conditions and probation and parole for juvenile delinquents
484.3 Community-based corrections (Table K11)
485 Criminal registers (Table K11)
Extradition see KL-KWX7 466
486 Costs (Table K11)
Victimology
487 General (Table K11)
488 Children and sexual crimes (Table K11)
Compensation to victims of crimes see KL-KWX7 97.74
Criminology and penology
see HV6001+

1 Bibliography

<1.2> Periodicals

For periodicals consisting predominantly of legal articles, regardless of subject matter and jurisdiction, see K1+

For periodicals consisting primarily of informative material (newsletters, bulletins, etc.) relating to a special subject, see the subject and form division tables for periodicals

For law reports, official bulletins or circulars intended chiefly for the publication of laws and regulations, see appropriate entries in the text or form division tables

1.3 Monographic series

Official gazettes

For departmental gazettes, see the issuing department or agency

For city gazettes, see the issuing city

1.4 Indexes (General)

1.5.A2-.A29 General

Arranged chronologically

Legislative and executive papers

Including historical sources

see class J

Legislation

Indexes and tables

1.55 Serials

1.6 Monographs. By

1.7 Abridgments and digests

Early territorial laws and legislation

Class here early sources not provided for elsewhere, e.g. custumals, privileges, edicts, mandates, etc.

2 Collections. Compilations

Individual

see the subject

Statutes

Including statutory orders and regulations

For statutes, statutory orders, and regulations on a particular subject, see the subject

Collections. Compilations

Including official and private editions with or without annotations

2.2 Serials

2.3 Monographs. By date

3.3 Codifications and related material

Class here collections of codes and codifications not limited to a subject

Including early codifications, and including enactments of codes

For codes on a subject, see the subject

Court decisions and related materials
Including historical sources, and authorized and private editions
For decisions on a particular subject, see the subject

3.33 Digests. Summaries
For indexes and digests relating to a particular publication, see the publication

3.4 Several courts. By date
Class here decisions of courts of several jurisdictions

Particular courts and tribunals
Including historical courts and tribunals not provided for by subject

3.43 Highest court of appeals. Supreme Court (Table K18)

Intermediate appellate courts. Courts of appeal
Including reports of the only or several intermediate appellate courts of a state and reports of national court of appeals in judicial districts

3.5 Collective (Table K18)

3.6.A-Z Particular courts, A-Z

Trial courts

3.7 Collective (Table K18)

4.A-Z Particular courts. By city, county, district, etc., A-Z

Local courts
Including justices of the peace courts, people's courts, magistrates' courts, etc.

4.2 General (Table K18)

4.4.A-Z Particular courts. By city, etc., A-Z

4.5.A-Z Other courts. By place or name, A-Z

Encyclopedias
see the numbers provided for encyclopedias at the national level

Dictionaries. Terms and phrases
see the numbers provided for dictionaries at the national level

Form books
see see the numbers provided for form books at the national level

Judicial statistics

5.2 General

5.3 Criminal statistics
Including juvenile delinquency

5.4.A-Z Other. By subject, A-Z

Directories
see the numbers provided for directories at the national level

Trials
see the numbers provided for trials at the national level

Legal research
see the numbers provided for legal research at the national level

Legal education
  see the numbers provided for legal education at the national level
The legal profession
  see the numbers provided for the legal profession at the national level
Legal aid
  see the numbers provided for legal aid at the national level
Bar associations. Law societies and associations
  see the numbers provided for bar associations and law societies at the national level
6 History of law
  For the history of a particular subject (including historical sources), see the subject
  For collections and compilations of sources see KL-KWX8 2+
7 Law reform. Criticism
  Including reform of general administration of justice
  For reform of criminal justice administration and criminal law see KL-KWX8 91+
8 General works
  Including compends, popular works, civics, etc.
Private law
11 General (Table K11)
  Private international law. Conflict of laws
    For works on conflict rules of branches other than private law and law of procedure (e.g. criminal law), see the subject
12 General (Table K11)
  Interlocal (interstate) law
    see KL-KWX4 483.5 ; KL-KWX6 483.5
13.A-Z Particular branches and subjects of the law, A-Z
13.2 Intertemporal law. Retroactive law (Table K11)
  Including conflict of laws
Civil law
13.3 General (Table K11)
  Persons
13.4 General (Table K11)
  Natural persons
13.5 General (Table K11)
  Personality and capacity
    Including incapacity
13.6 General (Table K11)
13.7 Absence and presumption of death (Table K11)
  Civil registers see KL-KWX8 38.2.R44
13.8 Citizenship (Table K11)

Civil law
Persons
Natural persons -- Continued
13.9 Personality rights (Table K11)
For protection of personality rights see KL-KWX8 20.5.P76
Juristic persons of private law
14.2 General (Table K11)
14.3 Personality and capacity (Table K11)
Including personality rights
For protection of personality rights see KL-KWX8 20.5.P76
14.4 Associations (Table K11)
Including unincorporated and incorporated societies
14.5 Foundations. Charitable trusts and uses (Table K11)
14.6.A-Z Other special topics, A-Z
Subarrange each by Table K12
Things
14.7 General (Table K11)
14.8.A-Z Special topics, A-Z
Subarrange each by Table K12
15 Rights (Table K11)
Including immaterial rights
Legal transactions
15.2 General (Table K11)
15.3.A-Z Special topics, A-Z
15.3.T78 Trusts and trustees (Table K12)
Domestic relations. Family law
15.4 General (Table K11)
15.5 Marriage (Table K11)
Including matrimonial actions and dissolution of marriage
15.6 Marital property and regime (Table K11)
Consanguinity and affinity
Including parent and child
15.7 General (Table K11)
15.8 Parental power (Table K11)
16 Adoption (Table K11)
16.2 Illegitimate children (Table K11)
16.3 Affiliation. Paternity (Table K11)
16.4 Guardianship. Curatorship (Table K11)
For guardianship courts see KL-KWX8 38.2.G82
Property
16.5 General (Table K11)
16.6 Possession and violation of possession (Table K11)

Civil law
Property -- Continued
16.7 Ownership. Acquisition and loss (Table K11)
Including coownership
Real property. Land law
17 General (Table K11)
Land registration law see KL-KWX8 19.2+
Public and private restraint on real property
17.2 General (Table K11)
Zoning laws see KL-KWX8 60.5
Fideicommissum see KL-KWX8 73
17.3 Ownership. Acquisition and loss (Table K11)
Including contractual acquisition and loss by judicial decree
Rights incident to ownership of land
17.4 General (Table K11)
17.5 Law of adjoining landowners (Table K11)
17.6.A-Z Special topics, A-Z
17.6.A57 Air and space above ground (Table K12)
17.6.R56 Riparian rights. Water rights (Table K12)
Space above ground see KL-KWX8 17.6.A57
Water rights see KL-KWX8 17.6.R56
17.7 Superficies (Table K11)
Rights as to the use and profits of another's land
18 General (Table K11)
18.2 Emphyteusis (Table K11)
18.3.A-Z Servitudes (real and personal), A-Z
18.3.C65 Conveyance and life annuities (Table K12)
Life annuities see KL-KWX8 18.3.C65
18.4 Right of preemption (Table K11)
18.5.A-Z Types of real property, A-Z
Subarrange each by Table K12
Hypothecation
18.6 General (Table K11)
18.7 Mortgage. Hypotheca (Table K11)
18.8 Land charge (Table K11)
19 Pledges (Table K11)
Land register and registration
19.2 General (Table K11)
19.3 Cadastral surveys. Cadasters (Table K11)
19.4.A-Z Other special topics, A-Z
Subarrange each by Table K12
Inheritance. Succession upon death
19.5 General (Table K11)
Intestate and testamentary succession
Including wills

Civil law
Inheritance. Succession upon death
Intestate and testamentary succession -- Continued
19.6 General (Table K11)
19.65 Executors and administrators (Table K11)
19.7 Contract of inheritance (Table K11)
19.8 Unworthiness of heirs. Disinheritance (Table K11)
19.9 Certificate of inheritance. Proof of heirship (Table K11)
Obligations
20 General (Table K11)
Nonperformance. Damages
20.2 General (Table K11)
20.3.A-Z Special topics, A-Z
Subarrange each by Table K12
Delicts. Torts
20.4 General (Table K11)
20.5.A4-Z Special topics, A-Z
20.5.P76 Protected rights (Table K12)
20.6.A-Z Individual torts, A-Z
20.6.A87 Automobile accidents (Table K12)
20.6.N43 Negligence (Table K12)
Contracts and transactions
20.8 General (Table K11)
Individual contracts and transactions
20.9 Sale (Table K11)
21 Exchange. Barter (Table K11)
Lease. Landlord and tenant
21.2 General (Table K11)
21.3 Protection of the tenant (Table K11)
21.4 Procedure and execution. Housing courts (Table K11)
Including eviction
Housing
21.5 General (Table K11)
21.6.A-Z Special topics, A-Z
Disaster relief see KL-KWX8 21.6.E45
21.6.E45 Emergency measures. Disaster relief (Table K12)
21.7 Land lease (Table K11)
Contracts of service and labor
21.8 General (Table K11)
21.9 Servants (Table K11)
Employees and labor contract see KL-KWX8 30.4
22.A-Z Other contracts, A-Z
Subarrange each by Table K12
Commercial contracts and transactions
22.2 General (Table K11)

Commercial contracts and transactions -- Continued
Commercial courts see KL-KWX8 31.8
22.3 Merchant and business enterprise (Table K11)
Including firma, good will, accounting, etc.
22.4 Agency (Table K11)
Including commercial agents
22.5 Commercial registers (Table K11)
22.6 Sale (Table K11)
22.7 Consignment (Table K11)
22.8 Warehousing (Table K11)
Freight forwarders and carriers see KL-KWX8 25+
Negotiable instruments. Titles of credit
23 General (Table K11)
23.2 Bills of exchange (Table K11)
23.3 Checks (Table K11)
Stock certificates and bonds see KL-KWX8 28.5.S86
23.4.A-Z Other special, A-Z
Subarrange each by Table K12
23.5 Criminal provisions (Table K11)
Banking. Stock exchange
23.6 General (Table K11)
23.7 State supervision (Table K11)
23.8.A-Z Types of banks and credit institutions, A-Z
23.8.M67 Mortgage banks (Table K12)
23.8.S29 Savings banks (Table K12)
24.A-Z Banking transactions, A-Z
24.A24 Account current (Table K12)
Credit see KL-KWX8 24.L6
24.D45 Deposit banking (Table K12)
24.L6 Loans. Credit (Table K12)
24.3 Investments (Table K11)
Carriers. Carriage of goods and passengers
For regulatory aspects of transportation see KL-KWX8 82.5+
25 General (Table K11)
25.3 Coastwise and inland shipping (Table K11)
Including passengers and goods
Bus lines see KL-KWX8 83.3.B88
Railroads see KL-KWX8 83.4+
Airlines
see KL-KWX4 3467+ ; KL-KWX6 1050+
25.5 Freight forwarders and carriers (Table K11)
26.A-Z Other special topics, A-Z
Subarrange each by Table K12
Insurance

Commercial contracts and transactions
Insurance -- Continued
26.5 General (Table K11)
26.8.A-Z Branches of insurance, A-Z
Subarrange each by Table K12
26.85.A-Z Individual risks and damages, A-Z
Subarrange each by Table K12
Business associations
27 General (Table K11)
Personal companies (Unincorporated business associations)
27.3 General (Table K11)
27.5.A-Z Special types of companies, A-Z
Subarrange each by Table K12
Stock companies (Incorporated business associations)
28 General (Table K11)
28.3.A-Z Particular types, A-Z
Subarrange each by Table K12
28.5.A-Z Special topics, A-Z
Bonds see KL-KWX8 28.5.S86
28.5.S86 Stock certificates. Bonds (Table K12)
28.7.A-Z Other types of companies, A-Z
Subarrange each by Table K12
28.8 Cooperative societies (Table K11)
29 Combinations. Industrial trusts (Table K11)
Including business concerns, consortia, etc.
Intellectual and industrial property
Including copyright, patents, trademarks, unfair competition, etc.
29.3 General (Table K11)
29.5.A-Z Special topics, A-Z
Subarrange each by Table K12
Labor law
Including works on both labor law and social insurance and private labor law as it applies to the labor contract and to the labor-management relationship
Criticism and reform
see KL-KWX4 1468 ; KL-KWX6 1208
30 General (Table K11)
30.3 Organization and administration (Table K11)
Including state and local departments and boards
30.4 Labor contract and employment (Table K11)
30.5 Labor-management relations (Table K11)
Collective bargaining and labor agreements
30.6 General (Table K11)
30.7.A-Z By industry, occupation, or group of employees, A-Z
Subarrange each by Table K12

Labor law -- Continued
Collective labor disputes
Including strikes
30.8 General (Table K11)
31.A-Z By industry, occupation, or group of employees, A-Z
Subarrange each by Table K12
31.2 Labor unions (Table K11)
31.3 Employers' associations (Table K11)
Protection of labor
31.4 General (Table K11)
31.5.A-Z Special topics, A-Z
31.5.C44 Child labor (Table K12)
Holidays see KL-KWX8 31.5.V32
31.5.H65 Home labor (Table K12)
31.5.H68 Hours of labor (Table K12)
31.5.L32 Labor hygiene and safety (Table K12)
Leave of absence see KL-KWX8 31.5.V32
Safety equipment see KL-KWX8 31.5.L32
Sick leave see KL-KWX8 31.5.V32
31.5.V32 Vacations. Holidays (Table K12)
Including leave of absence and sick leave
31.5.W35 Women's labor (Table K12)
31.6.A-Z By industry, occupation, or group of employees, A-Z
Subarrange each by Table K12
31.7 Labor supply. Manpower control (Table K11)
Including employment agencies
31.8 Labor courts and procedure (Table K11)
Social legislation
32 Social reform and policies (Table K11)
Including all branches of social legislation
32.2 General (Table K11)
32.3 Organization and administration (Table K11)
For department of labor and social affairs see KL-KWX8 30.3
Social insurance
32.4 General (Table K11)
32.5 Branches of social insurance, A-Z
32.5.H42 Health insurance (Table K12)
32.5.S62 Social security (Table K12)
32.5.U53 Unemployment insurance (Table K12)
32.5.W67 Workers' compensation (Table K12)
32.6.A-Z By industry, occupation, or group of employees, A-Z
Subarrange each by Table K12
Social services. Public welfare
33 General (Table K11)

Social legislation
Social services. Public welfare -- Continued
33.3.A-Z Services or benefits, A-Z
Subarrange each by Table K12
33.5.A-Z Beneficiary groups, A-Z
33.5.A88 Asocial types (Table K12)
33.5.C44 Children (Table K12)
33.5.D58 Disabled (Table K12)
33.5.E43 Elderly (Table K12)
33.5.F35 Families (Table K12)
Juveniles see KL-KWX8 33.5.C44
33.5.P45 Pensioners (Table K12)
33.5.P66 Poor (Table K12)
33.5.R43 Refugees (Table K12)
33.5.W37 War (Table K12)
(33.6) Disaster relief
see KL-KWX8 58.4
33.7 Social courts and procedure (Table K11)
Courts and procedure
The administration of justice. The organization of the judiciary
Administration of criminal justice see KL-KWX8 92.38+
Criticism and reform see KL-KWX8 7
34 General (Table K11)
34.2 Organization and administration (Table K11)
Including state and local departments and boards
Judicial statistics see KL-KWX8 5.2+
Courts
History
34.3 General (Table K11)
34.4.A-Z Particular courts, A-Z
34.4.F48 Feudal and servitary courts (Table K12)
Manorial courts see KL-KWX8 34.4.P38
34.4.P38 Patrimonial and manorial courts (Table K12)
Servitary courts see KL-KWX8 34.4.F48
35 General (Table K11)
35.2.A-Z Particular courts and tribunals, A-Z
Subarrange each by Table K12
35.2.D57 District courts (Table K12)
35.4.A-Z Courts of special jurisdiction, A-Z
For courts of special jurisdiction not listed below, see the subject, e.g. KL-KWX8 31.8 Labor courts; KL-KWX8 33.7 Social courts; etc.
35.4.C68 Courts of honor (Table K12)
35.4.J88 Justices of the peace (Table K12)

Courts and procedure -- Continued
The legal profession
Including judicial officers and personnel
35.6 General (Table K11)
Law school education
see KL-KWX4 50+ ; KL-KWX6 50+
35.7 Judicial personnel other than lawyers (Table K11)
36 Judges (Table K11)
36.2 Office of the public prosecutor. Procuratura (Table K11)
Notaries see KL-KWX8 38.2.N68
36.4 Practice of law (Table K11)
Including attorneys and legal consultants
Judicial assistance
36.5 General (Table K11)
36.6 International judicial assistance (Table K11)
36.7 Foreign judgments (Conflict of laws) (Table K11)
Judicial review see KL-KWX8 54
37 Procedure in general (Table K11)
Including all branches of the law
Civil procedure
37.2 General (Table K11)
37.3.A-Z Special procedures, A-Z
Subarrange each by Table K12
37.4 Remedies (Table K11)
37.5 Arbitration (Table K11)
Including commercial arbitration
Noncontentious jurisdiction
38 General (Table K11)
38.2.A-Z Branches of noncontentious jurisdiction, A-Z
Children (General) see KL-KWX8 38.2.D65
Civil registers see KL-KWX8 38.2.R44
38.2.D65 Domestic relations (Table K12)
Including children (General)
38.2.G82 Guardianship court (Table K12)
38.2.I54 Inheritance (Probate) court (Table K12)
Matrimonial property registers see KL-KWX8 38.2.R44
38.2.N68 Notaries (Table K12)
Probate court see KL-KWX8 38.2.I54
Recording see KL-KWX8 38.2.R44
38.2.R44 Registration. Recording (Table K12)
Including civil registers, registers of matrimonial property, etc.
Insolvency
38.5 General (Table K11)
38.6 Execution (Table K11)
Including procedures

Courts and procedure
Insolvency -- Continued
Bankruptcy
38.7 General (Table K11)
38.8.A-Z Special topics, A-Z
Subarrange each by Table K12
39 Debtors' relief (Table K11)
39.2 Costs (Table K11)
40 Public law
Constitutional law
Constitutional history
41 General
Estates. Classes
42 General
42.2 Nobility
Peasantry see KL-KWX8 71.4+
42.3.A-Z Other special topics, A-Z
Subarrange each by Table K12
Feudal law
43 General
43.2.A-Z Special topics, A-Z
Subarrange each by Table K12
43.3 Constitutional reform. Criticism (Table K11)
43.4 General (Table K11)
Sources
Including historical sources and related material
43.5 Collections. Compilations
Constitutions
Collections see KL-KWX8 43.5
44.5<date> Individual constitutions
Arrange chronologically by appending the date of adoption to this number and deleting any trailing zeros.
Subarrange each by Table K17
44.6<date> Individual sources other than constitutions
Arrange chronologically by appending the date of adoption or issuance to this number and deleting any trailing zeros.
Subarrange by main entry
44.7.A-Z Constitutional principles, A-Z
44.7.R85 Rule of law (Table K12)
44.7.S46 Separation of power (Table K12)
45 Territory (Table K11)
45.3 Foreign relations (Table K11)
Individual and state
45.5 General (Table K11)
46 Nationality and citizenship (Table K11)

| | |
|---|---|
| | Constitutional law |
| | Individual and state -- Continued |
| 46.2-46.2.Z | Particular groups, A-Z |
| | Subarrange each by Table K12 |
| | Fundamental rights and constitutional guaranties |
| 46.3 | General (Table K11) |
| 46.5.A-Z | Individual rights or guaranties, A-Z |
| | Subarrange each by Table K12 |
| 46.7 | Civic duties (Table K11) |
| 47 | Political parties (Table K11) |
| 47.2.A-Z | Other special topics, A-Z |
| | Subarrange each by Table K12 |
| | Election law see KL-KWX8 48 |
| 47.3 | Internal security (Table K11) |
| | Organs of government |
| 47.5 | General (Table K11) |
| | The people |
| 47.6 | General (Table K11) |
| 48 | Election law (Table K11) |
| | The legislature. Legislative power |
| 48.2 | General (Table K11) |
| 48.3 | Legislative bodies. Peoples' assembly (Table K11) |
| | Including bodies with one or two chambers |
| 48.4.A-Z | Special topics, A-Z |
| | Subarrange each by Table K12 |
| | The head of state |
| 48.5 | General (Table K11) |
| 48.6-.7 | Kings. Princes and other rulers |
| 48.6 | General (Table K11) |
| 48.7.A-Z | Special topics, A-Z |
| 48.7.B57 | Birth rights (Table K12) |
| 48.7.E43 | Election (Table K12) |
| | Emergency powers see KL-KWX8 48.7.W37 |
| 48.7.L44 | Legislative power (Table K12) |
| 48.7.S92 | Succession (Table K12) |
| 48.7.T73 | Treatymaking power (Table K12) |
| 48.7.W37 | War and emergency powers (Table K12) |
| 49-51 | The central government. Executive power |
| 49 | General (Table K11) |
| 49.3 | Prime minister and cabinet (Table K11) |
| 50 | The Governor (Table K11) |
| 50.5.A-Z | Other, A-Z |
| 50.5.C42 | Chancellery (Table K12) |
| 50.5.C68 | Councils (Table K12) |
| 50.5.P74 | Privy council (Table K12) |

Constitutional law
Organs of government
The central government. Executive power -- Continued
51.A-Z Executive departments, A-Z
Subarrange each by Table K12
Class here departments not provided for by subject
The judiciary see KL-KWX8 33.92+
52 Constitutional courts (tribunals) and procedure (Table K11)
State and religion
see KL-KWX4 2685+ ; KL-KWX6 2162+
Administrative law
53.3 General (Table K11)
Administrative process
53.4 General (Table K11)
53.5 Administrative acts and enforcement (Table K11)
53.6 Legal transactions and public contracts (Table K11)
54 Administrative courts and procedure (Table K11)
Including judicial review of administrative acts
Indemnification for acts performed by government
54.3 General (Table K11)
54.4 Eminent domain (Table K11)
54.5 Government liability (Table K11)
54.6.A-Z Other special topics, A-Z
Subarrange each by Table K12
Administrative organization
55 General (Table K11)
Executive departments. Ministries see KL-KWX8 51.A+
55.5 Administrative and political divisions. Local government other than municipal (Table K11)
Municipal government
56 General (Table K11)
56.4 Autonomy and self-government. State supervision (Table K11)
56.5 Constitution and organization of municipal government (Table K11)
Including city mayor, city director, councils, civic associations, elected and honorary officers, etc.
For works on municipal civil service (General), see KL-KWX4 2989 ; KL-KWX6 2424
For works on officers and employees of an individual municipality, see the municipality
56.6 Civil service. Functionaries (Table K11)
Police and public safety
57 General (Table K11)
57.3 Police magistrates (Table K11)

Police and public safety -- Continued
Public safety
57.4 General (Table K11)
57.5.A-Z Hazards and preventive measures, A-Z
Subarrange each by Table K12
Control of individuals
57.6 General (Table K11)
57.7 Identification and registration (Table K11)
58.A-Z Particular groups, A-Z
Subarrange each by Table K12
58.3 Control of social activities (Table K11)
58.4 Disaster control. Disaster relief (Table K11)
Public property. Public restraint on private property
59 General (Table K11)
59.3 Government property. Powers and control (Table K11)
59.4 Roads and highways (Table K11)
Water resources
Including rivers, lakes, water courses, etc.
59.5 General (Table K11)
59.6 Water resources development (Table K11)
State preserves. Forests
60 General (Table K11)
Wilderness preservation see KL-KWX8 63.6
Architectural and historic monuments see KL-KWX8 69
Public land law
Land reform and land policy legislation
For agricultural land law see KL-KWX8 73.4+
60.3 General (Table K11)
Regional planning
For jurisdiction and organization, see KL-KWX4 3057+ ; KL-KWX6 2570+
60.4 General (Table K11)
60.5 Land use. Zoning. Subdivision (Table K11)
60.6 Building laws (Table K11)
Entail see KL-KWX8 73
Fideicommissum see KL-KWX8 73
Public health
61 General (Table K11)
61.2.A-Z Special topics, A-Z
61.2.B87 Burial and cemetery laws (Table K12)
Cemetery laws see KL-KWX8 61.2.B87
61.2.C65 Contagious and infectious diseases (Table K12)
61.2.D78 Drug laws (Table K12)
Including pharmacists and pharmacies
Infectious diseases see KL-KWX8 61.2.C65

Public health
Special topics, A-Z -- Continued
Pharmacists and pharmacies see KL-KWX8 61.2.D78
Medical legislation
62.3 General (Table K11)
62.4.A-Z The health professions, A-Z
Subarrange each by Table K12
62.5.A-Z Auxiliary (paramedical) professions, A-Z
Subarrange each by Table K12
62.6 Veterinary medicine (Table K11)
Environmental law
63 General (Table K11)
63.3 Environmental planning and conservation of resources (Table K11)
Environmental pollution
63.4 General (Table K11)
63.5.A-Z Pollutants, A-Z
Subarrange each by Table K12
63.6 Wilderness preservation (Table K11)
Including plant and wildlife conservation
Cultural affairs. Cultural policy
64 General (Table K11)
64.3 Organization and administration (Table K11)
Including subordinate agencies, commissions, councils, boards, etc.
64.4 Language. Regulation of use, purity, etc. (Table K11)
Education
65 General (Table K11)
65.2 Teachers (Table K11)
65.3 Elementary and secondary education (Table K11)
65.4 Vocational education (Table K11)
66 Higher education (Table K11)
66.4 Private schools (Table K11)
66.5 Adult education. Continuing education (Table K11)
Special topics, A-Z
66.6.C65 Compulsory education (Table K12)
66.6.P37 Participation in school government (Table K12)
67 Physical education. Athletics (Table K11)
Science and the arts
67.2 General (Table K11)
67.3.A-Z Special topics, A-Z
Academies see KL-KWX8 67.3.P82
67.3.P82 Public institutions. Academies (Table K12)
67.3.S72 Statistical services (Table K12)
Public collections

Cultural affairs. Cultural policy
Public collections -- Continued
68 General (Table K11)
68.5 Archives (Table K11)
68.6 Libraries (Table K11)
68.7 Museums and galleries (Table K11)
69 Historic buildings (Table K11)
Economic law. Regulation of industry, trade, and commerce
70 General (Table K11)
70.3 Economic constitution (Table K11)
70.4 Organization and administration (Table K11)
Including departments of commerce, and subordinate agencies and courts
70.5 Corporate representation of industry, trade, and commerce. Guilds (Table K11)
Standards and norms
see KL-KWX4 3254+ ; KL-KWX6 981+
Labeling
see KL-KWX4 3268 ; KL-KWX6 981.7
71 Licensing. State supervision (Table K11)
Advertising
see KL-KWX4 3280+ ; KL-KWX6 982.4+
Agriculture
History
71.3 General
Rural (peasant) land tenure. Peasantry
71.4 General
71.5 Mark communities. Village communities
Manorial estates. Seigniories
72 General
72.3.A-Z Special topics, A-Z
72.3.M35 Manorial serfdom
72.3.S47 Serfs
Leasehold for years and inheritance
72.5 General
72.7.A-Z Special topics, A-Z
73 Entailed estates of the greater nobility. Fideicommissum
Land reform and agrarian land policy legislation
73.4 General (Table K11)
73.5 Restraint on alienation of agricultural land (Table K11)
73.6 Consolidation of land holdings. Commasation (Table K11)
74 General (Table K11)
74.3 Organization and administration (Table K11)
Including department of agriculture, viticulture, and forestry, and subordinate agencies and boards

Economic law. Regulation of industry, trade, and commerce
Agriculture -- Continued
74.5.A-Z Agricultural industries and trades, A-Z
Subarrange each by Table K12
74.6.A-Z Agricultural products, A-Z
Subarrange each by Table K12
75 Corporate representation. Agricultural societies (Table K11)
75.3 Agricultural courts (Table K11)
75.4 Viticulture (Table K11)
75.5 Apiculture. Beekeeping (Table K11)
76 Horticulture (Table K11)
76.3 Forestry (Table K11)
Including timber and game laws
77 Fishery (Table K11)
Mining and quarrying
77.3 General (Table K11)
77.4.A-Z By resource, A-Z
77.4.S34 Salt (Table K12)
Manufacturing industries
78 General (Table K11)
78.3.A-Z Types of manufacture, A-Z
Subarrange each by Table K12
Food processing industries
78.5 General (Table K11)
78.6.A-Z By industry, A-Z
Subarrange each by Table K12
79 Construction and building industry (Table K11)
79.3 International trade (Table K11)
Domestic trade
79.5 General (Table K11)
79.6 Wholesale trade (Table K11)
79.7 Retail trade (Table K11)
80.A-Z Modes of trading, A-Z
Subarrange each by Table K12
80.3.A-Z Products, A-Z
Subarrange each by Table K12
80.4 Second-hand trade (Table K11)
Including auction houses, pawnbrokers, etc.
80.5.A-Z Service trades, A-Z
Subarrange each by Table K12
Artisans
81 General (Table K11)
81.2 Corporate representation (Table K11)
81.3.A-Z Crafts, A-Z
Subarrange each by Table K12

Economic law. Regulation of industry, trade, and commerce -- Continued

Public utilities. Power supplies

81.5 General (Table K11)

81.6.A-Z By utility, A-Z

Subarrange each by Table K12

82 Industrial arbitral courts and procedure (Table K11)

82.3 Business ethics. Courts of honor (Table K11)

82.4 Criminal provisions (Table K11)

Transportation

82.5 General (Table K11)

Road traffic

82.6 General (Table K11)

82.7 Traffic regulations and enforcement (Table K11)

83 Carriage of passengers and goods (Table K11)

83.3.A-Z Special topics, A-Z

83.3.B88 Bus lines (Table K12)

Railroads

Including carriage of passengers and goods

83.4 General (Table K11)

83.5.A-Z Special topics, A-Z

Subarrange each by Table K12

Pipelines

see KL-KWX4 3466 ; KL-KWX6 1049

Aviation

see KL-KWX4 3467+ ; KL-KWX6 1050+

Water transportation. Domestic shipping

Including carriage of passengers and goods

83.6 General (Table K11)

83.7.A-Z Special topics, A-Z

Subarrange each by Table K12

Communication. Mass media

84 General (Table K11)

84.3 Postal services (Table K11)

84.4 Telecommunication (Table K11)

84.5 Radio communication (Table K11)

84.6 Press law (Table K11)

84.7.A-Z Special topics, A-Z

Subarrange each by Table K12

Professions

85 General (Table K11)

85.3.A-Z Individual professions, A-Z

Subarrange each by Table K12

85.4 Professional ethics. Courts of honor (Table K11)

For a particular court of honor, see the profession

Public finance
85.5 General (Table K11)
85.6 Organization and administration (Table K11)
86 Budget. Accounting and auditing (Table K11)
Including courts
86.3 Public debts. Loans (Table K11)
86.4 Money. Coinage (Table K11)
Including mint regulations
State revenue
86.5 General (Table K11)
Taxation
Including taxes shared by the state and municipality
For local ordinances and works on the taxation of a particular locality or municipality, see the locality or municipality
86.6 General (Table K11)
Income tax
see KL-KWX4 3573+ ; KL-KWX6 2832+
Sales tax
see KL-KWX4 3628+ ; KL-KWX6 3147+
86.7 Estate, inheritance, and gift taxes (Table K11)
Property tax. Taxation of capital
87 General (Table K11)
87.3.A-Z Special topics, A-Z
Subarrange each by Table K12
87.4 Taxation of motor vehicles (Table K11)
87.5 Taxes from gambling tables. Casinos (Table K11)
87.6.A-Z Other, A-Z
Subarrange each by Table K12
Customs. Tariff
87.7 General (Table K11)
87.8.A-Z Special topics, A-Z
Subarrange each by Table K12
88 Tax and customs courts and procedure (Table K11)
Tax and customs crimes and delinquency
see KL-KWX4 3693+ ; KL-KWX6 3315+
Government measures in time of war, national emergency, or economic crisis
88.3 General (Table K11)
88.4.A-Z Particular measures or claims, A-Z
88.4.I53 Industrial priorities and allocations (Table K12)
Legislation for economic and social recovery and restitution
89 General (Table K11)
89.3.A-Z Groups of victims or types of damage, A-Z
Subarrange each by Table K12

| | |
|---|---|
| | Government measures in time of war, national emergency, or economic crisis |
| | Legislation for economic and social recovery and restitution -- Continued |
| 89.5.A-Z | Special topics, A-Z<br>Subarrange each by Table K12 |
| | Military law |
| 89.6 | General (Table K11) |
| 89.7 | Compulsory service (Table K11) |
| 89.8.A-Z | Individual branches of service, A-Z<br>Subarrange each by Table K12 |
| 90 | Civil defense (Table K11) |
| | Military criminal law and procedure |
| 90.3 | General (Table K11) |
| 90.4.A-Z | Individual offenses, A-Z<br>Subarrange each by Table K12 |
| 90.5.A-Z | Special topics, A-Z<br>Subarrange each by Table K12 |
| | Criminal law |
| 91 | Reform of criminal law, procedure, and execution (Table K11) |
| 91.2 | General (Table K11) |
| | Philosophy of criminal law<br>see KL-KWX4 3812+ ; KL-KWX6 3812+ |
| 91.3 | Concepts and principles (Table K11) |
| | Punishment |
| 91.4 | General (Table K11) |
| 91.5.A-Z | Special topics, A-Z<br>Subarrange each by Table K12 |
| 91.6 | Criminal registers (Table K11) |
| 92.A-Z | Individual offenses, A-Z<br>Subarrange each by Table K12 |
| 92.B75 | Bribery. Corruption (Table K12) |
| 92.R33 | Racketeering (Table K12) |
| | Criminal courts and procedure |
| | Criticism and reform see KL-KWX8 91 |
| 92.3 | General (Table K11) |
| | Administration of criminal justice |
| | Criticism and reform see KL-KWX8 91 |
| 92.4 | General (Table K11) |
| | Department of justice see KL-KWX8 34.2 |
| | Judicial statistics see KL-KWX8 5.2+ |
| | Judicial assistance |
| 93 | General (Table K11) |
| 93.3 | International judicial assistance (Table K11) |
| 93.4 | Foreign judgments (Conflict of laws) (Table K11) |

Criminal law
Criminal courts and procedure
Administration of criminal justice -- Continued
Court organization
94 General (Table K11)
94.3.A-Z Particular courts, A-Z
Subarrange each by Table K12
94.5 Procedural principles (Table K11)
95 Pretrial procedures (Table K11)
95.3 Procedure at first instance (Table K11)
95.4 Judicial decisions and remedies (Table K11)
Execution of sentence
Criticism and reform see KL-KWX8 91
95.5 General (Table K11)
Imprisonment
96 General (Table K11)
96.3.A-Z Penal institutions, A-Z
Subarrange each by Table K12
96.4.A-Z Other special, A-Z
96.4.C36 Capital punishment (Table K12)

.A1A-.A1Z Bibliography

<.A15> Periodicals

For periodicals consisting predominantly of legal articles, regardless of subject matter and jurisdiction, see K1+

For periodicals consisting primarily of informative material (newsletters, bulletins, etc.) relating to a special subject, see the subject and form division tables for periodicals

For law reports, official bulletins or circulars intended chiefly for the publication of laws and regulations, see appropriate entries in the text or form division tables

.A17A-.A17Z Official gazettes

Including historical sources

Legislative documents

Including historical sources

Cf. JS300+ Municipal documents of local governments

.A2 Serials

.A25 Monographs. By date

Statutes (national and/or state) affecting cities, etc.

Including historical sources

.A29A-.A29Z Serials

.A3 Monographs. By date

Charters (Privileges), ordinances, and local laws

Including historical sources

.A4 Serials

.A45 Collections. By date

.A5 Individual charters or acts of incorporation. By date

Collections of decisions and rulings

Including historical sources

.A6 Serials

.A65 Monographs. By date

Judicial statistics. Surveys of local administration of justice

.A7 Serials

.A75 Monographs

.A8A-.A8Z Special agencies, courts or topics, A-Z

Subarrange by date

Directories

see the numbers provided for directories at the national level

Legal profession

see the numbers provided for the legal profession at the national level

Legal aid

see the numbers provided for legal aid at the national level

History

For the history of a particular subject, see the subject

.A85A-.A85Z Sources

Class here sources not falling under one of the categories above

History -- Continued
.A9-.AZ General works
Particular subjects
Not to be further subarranged by form
Private law
Including civil and commercial law
.12 General
.125 Persons. Status. Capacity and incapacity
Domestic relations. Marriage. Parent and child
.13 General
.14.A-Z Special topics, A-Z
Property. Law of things. Real property
.15 General
.18 Land register
.19.A-Z Special topics, A-Z
Inheritance. Succession upon death
.2 General
.23.A-Z Special topics, A-Z
Obligations
.24 General
.25.A-Z Special topics, A-Z
.25.L43 Leases. Rent
Rent see KL-KWX9 .25.L43
.26 Merchant and business enterprise
.27 Commercial registers
.28 Banking. Negotiable instruments. Insurance
.29 Business associations
Labor law. Social insurance. Public welfare
.3 General
.32.A-Z Particular groups, A-Z
.33.A-Z Particular agencies, institutions, or courts, A-Z
Courts and procedure see KL-KWX9 .38
City constitution and government
.34 General
.35 Legislative functions. City council, etc.
Including elections
.36 Executive functions. Mayor and administrative departments. Municipal civil service
Including elections
.38 Judicial functions. City courts and procedure
Municipal civil service see KL-KWX9 .36
Police and public safety. Police force
.4 General
.44.A-Z Particular safety hazards or preventive measures, A-Z
.44.F57 Fire
.46.A-Z Special topics, A-Z

Particular subjects
City constitution and government
Special topics, A-Z -- Continued
Flags see KL-KWX9 .46.N34
Insignia see KL-KWX9 .46.N34
.46.N34 Name. Flags. Insignia. Seals, etc.
Seals see KL-KWX9 .46.N34
Public property. Public restraint on private property
.47 General
.5.A-Z Special topics, A-Z
.5.B84 Building laws
.5.C84 City planning and redevelopment
Public health. Medical legislation
.54 General
.55 Burial and cemetery laws
.58.A-Z Special topics, A-Z
.58.D74 Drinking water
.6 Environmental laws
Cultural affairs
.63 General
.64 Education. Schools. Institutions
.65 Theater. Orchestra
.66 Public collections
.67 Historic buildings and monuments
.68.A-Z Special topics, A-Z
Industry, trade, and commerce
.7 General
.75.A-Z Artisans, A-Z
.76.A-Z Professions, A-Z
.78.A-Z Corporate representation, A-Z
.78.B62 Boards of trade
.78.C42 Chambers of commerce
.78.G55 Guilds
.78.T72 Trade associations
.8 Public utilities
Public finance
.83 General
Sources of revenue. Taxes, fees, and fines
.85 General works
.855.A-Z Particular taxes and other sources of revenue, A-Z
.855.S25 Sales tax. Value-added tax
.86 Offenses (Violation of ordinances) and administration of criminal justice. Correctional institutions

.xA-.xZ Legislation. By main entry, A-Z
.x2 Decisions
.x3 General works
Including comprehensive works and works on specific legal topics

0.1 Royal (Imperial) statutes. Code of law

0.2 Treaties

0.3 Royal (Imperial) privileges, decrees, mandates, etc., A-Z
Subarrange each by Table K21

0.4 Judicial decisions and opinions, A-Z
Subarrange each by Table K21

0.5 Contracts. Deeds, A-Z
Subarrange each by Table K21

0.6 Testaments. Wills, A-Z
Subarrange each by Table K21

0.7 Boundary stones (e.g. Kudurru), A-Z
Subarrange each by Table K21

Census lists
see PJ3851+

0.8 Inventories, A-Z
Subarrange each by Table K21

0.9 Formularies. Clauses and forms, A-Z
Subarrange each by Table K21

.xA3 Autobiography. Reminiscences. By date

.xA4 Letters. Correspondence. By date

Including individual letters, general collections, and collections of letters to particular individuals

.xA8-.xZ Biography and criticism

| | |
|---|---|
| | National (Federal) law |
| | Including treaties, statutes, regulations |
| .A2 | Serials |
| .A3 | Monographs. By date of publication |
| | Customary law |
| | Including treaties, constitutions, statutes |
| .A4 | Serials |
| .A5 | Monographs. By date of publication |
| .A6-.Z | General works |

| | |
|---|---|
| 1 | General works |
| 2 | Persons |
| | Domestic relations. Family law |
| 3 | General |
| 4 | Marriage. Dissolution of marriage |
| 5 | Matrimonial property |
| 6 | Consanguinity and affinity. Lineage. Kinship |
| | Property |
| 7 | General |
| 8 | Personal property |
| | Land law |
| 9 | General |
| 10 | Land tenure |
| 11 | Riparian rights. Water rights. Fishing rights |
| 12 | Grazing and hunting rights |
| 13 | Family property. Ancestral property |
| 14 | Contracts |
| 15 | Inheritance and succession |
| 16 | Customary (native) courts and procedure |
| 17 | Constitution. Political organization |
| | Criminal law and procedure |
| 18 | General |
| 19 | Particular crimes (not A-Z) |
| 20 | Particular punishments (not A-Z) |

| | |
|---|---|
| .xA11-.xA119 | General works |
| .xA1191-.xA11919 | Persons |
| | Domestic relations. Family law |
| .xA12 .xA129 | General |
| .xA13-.xA13 | Marriage. Dissolution of marriage |
| .xA14-.xA149 | Marriage. Matrimonial property |
| .xA15-.xA159 | Marriage. Consanguinity and affinity. Lineage. Kinship |
| | Property |
| .xA16-.xA169 | General |
| .xA17-.xA179 | Personal property |
| | Land law |
| .xA18-.xA189 | General |
| .xA19-.xA199 | Land tenure |
| .xA21-.xA219 | Riparian rights. Water rights. Fishing rights |
| .xA22-.xA229 | Grazing and hunting rights |
| .xA23-.xA239 | Family property. Ancestral property |
| .xA3-.xA39 | Contracts |
| .xA4-.xA49 | Inheritance and succession |
| .xA5-.xA59 | Customary (native) courts and procedure |
| .xA6-.xA69 | Constitution. Political organization |
| | Criminal law |
| .xA7-.xA79 | General |
| .xA8-.xA89 | Particular crimes (not A-Z) |
| .xA9-.xA99 | Particular punishments (not A-Z) |

A



INDEX

INDEX

INDEX

D

INDEX

INDEX

INDEX

INDEX

## F

INDEX

## G





INDEX

INDEX

INDEX

INDEX

N

INDEX

## O

INDEX

## P

INDEX

INDEX

## Q

INDEX

INDEX

## S

INDEX

INDEX

INDEX

T

INDEX

W

GPO U.S. GOVERNMENT PRINTING OFFICE: 2008–330–111/60016